DATE DUE

DE 28 99		
MY 20		
MY 20 03		
AG 7 05		

DEMCO 38-296

ADAPTED PHYSICAL EDUCATION AND SPORT

Second Edition

Joseph P. Winnick, EdD
State University of New York College at Brockport

Human Kinetics

ary of Congress Cataloging-in-Publication Data

ort / Joseph P. Winnick, editor. --
2nd ed.
   p. cm.
   Includes bibliographical references and index.
   ISBN 0-87322-579-1
   1. Physical education for handicapped persons.   2. Sports for the
handicapped.   I. Winnick, Joseph P.
GV445.A3   1995   95-1521
371.9'04486--dc20   CIP

ISBN: 0-87322-579-1

Acquisitions Editor: Richard D. Frey, PhD; **Developmental Editor:** Rodd Whelpley; **Assistant Editor:** Hank Woolsey, Dawn Roselund, Ed Giles, Jacqueline Blakley, Susan Moore, and Karen Bojda; **Copyeditor:** Elaine Otto; **Proofreaders:** Danelle Eknes and Gloria Jensen; **Indexer:** Theresa Schaefer; **Typesetting and Text Layout:** Yvonne Winsor; **Text Designer:** Stuart Cartwright; **Cover Designer:** Jack Davis; **Illustrator:** Beth Young and Jennifer Delmotte; **Printer:** Braun-Brumfield

Printed in the United States of America

10 9 8 7 6 5 4 3 2 1

Human Kinetics
P.O. Box 5076, Champaign, IL 61825-5076
1-800-747-4457

Canada: Human Kinetics, Box 24040, Windsor, ON N8Y 4Y9
1-800-465-7301 (in Canada only)

Europe: Human Kinetics, P.O. Box IW14, Leeds LS16 6TR, United Kingdom
(44) 1132 781708

Australia: Human Kinetics, 2 Ingrid Street, Clapham 5062
South Australia
(08) 371 3755

New Zealand: Human Kinetics, P.O. Box 105-231, Auckland 1
(09) 523 3462

Contents

Preface

During the past three decades, increasing attention has been given to the education of individuals with unique needs. Much of the impetus for high-quality education and sport participation has been sparked by federal legislation dealing with individuals with disabilities. With this increased attention has come the realization that individuals with disabilities are really individuals with *abilities* who are capable of much more than society has ever believed. In physical education and sport, persons with unique needs have been provided with increased opportunities, and the result has been an unbelievable demonstration of abilities and a virtual knowledge explosion in these fields. As opportunities are provided and more persons with unique needs participate, the value of physical activity is more clearly recognized and accepted. More parents, medical professionals, educators, and others recognize the tremendous value of physical education and sport today than ever before. This recognition and acceptance extends throughout the world, as clearly demonstrated at international symposia and international competition in sport.

The advances in adapted physical education and sport have become so pronounced that a series of recognizable subspecialties have emerged in connection with these areas. It has become very difficult, if not impossible, for one or two authors to write, keep current, and provide up-to-date revisions of quality texts on these topics. Thus, I have assembled the top people in their areas of expertise to serve as a textbook writing team. The result is a book that reflects the very sharply focused thinking of a team of specialists who draw on more than 350 years of experience in adapted physical education and sport.

This book has been designed as both a text and a resource in adapted physical education and sport. As a text it can be used to prepare students majoring in physical education, recreation, sport management, special education, and related disciplines. As a resource it can serve a variety of individuals and groups: teachers, administrators, parents, coaches, volunteers, and other professionals.

In both this and the first edition, emphasis has been focused on physical education and sport. This is evidenced by the number of chapter titles reflecting areas of physical education and sport. This emphasis is maintained as readers receive the essential educational and medical background necessary to work with individuals with disabilities. Emphasis is also placed on making this text comprehensive yet easy to read and understand. Although many of the strengths of the first edition of this text are retained in this second edition, some notable changes appear in this edition. The second edition presents updated information and expanded coverage in many topical areas and includes new topics as well. For example, this second edition adds information on individuals with traumatic brain injury, stroke, autism, and dwarfism. More information is provided relative to infants, toddlers, and preschoolers.

In this edition, key terms are highlighted throughout. The text is fully illustrated, concise, accessible, and practical. An instructor's guide accompanies the book. The instructor's guide provides suggestions for an introductory course in adapted physical education and subsequently provides chapter-by-chapter suggested objectives appropriate for students; enrichment or learning activities that instructors may use to supplement class lectures, discussions, and readings; study or test questions that instructors may use; and additional resources that might be helpful to amplify material included in each chapter.

I have divided the book into four parts. Part I, "Foundational Topics in Adapted Physical Education and Sport," presents information that introduces the reader to adapted physical education and sport. It includes a brief history and overview of adapted physical education and sport, information on the organization and management of programs, and information on developing and implementing individual education programs successfully.

In Part II, "Children and Youth With Unique Needs," seven chapters are devoted to disabilities associated with the Individuals With Disabilities Education Act (IDEA) and one chapter discusses nondisabled youngsters with unique needs in physical education. An important part of this section talks about understanding the nature of conditions that result in unique physical education and sport needs and implications for meeting these needs.

Part III, "Developmental and Early Childhood Topics in Adapted Physical Education," begins with three chapters discussing physical fitness development, motor development, and perceptual-motor development and concludes with two chapters discussing programs associated with early childhood; i.e., relating to infants, toddlers, and preschoolers. The latter two chapters are new and unique contributions to the body of knowledge in adapted physical education, and the writers of these chapters will be particularly interested in the professional response to the positions taken and the ideas presented.

Part IV, "Activities for Students With Unique Needs," describes physical education and sport activities in school and community contexts. It includes separate chapters on body mechanics and posture; developmental and remedial exercises; rhythms and dance; aquatics; team sports; individual, dual and cooperative sports; winter activities; and wheelchair sport performance. A key aspect of this part is the presentation of specific activity modifications for the various populations involved in adapted physical education and sport. This part concludes with a chapter related to the enhancement of wheelchair sport performance.

The book has been designed to be a comprehensive, high-quality introduction to adapted physical education and sport and to be interesting, relevant, and user friendly. I hope it will help to provide quality services to individuals with unique needs.

Joseph P. Winnick

Acknowledgments

Diane H. Craft—My thanks to Craig Smith for giving so freely of his time and experience.

Bobby L. Eason—To Dr. Jo E. Cowden, I appreciate you for sharing with me your vision and initiative concerning infants and toddlers and adapted physical education; you are the originator. To Ellen and Dr. Paul Surburg, thanks for reading and critiquing the chapter. Because you showed me patience, although expressed in different ways, thank you, Dr. Sandra Eason and Dr. Joe Winnick.

David L. Gallahue—Thanks to Sandy Smith for typing the manuscript and my colleagues at Indiana University dedicated to quality physical education and sport experiences for all.

Colin Higgs—Thanks to the Government of Canada, Fitness and Amateur Sport for funding racing wheelchair research, and to the Technical Services Division of Memorial University, St. John's, Newfoundland for building my experimental wheelchairs. Special thanks to athletes using wheelchairs for their cooperation with sport scientists.

Luke E. Kelly—I would like to thank Dr. Joseph P. Winnick for inviting me to participate and for his inspiration and dedication to improving the quality of services provided in adapted physical education and sport. I would also like to thank my graduate students at the University of Virginia, who have served as a sounding board for my ideas and who have spent countless hours reviewing the chapters I have written.

Ellen M. Kowalski—Special thanks to Joe Winnick for inviting me to participate in writing this book. Special thanks also to Pat Krebs and Bonnie Boswell for providing valuable feedback and information as I developed the chapter. Finally, I would like to extend my appreciation to my students and colleagues, from whom I continue to learn.

Patricia L. Krebs—On behalf of all people with mental retardation, I would like to thank Special Olympics for its extraordinary vision and service. My personal appreciation to my son, Greg Kaylor, Dr. Doreen Croser, Dr. Joe Winnick, and the staff,
athletes, coaches, volunteers, and families of Maryland Special Olympics.

E. Michael Loovis—I wish to express my gratitude to everyone who even in the smallest way contributed to the development and refinement of my chapters. Several individuals and institutions deserve special mention; these include Dr. Richard Lockwood from the University of Western Australia and Instructional Media Services at Cleveland State University, especially Michael Ludwig and Nathaniel Eatman.

David L. Porretta—Recognition goes to the following organizations for the preparation of photos used in my chapters: the Disabled Sports Association of North Texas, C.A. Blatchford & Sons, Ltd., and the Ohio State School for the Blind. Also, special thanks goes to participants in both the Adapted Physical Education Laboratory and the leisure programs at Ohio State University.

E. Louise Priest—My appreciation to Susan Grosse for reviewing and making suggestions on my chapter.

Francis X. Short—Appreciation is extended to the design and production staff at SUNY, College at Brockport for their assistance in developing the figures used in my chapters. I also want to thank Joseph P. Winnick for his feedback during the construction of my chapters.

Paul R. Surburg—Both chapters are dedicated to Dr. Luther C. Schwich, who was instrumental in guiding me into the field of physical education and who until his death provided me with insights into the role of physical activity for persons with cancer.

Dale A. Ulrich—I would like to thank the staff at the Center for Innovative Practices for Young Children at the Institute for the Study of Developmental Disabilities, Indiana University, for their excellent resources on preschool services.

Joseph P. Winnick—I wish to acknowledge the wonderful support and cooperation I have received from the outstanding authors involved in this edition. I very much appreciate the help and support I have received from many persons at the State University of New York, College at Brockport.

PART I

Foundational Topics in Adapted Physical Education and Sport

Part I of this book, consisting of six chapters, introduces you to adapted physical education and sport. The first chapter defines adapted physical education and sport and offers a brief orientation concerning its history, legal basis, and professional resources. In chapter 2, where the focus shifts to the organization and management of programs, topics include programmatic and curricular direction in adapted physical education, guidelines for administrative procedures and program implementation, human resources necessary for adapted physical education and sport programs, and program evaluation. Chapter 3 is a detailed discussion of individualized education programs developed for students with unique needs. Vital to the establishment of these programs are several concepts related to measurement and evaluation. These concepts are treated in chapter 4, which discusses various types of tests and standards, purposes of measurement and assessment, and tests and awards relevant to adapted physical education. Chapters 5 and 6 deal with instructional styles and strategies related to adapted physical education and basic concepts and approaches related to methods of managing behavior.

CHAPTER 1

An Introduction to Adapted Physical Education and Sport

Joseph P. Winnick

Many individuals who pursue a career of teaching physical education and coaching sports are skilled athletes. They have had a great deal of success and have probably earned letters in high school and college athletics. Many have interacted with high-level athletes like themselves. As they prepare for careers, they often become aware of the existence of adapted physical education and sport, which provides services to individuals with unique needs, who need activities adapted for them.

Although most individuals with unique needs remain rather obscure, some have become sport celebrities. For example, Wilma Rudolph—despite birth defects and polio—was a triple gold medalist in the 100m, 200m, and 400m relays in the 1960 Rome Olympics. Peter Gray, whose right arm was amputated, played centerfield for the St. Louis Browns in 1945. Others include Harry Cordellos, a sightless distance runner who ran the 1975 Boston Marathon with a sighted partner in 2 hours, 57 minutes, and 42 seconds; Tom Dempsey, born with only half a right foot, who set a National Football League record in 1970 for the longest field goal kicked (63 yards); and Jim Abbott, who became an award-winning lefthanded pitcher for the New York Yankees despite an impaired right hand. As Figure 1.1 shows, individuals with unique needs are capable of feats that many people would not think possible.

THE MEANING OF ADAPTED PHYSICAL EDUCATION

Because different terms and different definitions of the same term have been applied to physical education that meets unique needs, it is necessary to clarify some terms. Adapted physical education is an individualized program of developmental activities, exercises, games, rhythms, and sport designed to meet the unique physical education needs of individuals. As a subdiscipline of physical education (PE), it includes instruction individually planned to meet the needs of students who require adaptations in physical education for safe, satisfying, and successful participation.

Adapted physical education is generally designed to meet long-term (more than 30 days) unique needs. These include disabilities as specified in the Individuals with Disabilities Education Act (IDEA). According to this legislation, children with disabilities, ages 6–21, are those with mental retardation, hearing impairments, speech or language impairments, visual impairments, serious emotional disturbance, orthopedic impairments, autism, traumatic brain injury, other health impairments, or specific learning disabilities; for this reason, they need special education and related services. At a state's discretion, children with disabilities, ages 3–5, may include those who are experiencing developmental delays in one of the following areas: physical, cognitive, communication,

a   b

Figure 1.1 An elite performer with a lower limb impairment performing a handstand (a) in the early years and (b) as a teenager.

adaptive, social, or emotional development and who, by reason thereof, need special education and related services. Adapted physical education may also include infants and toddlers with disabilities who need early intervention services because they are experiencing delays in one or more of the following areas: cognitive, physical, communication, social, or emotional development or self-help skills or they have a diagnosed physical or mental condition that has a high probability of resulting in developmental delay. Adapted physical education may include pupils who are not identified by a school district as disabled under federal legislation, but who may have unique needs that call for a specially designed program. The latter group may include students of low fitness (including exceptional leanness or obesity), inadequate motor development, or low skill and those pupils with poor functional posture. These individuals may require individually designed programming to habilitate or remediate physical and motor functions required for continued physical education, functional skills, and physical well-being.

According to IDEA, students with disabilities, ages 3–21, must have an *individualized education program* (IEP) developed by a planning committee.

In developing an IEP, physical education needs must be considered, and the IEP developed may include specially designed instruction in physical education. Federal legislation also requires the development of an *individualized family service plan* (IFSP) for infants and toddlers with disabilities. Although physical education services are not required for this age group, they may be offered as part of an IFSP. Although not required by federal law, an *individualized physical education program* (IPEP) should also be developed for those who have a unique need but have not been identified by the school as disabled. It is recommended that each school have policies and procedures to guide the development of all individualized programs. More specific information on the development of programs and plans are presented in chapter 2.

Adapted physical education may take place in classes that range from those *mainstreamed* (i.e., regular physical education) to those *segregated* (i.e., only persons with unique needs). Although an adapted physical education program is individualized, it can be implemented in a group setting. It should be geared to each student's needs, limitations, and abilities. Whenever appropriate, students receiving an adapted physical education program should be included in regular physical education settings.

Adapted physical education is an *active* program of physical activity rather than a *sedentary* alternative program. It supports the attainment of the benefits of physical activity by meeting the needs of students who might otherwise be relegated to passive experiences associated with physical education. In establishing adapted physical education programs, educators work with parents, students, teachers, administrators, and professionals in various disciplines. Adapted physical education may employ developmental, community-based, or other orientations and may use a variety of teaching styles. It takes place in schools and other agencies responsible for educating individuals. Although adapted physical education is *educational*, it draws upon *related* services (more on related services later in this chapter), especially medically related services, to help meet instructional objectives and goals.

In this text, adapted physical education and sport are viewed as part of the emerging area of study referred to as **adapted physical activity**, a term used to encompass the comprehensive and interdisciplinary study of physical activity for the education, wellness, sport participation, and leisure of individuals with unique needs.

Adapted physical education can help to restore the individual's capabilities. Although it may exceed the minimal time required by policies or law, it should not be supplanted by related services, intramurals, sport days, athletics, or other experiences that are not primarily instructional.

Adapted sport programs are conducted in diverse environments and organizational patterns for a variety of purposes. Educational programs are generally conducted in schools and include intramurals, extramurals, and interschool activities. Intramural activities are conducted within schools, involve only pupils enrolled in that school, and are organized to serve the entire school population. Extramural sport activities involve participation of pupils from two or more schools and are sometimes conducted as play days or sport days at the end of instructional or intramural sessions. Interschool sports involve competition between representatives from two or more schools and offer enriched opportunities for selected and more highly skilled individuals. Adapted sport activity may also be conducted for leisure or recreational purposes within formal, open, or unstructured programs or as part of the lifestyle of individuals and/or groups. Adapted sport activity may also be conducted for wellness, medical, or therapeutic reasons. For example, sport or adapted sport may be used as part of recreational therapy, corrective therapy, sport therapy, or wellness programs. Finally, adapted sport may be conducted for team or self-actualization and/or pursuit of excellence; that is, be all you can be in a particular sport. In general, one's involvement in sport or adapted sport serves several purposes. This text will focus on adapted sport in educational settings and in regional, national, and international competition under the governance of formalized organizations promoting sport for individuals with disabilities.

ADAPTED SPORT

Adapted sport refers to sport modified or created to meet the unique needs of individuals with disabilities. Adapted sport may be conducted in a variety of settings, ranging from integrated settings in which individuals with disabilities interact with nondisabled participants to segregated environments in which play in sport includes only persons with disabilities (see Figure 2.4). Based on this definition, for example, basketball is a sport and wheelchair basketball would be considered an adapted sport. Special Olympic sport participation would be considered adapted sport if rules were modified, and goal ball (a game in which players with visual impairments attempt to roll a ball that emits a sound across their opponents' goal) would be considered an adapted sport.

BRIEF HISTORY OF ADAPTED PHYSICAL EDUCATION

Although significant progress concerning educational services for persons with disabilities is relatively recent, the use of physical activity or exercise for medical treatment and therapy is not new. Therapeutic exercise may be traced in China to 3000 B.C. It is known that the ancient Greeks and Romans recognized the medical and therapeutic value of exercise. However, the provision of physical education or physical activity to meet the unique needs of persons with disabilities is a recent phenomenon. Efforts to serve these populations through physical education and sport has only been given significant attention during the twentieth century, although they began in the United States in the nineteenth century.

Beginning Period

In 1838, physical activity began receiving special attention at the Perkins school for pupils with visual disabilities in Boston. According to Charles E. Buell (1983), a noted physical educator with a visual impairment, this special attention resulted from the fact that Samuel Gridley Howe, the school's director, advocated the health benefits of physical activity. For the first eight years, physical education consisted of compulsory recreation in the open air. In 1840, when the school was moved to South Boston, boys participated in gymnastic exercises and swimming. This was the first physical education program for students who are blind in America, and, by Buell's account, it was far ahead of most of the physical education in public schools. Buell was a leader in providing physical education for persons who are blind and the author of several books and articles.

Medical Orientation

Although physical education was provided to persons who are blind as well as individuals with other disabilities in the early 1800s, most students of the history of adapted physical education generally recognized medically oriented gymnastics and drill begun in the latter part of the century as the forerunner of modern adapted physical education in the United States. Sherrill (1993) states that physical education prior to 1900 was medically oriented and preventive, developmental, or corrective in nature; its purpose was to prevent illness and/or to promote the health and vigor of the mind and body. Strongly influencing this orientation was a system of medical gymnastics developed in Sweden by Per Henrick Ling and introduced to the United States in 1884.

Shift to Sports and the Whole Person

Toward the end of the nineteenth century and into the 1930s, programs began to shift from medically oriented physical training to sports-centered physical education, and concern for the whole child emerged. Compulsory physical education in public schools increased dramatically, and physical education teacher training developed rather than medical training for the promotion of physical education (Sherrill, 1993). This transition resulted in broad mandatory programs consisting of games, sports, rhythmic activities, and calisthenics designed to meet the needs of the whole person. Individuals unable to participate in regular activities were provided corrective or remedial physical

Figure 1.2 Claudine Sherrill, a leader in the field of adapted physical education and sport.

education. According to Sherrill (see Figure 1.2), physical education programs between the 1930s and 1950s consisted of regular or corrective classes for students who today would be considered normal. Sherrill has succinctly described adapted physical education during this period:

Assignment to physical education was based upon a thorough medical examination by a physician who determined whether a student should participate in the regular or corrective program. Corrective classes were comprised primarily of limited, restricted, or modified activities related to health, posture, or fitness problems. In many schools students were excused from physical education. In others, the physical educator typically taught several sections of regular physical education each day. Leaders in corrective physical education continued to have strong backgrounds in medicine and/or physical therapy. Persons preparing to be physical education teachers generally completed one university course in corrective physical education. (p. 19)

The Emerging Comprehensive Subdiscipline

During the 1950s, more and more pupils described as handicapped were being served in public schools, and the outlook toward them was becoming increasingly humanistic. With a greater diversity in pupils came a greater diversity in programs to meet their needs. In 1952, the American Association for Health, Physical Education and Recreation (AAHPER) formed a committee to define the subdiscipline and give direction and guidance to professionals. This committee defined adapted physical education as "a diversified program of developmental activities, games, sports, and rhythms suited to the interests, capacities, and limitations of students with disabilities who may not safely or successfully engage in unrestricted participation in the rigorous activities of the general physical education program" (Committee on Adapted Physical Education, 1952). The definition retained the evolving diversity of physical education and specifically included students with disabilities. *Adapted physical education* serves today as the comprehensive term for this subdiscipline.

Recent and Current Status

With the impetus provided by a more humanistic, more informed, and less discriminatory society, major advances continued in the 1960s. Many of these advances were associated with the Joseph P. Kennedy family. In 1965, the Joseph P. Kennedy, Jr. Foundation awarded a grant to the American Alliance for Health, Physical Education, Recreation, and Dance to launch the Project on Recreation and Fitness for the Mentally Retarded. The project grew to encompass all special populations, and its name was changed in 1968 to the Unit on Programs for the Handicapped. Its director, Dr. Julian Stein (Figure 1.3), was able to influence adapted physical education throughout the United States at every level in the late 1960s and 1970s.

In 1968, the Kennedy Foundation exhibited further concern for individuals with mental retardation with the establishment of the Special Olympics. This grew rapidly, with competition held at local, state, national, and international levels in an ever-increasing range of sports.

During the mid-1960s, concern for people with emotional and/or learning disabilities had a significant effect on adapted physical education in the United States. The importance of physical activity for the well-being of those with emotional problems was explicitly recognized by the National Institute of Mental Health, U.S. Public Health Service, when it funded the Buttonwood Farms Project. The project, conducted at Buttonwood Farms, Pennsylvania, included a physical recreation component. This project was valuable for

Figure 1.3 Julian "Buddy" Stein has provided sustained leadership in the field of adapted physical education and sport.

recognizing the importance of physical activity in the lives of persons with disabilities, bringing the problems of seriously disturbed youngsters to the attention of educators, and developing curricular materials to prepare professionals in physical education and recreation for work with this population. During the same era, adapted physical education gained much attention with the use of perceptual-motor activities as a basis or modality for academic and/or intellectual development, particularly with students with learning disabilities. Newell C. Kephart, Gerald N. Getman, Raymond H. Barsch, Marianne Frostig, Phyllis Maslow, Bryant J. Cratty, and Jean A. Ayres were major authors who recommended motoric experiences as a basis or modality for perceptual and/ or academic development. This influence was particularly strong in the 1970s and continues with varying degrees of emphasis today.

Contemporary direction and emphasis in adapted physical education are heavily associated with the individual's right to a free and appropriate education. Because of litigation and the passage of various federal laws and regulations (the Individuals with Disabilities Education Act, Section 504 of the Rehabilitation Act of 1973, the Amateur Sports Act of 1978, and the Americans with Disabilities Act of 1990), change and progress have occurred in both adapted physical education and sport. The legal impetus has improved programs in many schools and agencies, extended mandated physical education for persons ages 3–21, stimulated activity programs for infants and toddlers, and resulted in dramatic increases in participation in sport programs for individuals with disabilities. Legislation has also resulted in funds for professional preparation, research, and other special projects relevant to the provision of full educational opportunity for persons with unique needs.

LITIGATION

Much has and can be written about the impact of litigation on the guarantee of full educational opportunity in the United States. The most prominent of cases, which has served as an important precedent for civil litigation, was *Brown v. Board of Education of Topeka, Kansas* (1954). This case established that the doctrine of *separate but equal* in public education resulted in segregation that violated the constitutional rights of black persons. Two landmark cases also had a heavy impact on the provision of free, appropriate public education for all handicapped children. The first was the class action suit of the *Pennsylvania Association for Retarded Children v. Commonwealth of Pennsylvania (1972)*. Equal protection and due process clauses associated with the Fifth and Fourteenth Amendments served as the constitutional basis for the court's rulings and agreements. The following were among the rulings or agreements in the case:

- Labeling a child as mentally retarded or denying public education or placement in a regular setting without due process or hearing violates the rights of the individual.

- All mentally retarded persons are capable of benefiting from a program of education and training.

- Mental age may not be used to postpone or in any way deny access to a free public program of education and training.

- Having undertaken to provide a free, appropriate education to all its children, a state may not deny mentally retarded children the same.

A second important case was *Mills v. Board of Education of the District of Columbia* (1972). This action, brought on behalf of seven children, sought to restrain the District of Columbia from excluding children from public schools or denying them publicly supported education. The district court held that, by failing to provide the seven handicapped children and the class they represented with publicly supported specialized education, the district

violated controlling statutes, its own regulations, and due process. The District of Columbia was required to provide a publicly supported education, appropriate equitable funding, and procedural due process rights to the seven children.

From 1972 to 1975, 46 right-to-education cases related to persons with disabilities were tried in 28 states. They provided the foundation for much of the legislation to be discussed in the next section.

LAWS IMPORTANT TO ADAPTED PHYSICAL EDUCATION AND SPORT

Laws have had a tremendous influence on educational programs for individuals with disabilities. With legislation supported by Senator Ted Kennedy in the late 1960s, the federal government began to fund various projects in adapted physical education and therapeutic recreation. Since 1969, colleges and universities in many states have received federal funds for professional preparation, research, and other projects to enhance programs for individuals with disabilities. Although the amount of money has been relatively small, physical educators have gained a great deal from that support. Several well-known projects have been associated with federal funding. The government agency that has been most responsible for administering federally funded programs related to adapted physical education is the Office of Special Education and Rehabilitative Services within the Department of Education.

Four laws or parts of laws have impacted greatly on adapted physical education and/or adapted sport: the Individuals with Disabilities Education Act (IDEA), Section 504 of the Rehabilitation Act of 1973, the Americans with Disabilities Act, and the Amateur Sports Act.

Individuals with Disabilities Education Act (IDEA)

A major force is the Individuals with Disabilities Education Act of 1990 (Public Law 101-476 and subsequent amendments). This act expanded upon the previous Education for the Handicapped Act and amendments, including PL 91-230 in 1970, PL 94-142 in 1975, PL 98-199 in 1983, and PL 99-457 in 1986. Each of these pieces of legislation has contributed to the education of individuals with disabilities. However, IDEA reflects the composite and the most recent version and amendments of

Table 1.1 Highlights of the Individuals With Disabilities Education Act (IDEA)

IDEA and its rules and regulations require:

A right to a free and appropriate education

Physical education be made available to children with disabilities

Equal opportunity in athletics and intramurals

An individualized program designed to meet unique needs for children with disabilities

Programs conducted in the least restrictive environment

Nondiscriminatory testing and objective criteria for placement

Due process

Related services to assist in special education

these laws (see Table 1.1). This act was designed to ensure that all children with disabilities have available to them a free appropriate public education that emphasizes *special education* and *related services* designed to meet their unique needs. In this legislation, the term *special education* was defined to mean specially designed instruction at no cost to parents or guardians to meet the unique needs of a child with a disability, including instruction conducted in the classroom, in the home, in hospitals and institutions, and in other settings, and instruction in physical education. IDEA specifies that the term *related services* was designated to mean transportation and such developmental, corrective, and other supportive services (including speech pathology and audiology, psychological services, physical and occupational therapy, recreation including therapeutic recreation, social work services, and medical service except that such medical services shall be for diagnostic and evaluating purposes only) as may be required to assist the child with a disability to benefit from special education, and includes early identification and assessment of disabling conditions in children. The act also ensures that the rights of children with disabilities and their parents or guardians are protected, and it helps states and localities provide education for all individuals with disabilities. IDEA has also established a policy to develop and implement a program of early intervention services for infants and toddlers and their families.

Definition and Requirements of Physical Education

The Education for the Handicapped Act, PL 94-142, a precessor to IDEA, defined physical education as the "development of (a) physical and motor fitness, (b) fundamental motor skills and patterns, and (c) skills in aquatics, dance, and individual and group games and sports (including intramural and lifetime sports)" (Department of Health, Education, & Welfare, 1977a, p. 42480). This term includes special physical education, adapted physical education, movement education, and motor development.

IDEA requires that special education, including physical education, be made available to children with disabilities and that it include physical education specially designed, if necessary, to meet their unique needs (see Figure 1.4). This federal legislation, together with state requirements for physical education, impacts significantly upon adapted physical education in schools.

Free Appropriate Public Education Under the IDEA

The term *free appropriate public education* means special education and related services that are provided at public expense in conformity with an IEP. The IEP is developed by a representative of the local education agency or an intermediate educational unit qualified to provide or supervise the provision of specially designed instruction and by the teacher, the parents or guardians, and—where appropriate—the child. The statement must include present levels of educational performance, annual goals (including short-term instructional objectives), specific educational services to be provided, the extent to which the child will be able to participate in regular educational programs, the projected date for initiation and anticipated duration of such services, and appropriate objective criteria and evaluation procedures and schedules for determining, on at least an annual basis, whether instructional objectives are being achieved. The development of an IEP, a crucial element of IDEA, is discussed in detail in chapter 3.

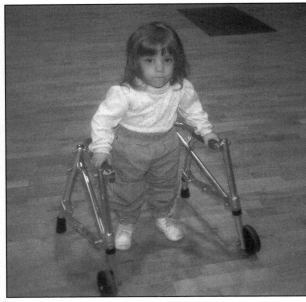

a   b

Figure 1.4   Physical education is for all pupils.

Least Restrictive Environment

IDEA also requires that education be conducted in the least restrictive environment. According to this law, each child with a disability must have the opportunity to participate in the regular physical education program available to nondisabled children, unless the child is enrolled full-time in separate facilities or needs specially designed physical education as prescribed in the IEP.

Basic to education in the most appropriate setting is a continuum of instructional placements (see Figure 2.3), which range from a situation in which children with disabilities are integrated into a regular class to a very restrictive setting (out-of-school segregated placement).

Focus on Pupil Needs and Opportunity

IDEA implicitly, if not explicitly, encourages educators to focus on the educational needs of the student instead of upon clinical or diagnostic labels. For example, as the IEP is developed, concern focuses on present functioning level, objectives, annual goals, etc. IDEA does not require that disability labels be identified on an IEP. The associated rules and regulations also indicate that children with disabilities must be provided with an equal opportunity for participation in nonacademic and extracurricular services and activities, including athletics, intramurals, and recreational services.

Section 504 of the Rehabilitation Act

The right of equal opportunity also emerges from another legislative milestone which has had an impact on adapted physical education and sport. Section 504 of the Rehabilitation Act of 1973, PL 93-112, provides that "no otherwise qualified handicapped individual . . . solely by reason of his handicap, be excluded from participation in, be denied the benefits of, or be subject to discrimination under any program or activity receiving Federal Financial assistance" (Department of Health, Education, and Welfare, 1977b).

As identified in a position statement developed by Winnick, Auxter, Jansma, Sculli, Stein, and Weiss (1980), an important intent of Section 504 is to ensure that individuals with handicapping conditions or disabilities receive intended benefits of all educational programs and extracurricular activities. Two specific conditions are prerequisite to the delivery of services that guarantee benefits to those individuals: programs must be equally effective, and they must be conducted in the most normal and integrated settings possible. To be equally effective, a program must offer individuals with disabilities equal opportunity to attain the same results, gain the same benefits, or reach the same levels of achievement as peers without disabilities.

To illustrate the basic intent associated with Section 504, let us consider a totally blind student enrolled in a college course in which all other students in the class are sighted. A written test given at the end of the semester would not provide the blind student equal opportunity to demonstrate knowledge of the material, and this approach would not be equally effective. By contrast, on a test administered orally or in braille, the blind student would have an equal opportunity to attain the same results or benefits as the other students. In giving an oral exam, the instructor would be giving equivalent, as opposed to identical, services. (Merely identical services, in fact, would be considered discriminatory and not in accord with Section 504.) It is neither necessary nor possible to guarantee equal results; what is important is the equal opportunity to attain those results. For example, a recipient of federal funds offering basketball to the general student population must provide wheelchair basketball for students confined to wheelchairs, if a need exists.

A program is not equally effective if it results in indiscriminate isolation or separation of individuals with disabilities. To the maximum degree possible, individuals with disabilities should participate in the least restrictive environment as represented by a continuum of alternative instructional placements (see chapter 2).

Compliance with Section 504 requires program accessibility; its rules and regulations prohibit exclusion of individuals with disabilities from federally assisted programs because of architectural or other environmental barriers. Common barriers to accessibility include facilities, finances, and transportation. Money available for athletics within a school district cannot be spent in a way that discriminates on the basis of disability. If a school district lacks sufficient funds, then it need not offer programs; however, it cannot fund programs in a discriminatory manner.

The Amateur Sports Act

In 1978, the Amateur Sports Act (PL 95-606) was passed to coordinate national efforts concerning amateur athletic activity, including competition for athletes with disabilities. This legislation led to the establishment of the Committee on Sports for the Disabled (COSD), a standing committee of the United States Olympic Committee (USOC) representing the following sport organizations: American Athletic Association for the Deaf (AAAD), National Wheelchair Basketball Association (NWBA), Wheelchair Sports, USA, United States Cerebral Palsy Athletic Association (USCPAA),

United States Les Autres Sports Association (US-LASA), National Handicapped Sports and Recreation Association (NHSRA), and the United States Association for Blind Athletes (USABA). The COSD coordinates American efforts for the Paralympics and stimulates sports for athletes with disabilities by obtaining facilities and other services for training.

Americans With Disabilities Act

In 1990, PL 101-336, Americans with Disabilities Act was passed. Whereas Section 504 focused on educational rights, this legislation extended civil rights protection for individuals with disabilities to all areas of American life. Provisions include employment, public accommodation and services, public transportation, and telecommunications. Related to adapted physical education and sport, this legislation has required that community recreational facilities including health and fitness facilities be successful and accessible and, where appropriate, that reasonable accommodations be made for persons with disabilities. One implication of this enhanced accessibility is the need for physical educators to develop programs that link skills learned in school with meaningful recreational experiences with the community (Auxter, Pyfer, Huettig, 1993).

HISTORY OF ADAPTED SPORT

Deaf athletes were among the first Americans with disabilities to become involved in organized sports at special schools. As reported by Gannon (1981), in the 1870s, the Ohio school became the first school for the deaf to offer baseball, and the state school in Illinois introduced football in 1885. Football became a major sport in many schools for the deaf around the turn of the century, and basketball was introduced at the Wisconsin School for the Deaf in 1906. Teams from schools for the deaf have continued to compete against each other and against athletes in regular schools.

Beyond interschool programs, formal international competition was established in 1924, when competitors from nine nations gathered in Paris for the first international silent games. In 1945, the AAAD was established to provide, sanction, and promote competitive sport opportunities for Americans with hearing impairments. In 1965, the United States hosted the International Summer Games for Athletes with Hearing Disabilities in Washington, DC.

The earliest formal, recorded athletic competition in the United States for individuals with visual disabilities was a telegraphic track meet between the Overbrook and Baltimore schools for the blind in 1907. In a telegraphic meet, local results are mailed to a central committee, which makes comparisons to determine winners. From this beginning, athletes with visual disabilities and their schools have competed against each other and against sighted peers and their schools. With the emphasis on integration since the 1970s, the amount and level of competition have diminished because of greater severity of disability in special schools.

Since the 1900s, wars have provided impetus for competitive sport opportunities. Sir Ludwig Guttman of Stoke Mandeville, England, is credited with introducing competitive sports as an integral part of the rehabilitation of veterans with disabilities; in the late 1940s, Stoke Mandeville Hospital sponsored the first recognized games for wheelchair athletes. In 1949, the University of Illinois organized the first national wheelchair basketball tournament; it resulted in the formation of the NWBA. To expand sport opportunities, Ben Lipton founded the NWAA in the mid-1950s. This organization sponsors various competitive sports on state, regional, and national levels for individuals with spinal cord conditions and other conditions requiring wheelchair use.

Another recent advancement was the creation of the NHSRA. The organization, now entitled National Handicapped Sports (NHS), was formed by a small group of Vietnam veterans. It has been dedicated since 1967 to providing year-round sport and recreational opportunities for persons with orthopedic, spinal cord, neuromuscular, and visual disabilities.

Special Olympics was created by the Joseph P. Kennedy, Jr., Foundation to provide and promote athletic competition for persons with mental retardation. This organization held its first international games at Soldier Field in Chicago in 1968. (A symbol for Special Olympics is shown in Figure 1.5). Special Olympics has served as the model sport organization for persons with disabilities through its leadership in direct service, research, training, advocacy, education, and organizational leadership.

In 1976, the USABA was created to provide competitive opportunities for legally blind athletes. USABA members compete against athletes with and without visual disabilities. USABA leadership facilitates member participation in sports on state, regional, national, and international levels.

Figure 1.5 This symbol of the Special Olympics was a gift from the Union of Soviet Socialist Republics on the occasion of the 1979 International Special Olympic Games hosted by the State University of New York, College at Brockport. The artist is Zurab Tsereteli.

To govern sport programs in the United States for individuals with cerebral palsy and similar neurological conditions, the NASCP was formed in 1978. In that year, the first national cerebral palsy games were held in Detroit and the first U.S. team attended the fourth international games for individuals with cerebral palsy in Scotland. The United States Cerebral Palsy Athletic Association (USCPAA), which has replaced NASCP, currently organizes sports for athletes with cerebral palsy, closed head injury, or stroke.

Although evolving programs were increasingly meeting the needs of athletes with disabilities, there were still many youngsters not eligible in the 1970s and 1980s. To address this situation, sport competition for Les Autres (the others) was developed. Athletes designated as Les Autres competed in the 1984 International Games for the Disabled and in the 1985 Cerebral Palsy/Les Autres games. USLASA was founded in 1985, and in 1986 the Dwarf Athletic Association of America (DAAA) formed.

Important to emphasize is the availability of international competition. Especially notable in this regard and centered around physical disabilities are the Paralympics and international competition arranged by the International Stoke Mandeville Wheelchair Sports Federation (ISMWSF), the International Sports Organization for the Disabled (ISOD), Cerebral

Table 1.2   Relationship Among Disabled Sport Organizations Under the U.S. Olympic Committee and International Sport Organizations

American sport organizations	International counterparts	Disability areas
American Athletic Association for the Deaf (AAAD)	World Games for the Deaf	Deafness
*Wheelchair Sports, USA	International Stoke Mandeville Wheelchair Sports Federation (ISMWSF)	Spinal cord conditions and other conditions resulting in wheelchair use
*National Handicapped Sports	International Sports Organization for the Disabled (ISOD)	Amputations, paralympics for les autres, winter sports for several disability areas
Special Olympics	Special Olympics International	Mental retardation
*U.S. Cerebral Palsy Athletic Association (USCPAA)	Cerebral Palsy–International Sports and Recreation Association (CP–ISRA)	Cerebral palsy, closed head injury, stroke
*Dwarf Athletic Association of America (DAAA)	International Sports Organization for the Disabled (ISOD)	Dwarfness
*U.S. Association for Blind Athletes (USABA)	International Blind Sports Association (IBSA)	Blindness

*Participate in Paralympics.

Palsy–International Sports and Recreation Association (CP–ISRA), and the International Blind Sports Association (IBSA). The Paralympics are counterparts of the regular Olympics for athletes with disabilities. The summer and winter Paralympics are held the same year as the regular Olympics and, to the extent possible, in the same country. In 1992, Madrid hosted the first Paralympic Games for the mentally handicapped. The competition was designed to provide international competition for elite athletes who could meet minimum qualifying standards. Table 1.2 lists American organizations that participate in the Paralympics, World Games for the Deaf, and Special Olympics International. These organizations as well as USLASA are multisport programs; that is, several sports are included as a part of their programs. There are also several single sport organizations, including the American Blind Bowling Association and the National Wheelchair Basketball Association. Some of these programs also are associated with international competition. These unisport organizations provide excellent opportunities for athletes with disabilities, and several are discussed in other parts of this book.

In the past few years, much of the impetus for sports for athletes with disabilities has been provided by out-of-school sport organizations. Although developing at a slower rate, other opportunities have begun to surface throughout the United States in connection with public school programs. An important milestone came on November 11, 1992, when Minnesota became the first state to welcome athletes with disabilities into its state high school association. This made Minnesota the first in the nation to sanction interschool sports for junior and senior high school students with disabilities. Prior to this time (since 1981) athletics for students with disabilities in Minnesota were established and conducted by the Minnesota Association for Adapted Athletes. MAAA welcomed the development of incorporation into the Minnesota High School League. This program undoubtedly serves as a model for the rest of the country.

New York State offers regional and statewide competition for individuals with disabilities (other than mental retardation) in connection with its State Parks Games for the Physically Challenged. These games, conducted with government financing, serve as an alternative to New York's Empire

Figure 1.6 Three important periodicals in physical education and sport.

State Games designed for able-bodied athletes. A few other states now provide statewide competition for athletes with disabilities.

PERIODICALS

The increased knowledge base and greater attention to adapted physical education and sport in recent years has been accompanied by the founding and development of several periodicals devoted to the subject. Among the most relevant of these are the *Adapted Physical Activity Quarterly, Palaestra, and Sports 'N Spokes* (see Figure 1.6). Through his former role as editor of *Adapted Physical Activity Quarterly*, Dr. Geoffrey G. Broadhead has contributed significantly to the body of knowledge. The current editor is Greg Reid, McGill University, in Montreal (see Figure 1.7). Other periodicals that publish directly relevant information from time to time include *Journal of Physical Education, Recreation and Dance, Research Quarterly for Exercise and Sport, Journal of Visual Impairment and Blindness, Journal of Learning Disabilities, American Annals of the Deaf, Teaching Exceptional Children,*

Figure 1.7 Greg Reid from McGill University in Canada has contributed substantially to the body of knowledge in adapted physical education and sport as editor of the *Adapted Physical Activity Quarterly*. Photo by Peter Cashin.

American Journal of Mental Deficiency, Journal of Special Education, Therapeutic Recreation Journal, Journal of the Association for the Severely Handicapped, Education and Training of the Mentally Retarded, and *Clinical Kinesiology.*

ORGANIZATIONS

The American Alliance for Health, Physical Education, Recreation and Dance (AAHPERD) is an important national organization which makes significant contributions to programs for special populations. AAHPERD (called AAHPER before the dance discipline was added) has many members whose primary professional concern lies in adapted physical education and sport. AAHPER established a definition of adapted physical education in 1952. Over the years, its many publications, conferences, and conventions have given much attention to adapted physical education—not only on the national level, but within the organization's state, district, and local affiliates. Its professional conferences and conventions are among the best sources of information on adapted physical education and sport. At the national level, AAHPERD continues to advocate physical education and fitness for persons with disabilities. It has also been a leader in defining competencies required for quality professional preparation in adapted physical education. In the past few years AAHPERD has reorganized to better serve persons with disabilities.

An organization within AAHPERD, the Adapted Physical Activity Council, is now directly associated with adapted physical education. It is expected that this council, established in 1985, will continue to provide key professional services and leadership.

The National Consortium for Physical Education and Recreation for Individuals with Disabilities (NCPERID, or the Consortium) was established to promote, stimulate, and encourage professional preparation and research. It was started informally in the late 1960s by a small group of college and university directors of federally funded professional preparation and/or research projects seeking to share information. Its members have extensive backgrounds and interest in adapted physical education and/or therapeutic recreation. They have provided leadership and input on national issues and concerns including the development of IDEA and its rules and regulations, federal funding for professional preparation, research, demonstration projects and other special projects, and the monitoring of

legislation. The Consortium holds an annual meeting and publishes a newsletter.

The International Federation for Adapted Physical Activity (IFAPA), which originated in Quebec, has expanded to a worldwide organization with an international charter. Its primary service has been to sponsor a biennial international adapted physical activity symposium, held in Quebec (1977), Brussels (1979), New Orleans (1981), London (1983), Toronto (1985), Brisbane (1987), Berlin (1989), Miami (1991), Yokohama (1993), and Oslo (1995). Symposia are also conducted in years alternating with the IFAPA Symposium in regions throughout the world organized by IFAPA. The organization primarily solicits memberships from allied health therapists, therapeutic recreators, and adapted physical educators. With its international dimensions, IFAPA can disseminate valuable knowledge throughout the world. Gudrun Doll-Tepper is heavily involved in the advancement of IFAPA and the development of adapted physical activity in Europe (see Figure 1.8).

The Office of Special Education and Rehabilitation Service, within the Department of Education, is responsible for monitoring educational services for individuals with disabilities and for providing grants to colleges and universities to fund professional preparation, research, and other special projects.

Figure 1.8 Gudrun Doll-Tepper. Dr. Doll-Tepper, Berlin, Germany, is one of the significant persons involved in beginning and developing the International Federation for Adapted Physical Activity.
© Frank Donati Photographie. Used by permission.

A private organization which has made a monumental contribution to both adapted physical education and sport is Special Olympics, Inc., founded by Eunice Kennedy Shriver. Although its leadership in providing sport opportunities for persons with mental disabilities is well known, this organization has provided much more to adapted physical education and sport. Specifically, it has played a key role in the attention to physical education in federal legislation and the provision of federal funding for professional preparation, research, and other projects in federal legislation through its advocacy activities. The organization has provided a worldwide model for the provision of sport opportunities; its work is acknowledged in several sections of this book.

SUMMARY

Gradually there has evolved an awareness that there are individuals with unique needs related to physical education and sport, needs that require special provisions or adaptations for fulfillment. This chapter has introduced adapted physical education and sport and highlighted factors that have affected their development.

BIBLIOGRAPHY

Amateur Sports Act of 1978, 36 U.S.C. 371 (1978).

Auxter, D., Pyfer, J., & Huettig, C. (1993). *Principles and methods of adapted physical education and recreation* (7th ed.). St. Louis: Mosby.

Buell, C.E. (1983). *Physical education for blind children* (2nd ed.). Springfield, IL: Charles C Thomas.

Brown v. Board of Education of Topeka, Kansas 347 U.S. 483 (1954).

Committee on Adapted Physical Education. (1952). Guiding principles for adapted physical education. *Journal of Health, Physical Education and Recreation*, **23**, 15.

Department of Health, Education, & Welfare (1977a). Education of handicapped children. *Federal Register*, **42**(163), 42434–42516.

Department of Health, Education, & Welfare (1977b). Nondiscrimination on basis of handicap. *Federal Register*, **42**(86), 22676–22702.

Education for the Handicapped Act Amendments of 1986, 20 U.S.C. 1400 (1986)

Gannon, J.R. (1981). *Deaf heritage: A narrative history of deaf America*. Silver Spring, MD: National Association for the Deaf.

Individuals with Disabilities Education Act of 1990, 20 U.S.C. 1400 (1990)

Individuals with Disabilities Education Act Amendments of 1991 20 U.S.C. 1400 (1991) Department of Education (1991)

Mills v. Board of Education of the District of Columbia, 348 F. Supp. 966 (1972).

Pennsylvania Association for Retarded Children v. Commonwealth of Pennsylvania, U.S. District Court, 343 F. Supp. 279 (1972).

Sherrill, C. (1993). *Adapted physical activity, recreation and sport: Crossdisciplinary and lifespan*. (4th ed.). Madison, WI: Brown & Benchmark.

Winnick, J.P., Auxter, D., Jansma, P., Sculli, J., Stein, J., & Weiss, R.A. (1980). Implications of Section 504 of the Rehabilitation Act as related to physical education instructional, personnel preparation, intramural, and interscholastic/intercollegiate sport programs. *Practical Pointers*, **3**(11): 1–20.

RESOURCES

Block, M.E. (1995). Americans with disabilities act: Its impact on youth sports. *Journal of Education, Recreation and Game*, **66**(1), 28-32. This article summarizes major parts of the Act and answers questions on how it affects youth sports.

Buell, C.E. (1983). *Physical Education for Blind Children* (2nd ed.). Springfield, IL: Charles C Thomas. This book is an excellent resource on the topic of physical education for blind children to the 1980s.

Minnesota Association for Adapted Athletics. P.O. Box 357, Golden Valley, MN 54427-0357. This organization provides information about the Minnesota Association for Adapted Athletics. Information and consultation can also be received from George Hanson, Physical Education Specialist, Minnesota Department of Education, St. Paul, MN 55101.

Winnick, J.P., Auxter, D., Jansma, P., Sculli, J., Stein, J., and Weiss, R.A. (1980). Implications of Section 504 of the Rehabilitation Act as related to physical education instructional, personnel preparation, intramural, and interscholastic/intercollegiate sport programs. In J.P. Winnick & F.X. Short, *Special athletic opportunities for individuals with handicapping conditions* (pp. 1–17). Brockport, NY: SUNY College at Brockport. (ERIC ED 210 897). This resource provides a full position paper related to Section 504 of the Rehabilitation Act of 1973.

CHAPTER 2

Program Organization and Management

Joseph P. Winnick

Jimmy, an elementary student with cerebral palsy, definitely could benefit from an individualized program to meet his physical education needs. Unfortunately for Jimmy, there is a great deal of confusion at his school. Is he eligible for adapted physical education? In what setting should his program be implemented? How much time should he receive in physical education? Should he receive physical therapy? In his school, confusion occurs whenever a student with a unique need enrolls. Should this school have a plan to enhance the educational process for such students? The answer is yes.

This chapter describes developing such a plan. For effective organization and management, schools are advised to write detailed guidelines for their adapted physical education and sport programs. The guidelines can serve as an operating code that reflects laws, regulations, policies, procedures, and practices.

CURRICULAR AND PROGRAMMATIC DIRECTION

One necessary step in developing a school's adapted physical education program is to clearly identify programmatic and curricular direction. Because there is no universal model, each school or educational program must establish or adopt its own. A framework may include a philosophical statement, a curricular aim, program goals, and content goals. The skeletal curricular framework in Figure 2.1 can serve as a reference for school

programs and as an organizational model for this book. This framework assumes that the adapted program is part of the total physical education and sport program and that adapted physical education contributes to the same curricular aim and program goals. In essence, the program strives to develop people to their maximum, serving the needs of both the individual and society. This is accomplished by maximizing the integrated cognitive, psychomotor, and affective development of each person. The aim of the curriculum occurs through development in the psychomotor, affective, and cognitive domains. Program goals are accomplished by development *of* and *through* the psychomotor domain. In Figure 2.1, education *of* the psychomotor domain is represented by solid lines connecting content and program goals. Development *through* the psychomotor domain is represented by dotted lines among cognitive, affective, and psychomotor developmental areas.

The general content areas related to psychomotor development can be grouped in many ways. Figure 2.1 shows four general areas: physical fitness, motor development and skill, posture and body mechanics, and community and sport-related activities. Each of these content areas includes specific sport skills or developmental areas. For example, the larger content area of motor development includes walking as a developmental area. Age-appropriate neighborhood skills like those shown in Figure 2.2 can be included in one or more of the content areas.

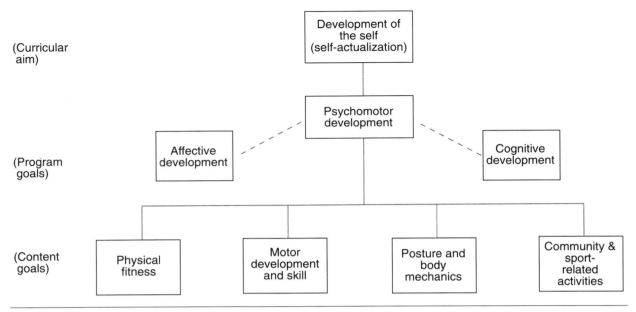

Figure 2.1 Aims and goals for an adapted physical education program.

The psychomotor content goals shown in Figure 2.1, as well as goals in affective and cognitive areas, may serve as annual goals for individualized programs, whereas specific skills and developmental areas associated with these goals may be used to represent short-term objectives. For example, an annual goal for a student might be to improve physical fitness; the corresponding specific short-term objective might be to improve flexibility by obtaining a score of 25 centimeters on a sit-and-reach test. Objectives can be expressed on several levels to reflect the specificity desired by a teacher. The emphasis given to the three developmental domains and their objectives and goals in individualized programs should be based upon students' needs as well as the unique contributions of a curricular area in the school curriculum.

ADMINISTRATIVE PROCEDURES AND PROGRAM IMPLEMENTATION

School administrators who create and implement sound adapted physical education programs must ensure that the resources at their disposal adequately meet the needs of the pupils they serve. First they must identify pupils for their adapted physical education programs, then they must place them in an appropriate setting. Mandated time requirements and challenging activities should be offered to all students with unique needs. Administrators need to be sure that the adapted programs fit into the students' and the school's schedules, that the facilities are up to the task of housing adapted programs (or they must seek additional facilities), and that the adapted physical education program is appropriately funded. The next few pages will address these areas in more detail.

Identifying Pupils for Adapted Physical Education

In identifying students for adapted physical education, it is important at the outset to determine who is qualified. In some instances, the decision is obvious and an elaborate system of identification is not necessary. In other instances, students will have unique needs that are not readily apparent.

Essentially, adapted physical education is for students with unique needs who require a specially designed program exceeding 30 consecutive calendar days. In selecting candidates for such a program, procedures, criteria, and standards for determining unique needs are important (they are discussed in chapters 3 and 4). Placement in the lowest tenth percentile on a physical fitness test is an example of one criterion and standard for establishing unique need.

Searching for adapted physical education students involves one or more important activities associated with *child find*. These include screening

a

b

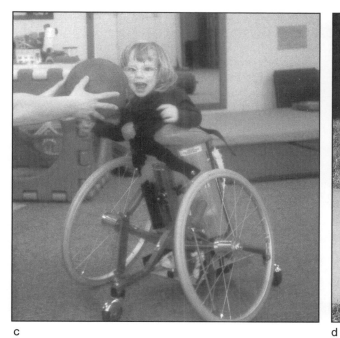

c

d

Figure 2.2 Age-appropriate neighborhood skills, an important part of physical education: a) pushing a prewheel-chair mobility device, (b) batting a softball, (c) catching a ball, (d) riding a tricycle.

- all new school entrants
- pupils with disabilities
- *all* pupils annually
- referrals
- pupils requesting exemption from physical education

An important child-find activity is the screening of all new entrants to the school. For transfer students, records should be checked to determine whether unique needs in physical education have been identified. In the absence of such information, the school, as part of its procedures, may decide to administer a screening test if a unique physical education need is suspected.

A second child-find source is a list of enrolled students who have been identified as having a disability in accordance with IDEA. Every student who has been so identified and whose disability is frequently associated with unique physical education needs should be routinely screened. Many children with disabilities have participated in preschool programs, and records from these programs may indicate those children with unique physical education needs. In some school districts, all students identified as disabled must undergo a screening test to determine if a unique physical education need exists. In other districts, only pupils who are mentally retarded or have orthopedic, visual, learning, or other health impairments are routinely tested. For example, a speech-impaired student classified as disabled by a school district would not be routinely tested unless a unique need in physical education were suspected.

A third source is the annual screening of all those enrolled in school. Such screening might involve informal observation as well as a test. Conditions that may be detected through informal screening and may warrant in-depth evaluation include (but are not limited to) disabling conditions, obesity, clumsiness, aversion to physical activity, and postural deviations.

Many students are referred to adapted physical education. School guidelines should permit referrals from parents or guardians; professional staff members in the school district; physicians; judicial officers; representatives of public agencies with responsibility for the student's welfare, health, or education; or the student if at least 18 years of age or an emancipated minor. Referrals for adapted physical education should be received by one specifically designated person in each school.

Medical excuses or requests for exemption from physical education are a common source of adapted physical education referrals. When an excuse or request is made, immediate discussion with the family physician may be necessary to help determine the needed duration of the adaptation. For a period shorter than 30 consecutive days, required adjustments can be determined by the regular physical education teacher following established local policies and procedures. If the period is longer than 30 consecutive days, the procedure for identifying pupils in adapting physical education should be followed.

Alternative Instructional Placements in Physical Education

Individuals who are referred or are otherwise identified as possibly requiring a specially designed program should undergo thorough assessment to determine whether a unique need exists. Chapters 3 and 4 deal with the procedures for assessment.

Once it is established that students have unique physical education needs, they must be placed in appropriate instructional settings. To the extent possible, the most normal/integrated setting should be provided. Typical (although not all-inclusive) options on a continuum of instructional arrangements appear in Figure 2.3. The number of options available is less important than the concept that students will be educated in the environment most conducive to their advancement. The continuum clearly depicts more possibilities than regular or segregated adapted physical education. Although these two placements may be appropriate for some students with unique needs, they are not sufficient to meet the needs of all members of this population.

The three levels at the base of the continuum include placement in a regular class. It is within these levels that forms or degrees of mainstreaming or inclusion take place. Level 1 placement is for students without unique needs or those whose short-term needs are met in the regular physical education program. This placement is also appropriate for individuals with long-term needs that can be met in the regular physical education setting.

Level 2 is for students whose unique needs can be met in a regular class placement with support service assistance. For example, some students may function well in a regular class if consultation is available to teachers and parents. In another instance, regular class placement may be warranted if a paraprofessional or an adapted physical education teacher can work with the individual with unique needs.

Level 3 is a regular class placement with supplementary and/or resource room assistance, as appropriate. Supplementary services can be

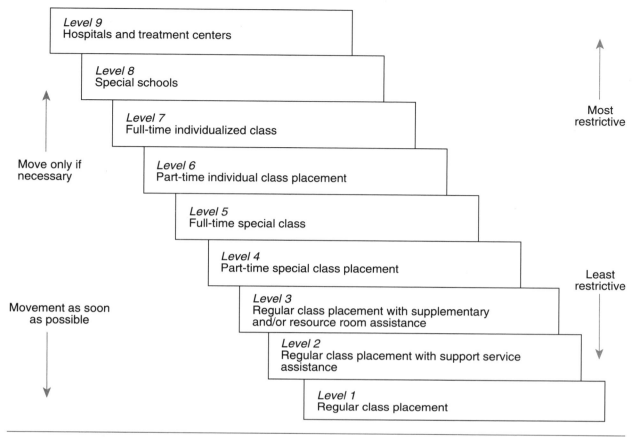

Figure 2.3 Continuum of alternative instructional placements in physical education.

provided each day or several times weekly, as a part of or in addition to the time scheduled for physical education. Where indicated, the student may spend a portion of physical education time in a resource room.

Students who require part-time special class placement represent Level 4. Their needs might be met at times in a regular class and at times in a special physical education class. To a great extent, the choice of setting would be determined by the nature of the class activity.

Level 5—full-time placement in a special class—is appropriate for those whose unique needs may not be met in the regular physical education setting. Levels 6 and 7 are appropriate when part- or full-time individualized instruction is necessary because the student's needs cannot be appropriately met in other settings.

Levels 8 and 9 reflect instructional placements in which needs must be met outside the regular school. In level 8, instruction is given in special schools; in level 9, instruction may be given in hospitals, treatment centers, and even at the student's home. Students in levels 8 and 9 may be

placed outside the school district. In such cases, it is important to remember that the local school system is still responsible for ensuring that appropriate education is provided.

Many schools are incorporating "inclusion" in their physical education programs. Physical educators with minimal training in adapted physical education are teaching or sharing responsibility for teaching students with diverse abilities (Craft, 1994). The January 1994 issue of the *Journal of Physical Education, Recreation & Dance* presents a feature on inclusion that is designed to provide ideas and strategies for teaching all children in regular physical education. In addition, several chapters in this text provide helpful suggestions.

Class size is another variable that must be considered in placement. Special classes should not exceed 12 students; this number should be reduced to six homogeneous students when extraordinary needs are exhibited. In certain instances, individualized instruction may be warranted. Chronological age affects placement as well. *Age differences within a class should never exceed three years unless students are 16 or older.* In any case, school officials should know and comply with their state laws and regulations governing size and composition.

Scheduling

Scheduling becomes an important matter as placement decisions are made. There are many approaches to scheduling that can accommodate various instructional arrangements. One effective method is to schedule supplementary and resource services and adapted physical education classes at the same time as regular physical education. A large school might have four physical education teachers assigned to four regular classes during a single period with a fifth teacher assigned to adapted physical education. Other instructional arrangements might provide extra class time on alternative days from regular physical education classes, alternate periods, or opportunities during elective periods. In one scheduling technique used in elementary schools, a youngster placed in a special academic class joins an appropriate regular physical education class. This arrangement meets the student's need to be integrated in physical education while receiving special support in academic areas. Too often, students who could have been integrated in a regular physical education class are placed in a special class primarily on the basis of academic or other performance unrelated to physical education. Schools in which students are permitted to elect courses or units often find scheduling problems reduced because students may choose activities in which they can participate with little or no adjustment and that fit their schedule.

Time Requirements

In a program of adapted physical education, it is important to clearly specify time requirements for the instructional phase. The frequency and duration of the required instructional program should at least equal those of regular physical education classes. If state time requirements for regular physical education instruction are specified for various grade levels and if adapted physical education students are placed in ungraded programs, the school's guidelines should express equivalent time requirements using chronological age as the common reference point. In accordance with federal legislation, a local school district plan should state that physical education, specially designed, must be made available to all students ages 3 to 21 identified as having a disability.

Physical education should be required of all students and should be adapted to meet unique needs. In cases of temporary disability, it is important to ascertain how long the student will require an adapted physical education program and to set a standard to distinguish temporary and long-term conditions. For this book, a short-term condition ends within 29 consecutive calendar days and can be accommodated by the regular classroom teacher. To the extent possible and reasonable, participation in physical activity rather than alternative, sedentary experiences should be required. For evaluation purposes, schools should set standards concerning the proportion of their students who participate in physical education but not physical activity. When many students meet physical education requirements through inactivity, it is time to reassess the local program.

School districts also need to clearly deal with the issue of permitting participation in athletic activities as a substitute for physical education. Although coordination of instruction and sport participation (regular or adapted) is necessary, substitution should not be made unless it is approved in the student's IEP and the practice fits in with the school district's overall physical education plan. Ordinarily, substitution should not be permitted.

School districts must also clarify and coordinate instructional time requirements with related services. For instance, time spent in physical therapy must not supplant time in the physical education program. If appropriate guidelines are developed, few, if any, students should be exempt. Physical education will mean physical activity and will not be replaced by related services or extracurricular activities.

Sports

An adapted physical education plan should include general guidelines on sports participation and its relationship to the physical education program. In view of the detail involved in implementing a comprehensive extraclass sport program, a specific operating code should also be developed for local use. It is recommended that the extraclass sport program be established on the assumption that the sport program and the adapted physical education program are interrelated and interdependent. The extraclass program should build upon the basic instructional program in adapted physical education and should be educational in nature.

Guidelines for Sport Participation

A sport program should emphasize the well-being of the participants in the context of games and sports. It is also important to ensure participation to the extent possible and reasonable. Health examinations before participation in strenuous activities and periodically throughout the season, if necessary, will also enhance safe participation. Athletes with disabilities should receive, at minimum, the same medical safeguards as other athletes.

For an interscholastic program, it is important to have a written statement of the principal educational goals as agreed to by the board of education, the administration, and any other relevant individuals or groups. The statement should reflect a concern with student welfare, an interest in the educational aspects of athletic competition, and a commitment to the development of skills that will yield health and leisure benefits during as well as after school years.

Integration Continuum

In the past few years, increasing attention has been given to providing sport opportunities for individuals with disabilities. In response to the intent of Section 504 of the Rehabilitation Act of 1973, educational and extracurricular opportunities must be provided in the least restrictive (most normal/integrated) setting possible, on the basis of a continuum of setting ranging from the most restrictive (segregated) to the least restrictive (integrated). Figure 2.4 presents a framework for a sport continuum to help enhance integration to the maximum extent possible, help guide decisions on sport participation, and help stimulate the provision of innovative opportunities. The continuum and the related material in this section were published originally by Winnick (1987).

The continuum, which relates to the provision of programs in the least restrictive environment, encompasses opportunities in intramural, extramural, and interschool programs and out-of-school sport programs. (For purposes of this book, all are encompassed under the designation of sport.)

Levels 1 and 2 of the continuum are essentially regular sport settings, distinguished only by a need for accommodation. In regular sport, the setting is integrated. Individuals with disabilities should be given equal opportunities to qualify for participation at these levels. An example at level 1 participation would be an athlete with mental retardation running the dash for a regular high school track team. According to the framework, if the individual qualified for regular sport competition, Special

Olympics competition would not be appropriate because competition occurs in a more segregated (restrictive) setting. Regular participation in a particular sport should not be supplemented or supplanted by more restrictive participation in the same sport.

In accordance with Section 504, schools and agencies should provide modified or special activities only if (a) they operate programs and activities in the most normal and appropriate setting, (b) qualified students with disabilities are not denied opportunity to participate in programs and activities that are not separate and different, (c) qualified students with disabilities are able to participate in one or more regular programs and activities, and (d) students with disabilities are appropriately placed in full-time special facilities (Department of Health, Education, and Welfare, 1977; Winnick et al., 1980).

A bowler who is blind competing in regular sport competition with only the accommodation of a guide rail exemplifies level 2. In making accommodations at level 2, Section 504 rules and regulations require that any accommodation provided be reasonable and allow individuals with disabilities equal opportunity to gain the same benefits or results as other participants in a particular activity. At the same time, accommodations should not confer an unfair advantage on an individual with a disability. In the case of the bowler who is blind, the guide rail serves as a substitute for vision for the purpose of orientation to the target. Because the activity remains essentially unchanged for all participants and no undue advantage is given, this accommodation constitutes regular sport participation.

Level 3 includes both regular and adapted sport conducted in settings that are partly or fully integrated. Those with a disability may compete against or coact with all participants in a contest including both disabled and nondisabled competitors. For instance, an athlete participating in a wheelchair (adapted sport) may compete against all runners in a marathon, including athletes with and without disabilities; nondisabled athletes run on foot (regular sport). In another level 3 example, a nondisabled athlete and an athlete with a disability may cooperate as doubles partners in wheelchair tennis. The nondisabled partner is permitted one bounce before returning the volley (regular sport), whereas the athlete with a disability is permitted two bounces (adapted sport).

Level 3 also includes situations in which an athlete participates part-time in regular sport and part-time in adapted sport. For example, a person

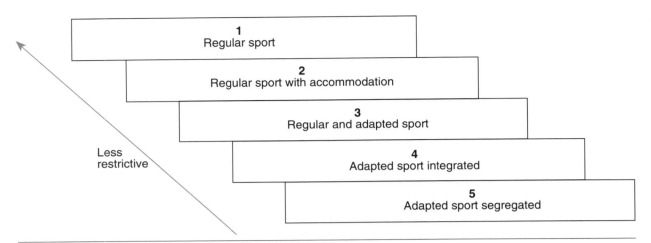

Figure 2.4 Sport integration continuum.
From ''An Integration Continuum for Sport Participation'' by J.P. Winnick, 1987, *Adapted Physical Activity Quarterly*, **4**, p. 158. Copyright 1987 by Human Kinetics. Reprinted by permission.

who is blind may participate in regular competition for weightlifting, but in adapted sport competition for goal ball. Level 3 activities show either (a) athletes with and without disabilities integrated and participating in regular sport and adapted sport, respectively, or (b) athletes with disabilities participating part-time in adapted sport and part-time in regular sport.

At level 4 athletes both with and without disabilities participate in a modified version of the sport. At this level, competition or coaction must include both an individual with a disability and a nondisabled participant. One example is a game of tennis in which athletes with and without disabilities use wheelchairs in their competition against opponents who are likewise in wheelchairs.

At level 5, athletes with disabilities participate in adapted sport in a totally segregated setting; for example, athletes with mental retardation competing against each other in the Special Olympics program or two teams of youngsters who are blind competing in goal ball.

The conceptual framework for the sport continuum is primarily based on degree of integration (with cooperator/coactor and/or competitor) and sport type (regular, adapted). The continuum stresses association or interaction between athletes with and without disabilities, the key ingredient in *integration*. To some extent, the continuum reflects severity of disability and ability to compete, but at other times it appears less responsive to this concern. This is because *nature* of disability and *ability* to perform, as related to a specific sport, are greater factors than *severity* of condition.

Facilities

The facilities available to conduct programs in adapted physical education and sport may significantly affect program quality. A school's overall athletic facilities should be operated in a way that makes them readily accessible to individuals with disabilities. In fact, Section 504 rules and regulations prohibit exclusion of individuals with disabilities from federally assisted programs because of architectural, program, or other environmental barriers. Provision of access may dictate structural changes in existing facilities. All new facilities should be constructed to ensure accessibility and usability.

In planning facilities related to adapted physical education and sport, attention must be given to indoor and outdoor facilities, including teaching stations, lockers, and restrooms (see examples in Figure 2.5 and 2.6). Indoor facilities should have adequate activity space that is clear of hazards or impediments and is otherwise safe. The environment must have proper lighting, acoustics, and ventilation. Ceiling clearance should permit appropriate play. Floors should have a finish that enables ambulation in a variety of ways for individuals with disabilities. When necessary, protective padding should be placed on walls. Space should be allotted for wheelchairs to pass and turn.

Like indoor areas, outdoor areas should be accessible and properly surfaced. Facilities should be available and marked for various activities including special sports. Walkways leading to and from outdoor facilities should be smooth, firm, and free of cracks and at least 48 inches wide. Doorways leading to the facilities should have at least a

36-inch clearance and be light enough to be opened without undue effort; if possible, they should be automatically activated. Water fountains with both hand and foot controls should be located conveniently for use by persons with disabilities. Colorful signs and factual orientation maps of facilities should be posted to assist individuals with visual disabilities.

Participants in adapted physical education and athletics need adequate space for dressing, showering, and drying. Space must be sufficient for peak periods. The design of the locker rooms should facilitate ambulation and the maintenance of safe and clean conditions; adequate ventilation, lighting, and heating are necessary. The shower room should be readily accessible and should provide a sufficient number of shower heads; the facilities should be equipped with grab rails. Locker rooms should include adequate benches, mirrors, and toilets. Person with disabilities frequently prefer horizontal lockers and locks that are easy to manipulate. Planning must ensure that lockers are not obstructed by benches and other obstacles. All facilities should, of course, be in operable condition. Well-designed restrooms should have toilets at floor level, adequate space for manipulation of wheelchairs, easily activated foot and/or hand flush mechanisms, grab rails, and toilet and urinal levels to meet the needs of the entire school population.

Swimming pools are among the most important facilities. Pool design must provide for safe and quick entry and exit (see Figure 2.7). Water depth

Figure 2.6 Accessible sinks and a tilted mirror.
Photo courtesy of New York State School for the Blind, Robert Seibold, superintendent and coordinator. Printed with permission.

and temperature should be adjustable to meet learning, recreational, therapeutic, and competitive needs. Careful coordination of pool use is usually necessary to accommodate varying needs. Dressing, showering, and toilet facilities must be close by, with easy access to the pool.

Students in adapted physical education and sport programs must have equal opportunity to use normal/integrated facilities. Too often, physical education for individuals with disabilities is conducted in boiler rooms or hallways. Small class size should not be used as a reason to exclude persons with disabilities from equitable use of facilities; such a practice is discriminating and demeaning to both pupils and school personnel.

Budget

If the education is equitable, it will cost more to educate students with disabilities than students without disabilities. To supplement local and state funds, the federal government, through a variety of programs, provides money for the education of people with unique needs. Funds associated with IDEA are specifically earmarked. To ensure receipt of federal funds for physical education, planners must be sure that it is included in IEPs. This inclusion is more likely to occur if physical education personnel are involved in IEP development.

Figure 2.5 An accessible drinking fountain.
Photograph courtesy of New York State School for the Blind, Robert Seibold, superintendent and coordinator. Printed with permission.

Figure 2.7 Pool with easy access and an adjustable bottom.
Photo courtesy of New York State School for the Blind, Robert Seibold, superintendent and coordinator. Printed with permission.

Funds associated with IDEA are available to help provide excess costs of special education (i.e., costs that exceed student expenditure in regular education). These funds "flow" through state education departments (which are permitted to keep a certain percentage) and on to local education agencies. The flow-through money can be used to help cover excess costs already met by states. Because adapted physical education deals with students who are not disabled as well as those who are, it is advantageous for schools to fund teachers in physical education, whether regular or adapted, from the same local funding source rather than to rely on federal money. This is justifiable, since states are responsible for the education of all their students.

In addition to meeting needs identified in IEPs, funding must support the preparation of teachers to provide quality services in adapted physical education and sport. For example, funds are needed for in-service education, workshops, clinics, local meetings, professional conferences and conventions, program visitations, and so on. Schools also need funds to maintain up-to-date libraries and other reference materials.

Interscholastic teams made up of students with disabilities must receive equitable equipment, supplies, travel expenses, officials, and so on. While the funding level for a local community is not externally dictated, available funds cannot be used in a discriminatory fashion (e.g., available to males but not females, or available to students without disabilities but not to students with disabilities).

HUMAN RESOURCES

A quality program in adapted physical education and sport depends to a great extent on the availability of quality human resources and the ability of involved personnel to perform effectively as members of a group. People are needed to coordinate and administer services, fulfill technical and advocacy functions, and provide instruction. Many of these functions are carried out in important committees. To provide high-quality services for adapted physical education and sport, the teacher must work with various school and IEP committees. In doing so, it is helpful to understand roles and responsibilities and to realize that the concern for students with unique needs is shared by many. This section identifies key personnel and discusses their primary roles and responsibilities. Many perform their responsibilities by serving on committees identified in chapter 3.

Director of Physical Education and Athletics

Although not a universal practice, it is desirable for all aspects of physical education and sport programs to be under the direction of an administrator certified in physical education. Such centralization enhances coordination and efficiency in regard to personnel, facilities and equipment, budgeting, professional development, and curriculum. The director of physical education and athletics should oversee all aspects of the program, including the work of the coordinator of adapted physical education if that position exists.

Because adapted physical education and sport are often in the developmental stage and not a well-advocated part of the total program, the physical education director needs to demonstrate genuine concern and commitment to this part of the program. A positive attitude will serve as a model for others to emulate. With the help of other administrative personnel, the director can help the program in adapted physical education and sport by ensuring adequate funding, employing qualified teachers, and providing support services. The director must also be knowledgeable about adapted physical education and sport to work effectively with individuals and groups outside the department. The director must work with other directors, coordinators, building principals, superintendents, and school boards and must form positive professional relationships with medical personnel, including physicians, nurses, and therapists. Other important relationships are those with parents, teachers, students with disabilities, and advocacy groups. For this reason, it is important that the director of physical education and sport be kept informed about all students who are identified as having unique needs.

Adapted Physical Education and Sport Coordinator

To provide a quality comprehensive school program in adapted physical education and sport, schools are advised to name a coordinator. In a small school, this might be a part-time position; in larger schools, a full-time adapted physical education coordinator may be needed. Although most states do not require a special endorsement, credential, or certification in adapted physical education, it is best to select an individual who has considerable professional experience. If possible, the coordinator should have completed a recognized specialization or concentration in adapted physical education and, where applicable, should meet the state competency requirements for certification. A person demonstrating these competencies is likely to be knowledgeable and genuinely interested in serving in that particular role. If a school cannot employ a person with preparation

in adapted physical education, the coordinator's duties should be entrusted to someone who demonstrates genuine interest.

The particular role and functions of the coordinator will depend upon the size of the school, the number and types of students with disabilities within the school population, and the number and types of students in adapted physical education and sport. Generally, however, the coordinator will need to assume a leadership role in various functions associated with adapted physical education and sport. The specific functions often differ more in degree than in kind with those performed by regular physical educators. Table 2.1 identifies typical functions associated with adapted education and sport and indicates who is responsible for those functions. Functions may overlap or be shared; specific lines of demarcation should be drawn to suit local conditions.

Some schools may employ adapted physical education teachers who are not needed to assume the position of adapted physical education and sport coordinator. Although these teachers will certainly provide support function to the coordinator, they are primarily involved in carrying out instructional programs in a variety of settings. In addition, they may help to implement adapted sport programs, for example, by developing and implementing sport days, arranging competition in out-of-school programs, preparing participants, and coaching teams. Most adapted physical education teachers will be very much involved in working with IEP committees.

Regular Physical Educator

Although adapted physical educators may be employed by a school, the regular physical educator plays an extremely important role in implementing quality programs in adapted physical education and sport. Table 2.1 presents several functions that are shared by or are the primary responsibility of regular physical educators. For example, they play an important role in screening. They may also be called on to implement instructional programs for students with short-term needs, to implement adapted physical education programs in integrated environments, and to help implement sport programs. One of the most important tasks is referral. In the area of management/leadership, the regular physical educator will generally play a secondary role. With the present-day trend of including more and more students with disabilities (with or without unique needs) in regular classes,

Table 2.1 Primary Responsibility for Functions Relevant to Adapted Physical Education and Sport

Functions	Responsibility	
	Regular physical educator	Adapted physical educator/coordinator
Measurement, assessment, evaluation		
• Student screening	X	X
• In-depth testing		X
• Student assessment and evaluation		X
• APE/S program evaluation		X
Teaching/coaching		
• Implement instructional programs for students with short-term unique needs	X	
• Implement instructional program to meet long-term unique needs in integrated environments	X	X
• Implement instructional program to meet long-term unique needs in segregated environments		X
• Implement instructional and sport programs with guidance of adapted physical educator	X	
• Implement adapted sport program		X
Management/leadership		
• Consultation		X
• In-service education		X
• Advocacy/interpretation		X
• Recruitment of aides/volunteers		X
• Chair adapted physical education committee		X
• Liaison with health professionals	X	X
• Referral and placement	X	X
• Organization of adapted sport program		X

it is often the responsibility of regular physical educators to implement such programs.

Nurse

An allied health professional with an important part in the successful development of and implementation of adapted physical education and sport programs is the nurse. The school nurse must be knowledgeable about the adapted physical education and sport program and, ideally, should serve on its committee on adapted physical education. The nurse can be a valuable resource. She or he can help in interpreting information that is required for IEP or IPEP planning.

If time permits, the school nurse can assist the physical education staff in testing students, particularly in the case of postural screening. The nurse can also provide a valuable service in keeping medical records, communicating with physicians, and helping parents and pupils to understand the importance of exercise and physical activity.

Physicians

Physicians are among the allied health professionals who have an important relationship to the school's adapted physical education and sport program. The physician's role is so important that it is often addressed in federal, state, or local laws, rules, and regulations. In some instances, states look to the school physician for the final decision on participation in athletic opportunities. Also very important, physicians should provide and interpret medical information on which school programs are based. Using this information, the groups responsible plan appropriate programs. The school physician also has an important responsibility for interpreting the adapted physical education and sport program to family physicians and other medical personnel.

In states where physical education is required of all students, physicians must know and support laws and regulations. Also, they must be confident that if a student is unable to participate without restriction in a regular class, adaptation will be made. Physicians should be aware that quality physical education and adapted physical education have changed considerably since many of them attended school, and they need to understand the nature of these changes. In other words, they need to be aware of their role and responsibility in well-established modern programs.

One of a physician's important functions is to administer periodic physical examinations. Examination results are used as a basis for individualized pupil evaluation, program planning, placement, and determination of eligibility and qualification for athletic participation. It is desirable for each student to receive an exam every three years, beginning in the first grade. Examinations should be annual for those assigned to adapted physical education because of medical referrals. School districts that do not provide physical examinations should require adequate examination by the family physician. For athletic participation, annual exams should be administered.

Coaches

Adapted sport programs should be operated under the direction of qualified school personnel. Where an adapted program includes interschool athletic teams, standards for coaches must be consistent with those for the regular interschool athletic program. Teachers certified in physical education should be permitted to coach any sport including those whose participants have disabilities. Ideally, coaches of teams composed primarily of individuals with unique needs should have additional expertise in adapted physical education.

Coaches must follow acceptable professional practices, including maintaining a positive attitude and insisting upon good sportsmanship, respect, personal control, and willingness to improve professionally through in-service programs, workshops, and clinics.

Related Service Personnel

Under IDEA, **related services** means transportation and such developmental, corrective, and other supportive services that are required to assist children with disabilities to benefit from special education. Related services include speech pathology and audiology; psychological services; physical and occupational therapy; recreation, including therapeutic recreation; social work services; counseling services, including rehabilitation counseling; and medical services for diagnostic or evaluation purposes. Related service providers who often impact on physical education include occupational and physical therapists. According to the rules and regulations for the implementation of IDEA, occupational therapy includes (a) improving, developing, or restoring functions impaired or lost through illness, injury, or deprivation; (b) improving ability to perform tasks for independent functioning when functions are impaired or lost; and (c) preventing, through early intervention, initial or further impairment or loss of functioning. The same rules and regulations define physical therapy as services provided by a qualified physical therapist. These services have traditionally included the provision of physical activities and other physical means for rehabilitation as prescribed by a physician. The rules and regulations specify that recreation includes assessment of leisure function, therapeutic recreation services, recreation programs in schools and community agencies, and leisure education.

Much has been written about the relationship of adapted physical education and the related services of physical and occupational therapy. Often the lines of responsibility between these areas are blurred. What is clear and not controversial is the fact that related services must be provided if a student requires them to benefit from direct services. For example, both physical and occupational therapy must be provided to the extent the student needs them to benefit from physical education or other direct services in the school program. IDEA specifies that physical education must be made available to children with disabilities. Also, states have their own requirements concerning the provision of physical education. Clearly, physical therapy and adapted physical education are not identical, and related services should not supplant physical education or adapted physical education (which are direct services under IDEA).

Several assumptions about the role of physical education may underlie the assignment of responsibility to design programs to improve the physical fitness of students with disabilities. First, it is clearly the physical educator's responsibility to design programs to improve the physical fitness of individuals with disabilities. Thus, the physical educator is involved with the development of strength, endurance, cardiorespiratory endurance, and flexibility (range of motion). His or her responsibility concerns *both* affected and unaffected parts of the body. For example, individuals with cerebral palsy should be helped to maintain and develop their physical fitness. To deal with affected parts, the physical educator should cooperate with medical and/or related service personnel in program planning.

Sometimes improvements in physical development cannot be attained by a physical educator using the usual time allotments, methods, or activities associated with physical education. In such cases, the inclusion of physical or occupational therapy can enhance physical fitness development. Activities included in the physical education programs of youngsters with disabilities should be those which are typically within the scope of physical education. These are the kinds of activities subsumed under the definition of physical education in the rules and regulations of IDEA and included in the scope of physical education as described in Figure 2.1. Although the physical educator involves children in exercise, it is important *not* to limit physical education to an exercise prescription program. Instead, it is important for the physical educator to offer a broad spectrum of physical education activities. A youngster who requires a specific exercise to the extent that it would encompass an entire physical education period should meet this need in an extended physical education program or be provided related services. This approach would permit use of a broad spectrum of activities within the regularly scheduled physical education class. Physical educators should help students appropriately use wheelchairs and supportive devices in physical education activities. They must, therefore, be knowledgeable about wheelchairs and other assistive devices. However, it is not their responsibility to provide functional training in the use of those aids for basic movement or ambulation.

It is vital that physical educators coordinate their programs with physicians and other medical personnel. It is important to establish and follow the procedures in a school district associated with planning programs, as described in chapter 3.

Although much can be written and discussed concerning roles and responsibilities, very often the quality of services provided depends on the interpersonal relationships of service providers. Successful situations are those in which professionals have discussed roles and responsibilities and work hard to deliver supportive services to benefit individuals with unique needs.

PROGRAM EVALUATION

At the beginning of this chapter, the importance of an adapted physical education and sport plan to serve as an operating code was stressed. Once in place, the plan can serve as a basis for program evaluation. The implementation aspects of adapted physical education should be evaluated annually and the total plan evaluated at five-year intervals. Program evaluation should draw upon data collected from a variety of relevant sources. Helpful to evaluation is use of a rating scale or checklist. A rating scale develop by Winnick (1994) is presented in an appendix of this text. This scale may be modified for local use or be used in its entirety. An instrument for evaluation is least threatening if used for self-appraisal. Evaluation provides a point of departure for identifying and discussing strengths and weaknesses and upon which to develop a schedule to remedy weaknesses.

SUMMARY

Well-conducted programs in adapted physical education start with strong curricular and programmatic direction. They are also characterized by sound guidelines for student identification, placement, scheduling, participation, facilities, and budget. They depend on the cooperation of professionals from many disciplines. Schools should write detailed guidelines to help them improve organization and management to provide quality services and evaluate program effectiveness.

BIBLIOGRAPHY

Craft, D.H. (1994). Inclusion: Physical education for all. *Journal of Physical Education, Recreation & Dance,* **65**(1), 22–23.

Department of Health, Education, and Welfare. (1977). Nondiscrimination on basis of handicap. *Federal Register, 42*(86), 22676–22702.

Winnick, J.P., Auxter, D., Jansma, P., Sculli, J., Stein, J., & Weiss, R.A. (1980). Implications of Section 504 of the Rehabilitation Act as related to physical education instructional, personnel preparation, intramural, and interscholastic/intercollegiate sport programs. *Practical Pointers, 3*(11), 1–20.

Winnick, J.P. (1987). An integration continuum for sport participation. *Adapted Physical Activity Quarterly, 4,* 157–161.

RESOURCES

Auxter, D., Pyfer, J., & Huettig, C. (1993). *Principles and methods of adapted physical education and recreation* (7th ed.). St. Louis: Mosby. This book describes and effectively applies community-based programming to adapted physical education and sport. It also includes an excellent chapter on facilities and equipment.

Flynn, R.B. (Ed.) (1985). *Planning facilities for athletics, physical education, and recreation.* Reston, VA: American Alliance for Health, Physical Education, Recreation and Dance. This comprehensive resource for planning facilities includes one chapter on planning facilities usable and accessible for individuals with disabilities and refers to adapted physical education in other chapters.

Seaman, J.A., & DePauw, K.P. (1989). *The new adapted physical education: A developmental approach.* Palo Alto, CA: Mayfield. Describes and applies the developmental approach for programming.

Sherrill, C. (1993). *Adapted physical activity, recreation, and sport: Crossdisciplinary and lifespan* (4th ed.). Madison, WI: Brown & Benchmark. Includes a checklist for evaluating a school district adapted physical education program.

Winnick, J.P. (1994). Rating scale for adapted physical education. This rating scale can be used as one self-assessment instrument on which to base evaluation of a school's adapted physical education program. The survey presents criteria statements reflecting guidelines implicitly suggested in this chapter. It appears in Appendix A.

CHAPTER 3

Individualized Education Programs

Francis X. Short

When President Ford signed Public Law 94-142, the Education for All Handicapped Children Act of 1975, the provision of special education in the United States was significantly changed in a number of ways. One significant change was the provision that every student with a disability should have an individualized education program, or as it is more commonly known, an IEP. More recent legislation, culminating with the Individuals with Disabilities Education Act (IDEA) has reaffirmed the importance of the IEP in developing an appropriate education for students with disabilities. An IEP is a written document that essentially describes the student's current level of educational achievement, identifies goals and objectives for the near future, and lists the educational services to be provided to meet those goals. IDEA requires that IEPs be developed for all disabled students with unique needs between the ages of 3 and 21.

IDEA also has provisions for addressing the developmental needs of infants and toddlers with disabilities. Local agencies may provide early intervention services for infants/toddlers and their families who request them. These services are detailed in an individualized family service plan (IFSP), a document written for all eligible participants. The Individuals with Disabilities Education Act therefore addresses the needs of students (aged 0–21) who are identified as disabled by a particular school district. Occasionally, however, students who are not identified or labeled as disabled under IDEA may have a unique need in physical education. Students recuperating from injuries or accidents, those convalescing from noncommunicable diseases, and those who are overweight or have low skill levels or low levels of physical fitness may fall into this category. Schools, therefore, must have procedures for arranging appropriate physical education experiences for students who are not covered by IDEA but who require an adapted physical education program.

This chapter discusses the development of individualized education programs in physical education. It addresses the requirements for the development of an IEP for students with disabilities aged 3–21 and makes recommendations for the construction of individualized programs for nondisabled students with unique needs in physical education. It also describes requirements for the development of an IFSP for infants and toddlers with disabilities.

THE STUDENT WITH A DISABILITY

The specially designed program for any child who has been identified as disabled by the school district is dictated by the IEP. Local districts may determine and design their own IEP format. Consequently, it is not unusual for neighboring school districts to use different IEP forms.

Components of the IEP

While formats vary, each IEP form must contain six components. Sample physical education information that might be included in an IEP is shown in Figure 3.1.

Student's Name: Grace   **Age:** 15

I.   Present Level of Performance

1.   Makes 4 out of 20 shots from the free throw line in basketball.

2.   Scores 19 points (5th percentile) on the AAHPERD basketball passing test.

3.   Completes the AAHPERD basketball control dribble test in 17.2 s (< 5th percentile).

4.   Runs one mile in 11:52 (FITNESSGRAM standard is 10:30).

5.   Has 38% body fat calculated from triceps and calf skinfolds (FITNESSGRAM standard ranges from 17-32).

6.   Performs 15 curl-ups in 60 s. (FITNESSGRAM standard is 18).

II.   Annual Goals and Short-Term Objectives

1.0   Grace will improve her basketball skills.

1.1   Grace will make 8 out of 20 shots from the free throw line.

1.2   Grace will score 28 points on the AAPHERD basketball passing test.

1.3   Grace will complete the AAHPERD control dribble test in 12.0 s.

2.0   Grace will improve her scores on selected measures of physical fitness.

2.1   Grace will run one mile in 11:00
2.2   Grace will have 32 percent body fat.
2.3   Grace will perform 18 curl-ups.

III.   Statement of Services and Extent of Integration

In addition to her regularly scheduled physical education class, Grace will participate with the Fitness Club three days per week. No special equipment or materials required. Grace's program will be conducted completely (100%) in regular class placements.

IV.   Transition Services

Results of the vocational assessment scheduled for December should be shared with the physical education staff to identify any physical development problems which might be remediated to potentially enhance vocational training.

V.   Schedule of Services

Grace will participate in regular physical education during third period on Mondays and Thursdays. Fitness Club meets after school from 2:30-3:15 Mondays, Wednesdays, and Fridays. This schedule will go into effect on September 15 and end on June 1.

VI.   Criteria, Procedures and Schedule for Evaluation

Criteria for evaluation are specified in the short-term objectives. Progress on objectives will be monitored periodically and final evaluation on all objectives will be conducted during the week of June 4.

Figure 3.1   Sample physical education information for the IEP.

Present Level of Performance

The present level of performance (PLP) component is the cornerstone of the IEP. The information presented in all subsequent components is related to the information set forth here. If the PLP is not adequately and properly determined, chances are the student's specially designed instructional program will not be the most appropriate. PLP statements should be objective, observable, and measurable; they should accurately reflect the child's current educational abilities. Ordinarily the PLP component will consist primarily of test results. These results could come from standardized tests with performance norms or criteria or from less formal teacher-constructed tests. Although both types of results are appropriately included in the IEP, it is recommended that, when possible, the PLP contain at least some standardized test results. Standardized results can help determine a unique need in a particular area and can provide stronger justification for an educational placement.

PLP information should be presented in a way that places the student on a continuum of achievement—that is, the test results shown should discriminate among levels of ability. For this reason, tests on which students attain either minimum (0 out of 10) or maximum (10 out of 10) scores are not helpful in determining PLP. Also, in situating a student on this continuum, the PLP component should note, to the extent possible, what the individual *can* do, not what he or she cannot do. Finally, PLP information should be presented in a way that is immediately interpretable; it should not require additional explanation from the teacher. When standardized test results are included, percentiles, criterion-referenced standards, or other references should be presented as well as the raw scores, and teacher-constructed tests should be adequately described so the conditions can be replicated at a later date. (See chapter 4 for more information on measurement in adapted physical education.)

Annual Goals and Short-Term Objectives

An annual goal is a broad or generic statement designed to give direction to the instructional program. Once the PLP information has been obtained and studied, the teacher should identify one or more content areas to be emphasized in the student's program. Usually an annual goal focuses on the student's area of weakness as identified in the PLP. In fact, this linkage is a key element in writing an annual goal statement. The annual goal must clearly relate to information presented in the PLP component. For instance, if the PLP contains only information on ball handling skills, it would be inappropriate to write an annual goal for swimming, physical fitness, or any other content area unrelated to ball handling skills. The need for emphasis on a particular content area must be documented in the PLP.

While the annual goal is broad or generic, a short-term objective (STO) is narrow and specific. An STO is a statement that describes a skill in terms of *action, condition*, and *criterion*. Action refers to the type of skill to be performed (e.g., *run*). Condition indicates the way the skill is to be performed (e.g., run *50 yards*). Criterion refers to how well the skill is to be performed (e.g., run 50 yards *in 8.5 seconds*). Conditions and criteria used in physical education usually relate to such concepts as "how fast," "how long," "how far," or "how many," although it is also appropriate to describe "how mature." For instance, a 10-year-old student may throw a ball into a wall target 9 out of 10 times from a certain distance. The teacher may be pleased with the accuracy score ("how many"), but if the student does not step with the opposite foot when throwing, the teacher may not be pleased with the quality of the movement pattern ("how mature"). In this case the teacher might write an STO that describes a movement pattern, rather than an accuracy score, to be attained.

Just as an annual goal must relate to PLP information, STOs must relate to an annual goal. If an annual goal stresses the content area of "eye-hand coordination," the STOs should include skills such as throwing, catching, and striking. Furthermore, it is important that the student's baseline (pretest) ability appear in the IEP, usually in the PLP component. For example, a short-term objective might specify that a student will be expected to do 15 sit-ups in 60 seconds at some future date; this statement has little meaning unless it is known how many sit-ups the student can do now. In fact, the easiest way to write an STO is to take a well-written PLP statement, copy the action and condition elements verbatim, and make a reasonable change in the criterion. (The teacher must use professional judgment to determine what constitutes a "reasonable" expectation for improvement.) It should be noted that, although STOs are helpful in identifying activities to be conducted in class, they are not meant to supplant daily, weekly, or monthly lesson plans.

Statement of Services and Extent of Integration

Once the present level of performance is determined and annual goals and short-term instructional objectives are written, decisions must be made regarding the student's educational placement, additional services (if any) to be provided, and the use of special instructional media and materials as necessary. The placement agreed upon should be considered the least restrictive environment for the student.

In addition to appropriate placement, other special education and related services may be prescribed. A special education service is one that makes a direct impact on educational objectives—for example, physical education. Provisions for this service should be specified in this component of the IEP. A related service makes an indirect impact on educational objectives and therefore should be presented only to the extent that it will help the student benefit from a special education service. Examples include physical therapy, therapeutic recreation, occupational therapy, psychological services, and speech, language, and/or hearing therapy.

In some cases special instructional materials may be required for the education of children with disabilities. These materials should also be listed in this IEP component. Modified pieces of equipment such as a beep baseball, an audible goal locator, a snap-handle bowling ball, or a bowling ramp are examples. The IEP must specify the extent to which the student with a disability will be educated with nondisabled students. Often this is expressed as the percentage of time the student is included in a regular educational program.

Transition Services

By the time a student is 16, the IEP must address issues pertaining to when the student leaves the school-based educational program at age 22. This component should include goals and specific actions to help the student make a successful transition from the school to another available option. Many students, for instance, eventually may be enrolled in vocational training programs, some may have the opportunity to go on to college, and others may enter alternative adult service programs (e.g., group homes, sheltered workshops). School personnel attempt to prepare the student for entrance into the most appropriate option when he or she "ages out" of school.

Schedule of Services

The IEP must indicate when all special education and related services will begin and end and how often they will be provided to the student.

Criteria, Procedures, and Schedule for Evaluation

This component is used to specify how and when the student's progress will be evaluated. In most cases progress is determined by testing the objectives written earlier. Evaluation can be scheduled to occur at any time within 12 months from the time the IEP takes effect; the IEP *must* be reviewed at least annually.

Development of the IEP

Procedures for developing an IEP vary slightly from state to state, but essentially the process involves two steps. The first is to determine if the student is eligible for special education services; if so, the second step is to develop the most appropriate program including the establishment of goals and objectives and the determination of an appropriate placement. The process that results in the development of an IEP usually begins with a referral. Any professional staff member at a particular school who suspects that a child might possess a disability can refer the child for an evaluation to determine eligibility for special education. A referral should outline reasons for suspecting a disability, including test results, records or reports, attempts to remediate the student's performance, and the extent of parental contact prior to the referral (New York State Education Department, 1992).

A sample referral form is shown in Figure 3.2. Parents may refer their own children for evaluation when they suspect a problem. In fact, when parents enroll a youngster in a new school, the district will frequently ask if they feel their child might possess a disability.

In many states a standing multidisciplinary team consisting of a special educator, a psychologist, a physician, a parent, and/or other individuals, is charged with the responsibility of determining special education eligibility. This diagnostic team has different names in different states. In New York, for instance, it is called the Committee on Special Education, while in Louisiana it is known as the Pupil Appraisal Team. Regardless of name, however, the team's primary purpose is to determine whether a particular student has a unique educational need (or needs). In many cases the diagnostic team will determine unique need by assessing the results of standardized tests. But the team will also consider other information, such as samples of current academic work and anecdotal accounts, including parental input, before reaching a final decision. On the basis of the information gathered and the ensuing discussion, the diagnostic team will decide if the youngster qualifies for special education; if so, the team will recommend a program based on an IEP it has developed.

It should be emphasized that the IEP is a negotiated document; both the school and the parents have input into its development and must agree on its contents before it is signed and implemented. In the event the two parties cannot agree on the content of a student's IEP, IDEA provides procedures for resolving the disagreement. These due process procedures are designed to protect the rights of the child, the parents, and the school district (see Figure 3.3).

The Role of the Physical Educator

Historically, physical educators have not been actively involved in the IEP development process. Churton (1987) indicates that relatively few IEPs contain physical education entries. He points out that, according to 1980 Department of Education data, fewer than 3% of the IEPs surveyed mentioned physical education. It is clear that if students with disabilities are to receive the free, appropriate education guaranteed by IDEA, physical education must be included in their IEPs. It is also clear that this will be accomplished only if physical educators make sure that they are involved in IEP development.

DEPARTMENT OF PHYSICAL EDUCATION
Referral Form

This form should be used by teachers or administrators of physical education to refer pupils with unique needs to chairpersons of CSE, CPSE, CAPE, or the school building administrator. Referrals should be processed through the office of the APE Coordinator to the Director of Physical Education who shall forward the referral to appropriate individuals. Referrals may be made to change the program and/or placement of the student or for any other action within the jurisdiction of the CSE, CPSE, or CAPE.

Faculty member making referral _____ **Date** _____

Student referred _____ **Age** _____ **Gender** _____

Present physical education class (if any) _____

Student's primary or homeroom teacher _____

A unique physical education need has been identified for the student:

By the CSE? _____ Yes _____ No

By the CPSE? ____ Yes _____ No

By the CAPE? ____ Yes _____ No

If no, give reasons for believing a unique physical education need exists _____

_____

_____

_____

Give test results, records, or reports upon which a referral is based _____

_____

_____

_____

Describe prior attempts to remediate student's performance _____

_____

_____

Has parental contact been made? _____ Yes _____ No **If yes, describe:** _____

_____

_____

If a recommendation for placement or other action is included as a part of this referral, indicate the recommendation: _____

_____

_____

Referral processed by: **Referral initiated by:**

_____   _____

(Director of Physical Education)   **(Staff member)**

Legend: **CSE - Committee on Special Education**

CPSE - Committee on Preschool Education

CAPE - Committee on Adapted Physical Education

Figure 3.2 Sample referral form for adapted physical education.

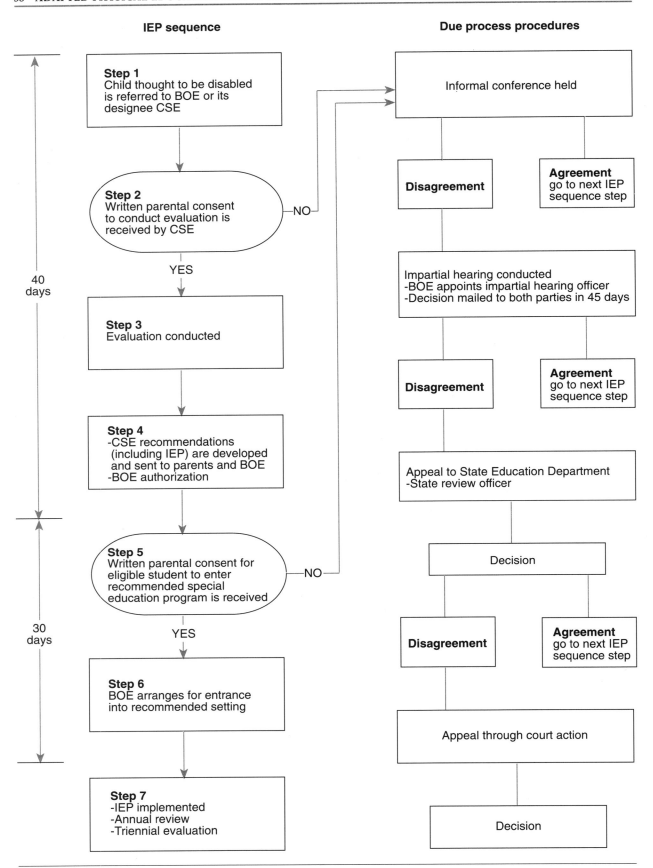

Figure 3.3 Sample IEP sequence and due process procedures.

Unfortunately, many students are assigned to physical education settings more as a function of convenient scheduling than as a function of educational needs. It is not unusual for students to be evaluated by the multidisciplinary diagnostic team without a physical education assessment being performed. Consequently, students may be assigned to inappropriate physical education programs or placements, and physical education teachers may be assigned students for whom there are no assessment data, long-term goals, or short-term objectives. It is therefore recommended that school districts include an adapted physical education teacher on the multidisciplinary diagnostic team. This educator would determine if the student qualifies for an adapted program and would help write the eligible student's initial IEP.

In determining eligibility for adapted physical education, it is necessary to have a strong assessment program in place. Assessment should reflect as many content areas of physical education as possible. The Education for the Handicapped Act, Public Law 94-142 (1975), defined physical education as follows: "The term means the development of (a) physical and motor fitness, (b) fundamental motor skills and patterns; and (c) skills in aquatics, dance, and individual and group games and sports (including intramural and lifetime sports)." (Department of Health, Education, and Welfare, 1977, p. 424807). The physical educator therefore should select assessment instruments that reflect these components. Deficient scores would help the physical educator to determine unique need and justify an adapted program.

Although documentation of subaverage test performance is important in determining an adapted program, it is not the only criterion to use in making such a decision. For instance, an emotionally disturbed child might be placed in a segregated, adapted physical education class even though the child's physical and motor skills are age appropriate. A unique need in the affective domain might prevent safe and successful participation in an integrated physical education class. In this case, a placement in a segregated setting might be justified on the basis of behavioral concerns; a large class size or an emphasis on competitive activities might make a regular physical education class inappropriate for such a child.

THE NONDISABLED STUDENT WITH UNIQUE NEEDS

As mentioned at the outset of this chapter, nondisabled pupils who have unique needs in physical education are not covered by IDEA. School districts, however, still must provide an appropriate education for these students.

Committee on Adapted Physical Education

It is recommended that school districts establish a Committee on Adapted Physical Education (CAPE) to address the unique needs of the nondisabled student in physical education. This committee should consist of at least three members: the director of physical education or designee, the school nurse, and an adapted physical educator. When possible, the student's regular physical education teacher should also be a member of the committee, and a school administrator should be available for consultation. The function of CAPE is to determine the student's eligibility for an adapted program; define the nature of that program, including placement; and monitor the student's progress.

Formulation of the Physical Education Program

A process for providing an appropriate adapted program for nondisabled students is illustrated in Figure 3.4 and defined in the following paragraphs.

Step 1

Referrals to CAPE will ordinarily be made to the chairperson of the committee by a physical educator, a family physician, a parent, or even the student, when it is felt that the student has a unique need in physical education. CAPE should consider only those referrals where the needs are thought to be long-term (more than 30 days).

Step 2

When CAPE receives a referral (from a source other than the parents), it should notify the parents of the referral and indicate that the committee will be considering an adapted program. The notification should point out that physical education is a required subject area under state law (where applicable) and that "blanket" excuses, waivers, or substitution are not appropriate options; that development of an "adapted" program would not mean that the district considers the student to be "disabled" under IDEA; and that any change in program will be reviewed periodically (at least

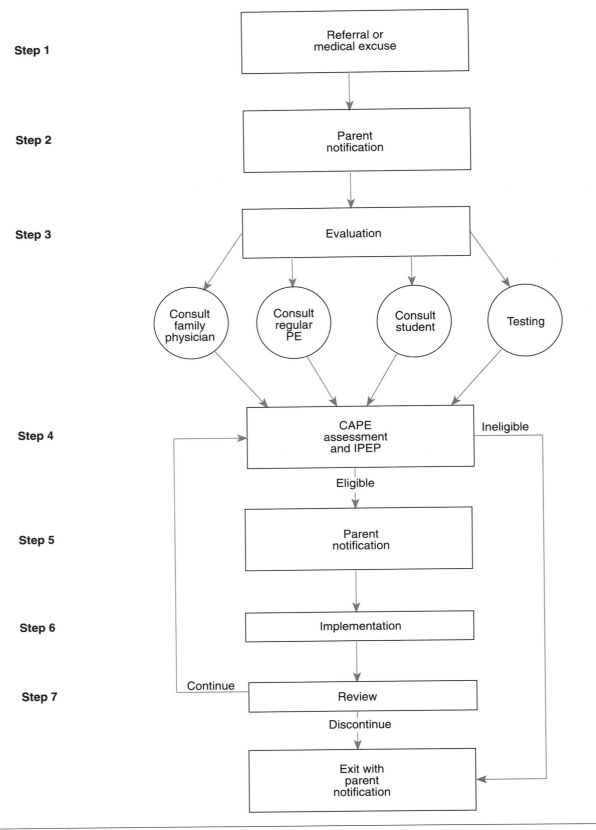

Figure 3.4   A recommended procedure for providing adapted physical education services to nondisabled students.

annually). Parents should also be invited to submit their own concerns or aspirations for their child's physical education program.

Step 3

In the case of a medical excuse or referral, CAPE should contact the family physician to determine the nature of the condition or disease and the impact on physical education. A sample form to be used for this purpose is shown in Figure 3.5. CAPE should also consult the student's regular physical education teacher (to determine the student's performance level and any difficulties the student experiences in his or her current program) and the student (to discuss the basis for the referral and goals of a possible adapted program). It also may be necessary to conduct additional testing to better understand the student's strengths and weaknesses.

Step 4

After considering all the information collected in step 3, CAPE must decide if an adapted program is most appropriate for this student. If the student does not have a unique need, the parents are informed and the process is over. If, however, the student is eligible for an adapted program, CAPE must develop an individualized physical education program (IPEP) for the student. The IPEP is similar to the IEP and should include program goals, present levels of performance (including any medical limitations), short-term objectives, placement and schedule of services, and a schedule for review.

Step 5

Parents are notified of CAPE's decision. If the student is eligible, parents should receive an explanation of the adapted program and a copy of the IPEP. It is also recommended that the regular physical education teacher and, in the case of a medically initiated referral, the family physician receive copies of the IPEP as well. (The district should have due process procedures comparable to those depicted in Figure 3.3 in place in the event the parents do not agree with CAPE's decision or with the program outlined in the IPEP.)

Step 6

The adapted program described in the IPEP is implemented. Most IPEPs can probably be implemented in an integrated placement. In cases where a segregated placement is required, however, districts should seek parental permission prior to changing the placement unless the board of education has different procedures.

Step 7

The IPEP will be in effect for the period of time specified under "schedule for review." At the conclusion of this time period CAPE evaluates the student's progress and decides whether to continue or discontinue the program.

INFANTS AND TODDLERS WITH DISABILITIES

The Individuals with Disabilities Education Act encourages states, through a grant program to provide early intervention services to infants and toddlers who are experiencing developmental delays or who are at risk for developmental delays and their families (EDLAW, 1992). These early intervention services are outlined in the individualized family service plan. Although somewhat analogous to the IEP, the IFSP focuses on broader, developmental needs. Consequently, while the IEP tends to be student-centered and school-based, the IFSP tends to be more family-centered and community-based (although schools certainly can be a part of the community-based program). The eight components of the IFSP are described in the following paragraphs.

- **Present level of development**

  Information, based on objective criteria, is provided on the infant/toddler's developmental status. Areas to be stressed include physical development, cognitive development, communication development, social/emotional development, and adaptive development (i.e., self-help skills).

- **Family information**

  This component contains statements pertaining to the family's resources, priorities, and concerns relative to the infant/toddler's development. Essentially family strengths and needs for enhancing the child's development are described here.

- **Outcomes**

  Major outcomes expected for the infant/toddler and the family are written in this section. Outcome statements should include criteria,

Ocean Bay Park Central School District
Physical Activity Form

TO: _____ , MD

FROM: _____ Chair, Committee on Adapted Physical Education

_____
Address

RE: _____   _____
          Name of pupil   Grade in school

    The Committee on Adapted Physical Education (CAPE) has received a medical excuse (or referral) regarding this student. All pupils registered in the schools of New York are required by IDEA to attend courses of instruction in physical education. As necessary, it is required that courses are modified to meet individual pupil needs. The physical education classes are approximately _____ minutes in length and are held _____ times a week.

    The final responsibility for the determination of a student's individualized program rests with the Committee on Adapted Physical Education. Medical information from you will assist the Committee in making a decision. If further clarification is needed, the school physician will arrange a conference with you.

Diagnosis: _____

Specific physical limitations: _____

_____

Within the physical limitations listed, this student can otherwise engage in: (check one)

_____ Vigorous physical activity   _____ Mild physical activity
_____ Moderate physical activity   _____ Minimal physical activity

Other recommendations for program modification: _____

_____

Do you wish student to return for reevaluation? Yes _____ No _____
If so, when? _____

This is to certify that I have examined _____
and recommend that he/she participate in a physical education program within the guidelines specified above for a period of _____ weeks/months.

                                                    Physician's
                                                    signature: _____

                                                    Date: _____

White: APE   Yellow: CAPE file Pink: Physician

Figure 3.5 Sample physician form.

procedures, and timelines to determine the extent of progress.

- **Early intervention services**

  Specific services to be provided to meet the needs of the infant/toddler and the family are listed in this component. Descriptions of the frequency, intensity, and method of delivery of the services are included.

- **Natural environments**

  Efforts should be made to provide early intervention services in the most appropriate location. Possible natural environments include hospitals, homes, child-care centers, and schools.

- **Schedule**

  Projected dates for initiation and duration of the early intervention services are provided here.

- **Case manager**

  The name of the person who will coordinate the early intervention services is contained in the IFSP. It is recommended that the case manager come from the profession that is most relevant to the infant/toddler's and family's needs.

- **Transition plan**

  The infant/toddler will "age out" of this program at 3. Consequently, the IFSP should include steps to be taken to support the child's transition to the next option. Many children, for instance, will be referred to the school district's multidisciplinary diagnostic team for evaluation.

At this time, as strategies for meeting the specifications in IDEA emerge, the extent of involvement of physical education personnel in programming for infants and toddlers with disabilities is unclear for a few reasons. First of all, state participation is not mandated by IDEA; states have the option to participate in the grant program provided in the legislation. Second, those states choosing to participate must develop plans to coordinate the *interagency* early intervention services to be provided; the department of education may be only one of the agencies involved. In New York State, for example, the State Education Department provides some support for infant/toddler programs, but the lead agency is the Department of Health. Finally, IFSPs are not coordinated by school districts (at least there is no such mandate in IDEA); in New York, the IFSP is coordinated by the county health department. Consequently, schools may not play a

dominant role in providing the early intervention services. So, there are a number of variables that will affect physical education's involvement with children under the age of 3. It *is* clear, however, that motor experiences are *critical* to the development of infants and toddlers and that physical educators, as a result of their training, are logical choices for providing those experiences. Indeed, many private schools and agencies and public "cooperative" schools (i.e., special education facilities) provide infant and toddler programs in which physical education personnel play a central role.

SUMMARY

Students may be eligible for adapted physical education, regardless of disability, if they exhibit a unique need. Procedures for program development for students (aged 3–21) who are considered disabled by a school district are governed by the Individuals with Disabilities Education Act (IDEA). These procedures include the determination of program eligibility and program design as defined by an individualized education program (IEP). The procedures for program development for students who are not considered disabled by a school district are not governed by federal legislation. Districts must develop their own procedures for determining program eligibility and design. It is recommended that districts establish a Committee on Adapted Physical Education (CAPE) to perform these functions, including the development of an individualized physical education program (IPEP) for each eligible nondisabled student. Infants and toddlers and their families may receive early intervention services under IDEA. These services are described in the individualized family service plan (IFSP).

BIBLIOGRAPHY

Churton, M. (1987). Impact of the Education of the Handicapped Act on adapted physical education: A 10-year review. *Adapted Physical Activity Quarterly*, **4**, 1–8.

Department of Health, Education, and Welfare. (1977). Education of handicapped children. *Federal Register*, **42**(163), 42434-42516.

EDLAW. (1992). *Individuals with Disabilities Education Act*. Alexandria, VA: National Association of State Directors of Special Education.

New York State Education Department. (1992). *A parent's guide to special education for children ages 5–21*. Albany, NY: University of the State of New York.

RESOURCES

Written

American Alliance for Health, Physical Education, Recreation and Dance. *Update*. Answers to often-asked questions related to P.L. 94-142, especially as they relate to physical education. Relevant issues include November 1977, January 1978, February 1978, June 1978, October 1978, November 1978, January 1979, May 1979, and July-August 1979.

American Alliance for Health, Physical Education, Recreation and Dance. *Journal of Physical Education, Recreation and Dance*, August 1991. A series of articles relating Public Law 99-457 to preschool physical education programs; John M. Dunn, feature editor.

Audiovisual

Bowers, L. & Klesius, S. (1982). *I'm Special*. Tampa: University of South Florida. A series of 15 videotapes related to adapted physical education. Modules 2 and 3, "Score One for Physical Education" and "On the Edge of Light," are specifically related to P.L. 94-142 and the IEP. Each module is approximately 15 minutes long. Contact Dr. Lou Bowers, School of Physical Education, Wellness, and Sport Studies, University of South Florida, Tampa, FL 33620.

CHAPTER 4

Measurement and Assessment

Francis X. Short

At a recent physical education staff meeting, teachers were discussing some of their frustrations about how students are assigned to physical education classes. "Something's definitely wrong," said Mr. Webb. "I seem to have three or four kids in every regular class who can't keep up with their classmates and should probably be learning more elementary skills than the others. Then my special education class comes into the gym, and two or three of those kids could handle the regular class, no sweat."

"That's because kids are assigned to PE without any prior consideration of their ability," said Mrs. Nelson. "What we need to do is establish some kind of a testing program to help get these students into the most appropriate program."

*"O.K., but **what** should we test and **which** tests should we use?" asked Ms. Mestre.*

"Not only that," said Mr. Ferruggia, "but what cut-off scores would we use to decide on the best program for each youngster?"

Measurement and assessment serve a number of purposes in physical education. One of the more critical purposes in adapted physical education, the question of program eligibility, is characterized above. The goal of this chapter is to familiarize the reader with many of the important concepts of measurement and assessment as they relate to adapted physical education. Types of tests and standards, purposes of testing, tests for use in adapted physical education, award programs, and computer aids are the major topics covered.

TESTS AND STANDARDS

Many types of tests with different types of standards are used in adapted physical education and

sport as well as in other professional settings. Each test has its own relative strengths and weaknesses, and physical educators need to be aware of these characteristics prior to selecting a test instrument. Some of these strengths and weaknesses relate to the types of standards associated with the test. Three types of standards—norm-referenced, content-referenced, and criterion-referenced—are discussed in the following paragraphs. Relative strengths and weaknesses of each are given in Table 4.1.

Norm-Referenced Tests

A norm-referenced test provides the tester with standards that can be used to compare a particular individual's performance with that of other individuals from a specifically defined group. These standards, or norms, may be presented in a variety of ways, although percentiles, standard scores, and age norms are the most popular. When norms are provided, they reflect research done by the test developer on a standardized sample. It is assumed that the sample is representative of the population from which it was selected. Using scores obtained by the standardization sample, the test developer calculates and presents statistics (e.g., percentiles, standard scores, or age norms) to indicate certain levels of performance that compare individuals with certain characteristics (e.g., age, gender, disability). Many commercially available physical fitness tests and motor ability tests are norm-referenced.

Content-Referenced Tests

Content-referenced tests are used to place a student on a continuum of achievement; the test score

Table 4.1 Relative Strengths and Weaknesses of Tests With Three Types of Standards

Reference	Strengths	Weaknesses
Norm	Compares student scores (average, below average, etc.) with others from a similarly defined group; particularly helpful in summative evaluation (unique needs determination, placement, awards, etc.).	Teacher is limited to specific items on the test; therefore, strong relationship to the curriculum is not guaranteed; limited applicability for formative (ongoing or corrective) evaluation; information on skill "mastery" (competent vs. noncompetent) is lacking.
Content	Places student on an achievement continuum; teacher-constructed, therefore, test has the potential to be highly related to the curriculum; ideal for formative evaluation because it has day-to-day applicability.	Comparisons with established standards or performance are not possible; therefore, the *significance* of a test score may not be known.
Criterion	Compares score to standards for "mastery" (an acceptable level of performance); the evaluation of one student is not influenced by the performance of other students.	If standards for "mastery" are established capriciously, interpretation of the significance of the score may be meaningless or erroneous.

is "interpreted in terms of performance at each point on the achievement continuum being measured" (Joint Committee, 1974, p. 19). In contrast to the norm-referenced test, the primary strength of a content-referenced test is flexibility. Unlike most norm-referenced tests, content-referenced tests generally are not "store bought" but developed by the user. Consequently, the user has the flexibility to devise a test to measure exactly what is being taught in the gymnasium. Virtually any observable skill being taught in the curriculum can be measured using a content-referenced test. For instance, free throw shooting accuracy can be easily tested by giving each student 20 shots from the foul line and counting how many go in the basket. Serving in volleyball can be measured by counting the number of times out of 10 a student can serve the ball into the opponent's court. In this case, the continuum of achievement ranges from 0 to 10 successful serves, and each student will fall somewhere along that continuum. The interpretation is that a higher score is associated with a more advanced level of functioning.

Criterion-Referenced Tests

Criterion-referenced tests are very similar to content-referenced tests in that both types place persons on an achievement continuum. The primary difference between the two is that criterion-referenced tests specify performance criteria that may be used to appraise performance. For instance, where a content-referenced test asks, "How far can you jump?" a criterion-referenced test asks, "Can you jump 30 inches?" The distance of 30 inches represents the criterion by which performance can be assessed; in this case, 30 inches is the standard that defines "good jumping." Behavioral objectives, such as those found in an IEP, therefore very often reflect criterion-referenced standards. The objectives specify a level of mastery that the student must attain (e.g., "Ralph will make 5 out of 10 baskets from the free-throw line"). Criterion-referenced tests are popular in competency-based programs such as those sponsored by the American Red Cross. Participants must meet specific standards to gain Lifeguard or Water Safety Instructor certification.

More recently attention has been given to the development of criterion-referenced tests such as FITNESSGRAM (1993). The standards associated with FITNESSGRAM are those that are thought to be necessary to attain objectives related to good health and improved function. For each test item (see Table 4.2) standards for a "healthy fitness zone" are provided by gender and age (5 to 17+). The healthy fitness zone is defined by a lower-end score and an upper-end score. All students are encouraged to achieve at least the lower-end criterion. There is little emphasis placed on going *beyond* the upper-end criterion, however, since

Table 4.2 FITNESSGRAM Components and Test Items

Aerobic capacity (select one)

- One-mile walk/run
- The PACER (a multistage 20-meter shuttle run)

Body composition (select one)

- Percent fat (triceps and calf skinfolds)
- Body mass index (calculated from height and weight)

Muscle strength, endurance and flexibility

Abdominal strength (must select)

- Curl-ups

Trunk extensor strength and flexibility (must select)

- Trunk lift

Upper body strength (select one)

- Push-up
- Modified pull-up
- Pull-up
- Flexed arm hang

Flexibility (may select one)

- Back-saver sit and reach
- Shoulder stretch

---

health-related objectives can be attained by simply staying within the healthy fitness zone.

Test Applications

The usage in the present discussion of such terms as **norm-referenced test** and **criterion-referenced test** appears consistent with professional vocabulary. The reader should recognize, however, that the test per se is not norm referenced; rather, the standards are. It is possible, for instance, that a single test could be considered content-referenced, criterion-referenced, or norm-referenced depending on the standards that are available and/or utilized by the teacher. As an example, consider a standing broad jump score of 35 inches. If the teacher reports or utilizes only the raw score (35 inches), the standing broad jump becomes a content-referenced test. If the 35 inches is compared to a predetermined standard of competence (e.g., students who jump at least 35 inches qualify for the "Kangaroo Klub"), then it becomes a criterion-referenced test. And finally, if the teacher compares the score of 35 inches to scores obtained by

other students who are similarly defined by using, say, a percentile table, the test is considered to be norm-referenced.

PURPOSES OF MEASUREMENT AND ASSESSMENT

While there are numerous reasons for assessment in physical education in general (see Safrit, 1990), there are three primary purposes in adapted physical education: screening, determination of unique need, and instruction. The relationship of measurement and assessment to each of these functions is discussed next.

Screening

As discussed in the preceding chapters, students who are suspected of having unique physical and motor needs should be referred to the special education diagnostic team or a Committee on Adapted Physical Education (CAPE). Referrals must document the reasons why the student should be considered for an adapted physical education program. Measurement and assessment at the referral level is usually called screening. The primary purpose of screening is to document the need for an in-depth evaluation for adapted physical education services. A screening test can be any test that is routinely administered as part of the regular physical education program. Screening tests therefore can range from more formal, norm-referenced or criterion-referenced tests to less formal, content-referenced tests.

Assessment for the purpose of screening also may include the use of checklists, rating scales, and informal observation techniques. Although each of these is typically less objective than tests with standardized conditions, directions, and scoring procedures, checklists and rating scales usually have more objectivity than informal observation because these techniques provide the tester with some guidelines for the evaluation of performance. In evaluating the volleyball serve with a 1–5 rating scale, for instance, the tester might award a 5 if the ball has "good velocity *and* good placement" or perhaps a 4 if the ball has "good velocity *or* good placement." Still, there is a sufficient degree of subjectivity in this approach since the tester must decide what constitutes good velocity and good placement.

With informal observation, teachers do not have any specific guidelines by which to judge performance. Rather, they must rely upon their powers of observation and professional judgment. Knowing at what age a youngster should be able to perform a particular skill and being able to detect deficiencies in mature movement patterns are examples of abilities that teachers must possess. Although largely subjective, informal observation is still an important assessment device, particularly for the purposes of screening, for a couple of reasons. First, observation can be unobtrusive; students can be observed in "natural" physical activity settings without feeling that they are being tested. A second reason is that a good observer can evaluate a relatively large number of students in a relatively short period of time. Formal testing techniques, on the other hand, frequently require the construction of artificial conditions and one-on-one testing.

It is important to note that the purpose of screening is to guarantee that every student who might be eligible for adapted physical education services is identified. For this reason, information collected in a variety of formal and informal ways should be considered, and when standards are used for appraisal purposes, they should be sufficiently high to prevent borderline students from "falling through the cracks." A school district might decide, for instance, to use a norm-referenced standard for screening and to refer for in-depth testing any youngster who falls below the 25th percentile on one or more measures.

Determination of Unique Need

Determining unique need is critical for two reasons. First a student must have a unique need to be eligible for adapted physical education services. This is true both for students who are considered to be disabled under the Individuals with Disabilities Education Act (IDEA) and for nondisabled students who are low in physical education–related abilities. Second, once a unique need is determined, that need serves as the basis for establishing appropriate goals and objectives for the student. These aspects of unique need—eligibility and goals and objectives—are discussed in the following paragraphs.

In dealing with the question of eligibility, a distinction must be made between an adapted physical education program and the placement to which a student is assigned. A student might qualify for an adapted program, but receive that program in a regular class placement. Placement therefore is established after the appropriate program has been determined. When a student is referred to CAPE or the special education diagnostic team on the basis of preliminary screening, the committee must first determine whether the student is eligible for the adapted physical education program. It will probably be necessary for the adapted physical educator to conduct more assessment to determine whether or not the student has a unique need. A long-term unique need, therefore, must be established in order for a student to qualify for adapted physical education. In the absence of a medically based referral, the criteria for entry into the adapted program generally should be based on performance. Usually measurement and assessment for the purpose of determining program eligibility should focus, to the extent possible, on norm-referenced testing.

A number of states, including Georgia, Minnesota, and Louisiana, have developed specific criteria for admission into adapted physical education. In the absence of statewide criteria, it is recommended here that school districts adopt local criteria for admission into adapted physical education. It is further recommended that districts consider the following standards for admission based upon test results that measure developmental aspects of physical education:

- the student scores below the 15th percentile when percentile ranks are used;

- the student scores more than one standard deviation below the mean (e.g., a T score less than 40) when standard scores are used; or

- the student exhibits a developmental delay of at least two years when age norms are used (although the use of age norms is not recommended for students beyond seven years of age).

Inasmuch as formal testing often takes place under "artificial" conditions, districts might also consider additional criteria. For example, corroboration of test results through observational techniques or a temporary trial placement might also be required.

Although preference should be given to the use of norm-referenced standards in documenting unique need, criterion-referenced tests also can be used, particularly in competency-based programs. In Louisiana, for instance, failure to meet 70% or more of the competencies in the physical education curriculum can serve as a criterion for entrance into adapted physical education. Failure to meet the criterion-referenced standards of a health-related physical fitness test might be another way of establishing unique need.

Once eligibility has been established, based on a documented unique need, appropriate goals and objectives must be written. Typically, annual goals and short-term objectives are selected to improve the area(s) of unique need. Students in adapted physical education often will have the same goals as the regular program (e.g., to improve physical fitness, ball handling skills, etc.), but the specific objectives usually will be different. Objectives will be different for a student with a unique need because different activities may have to be substituted for those in the regular program or perhaps because different performance criteria will have to be adopted. While teachers will have to rely on their professional judgment in setting appropriate performance criteria, these standards always should consider the student's current level of performance. In some cases the teacher may wish to use normative data to help establish reasonable criteria. For instance, if a student has a spinal cord injury, the teacher might consult the percentile tables in the Project UNIQUE Physical Fitness Test (Winnick & Short, 1985) to determine a reasonable 50-yard dash time for an 11-year-old girl using a wheelchair. The teacher may decide that the 50th percentile (in this case a test score of 24.2 seconds) constitutes a reasonable expectation.

After the goals and objectives have been determined, the most appropriate placement for obtaining them must be selected. It should be kept in mind, however, that *every effort should be made to keep the student in the regular class placement*. Teachers should attempt to modify activities and methodologies so that the student's objectives can be met in the regular class. While there was one primary criterion for admission into the program (i.e., performance), there are a number of considerations in the selection of the appropriate placement. Students, for instance, may have to be assigned to a more restrictive placement (see continuum of alternative placements) if they are unable to understand concepts or safety considerations being taught in the regular class placement, or if they are unable to maintain appropriate peer relations or engage in other forms of acceptable social behavior.

In instances where students are referred for behavioral reasons, measurement should focus on affective behaviors. These behaviors might include tantrums, physical aggression, and noncompliance. Once these behaviors are defined, baseline data can be collected to show how often a behavior occurs ("Joe averages 1.25 physical provocations a day in physical education"), how long it lasts ("Barbara's tantrums last, on the average, 4.5 minutes per occurrence"), or what percentage of time it occurs ("Sean is compliant with teacher directions approximately 67% of the time").

Placement also may depend, at least in part, on what is being taught in the regular class. A student who uses a wheelchair, for example, could probably meet appropriate goals and objectives for individual sports such as swimming, weight lifting, and track and field in a regular placement (see Figure 4.1). Conversely, the same student might be assigned to a more restrictive setting when team sports such as basketball, soccer, or football are being taught in the regular class. A third important consideration in placement is the input received from the student or the student's parents.

Instruction

The role of measurement and appraisal does not stop after the student has been assigned to an appropriate physical education program. Progress on the goals and objectives should be monitored closely. As suggested earlier, content- or criterion-referenced tests can be designed and utilized for this purpose. Another technique, called **task analysis,** can help monitor progress during instruction. Although there are different approaches to task analysis, the one often used in physical education involves listing, usually in sequential order, the subtasks or subskills necessary for successful performance of the skill in question. When skills are analyzed in this fashion, the teacher has essentially developed a criterion-referenced checklist that can be used to teach and evaluate progress on a particular skill. Although teachers can develop their own task analyses, task-analytic curricula in physical education are available. (Chapter 5 presents more information on task analysis.)

At the conclusion of the instructional program or unit, the teacher should conduct final testing to determine the student's "exit abilities." In some cases, grades will be awarded based upon this final assessment. Whether the program is graded or nongraded, however, progress should be evaluated in terms of the written objectives. As mentioned earlier, the objectives can be tested as a series of criterion-referenced tests. Occasionally teachers may wish to give awards to students on the basis of their final test performance. Some existing award programs are discussed later in this chapter.

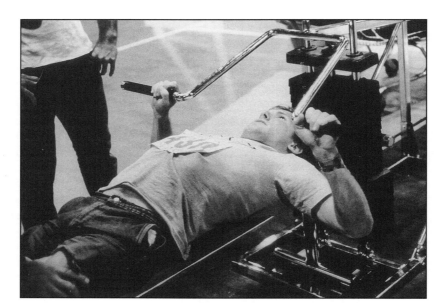

Figure 4.1 A person with a lower limb disability could meet goals and objectives in many individual activities in a regular class placement.
Photo by Craig Huber.

TESTS FOR USE IN ADAPTED PHYSICAL EDUCATION

The problem of selecting a test or tests for use in adapted physical education is not insignificant. Davis (1984) has reported that over 250 tests exist for use in the motor assessment of disabled populations. In choosing test instruments, teachers should consider the following criteria:

- **Economy**. Tests selected should be economical in terms of both time and money.
- **Validity**. Test users should be provided with evidence that the test actually measures what it was designed to measure.
- **Reliability**. Teachers should have confidence that a test yields consistent scores.
- **Purpose**. Teachers should consider *why* they are testing, *whom* they are testing, and *what* they are testing.

In regard to purpose, if the test is being conducted to determine eligibility for adapted physical education, for instance, the test selected should have some external standards by which to judge performance. Norm-referenced measures and health-related criterion-referenced fitness standards are most applicable in this context, and content-referenced measures are least applicable. After the *why* has been determined, the teacher must ascertain that the test is cognitively, af-

fectively, and physically appropriate for the students being assessed. For example, teachers should determine if students in wheelchairs or those who use crutches can participate in the test items and have their performances validly assessed. Similarly, teachers should be assured that students with mental retardation understand the items or directions. Finally, the teacher has to decide *what* to test; physical education is a fairly broad subject area and different tests measure different aspects of the subject. Most standardized tests used in physical education seem to fall into one of six general areas: reflexes and reactions, rudimentary movements, fundamental movements, perceptual-motor abilities, physical fitness, and specialized movements including sport skills, aquatics, and dance. From a developmental perspective there are periods of time when the measurement of each of these six areas would be optimal. These time frames are represented in Figure 4.2. The information in Figure 4.2 provides a practical guideline when choosing *what* to test. Readers should remember, however, that the time frames depicted are somewhat arbitrary and are influenced by the availability of standardized test instruments. For example, the figure should not be interpreted to mean that physical fitness is not important prior to age 5. It only suggests that as a matter of practice teachers usually do not conduct standardized fitness assessment until at least that age. Furthermore, readers are reminded that the ages are *developmental* ages

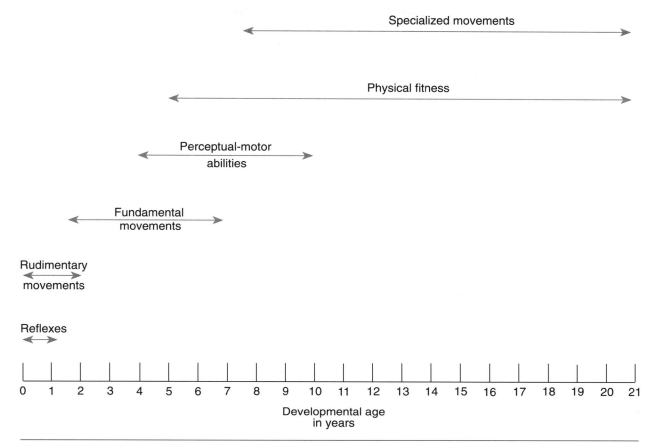

Figure 4.2 Recommended areas for testing based on developmental age.

and represent a general level of functioning rather than a chronological age.

The remainder of this section of the chapter is devoted to a discussion of tests from each of these six areas. One test from each area is highlighted. The highlighted tests are meant to be representative of a particular content area and are recommended or used by many adapted physical educators. Additional tests are listed at the end of this chapter in the Resources section.

Testing Reflexes and Reactions

The assessment of primitive reflexes and postural reactions is becoming increasingly common in adapted physical education. (See chapter 16 for more information on reflexes and reactions.) As educational services are extended to infants and toddlers as well as to those with more severe disabilities (especially those that are neurologically based, such as cerebral palsy), physical educators will need to understand the role of reflexes and reactions on movement.

Since primitive reflexes normally follow a regular sequence for appearing, maturing, and eventually disappearing, they are particularly helpful in providing information on the level of central nervous system maturation. If a primitive reflex persists beyond schedule, presents an unequal bilateral response (e.g., present on one side, but absent or not as strong on the other), is too strong or too weak, or is completely absent, neurological problems may be suspected. When primitive reflexes are not inhibited, they will undoubtedly interfere with voluntary movement as muscle tone involuntarily changes when reflexes are elicited. The Milani-Comparetti Motor Development Screening Test is a good example of an instrument that assesses reflexes and reactions.

**Milani-Comparetti
Motor Development Screening Test
for Infants and Young Children**

(Meyer Rehabilitation Institute, 1992)

Purpose: Designed to assess motor development in young children, birth to 24 months. Although the instrument has obvious utility for infant and toddler programs, the inclusion of a number of reflexes and reactions in the battery makes it appropriate for older developmentally delayed individuals as well, especially those with cerebral palsy.

Description: In all there are 27 items associated with this test. Nine of the items are classified as "spontaneous behaviors" which test for head control in four postures (vertical, prone, supine, and pulled from supine); body control in three postures (sitting, all fours, and standing); and two "active movements" (standing from supine and locomotion). The remaining 18 items are called "evoked responses" and test five primitive reflexes (hand grasp, asymmetrical tonic neck, moro, symmetrical tonic neck, and foot grasp) and 13 righting, parachute, or tilting reactions. In evaluating most of the spontaneous behaviors, testers are required to evaluate the progression of development. For instance, for "all fours" the child will progress from a prone position propped up by forearms and hands, to hands and knees, and finally to hands and feet (i.e., "plantigrade"). For evoked responses, the tester need only note whether the reflex or reaction was absent or present. Age norms are associated with each of the test items.

Validity and Reliability: Inter-observer and test-retest data provide evidence of acceptable levels of reliability. Age norms were established based on the performance of 312 subjects. Content validity is claimed based upon general acceptance of test items by physicians and therapists.

Comment: The primary advantage of the Milani-Comparetti is its relative ease of administration, which is due, in part, to the limited number of test items. If a more extensive assessment of reflexes and reactions is necessary, the reader is referred to Fiorentino (1963).

Availability:
Meyer Rehabilitation Institute
University of Nebraska Medical Center
600 South 42nd Street
Omaha, NE 68198-5450

Testing Rudimentary Movements

Rudimentary movements are the first voluntary movements (see chapter 16). Reaching, grasping, sitting, crawling, and creeping are examples. Most instruments that assess rudimentary movements do so in some kind of *developmental milestone* format; that is, a series of motor behaviors that are

associated with specific ages are arranged chronologically and tested individually. By determining which behaviors the child can do, the teacher can estimate the child's developmental age (since each milestone has its own "age norm") and can provide future learning activities (i.e., the behaviors in the sequence that the child cannot currently do). The Peabody Developmental Motor Scales is an example of this approach with some additional enhancements.

Peabody Developmental Motor Scales

(Folio and Fewell, 1983)

Purpose: To assess the motor development of children aged birth to 6 years 11 months in both fine and gross motor areas. Gross motor items are subcategorized into the following five areas: reflexes, balance, nonlocomotor skills, locomotor skills, and receipt and propulsion of objects.

Description: The gross motor scale comprises 170 developmental milestones that serve as the test items. The items are arranged chronologically (in groups of 10) in age levels (e.g., 0–1 month, 6–7 months, 18–23 months, etc.) and each is identified as belonging to one of the five categories being assessed (e.g., reflexes, balance, etc.). It is recommended that testers begin administering items one level below the child's expected motor age. Items are scored on a 0, 1, or 2 basis according to specified criteria. Testing continues until the "ceiling age level" is reached (a level for which a score of 2 is obtained for no more than 1 of the 10 items in that level). Percentiles, z-scores, T scores, and "Developmental Motor Quotients" are provided; all norms are based on the performance of nondisabled children.

Reliability and Validity: Standard errors of measurement, test-retest reliability coefficients (.95 for the gross motor scale), and interrater reliability coefficients (.97 for the gross motor scale) all indicate very good reliability for nondisabled children. Evidence for content, construct, and criterion-related forms of validity are provided.

Comment: The PDMS appears to have certain advantages over other rudimentary movement tests. First, the 170 gross motor items (90 of which are associated with birth to age 2) represent a larger sample of behaviors than exist in many other tests. Second, the five categories help teachers to pinpoint exactly which areas of gross motor development are particularly problematic. Finally, the scoring system and availability of normative data provide the teacher with more information on student performance than many other tests. One criticism of the instrument is its reliance on product-oriented measures (Ulrich, 1984).

Availability:
Riverside Publishing Co.
8420 Bryn Mawr Ave.
Chicago, IL 60631

Testing Fundamental Movements

The fundamental movements are those typically associated with early childhood (see chapter 16). Examples include throwing, catching, skipping, and hopping. Some fundamental movement test instruments utilize the developmental milestone approach discussed under rudimentary movements, but most utilize some type of point system to evaluate either the *process* of the fundamental movement or its *product*. Process-oriented approaches generally attempt to break down (or task-analyze) a movement into its component parts, and then each component is evaluated individually. This approach assesses the *quality* of the movement, not its result. Product-oriented approaches, on the other hand, are concerned primarily with outcome. Product-oriented assessment is more concerned with the *quantity* of the movement (e.g., how far? how fast? how many?) than with its execution. The Test of Gross Motor Development employs a process-oriented approach to the assessment of fundamental movements.

Test of Gross Motor Development

(Ulrich, 1985)

Purpose: According to Ulrich, his four purposes were (1) to design a test representing gross motor content frequently taught in preschool and early elementary grades including special education, (2) to develop a test that could be used by various professionals with a minimum amount of training; (3) to design a test with both norm-referenced and criterion-referenced standards; and (4) to place a priority on the gross motor skill sequence rather than the product of performance.

Description: The test measures ability in 12 gross motor areas divided into two subtests. The Locomotion subtest is comprised of the run, gallop, hop, leap, horizontal jump, skip, and slide. The Object Control subtest consists of the two-hand strike, stationary bounce, catch, kick, and overhand throw. For each skill the tester is provided

with an illustration, equipment/condition requirements, directions, and performance criteria. Children receive one point for meeting each of the performance criteria given. These criterion-based scores can be added and compared to norm-referenced standards.

Reliability and Validity: Reliability as evidenced by test-retest coefficients, inter-score coefficients, and Kappa statistics are quite high. Validity is documented based upon various criteria. Most notably, content validity is claimed for the selection of the 12 tests as representing skills frequently taught in the preschool and early elementary grades and for the selection of the performance criteria. Construct validity was determined by statistical analysis which indicated that (a) the skills all seem to relate to a "gross motor" construct, (b) the tests are highly related to age, and (c) nonhandicapped children do better on the test than mentally retarded children.

Comment: The sound process of test construction should provide the user with a good deal of confidence that scores obtained by children accurately reflect their fundamental movement abilities. The fact that both criterion-referenced and norm-referenced standards are provided increases the test's utility.

Availability:
Pro-Ed Publishing Co.
5341 Industrial Oaks Blvd.
Austin, TX 78735

Testing Perceptual-Motor Abilities

In a broad sense, virtually any test of gross motor ability is a perceptual-motor test, since movement success is influenced by perception, an analysis of the environmental conditions related to the movement problem. (See chapter 17 for more information on perceptual-motor abilities.) Over time, however, perceptual-motor assessment has come to refer to those test instruments that purport to evaluate the precision of the various sensory systems (visual, auditory, kinesthetic, vestibular, tactual) or the "processing" ability of the central nervous system (the integration, comparison, and storage of sensory information). There are a wide variety of perceptual-motor tests on the market. Many of these tests are "paper and pencil" tests and have their roots in the 1960s belief that academic success could be enhanced by improving perceptual-motor abilities. These tests might be thought of as *perceptual*-motor tests because they put a premium on perception and reduced the motor response to manipulating a pencil. The more contemporary view is to evaluate the interaction between perception and movement (Burton, 1990). Although a product of the 1960s, most of the items of the Southern California Perceptual-Motor Tests require perceptual-motor integration.

Southern California Perceptual-Motor Tests

(Ayres, 1969)

Purpose: To evaluate aspects of perceptual-motor functioning in children 4 to 8 years old.

Description: The test battery consists of six test items: imitation of postures (the child attempts to mirror 12 body positions modeled by the tester); crossing the mid-line of the body (the child attempts to mirror the tester as the tester touches either their left or right eye/ear with their right or left hand); bilateral motor coordination (the child attempts to replicate eight rhythmical cadences with the hands); right-left discrimination (the child responds to 10 commands/questions requiring "right" and "left" distinctions); standing balance—eyes open, and standing balance—eyes closed (the child is asked to maintain balance first on one foot and then the other both with eyes open and eyes closed). The battery takes about 20 minutes to administer. Raw scores can be converted to standard scores for each test item categorized by age and gender.

Reliability and Validity: Validity for the battery is claimed, in part, due to the similarity of these tests with those in the "clinical literature." Criterion-related validity is also claimed although no specific data are provided in the manual. Test-retest reliability coefficients range from a quite low .12 to a moderately high .78. Ayres suggests that relatively small standard errors of measurement help to establish acceptable levels of reliability.

Comment: Although the SCPMT has advantages over the "paper and pencil" or "motor-free" perception tests, the movement responses required of the child are limited (all responses are made from either a sitting or standing posture). Still, many of the perceptual-motor abilities evaluated by this test remain prominent in the professional literature.

Availability:
Western Psychological Services
12031 Wilshire Boulevard
Los Angeles, CA 90025

Testing Physical Fitness

There are numerous physical fitness tests from which teachers can choose. Some measure health-related physical fitness, others measure skill-related physical fitness (or motor fitness), and still others measure some combination of the two. (See chapter 15 for a discussion of physical fitness.) Although some similarity among test items can be noted from battery to battery, few batteries are identical. Some of the tests provide norm-referenced standards, and others provide criterion-referenced standards. Of those that provide criterion-referenced standards, the Prudential FIT-NESSGRAM is growing in popularity among physical educators, but readers should recognize that those standards have been established for non-disabled youngsters. Teachers who work with disabled students may wish to administer FITNESSGRAM test items, but compare the scores to modified standards they develop or select. Project Target, a national study to develop criterion-referenced, health-related physical fitness standards for adolescents with disabilities, has been federally-funded under the direction of Dr. Joseph P. Winnick in Brockport, NY. A goal of the project is to have the standards available by 1999. Of those that provide norm-referenced standards, most are limited to the nondisabled population, although some provide norms for specific disability groups. Whether teachers select criterion-referenced or norm-referenced tests, it is recommended that they give preference to those instruments that can be "mainstreamed" (i.e., the test items given to both disabled and nondisabled students are the same, but the standards used for assessment may be different). The Project UNIQUE Physical Fitness Test is an example of a norm-referenced test with standards for nondisabled and disabled groups of students.

Project UNIQUE Physical Fitness Test

(Winnick and Short, 1985)

Purpose: To provide a test of physical fitness appropriate for adolescents (aged 10–17) with orthopedic and sensory disabilities as well as for those who are not disabled.

Description: Depending upon the disability, the test battery consists of between four and six items measuring either three or four components of fitness. The components and the items that comprise them are as follows: body composition—sum of the triceps and subscapular skinfolds; muscular strength/

endurance—situps, grip strength, 50-yard dash; flexibility—sit and reach; cardiorespiratory endurance—long distance run. Items are appropriate for individuals with auditory impairments, visual impairments, cerebral palsy, spinal neuromuscular conditions, and anomalies/amputations. Items are selected or modified based upon the student's disability. Among the modifications is the allowance for different running methods (wheelchair, crutches, guidance, etc.). Test scores can be compared to "regular" and/or "adapted" percentile tables.

Reliability and Validity: In addition to reporting acceptable reliability coefficients found in the literature, alpha coefficients based on the standardization samples for selected items range from .84 to .99. Information on criterion-related, construct, and content validity is provided. Construct validity was determined primarily by a series of factor analyses that provide evidence that the test items measure the components of fitness listed above (Winnick and Short, 1984).

Comment: Advantages of the Project UNIQUE test include sound test development procedures (Safrit, 1990), publication of the only available fitness norms for students with cerebral palsy or spinal neuromuscular conditions, and the provision of norms for nondisabled adolescents that helps to "mainstream" the test and allows for multiple test score comparisons.

Availability:
Human Kinetics
P.O. Box 5076
Champaign, IL 61820

Testing Specialized Movements

Of the six content areas described in this section, specialized movements (see chapter 16) presents the greatest challenge for making summary statements relative to assessment and for choosing one test instrument as an example. This is due to the wide variety of possible activities that could be tested under this heading. Safrit (1990), for instance, lists 185 different skills tests across 25 different sports. Sports skills tests can take many forms, but frequently they are criterion-referenced. Teachers who work with disabled students who compete in special sport programs, such as those sponsored by Wheelchair Sports, USA, the United States Association of Blind Athletes, or the United States Cerebral Palsy Athletic Association, are encouraged to develop their own criterion-referenced tests specific to the event in which the

athlete competes. One example of a criterion-referenced sports skills test that can be used with disabled athletes comes from the Special Olympics Sports Skills Instructional Program.

Sports Skills Instructional Program

(Special Olympics, c. 1982)

Purpose: To complement or supplement existing physical education and recreation programs for the disabled in sports skills instruction.

Description: The Sports Skills series is a curriculum that includes 39 sports divided into three categories: "Special Olympic Sports," "Olympic Sports," and "Lifetime Sports." Although not a test instrument per se, assessment is a critical aspect of the program. The assessment is criterion-referenced and testers check off those skills which the student is able to perform. For instance, in Level II Soccer, the test consists of 34 separate skills (e.g., "Dribbles and controls ball while running the length of the field"). The scoring system rates the athlete as either a "Star," "Super Champ," or "Superstar." The program is designed for youngsters possessing primary motor skills and sufficient levels of physical fitness to participate in the program.

Reliability and Validity: No information reported, but content validity probably could be claimed, since the tests reflect task analyses of sports skills completed by "experts" in the field.

Comment: A primary advantage of the SSIP is its convenience; a teacher or coach can adopt the existing task analytic curricula for a wide variety of sport activities. The program has been in use with mentally retarded participants for some time and has been shown to have good utility for that group. A disadvantage of the SSIP is that neither reliability nor validity of the various test instruments has been formally established.

Availability:
Special Olympics, Inc.
1350 New York Ave.
Washington, DC 20006

Selecting Alternative Test Items

In each of the previous sections, a standardized test battery was recommended for the various content areas of physical education. Frequently in adapted physical education settings, however, specific test items may not be appropriate for a youngster given his or her unique needs. In those cases the teacher should attempt to find a substitute or alternative test item that measures, as closely as possible, the same content area or component as the original. As an example, alternative test items for various components of fitness are provided in Table 4.3. The teacher would have a reasonable assessment of a student's fitness by selecting and administering the most appropriate test item from each of the components listed. For instance, the shoulder stretch is a more appropriate measure of flexibility than the sit-and-reach for a youngster with a disability that involves the lower limbs. Similarly, the PACER (a multistage shuttle run) might be a better choice than a mile run as a measure of aerobic capacity for students who are mentally retarded. The PACER provides auditory feedback on pacing, something that is frequently a problem when students with mental retardation perform distance runs. Ultimately, teachers should attempt to "personalize" test item selection and associated standards as much as possible. (Readers are referred to chapter 15 for more information on personalizing.)

AWARDS

Traditionally teachers have used award programs to motivate students to improve their physical and motor performance or to attain standards of excellence. These award programs have ranged from a teacher simply placing a star next to a student's name on a chart in the gym to adopting the criteria of an established award program. Although subject to change in 1995, both AAHPERD and the Cooper Institute for Aerobics Research (CIAR) sponsor award or recognition programs associated with the criterion-referenced health-related test FITNESSGRAM. The AAHPERD program includes the Fitness Activity Award (for participation), the Fitness Goals Award (for achieving personal goals), and the Health Fitness Award (for meeting the standards in the test manual). The Health Fitness Award standards may be inappropriate for students with certain kinds of disabilities, but the Fitness Activity Award and the Fitness Goals Award are appropriate for all students. As with the AAHPERD program, most of the incentives associated with the CIAR program (Fit for Life, Get Fit, and the SMARTCHOICE incentive) are appropriate for all students. Only the I'm Fit incentive that requires students to achieve standards published in the manual may be inappropriate for some students with disabilities.

The President's Council for Physical Fitness and Sports also sponsors an award program. The President's Council offers the Presidential Physical Fitness Award to students who can achieve the 85th percentile on each of the five items of the President's Challenge Fitness Test; the National Physical Fitness Award for students who can achieve the 50th percentile for each item; and the Participant

Table 4.3 Sample Alternative Test Items Categorized by Components of Fitness

Body size and composition
- ❑ Height and weight
- ❑ Skinfolds
- ❑ Body mass index
- ❑ Girth measurements

Muscular strength and endurance
- ❑ Grip strength
- ❑ Modified pull-ups
- ❑ Flexed arm hang
- ❑ Sit-ups
- ❑ Bench press
- ❑ Wheelchair dips

Power
- ❑ Standing long jump
- ❑ Vertical jump
- ❑ Medicine ball throw
- ❑ Softball throw
- ❑ Club throw

Agility and speed
- ❑ Shuttle run
- ❑ Side step
- ❑ 50-yard dash
- ❑ Mat creep

Aerobic capacity
- ❑ Arm ergometry
- ❑ Swimming
- ❑ Walking
- ❑ Running
- ❑ Bench step
- ❑ PACER

Flexibility
- ❑ Sit and reach
- ❑ Trunk twist
- ❑ Lateral bends
- ❑ Trunk raise
- ❑ Shoulder stretch

Physical Fitness Award for students whose scores fall below the 50th percentile on one or more of the five items. The President's Council provides criteria by which students with special needs may qualify for any of these rewards.

SUMMARY

Measurement serves a number of functions in adapted physical education. It can take many forms including the administration of tests with norm-referenced, content-referenced, and criterion-referenced standards, or the use of task analyses, checklists, rating scales, or informal observation. These approaches can also be combined to yield a more complete picture of the student. Careful observation by the tester, for example, might help to explain a curious test score on a norm-referenced test. Each of these approaches has various strengths and weaknesses and should be selected in accordance with the purpose of the assessment. Some of the major purposes include preliminary screening, determination of unique need, and the establishment and maintenance of reasonable goals and objectives. Ordinarily, assessment will focus on physical fitness, motor ability, sport skills, aquatics, dance, and perceptual-motor ability. Occasionally it may be necessary to supplement this information with data from the affective and cognitive domains. Finally, it should be emphasized that, although some tests have been designed to serve a summative evaluation function, formative evaluation is critical and teachers should make every effort to integrate measurement with their daily instruction.

BIBLIOGRAPHY

Ayres, A. (1969). *Southern California perceptual-motor tests.* Los Angeles: Western Psychological Services.

Burton, A. (1990). Assessing the perceptual-motor interaction in developmentally disabled and nondisabled children. *Adapted Physical Activity Quarterly,* 7(4), 325–337.

Davis, W. (1984). Motor ability assessment of populations with handicapping conditions: Challenging basic assumptions. *Adapted Physical Activity Quarterly,* 2, 125–140.

Folio, M., & Fewell, R. (1983). *Peabody developmental motor scales and activity cards.* Chicago: Riverside.

Joint Committee of the American Psychological Association, the American Educational Research Association, and the National Council on Measurement in Education. (1974). *Standards for Educational and Psychological Tests.* Washington, DC: American Psychological Association.

Meyer Rehabilitation Institute. (1992). *Milani-Comparetti motor development screening test for infants and young children: A manual.* Omaha: Author.

Safrit, M.J. (1990). *Introduction to measurement in physical education and exercise science.* St. Louis: Times Mirror/Mosby.

Special Olympics. (c. 1982). *Sports skills instructional program.* Washington, DC: Kennedy Foundation.

Ulrich, D. (1984). Book review: Peabody developmental motor scales and activity cards. *Adapted Physical Activity Quarterly,* 1(2), 173–178.

Ulrich, D. (1985). *Test of gross motor development.* Austin, TX: Pro-Ed.

Winnick, J., & Short, F. (1984). Test item selection for the Project UNIQUE physical fitness test. *Adapted Physical Activity Quarterly,* 1(4), 296–314.

Winnick, J., & Short, F. (1985). *Physical fitness testing of the disabled.* Champaign, IL: Human Kinetics.

RESOURCES

Written

American Alliance for Health, Physical Education and Recreation. (n.d.). *Testing for impaired, disabled, and handicapped individuals.* Washington, DC: Author. This handbook provides an overview on testing and a summary of over 50 tests related to physical education.

Werder, J., & Kalakan, L. (1985). *Assessment in adapted physical education.* Minneapolis: Burgess. A textbook designed to clarify "issues regarding the physical and motor assessment of students who are handicapped."

Software

Cooper Institute for Aerobics Research (1993). FITNESSGRAM [Computer program]. 12330 Preston Road, Dallas, TX 75230. A computer software program that will generate fitness report cards on each student in the class.

Kelly, L.E. (1987). *Physical education management system.* Hubbard Scientific, P.O. Box 104, Northbrook, IL 60062. This computer software program will manage data on up to 15 teacher-specified objectives for each class. Summarizes data for individual students or specific classes.

Tests

AAU Physical Fitness Program (1993). Poplars Building, Bloomington, IN 47405. A five-item criterion-referenced fitness test for boys and girls aged 6–17. Additional items are optional, and an award program is provided.

Brigance Diagnostic Inventory (1978). Curriculum Associates, Inc., 5 Esquire Road, North Billerica, MA 01862. Developmental ages provided for normal development of preambulatory and gross motor skills up to age 7.

Bruininks-Oseretsky Test of Motor Proficiency (1978). American Guidance Services, Publisher's Building, Circle Pines, MN 55014. Norm-referenced test of motor ability for youngsters aged 4-1/2 to 14-1/2.

Callier-Azusa Scale (1978). Callier Center, University of Texas, 1966 Inwood Road, Dallas, TX 75235. Developmental scale from birth to age 7; includes posture, locomotion, and visual motor items.

Carolina Curriculum (1986). Paul H. Brookes Publishing Co., P.O. Box 10624, Baltimore, MD 21285. Milestone-based age norms; designed to be used with a curriculum for disabled and at-risk infants.

Denver II (1990). Denver Developmental Materials, Inc., P.O. Box 6919, Denver, CO 80206. Developmental milestones for normal gross motor development; age norms up to 6 years.

Fiorentino, M. (1963). *Reflex testing methods for evaluating C.N.S. development.* Springfield, IL: Charles C Thomas. A complete text of reflex and reaction testing.

FITNESSGRAM (1987). Institute for Aerobics Research, 12330 Preston Road, Dallas, TX 75230. A criterion-referenced test of health-related fitness (5 items); standards are for nondisabled with some recommendations for disabled students.

I CAN (1978). Hubbard Scientific Co., P.O. Box 104, Northbrook, IL 60062. Criterion-referenced, curriculum-imbedded tests; part of an extensive physical education curriculum.

Learning Accomplishment Profile (1974). Kaplan Press, P.O. Box 5128, Winston-Salem, NC 27113. Milestone-based test of motor ability for ages 1 month to 6 years.

McClenaghan, B., and Gallahue, D. (1978). *Fundamental movement: A developmental and remedial approach.* Philadelphia: Saunders. Fundamental movements are evaluated as "initial," "elementary," or "mature" based on specified criteria.

Ohio State SIGMA (1979). Mohican Publishing Co., P.O. Box 295, Loudonville, OH 44842. Criterion-referenced test of fundamental movements; designed primarily for use with students with mental retardation.

President's Challenge (1987). President's Council on Physical Fitness and Sports, Washington, DC 20001. Standards for the 85th percentile are presented for five measures of fitness; students aged 6–17 who meet the criteria for all five items qualify for the Presidential Physical Fitness Award.

Project ACTIVE (1974, 1978). Joe Karp, 13209 NE 175th St., Woodinville, WA 98072. Norm-referenced tests of physical fitness and motor ability are available as part of an extensive physical education curriculum.

Purdue Perceptual-Motor Survey (1966). Charles E. Merrill Publishing Co., 936 Eastwind Drive, Westerville, OH 43081. Norm-referenced test for children aged 6–10; balance, posture, perceptual-motor match, body image, and ocular pursuit are measured.

CHAPTER 5

Instructional Styles and Strategies

Sarah M. Rich

In the preface to their 1977 book, *An Exceptional View of Life*, McGrath and Krauss, who are children with disabilities, present a challenge when they ask:

What if you have never been able to walk or dress yourself? What if your eyes couldn't focus properly, or your speech slurred, or you took so long to express your thoughts that you were always left far behind?

What if your parents worried that you might hurt yourself, wouldn't let you play with your friends and you always had to watch from the sidelines? Because you were you, you felt left out—angry, helpless—a loser.

And then, one day someone said, "You're not a loser!" Some people offered to help you learn how to move and strengthen those legs and arms. They showed you how to practice so that you could speak more distinctly. They helped you find ways to cope with your handicaps and to overcome them.

And when it seemed that you couldn't possibly do it, there was always the touch of a hand or a warm voice telling you that you could, and you did! And you began to feel like a winner.

How can physical educators meet these challenges and assist students with disabilities to develop their motor skills most effectively? This chapter will provide information about developing an appropriate philosophy, providing challenging learning environments, and utilizing effective instructional approaches and models to facilitate learning. This information will assist the teacher to structure a learning environment that optimizes the learning of motor skills and sport activities. It will also assist teachers in interacting effectively and efficiently with their students.

As this information is used, it may be necessary to modify some of the principles presented based on your unique abilities as a teacher and the specific needs of your students. By understanding the variables that impact on learning, the teacher can enhance the learning process, allowing each student to reach his/her maximum potential.

EDUCATIONAL APPROACHES TO ADAPTED PHYSICAL EDUCATION AND SPORT

Modern physical education programs, including adapted programs, follow educational approaches that recognize students' individual needs. The philosophical approaches that have most influenced adapted physical education are the humanistic and behaviorist.

Some persons find it difficult to accept all of the tenets of one of these approaches and are more comfortable combining some of the philosophical concepts of each to form a set of compatible beliefs that provide them with a sound approach. The combination of philosophies in this manner is known as the eclectic approach.

Humanism

Humanism is a philosophical approach that emphasizes the development of self-concept, positive interpersonal relationships, intrinsic motivation, and personal responsibility (Sherrill, 1993). Humanistic physical education uses physical activity to help individuals in developing self-esteem, self-understanding, and interpersonal relations. It attempts to identify and meet unique needs, abilities, and interests through individualized instruction that incorporates student choice. Sherrill believes that adapted physical educators who employ a humanistic approach will assist their students to develop positive self-concepts so that they will become intrinsically motivated and achieve their highest potential in physical education and sport.

Humanistic theory became popular in the 1950s. The humanistic movement resulted mainly from the works of Abraham Maslow (self-actualization theory), Carl Rogers (fully functioning self-theory), and their followers. Maslow, Rogers, and their disciples espoused the theory that development occurs naturally and results in a healthy self-actualized person.

Since students and athletes with disabilities often begin physical activity with low levels of self-esteem, skill, fitness, and motivation, many adapted physical education teachers and coaches employ humanistic principles to assist in the development of these attributes. They develop programs that allow individuals to build confidence in their abilities, experience success, enjoy physical activities, and develop healthier lifestyles while valuing individual differences (see Figure 5.1).

Sherrill (1993) suggests that a humanistic philosophy will assist individuals to reach their fullest potential by offering learning, living, and work opportunities that are congruent with those of society in general. At the same time, individual needs are met through a continuum of services.

Sherrill (1993) believes that the characteristics of a self-actualized person, particularly self-concept and body image, are those that adapted physical educators should strive to develop through movement experiences. She feels that nondisabled students tend to develop positive affective behaviors

Figure 5.1 Developing a positive self-concept about physical abilities is important for all individuals regardless of age or disability as depicted by a deaf athlete from Niger, West Africa, practicing the long jump.

without planned intervention by their teachers, but children with disabilities need special help to develop these attributes. It is, therefore, important that physical education teachers help students to develop positive body images and self-concepts so that they will be intrinsically motivated to become all that they can be in physical education and sport activities.

In order to reach affective domain goals in physical education, students need to feel good about themselves. Teachers play an important role here. A success-oriented program is instrumental in improving self-concept. Teachers must create a climate of success by adapting approaches and methods to meet the needs, interests, and abilities of all students. Successful experiences in physical education will promote positive social interaction.

This is accomplished through providing positive feedback and praise, using appropriate task and activity analyses, assisting the students to perceive their skill development as important, and assisting students through leisure counseling to identify activities they will continue to enjoy after their school years are completed.

Hellison (1985) has also worked on a framework to demonstrate the essence of humanistic goals for physical education. These goals, he believes, focus on human needs rather than on such things as fitness or sports skill development. These goals are developmental and hierarchical in nature. They include self-control, involvement, self-responsibility, caring, student sharing, and specified strategies. (See chapter 6 for a more detailed discussion.)

One recurring theme of humanistic philosophy is to meet the unique needs and interests of each student through individualized instruction. Its emphasis on sensitivity to individual differences and the development of the total person makes humanism a viable philosophy upon which to base adapted physical education programs.

Behaviorism

The **behavioral approach** advocates a systematic planned organization of the environment to achieve a desired behavioral response from an individual. It can be used to facilitate learning and enhance social behavior. Cooper, Heron, and Heward (1987) describe this approach as utilizing procedures derived from the principles developed by psychologists such as B.F. Skinner and Bandura to systematically change performance. This approach is based on the premise that the teacher can best ensure that learning occurs by structuring the environment.

A behavior modification orientation is advocated. Behavior modification is used in adapted physical education to help students learn control and maintain appropriate behavior by

- defining the specific behavior to be developed or changed,
- determining a baseline or present level of performance,
- establishing one or more terminal goals, and
- implementing a behavioral intervention program.

The use of behavior modification will be discussed in more detail in chapter 6.

Auxter, Pyfer, and Huettig (1993) are among the leaders in adapted physical education who espouse this approach. They suggest that behavior can be changed through the application of behavioral principles. They postulate that if adapted physical educators are going to apply behavioral principles, they must have precise behaviorally stated objectives and the learner must have a reason for wanting to meet these objectives. If these prerequisites are present, then it is possible to promote effective learning by applying systematic behavioral techniques.

One example of the behavioral approach being used to facilitate skill acquisition and develop appropriate social behaviors is the Data Based Gymnasium Model (discussed later in this chapter) (Dunn, Morehouse, & Fredericks, 1986). This approach requires teachers to task-analyze motor skills and social behaviors, develop specific objectives, and enhance their development using instructional procedures based on behavioral principles.

The main focus of behaviorism is to promote the attainment of skills that will make an individual self-sufficient. In the adapted physical education setting, a behaviorist philosophy results in a program that is very goal oriented and structured. It strives to minimize incorrect responses by providing a highly structured learning environment that is oriented toward functional skill development and success. This orientation makes behaviorism a popular and appropriate approach in the adapted physical education setting.

Eclectic Approach

Both the humanistic and behavioristic approaches along with other educational philosophies are relevant to skill facilitation and behavioral management in adapted physical education. However, the greatest value of these philosophies for the physical educator may be best realized by taking the best elements of each. This is known as the **eclectic approach**.

There are times when, because of the variety of individual needs, a humanistic approach is preferable. At other times, such as when there is a severe developmental delay, the behavioristic approach is more expedient and effective. By integrating several philosophical approaches into an eclectic approach, the physical educator can ensure that each student experiences success through facilitating optimal achievement.

TEACHING STYLES

Another choice crucial to successful teaching is to match the learning styles and the characteristics of the learners. A teaching style is a method of presenting material. Mosston (1981) has described several strategies and classified them on a continuum, from direct teacher-centered styles to indirect student-centered styles. The continuum reflects the amount of decision-making responsibility allocated to the teacher and to the learner. In a teacher-centered approach, the teacher makes most of the decisions on such matters as the structure of the learning environment, lesson content, entry level of the students, and starting and stopping times. As one moves along the continuum, decision-making responsibility is shifted increasingly to the student. Decisions assumed by students include solving movement problems, finding a beginning level for a task, and determining the amount of time to be spent on each problem. While Mosston identified eight teaching styles, only four will be discussed in this chapter: command, task, guided discovery, and problem solving. These styles appear to have the greatest utility for providing adapted physical education students with a challenging learning experience.

Command Style

The command style is probably the most common teaching style in adapted physical education. Decisions are made predominately by the teacher concerning lesson content, organization of the learning environment, and acceptable standards of performance.

Use of the command style can be illustrated in an adapted physical education setting by a class of students, all of whom are in wheelchairs. The group is gathered around the teacher, who explains how to execute the overhand throw. A demonstration follows, with the teacher using a chair or wheelchair to make the demonstration more relevant for the class. The students are then sent to practice the skill using tethered balls or rebounders with ball returners attached, so that the individual can retrieve the ball easily and have maximum continuous practice. The teacher moves from student to student, assisting each one with ball control, skill improvement, and motivation. At the end of the lesson, the teacher asks questions to review the major aspects of throwing and to measure the students' comprehension of the skill.

Advantages associated with the command style are

- teacher control,
- minimal investment of time in group organization, and
- knowledge of the expected outcomes.

This is an effective style for use with large groups, in one-on-one instruction, or when the teacher wants all of the students to practice the same task at the same time. It is particularly effective for children with behavioral problems, those with severe/profound mental retardation, and those who require external control.

Disadvantages of the command style are

- little thought about how to accomplish the skill is required on the part of the learner,
- little creativity is allowed in terms of motoric response, and
- little variation of response is permitted.

Also, because this method stresses the attainment of one correct response, it is generally insensitive to individual differences. This is a severe limitation when working with individuals whose motor abilities may vary greatly or whose impairment inhibits production of the one correct response. For example, when working with a class of children with orthopedic impairments, it may be impossible for all children in the class to execute an overhand tennis serve upon command by the teacher.

Task Style

The task style of instruction requires the teacher to develop a series of tasks that progressively lead to the achievement of an instructional objective. The teacher develops task cards, which are given to the students. For learners who are unable to read, task cards can be made with pictures or braille writing or even recorded on audio cassettes to meet individual needs. Additional resources such as filmstrips, posters, videotapes, books, and three-dimensional models can assist learners in mastering tasks. The tasks must be presented in a manner that allows the learner to determine when the assignment has been successfully completed. For example, in a lesson using a task approach to teach basketball dribbling, a task card may instruct the student to dribble through a five-cone obstacle course without losing control of the ball. After a successful evaluation is completed by the teacher, the learner, or a peer, the learner moves on to the next task in the sequence (for example, negotiating the same obstacle course while dribbling with the other hand). This method allows the teacher to organize the learning setting so that all students can be working on individual tasks concurrently in a safe environment. Examples of the task method specifically designed for learners with disabling conditions include the I CAN curriculum (Wessel, 1979), the Data Based Gymnasium (Dunn et al., 1986), and the Special Olympics Sports Skills Program (1985).

Advantages of the task method are numerous. This style

- encourages individuals to work at their own pace,
- allows individuals to practice tasks appropriate to their abilities,
- diminishes competition with others,
- allows the teacher to control the difficulty of the task,
- enhances success for each student,
- enables the teacher to work with students on an individual basis, and
- encourages the maximum use of equipment, facilities, and aides or volunteers.

The task method can be used effectively with children who can work independently on their own, who may need extra time to master tasks, and who can be assisted in tasks by peers, aides, or paraprofessionals.

Disadvantages of the task style include

- less structure in the learning setting than in the command style,
- possible increase in safety concerns,
- possible increase in distractions, and
- appearance of disorganization because many activities are going on simultaneously.

Guided Discovery Style

Guided discovery uses teacher-designed movement challenges to help students attain a specific movement goal. Students are encouraged to discover movement solutions that meet the criteria stated by the teacher. Using questions or short statements, the teacher guides the student in a progressive series of steps or subchallenges toward the desired outcomes or challenge goal (Nichols, 1986).

Following is an example of the use of guided discovery in teaching a class of students with emotional disturbances to throw a softball for distance. The teacher breaks the skill down into subchallenges.

Challenge:
"How far can you throw the softball using the overhand throw?"

Subchallenge 1:
"How should you stand to get the most distance?" If students do not respond motorically, the teacher can cue the response by giving them ideas such as (a) feet together behind the line, (b) feet parallel but wide apart, or (c) stride position—"Which foot should be forward?"

Subchallenge 2:
"How high should the ball go to travel the farthest?" Possible cues for this subchallenge would be, "Will it travel farther close to the ground?" "If you throw the ball as high as you can, will it travel a long distance?"

These are examples of subchallenges that would help a student find the answer to the teacher's challenge, "How do you throw the softball the greatest distance."

Advantages of the guided discovery style are that it

- encourages creativity,
- allows students to discover how various parts of the body contribute to movement patterns, and
- enhances self-concept as students receive positive feedback while shaping their response to obtain the desired outcome.

This method is appropriate with mature students and students whose cognitive ability permits the required thought processes. According to Gallahue (1993), it is also appropriate for toddlers and preschoolers who are experimenting or are not yet ready to give one correct response.

Disadvantages of the guided discovery style are that it may require

- more time to achieve movement goals,
- more preparation on the part of the teacher, and
- more patience and a great deal of feedback by the teacher to bring about the same level of performance as the command style.

Problem-Solving Style

This method resembles the guided discovery method in presenting a series of movement challenges to the learner. However, in contrast to guided discovery where one specific movement is the goal, the problem-solving style emphasizes the development of multiple solutions to a given problem posed by the teacher. This style encourages students to develop as many solutions as possible, provided that the solutions meet the criteria stated by the teacher.

In an instructional episode in which students are encouraged to display different ways of rolling effectively, the teacher might pose the following challenges:

1. "Staying within the mat areas and not getting into another child's self-space, roll in as many different ways as you can."

2. "Roll with your body as long as possible."

3. "Can you find a way to roll with your arms out to the side?"

4. "Can you combine three different rolls and roll in a circle?"

After each challenge the teacher lets students experiment with a variety of movement solutions. Often, additional questions are needed to elicit a variety of responses, especially with students who learn primarily by imitation and those who have had limited motor experience. Children who have spent most of their time in wheelchairs, toddlers, and preschool children may benefit from being taught by this method.

Advantages of the problem-solving style include

- wide allowances for individual differences,

- emphasis on cognitive process and creativity, and

- acceptance of skill execution that varies from the expected norm.

It treats as correct any response to the movement challenge that meets the criteria; this is important in cases where disabling conditions inhibit a particular response. Problem solving boosts learners' self-esteem by allowing them to experience success.

Disadvantages of the problem-solving style are

- the great amount of time required for students to fully explore possible movement solutions,

- the lack of structure, and

- the absence of an absolute outcome.

Direct vs. Indirect Styles

Teaching styles can also be described as direct and indirect. Direct teaching styles are the more traditional teacher-centered styles where the teacher makes most of the decisions about performance. These styles are recommended for individuals functioning at the severe/profound level, students who benefit from structure (e.g., those with autism), and students with behavioral disabilities.

Individuals who are learning at an advanced skill level also may profit from these methods. Teachers who follow a behaviorist philosophy generally prefer utilizing direct teaching styles.

Indirect styles are more child centered. They permit the learner to take an active role in the learning process through problem solving, experimentation, and self-discovery. The indirect styles are most beneficial for students in adapted physical education who are high-functioning, preschool infants and toddlers, those learning basic motor skills, or those learning skills not requiring one correct response.

The range of instructional styles allows educators to teach the same content using a variety of methods. In selecting a style, the teacher should consider its appropriateness for the desired objectives. The choice of teaching style should also reflect such factors as the teacher's preferences and personality; the students' ages, experience, learning style, and disabling conditions; the stage of learning; and the skills to be taught. The learning environment may also influence the choice of style. Practical considerations such as equipment, space, available time, and number of students may make one teaching style preferable to the others.

MOTOR LEARNING

Research supports the assertion that, when students are taught by methods that complement their learning characteristics, they are motivated and learn more easily (Webster, 1993). By understanding how a student learns best, the educator can facilitate the learning process considerably. Material may be presented in one of three approaches: the *whole*, the *part-whole*, and the *progressive-part*.

Whole Method

The whole method of learning should be used when the skill to be learned is relatively simple or made up of few parts. An example utilizing this method to teach the skip to an elementary school student with learning disabilities would involve the teacher demonstrating the skill and then taking the child by the hand and skipping together. For this child the whole approach might be more successful than having the child practice a step-hop with one foot and a step-hop with the other foot.

This method may be preferable for students who have difficulties in conceptual learning and are unable to relate the several parts of a skill to its whole. It is also the method of choice for students with short attention spans and students who learn best by imitation. However, one requirement is that the learner be able to remember the skill to be learned, its specific movements, and its sequence. Motor skills that can be presented through the whole approach include running, catching, striking, and jumping.

Part-Whole Method

The part-whole method requires individuals to learn skills by practicing one part at a time and then combining them to perform the whole skill. This method works best for individuals who can concentrate on and accomplish small tasks. It may not be desirable for those who have difficulty integrating various parts into a whole, even with the guidance of the instructor. In using this method, the physical educator breaks down the complete task into meaningful parts; this process is known as task analysis. The teacher should make each part an end in itself, thus providing a sense of accomplishment even though the learner may not be able to master the entire task or terminal objective.

The individual parts of the developmental sequence or the task analysis can be taught using a concept known as *chaining*. Chaining refers to the successful learning of a task or part, which is then combined with other parts to master a skill. Chaining can be completed in a forward or backward direction. *Forward chaining*, the traditional method, involves starting with the first or most basic step or level and building toward the end product. *Backward chaining* involves starting with the end product and working backward toward the basic parts.

An example of a skill that can be analyzed into meaningful tasks and thus is amenable to the part-whole method is the beginner's backstroke in swimming. The skill can be divided into the back float, back glide, back glide with flutter kick, arm action, and leg action. Each of these tasks can give the learner a feeling of accomplishment and lead to successful movement in the water. Many individuals with disabilities may not master the elementary backstroke in its entirety, yet they can succeed in mastering its various elements. This is an example of forward chaining. Skills that are more effectively taught using backward chaining are kicking an object or throwing.

Progressive-Part Method

The progressive-part approach involves teaching the most fundamental part of the skill first and then building on this base to present the next part. When the first two parts are learned, they are combined, and succeeding parts are added until the whole skill is mastered.

Special Olympians might use this method in learning the triple jump. The coach would first work to develop the athlete's hopping ability, then combine the hop with a step. When the athlete mastered these two skills, the final skill, jump, would be added.

With the progressive-part method, the teacher or coach should be alert to problems that can occur if an individual fails to learn one part of the progression and should take care to provide the opportunity for success at each part level. This method lets individuals master a skill at their own pace, practicing the most difficult parts while still progressing toward the overall objective. Programs that incorporate the principles of task analysis and employ the part-whole and the progressive-part methods include the Data Based Gymnasium (Dunn et al., 1986), and I CAN (Wessel, 1979).

Principles of Motor Learning

Application of the principles that form the scientific foundations of physical education can result in better learning experiences for children with special needs. To ensure success, the physical educator or coach must understand the learning process, know how to adapt it to meet individual needs, and promote the learner's active involvement in the process.

Learning can be enhanced by applying the principles of motor learning. These focus on the process by which people acquire motor skills. By understanding and applying the motor learning guidelines listed below, the teacher or coach may help students with unique needs to achieve their maximum potential.

Guidelines for Teaching
Based on Principles of Motor Learning

1. To accommodate differences in learning styles, use a variety of teaching techniques.

2. To facilitate learning, present skills to individuals when they have reached the appropriate developmental level.

3. To increase the likelihood of continued participation, provide enjoyable experiences in which the individuals succeed.

4. To motivate individuals to continue their participation, reinforce their efforts.

5. To increase learning, present the principal focus of the lesson early.

6. To enhance performance, provide appropriate practice opportunities.

7. To accommodate differences in individuals' rates and amounts of learning, individualize instruction.

8. To encourage individuals to persist in their skill acquisition efforts, provide appropriate feedback.

9. To assist individuals in transferring previously learned skills to new learning situations, identify common aspects of the situations.

10. To help individuals make more rapid progress in learning, set meaningful and realistic goals.

11. To increase the retention of skills, provide opportunities for mastery and select skills that have personal meaning to the individual.

FACILITATING SKILL DEVELOPMENT

There are three ways of facilitating skill development. *Task analysis* allows the teacher to identify and sequentially develop the components inherent in various skills. *Activity analysis* assists the teacher in selecting activities by identifying the physical, cognitive, affective, and social components that will contribute to student success. Once an appropriate activity has been selected, functional adaptations and *activity modifications* may be necessary to meet the special needs of the learner.

Task Analysis

Task analysis can facilitate the acquisition of a skill by separating it into meaningful components. These components can be arranged in sequence, from easy to difficult, and can serve as the basis for short-term performance objectives. Before introducing a specific task, the teacher should determine where on the developmental continuum the learner is functioning and whether the child has met all relevant developmental prerequisites. Teachers should include prerequisite skills in the task analysis for a particular skill and should consider developmental, environmental, and biomechanical factors. Task analysis provides a

systematic, hierarchical method for analyzing skill mastery, from the fundamental level to the advanced level. It offers a way of breaking a skill down into its related subtasks, with each subtask more challenging than the previous one. An example is presented in Figure 5.2. In writing a task analysis, it is important to include all steps describing each component in observable behavioral terms. This thoroughness will facilitate the identification of short-term behavioral objectives and thus simplify the process of IEP development.

An **ecological task analysis** (ETA) has recently been advocated as an alternative to the traditional type. Balan and Davis (1993) describe the ETA as a model that "provides a framework for the process of assessment and instruction" (p. 54). The ETA provides methods for individualizing instruction, which allows students to make decisions and encourages creativity and discovery. It allows the teacher to structure the learning environment to stimulate participation by providing students with many movement alternatives. The ETA is a viable option for teachers seeking to encourage students "to expand their skills through a series of conditions, challenges, and competitions" (p. 61).

Activity Analysis

Activity analysis is a technique for determining the basic characteristics of an activity and relating them to desired student outcomes. By breaking an activity into components, the teacher can better understand the specific value of a certain activity and modify it to fit an individual learner's needs, if necessary. Thus, once a student's needs have been determined, the teacher can use activity analysis to assess whether a specific activity can meet those needs.

Activity analysis facilitates the selection of program content to meet stated objectives. In making the analysis, the teacher must consider how the activity contributes to learning in the physical, cognitive, affective, and social domains. When analyzing an activity from a physiological perspective, the teacher should examine such factors as basic body positions required, body parts utilized, body actions performed, fundamental movement patterns incorporated, coordination needed, fitness level required, and sensory systems used. Cognitive factors that should be evaluated include the number and complexity of rules and the need for memorization, concentration, strategies, and perceptual and academic skills. Affective factors to consider in the activity analysis include the emotional effect of participation and the amount of

Main Task: For Mary to jump rope for a full (overhead) turn 4 times without verbal cue.

Prerequisite Skills: Ability to jump. Ability to stand erect.

I. **Jump over painted line once over and back without verbal cue.**

   a. Walk line down and back heel-toe with verbal cue.
   b. Face rope with toes, jump over once with verbal cue.
   c. Stand parallel to rope, jump over and back without verbal cue.

II. **Jump over still rope over and back twice without verbal cue.**

   a. Face rope with toes, jump over once with verbal cue.
   b. Stand parallel to rope, jump over and back with verbal cue.
   c. Stand parallel to rope, jump over and back twice without verbal cue.

III. **Jump over wiggly (snake) rope 2" off ground without verbal cue.**

   a. Jump wiggly rope on ground once with verbal cue.
   b. Jump wiggly rope 1" off ground over and back with verbal cue.
   c. Jump wiggly rope 2" off ground over and back without verbal cue.

IV. **Jump over 1/2 turned rope without verbal cue 4 times.**

   a. Stand and jump on the back swing twice with verbal cue.
   b. Stand and jump on the forward and back swing twice with verbal cue.
   c. Stand and jump on the forward and back swing 4 times without verbal cue.

V. **Jump rope a full turn overhead 4 times without verbal cue.**

   a. Stand and jump once as the rope makes a full turn with verbal cue.
   b. Stand and jump twice as the rope makes a full turn with verbal cue.
   c. Stand and jump 4 times as the rope makes a full turn without verbal cue.

Figure 5.2 Example of a task analysis for rope jumping.

emotional control required. The social interaction required for successful participation in the activity must also be ascertained. Table 5.1 provides an example of an activity analysis for table tennis.

Activity Modifications

Task analysis and activity analysis provide the basis for activity or game selection. After choosing the most appropriate activities, the educator must then modify them to the extent necessary. A softball game in an adapted physical education class provides an example. Activity modification for students with below-average mental abilities may include simplifying the rules or practicing lead-up activities. For those with visual impairments, the playing field might be made smaller, with base paths having a different texture than the field. Equipment might be adapted to include sound devices in the ball and in the bases to aid players with visual disabilities and lighter balls and batting tees for those with physical disabilities.

Modified rules for making "outs" or a change in the number of participants may be required for players with limited mobility. When modifying an activity, the educator should try to maintain its inherent nature so that it is as close to the traditional activity as possible.

Modifications need not affect every component of an activity; they should be limited to those that are necessary to meet individual needs. It may be necessary to modify the rules to make them more easily understandable, facilities to make them accessible, scoring to equalize competition, the number of participants to ensure maximum participation, or modifications of equipment.

ORGANIZATIONAL AND METHODOLOGICAL TECHNIQUES

Various organizational and methodological techniques may be employed to individualize instruction. They include team teaching, supportive teaching, peer and cross-age tutoring, and independent learning.

Team Teaching

It is often best for two or more teachers to instruct an adapted physical education class together so that individual differences can be accommodated. This approach, called team teaching, is especially

Table 5.1   An Activity Analysis for Table Tennis

Activity demands	Activity	Table tennis
Physical demands	1. Primary body position required?	Standing
	2. Movement skills required?	Bending, grasping, catching, hitting
	3. Amount of fitness required?	Minimal fitness level
	a. Strength	Low ability to hold paddle
	b. Endurance	Low cardiovascular requirements
	c. Speed	Quickness is an asset
	d. Flexibility	Moderate
	e. Agility	High level desirable
	4. Amount of coordination required?	Important, especially eye-hand coordination
	5. Amount of energy required?	Little
Social demands	1. Number of participants required?	2 persons, 4 for doubles
	2. Types of interaction?	Little; 1 to 1
	3. Type of communication?	Little verbal, opportunity for nonverbal
	4. Type of leadership?	None
	5. Competitive or cooperative activity?	Competitive mainly, cooperative if doubles
	6. Amount of physical contact required?	None in singles, much in doubles
	7. Noise level?	Minimal
Cognitive demands	1. Complexity of rules?	Moderate
	2. Level of strategy?	Moderate
	3. Concentration level?	Moderate
	4. Academic skills (reading, etc.) needed?	Ability to count to 21 and to add
	5. Verbal skills needed?	None
	6. Directional concepts needed?	Yes
	7. Complexity of scoring system?	Simple
	8. Memory required?	Little
Administrative demands	1. Time required?	Can be controlled by score or time
	2. Equipment needed?	Paddles, balls, tables with nets
	3. Special facilities required?	Area large enough to accommodate tables
	4. Type of leadership required?	Ability to instruct small group
	5. Safety factors to be considered?	Space between tables

important in settings where educators are not well prepared to work with students who have unique needs.

Supportive Teaching

Often when students with disabilities are integrated into regular physical education classes, it is necessary for the child's aide or a volunteer assistant to participate or help the student. This assistance supports the physical education teacher's efforts to include the child fully in the activity of the regular class and promotes successful participation by the student. The supportive teaching approach is extremely valuable to a student who is just beginning the integration process. It eases the adjustment process and allows the student to concentrate on the material being taught.

Peer and Cross-Age Tutoring

Peer tutoring involves same-age students helping with instruction. Peer tutors can be used to reduce the student-teacher ratio. Cross-age tutoring programs enlist students of different ages (such as high school juniors or seniors) to work with the young children in adapted physical education. Cross-age tutoring can provide satisfaction to the tutors while increasing the level of learning for students with disabilities (see Figure 5.3).

Independent Learning

Independent learning gives students the opportunity to progress at their own rate. This technique is particularly useful when the educator is obliged to exclude a student from certain activities. Independent learning materials may take several forms. For example, the teacher may prepare a series of task cards for the student, specifying skills to be accomplished.

Sometimes the student and the educator might make a formal agreement designating the tasks the student must master to earn a certain grade. This is known as a learning contract. Such contracts allow teachers to personalize grading to reflect the unique conditions of each learner.

Figure 5.3 Using an older athlete with a disability for one-on-one instruction provides a role model for the young athlete and satisfaction to the instructor.

Computer-assisted instructional modules also allow students with disabilities to learn at their own pace. They progress through the use of interactive episodes and programmed learning.

PRESCRIPTIVE PLANNING AND INSTRUCTIONAL MODELS

Several curricular models have proven to be successful in providing a quality physical education experience for individuals with disabilities. When used as guides, these models can help enhance the teaching process and ensure that students with unique needs are taught in an efficient and effective manner. They include the Achievement-Based Curriculum developed by I CAN (Wessel & Kelly, 1985), the Data Based Gymnasium (Dunn et al., 1986), the Motor Development Curriculum for Children (Werder & Bruininks, 1988), the PREP Program Instructional Model (Watkinson & Wall, 1979), and the TAPE instructional model advocated as part of Project ACTIVE (Vodola, 1976).

I CAN and the Achievement-Based Curriculum Model

I CAN (Individualize instruction, Create social leisure competence, Associate all learnings, Narrow the gap between theory and practice) is a comprehensive physical education and leisure skills program appropriate for children with unique needs. It is developmental in nature and provides a continuum of skills, from preprimary motor and play skills to sport, leisure, and recreation skills. The I CAN program offers a balance between the development of psychomotor skills and affective and social development. It provides for individualized instruction at each student's level of ability and lets learners progress at a rate and in a manner appropriate to their learning styles and motivation/interest levels. I CAN is particularly useful for children whose developmental growth is slower than average, including those with physical and mental disabilities as well as those with specific learning disabilities and social-emotional behavior problems.

The I CAN program comprises three major areas: preprimary motor and play skills, primary skills, and sport, leisure, and recreation skills (some I CAN curricular materials are shown in Figure 5.4). The program is designed for use by physical education specialists and special education or classroom teachers.

The Achievement-Based Curriculum model (ABC) includes a systematic, sequential process

Figure 5.4 Some available I CAN curriculum materials.
From Brochure No. 335, Northbrook, IL: Hubbard. Used with permission of Pro-Ed, Austin, TX.

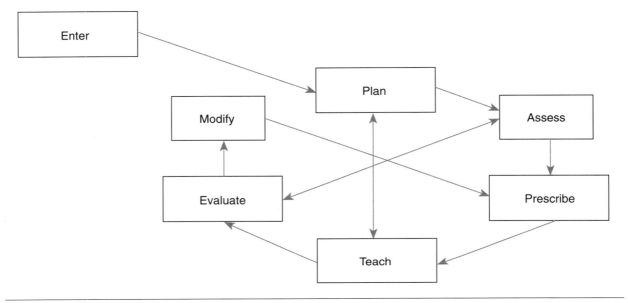

Figure 5.5 ABC Model used by I CAN.
Adapted from *Leadership Training Guide* by L. Burkett and J.A. Wessel, 1984, Tempe: Arizona State University. Adapted with permission of Pro-Ed, Austin, TX.

that enables teachers to plan, implement, and evaluate instructional programs for individuals based on selected goals and objectives (Kelly, 1989).

Figure 5.5 represents the ABC model, developed by I CAN, which includes perspective methods for planning and programming.

The ABC model assists the teacher in developing instructional strategies in a systematic manner while being sensitive to individual needs. The model involves five steps:

1. *Plan.* The planning step includes defining the program goals; determining community, school, and student interests; and creating a developmental sequence that will permit achievement of the stated goals.

2. *Assess.* Assessment is continuous. Criterion-referenced tests are used to assess the student's

level of skill and to document improvement. Norm-referenced tests may also be employed to assess a student's performance in comparison with that of designated groups.

3. *Prescribe.* Using the assessment results, the teacher selects specific skills to be included in the physical education program for each individual and indicates what teaching methods, groupings, and equipment are necessary to ensure optimal student achievement.

4. *Teach.* Teaching is the implementation of the prescription. It is based on the instructional techniques previously discussed: motivation, feedback, maximizing on-task time, managing disruptive behaviors, and so on.

5. *Evaluate.* The evaluation step allows the teacher to determine the student's level of

functioning at the completion of the instructional process. The teacher can then modify expectations, techniques, or the environment to improve future efforts and responses.

The Data Based Gymnasium Instructional Model

The Data Based Gymnasium (DBG) provides ways to initiate and analyze behavior, emphasizes provision of feedback, and recommends ways to manage the learning environment (Dunn et al., 1986). The DBG also provides an exercise, sport, and leisure curriculum. Specific skills are task-analyzed, and the tasks are sequenced as phases that represent shaping behaviors. Although the DBG is similar in design to many other instructional models, it is unique in its specific delineation of behavior modification techniques as a means of accomplishing task and terminal objectives.

Originally, the DBG model, as illustrated in Figure 5.6, was designed to provide a physical education program for individuals with severe disabilities. However, its principles are applicable in some form to many instructional situations involving students with a variety of unique learning needs.

The DBG instructional model emphasizes three essential elements:

1. *Cue.* The cue is a condition, signal, or request to the learner designed to influence the occurrence of a behavior. Cues can be verbal, like the command "Stand up," or nonverbal, like printed directions or a demonstration of the desired activity.

2. *Behavior.* Behavior is what a person does in response to a cue. In the DBG model it is a component of the task that the student is to learn or the skill that the student is being asked to master. The teacher presents cues that will result in the performance of the targeted behavior. If the desired terminal behavior is too complex for the student to achieve, it must be broken down into simpler enabling behaviors. When the enabling behavior is accomplished (forward chaining), the student may then be capable of the more complex terminal behavior. With moderately and severely disabled individuals, backward chaining may be used. In the DBG model, this means providing assistance with the initial parts of the task but letting the student perform the last component independently. Progressing, the student is allowed to perform additional components of the task unaided. The sequence thus builds systematically from the final component to the initial one.

3. *Consequence.* After a behavior is performed, the student must receive information about its success or failure. Feedback, or consequences, can be positive or negative in nature. Positive feedback is called a reinforcer, while negative feedback is a punisher. The model stresses the delivery of appropriate positive consequences to increase the probability of behavior being repeated.

The Data Based Gymnasium includes a task-analyzed game, exercise, and leisure sport curriculum. Figure 5.7 presents an example of the instructional procedures for teaching the skill of sliding down a slide. Utilizing the DBG model, the instructor demonstrates the skill and tells the student to "slide down the slide" (cue). Depending upon the student's response, (behavior), the instructor uses reinforcers and/or physical assistance to ensure successful completion of the task. In addition, the DBG model provides examples of systematic data collection techniques that can help the instructor to successfully implement the program.

Although I CAN and DBG are probably the best-known models, three others should be included in an overview of quality instructional delivery systems.

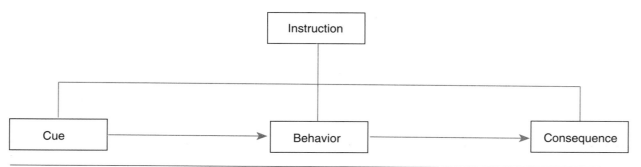

Figure 5.6 The data based gymnasium instructional process.

Program Cover Sheet

Pupil: Jim
Date started: April 3, 1996
Date completed:

Program: Leisure Skills
Go down a slide

Verbal cue:
"Jim, slide down the slide."

Materials:
1. Clipboard
2. Pencil
3. Slide
4. Reinforcer

Instructional setting:
Position Jim so he can see the demonstration.

Reinforcement procedure:
Give social reinforcement on completion of task.

Correction:
"No, Jim." Model, recue, give mild social reinforcement if correct.
If not, go to next level of assistance.
"No, Jim."
Cue. "Jim, slide down the slide."
Physically assist Jim as he slides.
Socially reinforce on completion of the task.

Criterion:
Three consecutive correct responses before going to next step

Figure 5.7 Example of the instructional procedure for teaching a skill according to the DBG model.
From *Physical Education for the Severely Handicapped: A Systematic Approach to a Data Based Gymnasium* (p. 53), by J. Dunn, J. Morehouse, and H.D. Fredericks, 1986, Austin, TX: Pro-Ed. Reprinted by permission.

Body Skills: A Motor Development Curriculum for Children

Body Skills is a motor development curriculum for children aged 2 to 12 years (Werder & Bruininks, (1988). It can be used in preschool, special education, and elementary school settings. It provides a systematic procedure for assessing, planning, and teaching gross motor skills. It provides units in body management, locomotion, body fitness, object movement, and fine motor development.

Body Skills consists of a series of folders, one for each of the 31 skill areas covered. Each folder has a pictorial developmental sequence of the skill for criterion-referenced assessment purposes. It also provides a series of activities that utilize the skill, and suggestions for adaptations, and record forms.

The strongest asset of this program is the formal assessment, The Motor Skills Inventory (MSI). It provides a criterion-referenced test for measuring a student's prestart developmental level. Using the record forms, the teacher relates the scores from the MSI

to a standardized measure, the Bruininks-Oseretsky Test of Motor Proficiency (Bruininks, 1978). This can be very helpful when developing IEPs.

Project ACTIVE

The ACTIVE program (**All Children Totally Involved Exercising**) was designed by Dr. Thomas Vodola (1976) to ensure that every child, regardless of disability, would have a chance to participate in a quality physical education program. Project ACTIVE incorporates a test-assess-prescribe-evaluate planning process and includes normative as well as criterion-referenced tests in the areas of motor ability, nutrition, physical fitness, and posture. These are specially designed instructional programs for individuals with mental retardation, learning disabilities, orthopedic impairments, sensory impairments, eating disorders, and breathing problems. They also include activities for postoperative convalescent, normal, and gifted children. Karp and Adler

(1992) have revised and updated the ACTIVE materials. Project ACTIVE is an innovative, cost-effective program that has been used throughout the United States.

PREP Play Program

The goal of the PREP Play Program, designed in 1974 in Edmonton, Alberta, is to develop the play skills of moderately mentally retarded children aged 3 to 12 (Watkinson and Wall, 1979). It is based on the belief that improving individual play skills will enable children to participate more success-fully in a nonstructured play environment.

The most helpful feature of the PREP Program is the set of task-analyzed, instructionally sequenced skills that are used for assessing the level of func-tioning of each individual, determining teaching objectives, and carrying out the instructional pro-cess. This model, if modified, can be used for teach-ing other physical skills.

The PREP Program is carried out during free play periods. The teacher interacts with one child at a time while the others continue their free play. In-structional episodes are short and focus on a specific task (e.g., learning to jump down). Although most of the teaching is done on a one-on-one basis, the teacher spends part of the time with small groups. These groups are composed of children with similar motor abilities, and they allow practice in a group context of the skills learned individually. An im-portant underlying requirement of the PREP Play Program is an environment that is conducive to stim-ulating and purposeful play.

The instructional systems just described are pri-marily behavioral in nature. Although there are also instructional systems based on humanistic principles, they have not yet been developed to the same extent.

SUMMARY

Many factors affect teaching effectiveness in the adapted physical education and sport setting. Edu-cators who are capable of employing a variety of approaches and teaching methods and matching them to the learning needs of individuals can better structure the learning environment to ensure stu-dent satisfaction and success. Their flexibility per-mits them to teach the same content in different ways, thus allowing them to more fully adapt their teaching to meet individual needs. It also allows teachers to optimize student skill development by

successfully implementing the principles of motor learning.

Teachers can facilitate learning by employing task analysis, activity analysis, and activity modifi-cation. These techniques are valuable in helping educators to meet learners' goals and accommo-date their needs.

Organizational and methodological techniques allow teachers to maximize learning opportunities by decreasing the teacher-student ratio and struc-turing independent learning experiences.

Several instructional planning models have been developed to meet individual needs. They include the Achievement-Based Curriculum and I CAN, the Data Based Gymnasium, Body Skills: A Motor Development Curriculum for Children, Project ACTIVE, and the PREP Play Program. In addition to these behaviorally oriented models, teachers may draw on the humanistic orientation to physi-cal education. These resources offer valuable assis-tance to physical educators in designing quality physical education programs to optimize learning for individuals with unique needs.

BIBLIOGRAPHY

Auxter, D., Pyfer, J., & Huettig, C. (1993). *Principles and methods of adapted physical education and recreation* (7th ed.). St. Louis: Mosby.

Balan, C., & Davis, W. (1993). Ecological task analysis: An approach to teaching physical education. *Journal of Physical Education, Recreation and Dance*, **64**(9), 54–61.

Bruininks, R.H. (1978). *Bruininks-Oseretsky test of motor proficiency: Examiners manual*. Circle Pines, MN: American Guidance Service.

Burkett, L., & Wessel, J.A. (1984). *Leadership Training Guide*. Tempe, AZ: Department of Health and Physi-cal Education, Arizona State University.

Cooper, J.O., Heron, T.E., & Heward, W.L. (1987). *Applied behavior analysis*. Columbus, OH: Merrill.

Dunn, J.M., Morehouse, J.W., & Fredericks, H.D. (1986). *Physical education for the severely handicapped: A sys-tematic approach to a data based gymnasium* (2nd ed.). Austin, TX: Pro-Ed.

Gallahue, D.L. (1993). *Developmental physical education for today's children* (2nd ed.). Madison, WI: Brown & Benchmark.

Hellison, D.R. (1985). *Goals and strategies for teaching phys-ical education*. Champaign, IL: Human Kinetics.

Karp, J., & Adler, A. (1992). *ACTIVE*. (Available from: J. Karp, 20214 103rd Place, NE, Bothell, WA 98011-2455).

Kelly, L.E. (1989). *Project I CAN-ABC*. Charlottesville: University of Virginia.

McGrath, R., & Krauss, B. (Eds.). (1977). *An exceptional view of life*. Washington, DC: Potomac.

Mosston, M. (1981). *Teaching physical education* (2nd ed.). Columbus, OH: Merrill.

Nichols, B. (1986). *Moving and learning: The elementary school physical education experience*. St Louis: Times Mirror/Mosby.

Sherrill, C. (1993). *Adapted physical activity, recreation, and sport: Crossdisciplinary and lifespan* (4th ed.). Madison, WI: Brown & Benchmark.

Special Olympics sport skill guides. (1985). Washington, DC: Special Olympics.

Vodola, T. (1976). *Project ACTIVE maxi-model: Nine training manuals*. Oakhurst, NJ: Project ACTIVE.

Watkinson, E.J., & Wall, A.E. (1979). *The PREP Play Program: Skill instruction for young mentally retarded children*. Edmonton, AB: Physical Education Department, University of Alberta.

Webster, G.E. (1993). Effective teaching in adapted physical education: A review. *Palaestra* **9**(3), 25–31.

Werder, J.K., & Bruininks, R.H. (1988). *Body Skills: A motor development curriculum for children*. Circle Pines, MN: American Guidance Service.

Wessel, J.A. (1979). *I CAN—Sport, leisure and recreation skills*. Northbrook, IL: Hubbard.

Wessel, J.A., & Kelly, L.E. (1985). *Achievement-based curriculum development in physical education*. Philadelphia: Lea & Febiger.

RESOURCES

Auxter, D., Pyfer, J., & Huettig, C. (1993). *Principles and methods of adapted physical education and recreation* (7th ed.). St. Louis: Times Mirror/Mosby. This book provides comprehensive information about adapted physical education and advocates the task-specific approach. It also provides various approaches to task analysis and compares the developmental and task-specific approaches.

Gallahue, D.L. (1993). *Developmental physical education for today's children*. Madison, WI: Brown & Benchmark. The development process from the prenatal period through age 12 is discussed. This book treats psychomotor, cognitive, and affective factors that influence the motor development of children and also describes teaching behaviors and styles that promote effective teaching of students with special needs. It would be helpful in working with developmentally delayed children.

Magill, R.A. (1985). *Motor learning: Concepts and applications*. Dubuque, IA: Brown. This book explains the scientific foundations of motor learning while stressing practical applications. It offers an introduction to motor learning followed by information on both the learner and the learning environment.

Mosston, M., & Ashworth, S. (1986). *Teaching physical education* (3rd ed.). Columbus, OH: Merrill. This book provides a comprehensive discussion of various teaching styles as well as excellent examples of their application.

Sherrill, C. (1993). *Adapted physical activity, recreation, and sport: Crossdisciplinary and lifespan* (4th ed.). Madison, WI: Brown & Benchmark. This is an excellent source of information on the philosophy of humanism as it is applied to adapted physical education and the developmental approach to teaching. It also provides examples of teaching to meet individual needs through task analysis, activity analysis, and activity modification.

CHAPTER 6

Behavior Management

E. Michael Loovis

Lack of discipline continues to be one of the greatest problems in the public schools (Elam, Rose, & Gallup, 1992). For years, educators confronting problems of inappropriate behavior have employed several remedial practices, including corporal punishment, behavior management techniques, suspension, and expulsion. In most cases use of these practices has been and continues to be *reactive:* a particular method is applied after some misbehavior has occurred. However, many of the problems that educators face on a daily basis could be prevented if they took a more *proactive* stance toward managing student behavior. Implicit in this statement is the prevention of misbehavior before it occurs. For example, it will be difficult for a physical educator to establish an appropriate instructional climate in a self-contained class for students with behavior disabilities when several students persist in being verbally and physically abusive toward the teacher and other class members.

From another perspective, behavior management approaches have been used successfully to facilitate skill acquisition—either directly, through systematic manipulation of content, or indirectly, through arrangement of the consequences of performance to produce greater motivation. For example, a behavior management approach can help a physical educator to determine the appropriate level at which to begin instruction in golf for students with mental retardation and to maintain the students' enthusiasm for learning this activity over time. Behavior management has also been used to teach those

appropriate social behaviors considered essential to performance in school, at home, and in other significant environments. This chapter offers several proactive systems to help teachers and coaches achieve the goals and objectives of their programs in a positive learning environment.

BEHAVIOR MODIFICATION

Behavior modification is a systematic process in which the environment is arranged to facilitate skill acquisition and/or shape social behavior. More specifically, it is the application of reinforcement learning theory derived from operant psychology. Behavior modification includes such procedures as respondent conditioning (the automatic control of behavior by antecedent stimuli), operant conditioning (the control of behavior by regulating the consequences that follow a behavior), contingency management (the relationship between a behavior and the events that follow behavior), and behavioral modeling, also called observational learning (learning by observing another individual engaged in a behavior). All have one thing in common: the planned systematic arrangement of consequences to alter an individual's response or at least the frequency of that response. In adapted physical education, this arrangement could involve the use of rewards to cause mentally retarded students to engage in sustained exercise behavior when riding stationary bicycles. It could also mean establishing a contract with a student who has cerebral palsy to define a number of tasks to be completed in a unit on throwing and catching skills.

To understand behavior modification, it is necessary to know some basic terminology. On the assumption that behavior is controlled by its effect on the environment, the first step toward understanding the management of human behavior is to define the stimuli that influence people's behavior. A measurable event that may have an influence on behavior is referred to as a *stimulus*. **Reinforcement** is a stimulus event that increases or maintains the frequency of a response. In physical education, reinforcement may be thought of as feedback provided directly or indirectly by the teacher or coach. Reinforcers can be physical, verbal, visual, edible, or active in nature. Examples of reinforcers include

- a pat on the back (physical),
- an approving comment like "Good job!" (verbal),
- a smile (visual),
- a piece of candy (edible), and
- a chance to bounce on a trampoline (active).

All of these examples are usually considered positive reinforcers. Positive reinforcers, or rewards, are stimuli that individuals perceive as good, that is, as something they want. If a response occurs and it is positively reinforced, the likelihood of its recurring under similar circumstances is maintained or increased. For example, a teacher might praise a student who demonstrates appropriate attending behavior during instruction in the gymnasium. If praise is positively reinforcing to that student, then the chances of the student's attending to instruction in the future are strengthened. **Positive reinforcement** is one of the basic principles of operant conditioning described in this section. Figure 6.1 illustrates this, and the other principles that this chapter examines. The presence of aversive or "bad" stimuli—something that individuals wish to avoid—is commonly called **negative reinforcement**. If a response occurs and if it successfully averts a negative stimulus, the likelihood of the desired response recurring under similar circumstances is maintained or increased.

Because positive and negative reinforcement may produce similar results, the distinction between them may not be readily apparent. An example may clarify the difference. Suppose that the student mentioned in the previous paragraph had been talking to a friend while the teacher was explaining the lesson, and that this talking was distracting to the teacher and the rest of the class.

If the teacher had warned that continual talking would result in after-school detention or a low grade for the day (possible aversive stimuli) and if the student perceived the stimuli as something to avoid, then the likelihood that the student would attend to instructions would increase. By listening in class the student would have avoided staying after school or having the grade reduced. This is an example of negative reinforcement because the stimulus increased the likelihood of a desired behavior through the avoidance of an aversive consequence rather than the presence of a positive one.

Just as teachers and coaches seek to maintain or increase the frequency of some behaviors, they may wish to decrease the occurrence of others. When the consequence of a certain behavior has the effect of decreasing its frequency, the consequence is called **punishment**. Punishment can be either the presentation of an aversive stimulus or the removal of a positive stimulus. The intention of punishment is to weaken or eliminate a behavior. The following scenario illustrates the effect of punishment on the student in our previous example. The student has been talking during the instructional time. The teacher has warned the student that continual talking will result in detention or a grade reduction. The student ignores the warning and continues to talk. The consequence for talking when one is supposed to be listening, at least in this situation, will be the presentation of one of the two aversive stimuli.

A slightly different scenario illustrates the notion of punishment as the removal of a positive stimulus. Our student, still talking after the teacher's warning, is punished by being barred from a 5-minute free-time activity at the end of class—an activity perceived as a positive stimulus. The removal of this highly desirable activity fits the definition of punishment and will weaken or eliminate the disruptive behavior in future instructional episodes.

In contrast to punishment, *withholding of reinforcement* from a response that has previously been reinforced results in **extinction** or cessation of a behavior. Extinction differs from punishment in that no consequence follows the response; a stimulus (aversive or positive event) is neither presented nor taken away. For example, teachers or coaches who pay attention to students when they clown around may be reinforcing the very behavior they would like to see extinguished. If they ignore (i.e., stop reinforcing) the undesirable behavior, it will probably decrease in frequency.

Table 6.1 summarizes the basic principles of behavior modification. Each principle has a specific purpose; application of the principles requires that

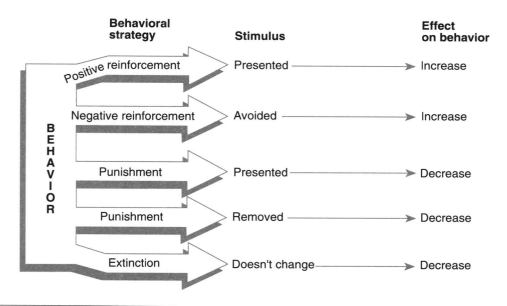

Figure 6.1   Principles of operant conditioning.

Table 6.1   Behavior: Consequences, Classification, and Probable Effect

Behavior exhibited	Consequence	Classification	Effect
Jane pays attention during instruction.	Teacher praises Jane.	Positive reinforcement	Jane will continue to pay attention.
Bob forgets to wear his tennis shoes to gym.	Teacher suggests that next time he will lose 5 points.	Negative reinforcement	Bob wears his shoes.
Joyce fails to submit her class assignment on time.	Teacher deducts 5 points for late assignment.	Punishment	Joyce will not turn in late assignments.
Bill requests unneeded special help from the teacher every day.	Teacher ignores Bill's requests.	Extinction	Bill will stop requesting unneeded help.
Sue demonstrates poor sportsmanship during a game.	Teacher eliminates participation in free time activity at end of class.	Punishment	Sue functions as a good sport.

teachers or coaches analyze behaviors carefully before attempting to change them.

The examples just provided illustrate the range of learning principles available to teachers and coaches who wish to change the behavior of students. No one principle is necessarily the best choice all the time; the principle applied will depend on the specifics of the situation. Later in this chapter and again in chapter 9, recommendations are provided that originate from the work of Dunn, Morehouse, and Fredericks (1986). After reading the section on their rules of thumb (in chapter 9), readers are encouraged to review Table 6.1 to better understand the place of selected learning principles in behavior modification strategies.

Types of Reinforcers

Several types of reinforcers can be used in behavior management. These include primary (unconditioned), secondary (conditioned), and vicarious reinforcers. The use of highly preferred activities to control the occurrence of less preferred responses, known as the Premack Principle, is another reinforcer.

Primary Reinforcers

Primary or unconditioned reinforcers are stimuli that are necessary for survival. Examples include food, water, and other phenomena that satisfy biological needs such as the needs for sleep, warmth, and sexual stimulation.

Secondary Reinforcers

Secondary or conditioned reinforcers acquire their reinforcing properties through learning. A few examples are praise, grades, money, and completion of a task. Because secondary reinforcers must be learned, stimuli or events often must be paired repeatedly with other primary or secondary events before they will become reinforcers in their own right.

Vicarious Reinforcers

The essence of vicarious reinforcement consists in observing the reinforcing or punishing consequences of another person's behavior. As a result of vicarious reinforcement, the observer will either engage in the behavior to receive the same positive reinforcement or avoid the behavior to avert punishment.

Premack Principle

According to the Premack Principle (Premack, 1965), activities that have a high probability of occurrence can be used to elicit low-probability behaviors. To state it another way, Premack implies that activities in which an individual or group prefers to engage can be used as positive consequences or reinforcers for activities that are not especially favored.

Schedules of Reinforcement

When using the behavior modification approach, the teacher or coach must understand when to deliver a reinforcer to attain an optimal response. During the early stages of skill acquisition or behavior change, it is best to provide reinforcement after every occurrence of an appropriate response. This is called continuous reinforcement. After a behavior has been acquired, continuous reinforcement is no longer desirable or necessary. In fact, behavior is best maintained not through a process of continuing reinforcement but through a schedule of intermittent or partial reinforcement. Several types of reinforcement schedules exist; however, the two most commonly used are ratio and interval schedules.

In ratio schedules, reinforcement is applied after a specified number of "defined" responses occur. Interval schedules, on the other hand, provide reinforcement when a specified time has elapsed since the previous reinforcement. A ratio schedule, therefore, is based on some preestablished number of responses, while an interval schedule is based on time between reinforcements. Associated with each of these major schedule types are two subtypes, fixed and variable, When these types and subtypes are combined, four alternatives for dispensing reinforcement are available. Table 6.2 presents the intermittent reinforcement schedules and provides a short description of their operation and possible effect on behavior.

Procedures for Increasing Behavior

Once it is determined that either a behavior not currently in a student's repertoire is desired or that the frequency of a given behavior needs to be altered, it is necessary to define the targeted response in measurable and observable terms. That response will be an observable instance of performance having an effect on the environment. After clear identification has been made, behavioral intervention can begin. The following discussion highlights several of the more commonly used behavioral strategies. These include shaping, prompting, forward and backward chaining, modeling, token economy, fading, and contingency management.

Shaping

Shaping involves administering reinforcement contingent upon the learning and performing of sequential steps leading to development of the desired behavior. Shaping is most often employed in the teaching of a new skill. The use of shaping to teach a dive from a 1-meter board could include the following progression of steps: kneeling dive from a 12-inch elevation, squat dive from 12-inch elevation, standing modified dive from 12-inch elevation, squat dive from diving board, and standing modified forward dive from the diving board.

Prompting

Events that help initiate a response are called prompts. These are cues, instructions, gestures, directions, examples, and models that act as antecedent events and trigger the desired response. In this

Table 6.2   Intermittent Schedules of Reinforcement

Type	Operation	Effects on behavior	Example
		Ratio	
Fixed	Reinforcer is given after each predetermined response.	High response rate	Praise every second successful throw
Variable	Reinforcer is given after *x* responses on the average.	High response rate	Praise every third successful throw on average
		Interval	
Fixed	Reinforcer is given after first response that occurs after each predetermined interval.	Cessation of response after reinforcement; high response rate just prior to time for next reinforcement	Praise first successful throw at end of each 1-minute interval
Variable	Reinforcer is given after first response that occurs after each predetermined interval on the average.	Consistent response rate	Praise first successful throw at end of an average 3-minute interval

way the frequency of responses and, subsequently, the chances of receiving reinforcement are increased. Prompting is very important in shaping and chaining procedures.

Fading

The ultimate goal of any procedure to increase the frequency of a response is for the response to occur without the need for a prompt or reinforcer. The best way to reach this goal is with a procedure that removes or fades the prompts and reinforcers gradually over time. Fading reinforcers means stretching the schedule of reinforcement so that the individual has to perform more trials or demonstrate significantly better response quality in order to receive a reinforcement. For example, a person who has been receiving positive reinforcement for each successful basket must now make two baskets, then three baskets, and so forth before reinforcement is provided.

Chaining

Unlike shaping, which consists of reinforcing approximations of a new terminal behavior, chaining

develops a series of discrete portions or links which, when tied together, lead to enhanced performance of a behavior. There are two types of chaining: forward and backward. In forward chaining, the first step in the behavioral sequence occurs first, followed by the next step, and so forth until the entire sequence has been learned. A student learning to execute a lay-up from three steps away from the basket would (a) take a step with the left foot, (b) take a step with the left foot while dribbling once with the right hand, (c) repeat previous step and add a step with the right foot, and (d) repeat previous step with an additional step and jump off the left foot up to the basket for lay-up attempt. In some cases it is necessary to teach the last step in a behavioral sequence first, followed by the next-to-last step, and so on until the entire sequence is learned. This is called backward chaining.

Modeling

Modeling is a visual demonstration of a behavior that students are expected to perform. From a behavioral perspective, modeling (cf. vicarious reinforcement) is the process in which an individual watches someone else respond to a situation in a way that produces reinforcement or punishment. The observer thus learns vicariously.

Token Economy

Tokens are secondary reinforcers that are earned, collected, and subsequently redeemed for any of a variety of backup reinforcers. Tokens, which could be poker chips or checkmarks on a response tally sheet, are earned and exchanged for consumables, privileges, or activities—the backup reinforcers. A reinforcement system based on tokens is called a token economy. Establishment of a token economy includes a concise description of the targeted behavior or behaviors along with a detailed accounting of the numbers of tokens administered for performance of targeted behaviors.

Contingency Management

Contingency management means changing behavior by controlling and altering the relationship among the occasion when a response occurs, the response itself, and the reinforcing consequences (Walker & Shea, 1988). The most sophisticated form of contingency management is the behavioral contract. Basically, the contract (which is an extension of the token economy) specifies the relationship between behaviors and their consequences. The well-developed contract contains five elements: (a) a detailed statement of what each party expects to happen; (b) targeted behaviors that are readily observable; (c) a statement of sanctions for failure to meet the terms of the contract; (d) a bonus clause, if desirable, to reinforce consistent compliance with the contract; and (e) a monitoring system to keep track of the rate of positive reinforcement given (Kazdin, 1984).

Procedures to Decrease Behavior

There will be occasions when some behavior of an individual or a group should be decreased. Traditionally, decreasing the frequency of behavior has been accomplished using extinction, punishment, reinforcement of alternative responses, and time out from reinforcement. This section will stress the management techniques that are positive in nature because they have been successful in reducing or eliminating a wide range of undesirable behaviors. Moreover, they model more socially appropriate ways of dealing with troublesome behaviors and are free of the undesirable side effects of punishment. Reinforcement is ordinarily thought of as a process to increase, rather than decrease, behavior.

Consequently, extinction and punishment are most often mentioned as methods for decreasing behaviors. This section highlights the use of reinforcement techniques to decrease behavior (Auxter, Pyfer, & Huettig, 1993).

Reinforcement of Other Behavior

Reinforcing an individual for engaging in any behavior other than the targeted behavior is known as differential reinforcement of other behavior. The reinforcer is delivered as long as the targeted behavior (e.g., inappropriate running during the gym class) is not performed. This reinforcement has the effect of decreasing the targeted response.

Reinforcement of Incompatible Behavior

This technique reinforces behaviors that are directly incompatible with the targeted response. For example, a student has a difficult time engaging cooperatively in games during the physical education class. The opposite behavior is playing cooperatively. The effect of reinforcing cooperation during game playing is the elimination of the uncooperative response.

Reinforcement of Low Response Rates

With a technique known as differential reinforcement of low rates of responding, a student is reinforced for gradually reducing the frequency of an undesirable behavior or for increasing the amount of time during which the behavior does not occur. For instance, a student who swears on the average of five times per day would be reinforced for swearing only four times. This schedule would be followed until swearing was eliminated completely.

The three techniques just discussed use positive reinforcement to decrease the frequency of undesirable behavior. More traditional methods of decreasing such behaviors are described below, in recognition of the breadth and diversity of behavior management techniques.

Punishment

Normally, punishment is thought of as the presentation of an aversive consequence contingent upon the occurrence of an undesirable behavior. In the Skinnerian (or operant psychology) tradition, punishment also includes the removal of a positively reinforcing stimulus or event, which is referred to as response cost. In either case, the individual is presented with a consequence that is not pleasing or is deprived of something that is very pleasing.

The student who is kept after school for being disobedient is most likely experiencing punishment. Likewise, the student who has failed to fulfill a part of the contingency contract in the class and thus has lost some hard-earned tokens that "buy" free time in the gymnasium is experiencing punishment. In each case the effect is to reduce the frequency of the undesirable behavior. Walker and Shea (1988) detail the advantages and disadvantages of using punishment. One advantage is the immediacy of its effect: Usually there is an immediate reduction in the response rate. In addition, punishment can be effective when a disruptive behavior occurs with such frequency that reinforcement of an incompatible behavior is not possible. Punishment can also be effective for temporarily suppressing a behavior while another behavior is reinforced. The disadvantages are several: undesirable emotional reactions, avoidance of the environment or person producing the punishment, aggression toward the punishing individual, modeling of punishing techniques by the individual who is punished, and reinforcement for the person who is delivering the punishment. Additionally, physical punishment may result in physical abuse to the person, although that may not have been the intent.

Time-Out

Time-out is an extension of the punishment concept. We have mentioned that punishment often involves the removal of a positive event. The time-out procedure is based on the assumption that some positive reinforcer in the immediate environment is maintaining the undesirable behavior. In an effort to control the situation, the individual is physically removed from the environment and consequently deprived of all positive reinforcement for a specified time.

IMPLEMENTING A BEHAVIOR MODIFICATION PROGRAM

On a daily basis, behavior modification is used in some form by most people—parents, teachers, coworkers, and students. In ordinary situations, however, its use may not be thorough and regular. On the other hand, the deliberate actual application of reinforcement learning principles in an attempt to change behavior is a systematic, step-by-step procedure. Minimally there are four steps that, if implemented correctly, provide a strong basis

for either increasing or decreasing the frequency of a particular behavior.

Identifying the Behavior

The first step is to identify the behavior in question. This is not as easy as it may sound because it entails fulfillment of two criteria. The first criterion is that the behavior must be observable; specifications that distinguish one behavior from another are clearly established. Measurability is the second criterion; it assumes that the frequency, intensity, and duration of a behavior can be quantified. Sportsmanship, for example, could be defined as the number of times students compliment their opponents for good performance during a game.

Establishing Baseline

With the targeted behavior identified, it is necessary to determine the frequency, intensity, and duration of its occurrence. This process, known as establishing baseline, consists of observing the individual or group in a natural setting with no behavioral intervention taking place. Baseline determination should occur across a minimum of three sessions, days, periods, classes, or trials. Baseline is important as the comparison against which any programmatic gains are measured; it requires precise and accurate recording based on the criteria described in the preceding step. There are several recording systems; the choice depends on the nature of the behavior being observed. The most frequently used recording systems note event, duration, and interval. Event recording entails counting the exact number of times a clearly defined behavior occurs during a given period (e.g., the number of acts of good sportsmanship during a game or class period). Duration recording, on the other hand, measures the amount of time a student spends engaged in a particular behavior (e.g., cumulative time demonstrating good sportsmanship during a game). When reliable estimates of behavior are desired and when these observations are made during specific time periods, interval recording may be used. An example of interval recording is counting the number of 10-second intervals during which students demonstrate good sportsmanship, as defined in the first (identification) step of the behavior management program.

Choosing the Reinforcer

Once it has been determined that a behavior requires modification and the baseline data confirms this suspicion, it is essential to the success of the behavior modification program to choose the most effective reinforcer. Two important factors influence this choice. First, the **type** of reinforcer that will be effective in a given situation depends on the individual. Not all potential reinforcers work with all people; therefore, it is necessary to ascertain which is best. A second factor is **quantity**. Within limits, more reinforcement is probably better. However, when teachers and coaches reinforce in excessive amounts, satiation results and the reinforcer loses its value and effectiveness.

Scheduling the Reinforcer

With the reinforcer chosen, the next step is to schedule its use. The previous discussion of schedules is applicable here, with one very important reminder. When initiating a behavior change strategy, it is advisable to reinforce continuously. Once the behavior has shown desired change, reinforcement should be reduced gradually. It is this shift that maintains the new behavior at a desirable rate. One last word on scheduling: The longer reinforcement is delayed, the less effective it becomes.

USES OF BEHAVIOR MODIFICATION IN PHYSICAL EDUCATION/SPORT

Dunn and Fredericks (1985) suggest that evidence supports the use of behavior modification in both segregated and mainstreamed programs for students with special needs. Dunn, Morehouse, and Fredericks (1986) have developed a Data Based Gymnasium (DBG) for teaching students with severe and profound disabilities in physical education. Successful implementation of the DBG is dependent on systematic use of the behavioral principles discussed in this section. Additionally, Dunn et al. have provided rules of thumb that guide the use of behavioral techniques in teaching skills and/or changing social behaviors. These include the use of naturally occurring reinforcers such as social praise or an extinction (i.e., ignoring a behavior). Tangible reinforcers such as food, toys, or desirable activities, which are earned as part of a token economy system, are not instituted until it has been demonstrated that the consistent use of social reinforcement or extinction is ineffective.

In skill acquisition programs, task-analytic phases and steps are individually determined, and students move through the sequence at a rate commensurate with their ability. For example, a *phase* for kicking with the toe of the preferred foot consists of having students "perform a kick by swinging the preferred leg backwards and then forwards, striking the ball with the toe of the foot, causing the ball to roll in the direction of the target" (Dunn et al., 1986, p. 81). *Steps* represent distances, times, and/or number of repetitions that may further subdivide a particular phase (e.g., kicking the ball with the toe of the preferred foot a distance of 10, 15, or 20 feet). Decisions about program modifications or changes in the use of behavioral strategies (rules of thumb) are made on an individual basis after each student's progress is reviewed. Further discussion of the DBG and the specific rules of thumb for managing inappropriate behavior in physical education with students with severe disabilities are presented in chapter 9.

Advantages of using behavior modification are:

- it considers only behaviors that are precisely defined and capable of being seen,

- it assumes that knowing the cause of a particular behavior is not a prerequisite for changing it,

- it encourages a thorough analysis of the environmental conditions and factors that may influence the behavior(s) in question,

- it facilitates functional independence by employing a system of least prompts, that is, a prompt hierarchy is used that is ordered from least to most intrusive, and

- it requires precise measurement to demonstrate a cause-and-effect relationship between the behavioral intervention and the behavior that is changed.

Disadvantages should be considered before a behavior management program is implemented:

- actual use of behavioral principles in a consistent and systematic manner is not as simple as it might seem,

- behavioral techniques may fail because what is thought to be the controlling stimulus may not be so in reality, and

- behavioral techniques may not work initially, requiring more thorough analysis by the teacher to determine if additional techniques would be useful and to implement a new approach immediately, if necessary.

Example of Behavior Analysis

The process for implementing a behavioral system, which is commonly referred to as behavior analysis, requires reasonably strict adherence to a number of well-defined steps. The following example illustrates the teaching of a skill using a limited number of concepts.

Skill: Standing long jump

Objective: When requested to perform a standing long jump, the student will jump a minimum of 3 feet, demonstrating appropriate form on take-off, in the air, and on landing.

Prompt: Using the system of least prompts, the instructor would employ prompts in the order presented from least to most intrusive depending on the ability of the student to perform the task: (a) "Please stand behind this line and do a standing long jump" (verbal prompt), (b) "Please stand behind this line, bend your knees, swing your arms backward and forward like this, and jump as far as possible" (verbal plus visual prompt), and (c) "Please stand behind this line, bend your knees, feel how I'm moving your arms so they swing back and forth like this, and jump as far as possible" (physical guidance).

Behavior: Student acknowledges prompts, correctly assumes long jump position, and executes long jump as intended.

Reinforcement: Teacher says, "Good job!" (verbal reinforcement).

Subsequent Behavior: Student is likely to maintain or improve on the performance as defined.

OTHER APPROACHES

The management of behavior has been the concern of individuals and groups with various theoretical and philosophical views. No fewer than five major approaches have been postulated to remediate problems associated with maladaptive behavior. One of these approaches, behavior modification, has already been discussed. Other interventions include the *psychodynamic, psychoeducational, ecological, psychoneurological*, and *humanistic* approaches. These interventions will be discussed only briefly here. Resources will be suggested for those who wish to further explore a particular intervention and its primary proponents.

Psychodynamic

Most closely associated with the work of Freud, the psychodynamic approach has evolved as a collection of many subtheories, each with its own discrete intervention. The focus of this approach, in any case, is psychological dysfunction. Specifically, the psychodynamic approach strives to improve emotional functioning by helping students understand *why* they are functioning inappropriately. This approach encourages teachers to accept students but not their undesirable behavior. It emphasizes helping students to develop self-knowledge through close and positive relationships with teachers. From the psychodynamic perspective, the development of a healthy self-concept, including the ability to trust others and to have confidence in one's feelings, abilities, and emotions, is basic and integral to normal development. If the environment and the significant others in it are not supportive, then anxiety and depression may result. Self-perceptions as well as perceptions of others can become distorted, and the result can be impaired personal relationships, conflicting social values, inadequate self-image, ability deficits, and maladaptive habits and attitudes.

In an attempt to identify the probable cause(s) of inappropriate behavior, the psychodynamic approach uses various diagnostic procedures such as projective techniques, case histories, interviews, observational measures of achievement, and measures of general and specific abilities. Through interpretation of diagnostic results and an analysis of prevailing symptoms, the cause of the psychic conflict is, ideally, identified. Once the primary locus of the emotional disturbance is known, an appropriate treatment can be determined.

Conventional *psychodynamic treatment modalities* include

- psychoanalysis,
- counseling interviews, and
- psychotherapeutic techniques (such as play therapy and group therapy).

Treatment sessions involve the student alone, though some therapists see only the parents. Recently, family therapy has become popular, with students and parents attending sessions together. However the session is configured, it is designed to help students develop self-knowledge. Two of the more commonly used and understood interventions are reality therapy (Glasser, 1965, 1969) and transactional analysis (Harris, 1969). These interventions have been evaluated for use in physical education by Jansma (1980) and Jansma and French (1979), respectively.

The psychodynamic approach, including psychoanalysis and psychotherapy, is regarded as moderately effective. Its inadequacies include the following: (a) diagnostic study is time-consuming and expensive, (b) the results of diagnostic study yield only possible causes for emotional conflict, and (c) therapeutic outcomes are similar regardless of the nature of the intervention—whether the students are seen alone or with their parents, or are seen in play therapy or in group counseling.

Teachers should be aware that implementation of psychodynamic theory as a means to manage behavior does not preclude working with groups. It need not have as its primary goal increasing students' personal awareness. It also does not imply that teachers should be permissively accepting, deal with the subconscious, or focus on problems other than those presenting real concerns in the present situation. The preceding are prevalent misconceptions about the psychodynamic approach.

Psychoeducational

The psychoeducational approach assumes that academic failure and misbehavior can be remediated directly if students are taught how to achieve and behave effectively. It balances the educational and psychological perspectives. This approach focuses on the affective and cognitive factors associated with development of appropriate social and academic readiness skills useful in home, school, and community. Its proponents recognize that some students do not understand why they behave

as they do when their basic instincts, drives, and needs are not satisfied. The cause of inappropriate behavior, however, is of minimal importance in the psychoeducational approach; it is more important to identify students' potential for education and to emphasize their learning abilities. Diagnostic procedures include

- case histories,
- observational data,
- measures of achievement,
- performance in specific situations requiring particular skills, and
- consideration of measures of general abilities.

The psychoeducational approach focuses on strengthening the person's ego and teaches self-control through self-knowledge. This is accomplished through compensatory educational programs that encourage students to acknowledge that what they are doing is a problem, to understand their motivations for behaving in a certain way, to observe the consequences of their behavior, and to plan alternate responses or ways of behaving in similar circumstances.

When a behavioral crisis occurs (or shortly thereafter), a teacher prepared in the psychoeducational approach conducts a life-space interview (LSI), a term first used by Redl (1952). The purpose of LSI is to help the student either overcome momentary difficulties or work through long-range goals.

The psychoeducational approach assumes that making students aware of their feelings and having them talk about the nature of their responses will give them insight into their behavior and help them develop control. This approach emphasizes the realistic demands of everyday functioning in school and at home as they relate to the amelioration of inappropriate behavior.

There are several strategies that teachers can use to implement the psychoeducational approach. These include *self-instruction, modeling and rehearsal, self-determination of goals and reinforcement standards,* and *self-reward.*

Teachers are in an advantageous position to encourage students to use self-instructional strategies. This means helping students to reflect on the steps in good decision making when it is time to learn something new, solve a problem, or retain a concept. Fundamentally, the process involves teaching students to listen to their private speech, that is, those times when people talk either aloud or subvocally to themselves. For example, a person makes a faulty ceiling shot in racquetball and says,

"Come on, reach out and hit the ball ahead of the body!" Self-instruction can be as simple as a checklist of questions for students to ask themselves when a decision is required. The following questions represent an example of the self-instructional process:

- What is my problem?
- How can I do it?
- Am I using my plan?
- How did I do?

In the modeling strategy, students who have a difficult time controlling their behavior watch others who have learned to deal with problems similar to their own. Beyond merely observing the behavior, the students can see how the models respond in a constructive manner to a problematic situation. Modeling could include the use of relaxation techniques and self-instruction. Students can also learn appropriate ways of responding when time is provided to mentally rehearse or practice successful management techniques.

Another strategy that has proven effective in helping students control their behavior works by including them in the establishment of goals, reinforcement contingencies, or standards. I observed this process as a group of adolescents with behavior disabilities determined which prosocial behaviors each member needed to concentrate on while on an overnight camping trip. Likewise, the group established the limits of inappropriate behavior and decided what the consequences would be if someone exceeded the goal.

A fine strategy used in the psychoeducational approach is self-reward. It involves preparing students to reward themselves with some preestablished reinforcer. For example, a student who completes the prescribed tasks at a practice station immediately places a check on a recording sheet posted at that station. When the check marks total a specified number, the student is thus instrumental not only in seeing that the goal of the lesson is achieved but also in implementing the reinforcement process in an efficient manner.

Ecological

The ecological approach has as its basic assumption a disturbance in the student's environment or ecosystem. In effect, the student and the environment affect each other in a reciprocal and negative manner (i.e., some characteristic of the student disturbs the ecosystem, and the ecosystem responds in a way that causes the student to further agitate it). The problem has been and continues to be that the student is typically the one who is blamed for disturbed behavior with little or no consideration given to the context in which the disturbed behavior occurs.

Evaluative procedures for assessing the cause(s) of disturbed behavior are difficult at best. Educators have purported to use a five-phase process for collecting ecological data:

1. describing the environment,
2. identifying expectations,
3. organizing behavioral data,
4. summarizing the data, and
5. establishing goals.

Additionally, the Behavior Rating Profile (BRP-2) examines behaviors in several settings from several different points of view. It consists of three student rating subscales, one teacher rating scale, one parent rating scale, and a sociogram (a diagram or chart that uses connecting lines to indicate choices made in groups). Its purpose is to define deviant behavior specific to one setting or to one individual's expectations (Coleman, 1992).

The goal of the ecological approach is not just to stop some disturbed or unwanted behavior but to change the environment in substantive ways so that it will continue to support desirable behavior once the intervention is withdrawn (Hallahan & Kauffman, 1991). Generally speaking, the focus of intervention within the ecological approach is on a single ecosystem or on a combination of ecosystems. Interventions that focus on single ecosystems, however, are frequently unsuccessful given the interrelatedness and interdependence of each unit or subsystem as it operates within the larger ecosystem (Cullinan, Epstein, & Lloyd, 1991).

Educational applications of the ecological approach are designed to make environments accommodate individuals rather than having individuals fit environments. In a classroom this could require physical and psychological adaptations such as individual or small group work areas, time-out areas, or reinforcement centers. It means having teachers create environments where students succeed rather than anticipate failure. Changes in the home ecosystem might require parental involvement, respite care, or family therapy. At times, changes in several ecosystems are required (e.g., home, school, and community).

The most notable ecologically based program was Project Re-ED funded by the National Institute for Mental Health and headed by Nicholas Hobbs. This model used a short-term residential placement. Its philosophy posited that children are capable of controlling and changing their own behavior in adaptive ways. School interventions were implemented by teacher-counselors. Daytime teacher-counselors not only worked on academic areas but also modified maladaptive behaviors and provided counseling. Night teacher-counselors took over after school hours and provided supervision of extracurricular activities. A liaison teacher-counselor served as the conduit for reentry into school. This individual performed extensive assessment of home, school, and community in an effort to make reentry as comfortable as possible. The liaison-teacher counselor provided a supportive network in the student's major ecosystems (Coleman, 1992).

Psychoneurological

The central focus of the psychoneurological approach is *neurophysiological dysfunction*. Identification of students with disabilities in this realm is made on the basis of general behavioral characteristics and specific functional deficits. *General behavioral characteristics* include

- hyperactivity,
- distractibility,
- impulsiveness, and
- emotional lability.

Specific functional deficits, on the other hand, include disorders in

- perception,
- language,
- motor ability, and
- concept formation and reasoning.

The manifestation of these characteristics and deficits is attributable to injury or damage to the central nervous system.

The psychoneurological approach places considerable importance on etiological factors. The integrity of the central nervous system is assessed on the basis of performance in selected activities or tests such as walking a line with eyes closed, touching finger to nose, and reacting to various stimuli such as pain, cold, and light. Additionally, a neurological examination including an electroencephalogram (EEG) is often a part of the diagnosis. Following diagnosis, treatment can include *drug*

therapy, surgical procedures, physical therapy, sensory integrative therapy, and *developmental training*. The closest that physical education comes to applying the psychoneurological approach is in implementing perceptual-motor programs (e.g., Kephart [1960] and Frostig, Lefever and Whittlesey [1966]). In such cases, the management of social behavior is secondary to the training program; however, an inability to control the behavior could reduce the effectiveness of the program considerably.

A major trend associated with the psychoneurological approach is drug therapy, although the use of drugs as a means of controlling or modifying behavior cuts across several behavioral approaches. Students are medicated for the management of such behaviors as short attention span, distractibility, impulsiveness, hyperactivity, visual motor impairments, and large motor coordination problems. Two major categories of drugs, psychotropic and anticonvulsant, are used to manage the behavior of school-aged children. According to Gadow (1986) the psychotropic drugs are prescribed primarily to alleviate certain behavior problems, improve academic performance, and enhance social behavior in school, whereas the anticonvulsant drugs are used to control convulsive disorders. The most common categories of psychotropic drugs are stimulants, tranquilizers, and antidepressants.

Stimulants

Stimulants are administered primarily for the management of hyperactivity. Dexedrine and Ritalin, the most frequently prescribed stimulants, are adjunctive therapy and are used with students who experience moderate to severe hyperactivity, short attention span, distractibility, emotional lability, and impulsiveness. Possible side effects include loss of appetite, weight loss, and insomnia.

Tranquilizers

Tranquilizers are used to control bizarre behavior in psychotic adults. In children they are used to control hyperactivity, aggression, self-injury, and stereotypic behavior. Tranquilizers are classified as either major or minor. Major tranquilizers include such drugs as Mellaril and Thorazine, both of which are prescribed for the management of psychotic disorders, including severe behavior disorders marked by aggressiveness and combativeness. Valium, Miltown, and Librium are considered minor tranquilizers; they are used to relieve mild tension and anxiety in children (Gadow, 1986). Possible side effects of the major and minor tranquilizers, include dizziness, drowsiness, vertigo, fatigue, and diminished mental alertness that could impair performance in physical activities.

Antidepressants

Antidepressants are prescribed to adults to alleviate depression. In children they have a more diverse function, including the treatment of enuresis and, occasionally, hyperactivity. Perhaps because of the documented side effects of the antidepressant drugs—ataxia, muscle weakness, drowsiness, and mental dullness—physical educators and coaches should know when students are receiving such medication (Gadow, 1986). Tofranil and Dilantin are two commonly used antidepressants; Dilantin is administered mainly as an anticonvulsant in generalized tonic-clonic (grand mal) seizures and partial (psychomotor) seizures.

Humanistic

Based on the work of Maslow (1970), the humanistic approach has as its basis self-actualization theory—the basis of which is Maslow's hierarchy of human needs. In the hierarchy, five primary human needs are identified and arranged in ascending order, from the most basic to the most prepotent. According to this theory of motivation, the human, who seeks to meet unsatisfied needs, will satisfy lower-level needs first and then satisfy needs at progressively higher levels as lower ones are met. A person lacking food, safety, love, and esteem would probably hunger for food more strongly than for anything else. But when the need for food was satisfied, the other needs would become stronger. In the needs hierarchy, self-actualization is the fulfillment of one's highest potential. Maslow considered the following to be some of the attributes of self-actualized people: accepting, spontaneous, realistic, autonomous, appreciating, ethical, sympathetic, affectionate, helpful, intimate, democratic, sure about right and wrong, and creative.

Self-actualization is the process of becoming all that one is fully and humanly capable of becoming. In large measure this is developed naturally by nondisabled persons. Disabled persons, on the other hand, may not achieve the same relative status as their nondisabled peers without the intrinsic motivation to become all they are capable of becoming. The desire to move disabled persons toward self-actualization is supplied, at least

initially, by persons who care about these individuals as persons first and only then as persons with disabilities.

In the fourth revision of her text on adapted physical education, Sherrill (1993) has continued to draw extensively and build upon self-actualization theory to guide a humanistic orientation to adapted physical education in general and to affective development in particular. She is not only the spokesperson for the humanistic philosophy but also its instrumentalist in that she applies its concepts in the gymnasium and on the sports field. In an effort to demonstrate how the humanistic philosophy can be translated into action, Sherrill suggests that teachers and coaches of students with disabilities do the following:

1. To the degree possible, use a teaching style that encourages learners to make some of the major decisions during the learning process. This implies that students should be taught with the least restrictive teaching style or the one that most closely matches their learning styles.

2. Use assessment and instruction that are success oriented. No matter where students score in terms of the normal curve, they have worth as human beings and must be accepted as such.

3. Listen to and communicate with students in an effort to encourage them to take control of their lives and make personal decisions affecting their physical well-being. Counseling students to become healthy, fit, and self-actualized requires the skills of active listening, acceptance, empathy, and cooperative goal setting. Such interaction helps persons with disabilities reinforce their internal locus of control.

4. Use teaching practices that enhance self-concept. The following practices are recommended: (a) Show students that someone genuinely cares for them as human beings, (b) teach students to care about each other by modeling caring behavior in daily student and teacher interactions, (c) emphasize social interaction by using cooperative rather than competitive activities, and (d) build success into the instructional plan through the careful use of task and activity analysis.

Hellison is another physical educator who has been instrumental in disseminating the humanistic viewpoint (Hellison, 1985; Hellison & Templin, 1991). He has developed a set of alternative goals for physical education that he believes focus on human needs and values rather than on fitness and sport skill development per se. The goals are developmental in nature and reflect a level-by-level progression of attitudes and behaviors. Specifically, they include self-control and respect for the rights and feelings of others, participation and effort, self-direction, and caring and helping.

Level I: Self-Control and Respect for the Rights and Feelings of Others. The first level deals with the need for control of one's own behavior. Self-control should be the first goal, according to Hellison, because learning cannot take place effectively if one cannot control impulses to physically or verbally harm other students.

Level II: Participation and Effort. Level II focuses on the need for physical activity and offers students one medium for personal stability through experiences in which they can engage on a daily basis. Participation involves getting uninterested students to at least "go through the motions," experiencing different degrees of effort expenditure to determine if effort leads to improvement, and redefining success as a subjective accomplishment.

Level III: Self-Direction. Level III emphasizes the need for students to take more responsibility for their choices and to link these choices with their own identities. Students at this level can work without direct supervision and can take responsibility for their intentions and actions. At this level, students begin to assume responsibility for the direction of their lives and to explore options in developing a strong and integrated personal identity. This level includes developing a knowledge base that will enhance achievement of their goals, developing a plan to accomplish their goals, especially more difficult ones, and evaluating their plan to determine its success.

Level IV: Caring and Helping. Level IV is the most difficult for students; it is also not a requirement for successful engagement in the responsibility model. At Level IV students reach out beyond themselves to others, to commit themselves genuinely to caring about other people. Students are motivated to give support, cooperate, show concern, and help. Generally speaking, the goal of Level IV is the betterment of the entire group's welfare.

Hellison recognizes that the goals only provide a framework and that strategies must be employed to cause students to interact with self-control and respect for the rights and feelings of others, to participate and show effort, to be self-directed, and to demonstrate caring and helping behavior on a regular basis. He suggests six general interaction strategies to help reach the goals. These include *awareness* (students engage in sharing sessions), *experience* (students can be invited to play in a cooperative game), *choice* (students are permitted to redefine success or negotiate an alternative to a planned activity), *problem solving* (students discuss issues of low motivation or difficulty in being self-directed), *self-reflection* (students record in a journal or discuss how they did during class in relation to the goals they had established), and *counseling time* (students discuss their pattern of abusive behavior and possibly their underlying motives for such behavior). This last strategy gives students the opportunity to talk with the teacher about specific problems that may be preventing them from achieving their goals within specified levels of the responsibility model.

SUMMARY

Lack of discipline has been identified as one of the most significant problems confronting public school teachers. A number of behavior management systems are available that can significantly reduce the need to discipline students. If students with behavior disabilities are integrated into a regular class and demonstrate persistent disruptive behavior, a behavior management program designed to alleviate the problem might include any of the following: (a) behavior modification using a token economy system, (b) a psychoeducational approach using the life-space interview, (c) a psychodynamic approach incorporating play therapy, (d) an ecological approach using family therapy, (e) a psychoneurological approach using medication, (f) a humanistic approach using listening and counseling skills, or (g) a combination of approaches. Behavior management has also been used to promote skill acquisition and prosocial behaviors.

Physical educators and coaches have traditionally employed an eclectic approach in managing behavior. They have chosen the best that each approach has to offer and modified it to suit their particular situations. It is not uncommon to see teachers and coaches with strong backgrounds in behavior modification, for example, who also draw on the humanistic skills of listening and counseling to manage the behavior of their students and players. The eclectic approach is less likely to be used in special schools or other specialized settings, such as hospitals, where a particular approach or management orientation is implemented by an entire staff.

BIBLIOGRAPHY

Auxter, D., Pyfer, J., & Huettig, C. (1993). *Principles and methods of adapted physical education and recreation* (7th ed.). St. Louis: Mosby.

Coleman, M.C. (1992). *Behavior disorders: Theory and practice* (2nd ed.). Needham Heights, MA: Allyn & Bacon.

Cullinan, D., Epstein, M.H., & Lloyd, J.W. (1991). Evaluation of conceptual models of behavior disorders. *Behavioral Disorders*, **16**, 148–157.

Dunn, J.M., & Fredericks, H.D.B. (1985). The utilization of behavior management in mainstreaming in physical education. *Adapted Physical Activity Quarterly*, **2**, 338–346.

Dunn, J.M., Morehouse, J.W., & Fredericks, H.D.B. (1986). *Physical education for the severely handicapped: A systematic approach to a data based gymnasium.* Austin, TX: Pro-Ed.

Elam, S.M., Rose, L.C., & Gallup, A.M. (1992). The 24th Gallup poll of the public's attitudes toward the public schools. *Kappan*, **74**(1), 41–53.

Frostig, M., Lefever, D., & Whittlesey, J. (1966). *The Marianne Frostig developmental test of visual perception.* Palo Alto, CA: Consulting Psychology Press.

Gadow, K.D. (1986). Fundamental concepts in pharmacotherapy: An overview. In K.D. Gadow (Ed.), *Children on medication: Epilepsy, emotional disturbance, and adolescent disorders* (99–135). San Diego: College-Hill.

Glasser, W. (1965). *Reality therapy: A new approach to psychiatry.* New York: Harper & Row.

Glasser, W. (1969). *Schools without failure.* New York: Harper & Row.

Hallahan, D.P., & Kauffman, J.M. (1991). *Exceptional children: Introduction to special education* (5th ed.). Englewood Cliffs, NJ: Prentice Hall.

Harris, T.A. (1969). *I'm OK, you're OK.* New York: Harper & Row.

Hellison, D.R. (1985). *Goals and strategies for teaching physical education.* Champaign, IL: Human Kinetics.

Hellison, D.R., & Templin, T.J. (1991). *A reflective approach to teaching physical education.* Champaign, IL: Human Kinetics.

Jansma, P. (1980). Reality therapy: Another approach to managing inappropriate behavior. *American Corrective Therapy Journal*, **34**, 64–69.

Jansma, P., & French, R. (1979). Transactional analysis: An alternative approach to managing inappropriate behavior. *American Corrective Therapy Journal*, **33**, 155–162.

Kazdin, A.E. (1984). *Behavior modification in applied settings* (3rd ed.). Homewood, IL: Dorsey Press.

Kephart, N. (1960). *The slow learner in the classroom.* Columbus, OH: Merrill.

Maslow, A.H. (1970). *Motivation and personality* (2nd ed.). New York: Harper & Row.

Premack, D. (1965). Reinforcement theory. In D. Levine (Ed.), *Nebraska symposium on motivation.* Lincoln: University of Nebraska Press.

Redl, F. (1952). *Controls from within.* New York: Free Press.

Sherrill, C. (1993). *Adapted physical activity, recreation, and sport: Crossdisciplinary and lifespan* (4th ed.). Madison, WI: Brown & Benchmark.

Walker, J.E., & Shea, T.M. (1988). *Behavior management: A practical approach for educators* (4th ed.). Columbus, OH: Merrill.

RESOURCES

Written

French, R., & Lavay, B. (Eds.). (1990). *A manual of behavior management techniques for physical educators and recreators.* Kearney, NE: Educational Systems Associates. This manual provides professionals with an overview of the research and discusses effective behavior management techniques related to persons with disabilities. Readings address justification and importance, critical analysis, research designs, general techniques and strategies, and techniques applied to specific populations.

French, R.W., Henderson, H.L., & Horvat, M. (1992). *Creative approaches to managing student behavior.* Park City, UT: Family Development Resources. This text was written to help teachers manage behavior effectively to assure that learning can occur. The first part of the text is dedicated to a clear exposition of the major principles of operant conditioning. This enables the reader to comprehend the second section, which analyzes the most common behavioral profiles identified in physical education, recreation, and coaching and suggests prevention and intervention strategies.

Audiovisual

Almost everything you ever wanted to know about motivating people: Maslow's hierarchy of needs [Film]. (1975). Santa Monica, CA 90404: Salenger Educational Media, 1635 12th Street. Basic needs such as food, shelter, security, recognition, and achievement are reviewed in light of Maslow's hierarchy of needs; their meaning for motivation in organizational settings is analyzed and illustrated using dramatized incidents.

Bell, D. (Producer). (1976). *Reality therapy approach* [Film]. Chicago, IL 60640: Film, Inc., 5547 Ravenswood Avenue. This film observes elementary teachers successfully using concepts developed by Dr. William Glasser to achieve effective school discipline. It explains Dr. Glasser's approach to discipline and the seven steps of reality therapy.

O'Leary, K.D., & Schneider, M.R. (Producers). (1980). *Catch'em being good: Approaches to motivation and discipline* [Film]. Champaign, IL 60820: Research Press, Box 31775. This film presents methods for helping children with emotional, behavioral, and academic problems and shares the more rewarding application of positive discipline based on warm teacher-child interaction.

Reinforcement theory for teachers [Film]. (n.d.). Aptos, CA 95003: Special Purpose Films, 416 Rio Del Mar. Dr. Madeline Hunter discusses various aspects of reward and punishment, including positive reinforcement, negative reinforcement, extinction, and schedules of reinforcement.

PART II

Children and Youth With Unique Needs

Seven chapters in Part II relate to individuals with disabilities who are specially categorized in accordance with the Individuals with Disabilities Education Act (IDEA). Chapter 14 relates to children with unique physical education needs who have not been classified as disabled by IDEA.

The disabilities discussed in Part II include mental retardation, learning disabilities, behavioral disabilities, visual impairments, hearing losses, cerebral palsy, traumatic brain injuries, strokes, amputations, dwarfism, orthopedic impairments, spinal cord disabilities, and other health-impaired conditions. The chapters typically define terms and classifications, examine the causes and types of conditions, and describe characteristics of affected groups. Particular attention is given to teaching methods and activities that meet a variety of unique needs.

CHAPTER 7

Mental Retardation

Patricia L. Krebs

"When I was in school I sat in the back of the room and looked out the window at schoolmates having fun in sports. They said I was mentally retarded and couldn't compete. Then Special Olympics came and I began to run. My coach taught me to go further and faster, and now I can run the marathon in just over three hours. I have confidence in myself and know I can do almost anything I set out to do. Thanks, Special Olympics."

Loretta Claiborne, Special Olympics athlete.
(Special Olympics International, p. 17)

DEFINITION, CLASSIFICATION, AND INCIDENCE

Mental retardation is a concept. It is not a physiological impairment like blindness, deafness, or cerebral palsy. What then is mental retardation? What causes it? How many people have it and why is it so difficult to diagnose and classify?

Definition

In 1959, the American Association of Mental Deficiency (AAMD) established that those who, prior to their sixteenth birthday, scored more than one standard deviation below the mean (average) on a standardized intelligence test (yielding an IQ score) and evidenced impaired adaptive behavior were classified as having mental retardation. On most intelligence tests, the mean is 100 and the standard deviation is 15 or 16 points. Therefore, anyone who scored below 85 (100 − 15 = 85) on an intelligence test had mental retardation. At that time, those who scored between 70 and 85 were classified as having borderline mental retardation. In 1973, AAMD redefined mental retardation to include those who, prior to their eighteenth birthday, scored *two* or more standard deviations below the mean. This lowered the intelligence test ceiling to 70. Individuals who scored between one and two standard deviations below the mean were generally reclassified. Then in 1983, AAMD further clarified that the upper IQ range for the diagnosis was a guideline and with clinical judgment could extend to 75.

The American Association on Mental Retardation (AAMR) adopted a new definition in May 1992: *Mental retardation refers to substantial limitations in present functioning. It is characterized by significantly subaverage intellectual functioning, existing concurrently with related limitations in two or more of the following applicable adaptive skill areas: communication, self-care, home living, social skills, community use, self-direction, health and safety, functional academics, leisure, and work. Mental retardation manifests before age 18.*

Thus, three criteria must be met for an individual to be diagnosed as having mental retardation:

1. A person scores below 70–75 on an intelligence test (significant subaverage intellectual

functioning). Two intelligence tests are used extensively throughout the world: the Stanford-Binet Intelligence Scale and the Wechsler Intelligence Scale for Children–Revised (WISC–R).

2. Significant limitations must exist in 2 or more of the 10 adaptive skill areas listed. Adaptive skills refer to the individual's ability to mature personally and socially with age. Maturity is measured according to the individual's development in each of the 10 skill areas listed.

3. Mental retardation manifests before age 18.

Classification

Many systems exist for classifying mental retardation: behavioral, etiological, and educational. Until 1992, intelligence test scores also determined the severity level of mental retardation as shown in Table 7.1.

In 1992, AAMR changed its classification from four levels based on IQ score to two levels based on functioning levels and intensity of needed supports within the adaptive skill areas. Under the new classification system, one either does or does not have mental retardation. There are no levels of mental retardation based on IQ score. This represents a diminished role for the IQ score in definition of and classification for mental retardation. Rather, there are only two levels—mild and severe—classifying the degree of limitation. These levels are based on functioning in the 10 adaptive skill areas listed in the definition and on the amount of support the individual needs in a particular environment (i.e., school, home, community, etc.). There are four levels of support defined in the new classification system:

- *Intermittent:* short-term supports needed during lifespan transitions (e.g., job loss)
- *Limited:* support on regular basis for a short period of time; (e.g., job training)
- *Extensive:* ongoing, regular involvement; not time-limited (e.g., long-term work or home living support)
- *Pervasive:* constant and intense; potentially life-sustaining support

A problem with classification systems is that they assign labels to people. These labels tend to trigger absolute behavioral expectations and negative emotional reactions by society. Labels also provoke preconceived ideas about individuals' abilities, disabilities, and potential. Many urge the elimination of the term mental retardation because it is stigmatizing and erroneously used as a global summary. Individuals with mental retardation present a diversity of abilities and potential, which the educator must be prepared to accept.

Incidence

According to normal probability theory, it is estimated that 2.28% of the total population (with no known organic dysfunction) of any society has mental retardation. This figure is based on the distribution shown in Figure 7.1 that shows 2.28% (.13% + 2.15%) of the population scores below 70 on the two most prominent IQ tests. It is also estimated that .76% of the total population has known organic dysfunctions that cause mental retardation. These figures (2.28% plus .76% rounded to 3.0%) are used to estimate the incidence of individuals with mental retardation in a particular geographic area.

CAUSES OF MENTAL RETARDATION

There are over 350 disorders in which mental retardation may occur as a specific manifestation. These disorders are categorized according to when in the gestation period they occur—prenatally, perinatally, or postnatally. While the most prevalent known cause of mental retardation is fetal alcohol syndrome, sophisticated genetic mapping research has recently determined that X-linked disorders are the most prevalent genetic disorders manifesting mental retardation (1 in 550 births). X-linked disorders are caused

Table 7.1   Pre-1992 Classifications of Severity of Mental Retardation Based on IQ Scores

Intelligence test score	Mental retardation level
50–55 to 70–75	Mild
35–40 to 50–55	Moderate
20–25 to 35–40	Severe
Below 20–25	Profound

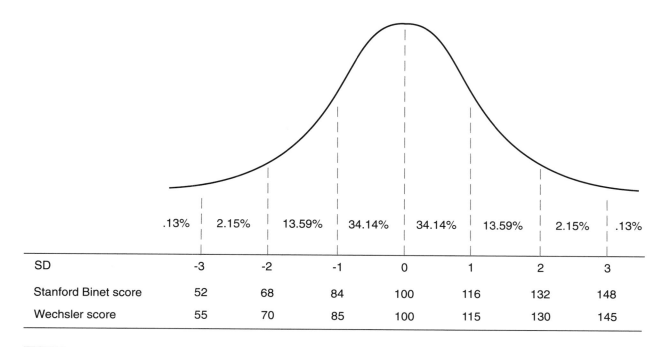

SD	-3	-2	-1	0	1	2	3
Stanford Binet score	52	68	84	100	116	132	148
Wechsler score	55	70	85	100	115	130	145

Figure 7.1 The normal curve and intelligence quotient scores.

by a recessive sex gene defect expressed in twice as many males as females. This is because males inherit one X chromosome and one Y chromosome. Females inherit two X chromosomes. Therefore, a male who receives the defective X gene will almost always display the disorder, whereas the female with a normal dominant X gene to oppose the abnormal recessive X gene will be clinically normal. However, she risks transmitting the defective gene to half her offspring, including the sons, all of whom will be affected. An affected male with an X-linked disorder will transmit the defective gene to all his daughters, who will be carriers. His sons will be both clinically and genetically normal.

About half of the population with mental retardation has more than one possible causal factor, and often it reflects the cumulative or interactive effects of these factors (McLaren & Bryson, 1987; Scott, 1988). For example, low birth weight is often considered to be an organic etiology, but other psychosocial factors such as maternal youth, poverty, lack of education, and inadequate prenatal care may have also contributed to the low birth weight. A multifactorial approach to etiology accounts for whether the causal factors affect the parents of the person with mental retardation, the person with mental retardation, or both; and it extends the types of etiology factors into four groupings:

- *Biomedical:* These relate to biologic processes, such as genetic disorders or nutrition.
- *Social:* These relate to social and family interaction, such as stimulation and adult responsiveness.
- *Behavioral:* These relate to potentially causal behaviors, such as dangerous (injurious) activities or maternal substance abuse.
- *Educational:* These relate to the availability of educational supports that promote the development of mental and adaptive skills (AAMR, 1992).

Similarly, prevention efforts are directed toward the parents and/or the person at risk for developing mental retardation. **Primary prevention efforts** are directed toward the parents of the person with mental retardation and aimed at preventing the problem from occurring (such as programs that prevent maternal alcohol abuse). **Secondary prevention efforts** are directed toward the person who is born with a condition that might result in mental retardation and aimed at limiting or reversing the effects of existing problems (such as dietary programs to treat persons born with phenylketonuria). **Tertiary prevention efforts** are directed toward the person who has mental retardation and aimed at improving the individual's level of functioning (such as programs for physical, educational, or vocational habilitation).

COGNITIVE DEVELOPMENT

The 1992 AAMR definition of mental retardation is functionally oriented. While this orientation is useful in determining individual limitations in present functioning, it is limited for understanding the dynamic nature of intellectual functioning and how it changes from age to age in the developmental process. Such a developmental orientation toward intelligence facilitates effective instruction and programming.

In order to establish developmental orientation, it is necessary to draw on the extensive work of Piaget (1952). In his vast writing, Piaget proposed that children move through four stages of cognitive development: the sensorimotor stage (ages 0 to 2), the preoperational stage (ages 2 to 7), the stage of concrete operations (ages 7 to 11), and the stage of formal operations (age 11 or 12 to adulthood). These stages are depicted in Table 7.2.

Sensorimotor Stage

During the sensorimotor stage, children develop, use, and modify their first schemata. For Piaget, schema or schemata (plural) are forms of knowing that develop, change, expand, and adapt. A schema may be a simple response to a stimulus, an overt action, a means to an end, an end in itself, an internalized thought process, or a combination of overt actions and internalized thought processes. Examples of schemata include grasping, sucking, and tossing a ball. During the sensorimotor stage, for example, the child develops the schema of grasping, which is internally controlled and can be utilized in grasping the mother's finger, picking up different objects, or picking up an object from various angles. A schema often will function in combination or in sequence with other schemata, as when the child throws the ball. In this activity the child combines the schemata of grasping and releasing.

To a great extent, the sensorimotor period is one in which the child learns about the self and the environment through the sense modalities. A great deal of attention is given to physically manipulating and acting on objects and to observing the effects of such actions. The child is stimulated by objects in the environment and observes how objects react to actions applied to them. Through exploration, manipulation, and problem solving, children gain information about the properties of objects such as texture, size, weight, and resiliency as they drop, thrust, pull, push, bend, twist, punch, squeeze, or lift objects that have various properties. At this stage, the functioning of the individual is largely sensorimotor in nature, with only rudimentary ability to manipulate reality through symbolic thinking.

Preoperational Stage

The preoperational stage includes the preconceptual substage, which lasts until about the age of 4, and the intuitive thought substage, which spans the ages of 4 to 7. Toward the end of the sensorimotor period, the child begins to develop the ability to symbolically represent actions before acting them out. However, the symbolic representation is primitive and limited to schemata associated with one's own actions. During the preoperational stage, progress occurs as the child is able to represent objects through language and to use language in thinking. The child now can think about objects

Table 7.2   Stages of Cognitive and Play Development

Age (years)	Piagetian cognitive developmental stage	Type of play	Play group
0–2	Sensorimotor	Practice play and ritualization	Individual
2–7	Preoperational	Symbolic	Egocentrism and parallel play
			Reciprocal play (progressive reciprocity in dyads, triads, etc.)
7–11	Concrete operations	Games with rules	Larger group play
11–adult	Formal operations		

and activities and manipulate them verbally and symbolically.

Concrete Operations Stage

During the stage of concrete operations, children achieve operational thought, which enables them to develop mental representations of the physical world and manipulate these representations in their minds (operations). The fact that operations are limited to those of action, to the "concrete," or to those that depend on perception distinguishes this stage from that of formal operations. The fact that the child is able to develop and manipulate mental representations of the physical world distinguishes this stage from earlier stages. In the stage of concrete operations, the child is able to mentally carry through a logical idea. The physical actions that predominated in earlier stages can now be internalized and manipulated as mental actions.

During the period of concrete operations, there is increased sophistication in the use of language and other signs. In the preoperational phase the child developed word definitions without full understanding of what the words meant. In the stage of concrete operations, language becomes a vehicle for the thinking process as well as a tool for verbal exchange. In this stage, children are able to analyze situations from perspectives other than their own. This decentering permits thinking to become more logical and the conception of the environment to be more coherently organized. During the period of concrete operations, children's thinking becomes more consistent, stabilized, and organized. At the same time, although children are able to perform the more complex operations just described, they are generally incapable of sustaining them when they cease to manipulate objects or when the operations are not tied to physical actions.

Formal Operations Stage

Children functioning at the stage of formal operations are not confined to concrete objects and events. They are able to think in terms of the hypothetical and to use abstractions to solve problems. They enter the world of ideas and can rely on pure symbolism instead of operating solely from physical reality. They are able to consider all possible ways a particular problem can be solved and to understand the effects of a particular variable on a problem. Individuals at this stage have the ability to isolate the elements of a problem and

systematically explore possible solutions. Whereas children at the stage of concrete operations tend to deal largely with the present, those functioning at the formal operations stage are able to be concerned with the future, the remote, and the hypothetical. They can establish assumptions and hypotheses, test hypotheses, and formulate principles, theories, and laws. They are able not only to think but to think about what they are thinking and why they are thinking it. During this stage, individuals are able to use systems of formal logic.

Piaget and Play

Piaget calls behaviors related to play ludic behaviors, which are engaged in to amuse or excite the individual. He holds that behaviors become play when they are repeated for functional pleasure. Activities pursued for functional pleasure appear early in the sensorimotor period. According to Piaget, the most primitive type of play is practice play or exercise play. The child repeats clearly acquired skills (schemata) for the pleasure and joy of it. The infant repeats movements such as shaking a rattle over and over and exhibits pleasure in doing so. This type of play does not include symbolism or make-believe.

Later in the sensorimotor period, the play in which the child engages is called ritualization. More and more schemata are developed and used in new situations. Play becomes a happy display of mastered activities. Gestures are repeated and combined as a ritual, and the child makes a motor game of them. As progress is made, the child forms still newer combinations from modified schemata. For example, a child may follow the ritual of sleeping after being exposed to the stimuli associated with sleeping (pillow, blanket, thumb sucking, etc.). Toward the end of the sensorimotor period, the child develops symbolic schemata and mental associations. These schemata enable a child to pretend. Some authors refer to symbolic play as make-believe play. Throughout the sensorimotor stage, play is individual or egocentric, and rules are not a part of it.

The preconceptual period within the preoperational stage marks the transition between practice play and symbolic play. At the preconceptual stage the child's play extends beyond the child's own actions. Also, new ludic symbols appear that enable children to pretend. At ages 4 through 7 (the intuitive thought stage), there is an advance in symbolic play. The child relates a story in correct order, is capable of a more exact and accurate imitation of reality, and uses collective symbolism (other people are considered in play). The child begins to play with one or more companions but also continues to display parallel play. The child can think in terms of others, and social rules begin to replace individual ludic symbols. For example, the child plays games of tag and games which involve hiding a moving object. Although play is egocentric, opportunities for free, unstructured, and spontaneous play are important. Children at this level are not positively responsive to intuitive thought. There is an advancement from egocentricity to reciprocity in play. Therefore, opportunities for cooperative play become appropriate. It should be remembered that the collective symbolism associated with cooperative play is at its beginning in this period. Guessing games, games based on looking for missing objects, games of make-believe, and spontaneous games are stimulating for children during this stage. The fact that children are responsive to tag games, for example, indicates that they are beginning to play with others and to think of others in their play.

At the stage of concrete operations, children's play exhibits an increase in games with rules. Such rules may be "handed down," as in cultural games, or developed spontaneously. In addition, there is an expansion of socialization and a consolidation of social rules. Thus, the playing and construction of group games with rules becomes very attractive to children. As the child enters and moves through this period, play becomes less concerned with make-believe and becomes more concerned with "real" games. At this stage, play may be structured, social, and bound by rules. Although some children may be ready for such games by the seventh birthday, children with retarded cognitive development may not be ready until after adolescence, if then.

Application of Cognitive Development to Teaching

There are many teaching implications associated with cognitive theory. Due to space considerations, only a few examples are presented. First, since language is more abstract than concrete, teachers need to reduce verbalization of instructions and emphasize tactile, kinesthetic, visual, and other more concrete forms of instruction. Children who can't readily transfer learning or apply past experiences to new situations need more gradual task progressions in smaller sequential steps and need to learn and practice skills in the environments in which they will be used. It is also important to

consider level of cognitive development in teaching rules and game strategies. As cognition develops, more complex rules and strategies can be introduced. Finally, language development should be considered in verbalization. For example, it is often helpful to emphasize action words and simple sentences when communicating instructions rather than multiple complex sentences. Feedback on quality of performance should be short and specific. Cognitive theory serves as a basis for some of the organizational and instructional methods suggested later in this chapter.

CHARACTERISTICS OF INDIVIDUALS WITH MENTAL RETARDATION

Mental retardation affects all aspects of an individual's life. The slower rate of learning and limited capacity to learn often affects the individual's ability to develop social competence and motor skills at the same rate and capacity as his or her nondisabled peers.

Learning Characteristics

The area in which individuals with mental retardation differ most from other individuals is in cognitive behavior. The greater the degree of retardation, the lower the cognitive level at which the individual functions. Most adults with severe limitations function at the sensorimotor cognitive stage. Adults with the mildest limitations may not be able to progress beyond the level of concrete operations. Others may be limited to simpler forms of formal operations or may be incapable of surpassing the preoperational substage.

Although the learning process and stages of learning are the same for both, children with mental retardation learn at a slower rate than nonretarded children and hence achieve less academically. The learning rate of children with mild limitations is usually 40–70% of the rate of nonretarded children. Children with severe limitations are often incapable of traditional schooling. Although self-contained classes and separate schools for children with severe limitations exist in most school systems, their primary educational objectives involve mastering basic life skills and communication skills needed for their care. Whereas adults with severe limitations who function at a higher level can learn to dress, feed, and toilet themselves properly and can even benefit from work activities, they will most likely need close supervision and care throughout their lives.

Social/Emotional Characteristics

Although children with mental retardation exhibit the same ranges of social behavior and emotion as other children, they more frequently demonstrate inappropriate responses to social and emotional situations. Because they have difficulty generalizing information or learning from past experiences at the same rate or capacity as nonretarded children, they are more often exposed to situations they are ill prepared to handle. Children with mental retardation often do not fully comprehend what is expected of them, and they may respond inappropriately because they have misinterpreted the situation rather than because they lack appropriate responses.

Educational programs for children with mental retardation should always include experiences to help them determine social behaviors and emotional responses for everyday situations. Personal acceptance and development of proper social relationships are critical to independence. As with nonretarded individuals, the reason most individuals with mild limitations lose jobs is inadequacy of social skills, such as poor work habits and the inability to get along with fellow workers.

Physical and Motor Characteristics

Children with mental retardation differ least from nonretarded children in their physical and motor characteristics. Although most children with mental retardation exhibit developmental motor delays, these seem to be related more to the cognitive factors of attention and comprehension rather than to physiological or motoric deficits.

Generally, the greater the intellectual deficit, the more lag in attaining major developmental milestones. As a group, children with mental retardation walk and talk later, are slightly shorter, and usually are more susceptible to physical problems and illnesses than other children. In comparative studies, children with mental retardation consistently score lower than nonretarded children on measures of strength, endurance, agility, balance, running speed, flexibility, and reaction time. Although many youngsters with mild limitations can successfully compete with their nonretarded peers, students with severe limitations tend to fall four or more years behind their nonretarded peers on tests of physical fitness and motor performance (health and safety adapted skill area).

In general, the fitness and motor performance of nonretarded children exceeds that of children with mild limitations, who in turn perform better than children with severe limitations. The performance of boys generally exceeds that of girls, with the differences between the sexes increasing as the degree of disability increases (Eichstaedt, Wang, Polacek & Dohrmann, 1991; Londeree & Johnson, 1974). Flexibility and balance seem to be the exceptions to the generalizations just stated. Whereas nonretarded girls show greater flexibility and balance than nonretarded boys, boys with mental retardation show greater flexibility and balance than girls with mental retardation. Also, children with Down syndrome exhibit more flexibility than other children with mental retardation (Eichstaedt, Wang, Polacek & Dohrmann, 1991; Rarick, Dobbins, & Broadhead, 1976; Rarick & McQuillan, 1977). Down syndrome children tend to have hypotonic musculature and hypermobility of the joints, which permits them greater than normal body flexibility, and because of weak ligaments and muscles, places them at greater risk of injury.

Many children with mental retardation are hypotonic and overweight or suffer other conditions (as shown in Figure 7.2). Disproportionate bodies pose many problems with body mechanics and balance. The "institutional" walk of the nonathletic child with mental retardation is characterized by a shuffling gait with legs wide apart and externally rotated for balance. Body alignment is in a total body slump. Club hands and feet, postural deviations, and cerebral palsy are all prevalent among youngsters with mental retardation; the physical educator must take them into consideration when planning the program for each child.

DOWN SYNDROME

Down syndrome is the most recognizable genetic condition associated with mental retardation. One in 700 children is born with Down syndrome. In the United States, approximately 5,000 such children are born each year. Although fathers are genetically responsible for the abnormality in about 25% of all cases, women over the age of 35 present the highest risk (1 in 290) of having a child with Down syndrome. At age 40 the risk increases to 1 in 150 births, and at age 45 the risk is 1 in 20 births (Cunningham, 1987).

Cause

Down syndrome results from one of three chromosomal abnormalities. The most common cause is

Figure 7.2   Many children with mental retardation have other conditions as well.
Photo by Stuart Rottor. Photo courtesy of Maryland Special Olympics.

trisomy 21, so named because of the presence of an extra #21 chromosome. This results in a total of 47 chromosomes instead of the normal 46 (23 chromosomes received from each parent). A second cause of Down syndrome is nondisjunction. This occurs when one pair of chromosomes fails to divide during meiotic cell division, resulting in 24 chromosomes in one haploid cell and 22 in the other. A third and rare cause of Down syndrome is translocation, which occurs when two chromosomes grow together so that, while appearing to be one chromosome, they actually contain the genetic material of two.

Characteristics

Although there are over 80 clinical characteristics associated with Down syndrome, the most common physical characteristics are the following (see also Figure 7.3):

- Short stature
- Poor muscle tone
- Hypermobility of the joints
- White spots in the iris of the eyes
- Transverse crease on the palms
- Small nose with a flat bridge
- Eyes slant upward and outward with exaggerated folds of skin
- Mild to moderate obesity

- Underdeveloped respiratory and cardiovascular systems
- Short neck; small lowset ears
- Small head; flat face and back of head
- Small mouth; thin lips
- Sparse, fine hair
- Protruding, fissured tongue
- Short legs and arms in relation to torso
- Broad hands and feet with stubby fingers and toes
- Poor balance
- Perceptual difficulties

Children with Down syndrome also tend to have many medical problems. Approximately 40% of these individuals develop congenital heart disease and have a greater risk of developing leukemia. Bowel defects requiring surgery and respiratory infections are also common. Down syndrome individuals age more rapidly, and almost half who live beyond age 35 develop Alzheimer's disease. All individuals with Down syndrome have mental retardation. Individuals with Down syndrome are becoming increasingly integrated into our society and institutions—schools, health care systems, community living, and the work force. While there is always a degree of slow development and learning difficulties associated with Down syndrome, attainment and functional ability is much higher

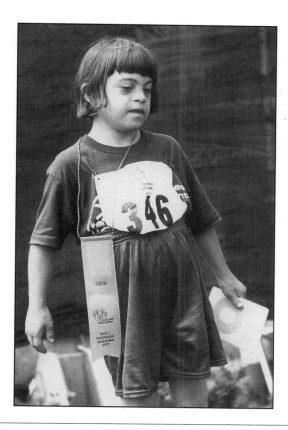

Figure 7.3 Special Olympics athlete with Down syndrome.
Photo by Mary Vane. Photo courtesy of Maryland Special Olympics.

than previously thought possible when individuals with Down syndrome have attended institutions and segregated schools.

Physical Education Programming

The many medical problems of individuals with Down syndrome require medical clearance for activity participation and careful planning of the physical education program. Muscle hypotonia (low muscle tone) and hypermobility (above normal mobility) of the joints often cause postural and orthopedic impairments such as lordosis, ptosis, dislocated hips, kyphosis, atlantoaxial instability, flat pronated feet, and forward head. Exercises and activities must not put undue stress on the body such that hernias, dislocations, strains, or sprains result.

TESTS

Assessment is necessary to determine the status of a student with mental retardation. Children with mild limitations who need only intermittent or limited supports in the health and safety and in the leisure adapted skill areas will, in many cases, be able to take the same tests as children without retardation. However, children with severe limitations who require extensive or pervasive supports in the health and safety or in the leisure adapted skill areas will often most appropriately be administered tests designed for their particular population.

Some norm-referenced tests have been developed specifically for use with people with mental retardation. Also, there are several appropriate content-and criterion-referenced tests that may be used to measure physical education abilities. These include tests associated with the Project ACTIVE Physical Fitness Test I (Vodola, 1978), the I CAN program (Wessel, 1979), the Ohio State University Scale of Intra-Gross Motor Assessment (Ohio State SIGMA) (Loovis & Ersing, 1979), the Special Olympics Sports Skills Guides (1985), and the Data Based Gymnasium (Dunn, Morehouse, & Fredericks, 1986). Consult chapter 4 for additional information dealing with testing.

ORGANIZATIONAL AND INSTRUCTIONAL METHODS

Although many of the organizational and instructional methods used in teaching nondisabled children can be applicable to those with mental retardation, certain methods are often stressed in the teaching of the latter. When employed, these methods ensure successful positive experiences for students with mental retardation in a physical education class where maximum participation takes place in a controlled environment.

Organizational Methods

Organizational methods are systems employed to group and manage students so that learning is maximized. How the learning environment is organized often greatly affects the amount of time the student is actively participating in tasks appropriate for his or her skill level. The following organizational methods will increase the amount of time students with mental retardation are learning appropriate skills.

Learning Stations

Learning stations divide the gymnasium/playing field into smaller units where each unit is designed for students to learn or practice a specific skill or sport. Students can be assigned to a specific learning station for the entire activity period or can rotate from station to station after a specific amount of time or a learning goal has been achieved. Learning stations permit flexibility and provide safe and successful learning experiences for students with mental retardation as well as nondisabled students in an integrated class. They allow students to progress at their own pace. Stations can focus on a theme such as physical fitness, tennis, or motor skills. Stations can enhance full integration while accommodating large numbers of students.

Peer Instruction and Cross-Age Tutoring

One of the most exciting developments in special education programs is the use of peers (other students) to help children with unique needs. It is common for young children to imitate slightly older peers. Cross-age tutoring is an excellent way of providing children with mental retardation with role models. Peer instruction and cross-age tutoring increases personalized instruction time.

Community-Based Instruction

Teaching skills in the "real" environment where the skills ultimately will be used is preferable to artificial environments such as the classroom or gymnasium. Students with severe disabilities do not generalize well from one environment to another. Thus, teaching skills in artificial environments forces a teacher to reteach these skills in community environments. It is, therefore, more efficient to teach skills in environments where they will be used. One of the critical steps in the process of teaching skills in natural environments is identifying and prioritizing environments in which these skills will actually be used. For example, teaching students to access and use community health clubs facilities, bowling facilities, or public pools is preferred to teaching these activities in school gymnasiums or pools. The availability of certain facilities in a particular community will determine whether a skill truly is functional.

Partial Participation

If a student with mental retardation can acquire some of the skills needed to participate in an activity, the parts of the skills that cannot be performed can be compensated through physical assistance or adaptations of equipment. Often, peer tutors can provide the physical assistance (see Figure 7.4),

while modified equipment and rule changes are adaptations that allow the student to participate in an integrated setting. For example, a student with cerebral palsy who uses a motorized wheelchair can be assigned a specially lined area of the soccer field. If the soccer ball enters this lined area, the peer tutor stops the ball. The student then has five seconds to maneuver his wheelchair to touch the ball. If the student is successful, the peer tutor then kicks the ball to a member of the student's team. If the student is unsuccessful, the peer tutor then kicks the ball to a member of the opposing team.

Instructional Methods

Instructional methods are teaching techniques used to maximize learning. How information is presented and skills are taught also greatly impacts the amount and quality of learning. The following instructional methods will facilitate learning for children with mental retardation.

Figure 7.4   Partial participation with physical assistance.
Photo by Mary Vane. Photo courtesy of Maryland Special Olympics.

Concrete and Multisensory Experiences

Because children with mental retardation are slower in cognitive development, their mental operations may be confined to concrete objects and events. Therefore, concrete tasks and information are more easily learned and utilized than their abstract counterparts. Instruction must therefore be concrete, emphasizing only the most important task cues. Because verbalization is more abstract, demonstration or modeling, physical prompting, and/or manipulation of body parts should accompany verbal instructions. Verbal instructions and cueing should be shortened and simplified and use specific action words (e.g., "run, walk, hop" as opposed to "go").

Data-Based Teaching

Data-based instruction involves carefully monitoring a student's progress and how such factors as environmental arrangement, equipment, task analysis, time of day, levels of reinforcement, and cueing techniques affect progress. By charting student progress, both teacher and student can often determine when an objective will be accomplished (e.g., complete two laps around the track). Cooperative charting by teacher and student can provide motivation and direction to help a student estimate how long it will take to accomplish any new task, set personal objectives to accomplish a task within a reasonable margin of error, and identify practice techniques for reaching the objectives set.

Task Analysis

Since children with mental retardation are generally unable to attend to as many task cues or pieces of information as children of normal or above normal intelligence, breaking down skills into sequential tasks is an important instructional approach. Many planned programs discussed later in the chapter employ task analysis.

Behavior Management

Applying the appropriate behavior management principles of cueing, reinforcing and punishing is critical to the success of task-analyzing skills and teaching all the smaller behaviors that enable the student to learn and perform the skill. Behavioral principles must be systematically employed and coordinated. Behaviors to be influenced must be pinpointed, and systems must be designed to promote change in the identified behaviors. The shorter the time lapse between student performance and feedback, the more learning is facilitated. This is especially true for persons with

severe limitations. An excellent example of a program that systematically employs behavioral principles in the teaching of children with severe limitations is the Data Based Gymnasium developed by Dunn et al. (1986).

Move from Familiar to Unfamiliar

Because students with mental retardation have difficulty applying past experience and previously learned information to new though similar tasks, they are more likely to view each new task as novel. Therefore, the progression from familiar to unfamiliar must take place gradually and be strongly reinforced. A teacher should begin to teach well within the range of student skill and comprehension. Tasks to be learned should be divided into small meaningful steps, presented and learned sequentially, and then rehearsed in total, with as little change in order as possible. A word of caution: Often, children with mental retardation have short attention spans, and although progression to new tasks should be gradual, the teacher should plan many activities to sustain the students' attention. For example, if the lesson is practicing the fundamental motor skill of hopping, the teacher may need to plan 10 different hopping activities in a 20-minute lesson!

Consistency and Predictability

Consistency of teacher behavior helps establish and maintain a sound working relationship between teacher and students. When students know what to expect, they can plan their behaviors with certainty of the consequences. Children with mental retardation are often less flexible in accepting or adapting to new routines. Therefore, day-to-day consistency of class structure, teacher behavior, and expectations is important in optimizing learning.

Choice Making

Activities for persons with mental retardation are often provided without considering individual preferences. Choice making allows students who often have very little control over their body and environment to have some control over their activity program. Choice making can consist of allowing students to choose which activity they want to play, which ball they prefer, how they would like to be positioned, who they would like to assist them, when they need to stop and rest, and so forth.

Activity Modifications

Often, students with mental retardation can successfully participate in physical education and sports alongside their nondisabled peers if challenging skills are modified to enable successful participation. This is particularly true for children who have associated health or physical impairments or who have more severe mental retardation. Activities can be modified by substituting fundamental motor skills and patterns for more highly developed sport skills, by reducing the speed of skill execution or the force required for successfully executing a skill, and/or by reducing the distance required for successful skill execution.

EDUCATION OF STUDENTS IN INTEGRATED SETTINGS

Approximately 27% of all students with mental retardation are receiving some support services while in an integrated class, and 61% are receiving specially designed instruction in separate classes within the school (U.S. Department of Education, 1992). Physical education teachers face the task of providing successful, enjoyable, and challenging learning experiences for all students in integrated classes. Their teaching strategies must ensure that students with mental retardation will comprehend instructions and achieve success in the integrated gymnasium. Teachers can enhance effective integration by using the teaching methods presented earlier, particularly

- employing the principle of partial participation,
- being consistent and reliable, thereby reducing the amount of uncertainty facing students who are integrated,
- shortening and simplifying instructions,
- using well-defined and distinctive cues,
- employing multisensory teaching strategies, and
- modifying instruction and activities by reducing the speed of skill execution and reducing the force required for successfully executing a skill.

ACTIVITIES

In selecting activities for students with mental retardation, the physical educator should be aware of the games, activities, and sports enjoyed by children within the neighborhood and offered by local recreation agencies. These activities are appropriate choices for the physical education class. Communication with local recreation agencies can result in cooperative programming and facilitate successful inclusion of students with mental retardation into structured community-based play groups.

Selection of Activities According to Chronological Age

Activities selected and skills taught should be appropriate to a student's chronological age and based on activities that the students' same-age peers enjoy. However, students' functional abilities and mental age must be considered when determining *how* to present skills and activities. Teaching chronologically age-appropriate skills minimizes the stigmatizing discrepancies between students with and without disabilities as well as teaching functional skills frequently used by all persons in natural, domestic, vocational, community, and recreational environments. Conversely, selecting activities based on mental age often involves keeping students with more severe limitations at the lower end of the developmental continuum working on "prerequisite skills" that often are nonfunctional and have an extremely low chance of being used in daily living or in community recreation and sport programs. Individuals with mental retardation particularly need to develop the motor skills and physical fitness levels they will require for optimal vocational training and successful use of leisure time.

Activities for Students With Mild Limitations

Often students with mild limitations excel in sports, and sports may be their primary avenue for success and self-esteem. Since students with mild limitations generally need only intermittent or limited support during physical education, they are more likely to be integrated in physical education classes than in any other subject. Their physical and motor needs are generally like those of nonretarded students; therefore, their physical education activities often will be the same as or similar to those for their nonretarded peers.

While students with very mild limitations often excel in physical education and sports, most generally do not achieve high skill levels. Still, basketball, soccer, hockey, baseball, and dancing are often popular among adolescents with mild limitations, even though concepts of team play, strategy, and rules are sometimes difficult for them to learn. Highly skilled people with mild limitations can learn strategy and rules through concrete teaching experiences. Skill and sport activities like those fostered by Special Olympics yield success and enjoyment for students with mental retardation.

Activities for Students With Severe Limitations

Individuals with severe limitations have not traditionally been placed into integrated public school classes, but rather into special classes, schools, or institutions because they generally require extensive or pervasive supports. However, more and more students with severe limitations are functioning successfully in integrated classroom settings when necessary and appropriate support systems are in place. Their level of mental and motor functioning is very basic. Their activity is generally characterized by little student interaction (i.e., parallel play), with most interaction occurring between teacher and student. They generally need an educational program that utilizes sensorimotor skills, fundamental skills, movement patterns, and physical and motor fitness development.

Sensorimotor programs stimulate a child's senses so that sensory channels are developed enough to receive information from the environment. Functional senses then permit the child to respond to the environment through movement and manipulation. In these programs, children are taught the normal infant motor progression of head control, crawling, grasping, releasing, sitting, creeping, and standing. Many students with severe limitations do not walk before the age of 9, and some never become ambulatory. Those with the most severe limitations may exhibit little or none of the curiosity that would motivate them to investigate the environment and learn. Even the most rudimentary skills must be taught. Through partial participation and activity modification, most can participate in physical education classes alongside their nondisabled peers.

Realistically, most students with severe disabilities are unable to independently perform most age-appropriate functional skills. However, the addition of physical assistance and technologies in the form of adapted equipment, switches, and computers enable many such students to participate in chronologically age-appropriate functional activities in natural environments.

PLANNED PROGRAMS

Several established programs are good resources for instructional processes and methods, assessment procedures, and activities relative to physical education and sport for individuals with mental retardation. Several of these, in fact, were originally designed for populations with mental retardation. In one of the first contributions, Thomas M. Vodola (1978) developed Project ACTIVE (All Children Totally InVolved Exercising). Project ACTIVE includes a systematic instructional process (test-assess-prescribe-evaluate), norm-referenced tests for measuring physical and motor ability, and a variety of other tests to help assess abilities in physical education. The project also provides many activity ideas for learning. Project ACTIVE was recently revised by Karp and Adler (1992).

Another notable program is I CAN, designed under the leadership of Janet Wessel (1979) of Michigan State University. I CAN uses an achievement-based curriculum (ABC) model designed to improve the quality of physical education services to all children, including those with mental retardation. The I CAN–ABC (Kelly, 1989) model provides criterion-referenced assessment evaluations in a variety of performance areas, as well as instructional resource materials to help children improve their abilities. The I CAN–ABC process consists of the following steps: plan, assess, prescribe, teach, evaluate, and modify. The program offers extensive resources including activities for preprimary motor and play skills, primary skills, and sport, leisure, and recreation skills. All have direct relevance to the physical education programs for students with mental retardation. The I CAN program is reviewed in greater detail in chapter 5.

The PREP Play Program (Watkinson & Wall, 1979) is designed to develop the play skills of young children with mental retardation. The program provides task-analyzed instructional sequences, curricular materials for the development of group play skills, and a systematic instructional model. The program is based on the assumption that, if play skills are developed, children will more likely become involved in play and reap the values of that involvement. Each target play skill is broken down into specific, sequenced tasks. The culminating step in the sequence is the actual target skill that, when attained, enables children to play well in most environments.

An important program with particular relevance for individuals with severe limitations is the Data

Based Gymnasium (Dunn et al., 1986). DBG offers a behaviorally oriented instructional model for teaching students with severe disabilities and a system for analyzing behavioral principles for the socialization of behaviors. Finally, DBG includes a game, exercise, and leisure sport curriculum. Specific skills within the curriculum are broken down into tasks and steps sequenced as phases representing shaping behaviors. Students are reinforced for successfully completing tasks that approximate the terminal or targeted behavior. The Data Based Gymnasium includes a clipboard instructional and management system that helps to identify present status, objectives, and progress on skill development.

Physical Education Opportunity Program for Exceptional Learners (PEOPEL) (Irmer, Glasenapp, Norenberg, & Odenkirk, 1983), a project began in Arizona, provides 36 units of instruction. These include basic performance objectives that have been task-analyzed for use in individualized physical education instruction. The task analysis and the use of student aids to individualize instruction make the program particularly suitable for teaching students with mental retardation.

The *Special Olympics Sports Skills Guides* are also helpful in sports skill development. Initially designed for children and adults with mental retardation, these guides offer long-term goals, short-term objectives, task-analyzed activities, sport-specific assessments, and teaching suggestions for various sports. Guides are now available for the following:

- alpine skiing
- aquatics (swimming and diving)
- athletics (track and field)
- basketball
- badminton
- bocce
- bowling
- canoeing
- croquet
- cross-country skiing
- cycling
- equestrian
- floor and poly hockey
- football (soccer)
- golf
- gymnastics
- horseshoes
- ice skating
- motor activities program
- powerlifting
- roller skating
- shuffleboard
- softball
- table tennis
- team handball
- tennis
- volleyball

The many planned programs discussed in this section are particularly relevant to people with mental retardation. However, because several have application for other populations in adapted physical education, they are discussed in more detail in other chapters throughout this book.

SPECIAL OLYMPICS

Special Olympics was created in 1968 by Eunice Kennedy Shriver and the Joseph P. Kennedy, Jr. Foundation. It is an international sports training and competition program open to individuals with mental retardation 8 years of age and older, regardless of their abilities. Children with mental retardation ages 5–7 may participate in Special Olympics training programs but not in competitions. The mission is to provide year-round quality training and competition in a variety of Olympic-type sports.

Special Olympics Summer and Winter Games are held annually as national, chapter (state or province), sectional, area or county, and local competitions. Special Olympics World Summer Games, which take place every 4 years, began in 1975. World Winter Games, also held every 4 years, began in 1977. Additional competitions that include two or more sports are defined as tournaments. To advance to higher levels of competition in a particular year (i.e., from local through area and sectional to chapter competition), an athlete must have trained for a minimum of 8 weeks in an organized program in the sport(s) in which he or she is entered for higher-level competition. To advance, an athlete must have placed first, second, or third at the lower level of competition in the sport(s). Instruction for 8-week training programs is provided in the *Special Olympics Sports Skills Guides*.

The showcase for acquired sports skills of Special Olympics athletes-in-training is the many competitions held throughout the year. These have the excitement and pageantry associated with Olympic Games—including a parade of athletes, lighting of the torch, an opening declaration, and reciting of the Special Olympics oath. In addition to showcasing their skills, athletes often have the opportunity to meet celebrities and community leaders, experience new sport and recreational activities through a variety of clinics, enjoy an overnight experience away from home, and develop the physical and social skills necessary to enter school and community sport programs.

Official Special Olympics summer sports include

- aquatics
- athletics
- basketball
- bowling
- cycling
- equestrian sports
- football (soccer)
- gymnastics (artistic & rhythmic)
- rollerskating
- softball
- tennis
- volleyball

Official winter sports include

- alpine and cross-country skiing
- figure and speed skating
- floor or poly hockey

Demonstration sports include:

- badminton
- golf
- powerlifting
- sailing
- table tennis
- team handball

To provide consistency in training, Special Olympics uses the sports rules of the International Sports Federation (given the responsibility by the International Olympic Committee for handling the technical aspects of Olympic Games) to regulate a sport, except when those rules conflict with *Official*

Special Olympics Sports Rules: 1992–1995 Revised Edition (1992).

Because of the wide range of athletic abilities among people with mental retardation, Special Olympics training and competition programs offer motor ability training, team and individual sports skills, modified competition, and regulation competition in most sports.

Special Olympics has developed three pioneer programs to help integrate its athletes into existing community and after-school sports programs. In the first program, Sports Partnerships, students with mental retardation train and compete alongside interscholastic or club athletes. Varsity and junior varsity athletes serve as peer coaches, scrimmage teammates, and boosters during competition. Athletes with mental retardation compete in existing interscholastic or club league competitions. For example, in a track and field meet, the varsity 100-meter race is followed by a Special Olympics 100-meter race. In distance races, all athletes start together. At the end of the meet, individual and school scores are tabulated for varsity and partnership teams. In team sports (soccer, softball, basketball, volleyball), partnership teams compete just prior to and at the same site as the varsity or junior varsity games.

The second program, Unified Sports, creates teams with approximately equal numbers of athletes with and without mental retardation of similar age and ability. Unified Sports leagues can be part of a school's interscholastic, intramural, or community recreation sports program. These leagues are established in six sports; bowling, basketball, softball, volleyball, soccer, and distance running.

The third program, Partners Club, brings together high school and college students with Special Olympics athletes to perform regular sports skills training and competition and to spend time enjoying other social and recreational activities in the school and community. The Partners Club should be a sanctioned school club with all the accompanying benefits.

All athletes with mental retardation should be able to earn school athletic letters and certificates, wear school uniforms, ride team buses to competitions, participate and be recognized in school award ceremonies, and represent their schools in Special Olympics local, area/county, and state competitions.

PARALYMPIC GAMES FOR THE MENTALLY HANDICAPPED

The Association Nacional Prestura de Servicio (ANDE) and the International Association of Sport for the Mentally Handicapped (INAS-FMH) held the first Paralympic Games for the Mentally Handicapped in September 1992 in Madrid. Unlike Special Olympics which provides competition for all trained athletes with mental retardation, 8 years and older, regardless of ability, the Paralympics for the Mentally Handicapped sponsors international competition for elite athletes with intellectual disabilities, 15 years and older, who can meet minimum qualifying sport standards.

Fourteen hundred athletes from 74 countries competed in five sports: athletics, aquatics, table tennis, indoor soccer, and basketball. In addition to competition, the Paralympic Games included opening and closing ceremonies, numerous recreational and cultural events, professional meetings and seminars, and receptions. Almost 200 medals were awarded during that week (DePauw & Rich, 1993). It is planned that the Paralympic Games will be held in the same year and same country as the Olympic Games.

SAFE PARTICIPATION

If the physical educator plans activities appropriate to the academic, physical, motor, social, and emotional levels of children with mental retardation, there will be few contraindications for activity. Special Olympics has prohibited training and competition in certain sports that hold unnecessarily high risk of injury, especially injury that could have lifelong deleterious effects. Prohibited sports are the javelin, discus, hammer throw, pole vaulting, boxing, platform diving, all martial arts, fencing, shooting, contact football and rugby, wrestling, judo, karate, nordic jumping, and trampolining. In addition, there is evidence from medical research that up to 10% of people with Down syndrome suffer from a malalignment of the cervical vertebrae C-1 and C-2 in the neck. This condition, called atlantoaxial subluxation, exposes affected individuals to the possibility of injury if they participate in activities that hyperextend or radically flex the neck and upper spine. The condition can be detected by a physician's examination that includes X-ray views of full flexion and extension of the neck. Physical education teachers are encouraged to follow the lead of Special Olympics in restricting individuals who have atlantoaxial subluxation from participating in activities that, by their nature, result in hyperextension, radical flexion, or direct pressure on the neck and upper spine. Such activities include the following:

- certain gymnastics activities
- butterfly stroke
- alpine skiing
- any warm-up exercises placing undue stress on the head and neck
- diving
- high jump
- heading the soccer ball

Because many children with mental retardation, particularly those with Down syndrome, are cardiopathic, students should receive activity clearance from a physician. Appropriate activities within the limitations specified by the physician should then be individually planned.

Another common condition of individuals with mental retardation is muscular hypotonia or flabbiness. Infants with this condition are often called floppy babies. Although hypotonia decreases with age, it never disappears, and hernias, postural deviations, and poor body mechanics are prevalent because of insufficient musculature. The physical educator again must be careful in planning exercises and activities that are beyond the capabilities of individuals with muscular hypotonia, because they can lead to severe injury. Abdominal and lower back exercises must be selected with care, and daily foot strengthening exercises are recommended.

SUMMARY

Mental retardation is one of the most prevalent disabilities. It is a condition that may be viewed from both functional and developmental perspectives. Mental retardation has numerous causes that result in varied characteristics influencing success and participation in physical education and sport. This chapter has suggested teaching methods, tests, and activities appropriate for this population and briefly reviewed selected planned programs relevant to students with mental retardation. One is Special Olympics, which has made a significant impact on both instructional and competitive opportunities for children and adults with mental retardation. The first Paralympic Games for the Mentally Handicapped were held during 1992 in Madrid. Most people with mental retardation have been and continue to be successfully involved in physical education and sport experiences.

BIBLIOGRAPHY

American Association on Mental Retardation. (1992). *Mental Retardation: Definition, classification, and systems of supports* (9th ed.). Washington, DC: Author.

Cunningham, C. (1987). *Down syndrome: An introduction for parents* (rev. ed.). Cambridge, MA: Brookline.

DePauw, K.P., & Rich, S. (1993). Paralympics for the mentally handicapped. *Palaestra, 9*(2), 59–64.

Dunn, J.M., Morehouse, J.W., & Fredericks, H.D.B. (1986). *Physical education for the severely handicapped: A systematic approach to a data based gymnasium.* Austin, TX: Pro-Ed.

Eichstaedt, C.B., Wang, P.Y., Polacek, J.J., & Dohrmann, P.F. (1991). *Physical fitness and motor skill levels of individuals with mental retardation: Mild, moderate, and individuals with Down syndrome, ages 6 to 21.* Normal: Illinois State University.

Irmer, L.D., Glasenapp, G., Norenberg, M., & Odenkirk, B. (1983). *PEOPEL: Physical education opportunity program for exceptional learners* (6th ed.). Phoenix: Arizona Department of Education.

Karp, J., & Adler, A. (1992). *ACTIVE.* (Available from J. Karp, 20214 103rd Place NE, Bothell, WA 98011-2455)

Kelly, L.E. (1989). *Project I CAN–ABC.* Charlottesville: University of Virginia.

Londeree, B.R., & Johnson, L.E. (1974). Motor fitness of TMR vs EMR and normal children. *Medicine Science and Sport, 6,* 247–252.

Loovis, E.M., & Ersing, W.F. (1979). *Assessing and programming gross motor development for children.* Cleveland Heights, OH: Ohio Motor Assessment Associates.

McLaren, J., & Bryson, S.E. (1987). Review of recent epidemiological studies of mental retardation: Prevalence, associated disorders, and etiology. *American Journal of Mental Retardation, 92,* 243–254.

Official Special Olympics sports rules: 1992–1995 revised edition. (1992). Washington, DC: Special Olympics.

Piaget, J. (1952). *The origins of intelligence in children.* New York: International Universities Press.

Rarick, G.L., Dobbins, D.A., & Broadhead, G.D. (1976). *The motor domain and its correlates in educationally handicapped children.* Englewood Cliffs, NJ: Prentice Hall.

Rarick, G.L., & McQuillan, J.P. (1977). *The factor structure of motor abilities of trainable mentally retarded children: Implications for curriculum development* (DHEW Project No H23-2544). Berkeley, CA: Department of Physical Education, University of California.

Scott, K.G. (1988). Theoretical epidemiology. Environment and life-style. In J.F. Kavanagh (Ed.), *Understanding mental retardation* (pp. 23–33). Baltimore: Brookes.

Special Olympics sports skills guides (1985). Washington, DC: Special Olympics.

Special Olympics International. (1991). *Keep the Flame Burning: Case Statement.* Lynchburg, VA: Progress Printing.

U.S. Department of Education. (1992). *Fourteenth annual report to Congress on the implementation of the Individuals with Disabilities Education Act* (DOE Publication No. 1992 0-328-452 QL 3). Washington, DC: U.S. Government Printing Office.

Vodola, T.M. (1978). *Developmental and adapted physical education: ACTIVE motor ability and physical fitness norms: For normal, mentally retarded, learning disabled, and emotionally disturbed individuals.* Oakhurst, NJ: Township of Ocean School District.

Watkinson, E.J., & Wall, A.E. (1979). *The PREP play program: Play skill instruction for young mentally retarded children.* Edmonton, AB: Physical Education Department, University of Alberta.

Wessel, J.A. (1979). *I CAN.* Northbrook, IL: Hubbard Scientific.

RESOURCES

Written

Dunn, J.M., Morehouse, J.W., & Fredericks, H.D.B. (1986). *Physical education for the severely handicapped: A systematic approach to a data based gymnasium.* Austin, TX: Pro-Ed. This book provides an instructional approach for teaching students with severe disabilities. To order, contact Pro-Ed, 5341 Industrial Oaks Blvd., Austin, TX 78735; (512) 451-3246.

Eichstaedt, C.B., & Lavay, B.W. (1992). *Physical activity for individuals with mental retardation: Infancy through adulthood.* Champaign, IL: Human Kinetics. A comprehensive up-to-date book that covers movement competency from infancy throughout adulthood for persons with mental retardation. To order, contact Human Kinetics, P.O. Box 5076, Champaign, IL 61825-5076; (217) 351-5076.

Special Olympics. (1981–1992). *Sports skills guides.* Washington, DC: Author. This is a series of sport-specific instructional manuals. Each manual includes long-term goals, short-term objectives, skill assessments, task analyses, teaching suggestions, progression charts, and related information. To order contact Special Olympics International, 1325 G Street, Washington, DC 20005; (202) 628-3630.

Audiovisual

ABC Wide World of Sports. (1991). [Videotape]. Washington DC: Special Olympics. Highlights of the 1991 International Summer Special Olympics Games, 33 minutes. Features various aspects of Special Olympics: competition, athlete profiles, volunteerism, family involvement and sponsorship, capturing the essence of Special Olympics. To order, contact Special Olympics International, 1325 G Street, Washington, DC 20005; (202) 628-3630.

Andrews, S., & Olsson, S. (Producers). (1988). *And then came John.* [Videotape]. New York: Filmakers Library. Movingly documents the importance of family and community support in the development of persons with disabilities. To order contact Filmakers Library, 124 East 40th Street, New York, NY 10016; (202) 808-4980.

CHAPTER 8

Learning Disabilities and Attentional Deficits

Diane H. Craft

A learning disability (LD) is characterized by a discrepancy between academic potential and achievement that is not caused by mental retardation, emotional disturbance, or environmental disadvantage but rather by a disorder in one or more of the basic psychological processes involved in understanding or in using language. Although a learning disability can be characterized and identified, it does not exist in isolation. It is only a part of all the strengths and challenges that characterize that individual who has learning disabilities.

Attention Deficit Disorder (ADD) and Attention Deficit Hyperactive Disorder (ADHD) are terms that apply to many, but certainly not all, students with learning disabilities. Children can have ADD without hyperactivity. While not overly active or disruptive, these students have difficulty focusing on tasks and activities. Deficits in attention can result in significant underachievement in school with resulting feelings of inadequacy. The overlap between ADD/ADHD and learning disabilities is enough that this chapter will address them together. The term ''LD/ADD/ADHD'' will be used to denote that the information presented may apply to children who have one or more of the three conditions.

It is possible for someone with LD/ADD/ADHD to meet the challenges or overcome the limitations imposed by others to excel in an area of his or her strength. Albert Einstein, Thomas Edison, Woodrow Wilson, and Greg Louganis are notable examples of people with learning disabilities who, as adults, have contributed successfully in their specialties. Thomas Edison, the inventor, was called abnormal, addled, and mentally defective. Woodrow Wilson, the scholarly 28th president, did not learn his letters until he was 9 years old and, like Einstein, did not learn to read until about age 11. It is important to underscore the notion that learning disabilities are found in an enormous variety and in many combinations of personal strengths and challenges. This means that physical education teachers need to work with each child to identify areas of learning disability and help the child develop accommodation and coping strategies. Consider the following biographies:

- Billy is a nine-year-old boy who is intellectually bright and artistically gifted. He can dash off a sketch that shows unusual artistic talent, but has great difficulty writing legibly, his letters seemingly strewn all over the page. When he can give an oral report instead of a written one, though, his excellent grasp of the subject matter becomes apparent. Billy also has difficulty skipping, walking a balance beam, or changing directions quickly in a tag game.

- Dashiki uses her well-developed imagination to tell delightful children's stories. She has a wonderful sense of humor, full of perceptive and witty insights. But most of the time she keeps these insights to herself, preferring to remain inconspicuous among her outgoing eighth-grade classmates. She struggles to hide the fact that she cannot yet read.

- Todd, a fifth grader, excels in athletic endeavors, with seemingly endless stamina and strength. Sitting still, though, for more than a few minutes is really difficult for him. Also, Todd is completely disorganized in his school work. He can rarely find his homework and struggles so hard today with math concepts that he had seemed to have finally grasped just yesterday. And when expected to do a task involving multiple steps, Todd frequently gives up on it almost immediately.

- José shows a mechanical aptitude well beyond his 10 years. He is always taking apart and reassembling household appliances to learn how they work. Yet José also shows inconsistencies in his academic performance. Socially, he has difficulty making and keeping friends. In conversation, he frequently makes inappropriate remarks, or his comments come at the wrong time. When other children are trying to be serious, José will often crack a joke. When teased playfully, José may cry or yell at his playmates. Such inappropriate reactions hurt his relationships and make other children want to exclude him from their play.

Whether destined for fame or not, students with learning disabilities or attention deficits have endured others' criticism and their own frustrations for their inability to master many things that come easily to most. They are the students most likely to be at risk to quit school, lose jobs, and experience difficult relationships throughout their lives. Further, they are more apt to have low self-esteem, painful memories of their childhood and schooling experiences, and more serious bouts of depression than students without learning disabilities or attention deficits.

The purpose of this chapter is to introduce physical educators to the area of LD/ADD/ADHD and to create an awareness of the realities faced by students with these disabilities. There are no "cures" for LD/ADD/ADHD, nor are these disabilities outgrown, although the characteristics may change over time. Fortunately, though, teachers can play a very important role in helping students like Billy, Dashiki, Todd, and José identify successful strategies to compensate and cope with their learning disabilities. Also, teachers can help them appreciate their strengths—and sometimes their giftedness—and value their uniqueness (Rief, 1993, p. v). "Getting the right kind of help from the professional field, especially understanding, flexibility, and determination from the child's teachers, is invaluable" (Rief, 1993, p. 148).

WHAT ARE SPECIFIC LEARNING DISABILITIES?

The most widely used definition of *specific learning disabilities* is found in the regulations of the Education for All Handicapped Children Act of 1975:

Specific learning disabilities means a disorder in one or more of the basic psychological processes involved in understanding or in using language, spoken or written, which may manifest itself in an imperfect ability to listen, think, speak, read, write, spell, or to do mathematical calculations. The term includes such conditions as perceptual handicaps, brain injury, minimal brain dysfunction, dyslexia, and developmental aphasia. The term does not include children who have learning problems that are primarily the result of visual, hearing, or motor handicaps; of mental retardation; of emotional disturbance; or of environmental, cultural, or economic disadvantage (Section 121a.5 [b] [9]).

Children with learning disabilities frequently also have difficulty with social skills. These difficulties may appear in four areas: starting relationships, keeping relationships, getting and using the right social feedback, and speaking and understanding social language (Levine, 1990).

All children, to some degree, and at one time or another, may have difficulty in some of these areas. Only when these behaviors *typify* the child, *persist* over an extended period of time, and *interfere* with learning do they need special attention. The term *specific* was added to learning disabilities to underscore that these children have learning difficulties only in specific areas (reading, speaking, calculating, etc.) and that there are other areas of learning where they are at least of average ability, and are sometimes gifted, in their learning.

WHAT IS ADD/ADHD?

Some of the behavioral characteristics of ADD that overlap with learning disabilities are as follows (modified from Rief, 1993, p. 1):

- distractibility
- difficulty attending to and following directions

- difficulty focusing and concentrating
- inconsistent performance in school work
- disorganization
- poor work habits and study skills
- difficulty working independently

Behavioral characteristics of ADHD that overlap with learning disabilities are as follows (modified from Rief, 1993, p. 2):

- high activity level, constant motion, fidgeting, squirming, restlessness, excessive talking, etc.
- impulsiveness and lack of self-control
- impatient
- intrusive
- risk-taking behavior leading to high frequency of injuries
- difficulty with transitions
- aggressive behavior
- social immaturity
- low self-esteem and high frustration

Any of the above behaviors are normal in childhood. Only when these behaviors typify the child and are developmentally inappropriate (because age mates have outgrown them) are the behaviors of concern. A child will display a particular combination of the above behaviors because of his/her unique combination of strengths, weaknesses, skills, and interests. There are also documented positive educational outcomes associated with ADHD. For example, the stories told by children with ADHD tend to be more creative than their classmates'. Individuals with ADHD can have the potential for energy, leadership, and spontaneity (Zentall, 1993, p. 150).

ADD/ADHD is conceptualized as an intrinsic disorder that is presumably caused by central nervous system dysfunction. It is often studied from three perspectives: neuroanatomical, neurochemical, or neurophysiological. The neuroanatomical approach studies brain areas thought to control attention and inhibit motor activity. The neurochemical approach studies specific neurotransmitters that aid communication among neural pathways thought to be involved in ADD/ADHD. The neurophysiological approach studies the dynamic interaction between the neurochemical and anatomical components of the brain (Riccio, Hynd, Cohen, & Gonzalez, 1993).

While ADD and ADHD are not categories recognized by IDEA for funding special education programs, these two represent a sizable group of children, many of whom are served under the learning disabilities provisions. This is no accident. ADD/ADHD and learning disabilities are two types of learning difficulties that appear to be similar in some respects. Attention deficit results from the brain's difficulty discriminating among situations that require focused, planned behaviors from situations where quick, impulsive actions are needed (Goldstein & Goldstein, 1989, p. 257). For example, playing on the playground after school is a setting in which quick, impulsive behaviors are appropriate, but completing a math test during school may require focused, planned behaviors. Children with ADD/ADHD may have difficulty with the tasks requiring focused, planned behaviors. With regard to teaching strategies, it is not important what label the child wears, be it LD or ADD or ADHD. What is important is to identify the child's strengths, needs, and behaviors of concern, then work with the child to develop successful learning strategies.

INCIDENCE OF LEARNING DISABILITIES

Children with specific learning disabilities (LD) form the largest group of learners with special needs in the United States. In addition, the learning disabilities category continues to outpace other exceptionalities with its rate of increase. And nearly all (98.4%) of the students with learning disabilities in the United States attend regular public schools either in regular or special education classes (Office of Special Education Programs, 1992). Thus, it is very likely that most physical education teachers will have the opportunity to teach many students with learning disabilities.

The U.S. Department of Education indicates that as of 1990 there were nearly two million children classified as having learning disabilities. (Some of these students may also have ADD/ADHD). This is just under 5% of all school-age children and represents 44% of all children receiving special education services. The ratio of learning disabilities among boys to girls is at least 3:1. Among the states, the bases for classification vary greatly. Kelly (1988) notes that the current definition includes learning disabilities caused by motivation, personality, environment—or any combination of these. This wide definition means that possibly 80% of all school-age youth could be eligible for special education.

WHAT ARE THE SUSPECTED CAUSES OF DISABILITIES THAT ARE SO PREVALENT?

The brain is responsible for perceiving, integrating, and/or acting on information. When one or more parts of the brain are not functioning optimally, this may contribute to one or more of the three conditions—LD/ADD/ADHD. The causes of LD/ADD/ADHD are largely unknown. Suspected causes include neurological, genetic, and environmental factors.

Neurological factors could include known or suspected brain damage due to infections, head injuries, anoxia, and fetal alcohol syndrome. There may or may not be signs of brain irregularities in neurological tests. Scientific research has not proven that prenatal exposure to drugs causes learning disabilities, but, based on the behavior of these children, such a link appears likely.

Genetic factors also are suspected of causing learning disabilities. The incidence is higher among children whose parents and grandparents also appeared to have learning disabilities.

Finally, the role of *environmental factors* such as toxins (e.g., lead poisoning) and inadequate nutrition (food additives, preservatives, refined sugar) in learning is not fully understood.

In summary, the causes of learning disabilities are largely unknown because the causes are probably multiple, cumulative, and interrelated, making them especially difficult to isolate and identify. Practitioners can only focus on the observed behaviors while researchers seek further knowledge about the underlying causes of learning disabilities.

WHY ARE THERE DIFFERENT CONCEPTUALIZATIONS OF LEARNING DISABILITIES?

Because the causes of learning disabilities remain unclear, the field of learning disabilities, as part of special education systems, has been fraught with a plurality of conceptualizations from its beginnings in the 1960s. Whether it is defined as a neurological dysfunction or as a behavioral phenomenon would reflect the perspective of the specialist developing the definition. In a manner as the blind men trying to describe an elephant, each observer ''sees'' learning disabilities his way. Moats and Lyon (1993) note the difficulties validating the learning disabilities construct. It is a young field with many different theoretical and conceptual views reflecting the learning disabilities field's multidisciplinary nature (e.g., psychology, education, neurology, and occupational therapy). Although a discrepancy between aptitude and academic achievement has become a widely accepted criterion, there is broad variation in the measurement of the discrepancy and serious concern about its validity. Separating children into a possibly artificial category prevents people from understanding how multiple and joint difficulties influence learning.

Increasingly, if a child is achieving at grade level, she or he is not considered to have learning disabilities and services are not provided, no matter how great the ability-achievement discrepancy. This denial of services to children with learning disabilities can be very damaging.

VIEWING LD/ADD/ADHD FROM AN INFORMATION PROCESSING PERSPECTIVE

Learning disabilities involve difficulty processing information. ADD/ADHD refer to attentional deficits. Any of these conditions can affect information processing. **Information processing** is the continuous cycle of four steps initiated by an external stimulus. These four steps are: (1) sensory input, (2) decision making, (3) output (doing the actual behavior), and (4) using feedback for the evaluation and planning of future sensory input and decision making. Thus, the fourth step, feedback, leads again to the first step, sensory input, restarting the cycle. The four events are diagrammed across the top of Figure 8.1.

Observation of the characteristics of individuals with LD/ADD/ADHD suggests that there is a breakdown in one or more of the steps of information processing. Only with attention, concentration, perception, organization, and self-control can information processing/learning proceed smoothly. Study Figure 8.1. Notice how a disruption in any one of these areas can affect the third step, behavior. Each child with a learning disability presents a unique combination of these behaviors. Refer back to the four students described earlier in the chapter. Different aspects of information processing may be affected in different individuals. Todd finds attending to the relevant stimuli very difficult while Billy attends easily but has

INFORMATION PROCESSING
An example of normal information processing

	1st step **Input**	2nd step **Decision making**	3rd step **Output**	4th step **Feedback**
External stimulus "Billy, throw me the ball."	Hears "Billy, throw me the ball."	I see the target. I will pick up the ball on my left. I will grasp it in my right hand, and step and throw the ball to Jane.	Execute motor plan—throw the ball to Jane.	The throw felt right; the ball went directly to Jane who caught it.

Examples of possible problems in information processing

One or more of these problems may occur:			
Inattention—not aware of the stimulus, "Billy, throw me the ball."		Does nothing	Inattention—does not attend to feedback and therefore does not use feedback to modify future throws
Distraction—hears the stimulus, looks at Jane, but also sees balance beam, thinks "I wonder how it feels to walk on that balance beam?"	Plans to walk over to the balance beam	Walks over to the balance beam	Distraction—does not continuously focus on the feedback, so does not learn to modify throw
Depth perceptual problem—does not correctly judge the distance between self and Jane		Throws ball over Jane's head	Haptic perceptual problems (including difficulty with laterality, directionality, and body awareness)—has difficulty judging how the ball was thrown and where the ball went in relation to Jane, so it is difficult to improve accuracy of throws with repetition
Visual figure-ground discrimination problem—cannot distinguish Jane from other children on the crowded playground	Guesses where to throw ball	Does not throw ball directly to Jane	
Auditory perceptual problem—hears "Bil me froh bal."	Does not understand what was said so plans to do nothing or	Does nothing or says "What?" or	
Auditory figure-ground perceptual problem—cannot hear "Billy, throw me the ball" because cannot distinguish request from competing noise in the hall	Guesses he heard "Kick the ball" so plans to kick ball Disorganization—lacks the cognitive strategies to identify what he needs to do and plan proper response	Guesses and kicks the ball Because he is disorganized, he feels pressure to act, so throws ball—in any direction	Disorganization—does use feedback but not in an efficient or effective way; does not develop appropriate cognitive strategies to be refined through feedback; processes feedback but within a disorganized, inappropriate learning strategy
		Impulsivity—spontaneously executes throw without pausing to reflect on decision making	Impulsivity—spontaneously executes next throw without pausing to modify throw based on feedback

Figure 8.1   The act of throwing a ball, viewed through an information processing model.

difficulty with directionality and in perceiving spatial relationships when planning a movement. Both students have learning disabilities but exhibit different characteristics because information processing is affected differently in each person. Todd may appear hyperactive but coordinated, while Billy may not be hyperactive but instead appear clumsy and disorganized when moving.

Teachers can help minimize the disruption of information processing among children with learning disabilities by using strategies to compensate for difficulties in the areas listed below. Further information on teaching methods is provided in the final section of this chapter.

1. *Attention* refers to focusing on the task at hand. An inattentive child may try to shoot a foul shot without really looking at the basket. After shooting, the child may not even look to see if the basket was made, thus not attending to the feedback that would facilitate refining the motor performance. When attempting to shoot a basket again, it may be as erratic as the first time because little use has been made of the feedback provided by previous experience shooting baskets. Inattentive children need help focusing.

2. *Concentration* on the relevant stimuli of the task at hand without being distracted by extraneous stimuli that compete for attention can be very difficult for some children. Children who are highly distractible may not finish a task because other things have captured their attention. Given the task of shooting foul shots, distractible children may shoot once and start to retrieve the ball. But when getting the ball, their attention may be diverted by the chart on the wall, a person passing by the gymnasium door, the child across the gym shooting baskets, or a comment made by an observer. The slightest extraneous stimulation seems to distract these children so that they are unable to focus on one task for any length of time, even when offered a very motivating reward for concentrating. With individuals who are highly distractible, there may be a neurological inefficiency in the area of the brain that controls impulses and aids in screening sensory input and focusing attention. During concentration, the brain may release neurotransmitters that enable an individual to focus on one task and block out competing stimuli. People who are highly distractible may have a shortage of these neurotransmitters (Rief, 1993, p. 4). They may return to shooting foul shots only

after the teacher refocuses their attention on the task.

3. *Perception* refers to the recognition and interpretation of stimuli received by the brain from the sense organs. Many, but not all, children with learning disabilities have difficulty with visual perception, auditory perceptions, proprioception. *Visual perception* involves figure-ground discrimination, spatial relationships, and/or visual-motor coordination. *Auditory perception* involves figure-ground perception, auditory discrimination, sound localization, temporal auditory perception, and auditory-motor coordination. *Proprioception* involves kinesthetic perception, including body awareness, laterality, and directionality.

4. *Organization* refers to a systematic approach to learning. Individuals with learning disabilities may show a haphazard approach to learning a task. According to Sutaria (1985, p. 146), students who are disorganized have difficulty with one or more of the following central processing tasks:

   (1) organizing thoughts and materials logically,

   (2) dealing with quantitative and spatial concepts,

   (3) seeing beyond the most superficial meanings or relationships, thus thinking only in concrete or stimulus-bound ways,

   (4) applying rules to problem solving,

   (5) arriving at logical conclusions or predicting outcomes,

   (6) making generalizations,

   (7) remaining flexible in their thinking, or

   (8) benefiting from experiences that do not mesh with their existing language system.

This significantly reduces their ability to deal with novel situations.

Many students with learning disabilities have difficulty *generating appropriate strategies* to guide their learning. Torgesen (1980) attributes the low task performance of children with learning disabilities to the use of inappropriate or inefficient learning strategies rather than to structural or capacity limitations. Capable learners may spontaneously generate appropriate learning strategies. Upon observing a new step, a folk dancer may develop verbal cues for each move that the dancer then repeats silently to guide learning the step. Many individuals with learning disabilities may not spontaneously generate or use strategies such as verbal mediation (saying cues aloud to one-self) to guide movement. Teachers can help provide these strategies.

5. *Self-control* refers to thinking before acting. Children who act before thinking about the consequences of the action, showing a lack of control or restraint on motor behavior or thought process, are acting impulsively. Impulsive children display little inhibition when they wish to speak or act. For these children it is very difficult to delay gratification and tolerate frustration. Upon arriving at the gymnasium door with the class, impulsive children may see a ball on the floor across the room, run over, pick it up, and throw it wildly in the direction of the basket before reflecting on the fact that they were to do warm-ups when first entering the gymnasium. There is little consideration of the consequences of the action. They behave first, then think.

OUTCOME/BEHAVIOR CHARACTERISTICS

Difficulties in information processing may result in observable performance characteristics of children with LD/ADD/ADHD. In the cognitive domain, two common difficulties are dyslexia and dysgraphia. Dyslexia, an inability to see words as written, contributes to reading achievement that is significantly below the level expected for the child's age, intelligence, and opportunities for reading instruction (Weiner, 1982, p. 139), and qualitatively different from that of even younger typical learners. "The normal interplay between visual and auditory processes never gets established" (Smith, 1983, p. 229). The delay occurs even with average or above intelligence and proper instruction. Dysgraphia is the written counterpart of dyslexia. Common problems in writing include the same kinds of disorganization, substitutes, and transpositions found among children with dyslexia. Difficulty with fine motor coordination also contributes to messy or illegible handwriting.

The motor behaviors among children with learning disabilities vary greatly. Some students with learning disabilities are average or even gifted athletes, such as Greg Louganis. Others are below average in motor behavior. Researchers studying the motor behavior of 369 students with learning disabilities found 12% were normal or above average, 75% had moderate difficulties, and 13% had

severe difficulties, averaging two to three years below the norm (Sherrill & Pyfer, 1985). Motor skills that included motor planning using the hands, perceptual-motor development, hand control and speed, and balance were especially challenging. Other researchers (Bruininks & Bruininks, 1977; Haubenstricker, 1983) have determined that motor skills involving balance, visual-motor, and bilateral coordination were areas of deficits.

Of the children with learning disabilities who do show difficulties with motor behavior, there are some areas that seem especially challenging. A descriptive summary of these motor behaviors follows.

A frequently documented characteristic of children with learning disabilities is difficulty with dynamic balance (Cinelli & DePaepe, 1984). Physical educators may observe children falling frequently and lacking coordinated movements as a reflection of difficulty in dynamic balance. There may be delays in motor development and basic motor skills such as the gallop, skip, or hop (Brunt, Magill, & Eason, 1983) perhaps also resulting from abnormal reflexes and perceptual deficits noted above. There may be delays in fine motor skills such as cutting with scissors, tying shoelaces, writing, and drawing. Extraneous movements such as flailing arms while skipping may be present (Haubenstricker, 1983, p. 43). Perseveration may be exhibited by some youngsters. Perseveration refers to continuing to perform a movement long after it is required. It is thought to be somewhat involuntary, rather than a voluntary action that can be unlearned once it is brought to the child's attention. For example, perseveration can compound the difficulty of jumping rope because the child may find it neurologically difficult to stop jumping or slow the pace of jumping. Arrythmical patterns during motor performance may be exhibited. These refer to the inability to maintain a constant rhythm during a repetitive task such as finger tapping or jumping rope. A child may begin jumping rope in a smooth manner but within the first six jumps will accelerate and add extraneous movements until the rope tangles in the feet. This is typical of many children as they first learn to jump rope, but it may be more difficult for some children with learning disabilities to develop the coordination to move past this stage. Motor planning contributes to smoothly executing skills involving balance, gross, and fine motor movements. Many children with learning disabilities find developing a plan before starting to execute the movement to be very challenging. Misapplied force (kicking a soccer ball too hard), premature or delayed responses (kicking too soon or too late), and inappropriate responses to complex sequences of stimuli (kicking the ball into one's own goal) all reflect problems in motor planning (Haubenstricker, 1983, p. 43). The variability of performance is at once the most frustrating and challenging aspect of learning disabilities. The motor behaviors of many children with learning disabilities are consistently inconsistent. A child who has worked very hard to learn the gallop one week may be unable to gallop the next week.

Behaviors of learning disabilities may also be observed in the affective domain. While studies have consistently found that individuals with learning disabilities perceive themselves less academically able than peers, a study by Bear, Juvonen, and McInerney in 1993 departed from other studies by looking at boys with learning disabilities who were fully integrated, with support services, and found that these boys were very aware of their own academic deficits. However, they appeared to have more favorable self-perceptions of social acceptance and peer relations than those with learning disabilities who were not fully integrated.

Physical fitness, motor skill, and athletic competence are key factors in determining the *self-concept* of children with disabilities (Kahn, 1982). Thus, athletic incompetence and academic failure can contribute to the low self-concept of uncoordinated children with learning disabilities. Typically, the uncoordinated child is selected last when teams are chosen, an embarrassing experience which does not make any child feel wanted or valued.

Social imperception has been found to characterize many children with learning disabilities. A child with perceptual problems may have difficulty interpreting facial expressions. Hence, that child can misread social cues and behave inappropriately. The imperceptive person may not note the cues of a furrowed forehead, sidelong glance, clenched jaw, or incline of the body away from the speaker that may communicate dissatisfaction and a desire to get away from the speaker. Frustrated because the speaker seems to be ignoring the listener's signals of displeasure with the conversation, the listener may finally walk away, leaving the imperceptive speaker at a loss to explain what happened.

Other perception problems may also lead to social difficulties. For example, one first-grader with learning disabilities was observed to score a point in a playground game (an infrequent event for this uncoordinated boy) after which he ran over to his cheering teammates and whacked two of them on the back with his hand. The teammates immediately stopped cheering the boy's play and instead yelled at him. It seems that the boy had seen ball players on television give each other congratulatory pats on the back after a good play. He was attempting to do the same but did not perceive the cue that the pats should be soft, not hard blows. Such social imperception does little to contribute to an individual's popularity. Given the emphasis on teaming and cooperation, physical education can serve as a laboratory in which to teach social skills to students with learning disabilities.

GENERAL APPROACHES TO LD/ADD/ADHD

Physical educators may be involved in some approaches, but others, such as the decision to prescribe medication, are beyond their responsibility. Yet it can be useful to understand these general approaches so that physical educators can support them as appropriate. Specific physical education teaching methods will be discussed at the end of the chapter.

Learning disabilities apparently have many different causes. It follows, therefore, that there would be many different ways of teaching children with learning disabilities. There is no one approach that is universally supported, but rather several, each of which has been successful with some students but unsuccessful with others. Six of these approaches are described briefly here: behavior management, cognitive behavior modification, applied behavioral analysis, perceptual-motor approach, multisensory approach, and a multifaceted approach. For the sake of consistency, the physical educator may wish to determine which approach is used successfully in the child's classroom and/or home and follow the same approach where practical.

Behavior Management

Behavior management refers to strategies that use reinforcement or punishment to increase desirable behaviors and decrease undesirable behaviors (Fiore, Becker, & Nero, 1993). This approach helps the teacher analyze the child in his/her environment and understand how specific behaviors function for the child in that environment. For example, Todd persists in talking while the teacher is instructing the group, and the teacher persists in telling Todd to be quiet each time he disrupts. In effect, Todd's disruptive behavior is reinforced by the teacher's attention. Understanding this, the teacher can modify his/her behavior and pay attention to Todd only when he quiet, thus rewarding him for the appropriate behavior instead of the inappropriate one. Use of the behavior management approach, then, helps the teacher analyze the situation and make modifications. For an extended discussion of behavior management, please refer to chapter 6.

Cognitive Behavior Modification (CBM)

CBM approaches learning and attentional difficulties as learning-strategy deficits. A basic premise of this approach is that cognition or thought (of which inner speech is a part) influences behavior. This method assumes that the way students think guides their behavior. Thus, this method seeks to change the way students think. It further assumes that students need to understand how they think and to take responsibility for changing how they think through monitoring, instructing, and recording their own behavior. CBM, then, helps students develop strategies to learn across every subject area, including physical education. Students are taught strategies that they may use to feel in charge of their own learning, which improves self-esteem.

One CBM training method is built around four main steps. The student is taught to verbalize in a modeling and rehearsal sequence.

1. Cognitive modeling: the teacher performs the task to be learned, talking aloud while the student watches and listens.

2. Overt guidance: the student performs the task using the same verbalizations that were demonstrated by the teacher, and the teacher assists as needed.

3. Faded self-guidance: the student performs the task, self-instructing in a whisper with no assistance from the teacher.

4. Covert self-instruction: the student performs the task guided by covert speech, that is, thinking the self-instruction but not saying it aloud.

Applied Behavioral Analysis (ABA)

ABA is an approach that is also based upon behavioral principles. This approach is even more precise in its application than either behavior management

or CBM. It involves identifying the precise behavior to be taught (the criterion); arranging situations in which the behavior can occur; obtaining baseline data; analyzing error patterns; applying interventions, stopping interventions when criteria are reached; and managing generalization of the learned behavior. Some practitioners of ABA conclude the process by teaching the student to self-manage the learned behavior, thus incorporating a feature of CBM. ABA, then, is based upon behavioral principles and requires analysis of behaviors and tasks into observable, teachable units (task analysis), pinpointing of specific problems, application of observable teaching strategies (interventions), and measurement of progress. Graphing and charting of student progress are used in the process.

Perceptual-Motor Approach

The perceptual-motor approach was developed by Kephart, Frostig, Barsch, Getman, Ayres, and other theorists who believe that higher-level mental processes develop out of and follow the consistent, integrated development of the motor system. To these theorists, early perceptual-motor abilities are the essential base for later conceptual abilities. Accordingly, they believe that movement experiences can help children develop perceptual-motor skills that, in turn, will enhance cognitive skills. While there is scant documentation that movement experiences will directly improve academic or cognitive performance (Kavale & Mattson, 1983), improvement of perceptual-motor skills is an important goal unto itself because it is vital to skilled motor performances. So, many physical educators include perceptual-motor activities in the curriculum for children with learning disabilities. Refer to chapter 17 for further discussion of perceptual motor development. The perceptual-motor approach has laid a foundation for later approaches to teaching children with learning or attentional difficulties

Multisensory Approaches

Multisensory approaches have developed from the perceptual-motor approach, as well as earlier approaches that attempt to teach new skills to young children and to remediate deficits in older children by teaching through areas of learning strengths. Multisensory approaches, then, focus on the use of three or more of the sensory channels in the teaching-learning process.

The sensory modalities that are typically used in this fusion are visual, auditory, kinesthetic, and tactile. A teaching method that integrates three of these modalities might have the child watch a demonstration of a movement (visual), listen to the teacher describe the specific movement (auditory), and be physically manipulated through the movement (kinesthetic). For example, a student might learn letters by looking at a printed letter, hearing its name, feeling its shape by tracing the letter in same or tracing on the palm of the hand, and moving the entire body to form the letter's shape.

The multisensory approach, in turn, influenced the "learning style" movement. Many modern special educators have promoted the idea that teaching children with learning and attentional difficulties is best accomplished by matching the teaching method to the child's preferred learning style. Skillful teaching has been affected by this movement; good teaching practice generally is thought to appeal to varied learning styles simultaneously. The multisensory approach has not only been utilized extensively to assist children with learning and attentional difficulties but has also become standard teaching practice.

Multifaceted Approach

A more eclectic approach to working with children with LD/ADD/ADHD is often more effective in schools than any single approach. A list of suggestions follows (modified from suggestions in Rief, 1993, p. 15):

- *Behavior management* is used both at school and at home. Avoid abandoning the behavior management technique if the first few reinforcers tried do not influence behavior. Continue to seek a strong reinforcer for this particular child.

- *Family counseling* is recommended with ADD/ADHD because the entire family is affected. It can be very reassuring to parents/caregivers to learn that they are not the cause of their child's difficulty and to learn strategies to help them cope with the daily challenges of the inattentive or hyperactive behavior of their child.

- *Individual counseling* helps the child to develop coping, stress reduction, and learning strategies and to build/maintain a positive self-concept. Counseling, an important source of training in *social skills*, may help the child learn to attend to social cues and thus decrease social imperception.

- *Cognitive therapy* teaches children with ADD/ADHD the skills to regulate their own behavior as well as to use "stop and think" techniques to counteract impulsivity.

- *Numerous school interventions* are used, including behavior management/therapy, cognitive-behavioral therapy, and applied behavioral strategies.

- *Medical intervention* may take the form of drug therapy.

- *Parent education* helps parents/caregivers learn all they can about LD/ADD/ADHD so they can better assist their child. Welcome and inform caregivers. Seek their assistance. Caregivers can be extremely important advocates for getting the support systems needed to teach children with special needs in physical education.

- *Physical activity* is an important intervention in that it can help reduce stress and focus attention. It also provides a socially appropriate outlet for energy in a child with ADHD. Noncompetitive activities that do not demand quick reaction and accuracy may work best.

Medication

Drug therapy is a treatment of last resort with ADD/ADHD, but, nonetheless, *stimulant medications* are widely used. Methylphenidate (Ritalin) and dextroamphetamine (Dexedrine) are relatively fast acting, taking effect within 1 to 4 hours for Ritalin and 4 to 8 hours for Dexedrine. It is suspected that the drugs affect the body's neurotransmitters. These drugs have been shown to increase attending behaviors and decrease impulsivity, thus requiring less need for teacher control (Forness & Kavale, 1988), but their use does not necessarily result in increased learning. When a child's medication wears off, mood swings or irritability may be observed during the "rebound." Teachers may observe changes in behavior during transition periods while the optimal dosage of a medication is determined. Physical educators and other teachers are important sources of information regarding the child's behavior while on or off medication. Teachers are encouraged to share their observations with the classroom teacher, parents, and school nurse.

TEACHING CHILDREN WITH LD/ADD/ADHD

Instruction is accomplished through a series of steps: assess, plan, implement, and evaluate. First, the children are assessed to identify learning strengths and weaknesses. Second, instruction is planned and instructional objectives are written. Third, the instructional program is implemented. Finally, the children's progress is measured and evaluated. Programs are modified based on the ongoing evaluation. The rest of this chapter provides information useful in assessing the motor performance and planning appropriate teaching methods for children with LD/ADD/ADHD.

Assessing Skills

The first step in teaching and in writing an IEP is determining the student's present level of performance. Administering perceptual and motor tests is particularly useful. The Bruininks-Oseretsky Test of Motor Proficiency may be used to measure fine and gross motor coordination. The Ohio State University Scale of Gross Motor Development (OSU SIGMA) and Ulrich's Test of Gross Motor Development are both suitable for measuring the maturity of basic motor patterns. Other tests that have been used include Ayres's Southern California Perceptual Motor Tests and the Purdue Perceptual Motor Survey (measures the four components of perceptual-motor development). Additional information on each of these tests may be found in chapter 4.

Specific Teaching Methods

Recall that 98.4% of the students with learning disabilities in the United States attend regular public schools either in regular or special education classes. "Children with ADHD in the regular classroom face a risk of school failure two to three times greater than that of other children without disabilities but with equivalent intelligence" (Rubinstein & Brown, 1981). Thus, it is important that physical education teachers make the extra effort to reach and teach children with LD/ADD/ADHD. Many of the following suggestions are sound teaching techniques for *all* children. They are organized into four categories: focusing and maintaining attention, selecting appropriate curricula, teaching socialization and cooperation, and getting support systems.

Focusing and Maintaining Attention

Keeping students' attention is crucial for teaching. Obviously, for students with ADHD the task is more difficult than usual. The following paragraphs offer principles for maintaining students' attention.

1. *Use a highly structured, consistent approach to teaching.* Establish a routine and repeat it day after day. Students with ADHD have greater difficulty tolerating instructional delays. Prior organization and smooth transitions during instruction are essential teaching skills. For example, every day students enter the gym and go to their spots marked on the floor. Instruction begins with an established warm-up routine, followed by the introduction and practice of new skills, participation in a game or dance and a return to the same floor spots for the cool-down and review. The same warm-up may be used for several sessions to enable the child to learn it well and anticipate the structure of the class. The teacher may wish to create an audiocassette tape of the warm-up routine with music and verbal instructions and appoint a skilled student to lead and demonstrate each exercise. Thus freed from calling out instructions and demonstrating, the teacher may move among the students as they warm up, providing individual assistance to students with learning disabilities. Perceptual concepts, such as laterality, can be incorporated in the warm-up; for example, "Turn to the left as you run in place, twist to the right as you do sit-ups, stretch and reach to the ceiling with your left hand."

    There are few class rules, but these are understood and equally applied to all students. Sample rules for young children could include:

    - listen when others are speaking
    - keep your hands to yourself
    - wear sneakers
    - *try* every activity

    Posting these rules provides visual cues for children who do not process auditory information well or who are impulsive. Silently pointing toward the poster enables the teacher to prompt the child effectively.

2. *Use a behavior management program to teach children the sequence "attend-think-act" to decrease their hyperactivity.* Three common behavioral

interventions appear especially useful: positive reinforcement, short verbal reprimands, and response cost. Continuous positive reinforcement can reduce activity level, increase time on task, and improve academic performance of students with ADD. Short reprimands are often effective when they immediately follow the behavior. ("Billy, hands to yourself!") Avoid long or escalating reprimands. Short, quick reprimands work better. Response cost, a program in which a child can earn points/tokens for appropriate behavior (but can also lose them for inappropriate behavior), can help improve on-task behavior and task completion.

3. *Clarify all expectations.* Teach what is acceptable behavior in physical education through practicing, modeling, and reviewing behavioral expectations and rules. Follow through to consistently apply clear, fair consequences. Use proximity control to redirect students with attentional or behavioral problems. Stay close and use eye contact, a hand on the shoulder, or silent pointing to prompt students about appropriate behavior. Provide ample notice of transitions. For example, use the last minutes of class to practice relaxation techniques and calm the students before they leave. Chapter 21 provides additional information on relaxation.

4. *Select activities that emphasize moving slowly and with control to decrease hyperactivity and impulsivity.* Use "slow" races, with such challenges as, "How slowly can you do a push-up? A forward roll?" Include instruction in relaxation. For example, dim the lights and ask all students to go to their floor spots and lie on their backs with their eyes closed. Present relaxation activities through guided imagery ("Imagine that you are relaxing in a warm place under the hot sun.") or progressive relaxation ("Tense your right arm. Hold it. Now relax. Feel the tension flow from your arm. Feel how limp your arm has become."). Check that students are, in fact, relaxing by gently lifting a limb off the floor to see if it feels loose and heavy. If it does, then the person is probably relaxed. These activities may help children who only seem to know the feeling of "fast" and "tense" to learn the feeling of "slow" and "relaxed." Within each lesson, alternate active games with relaxation training or passive games, using a format of work, rest, work, rest. The periods of rest are designed to give hyperactive students a chance to slow down before they become so excited that they are out of control.

5. *Teach in a quiet, less stimulating environment to decrease distractibility.* Reduce background noise. Keep the gymnasium neat, clean, and well ordered, with unnecessary equipment stored out of sight. Facing distractible children toward the corner so that their backs are to the other activities in the gym also helps focus attention.

6. *Use verbal mediation to teach especially disorganized, distractible children.* Verbal mediation is a strategy in which children are encouraged to plan aloud what they will do to focus attention on the task at hand. Distractible children may be coached to repeat directions aloud; for example, "First, I will get the ball from the box, then I will shoot foul shots until I score 10 points." If the children are off-task, the teacher asks, "What is the task you are to do?" and prompts the children to refocus attention. On-task behavior is also reinforced. Praise children when they are attending to the task as expected. "Catch them being good."

7. *Provide appropriate learning strategies to help disorganized learners focus.* Plan the instructional objectives for each lesson and share these objectives with the students. This technique lets everyone know the behavior that is to be learned. For example, if the objective of the lesson is to throw a ball at one of several targets using a mature overhand pattern, tell this to the class. Together with the students, identify the critical elements of the mature throwing pattern. An example of a critical element may be "step with the other foot as you throw."

8. *Highlight relevant cues.* Many students with learning disabilities have difficulty selectively attending to the relevant aspects of the skill to be learned. For example, place footprints on the floor so that children standing in the footprints will have their sides to the target. Provide a visual cue by placing a third footprint where the children will step as they transfer their weight during the throw. Provide verbal cues as well. Teach children to say aloud, "Step and throw," as a cue to transfer weight while releasing the ball. Also, teach children how to use feedback. For example, after the ball is thrown, ask children to identify where the ball landed in relation to the target ("The ball hit below the target") and to identify what they

need to change in the next throw ("I need to release the ball sooner"). The intent is to help the children use feedback in perfecting future performances.

9. *Give instruction using more than one sense.* Some students' preferred mode of learning is visual, others is auditory, and still others is kinesthetic. To accommodate the variety of learners found in any class, and especially those classes with children who have learning disabilities, teach using all three modalities. Use short, clear directions that present the global information without using elaborate descriptions. Use demonstrations liberally to add visual cues to verbal directions. Physical educators may wish to show a picture of the skill to be learned in addition to explaining the skill. A photograph of the child putting away equipment may be placed next to the storage to visually illustrate what is expected at clean-up time. Physically assist the child through the skill to provide kinesthetic cues. Children with ADHD have difficulty attending to subtle cues, so highlight cues and teach children to look for subtle social cues.

If children are not following directions, it may be that they do not understand them. Some instruction in basic concepts may be necessary. Children may not follow the directions "skip around the outside of the circle" because they do not know how to skip, or they do not understand that the classmates holding hands form a circle, or they're not sure where the "outside" of the circle is located.

10. *Encourage motor planning.* Ask children to explain what they will do before they begin to move. This explanation will ensure that children give some advance thought to how and where they will move. "Students with ADHD are aware they fail to plan ahead or anticipate final steps. Their attempts to plan are disorganized in nature" (Zentall, 1993, p. 147). Teachers play a vital role in helping these students organize themselves. Teachers can provide a framework for organization and cue children to follow it. Physical educators may wish to use pictures, color codes, and short verbal cues to help these children organize themselves. And, as always, follow a routine that gives organization to the lesson.

11. *Change the task to add novelty.* Children with ADHD may have an attentional preference for novelty and active learning (Zentall, 1993). For example, if children are practicing striking objects, substitute a novel object before the child's attention wanes. If a child's attention wanes after five repetitions of striking a whiffle ball, then make the task novel every three or four repetitions by substituting a bean bag, then a nerf ball, then a balloon, then a koosh ball. In this manner the child may practice striking as many as twenty repetitions.

Select Appropriate Curricula

There are four key points in the selection of curricula appropriate for children with LD/ADD/ADHD.

1. *Teach to mastery to enhance students' self-efficacy and self-concept.* Avoid conducting a curriculum that only samples activities, rather than providing practice until skills are mastered. Task-analyze and use progressions to guarantee success at the early stages of learning. A data-based approach to instruction may be helpful. Daily or weekly progress is recorded so that, even when progress is slow and inconsistent, improvement over time can be demonstrated to the students.

2. *Review previously acquired basic skills before teaching more advanced skills.* Anticipate that children with learning disabilities may be inconsistent performers, particularly of skills taught during previous lessons. Daily review is important, as are opportunities for continued practice of newly acquired skills.

3. *Minimize highly competitive team games requiring precise skilled responses,* if these skills are beyond the capability of the child. Include team games only when the child has the skill to compete successfully. Forget hitting a pitched softball from the mound if the child with learning disabilities, or any child for that matter, does not have the prerequisite skills to be successful in this task. Noncompetitive activities that do not have high demands for quick reactions and accuracy may work better. Also, avoid elimination activities in which the skilled players get the most practice and unskilled players get the least practice. Reconsider teaching a competition-based curriculum that provides the most success for only the motor elite. Similarly, avoid team games that require some to be "losers." Many of these children already see themselves as losers; teachers have a responsibility to change, not reinforce, this concept. To decrease anxiety,

individualize instruction so that a child does not have to perform in front of classmates a skill that he or she has not yet mastered. Look to a curriculum that involves cooperative learning, group initiatives, or swimming, running, gymnastics, and perhaps yoga and martial arts such as aikido and tai chi. Focus on doing one's personal best.

4. *Include activities in perceptual-motor skills, gross and fine motor skills, and balance and body awareness in the curriculum.* Be alert to the role that perception plays in motor skill performance. If children have difficulty catching, it may be due to perceptual problems such as visual tracking or figure-ground discrimination, in addition to inadequate bilateral coordination or slow reaction times.

Teach Socialization and Cooperation

Teachers can use a number of strategies to foster students' cooperation and bolster the self-esteem of children with LD/ADD/ADHD.

1. *Use cooperative learning to increase students' social interactions and self-concepts.* In this approach, children succeed through working together. Cooperative games and competition against oneself may be more appropriate alternatives, especially in the elementary grades. Games such as Crossover Dodge Ball, Slowest Races, Cooperative Beach Ball and Volleyball, and Project Adventure Challenges may be more appropriate than the traditional team sports. Cooperative activities have been shown to increase social interaction. Further information on using cooperative learning in teaching may be found in Rief (1993) and Putnam (1993).

2. *Eliminate embarrassing teaching practices that force comparison among students.* Examples of such practices include posting the fitness scores of everyone in the class or "choosing up teams" in front of the class. No one enjoys knowing that he or she was the last choice. Instead, recognize the "most improved" and good performances of students with learning disabilities.

3. *Group students to maximize appropriate behavior.* Capitalize on the principle of imitation learning by putting students who show poor social skills with students who are good models. One student with poor social skills per group of 6 to 10 is a reasonable ratio.

Get Support Systems

Support systems are excellent for both teachers and students with special needs. But support systems don't happen by themselves. Teachers have to make them happen. Here's how:

1. *Use peer tutors to further individualize instruction.* A mature classmate, an upper-grade student or an adult volunteer may work with the one or two challenging children. The peer tutor helps children who are distractible remain focused on the task through verbal prompts, such as asking, "And what do you do now?" With peer tutors, the teacher can divide a large class into small groups that work in separate areas of the gym. This may help distractible children. Balance the number of hyperactive and hypoactive children in the group. Experiment with various combination of students to find the mix of personalities that works best. Also, seek opportunities for children with LD/ADD/ADHD to serve as peer tutors to their classmates or younger children. It builds self-esteem to be helpful to others.

2. *Enlist parent/caregiver assistance.* Caregivers can be important advocates in helping to get the support systems teachers need to successfully teach all children. Through the IEP mechanism, "caregivers can request support systems, such as the consultation services of an adapted physical educator or the assistance of a paraprofessional or the reduction in class size, be made available to their child's physical education teacher so that the child's needs and those of other classmates may be met in the regular physical education class" (Craft, in press).

3. *Work collaboratively with others.* Collaborate with students' other teachers, resource specialists, administrators, parents, physicians, school nurses, psychologists, and others who might share ideas they have found successful and unsuccessful in helping students.

Teachers Who Work Well With Students With LD/ADD/ADHD

Understanding students with learning disabilities and/or attentional difficulties is further helped by descriptions by adults of what teaching styles and approaches worked best for them as children. Adults have recounted the frustration and failure they experienced as children with learning disabilities. In addition to stories about teachers who accused them of laziness, there are stories about the teachers who really helped them or who served as mentors. These teachers shared the following characteristics (modified from Rief, 1993, pp. 5–10).

1. Teachers were flexible, committed, and willing to work with the student on a personal level. These teachers put a great deal of effort into teaching these children with learning disabilities and, in turn, reaped the rewards of knowing they had made a significant difference in the lives of these children.

2. Teachers sought training and knowledge about learning disabilities. Recognizing that the problems were more likely physiological and biological in nature, they avoided the interpretation "these children are out to get us deliberately" (Rief, 1993, p. 5). Instead, these teachers saw the talents of these people as children and worked with them in making changes and accommodations, plus identifying coping strategies so that the person's strengths could emerge, despite the learning disabilities.

3. These teachers cultivated administrative support. Administrators need to be aware of the behaviors and teaching strategies for working with children with LD/ADD/ADHD. Their help is essential in implementing behavior programs that might include removing a child from the class when the behavior is disrupting the teacher's ability to teach or other students' ability to learn. Educate administrators as to the importance of distributing children with learning challenges across classes and not scheduling large groups of students with ADD/ADHD in the same physical education class. Such "dumping" is unfair to all involved.

4. Teachers respected students and avoided embarrassing or humiliating them in front of others. The overriding characteristic of these teachers who really made a difference in the lives of people with learning disabilities is their belief in the student. When one approach did not work, the teachers tried a second, and a third, and a fourth, and a fifth, and so forth. "These children are worth the extra effort and time" (Rief, 1993, p. 10).

SUMMARY

Teachers can play a key role in helping children with learning and/or attentional problems develop compensatory strategies and coping skills. Also, teachers can promote a positive self-concept, enabling these children to develop confidence and satisfaction about their accomplishments and contributions. Many children with learning disabilities or attentional difficulties perform very well in physical education. For them it may be the one area where they can experience success during the school day, because there is seldom the requirement to sit still, read, or write in physical education. Physical educators can use this opportunity to showcase the motor skills of these children. For others with learning disabilities whose motor performances are not refined, physical education can still be an enjoyable experience. But it will only be enjoyable if conducted in a manner that does not dwell on the child's motor deficits.

In preparing to teach children with LD/ADD/ADHD, teachers may ask the following questions. What are the strengths and needs of *this* child? How does this child process information? Are there problems in any areas of processing information? How can I as the teacher help this child cope and compensate for these deficits in information processing? What approaches and programs are already in place for this child at school and at home? What support systems will I need, and how will I work to get them? How can I plan instruction in the child's physical education class to help the child succeed? And, finally, how can I collaborate with others to ensure this child's success?

ACKNOWLEDGMENT

The author gratefully acknowledges the contribution of C. Robin Boucher, PhD, Special Education Resource, Fairfax County, Virginia, Public Schools, for information and resources on learning disabilities in this chapter.

BIBLIOGRAPHY

Bear, G.G., Juvonen, J., & McInerney, F. (1993). Self-perception and peer relations of boys with and boys without learning disabilities in an integrated setting: A longitudinal study. *Learning Disability Quarterly*, **16**, 127–136.

Bruininks, V.L., & Bruininks, R.L. (1977). Motor proficiency and learning disabled and nondisabled students. *Perceptual and Motor Skills*, **44**, 1131–1137.

Brunt, D., Magill, R.A., & Eason, R. (1983). Distinctions in variability of motor output between learning disabled and normal children. *Perceptual and Motor Skills*, **57**, 731–734.

Cinelli, B., & DePaepe, J.L. (1984). Dynamic balance of learning disabled and nondisabled children. *Perceptual and Motor Skills, 58*, 243–245.

Craft, D.H. (in press). A focus on inclusion in physical education. In B. Hennessy, *Physical education teacher resource handbook.* Champaign, IL: Human Kinetics.

Education for All Handicapped Children Act of 1975, » 121a.5, U.S.C. » 1401 (1977).

Fiore, T.A., Becker, E.A., & Nero, R.C. (1993). Educational interventions for students with attention deficit disorder. *Exceptional Children, 60*(2), 163–173.

Forness, S.R., & Kavale, K.A. (1988). Psychopharmacological treatment: A note on classroom effects. *Journal of Learning Disabilities, 21*(3), 144–147.

Goldstein, S., & Goldstein, M. (1989). *Managing attention disorders in children.* New York: Wiley.

Haubenstricker, J.L. (1983). Motor development in children with learning disabilities. *Journal of Physical Education, Recreation and Dance, 53*, 41–43.

Kahn, L.E. (1982). *Self-concept and physical fitness of retarded students as correlates of social interaction between retarded and nonretarded students.* Unpublished doctoral dissertation, New York University.

Kavale, K.A., & Mattson, P.D. (1983). One jumped off the balance beam: Meta-analysis of perceptual-motor training. *Journal of Learning Disabilities, 16*, 165–173.

Kelly, E.B. (1988). Learning disabilities. In *The world and I.* Washington, DC: Washington Times.

Levine, M. (1990). *Keeping ahead in school.* Cambridge, MA: Educators Publishing Service.

Moats, L.C., & Lyon, G.R. (1993). Learning disabilities in the United States: Advocacy, science, and the future of the field. *Journal of Learning Disabilities, 26*(5), 282–294.

Office of Special Education Programs. (1992). *Fourteenth Annual Report to Congress on the Implementation of the Individuals with Disabilities Education Act.* Washington, DC: U.S. Department of Education, Office of Special Education and Rehabilitative Services.

Riccio, C.A., Hynd, G.W., Cohen, M.J., and Gonzalez, J.J. (1993). Neurological basis of attention deficit hyperactivity disorder. *Exceptional Children, 60*(2), 118–124.

Rief, S. (1993). *How to reach and teach ADD/ADHD children: Practical techniques, strategies, and interventions for helping children with attention problems and hyperactivity.* West Nyack, NY: Center for Applied Research in Education.

Rubinstein, R.A., & Brown, R.T. (1981). An evaluation of the validity of the diagnostic category of ADD. *American Journal of Orthopsychiatry, 54*, 398–414.

Sherrill, C., & Pyfer, J.L. (1985). Learning disabled students in physical education. *Adapted Physical Activity Quarterly, 2*, 283–291.

Smith, C.R. (1983). *Learning disabilities.* Boston: Little, Brown.

Sutaria, S.D. (1985). *Specific learning disabilities: Nature and needs.* Springfield, IL: Charles C Thomas.

Torgesen, J.K. (1980). Conceptual and educational implications of the use of efficient task strategies by learning disabled children. *Journal of Learning Disabilities, 13*, 364–371.

Weiner, I.B. (1982). *Child and adolescent psychopathology.* New York: Wiley.

Zentall, S.S. (1993). Research on the educational implications of attention deficit hyperactivity disorder. *Exceptional Children, 60*(2), 143–153.

RESOURCES

Written

Arrighi, M. (1985). Equal opportunity through instructional design. *Journal of Physical Education, Recreation and Dance, 56*(6), 58–64. Several ideas for individualizing instruction are presented that can be used in classes with a wide range of skills.

Decker, J., & Voege, D. (1992). Integrating children with attention deficit disorder with hyperactivity into youth sport. *Palaestra, 8*(4), 16–20. Contains the "Youth Sport Participation Profile" of potential use to coaches, parents and physical educators who seek to include children with ADHD in youth sports.

Lockavitch, J. (1983). The teaching connection: What to do with the kid who doesn't know his left from his right? Teach him! *Academic Therapy, 18*(3), 339–344. This article contains many practical suggestions for teaching the concepts of laterality and directionality.

McKinney, J.D., Hocutt, A., & Montague, M. (Eds.). (1993). Issues in the education of children with ADD. Special issue, *Exceptional Children, 60*(2).

Putnam, J.W. (1993). *Cooperative learning and strategies for inclusion: Celebrating diversity in the classroom.* Baltimore: Brookes. This book, along with Section 14 in Rief (1993), provide specific suggestions for teaching using cooperative learning. Both books address other academic subjects, so the reader needs to make the application to teaching physical education.

Rief, S. (1993). *How to reach and teach ADD/ADHD children: Practical techniques, strategies, and interventions for helping children with attention problems and hyperactivity.* West Nyack, NY: Center for Applied Research in Education. A practical resource for classroom teachers, but many of the ideas can be applied to teaching physical education.

Rockwell, S. (1993). *Tough to reach, tough to teach: Students with behavior problems.* Reston, VA: Council for Exceptional Children. This book is intended to serve as a resource of intervention strategies for regular education teachers, administrators, and support personnel. Practical suggestions and sample worksheets and charts are included. The book does not specifically address physical education as an instructional area, but presents intervention strategies that can be adapted for use by physical educators.

Shields, J.M., & Heron, T.E. (1989). Teaching organizational skills to students with learning disabilities. *Teaching Exceptional Children*, **21**(2), 8–13.

Smith, S.L. (1989). The masks that students wear. *Instructor* **98**(8), 27–28, 31–32.

Audiovisual

Barkley, R.A. (1992). *ADHD: What do we know?* (Film). Boston, MA: Fanlight Production, 47 Halifax Street, Boston, MA 02130; phone (800) 937-4113; FAX (617) 524-8838. This film outlines the history, etiology, and prevalence of ADHD and demonstrates the difficulties and heartbreak it has caused for three young people and their parents and teachers. Includes teacher's guide and program manuals.

Barkley, R.A. (1992). *ADHD: What can we do?* (Film). Boston, MA: Fanlight Production, 47 Halifax Street, Boston, MA 02130; phone (800) 937-4113; FAX (617) 524-8838. This film focuses on effective ways to manage ADHD at home and in the classroom. Parent interviews and demonstrations by teachers bring the problems and solutions to life. Includes teacher's guide and program manuals.

National Organizations

Children with Attention Deficit Disorders (CHADD)
499 NW 70th Avenue, Suite 308
Plantation, FL 33317
(305) 587-3700

Division on Learning Disabilities
Council for Exceptional Children (CEC)
1920 Association Drive
Reston, VA 22091-1589
(703) 620-3660

Learning Disabilities Association of America (LDAA)
4156 Library Road
Pittsburgh, PA 15234
(412) 341-1515

National Attention Deficit Disorder Association (NADDA)
P.O. Box 488
West Newbury, MA 01985
(800) 487-2282

CHAPTER 9

Behavioral Conditions

E. Michael Loovis

Mike, John, and Dan are standing together shooting basketballs. It is 9:10 a.m. Mr. Rogers, the physical educator, turns toward the students and says, "It's time for our lesson. Put your basketballs, away."

Mike says, "Not me."
John says, "Not me."
Dan says, "Not me."

Mr. Rogers moves toward Mike. Mike feints a throw at Mr. Rogers. Mr. Rogers jerks back. He then rushes forward and snatches the basketball from Mike. Mr. Rogers puts the basketball in the ball cart. Mike screams for the ball. "I want to play with it." He moves toward Mr. Rogers and tries to snatch the ball from the cart. Mr. Rogers pushes him away. Mike kicks Mr. Rogers on the leg twice and demands the return of his basketball. He kicks Mr. Rogers a third time. He pushes the metal ball cart at Mr. Rogers, who jumps out of the way. Mike picks up a small metal chair and throws it violently. Mr. Rogers cannot move in time, and the chair strikes his foot. He pushes Mike down on the floor. Mike starts up, pulling over the ball cart. Then he stops a moment. Mr. Rogers is picking up the ball cart. Mike looks at Mr. Rogers. Mr. Rogers moves toward him. Mike runs away. John decides he wants his basketball. Mr. Rogers shouts, "No!" John joins Mike in trying to pull over the ball cart and grabs basketballs from the cart. Mr. Rogers pushes John away roughly. John is screaming that he wants to play with the basketballs. He then pulls the cart over and lets it crash to the floor. Mike announces he is going to the bathroom. Mr. Rogers asks Dan to close the gymnasium door. Dan reaches the door at the same time Mike does. Mike hits him in the face, causing

his nose to bleed. Mr. Rogers then takes Dan to the lavatory. The time is now 9:14 a.m.

Mr. Rogers has had one of what may turn out to be many experiences with children with behavioral disabilities. The key to teaching these children effectively is first understanding the types of behavioral conditions that exist and then having a grasp of certain instructional considerations. This chapter encompasses two categories of behavioral conditions: autism and behavior disabilities (serious emotional disturbance). Even though these conditions represent separate categories in IDEA, the behavioral concerns that they produce relative to teaching and learning warrant their inclusion under the common label of behavioral conditions.

BEHAVIOR DISABILITIES

The fourth largest group of children and youth receiving special education are those with behavior disabilities (Council for Exceptional Children, 1994). In the past these students have been referred to as emotionally disturbed, socially maladjusted, behavior disordered, conduct disordered, and emotionally handicapped. Certain characteristics invariably associated with these students make them stand out. Not all of them exhibit the same characteristics; in fact, quite the opposite is true. Generally speaking, they can demonstrate behavior that is labeled hyperactive, distractive, and/or impulsive. Some of these students may exhibit aggression beyond what is considered normal or socially acceptable. Some may lie, set fires, steal, or abuse alcohol and/or drugs. Some may behave in a manner that is considered withdrawn; they may act immature or behave in ways that tend to highlight feelings of inadequacy. Another segment of this population may demonstrate behavior directed in a very negative way against society; these individuals are known as juvenile delinquents. Increasingly, others fit the category referred to as "at risk." These individuals are mired in an incompatibility between themselves and school resulting in low academic achievement and high dropout rates (Davis & McCaul, 1990).

According to IDEA, serious emotional disturbance is defined as follows:

(i) The term means a condition exhibiting one or more of the following characteristics over a long period of time and to a marked degree that adversely affects a child's educational performance:

(A) An inability to learn that cannot be explained by intellectual, sensory, or health factors;

(B) An inability to build or maintain satisfactory interpersonal relationships with peers and teachers;

(C) Inappropriate types of behavior or feelings under normal circumstances;

(D) A general pervasive mood of unhappiness or depression; or

(E) A tendency to develop physical symptoms or fears associated with personal or school problems. (*Federal Register,* September, 1992, p. 44802).

The terms *serious emotional disturbance* and *behavioral disability* (BD) are used synonymously in this chapter. Identification of individuals with serious emotional disturbance is perhaps the most perplexing problem facing school and mental health professionals. In addition, consideration is given to the ever expanding number of children and youth who are at risk. "In fact, the number of categories for 'at-risk' seems to increase as dramatically as the percentage of children that appear to need special consideration and attention: (Davis & McCaul, 1990, p. 1). Therefore, it is beneficial to understand the three qualifiers that appear in the first paragraph of the federal definition, namely, duration, degree, and adverse effects on educational performance.

- **Long period of time**

  This qualifier includes behavioral patterns that are chronic in nature, for example, a persistent pattern of physical and/or verbal attacks on a classmate. It excludes behaviors that conceivably could be construed as serious emotional disturbance but that are situational in nature and thus understandable or expected. For example, a death in the family, a divorce, or another crisis situation could alter a student's behavior in a way that makes it appear aberrant.

- **Marked degree**

  Under consideration here are the magnitude and duration of a behavior. Intensity of behavioral displays, such as intensity of an altercation with a classmate, is considered. For example, a violent physical and verbal attack on a fellow student that requires extensive crisis intervention from teachers and counselors in contrast to a "pushing and shoving" match would qualify under this criterion. Also noted is the amount of time a student engages in a particular behavior—for example, if these attacks occur frequently.

- **Adversely affects educational performance**

  There must be a demonstrable cause-and-effect relationship between a student's behavior and decreased academic performance. This requires, at the very least, determining if students are performing at or near the level they would be expected to attain without behavioral disability.

Behavioral Disabilities in Public School Settings

When endeavoring to understand students with mild and moderate BD, which is the group most likely to be found in an integrated classroom setting, a behavioral classification appears most serviceable. Perhaps the best work in dimensional classification has been done by Quay (1986). Studies have shown that several dimensions (i.e., conduct disorder, anxiety-withdrawal, immaturity, and socialized aggression) are consistently found in special education classes for students who are emotionally disturbed. In 1987, Quay and Peterson, using the Revised Behavior Problem Checklist, expanded the dimensions that had been identified previously. The six new dimensions (some of which are essentially the same as those listed above) include the following:

1. *Conduct disorder* involves attention-seeking behavior, temper tantrums, fighting, disruptiveness, and a tendency to annoy others.

2. *Socialized aggression* typically involves cooperative stealing, truancy, loyalty to delinquent friends, associating with "bad" companions, and freely admitting disrespect for moral values and laws.

3. *Attention problems-immaturity* characteristically involves short attention span, sluggishness, poor concentration, distractibility, lethargy, and a tendency to answer without thinking.

4. *Anxiety-withdrawal* stands in considerable contrast to conduct disorders, involving, as it does, self-consciousness, hypersensitivity, general fearfulness, anxiety, depression, and perpetual sadness.

5. *Psychotic behavior* insinuates saying things over and over and expressing strange, far-fetched ideas.

6. *Motor excess* suggests restlessness and an inability to relax. (pp. 20–22)

In similar fashion, Dunn, Morehouse, and Fredericks (1986) have identified four areas of inappropriate behavior—behaviors that are self-indulgent, noncompliant, aggressive, and self-stimulatory or self-destructive—that may require intervention.

Causes of Behavioral Disabilities

Several factors conceivably having a causal relationship to BD have been identified: biological, family, school, and cultural factors. In addition, society is slowly becoming aware of children and students who are at risk. Although space does not permit a detailed discussion of the forces or factors that place students at risk, it is sufficient to recognize that broad societal factors have been shown to correlate with poor educational performance. These include poverty, minority racial/ethnic group identity, non-English or limited-English language background, and specific family configuration (e.g., living in a single-parent household, limited education of mother) (Davis & McCaul, 1990).

Biological Factors

According to Kauffman (1989), several biological aberrations may contribute to the etiology of BD. These include genetic anomalies, difficult temperament, brain damage or dysfunction, nutritional deficiencies, physical illness or disability, and psychophysiological disorders. With these factors identified, it is important to reiterate Kauffman's assertion that "attractive as biological explanations may appear on the surface, however, the assumption that disordered behavior is simply a result of biological misfortune is misleading" (p. 142).

Family Factors

Family relationships are major contributory factors in the etiology of BD. Broken homes, divorce, chaotic or hostile family relationships, absence of mother or father, and parental separation may produce situations in which youngsters are at risk to develop BD. It is also clear that there is not a one-on-one relationship between disruptive family relations and BD. Many youngsters find parental discord more injurious than separation from one or both parents. Research also points to a multiplier effect: When two or more factors are present simultaneously, there is increased probability that a behavior disorder will develop.

School Factors

It has become increasingly clear that, besides the family, school is the most significant socializing factor in the life of the child. For this reason, the school must shoulder some of the responsibility for causing BD. According to Kauffman (1989, p. 192) schools contribute to the development of behavior disorders in several ways:

1. Insensitivity to students' individuality;
2. Inappropriate expectations for students;
3. Inconsistent management of behavior;
4. Instruction in nonfunctional and irrelevant skills;
5. Destructive contingencies of reinforcement; and
6. Undesirable models of school conduct.

Cultural Factors

Frequently, there exists a discrepancy between the values and expectations that are embraced by the child, the family, and the school. Consequently, there is an increased probability that the student will violate dominant cultural norms and will be labeled as deviant (Kauffman, 1989).

Part of the problem centers on conflicting cultural values and standards that society has engendered. For example, the popular media has elevated many high-status models whose behavior is every bit as violent as the villains they are apprehending; however, students who engage in similar behaviors are told that they are incompatible with society's expectations.

Another problem area involves the multicultural perspective or rather a lack of it. Teachers find it extremely difficult to eliminate bias and discrimination when evaluating a student's behavior. Consequently, students are labeled as deviant when, in fact, it is only at school that their behavior is considered inappropriate.

Other cultural factors include the peer group, neighborhood, urbanization, ethnicity, and social class. These factors are not significant predictors of disordered behavior by themselves; however, in combination and within the context of economic deprivation and family conflict, they can have an adverse affect on behavior (Kauffman, 1989).

A significant sociocultural factor that portrays the relationship between aberrant adult behavior and a spiraling incidence of behavioral disabilities is substance abuse. Children who are prenatally exposed to drugs and alcohol are affected in two ways. First, there is an increased incidence of neurological impairment since both drugs and alcohol can cross the placenta and reach the fetus, causing chemical dependency, congenital aberrations, neurobehavioral abnormalities, and intrauterine growth retardation. Second, these children are exposed to family situations that are, at best, chaotic. Typically, these children find themselves in the social service system bouncing from one substitute care situation to another (Bauer, 1991). The long-range effects of fetal alcohol exposure were reported by Van Dyke and Fox (1990). Their conclusions confirmed that a significant number of children who were diagnosed with fetal alcohol syndrome in the 1970s were having learning difficulties, behavioral problems, and attention deficits a decade later.

Cocaine is the number one drug used by women of child-bearing age in the United States (Schutter & Brinker, 1992). Much of the research has focused on prenatal and perinatal complications of cocaine use. The long-term effects of cocaine used during pregnancy are equivocal; apparently, most prenatally exposed children do not develop serious developmental disabilities (Hawley & Disney, 1992). Nevertheless, Cratty (1990) suggests that research is required that clearly identifies the nature of aberrant motor behavior in drug-stressed infants, especially as it relates to the appearance and disappearance of abnormal movements. Generally, more research is needed, especially research

that assesses the postnatal milieu in which these children are reared.

Approaches

The conceptual models that serve as the basis for understanding and treating or educating students with behavioral disabilities are discussed more comprehensively in chapter 6. The following paragraphs highlight the psychodynamic, psychoeducational, ecological, psychoneurological, and behavioral approaches to teaching students with BD.

Psychodynamic

The psychodynamic approach focuses on the improvement of psychological functioning. This improvement depends on helping individuals cope with deep-seated emotional problems that can result in impaired personal relationships, conflicting social values, poor self-concept, ability deficits, and antisocial habits and attitudes. Failure to alleviate the cause(s) of psychological dysfunction can lead to learning and behavioral difficulties. The psychodynamic approach uses a number of treatment modalities including psychoanalysis, counseling, play therapy, and group therapy. Because of its strong, primarily Freudian psychological orientation, this approach is less likely to be used by teachers, and consequently its potential benefits in the educational setting are at best speculative.

Psychoeducational

The psychoeducational approach assumes that making students aware of their feelings and having them talk about the nature of their responses will give them insight into their behavior and help them develop control. Academic failure and misbehavior are dealt with directly and therapeutically. Students are taught to

- acknowledge that they have a problem,
- understand why they are misbehaving,
- observe the consequences of their behavior, and
- plan an alternate response or way of behaving that is more appropriate.

Additionally, students are taught management procedures such as self-monitoring, self-assessment, self-instruction, and self-reinforcement as a means of promoting functional independence (Nelson, Smith, Young, & Dodd, 1991). Teachers are taught to anticipate a crisis and deal with it in an unemotional manner. In crisis intervention, they use the major tool of the psychoeducational approach: the life-space interview, which utilizes talking and experiencing to help students recognize and appreciate their feelings.

Ecological

Ameliorating disturbance in a student's environment or ecosystem is the focus of the ecological model. Intervening to stop unwanted behavior is only a secondary function of this model. Changing the environment in substantive ways to reduce the likelihood of the behavior recurring once intervention is withdrawn is the primary focus. To facilitate this objective, environments (i.e., the school, home, and community) are modified to accommodate students rather than expecting that students will always make the adjustment to the environment. Classrooms are converted into environments where the likelihood of success is greatly enhanced. It means using more nontraditional methods such as cooperative learning as a mechanism for psychological adaptation to the classroom. Teachers in the ecological model are also counselors. Beyond teaching academic subjects they also function as a supportive network when returning students to regular classrooms.

Psychoneurological

The use of the psychoneurological approach assumes the presence of neurological dysfunction, and the goal is to reduce those general behavioral characteristics such as hyperactivity, distractibility, impulsiveness, and emotional lability that make the management of behavior difficult at best. The prescribed treatment for such dysfunction within the psychoneurological model is drug therapy. The main category of medication used to manage behavior of school-aged children is the psychotropic drugs. Chapter 6 discusses drug therapy in depth; it is sufficient here to note that the primary advantage of drug therapy is its ability to make other interventions more effective.

Behavioral

The behavioral approach is an elaboration of learning principles such as those embodied in respondent conditioning, social learning theory, and operant conditioning. The term most commonly used to describe this approach is *behavior modification*. An extensive discussion of behavior modification and its principles, primarily reinforcement, is presented in chapter 6. The salient features of the behavioral approach are careful assessment of observable behavior; analysis of the effect of environmental stimuli, both those that precede a response (antecedents) and those that follow it (consequences); and systematic arrangement of the consequences in order to change a behavior, or at least its frequency. Within the behavioral model, the area having implications for students with behavioral disabilities is cognitive-behavior modification (Breen & Altepeter, 1990). With its emphasis on self-control techniques, it is a natural concomitant in programs that are attempting to move beyond the traditional Skinnerian concept of behavior management (e.g., in the psychoeducational approach described earlier).

The Student With a Behavioral Disability Integrated

At the very core of effective instruction with BD students is an examination of the ways people communicate. To communicate effectively individuals must be able to give and receive information clearly and use the information to achieve a desired result. Giving and receiving information clearly is a goal of effective interpersonal communication that results from active listening.

Active Listening

Three basic skills are essential to the technique of active listening. The first is attending, a physical act that requires the listener to face the person speaking, maintain eye contact, and lean forward, if seated. These actions communicate to the speaker that the listener is, in fact, interested in what is being said. Listening, the second component skill, means more than just hearing what is being said. It involves the process of "decoding," an attempt by the listener to interpret what has been said. Consider the following example:

Sender code:
   "Why must we do these exercises?"

Possible receiver decoding:
   a. "He doesn't know how to perform them and is embarrassed to admit it."
   b. "He's bored with the lesson and is anxious to get to the next class."
   c. "He's unclear about why the exercises are necessary and is seeking some clarification."

Suppose that the most accurate decoding was A or C, but the listener decoded the message as B.

A misunderstanding would result, and the communication process would start to break down. Situations like the one just portrayed occur frequently, with neither the speaker nor the listener aware that a misunderstanding exists. The question then becomes "What can be done to assure that the correct message is being communicated?" The answer is contained in the third and final step of the active listening process.

The third component of active listening is **responding**. The listener sends back the results of his or her decoding in an attempt to ascertain if there are any misunderstandings. In effect, the listener merely restates the interpretation of the sender's message.

The communication process called active listening can help prevent misunderstandings, facilitate problem solving, and demonstrate warmth and understanding. As with any new skill, it requires practice for maximum effectiveness.

Verbal Mediation

A second communication technique is **verbal mediation,** which involves having individuals verbalize the association between their behavior and the consequences of that behavior. Of particular importance in verbal mediation is having students taken an active role in the process rather than passively hearing teachers make the association for them. The following situation illustrates verbal mediation: A student has just earned 10 minutes of free time by successfully completing the assigned drill at a circuit training station.

Teacher:
"What did you do to earn free time?"

Student:
"I followed directions and completed my work."

Teacher:
"Do you like free time?"

Student:
"Yes, it's fun."

Teacher:
"So when you do your work, then you can have fun."

Student:
"Right."

Teacher:
"Good for you! Keep up the good work."

In this example, the teacher has facilitated the student's verbal mediation of the positive association between the appropriate behavior and the positive consequence.

Conflict Resolution

Teaching students with BD entails a greater than average risk of confrontation as a way of resolving conflict. This does not imply that interpersonal confrontation need be punitive or destructive. On the contrary, a healthy use of confrontation provides the opportunity to examine a set of behaviors in relation to expectations and perceptions of others as well as to establish rules.

The goal of confrontation is resolution of conflicts through constructive behavior change. Several steps are necessary in reaching this desired goal through confrontation:

- making an assertive, confrontive statement (one that expresses honestly and directly how the speaker feels about another's behavior),

- being aware of common reactions to confrontation, and

- knowing how to deal effectively with these reactions.

Although assertive confrontation can be an effective means of resolving conflicts, it requires skillful use of each step in the process. Without question the most crucial component of the conflict resolution process is the formulation of an effective confrontive statement. There are three main components, namely, a nonjudgmental description of the behavior causing the problem, a concrete effect that the behavior is having on the person sending the message, and an expression of the feelings produced from the concrete effect of the behavior. Together these components form what is referred to as an **I-message**. When combined with active listening, which further reduces defensiveness, the conflict resolution process can be an excellent means to avoid major conflicts, as exemplified in the following conversation:

Teacher:
"Robert, your disruptive behavior during class is causing me a problem. When you argue and fight with the other students in class, I have to stop teaching. It's distracting to me and I'm frustrated." (I-message)

Student:
"I get that stuff at home. I don't need it here."

Teacher:
"I see. Lately, you're having some problems at home with your parents." (active listening)

Student:

"My dad and I have been fighting all week."

Teacher:

"You're really upset about the problem you're having with your father." (active listening)

Student:

"Yeah! I don't know how much longer I can put up with his bulls—t."

Teacher:

"So you're angry because of the situation at home and it's carrying over into school." (active listening)

Student:

"Yeah! I know you're upset about me fighting and not getting along in class. You know I've tried to get along."

Teacher:

"You're a little surprised that it's such a problem for me even though the incidents are not always all that extreme." (active listening)

Student:

"Well, not really. I see what you're saying. You have to stop teaching and stuff. Mostly I'm taking my anger out on the guys in class. I'll just have to remind myself that it's not their fault that my old man and me are not getting along, and I'll just try harder not to get angry and fight with the guys, okay?"

Teacher:

"That would sure help me. Thanks, Robert."

Student:

"No sweat!"

In this example, the teacher has blended effectively the use of an I-message and the skill of active listening to diffuse a situation that could have erupted into a major confrontation between teacher and student.

Physical Education and Sport Activities

According to Steinberg and Knitzer (1992), effective physical education programs for students with emotional and behavioral disturbance are the exception rather than the rule. They suggest that this is especially perplexing in light of increased academic performance and decreased student absenteeism when students are involved in vigorous and systematic exercise program. Poor motor performance in BD students is often attributed to various indirect factors, such as attention deficits, poor work habits, impulsivity, hyperactivity, feelings

of inadequacy, and demonstration of aggressive behavior—rather than some innate inability to move well.

Exercise programs have been shown to exert a positive influence on disruptive behavior. As little as 10 or 15 minutes of jogging daily has produced a significant reduction in the disruptive behavior of children (Yell, 1988). Similar results with 11-year-old autistic children were confirmed in the study by Levinson and Reid (1993).

Depending on students' developmental abilities and behavioral characteristics, they should be placed in the class that can best meet their needs. Regardless of placement, the type of programming chosen and the degree of peer interaction are two variables of considerable import. The first area of concern is the program itself. Because some students with behavioral disabilities may demonstrate a lag in physical and motor abilities, the physical educator must provide them with appropriate developmental activities. The emphasis should be on physical conditioning, balance, and basic movement. The development of fundamental locomotor and nonlocomotor movements will also require attention. In addition, it may be necessary to emphasize perceptual-motor activities because students with behavioral disabilities often demonstrate inadequacies in this area.

Many physical education programs use games to accomplish goals and objectives established for individuals and classes. Because students with behavioral disabilities often lack fundamental skills, they frequently are incapable of demonstrating even minimal levels of competence in these games. As a result, they have an increased tendency to act out—perhaps with verbal and/or physical aggression—or to withdraw, which further excludes them from an opportunity to develop skills. In an effort to promote the most positive learning environment, Hellison (1993) and Hellison and Georgiadis (1992) have outlined a nontraditional approach to working with inner city, at-risk youngsters using basketball as the primary vehicle for empowering students to learn personal and social values. Employing Hellison's Responsibility Model (discussed in chapter 6) as the philosophical underpinning, the "coaching club" is a before-school program in Chicago's inner city. It offers students the opportunity to explore movement through a progression of five levels: self-control (control of one's body and temper), teamwork (full participation by all team members), self-coaching, coaching other team members, and applying skills learned in the program outside the gym to school, home, and neighborhood. Playing ability is not a prerequisite. This program exists to promote social responsibility. Likewise, extrinsic rewards were unnecessary, since students are motivated to reach Level IV (Coach) on the program's evaluation system (Hellison & Georgiadis, 1992, p. 7). Level IV consists of the following characteristics:

- Good attendance
- Is coachable and on task at practice
- Does not abuse others or interrupt practice
- Is able to set personal goals and work independently on these goals
- Possesses good helping skills: Can give cues, observe and give specific positive feedback as well as general praise
- Encourages teamwork and passing the ball
- Listens to his/her players; is sensitive to their feelings and needs
- Puts the welfare of his/her players above his/her own needs (such as the need to win or "look good")
- Understands that a coach's basketball ability is not the key to being a good coach, but the above characteristics are

Relaxation is another program component that deserves a special place in the normal movement routine of many students with BD. Making the transition from gymnasium to classroom can be difficult for students with hyperactive behavior. This difficulty is not a reason to eliminate vigorous activity from these students' programs; rather, it is a reason to provide additional time, a buffer, during which the students can use relaxation techniques they have been taught.

The ability *to play* effectively is crucial to success in physical education. Because games are a part of the physical education program for most students with BD, it is essential for teachers to be aware of the direct relationship between the type of activity chosen and the degree to which inappropriate behavior is likely to occur. The type of programming chosen directly relates to the amount of aggression demonstrated by students during activity. Some of the specific variables that seem to control aggression are reduced body contact, simpler rules, and fewer skill requirements. Not to be overlooked is

the New Games approach, which has a cooperative rather than a competitive orientation. In light of the problems surrounding self-concept and the antisocial behavior exhibited by some students with BD, the least desirable situation is one that prescribes winners and losers or that rewards overly aggressive behavior.

Instructional Considerations

There is not one consistently correct way of instructing children with behavior disabilities. Effective instructors will tailor their instruction techniques to the children they are teaching according to the students' types of BD.

Mild Behavior Disabilities

In physical education, students with behavior disabilities who function at higher levels can be taught with a humanistic approach. Generally speaking, some techniques suggested by Sherrill (1993, p. 146) for improving self-concept are singularly applicable with this population; for example, teachers should strive to

- Conceptualize individual and small group counseling as an integral part of physical education instruction,
- Teach students to care about each other and to show that they care,
- Emphasize cooperation and social interaction rather than individual performance,
- Stress the importance of genuineness and honesty in praise,
- Increase perceived competence in relation to motor skill and fitness, and
- Convey that they like and respect students as human beings, for themselves as whole persons, not just for their motor skills and fitness.

More specifically, the approach outlined by Hellison (1985) and further elaborated by Hellison and Templin (1991) has immediate relevance for practitioners confronted with students who lack self-control and consequently present management problems. Hellison's four primary goals or developmental levels—self-control and respect for the rights and feelings of others, participation and effort, self-direction, and caring and helping—are instrumental in overcoming many current discipline and motivation problems in schools. (Hellison's levels are discussed in chapter 6.) Hellison has likewise identified six basic strategies that foster attainment of the development levels: awareness, experience, choice, problem solving/student sharing, self-reflection, and counseling time. These strategies are "processes for helping students to become aware of, experience, make decisions about, and reflect on the model's goals" (Hellison & Templin, 1991, p. 108).

Because self-control is basic to Hellison's approach, *awareness* of the program's purpose is very important. Examples of this strategy include

- reminding students about the levels;

- illustrating attitudes and behaviors associated with levels as they occur; and

- conducting student sharing sessions regarding the importance of levels.

Experience is the second strategy that can be employed at each level of the model. For example, at level I students can be encouraged to play a cooperative game. At level IV students who know how to engage in a certain activity can help those who do not.

Choice is built into the model and confronts students at each level. At level I, abusive students can exercise choice by sitting out of an activity or modifying their unacceptable behavior. Level III choice could involve students analyzing the disparity between their program goals and the selection of activities they choose. For example, a student who wants to increase aerobic capacity but who chooses to participate in a game of table tennis with friends needs to be confronted with deciding what is more important.

Problem solving is the fourth strategy that is used at each level. Student sharing invites discussion of what constitutes self-control, and it encourages students to think about the consequences of violating the established self-control rules. It also provides students with the opportunity to evaluate aspects of the program.

Another strategy is *self-reflection*. At the conclusion of every class, students are given time to reflect on what occurred during the session, specifically as it related to their plans and the degree to which they were successful in accomplishing their goals. A variety of techniques are used for this purpose, including journals, checklists, and student discussions.

Counseling time is the final strategy. Time is allotted for discussions about specific problems, things that the teacher has observed, and/or general impressions of the program. Counseling is a part of each level; for example, at level I it could involve a discussion of a student's pattern of aggressive behavior. At level II it might involve a discussion of the degree of effort students are expending in relationship to the goals they have established for themselves.

Severe Behavior Disabilities

Students with severe behavior disabilities require more intense programming efforts. This group, which has been characterized by Dunn et al. (1986), includes students who are self-indulgent, aggressive, noncompliant, and self-stimulatory or self-destructive. Using the basic steps of behavioral programming discussed in chapter 6, Dunn and associates developed the Data Based Gymnasium. This program incorporates behavioral principles in a systematic effort to produce consistent behavior on the part of adults who work with students with BD and eventually to bring students' behavior under the control of naturally occurring reinforcers. To this latter end, instructors use natural reinforcers available in the environment—for example, praising a desirable behavior to strengthen it or ignoring an undesirable one to bring about its extinction. Tangible reinforcers such as token economies are introduced only after it has been demonstrated that the consistent use of social reinforcement or extinction will not achieve the desired behavioral outcome.

In an effort to equip teachers with a consistent treatment procedure, Dunn and associates have prescribed a set of consequences or rules of thumb that are applied to inappropriate behaviors. For each area of inappropriate behavior (e.g., self-indulgent behavior), there exists a specific rule of thumb. The intent of these rules is to make development and implementation of a formal behavioral program unnecessary.

Self-Indulgent Behavior

Behaviors in this category include crying, screaming, tantruming, and repetitive, irritating activities and noises. The rule of thumb for handling students who engage in self-indulgent behaviors is to ignore them until the behavior is discontinued and then socially reinforce the first occurrence of an appropriate behavior.

Noncompliant Behavior

Noncompliant behaviors include instances when students say no when asked to do something. They also include forgetting or failing to do something because students choose not to do what is asked. In addition, noncompliance includes doing what is requested but in a less than presentable way. The rule of thumb is that teachers should ignore noncompliant verbalizations, lead students physically through the task, or prevent students from participating in an activity until they follow through on the initial request. Compliance with any requests is immediately reinforced socially.

Aggressive Behavior

Verbal or physical abuse directed toward an object or a person is considered aggressive behavior. More specifically, hitting, fighting, pinching, biting, pushing, and deliberately destroying someone's property are examples of aggressive acts. The rule of thumb for aggressive behavior is that it is punished immediately with a verbal reprimand and the offending student is removed from the activity. Social reinforcement is given when students demonstrate appropriate interaction with other persons or objects.

Self-Stimulatory Behavior

This category includes behaviors that interfere with learning because students become engrossed in the persevering nature of the activities. Examples include head banging, hand flapping, body rocking, and eye gouging. As a rule of thumb, Dunn and associates recommend a formal behavioral program to deal with this type of behavior. An in-depth discussion of formal behavior modification principles and programs is presented in chapter 6.

AUTISM

IDEA prescribed autism as a separate category of disability and defined it as

a developmental disability significantly affecting verbal and nonverbal communication and social interaction, generally evident before age 3, that adversely affects a child's educational performance. Other characteristics often associated with autism are engagement in repetitive activities and stereotyped movements, resistance to environmental change or change in daily routines, and unusual responses to sensory experiences. The term does not apply if a child's educational performance is adversely affected primarily

because the child has a serious emotional disturbance. (*Federal Register*, September 29, 1992, p. 44801)

Generally recognized characteristics of autism span a wide range from

- being mute to verbal,
- exhibiting no affective response and resisting physical contact to physically clinging,
- failing to respond to perceptual stimuli to overreacting or being overwhelmed by physical stimuli,
- perseverating responses to fleeting from object to object,
- passivating to stereotyping, and
- having severe developmental deficits to possessing detailed knowledge in some specialized field, commonly referred to as *savant* (Silver & Hagin, 1990).

Autism has been included in this chapter because it is primarily the individual's aberrant behavior that causes teachers the most concern within the instructional setting.

According to the third edition of the *Diagnostic and Statistical Manual of Mental Disorders*, commonly referred to as DSM-III-R (American Psychiatric Association, 1987), autism, which is the most severe form of the category "pervasive developmental disorders," usually appears before the age of 30 months. The major developmental and behavioral characteristics associated with autism included the following (Sposato, 1993, p. 3):

1. Disturbances in the rate of appearance of physical, social, and language skills.

2. Abnormal responses to sensations. Any one or a combination of senses or responses are affected: sight, hearing, touch, balance, smell, taste, reaction to pain, and the way a child holds his or her body.

3. Speech and language are absent or delayed, while specific thinking capabilities may be present.

4. Abnormal ways of relating to people, objects, and events.

Students with autism generally demonstrate poor motor skills (Morin & Reid, 1985). Consequently, programs should emphasize fundamental motor skills and patterns, individual games and sports, and developmental activities that increase physical proficiency. In the physical education and sport setting, teachers and coaches who are going to work with students with autism should solicit as much information as they can about the student from teachers, counselors, psychologists, and parents before starting the program. To establish the most effective instructional situation, teachers and coaches should be provided with the most up-to-date information possible relative to changes in the student's schedule, medication, or behavior management program (Mangus & Henderson, 1988). Additionally, teachers and coaches should understand that students with autism require a structured teaching environment; therefore, activities such as entrance into the gymnasium, method of starting the class, and the conduct of the class itself should be consistent and predictable.

In terms of actually teaching a student with autism, a characteristic of major concern is stimulus overselectivity. As defined above, it means attending to narrowly defined aspects of relevant or irrelevant cues. This has implications for how teachers or coaches will provide sensory stimuli, how they will prompt an action, how they will fade a prompt once it is no longer necessary or appropriate, and how they will promote skill generalization.

Sensory Stimuli

A first step in dealing with stimulus overselectivity is to minimize or significantly reduce the amount of stimuli in the learning environment. Equipment that is not going to be used during the lesson should be removed from the surrounding environment. Even objects that conceivably are a normal part of a student's surroundings can have a deleterious effect on the lesson (e.g., a student's preoccupation with a digital wrist watch). What teachers say or do (sensory inputs) must be monitored. The use of simultaneous inputs, for example, giving a demonstration and also providing verbal directions or descriptions of the action, can produce stimulus overload and thereby reduce the effectiveness of instruction. As with all learners but especially with students with autism, it is important to ascertain their primary sensory modality and tailor the presentation to that modality. If a student learns best visually, then the teacher or coach should capitalize on that knowledge and provide instruction using that primary modality.

Prompting

Prompts are cues, instructions, demonstrations, or other events that signal the initiation of a response.

Two categories of prompting will be discussed. First, extrastimulus prompts exist as an explicit instructional/response hierarchy. For an example of response prompting, see chapter 6. The second category, within-stimulus prompting, involves tailoring specific stimuli related to the task itself, such as targets which have a high stimulus appeal. Extrastimulus prompting has been shown to be more effective than within-stimulus prompting for students with autism (Collier & Reid, 1987). Within the extrastimulus category, physical prompting has been shown to be slightly more effective than visual prompting (Reid, Collier, & Cauchon, 1991). When using physical prompting, teachers and coaches should use light touches and apply them in several locations (Connor, 1990). One also needs to be aware that some students with autism react negatively to being touched; consequently, physical prompting would be contraindicated with these students. When manipulating the within-stimulus properties of the task, the major problem is changing two or more stimuli at the same time. For example, if a striking task were planned, one would not introduce an oversized bat while at the same time using a batting tee for the first time. A final consideration is the use of similar prompts with different skills or tasks. Students with autism may have a difficult time distinguishing between tasks to be performed or actions to be used if the same prompt is used for both tasks. For example, kicking and throwing at the same target (within-stimulus prompt) or being touched on the elbow for both a throwing and a striking task (extrastimulus prompt) could produce difficulties with skill acquisition.

Generalization

Generalization, or the ability to demonstrate a skill in an environment different from the one in which the skill was learned, is difficult for students with autism (Mangus & Henderson, 1988). Teaching for generalization involves providing instruction in the most gamelike or natural environment possible (e.g., learning to bowl at the local bowling alley versus learning to bowl in a gymnasium). It likewise implies using equipment that resembles or closely approximates that which will be used in the final game or activity (e.g., learning to use an aluminum or wooden bat versus learning to play softball with a plastic bat). Additionally, adapted equipment should be faded as soon as possible (Connor, 1990).

Practice

The manner in which practice is organized is also an important consideration for students with autism. Practice that employs task variation or what is commonly referred to as distributed practice seems most beneficial when teaching skills (Weber & Thorpe, 1992). Task variation, or practicing a variety of tasks interspersed with periods of rest, serves two important functions for students with autism: it provides an opportunity to administer a higher frequency of reinforcement and it accommodates a short attention span that is characteristic of this population of students. In terms of student-teacher ratios, the ideal is a 1:1. Mangus and Henderson (1988) recommend the use of volunteers, teacher aides from special education, parents, and students from regular education in order to achieve as closely as possible the ideal ratio.

SUMMARY

Behavioral conditions as used in this chapter correspond to the categories of behavior disabilities (serious emotional disturbance) and autism as defined in IDEA. The psychodynamic, psychoeducational, ecological, psychoneurological, and behavioral approaches were examined for their effectiveness in habilitating students with behavioral disabilities. Suggestions were provided for teaching students with identified behavioral disabilities in integrated physical education classes; effective interpersonal communication was discussed, specifically, active listening, verbal mediation, and conflict resolution. The work of Hellison and the contributions of Dunn and his colleagues were cited as effective approaches to physical education for students with behavior disabilities and students considered "at risk." Autism was examined with special consideration given to "best practice" related to skill acquisition in the physical education and sport settings.

BIBLIOGRAPHY

American Psychiatric Association. (1987). *Diagnostic and statistical manual of mental disorders* (3rd ed. rev.). Washington, DC: Author.

Bauer, A.M. (1991). Drug and alcohol exposed children: Implications for special education for students identified as behaviorally disordered. *Behavioral Disorders*, **17**, 72–79.

Breen, M.J., & Altepeter, T.S. (1990). *Disruptive behavior disorders in children: Treatment-focused assessment.* New York: Guilford Press.

Collier, D., & Reid, G. (1987). A comparison of two models designed to teach autistic children a motor task. *Adapted Physical Activity Quarterly*, **4**, 226–236.

Connor, F. (1990). Combating stimulus overselectivity: Physical education for children with autism. *Teaching Exceptional Children*, **23**, 30–33.

Council for Exceptional Children. (1994). Statistical profile of special education in the United States, 1994. *Teaching Exceptional Children*, **26**(Suppl), 1–4.

Cratty, B.J. (1990). Motor development of infants subject to maternal drug use: Current evidence and future research strategies. *Adapted Physical Activity Quarterly*, **7**, 110–125.

Davis, W.E., & McCaul, E.J. (1990). *At-risk children and youth: A crisis in our schools.* Orono: University of Maine, Institute for the Study of At-Risk Students.

Dunn, J.M., Morehouse, J.W., & Fredericks, H.D.B. (1986). *Physical education for the severely handicapped: A systematic approach to a data based gymnasium.* Austin, TX: Pro-Ed.

Federal Register. (1992, September 29). Assistance to States for the Education of Children With Disabilities Program and Preschool Grants for Children With Disabilities; Final rules. Washington, DC: Department of Education.

Hawley, T.L., & Disney, E.R. (1992). *Crack's children: The consequences of maternal cocaine abuse* (Social Policy Report, Volume 6, Number 4). Ann Arbor, MI: Society for Research in Child Development.

Hellison, D.R. (1985). *Goals and strategies for teaching physical education.* Champaign, IL: Human Kinetics.

Hellison, D.R. (1993). The coaching club: Teaching responsibility to inner-city students. *Journal of Physical Education, Recreation and Dance*, **64**, 66–70.

Hellison, D.R., & Georgiadis, N. (1992). Teaching values through basketball. *Strategies*, **5**, 5–8.

Hellison, D.R., & Templin, T.J. (1991). *A reflective approach to teaching physical education.* Champaign, IL: Human Kinetics.

Kauffman, J.M. (1989). *Characteristics of children's behavior disorders* (4th ed.). Columbus, OH: Merrill.

Levinson, L.J., & Reid, G. (1993). The effects of exercise intensity on the stereotypic behaviors of individuals with autism. *Adapted Physical Activity Quarterly*, **10**, 255–268.

Mangus, B.C., & Henderson, H. (1988). Providing physical education to autistic children. *Palaestra*, **4**, 38–43.

Morin, B., & Reid, G. (1985). A quantitative and qualitative assessment of autistic individuals on selected motor tasks. *Adapted Physical Activity Quarterly*, **2**, 43–55.

Nelson, J.R., Smith, D.J., Young, R.K., & Dodd, J.M. (1991). A review of self-management outcome research conducted with students who exhibit behavioral disorders. *Behavioral Disorders*, **16**, 169–179.

Quay, H.C. (1986). Classification. In H.C. Quay & J.S. Werry, *Psychopathological disorders of childhood* (3rd ed., pp. 1–34). New York: Wiley.

Quay, H.C., & Peterson, D.R. (1987). *Manual for the revised behavior problem checklist.* Coral Gables, FL: Authors.

Reid, G., Collier, D., & Cauchon, M. (1991). Skill acquisition by children with autism: Influence of prompts. *Adapted Physical Activity Quarterly*, **8**, 357–366.

Silver, A.A., & Hagin, R.A. (1990). *Disorders of learning in childhood*. New York: Wiley.

Sherrill, C. (1993). *Adapted physical activity, recreation and sport: Crossdisciplinary and lifespan* (4th ed.). Madison, WI: Brown & Benchmark.

Schutter, S., & Brinker, R. (1992). Conjuring a new category of disability from prenatal cocaine exposure: Are the infants unique biological or caretaking casualties? *Topics in Early Childhood Special Education*, **11**, 84–111.

Sposato, B. (Ed.). (1993, Summer). *Newsletter of the Autism Society of America*. (Available from Autism Society of America, Inc., 8601 Georgia Ave., Suite 503, Silver Spring, MD 20910)

Steinberg, Z., & Knitzer, J. (1992). Classrooms for emotionally and behaviorally disturbed students: Facing the challenge. *Behavioral Disorders*, **17**, 145–156.

Van Dyke, D.O., & Fox, A.A. (1990). Fetal drug exposure and its possible implications for learning in the preschool and school-age population. *Journal of Learning Disabilities*, **23**(3), 160–163.

Weber, R.C., & Thorpe, J. (1992). Teaching children with autism through task variation in physical education. *Exceptional Children*, **59**, 77–86.

Yell, M.L. (1988). The effects of jogging on the rates of selected target behaviors of behaviorally disordered students. *Behavioral Disorders*, **13**, 273–279.

RESOURCES

Written Materials

Dunn, J.M., Morehouse, J.W., & Fredericks, H.D.B. (1986). *Physical education for the severely handicapped: A systematic approach to a data based gymnasium*. Austin, TX: Pro-Ed. This text is a "nuts and bolts" approach to working with severely handicapped students in the physical education setting. It combines detailed information on learning theory with a variety of examples to illustrate the principles that are advocated for use in the gymnasium.

Goldstein, A.P., Sprafkin, R.P., Gershaw, N.J., & Klein, P. (1980). *Skillstreaming the adolescent: A structured learning approach to teaching prosocial skills*. Champaign, IL: Research Press. This innovative program is designed to help adolescents develop competence in dealing with interpersonal conflicts, in increasing self-esteem, and in contributing to a positive classroom atmosphere.

Audiovisual

Foxx, R.M. (Producer). (1980). *Harry* [Videocassette and Film]. Champaign, IL 61820; Research Press, Box 31775. Dr. Richard M. Foxx demonstrates classic examples of fading, extinction, and time-out as well as almost every important principle of behavior modification during one-on-one treatment sessions with Harry. At the time this documentary was filmed, Harry was a 24-year-old mildly retarded person who had a history of severe self-abuse that had defeated all attempts to educate him.

Hurwitz, R., & Loovis, E.M. (1993). *Conflict Resolution* [Interactive Videodisc]. Tampa, Fl 33620-8600: University of South Florida, I'm Special Production Network. This Level III interactive application (external computer that uses a videodisc player as a peripheral device) teaches students how to send appropriate "I" messages, use active listening, and conduct the conflict resolution process. It is applicable to undergraduate students as well as to career teachers who will teach students with behavioral disabilities.

Peters, J. (Producer). (1988). *Autism: Breaking Through* [Film]. Princeton, NJ 08543-2053: Films for the Humanities & Sciences, Box 2053. This film highlights the Daily Life Therapy program at Boston's Higaski School. The school's curriculum is based upon the work of Dr. Kiyo Kitahara, who founded the first Higaski school in Tokyo, which serves 1,800 students, 25% of whom are autistic. The program emphasizes physical exercise as a means of tension release and as a way to enhance self-concept.

CHAPTER 10

Visual Impairments and Hearing Losses

Diane H. Craft

This chapter will describe both visual impairments and hearing losses. There are few similarities in teaching students with these two different sensory losses. Individuals with visual impairments usually remain integrated within sighted society, developing compensatory strategies for the lack of sight. In contrast, deaf individuals may or may not choose to integrate within hearing society. Many deaf individuals increasingly view themselves as possessing a unique culture and not as individuals who experience a disability. This chapter seeks to present information pertinent to teaching individuals with these two distinct and dissimilar sensory losses.

VISUAL IMPAIRMENTS

The educational definition from the regulations of Individuals with Disabilities Education Act (IDEA) states: ''Visually handicapped means a visual impairment which, even when corrected, adversely affects a child's educational performance. The term includes both partially sighted and blind children'' (Section 121a.5 [b] [1]).

Not every child with a visual loss needs special education. Special services are needed only when the visual loss interferes with the child's learning. There are at least three methods of classification that describe the remaining vision of individuals with visual impairments. These classifications are presented in Table 10.1.

Incidence

There are about 500,000 people in the United States who are legally blind. Most are over the age of 65 and have vision losses as a result of diseases associated with aging. Among individuals with visual losses, most continue to have some useful sight. Perhaps one in four individuals with visual impairments is totally blind. Of the children who are legally blind, about half of these children become blind before or at birth. The incidence of visual impairments among school-age children is low—17,749 children as of 1990–1991 (Office of Special Education Programs, 1992, p. A-25)—so low, in fact, that most physical educators will only teach a few students with visual impairments in their careers.

Causes of Visual Impairments

There are multiple causes for visual impairments. While most causes can be directly related to the effects of aging, occasionally blindness occurs before or at birth (congenital) or in childhood or later (adventitious). The causes of blindness affecting young people will be emphasized here.

Visual impairments may be caused by disorders of the *retina*, the nerve tissue at the back of the eye upon which the image of the outside world is focused for transmittal to the brain along the optic nerve. Retinas can be damaged by retinitis pigmentosa (an inherited, progressive disease leading

Table 10.1 Classifications of Visual Impairments

Classification based on ability to read print

Total blindness	is the inability to read large print even with magnification. Braille is usually used for written communication.
Partial sight	is the ability to read print through the use of large-print books and/or magnification.
Visual impairment	refers to the range of vision encompassing total blindness and partial sight.

Classification based on visual loss after correction

Legal blindness (20/00)	is visual acuity of 20/200 or less in the better eye even with correction, or a field of vision so narrowed that the widest diameter of the visual field subtends an angular distance no greater than 20°.
Travel vision (5/200 to 10/200)	is the ability to see at 5 to 10 ft what the normal eye can see at 200 ft.
Motion perception (3/200 to 5/200)	is the ability to see at 3 to 5 ft what the normal eye can see at 200 ft. This ability is limited almost entirely to perception of motion.
Light perception (<3/200)	is the ability to distinguish a strong light at a distance of 3 ft from the eye but the inability to detect a hand movement at 3 ft from the eye.
Total blindness	is the inability to recognize a strong light that is shone directly into the eye.

Classification for sport competition[a]

B1	From no light perception at all in either eye up to light perception and inability to recognize objects or contours in any direction and at any distance
B2	From ability to recognize objects or contours up to a visual acuity of 2/60 and/or limited visual field of 5°
B3	2/60 to 6/60 (20/200) vision and/or field of vision between 5° and 60°

[a]Classifications used by the United States Association for Blind Athletes (1986).

to tunnel vision and night blindness), **retinal detachment** (the separation of the layers of the retina), **retinal vascular diseases** (associated with sickle-cell anemia), injury, drugs, or poisons.

Light must pass from the outside world through the *cornea, lens,* and *uveal tract* to focus on the retina. These parts of the eye must remain absolutely clear and without distortion for optimal vision. Most **cataracts** (an opaque instead of clear lens) occur with aging, but can also occur in infants of mothers who are infected with rubella during the first trimester of pregnancy. **Uveitis,** an inflammation of the uveal tract, accounts for 12% of all visual impairments.

Glaucoma occurs when the *intraocular fluid* is unable to continuously drain from the eye. The resulting increase in pressure within the eye can lead to total blindness. The eye is designed so that the images from the environment are focused clearly on the retina. If the eye is shorter than normal (farsighted or **hyperopia**) or longer than normal (nearsighted or **myopia**) or irregularly

shaped (**astigmatism**), then vision needs to be corrected through glasses, contact lenses, or surgery. **Accommodative squint** occurs when a person's two eyes are not focusing together. With **double vision** or "lazy eye," the suppression of the image from one eye occurs. **Retinopathy of prematurity** is a form of blindness that can occur among infants born before their eyes are fully formed.

It is not possible to know what a person with a particular visual impairment can see based on the cause of the impairment. Figure 10.1 provides some idea. The best way to learn about what people can see is to discuss it with them.

Impact of Visual Impairments on Information Processing

Sight provides one of the main avenues for gathering information about the environment. As such, vision plays a prominent role in the **information processing model** described in chapter 8 and depicted in Figure 8.1. To the extent that vision is

a

b

c

Figure 10.1 Three photos of what a person with a visual impairment might see: (a) In age-related maculopathy (often called macular degeneration), central vision is impaired, making it difficult to read or do close work. (b) In retinitis pigmentosa, night blindness develops, and tunnel vision is another frequent result. (c) In cataract, a clouding of the lens causes reduced ability to see detail.
From *Visual Impairment: An Overview* by I. Bailey and A. Hall, 1990, NY: American Foundation for the Blind. Courtesy A.F.B.

necessary to input (step 1), decision making (step 2), output (step 3), and feedback (step 4), information processing in individuals with visual impairments will be disrupted. It is the task of the teacher to highlight other sources of sensory input, such as auditory, tactile, and kinesthetic, to compensate for the diminished or absent visual input.

Role of Incidental Learning

Any disruption in information processing among children who are blind can limit opportunities for incidental learning. Teaching students who are blind what sighted students learn incidentally by seeing needs to begin early in life. Information on early intervention programs may be found in the resources section at the end of this chapter.

Characteristics of People With Visual Impairments

There is tremendous diversity among individuals with visual impairments, but some characteristics in this group seem to occur with greater frequency than among sighted individuals. The following are some of these characteristics. The reader is cautioned to remember that any one student may differ considerably from these generalizations. Factors such as the amount of usable vision, the age at which vision was lost, the presence of other health problems and other disabilities can greatly influence the characteristics found among individuals with visual impairments.

Cognitive Characteristics.

Vision plays a key role in learning many basic perceptions, concepts, and motor skills. Before the age of 2, children develop the basis for body awareness, postural orientation, sensory integration, and motor patterns. If an infant who is congenitally blind is not stimulated to learn through senses other than vision, there may be subsequent problems in perception and later cognitive development. Many children who are born without vision show delays in these areas, delays that are not exhibited by children who lost their sight later in life.

Affective/Social Characteristics.

Stereotypic behaviors are seemingly purposeless movements that include rocking forward and backward while seated or standing, hand waving or finger flinging in front of the face, or digging the fingers into the eyes. These behaviors are more prevalent among children who are congenitally blind than those who are adventitiously blind. Stereotypic behaviors are thought to provide stimulation to the person who does not receive visual stimulation, but they are socially unacceptable. These behaviors may reflect nervousness, so calm reminders such as quietly placing a hand on the shoulder to stop a person who is rocking may be more effective than scolding. Also, substitute acceptable behaviors that are incompatible with the stereotypic behavior, such as playing with age-appropriate toys.

Three characteristics found among some individuals with visual impairments may present obstacles to socializing with sighted peers. Often individuals without vision display passive, expressionless faces because they cannot learn to animate their faces through watching others. Similarly, some individuals with visual impairments may at times appear insensitive to the concerns of others, particularly when in conversation with individuals who have no vision loss. This also reflects the fact that without sight, individuals cannot respond to the nonverbal cues (body language, facial expressions) that are used to communicate subtle feelings. Lastly, some individuals with visual impairments may appear very talkative. This may result from feeling uncomfortable with normal pauses in conversation that are customarily filled with nonverbal gestures. Socialization can be enhanced by helping individuals with sight understand and accept these subtle differences and by teaching individuals who have visual impairments to use their faces expressively and to allow for pauses in conversation.

Some individuals with visual impairments, regardless of whether they are congenitally or adventitiously blind, exhibit social behavior that is characterized by fearfulness and dependence. These characteristics develop, probably not as a result of the lack of vision, but rather as a result of the process of socialization experienced by the individual. Concerned parents and teachers may be overprotective of children with visual impairments. This overprotection usually leads to reduced opportunities for children to freely explore their environment, thus creating possible delays in perceptual, motor, and cognitive development.

Motor/Physical Characteristics.

The lack of sight does not directly cause any unique motor or physical characteristics. But the reduced opportunity to move, which often accompanies blindness, may result in many distinct characteristics. Developmental delays among children with visual impairments may be related to motor passivity (sitting more, moving less), stereotypic behaviors (self-manipulation rather than environmental manipulation), play and environmental interactions (immature play behaviors and the infrequent use of the environment as props for social and fantasy play), and limited experience with the environment through gross motor manipulation (Schneekloth, 1989, p. 197). As early as 12 weeks after birth, the movements of infants who are congenitally blind may differ significantly from their sighted peers. The reduced opportunity for rough-and-tumble play with parents, heightened protective instincts of parents/caregivers, the infant's own fear of being moved suddenly, the lack of vision that motivates movement, and the lack of the opportunity to observe others moving—all may contribute to motor delays among children who are blind. Children *must* be provided with the opportunity to move in a safe environment to minimize the development of motor delays. Enthusiastically encourage and positively reinforce movement by physically demonstrating and verbally reassuring them that it is safe to move.

Motor delays are not usually observed among individuals who are now blind but who were sighted for several years. These individuals need corrective feedback from observers, as a substitute for monitoring their own movements, so that skills once mastered are retained.

As a group, individuals with visual impairments show postural deviations. "To travel efficiently, the individual needs proper spatial and body awareness. Walking, posture, body control, and body management are all a part of orientation and mobility" (Chin, 1988). Again, this is more pronounced among individuals who have been blind since birth and never have had the opportunity to see how others sit, stand, and move. It is also pronounced among individuals with partial sight who may hold their heads in unique positions to maximize vision. Corrective postural exercises may help improve posture and thereby reduce stress on the body. Body image and balance may also be poor among pupils with visual impairments. This may be due to decreased opportunities for regular physical activity through which balance and body image are developed and refined. Activities such as dance, yoga, and movement education can be excellent means of developing body image and balance.

The walking gait of persons who are totally blind is characterized by shorter strides, a pronounced shuffle, slower pace, more time spent in the support phase, and a tendency, over distance, to veer away from the stronger leg. The running gait of sprinters who are totally blind (Class B1) is shorter in stride, exhibits less extension and flexion at the hip, and is half the speed of sprinters who are partially sighted (Class B2 and B3). Physical educators can increase stride length by generating greater hip extension during the drive phase and greater hip flexion during the recovery phase of the sprint run (Arnhold and McGrain, 1985).

The missing component in the development of normal patterns of movement among children with visual impairments is experience, not ability. Their fitness levels are below those of their sighted peers. Interestingly, Buell (1966) suggests that individuals with visual impairments need higher levels of physical fitness than their sighted counterparts. He notes that there are many instances in which they need to spend more energy to reach the same goals as those with sight. The relative performance on fitness test items of students with visual impairments varies with the degree of mobility required by a particular test. Winnick (1985) found the best performance among students with visual impairments was in flexibility, arm strength,

and muscular endurance, and the worst performance was in throwing. Gender and age are also factors that affect fitness level. Boys are more physically fit than girls with the exception of flexibility.

As a group, the fitness levels of students with visual impairments are below those of sighted students, but there are many students whose fitness levels exceed those of their sighted peers. On test items that do not require mobility, 25% of the youths who are blind are more fit than sighted youths (Winnick, 1985). Many individuals with visual impairments appear fully capable of developing fitness levels at least as high as those of sighted students, but perhaps they are not provided the opportunities to develop these higher fitness levels. The research by di Natale, Lee, Ward, and Shepard (1985) measured the fitness levels attained by students who participated in a vigorous fitness program during the academic year at a residential school for the blind. The researchers again measured the fitness level of these same students after the students spent 10 weeks of the summer at home, where they presumably did not have the opportunity to be physically active. After vacation, the students' fitness levels were now as unfit as other students with visual impairments. These findings underscore the importance of physical educators developing fitness programs for students with visual impairments and working with families to find fitness activities students can pursue at home. Harry Cordellos, an athlete who happens to be blind, scored among the very highest of all individuals assessed for cardiovascular fitness at the Cooper Institute for Aerobic Research in Texas. The opportunity and the will to move, not the degree of vision, are the important factors determining any individual's level of performance. Buell found that overprotected children with visual impairments scored lower in tests of running, jumping, and throwing than those who were neglected and not neglected. He concluded that neglect is preferable to overprotection in terms of motor performance (Winnick, 1985).

If it is lack of experience rather than lack of ability that delays motor development for individuals with visual impairments, then it is the physical educator's responsibility to provide movement experiences and to stimulate and motivate children to move. The physical educator must also encourage children to *feel safe and good about their movements*. This can be accomplished both through instruction in physical education and through collaboration with parents/caregivers and other influential persons in the child's life.

Teaching Students With Visual Impairments in Regular Classes

Students with visual impairments can be taught in regular physical education classes, with modifications. Generally, the same developmentally appropriate, individualized curriculum used for all physical education students can be used to meet the needs and allow the inclusion of a student with a visual impairment. Developmentally inappropriate curricula, such as those that emphasize competitive sports and focus only on "playing the game," showing preference to the "motor elite," cannot be readily adapted to include students with visual impairments. When students with visual impairments repeatedly serve as human cones, score keepers, or spectators or are excused from physical education to go to the library, they are not participating in meaningful ways. Physical educators may unwittingly do disservice to students who have visual impairments when segregating them from participation in class activities. Such an instance occurred when a girl who is blind was relegated to lifting weights throughout her years in high school physical education classes. Yet she was an exceptionally skilled goal ball player and could have performed successfully in physical education class if given the opportunity to participate in a meaningful way.

"Visually impaired youngsters share the same delight in and have the same need to use movement freely and imaginatively as do their sighted peers" (Chin, 1988). These can all be developed through active participation in physical education.

The following four sections will present ideas for adapting instruction for students with visual impairments based on

A. learning about the student's abilities,

B. fostering the student's independence,

C. teaching to the student's abilities, and

D. developing support systems for teaching the student.

A. Learn About the Student's Abilities

There are two steps involved in learning about a student's abilities: assessing the student's performance level and learning the answers to critical questions concerning the student's condition, history, and aptitudes.

1. Assess to determine each student's present level of performance.

Tests suitable for use with students with visual impairments are described in Table 10.2. Tests of physical fitness, such as FITNESSGRAM, can be taken by students with visual impairments. Except with test items requiring mobility, the students with visual impairments should be encouraged to take the same test items and attain the same standards as students with sight. In case of mobility limitations due to blindness, modify mobility test item standards and use assistive devices. For example, add auditory cues so students know where to throw, how far to skip or run, etc. Refer to chapter 4 for additional information on tests in the motor domain.

Using assessment as a basis for determining the motor needs, the physical education teacher plans goals and short-term instructional objectives with each student, modifying activities as needed.

2. Seek to learn the answers to the following five critical questions.

In addition to assessing current performance, ask:

- *What can the student see?*

  Ask the student, "What can you see?" rather than "How much you can see?" Ask the same question of others familiar with the student's vision including the student's previous teachers, parent/caregiver, and low-vision specialist. Read the student's educational file for further information regarding what the student can see.

- *When (at what age) was the loss of vision experienced, and over what period of time did it progress? Is it still progressing?*

  If a student gradually lost all vision due to disease between the ages of 8 to 10, that student may require less time preparing for specific activities, such as hitting a sound-emitting softball and running to a sound-emitting base, than a student who is congenitally blind and has never had the chance to see a game of baseball. A child with congenital blindness may need more detailed explanations that do not depend on analogies for which they have no basis of understanding. For example, the teaching cue "soar like a bird" may not be useful to a child who does not have any visual memory of birds in flight. The teacher may wish to teach the child how to "soar like a bird."

- *How can the teacher maximize use of existent sight?*

  For most visual impairments, bright lighting maximizes vision. For some conditions such as glaucoma and albinism, however, glare is a problem. Teaching these students in lighting free of glare enables maximum vision.

Table 10.2 Tests for Students With Visual Impairments

Test name	Area tested	Availability of norms
Physical fitness testing of the disabled: Project UNIQUE (Winnick & Short, 1985)	Fitness	Norms available for students with visual impairments, ages 10–17
Buell adaptation (1973) of AAHPERD youth fitness test (1965 version)	Fitness	Norms available for students with visual impairments, ages 10–17
Ohio State University scale of intra-gross motor assessment (Loovis & Ersing, 1979)	Motor skills[a]	No norms available
Callier Azusa (1978)	Motor development, perceptual skills, daily living skills, language socialization	No norms available

[a]This test has not been specifically adapted to assess the motor or sport skills of participants with visual impairments. No such tests currently exist.

- *Are there any contraindicated physical activities?*

To determine if there are any contraindicated (not recommended) physical activities, look for medical provider's notes in the student's educational file. Consult library reference texts on the etiology of visual impairments and read about the specific impairment the student has. There are few contraindications for individuals with total blindness, as there is no sight to preserve. For persons with partial sight, activity restrictions might be imposed in an effort to preserve the remaining sight. Discuss the condition with the student's eye specialist to determine what, if any, restrictions are necessary, especially following recent eye surgery. For example, jarring movements that could cause further detachment are usually contraindicated with a detached retina. Contact sports, as well as diving and swimming under water, may need to be avoided. Glaucoma occurs when the fluid within the eye is unable to drain and pressure increases within the eye, causing blindness. Inverted positions and swimming under water are often contraindicated with glaucoma because of increased pressure on the eye.

- *What are the student's favorite scholastic, social, and physical activities?*

Learn about the opportunities that exist for the child to participate in physical activities with family, friends, and in the community. Seek to incorporate these activities into the child's physical education program.

B. Foster the Student's Independence

There are six strategies for fostering independence.

1. Develop positive attitudes toward students with visual impairments.

The teacher's attitude is the determining factor in the classroom. If the teacher is truly interested in teaching all children, including a student with a visual impairment, and if this teacher makes accommodations for the diverse needs of all students without a fuss, students are more likely to also accept those with visual impairments or other challenging conditions.

2. Encourage participation of students with visual impairments in physical activities.

Discuss with students how they feel about various activities. Respect any fears they might express, and work with the children to create an environment in which they feel safe and are more willing to participate in physical activity. The following incident may help illustrate the importance of talking with one student to understand her concerns and encouraging her to participate. A young girl who had been totally blind since birth performed very well in swimming. But she seemed unable to learn to swim under water. When asked why, she replied, "No one will see me if I go under water. That scares me." After it was explained that water is clear, the girl was reassured and soon learned to swim under water.

3. Seek to avoid overprotection.

By maintaining expectations for students with visual impairments similar to those held for other students in the class, an instructor can avoid overprotection. Many individuals who work with individuals who are blind say that overprotection by teachers and parents is a major problem. It limits these individuals' opportunities to explore and contribute to their environment. Most of the individuals who have been noted for their achievements despite their lack of sight share a positive outlook on life and succeed in spite of others who tell them what they can't do. The reader is encouraged to read the biographies of Harry Cordellos, Charles Buell, and Helen Keller, as well as the controversial book by Robert Scott on socialized dependency of individuals who are blind, entitled *The Making of Blind Men*. Scott suggests that society treats individuals who are blind as though they were helpless and dependent. This treatment then teaches individuals who are blind to act in ways that are helpless and dependent. Based on this societal expectation of helplessness, when a person who is blind does otherwise perfectly ordinary things that show they are not helpless (get married, raise children, hold a job, etc.), such accomplishments may be seen as extraordinary. Both attitudes—viewing people with visual impairments as helpless and their accomplishments as extraordinary—patronize and limit opportunities for individuals with visual impairments. To counteract such patronizing societal attitudes, it is extremely important that physical educators teach independence and self-sufficiency to students who are blind and expect that these students will exhibit these qualities. In class, expect students with visual impairments to enter the gymnasium independently, participate with minimal assistance (e.g., play without someone standing next to them), run to a caller rather than be lead, and serve for themselves in volleyball. It is not always necessary to have a buddy throughout physical education class. Peer tutors are helpful at times, but continuous use can foster dependence.

4. Help parents see their children's ability.

Parents/caregivers are most children's biggest advocates. Based on their fears for the child who does not have use of a major sense organ, some caregivers may dwell on what the child can't do rather than on what they can do. In these cases the child will rarely have the opportunity at home to try new things, play games that sighted children play, or take risks. Teachers can educate parents about their children's capabilities by sending home notes or even newsletters describing students' accomplishments, photographs of the student doing activities, ribbons and certificates for accomplishments, and lists of the student's favorite physical activities. By learning about children's current performance and abilities, caregivers may have a better understanding of their children's potential and may allow or even encourage more opportunity for physical activity at home and in the community.

5. Challenge students with visual impairments so they might feel successful.

Reward and recognize all students' accomplishments to help improve self-esteem and motivate them to continue to work on their next goals. Teachers help as they

- work with the student to set realistic goals,
- keep caregivers informed of successes through sending notes home, and
- implement a reward system to recognize achievement, such as through bulletin boards, student newspapers, and announcements.

6. Expect the student to move as independently as possible during physical education.

At the beginning of the school year, thoroughly orient the person with a visual impairment to the playing fields, gymnasium, and equipment within it to increase independence and feelings of security. Together identify landmarks that can help students orient themselves. For example, a landmark might be the mats along either end of the gymnasium in contrast to the paneling along the sides. Enable individuals to walk around and touch everything as often as needed to create the mental map that will enable them to negotiate the area with confidence. Always keep equipment in the same position within the gymnasium. If a change is necessary, forewarn and reorient students. In the locker room, provide a lock that opens with a key rather than a combination for a student with a visual impairment.

C. Teach to the Student's Abilities

To keep visually impaired students participating, the teacher may be challenged to make some modifications in activities or in instruction style. Some of the possible modifications are described in the following paragraphs.

1. Modify a wide variety of activities.

Activities that do not depend heavily on throwing and catching objects are more easily adapted, but most activities can be modified so that a student with a visual impairment can participate in a meaningful way. The following activities are readily adapted:

- Dancing: folk, square dancing, jazz, creative, etc.

- Fitness activities: weight machines, free weights, stationary bicycle, rowing machine, rope jumping

- Tug-of-war and parachute play with young children, along with most movement education challenges

- Canoeing and tandem bicycling with a sighted partner in the front seat, crew with a sighted coxswain

- Swimming and wrestling

- Bowling and archery

- Water-skiing using whistle signals, and cross-country skiing with a sighted partner

- Relaxation training, Hatha yoga, and martial arts, such as Tai Chi, that include partner work providing continuous body contact.

Other activities require further modification, through adding kinesthetic and/or auditory cues and enhancing visual cues. Specific modifications follow.

2. Modify to provide kinesthetic cues.

Information processing can be facilitated by providing kinesthetic cues. The use of kinesthetic feedback is potentially a more efficient method of learning than the use of auditory feedback with students who are blind (Dye, 1983). Kinesthetic cues include the following examples:

- Physically guiding a child's body to the correct position when teaching a motor skill.

- Using a scale model such as a doll with movable joints that children can feel to convey the relationship of the body parts during a move such as a jumping jack, forward roll, or cartwheel.

- Teaching sighted students to guide students with visual impairments while walking and in activities. Allow the person who is blind to hold the sighted person's arm, just above the elbow, and walk a half step behind. In this way the person who is blind can get cues about changes in the terrain, stairs, and turns.

- Using different surfaces to mark playing areas and aid orientation. Mats can be placed on the floor in front of a wall to signal out of bounds.

- Using a fan or radio as feedback when a target is hit. Inexpensive mercury switches can be rigged to turn the fan or radio on when the target is hit. The blowing air or music tells students of a successful hit.

- Using a lightweight portable rail set up in line with the gutter to guide the bowler's approach.

- Stringing guide wires to orient a runner who is blind. Usually, though, it is more practical in integrated settings to run touching arms, or holding the other end of a short rope, with a sighted person who runs at a similar pace.

3. Modify to provide auditory cues.

Modify visually dependent activities to provide additional auditory information through sound devices and verbal cues.

- For baseball, use a large ball that is hit as it bounces off home plate or use a beeper ball (a ball with an audible buzzer inside). The first base coach calls to direct the batter to the base.

- Make playground balls audible by cutting the ball, inserting bells, then resealing the ball with a bicycle tire patch.

- Making scoring a goal audible by tying bells onto net goals. Everyone can hear the jingling sound when a goal is scored.

- Give feedback using precise descriptions. A statement such as "Hold the racket 3–4 inches above your left shoulder" provides more feedback than "Hold the racket like this." Use of precise language benefits all students, visually impaired and sighted.

- Include students with visual impairments during spectator events by assigning a student "announcer" to describe the action for spectators, much as a radio announcer describes a ball game. Select an announcer with a lively sense of humor to make the event more fun for everyone.

4. Enhance visual cues.

Most individuals with visual impairments do have some *residual vision*. Evaluate each activity to decide what type of visual cues are needed and how to highlight them. Color, contrast, and lighting are important (Tapp et al., 1991). Be sure to ask each student what enhances his or her vision. Examples include the following:

- Make the gymnasium lighting brighter (or darker for students who tend to self-stimulate on the bright lights)

• Use colored tape to increase the contrast of equipment with the background, such as high jump standards and poles or the edges of a balance beam.

• Use brightly colored balls, mats, field markers, and goals that contrast with the background for most students with visual impairments. Individuals with albinism and glaucoma, however, need solid-colored objects under nonglare lights.

D. Develop Support Systems

As students with more severe and/or multiple disabilities, such as visual impairments and severe retardation, are placed in regular physical education classes, support systems become a very necessary part of successful inclusion. Without these supports inclusion becomes dumping, a practice that is unfair to students with challenges, their peers, and teachers. Fortunately, the teacher is not the only source of ideas for adaptations. The child with the visual limitation is an excellent source, as are the other children in the class. Teachers have had much success in developing accommodations by making it a class effort. "How can we modify this game so that (child with visual impairment) can participate in a meaningful way?"

• Use peer tutors to assist in providing kinesthetic and auditory cues to students with visual impairments.

• If needed, request the services of a paraprofessional, mobility instructor, physical therapist, or low-vision specialist to involve a student with multiple challenges, including a visual impairment, in physical education.

• Enlist caregivers' assistance in advocating for appropriate support systems.

• Collaborate with others, such as a resource specialist in adapted physical education or physical education teachers at residential schools for students with visual impairments.

Refer to chapter 8 for other examples of support systems.

Teaching Children Who Are Deaf-Blind

Children called deaf-blind are really individuals with **multisensory deprivation (MSD)** who do not have effective use of the distance senses: vision and hearing. Even though the term *deaf-blind* suggests that these people can neither hear nor see, this is seldom accurate. The overwhelming majority of children who are deaf-blind receive both visual and auditory input, but information received through these sensory channels is usually distorted. It is more accurate to state that these people are both hard-of-hearing and partially sighted. Only in rare instances, such as with Helen Keller, is a person totally blind and profoundly deaf.

The challenges of MSD children are complex. They may

• communicate with their environment in ways that do not use vision and hearing,

• perceive their world in a distorted fashion,

• anticipate future events or the results of their actions in a different way,

• be deprived of many of the most basic extrinsic motivations,

• have medical problems that lead to significant developmental lags,

• be mislabeled as retarded or emotionally disturbed,

• develop unique learning styles to compensate for their multiple handicaps, or

• require a long period of time to establish and maintain interpersonal relationships (McInnes & Treffry, 1982, p. 2).

Multisensory deprivation presents many challenges to learning. Children with MSD can manipulate objects, but they do not get clear visual or auditory feedback, so it is difficult to anticipate consequences of an action. Until recently most of these children were assumed to be profoundly retarded, institutionalized, with few educational opportunities. Children with MSD have shown substantial lags in social, emotional, cognitive, and motor development. Results of recently developed programs demonstrate that many of these children are not inherently profoundly retarded but are only deprived of an opportunity to learn. But establishing an educational program for children with MSD is not a task that can be accomplished in a haphazard way. These children have almost no opportunity for incidental learning, so everything must be taught, including how to play. Activities should be planned to accomplish established objectives that require the child to solve problems, communicate appropriately, use residual vision and hearing, and exert control over the environment (McInnes & Treffry, 1982). Movement is at the base of the program because, through moving, deaf-blind children will learn about themselves and the environment.

Students with MSD can participate in most sports, whether on a competitive or recreational level. Athletes with MSD may choose to compete in sports for persons who are blind (USABA) or deaf (AAAD). Weight lifting, dance, roller skating, swimming, skiing, bowling, hiking, goal ball, track and field, cycling, and canoeing are some of the possibilities. But to enjoy these and other sports, students need the prerequisite skills and immediate feedback. McInnes and Treffry (1982) suggest the following steps be followed regardless of the child's current performance level.

1. Provide the opportunity to explore, manipulate, and become familiar with equipment and facilities.

2. Together with the child, demonstrate and model the response. For example, place the child's hand over the teacher's hands when paddling. Once the child can follow the motion, place the teacher's hands over the child's hands when paddling. This is analogous to demonstrating and modeling the desired behavior, and it is essential to provide security as well as skill development.

3. Provide immediate feedback so children can compare their performance with the model. Consider the following adaptation to provide feedback when a student has hit a target with an object. Instead of requiring that the teacher or another student provide feedback, rig a fan to a mercury switch on the target. When the object hits the target, it triggers the fan. The blowing air tells the student the target was hit!

4. Explain and give the child time to prepare for the coming action. Surprise moves do not foster security and confidence. For more complete teaching and curriculum suggestions with students with MSD, refer to books listed in the resource section at the end of this chapter.

An experience with a student named Eddie may illustrate the importance of not placing ceilings on expectations for students with MSD. Eddie is 15 years old, deaf, and blind. He asked to learn to ride a unicycle. Using the same task analysis his physical education teacher had used to learn to ride, Eddie learned independently. Teaching students with MSD challenges physical educators to adapt appropriately to enable these students to learn.

Sports for Athletes With Visual Impairments

It is the physical educator's responsibility to inform students with visual impairments about sport opportunities and encourage their participation. Students may wish to participate in integrated sports with their sighted peers or in sports exclusively for individuals with visual impairments, or both. Given the low incidence of blindness, many individuals with visual impairments enjoy participation in sport organizations for athletes who are blind because of the opportunity to meet others who are also blind. It is important that physical educators learn about and share information on blind sport organizations in their region so that students can choose to participate. Begin by calling the national organization and ask to be referred to the nearest local sport organization for athletes who are blind.

United States Association for Blind Athletes (USABA)

The motto of USABA is "If I can do this, I can do anything." It is the major sport organization in the United States for athletes of any age who are visually impaired and blind. USABA offers competition in the following sports:

- goal ball
- women's gymnastics
- men's wrestling
- track and field
- swimming
- tandem cycling
- judo
- Alpine and Nordic skiing and speed skating
- power and weight lifting
- road racing
- archery (currently a developmental sport)

USABA classification for competition is based on residual vision (see in Table 10.1). Rules for each sport are modified slightly from those established by the national sports organization. For example, track and field follows National Collegiate Athletic Association (NCAA) rules except that wire lane markers are used in sprints, sighted partners may be used on distance runs, hurdles are eliminated, and jumpers who are totally blind touch the high bar, then back off and use a one- or two-step approach.

Wrestling rules are modified slightly to require that opponents maintain physical contact throughout the match. Wrestlers with visual impairments have a long history of victories and state championships against sighted opponents (Buell, 1966).

Women gymnasts compete according to United States Gymnastics Federation rules except that vaulters who are totally blind may start with their hands on the horse and use a two-bounce takeoff, coaches on the balance beam may warn competitors when they near the end of the beam and no jumps are used, floor exercise competitors may count their steps to the edge of the mat, and music may be placed anywhere near the mat to aid directionality.

Swimming also follows NCAA rules. Athletes count their strokes so that they can anticipate the pool's edge. Coaches may also tap a swimmer, using a long pole with soft material at the end such as a tennis ball, to signal the upcoming end of the pool. On the backstroke, flags are hung low over the pool to brush the swimmers' arms to signal the end of the pool. When necessary a spotter may use a paddle board to protect a swimmer's head.

Goal ball (see Figure 10.2) is a sport unique to athletes who are blind. Two teams of three players compete on a rectangular playing area to stop a rolled ball from crossing their end line. All players wear blindfolds, so they must listen for the rolling ball filled with bells. It is a lively sport in which players stretch, dive, or lunge to stop the oncoming ball with any part of their bodies. Goal ball is a sport specifically designed to be played by athletes who are blind. Physical educators may wish to play goal ball in an integrated class to reverse the usual situation. Everyone wears blindfolds, so students with visual impairments may outperform students who are sighted due to increased opportunity to develop auditory perception. Ropes placed along the gymnasium floor and covered with wide tape create boundaries that players can feel. Additional information on goal ball is provided in chapter 24.

ISBA

The international counterpart of USABA is the International Blind Sports and Recreation Association. For international competition, USABA athletes participate in the Paralympic Games (Paciorek and Jones, 1994).

Other Sport Organizations for Athletes Who Are Blind

Beep ball is a popular modification of baseball, governed by the National Beep Baseball Association (NBBA). Competition culminates with the NBBA World Series. Beep Baseball is covered in more detail in chapter 24.

The 1980s witnessed a proliferation and tremendous growth among disabled sports. Opportunities for national and international competition are now available in numerous sports. But local opportunities for individuals who are blind remain limited. Perhaps this will be the area of growth in disabled sports during the 1990s.

Figure 10.2 Playing goal ball.

HEARING LOSSES

Being deaf in the United States today often means being a member of a subculture of American society that has its own language, its own customs, and its own way of perceiving the deaf person's role within the hearing world. Becoming aware of the deaf culture's perspective may be beneficial to the effective teaching of deaf students in physical education. Understanding this perspective might begin with the knowledge that many deaf people do not necessarily consider themselves disabled. Unlike members of most populations with disabilities, most who are deaf do not want "person first" terminology used to describe them. Many deaf individuals prefer to be called a "Deaf person" rather than a "person who is deaf." Dolnick (1993) notes that the use of the upper-case D in the word deaf is a succinct proclamation by the deaf that they share more than a medical condition; they share a culture. Hearing impairment, a term commonly used to describe some malfunction of the auditory mechanism, is not preferred by many deaf individuals because it also suggests that deafness is a disability.

Deaf refers to a hearing loss in which hearing is insufficient for comprehension of auditory information, with or without the use of a hearing aid. The federal law IDEA defines *deaf* as having a hearing loss that is so severe that the student is unable to process language through hearing, with or without the use of an amplification device. The loss must be severe enough to affect the student's educational performance adversely (Education for All Handicapped Children Act of 1975, Section 121a.5 [b] [1]).

Hard-of-hearing refers to a hearing loss that makes understanding speech solely through the ear difficult but not impossible. Hard-of-hearing persons usually use a hearing aid and/or remedial help in communication skills. IDEA defines *hard-of-hearing* as having a hearing loss that may be permanent or fluctuating and that adversely affects the student's educational achievement or performance (Education for All Handicapped Children Act of 1975, Section 121a.5 [b] [1]).

Most people with hearing losses are hard of hearing, not totally deaf. It is important to note that two children may have the same degree and pattern of hearing loss but may utilize their residual hearing differently due to differences in age when hearing loss occurred. Motivation, intelligence, presence of challenging conditions and response to a training program may also affect the degree to which residual hearing is utilized.

Amounts of hearing loss and residual hearing are both described in terms of decibel (dB) levels. The ability to detect sounds in the 0–25 dB range is considered normal for children. Ordinary conversation occurs in the 40–50 dB range, while noises in the 125–140 dB range are painfully loud. Degrees of hearing loss are presented in Table 10.3.

The age at which the hearing loss occurs can greatly influence the method of communication used by people with hearing losses. *Prelingual deafness* refers to the condition of persons whose deafness was present at birth or occurred at an age before the development of speech and language. *Postlingual deafness* refers to the condition of persons whose deafness occurred at an age after spontaneously developing speech and language. The first three years of life are when most children learn to understand and use language in the form of oral speech. If a person has a total hearing loss before learning to speak, the task of developing oral speech may be close to impossible. A prelingual deaf person with speechreading (lipreading) training is usually no more proficient at speechreading than an untrained hearing person. (Simulate this by turning off the sound while watching people on television and try to follow what is being said.) Due to the difficulty most prelingual deaf people have in speaking and speechreading, many use sign language in place of verbal communication. In contrast, people who have already developed speech before the hearing loss occurred usually can retain intelligible speech, often with the help of remedial training. It is usually possible for these people to speech read with proficiency.

Incidence

In 1990–1991 there were 42,161 school-aged children with hearing losses (Office of Special Education Programs, 1992, p. A-24). The incidence of profound deafness among children is approximately 1 in 1,000. However, as many as 1 in 16 children possess milder forms of hearing losses that can place them at a disadvantage in school. Sometimes these children are regarded as slow learners or behavior problems when their inappropriate behavior is actually due to an undetected mild hearing loss.

Among deaf children, approximately two thirds have congenital deafness (present at birth) and one third have acquired deafness (develops sometime after birth). At least two of the leading congenital causes of deafness (rubella, Rh incompatibility) are now preventable. However, the decrease in the incidence of deafness one might have expected has

Table 10.3 Degrees of Hearing Loss

Hearing threshold	Degree of impairment	Difficulty understanding the following speech
27–40 dB[a]	Slight impairment	Faint speech
41–55 dB	Mild impairment	Normal speech
56–70 dB	Marked impairment	Loud speech
71–90 dB	Severe impairment	Shouted speech
Greater than 90 dB	Profound impairment	Any speech, even amplified speech

[a]Decibels.

been offset by medical advances that enable more severely premature babies and children with meningitis and encephalitis to survive. These survivors may have multiple disabilities, including deafness.

Types and Causes of Hearing Losses

There are three major types of hearing loss: conductive, sensory-neural, and mixed. With a *conductive loss*, sound is not transmitted well to the inner ear. It is analogous to a radio with the volume on low. The words are faint, but there is no distortion. Conductive losses can be corrected surgically or medically because it is a mechanical problem in which nerves remain undamaged. A frequently observed cause of a conductive hearing loss is **serous otitis media**, or middle ear effusion. This condition is often treated by placing a plastic tube through the eardrum for several months to allow congealed fluid to drain away from sound-conducting inner ear bones.

A *sensory-neural loss* is much more serious and likely to be permanent. It is analogous to a radio that is not well tuned. Sensory-neural losses affect fidelity as well as loudness, so there is distortion. The words may be loud, but they are distorted and garbled. While raising one's voice or using a hearing aid may help the voice be heard, the words still may not be understood. Typically, low-pitched vowel sounds are heard, but the high pitch consonants such as *t, p,* and *k* are not heard clearly. This makes it difficult to distinguish words such as *pop* from *top*. A *mixed loss* is a combination of both conductive and sensory-neural losses. The conductive part of the loss may be permanent or temporary, as in the case of recurring ear infections. Injuries, infections, and allergies to drugs can all cause hearing loss, as can repeated exposure to loud music for more than a short time.

Implications of the Information Processing Model for Teaching Students With Hearing Loss

To the extent that information processing is dependent on auditory cues, hard-of-hearing and deaf students will have difficulty learning. Movement, however, is one area that is not heavily dependent on auditory cues. Usually visual cues can be substituted for the auditory cues that are distorted or absent. Few rules, equipment, facilities, or skills require modification. But deafness places profound limitations on verbal communication and thus requires that teaching methods be modified to provide nonverbal as well as verbal communication to accommodate hard-of-hearing and deaf students attending hearing schools.

Characteristics of Students With Hearing Losses

Individuals who are classified as **hard-of-hearing** typically share the same characteristics as the general population. Their hearing impairments are mild and do not present major obstacles to speech. But most people who are *postlingual profoundly deaf* or *prelingual severely* or *profoundly deaf* need to communicate through a means other than speech. These characteristics are the focus of the following section.

Language and Cultural Characteristics

''There is something about being Deaf that is quietly comforting to those who have this identity. It has to do, in part, with American Sign Language (ASL), a language oblivious to the rambling operations of speech. It has to do with experiences among deaf people that cannot be shared with hearing people. The resolve to be Deaf is steeped in hundreds of years of culture that has steadfastly evolved within a predominantly hearing society despite the interferences of educators, politicians, and a battalion of society's do-gooders." Preservation of a Deaf identity is fueled by the reassuring presence of a community of Deaf individuals (Stewart, 1991, p. 1).

The everyday language of an estimated half-million Americans is American Sign Language (ASL) (Dolnick, 1993). This is the basis of the shared identity, creating deaf culture. Just like English, ASL is a language used to communicate, having its own grammar and structure to convey subtle nuances of abstractions, in addition to describing concrete objects. Most hearing people only see the signs that name objects and directions, such as found in Figure 10.3, and are unaware of the subtleties of ASL.

Currently, *total communication* (a combination of speech, residual hearing, finger spelling, and sign language) is preferred in many residential schools for the deaf. American Sign Language is the preferred means of communication within the deaf culture. But the *oral-only method* (a combination of residual hearing, lipreading, and speech), and *cued speech* (spoken English accompanied by hand signals to help distinguish between words that look alike on the lips) also have their proponents. The bicultural and bilingual (BI/BI) education movement, in which ASL is the primary language with English taught as a second language, is gaining popularity.

Research has shown that a major factor in the development of language skills and social adjustment of prelingual deaf people is whether they are exposed to language (in this case, sign language) from birth. Significant language delays are found among deaf children with hearing parents. But language delays are not found among the 10% of deaf children who have deaf parents because they have the opportunity to learn sign language as rapidly as their hearing peers learn speech.

Currently, most prelingual deaf children do not develop intelligible speech despite the best known teaching methods. So, communication between hearing and deaf people remains a major problem.

Cognitive Characteristics

The difficulty and delay in acquiring language for deaf children raised in the hearing world are reflected in their reading achievement. ASL is a language without a written form, so for persons whose primary language is ASL, learning to read English is like learning to read a foreign language. This contributes to a situation in which the mean reading level of deaf high school graduates of average intelligence is found to be comparable to that of 9- or 10-year-old hearing children. Deaf students are substantially behind their hearing peers in other measures of achievement as well. Most tests are designed for hearing children and require a good working knowledge of written English. But even when appropriate tests are given, the performance of deaf students is still poor (Freeman, Carbin, and Boese, 1981, p. 245). One reason may be that test instructions are not clearly presented using the student's preferred mode of communication. Another reason is that deaf children in the hearing world have decreased opportunities for incidental learning because they cannot overhear conversations. Rarely do hearing parents, teachers, and friends sign when not addressing deaf children. So there is little opportunity to "oversee" conversations, and continuity with life's events is often missing. For example, there is no opportunity for a deaf child to overhear an argument that caused a classmate to cry.

Behavioral and Affective Characteristics

The incidence of impulsivity seems to be greater among deaf than among hearing children. This may be because there is a deprivation of communication and fewer incidental learning opportunities among deaf students living in the hearing community. Harris found that deaf children of deaf parents are significantly less impulsive than other deaf children. This suggests that a communication problem is at the root of impulsivity.

Studies show that 20–30% of deaf children have behavioral disorders, compared to 7–10% of hearing children. This greater incidence of behavioral disorders among deaf children may exist because these children have not learned enough about what is expected of them and why and how to behave in approved ways (Freeman et al., 1981, p. 178). This underscores the importance of establishing clear, concise classroom rules.

Research into the self-concept of deaf students is ambiguous. There is evidence that the self-esteem of deaf students in hearing public schools is lower than the self-esteem of both hard-of-hearing and hearing students in public schools; it is also lower than the self-esteem of deaf students in residential schools for the deaf. So the placement of deaf students in either deaf or hearing schools may be a significant factor. Other influential factors include communication skills, age at onset of hearing loss,

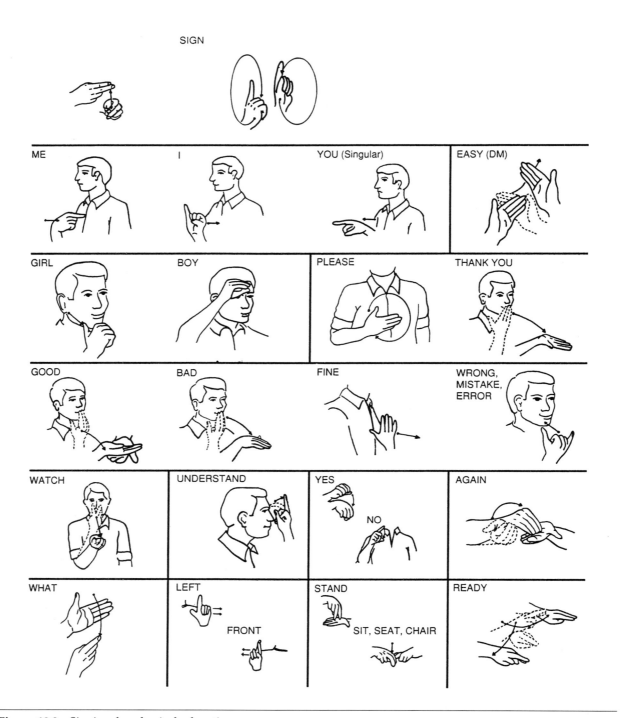

Figure 10.3 Signing for physical education.
Reprinted by permission of the American Alliance for Health, Physical Education, Recreation and Dance, 1900 Association Drive, Reston, VA 22091.

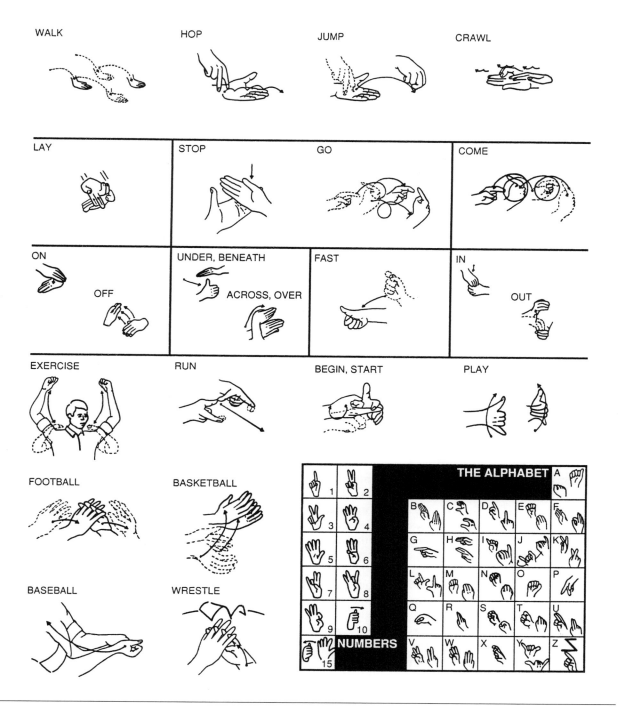

Figure 10.3 *(Continued).*

and whether the parents are hearing or deaf (Hopper, 1988, p. 296). "While it is difficult to infer causality, it seems likely that school success, sports skills, and physical attractiveness may lead to greater acceptance and popularity among one's peers" (Hopper, 1988, p. 299).

Motor Characteristics

The research on the motor performance of deaf students is somewhat ambiguous. Some studies find little difference among deaf and hearing children in static and dynamic balance, motor development, or motor ability. Other studies do find a difference. One possible explanation for the discrepancy in findings may be variation in the number of children with vestibular damage in each study. If the semicircular canals of the inner ear are damaged, balance problems are likely. These balance problems may, in turn, cause developmental delays and motor ability delays. Most studies on the motor performance of deaf children have not placed those with vestibular damage in a group separate from other deaf children. Results that show poor motor performance for deaf children as a group could reflect the very poor performance of those children with vestibular damage along with the average performance of the rest of the deaf children (Schmidt, 1985). For example, fewer deaf students showed mature basic gross motor patterns than found among hearing students (Butterfield 1986, 1989, 1990; Butterfield and Ersing, 1988). Butterfield found age-expected development in running, throwing, striking, and skipping. But he found delays in kicking, jumping, catching, and hopping. These delayed skills rely heavily on balance, raising the question of whether difficulties in balance can contribute to delays in developing mature patterns in kicking, jumping, and hopping. (Butterfield, 1986, 1988). Stewart, Dummer, and Haubenstricker (1990) found delays in stationary bounce, catch, kick, overhand throw, and two-hand strike among deaf children. They note that the difficulty in clearly communicating test directions to students with hearing losses may be another source contributing to the ambiguity in research results. They stress the importance of researchers using experts familiar with the linguistic and communication needs of a particular group of deaf subjects to help design and administer motor skill tests.

Deaf students do not seem to differ from hearing students with regard to physical fitness. There are no significant differences across age groups with regard to body composition, strength, flexibility, power-speed, and cardiorespiratory endurance measures of physical fitness (Winnick and Short, 1986; Hattin, Fraser, Ward, and Shepard, 1986). Only in the test's power-strength item (sit-ups) do hearing students perform significantly better than the deaf students. There are the usual performance differences according to gender and age. Boys are more fit than girls (except for tests of flexibility), and older children are more fit than younger children among hearing-loss as well as hearing populations. Based on these findings, physical educators could effectively evaluate deaf students against the same fitness norms used for hearing students and should expect that deaf children and youth can attain the same standards for health-related physical fitness as their hearing counterparts.

Schmidt (1985) and Winnick and Short (1985) compared the motor performances of deaf students educated in residential schools for the deaf with those of deaf students from hearing schools. Both studies found that the performance of deaf students in deaf schools was significantly better than that of students integrated into regular schools. While unproved, it is strongly suspected that deaf students in hearing schools are not provided with sufficient physical activity opportunities to allow them to achieve their potential. Thus, motor performance of deaf students attending hearing schools may be artificially limited by discriminatory attitudes and practices and inadequate communication, rather than by the students' lack of abilities.

Teaching Deaf Students in Physical Education

Over 75% of the students with hearing losses are educated in public schools (Office of Special Education Programs, 1992, p. I-1). The decision regarding whether to educate deaf students in schools for the deaf or in regular schools has far-reaching implications. Education in schools for the deaf provides the student with an important link to deaf culture. The student joins a world in which deafness predominates, yet most everyone can communicate freely, usually through ASL. Education in regular schools, in contrast, usually means living with one's family and remaining culturally within the hearing world, in an environment with limited opportunities for communicating with hearing individuals who do not sign. (Refer to Butterfield, 1991, for an excellent discussion of the placement issue.) Physical education is the one setting in the school day that does not rely heavily on spoken and written communication. Physical educators have the opportunity to accentuate the deaf student's abilities and help the student build self-concept and esteem. To accomplish this, the physical educator must give attention to the student's communication needs and social interaction skills, and must provide many opportunities for movement experiences.

When teaching deaf students, physical educators may find it helpful to learn the answers to the following three groups of questions. When seeking answers, ask the student, if possible. Look at the student's IEP. Ask the parent/caregiver and teacher.

1. What can the student hear? Knowing what, if anything, a person can hear enables the teacher to maximize the use of any remaining hearing.

2. What is the student's preferred mode of communication? And how can the teacher maximize communication with the student? If physical education teachers do not sign, they may request an interpreter through IDEA. If the teacher finds that physical education class serves as the interpreter's break period, the teacher has the right to request that the interpreter also be present during physical education class.

3. Are there any contraindications? Most individuals with hearing losses have no restrictions on their participation in physical education. Children with frequent ear infections may have tubes placed in their ears. These children may need to wear ear plugs when swimming to keep water from entering their ears. Children susceptible to earaches should avoid exposing unprotected ears to cold weather.

Due to balance problems and vertigo, individuals with damage to the semicircular canals of the inner ear should only climb to heights, jump on the trampoline, or dive into a pool if adequate safeguards have been taken to ensure they will not be hurt if they lose their balance during these activities. Tumbling activities that require rotation, such as dive forward rolls, cartwheels, and handsprings, should only be attempted with close spotting. Activities in a safe situation are recommended to teach individuals to make the maximum use of visual and kinesthetic cues in balancing. If a student exhibits a major deficit in balance, it should be addressed outside their regular physical education class. A student should *not* be pulled from regular physical education to work on balance. Learning

the age-appropriate skills in a particular unit may be just as important as improving balance skills.

Tests

Very few physical education tests are designed with norms specifically for hard-of-hearing and deaf students. Physical Fitness Testing of the Disabled: Project UNIQUE by Winnick and Short (1985) is the most current test available for this purpose. It has national norms established for 10- to 17-year-old hard-of-hearing and deaf students on fitness items that have been modified slightly to compensate for their lack of hearing. The fitness items are the same as those for hearing students, but hand signals have been added. The norms for deaf and hearing students are the same with the exception of the sit-ups.

Most other physical fitness tests can be administered to deaf students provided that visual cues are substituted for auditory cues in the test (e.g., dropping an arm in addition to shouting "go" to signal the start of an event). The only major modifications involve the instructions. Teachers must be very sure that deaf students understand each of the items on the tests so that their results reflect ability and not lack of understanding. ASL is not semantically similar to English, so care must be taken that, when signing instructions, the person signing be skilled in signing and give signed instructions that are semantically identical to the spoken instructions (Stewart et al., 1990. p. 232).

Balance may be difficult for some deaf children. Butterfield (1988) recommends screening deaf children for possible balance difficulties. Consider using the standardized Bruininks-Oseretsky Test of Motor Proficiency as well as informal teacher observation of the child in free play settings to gather information about balance. Refer to chapter 4 for additional information on tests in the psychomotor domain.

Teaching Suggestions

There are three basic suggestions for teaching students with hearing loss:

A. enhance communication,

B. promote social interaction, and

C. employ specialized curricular and teaching strategies.

These suggestions will be detailed in the paragraphs that follow.

A. Enhance Communication

Six methods of enhancing communication are listed below:

1. *Maximize hard-of-hearing students' opportunities to process auditory information by minimizing ambient noises while teaching.* For example, do not play recorded background music or allow students to talk while directions are being given to the class.

2. *Facilitate speechreading.* Provide bright lighting and face the students so that lips and facial expressions are fully visible to them. Position students who are speech reading directly in front of the teacher, taking care that the student does not face into the sun.

3. *Provide supplemental verbal input and feedback to a student who is speech reading.* Arrange for a hearing student to repeat or explain any instructions that might not have been heard. Use ample demonstrations, distribute written copies of games and even lesson plans, and utilize visual cues such as flashing the lights for getting the attention of deaf and hard-of-hearing students. When outside, stand near students with hearing losses and tap them on the shoulder to gain their attention. Develop highly recognizable and easily visible signals to communicate with students at a distance. Many teachers use arms in the air to signal the end of the lesson or change of activities.

4. *If the deaf students sign, learn as much sign language as possible.* Recognize, however, that unless a hearing person masters ASL, which requires as much effort as learning any other language, it will be difficult to communicate beyond a superficial level. Teachers can seek to learn signs for one unit at a time. In this manner they can gradually learn the necessary signs, simultaneously teaching them to interested hearing classmates. Request signing instruction so these hearing students can acquire the skills to communicate with deaf students on more than a superficial level. It is assumed that a physical education teacher in a school for the deaf would study to quickly acquire signing skills and employ the communication system used in the school. Typically, these teachers sign as well as speak most conversations. Signing continually enables deaf students to oversee conversations and thus gives them opportunities to gain incidental information important to the learning process. Signs

basic to physical education are presented in Figure 10.3.

5. *After giving directions, ask the deaf and hard-of-hearing students if they understand the activity.* Also, help hearing students to understand that if the deaf children do not follow the rules, it may be because they do not understand the rules, not because they are intentionally breaking them.

6. *Due to the teacher time needed to communicate with deaf children in regular class, the total class size should be reduced.* Request this support system through the individual education program (IEP) process.

B. Promote Social Interaction

An important objective of physical education for deaf students is to increase opportunities for social interaction. Physical education is the one area where verbal communication can be minimized and movement maximized. It is also an area where working together toward a common goal can be emphasized.

1. *Physical educators who use small, stable groups of students in instruction may play a key role in helping children with hearing losses socially interact with others, both during class and free play.* Research by Antia, Kreimeyer, and Eldridge (1993), conducted in class and free play settings, suggests that teachers can promote interaction among children with hearing losses and other deaf and hearing children by regularly placing students into the same small groups for physical education instruction and play. Keeping the composition of the groups of students constant enables children to really get to know each other and may result in increased interaction. This may facilitate social interaction among these same children during free play (Kreimeyer and Antia, 1988).

2. *Teach neighborhood games to further promote social interaction.* Hearing children learn games such as jumping rope, hopscotch, four-square, and softball mostly through watching and listening to others play. Such incidental learning through listening is not available to deaf children. Teaching these games in physical education class helps deaf children understand them, develop their playing skill, and enhance their chances of being included in neighborhood play.

3. *In elementary physical education, facilitate interaction by planning activities that encourage taking turns, guided problem-solving, and partner activities* (Butterfield, 1988). Cooperative learning is a teaching technique that also fosters social interaction. In intermediate and secondary physical education, few adaptations are usually required in lead-up games and team sports. Play these games only if all students have the prerequisite skills and understand the rules. It is especially important to check for understanding with deaf students. When asked if they understand, individuals might have a tendency to say yes even though understanding may not be complete. Go beyond asking students (hearing and deaf) whether they understand. Verify their understanding by asking them to explain the rules or to demonstrate them. Employing techniques to ensure that deaf students understand the rules increases their opportunities to succeed and be accepted by their hearing peers.

4. *Enable deaf students to work together.* One practicum supervisor observed an integrated physical education class in which the three deaf students used sign as their primary means of communication. The teacher decided to move the deaf students away from one another, reasoning that working with hearing students would help with the deaf students' communication and social interaction skills. Each time the students were moved apart, however, they managed to reunite by the end of the lesson. Why? They wanted to communicate and socialize in their primary language, something they could not do with the hearing students. Allow deaf students to socialize and communicate with each other, just as hearing students do.

5. *Hold the same expectations for hearing and deaf students with regard to motor performance, fitness, and behavior.* Clearly communicate these expectations to deaf students, beginning with the first day of the school year. As with all children, "Set up environments to promote the development of responsibility. . . . Recognize and reinforce responsibility when it occurs. . . . Simultaneously, refrain from reinforcing dependent behaviors" (Luckner, 1993, p. 14). Educators who are unusually understanding, or who offer excessive assistance when students are not prepared for class, teach these students that they can rely on others rather than accept responsibility for their own actions. Teachers should

ask themselves, "Am I really helping? Is the assistance I am giving helping students to cope more effectively with the world that they will be living in after graduation? Or is it better to let them experience the real consequences of their behavior?" (Luckner, 1993, p. 14).

6. *Exhibit a positive, welcoming attitude toward deaf students.* This attitude will be observed and adopted by most students. Enforce classroom rules fairly and uniformly for all students, including those with hearing losses. Avoid offering preferential treatment. Receiving special treatment does not endear hard-of-hearing or deaf students to their classmates.

C. Employ Specialized Curricular and Teaching Strategies

Physical educators have found the following strategies successful when working with hearing-impaired students.

1. *Select physical education activities to emphasize the development of social skills.* "Deaf children living in the hearing culture exhibit a low self-concept in this area" (Hopper, 1988, p. 302).

2. *Use the environment to communicate information* (Butterfield, 1988). For example, use footprints to provide positioning cues in throwing and striking (Butterfield, 1988). Use obstacle courses to provide motor challenges that are not heavily dependent on verbal cues. Also, consider using an ecological task-analysis (ETA) approach to teaching, as proposed by Davis. (Refer to Balan and Davis, 1993, for a more complete discussion of ETA). Manipulating the environment while encouraging student choice of activities reduces the need for verbal communication.

3. *Work to improve balance by offering elementary students many opportunities to experience static, dynamic, and inverted balance activities* (Butterfield, 1988). Step over, crawl across, walk through ladders, walk backwards and sideways on balance beams, change direction quickly in tag games, and balance while inverted in tripods, headstands, and handstands to develop balance (Butterfield, 1988).

4. *Use dance and rhythms.* To enable deaf students to feel the vibrations of music, place speakers on a wooden floor and have them dance in bare feet. Add strobe lights that flash in rhythm with the music to provide visual cues (Butterfield, 1988).

5. *Provide extra supervision when swimming under water for students with vestigular damage.* Butterfield suggests teachers pair deaf students with hearing partners and use signals developed for communication between the teacher and the class. Flashing the lights may be a quick way to gain student attention.

Deaf Sport

For many deaf students attending hearing schools, the majority of their exposure to deaf culture will be through deaf sport. *Physical educators have the extremely important role of introducing deaf students to sport, both hearing and deaf sport.* Many deaf athletes choose to compete against one another under the auspices of the American Athletic Association of the Deaf (AAAD). Persons with moderate or severe hearing losses (55 dB or greater in the better ear) are eligible for AAAD competition. AAAD currently has 200 member clubs and affiliated organizations, with membership approaching 25,000 (Paciorek and Jones, 1994).

The worldwide counterpart of AAAD is the Comité International des Sports des Sourds (CISS), or the International Committee of Silent Sports. The desire of deaf sports organizations to continue self-government and to avoid being viewed as organizations for persons with disabilities sparked controversy when CISS decided to join the international disabled sport organization, International Paralympic Committee. Instead of participating in the Paralympic, though, deaf sport continues to hold its own summer and winter World Games for the Deaf (WGD) for men and women every four years. Winter events include the following:

- alpine and Nordic skiing
- ice hockey
- speed skating

Summer events include:

- badminton
- basketball
- cycling
- men's wrestling
- shooting
- soccer
- swimming
- table tennis
- team handball
- tennis
- track and field
- volleyball
- water polo (Paciorek and Jones, 1994)

The rules followed by AAAD and CISS are nearly identical to those used in other hearing national and international competitions. A few changes have been made to use visual rather than auditory cues. For example, a whistle is blown *and* a flag is waved in team sports to stop play. In track, lighting systems, placed 50 meters in front of the starting blocks and to the side of the track, are used to signal the start of a race (Bessler, 1990).

Involving youth in deaf sport is an important objective of AAAD. The Annual Mini Deaf Sports Festival, held in Louisville, Kentucky, is specifically designed for the participation of 6 to 18 year olds (Paciorek and Jones, 1994). Physical educators are encouraged to refer to the resource section of this chapter to learn more about student involvement in deaf sport and to share this information with their deaf students.

The sport skills of deaf athletes span the range found in the hearing population, from unskilled to highly skilled. Deaf athletes are capable of competing as equals among hearing athletes, and some do so with much success. As far back as 1883, deaf athletes were competing professionally in this country. In that year Edward Dundon became the first recorded deaf professional baseball player. Scores have followed his example. Deaf athletes have also excelled in sports such as swimming, wrestling, football, and bowling. At least eight deaf bowlers have bowled a sanctioned perfect 300 game. Deaf women have also excelled in sports. Kitty O'Neal has earned the title of "Fastest Woman on Earth" for her women's world speed records in waterskiing (104.85 mph), rocket-powered car driving (512.083 mph), and quarter-mile car speed record (395.54 mph). Some deaf athletes have gone on to coach hearing teams, such as Albert Berg, who became the first football coach at Purdue University in 1887.

Deaf sport can be thought of as a vehicle for understanding the dynamics of being deaf. It facilitates a social identification among deaf people that is not easily obtained in other sociocultural contexts. . . . It relies on a deaf perspective to define its social patterns of behaviors, and it presents an orientation to deafness that is distinctly different from that endorsed by hearing institutions. Essentially, deaf sport emphasizes the honor of being Deaf, whereas society tends to focus on the adversity of deafness. (Stewart, 1991, p. 1).

SUMMARY

There is much variation among individuals with visual impairments or hearing losses. The characteristics of individuals with visual impairments depend in large part on the age at which sight was lost and the degree of loss. Most of the half million people in the United States who are legally blind have some sight remaining. To aid learning, physical educators need to enhance the visual cues while augmenting them with kinesthetic and auditory cues. Characteristics of individuals with hearing loss depend in large part on the degree of loss. To aid learning, physical educators need to enhance communication and promote social interaction, while holding high expectations for the person's motor performance. The physical educator has the important role of introducing individuals to sports and encouraging their participation, allowing each to choose whether to participate through the auspices of USABA, AAAD, or integrated sports.

ACKNOWLEDGMENT

The author gratefully acknowledges the contribution of Lauren Lieberman to content in this chapter. Lauren has worked extensively with individuals who are deaf, blind, and deaf-blind through her teaching at Perkins School for the Blind.

BIBLIOGRAPHY

Antia, S.D., Kreimeyer, K.H., & Eldridge, N. (1993). Promoting social interaction between young children with hearing impairments and their peers. *Exceptional Children*, **60**(3), 262–275.

Arnhold, R.W. & McGrain, P. (1985). Selected kinematic patterns of visually impaired youth in sprint running. *Adapted Physical Activity Quarterly*, **(2**(3), 206–213.

Balan, C.M. & Davis, W.E. (1993). Ecological task analysis: An approach to teaching physical education. *Journal of Physical Education, Recreation and Dance*, **64**(9), 54–61.

Bessler, H. (1990). The deaf sprinter: An analysis of starting techniques. *Palaestra*, **6**(4), 32–37.

Buell, C.E. (1966). *Physical education for blind children*. Springfield, IL: Charles C Thomas.

Butterfield, S.A. (1986). Gross motor profiles of deaf children. *Perceptual and Motor Skills*, **62**, 68–70.

Butterfield, S.A. (1988). Deaf children in physical education. *Palaestra*, **6**(4), 28–30, 52.

Butterfield, S.A. (1989). Influence of age, sex, hearing loss, and balance on development of throwing by deaf children. *Perceptual and Motor Skills*, **69**, 448–450.

Butterfield, S.A. (1990). Influence of age, sex, hearing loss, and balance on development of sidearm striking by deaf children. *Perceptual and Motor Skills*, **70**, 361–362.

Butterfield, S.A. (1991). Physical education and sport for the deaf: Rethinking the least restrictive environment. *Adapted Physical Activity Quarterly*, **8**, 95–102.

Butterfield, S.A. & Ersing, W.F. (1988). Influence of age, sex, hearing loss, and balance on development of catching by deaf children. *Perceptual and Motor Skills*, **66**, 997–998.

Chin, D.L. (1988). Dance movement instruction: Effects on spatial awareness in visually impaired elementary students. *Journal of Visual Impairment and Blindness*, **82**(5), 188–192.

di Natale, J., Lee, M., Ward, G., & Shepard, R.J. (1985). Loss of physical condition in sightless adolescents during a summer vacation. *Adapted Physical Activities Quarterly*, **2**, 144–150.

Dolnick, E. (1993). Deafness as culture. *Atlantic*, **272**, (3), 37–53.

Dye, L.A. (1983). *A study of augmented modes of feedback used by blind children to learn a selected motor task*. Unpublished doctoral dissertation, New York University.

Education for All Handicapped Children Act of 1975, § 121a.5, U.S.C. § 1401 (1977).

Freeman, R.D., Carbin, C.F., & Boese, R.J. (1981). *Can't your child hear? A guide for those who care about deaf children*. Austin, TX: Pro-Ed.

Hattin, H., Fraser, M., Ward, G.R., & Shepard, R.J. (1986). Are deaf children unusually fit? A comparison of fitness between deaf and blind children. *Adapted Physical Activity Quarterly*, **3**, 268–275.

Hopper, C. (1988). Self-concept and motor performance of hearing-impaired boys and girls. *Adapted Physical Activity Quarterly*, **5**(4), 293–304.

Kreimeyer, K., & Antia, S. (1988). The development and generalization of social interaction skills in preschool hearing-impaired children. *Volta Review*, **90**(4), 219–231.

Luckner, J. (1993). Developing independent and responsible behaviors in students who are deaf or hard of hearing. *Teaching Exceptional Children*, **26**(2), 13–25.

McInnes, J.M., & Treffry, J.A. (1982). *Deaf-blind infants and children: A developmental guide*. Toronto: University of Toronto Press.

Office of Special Education Programs (1992). *Fourteenth Annual Report to Congress on the Implementation of the Individuals with Disabilities Education Act.* Washington, DC: U.S. Department of Education.

Paciorek, M.J., & Jones, J.A. (1994). *Sports and recreation for the disabled.* Carmel, IN: Cooper.

Schmidt, S. (1985). Hearing-impaired students in physical education. *Adapted Physical Activity Quarterly,* **2**, 300–306.

Schneekloth, L.H. (1989). Play environments for visually impaired children. *Journal of Visual Impairment and Blindness,* **83**(4), 196–201.

Scott, R.A. (1969). *The making of blind men: A study of adult socialization.* New York: Russell Sage Foundation.

Stewart, D.A. (1991). *Deaf sport: The impact of sports within the deaf community.* Washington, DC: Gallaudet University.

Stewart, D.A., Dummer, G.M., & Haubenstricker, J.L. (1990). Review of administration procedures used to assess the motor skills of deaf children and youth. *Adapted Physical Activity Quarterly,* **7**, 231–239.

Stillman, R. (1978). *Callier Azusa Scale.* Dallas: South Central Center for Communication Disorders, University of Texas at Dallas.

Tapp, K.L. et al. (1991). *A guide to curriculum planning for visually impaired students* (Bulletin No. 91540.1). Madison: Wisconsin State Department of Public Instruction.

Winnick, J.P. (1985). The performance of visually impaired youngsters in physical education activities: Implications for mainstreaming. *Adapted Physical Activity Quarterly,* **2**, 292–299.

Winnick, J.P., & Short, F.X. (1985). *Physical fitness testing of the disabled: Project UNIQUE.* Champaign, IL: Human Kinetics.

Winnick, J.P., & Short, F.X. (1986). Physical fitness of adolescents with auditory impairments. *Adapted Physical Activity Quarterly,* **3**, 58–66.

RESOURCES ON VISUAL IMPAIRMENTS

International Blind Sports Association (IBSA)
Enrique Sanz Jimenez
Diego de Lion
58-Baja DCHA 28006 Madrid, Spain

Lieberman, L. and Cowart, J. (In press). *Motivational adapted activities: Games and activities for individuals who are blind or multihandicapped.* Reston, VA: American Alliance for Health, Physical Education, Recreation and Dance.

National Beep Baseball Association (NBBA)
9623 Spencer Highway
La Porte, TX 77571
(713) 476-1592

United States Association for Blind Athletes (USABA)
33 North Institute Street
Colorado Springs, CO 80903
phone (719) 630-0422
FAX (719) 630-0616

RESOURCES ON HARD OF HEARING AND DEAFNESS

American Athletic Association of the Deaf (AAAD)
3607 Washington Boulevard, Suite 4
Ogden, UT 84403-1737
(801) 393-7916 TDD
(801) 393-8710 Voice
(801) 393-2263 FAX

Comité International des Sports des Sourds (CISS)
Jerald M. Jordan
826 Locust Drive
West River, MD 20778
FAX (410) 867-1310

Grupp, M. (Producer). (1981). *Sign of victory* (Film). Film-Makers Library
124 East 40th Street
New York, NY 10016
phone (212) 808-4980
FAX (212) 808-4983
The movie presents the story of the championship girls' basketball team from Rhode Island School for the Deaf.

Mini Deaf Sports Festival
Tim Owens
P.O. Box 5455
Louisville, KY 40205

RESOURCES ON DEAF-BLIND IMPAIRMENTS

Cooley, E. (Producer) (1987). *Getting in touch: Communicating with a child who is deaf-blind.* Oregon Research Institute. Available through Research Press, Department J, P.O. Box 9177, Champaign, IL 61826; phone (217) 352-3273; FAX (217) 352-1221. This 19-minute video describes and demonstrates basic procedures that can be used to help deaf-blind children understand.

Lange, E. (Baud, H., Ed.) (1975). *Adapted physical education for the deaf-blind child.* Raleigh, NC: Department of Public Instruction. This curriculum guide addresses teaching physical education to deaf-blind children.

CHAPTER 11

Cerebral Palsy, Traumatic Brain Injury, Stroke, Amputations, Dwarfism, and Other Orthopedic Impairments

David L. Porretta

Individuals with cerebral palsy (CP), traumatic brain injury (TBI), stroke, dwarfism, and Les Autres (a French term meaning "the others") impairments were at one time restricted from physical activity for fear that it would aggravate their conditions. Now, these persons are encouraged to participate in a great variety of physical education and sport activities. Educators and medical specialists alike now realize the benefits of physical activity for the development of physical and motor fitness, self-image, and socialization especially for children and youth possessing these disabilities.

CEREBRAL PALSY

Cerebral palsy (CP) is a group of permanent disabling symptoms resulting from damage to the motor control areas of the brain. It is a nonprogressive condition that may originate before, during, or after birth and that manifests itself in a loss or impairment of control over voluntary musculature. Depending on the location and the amount of damage to the brain, symptoms may vary widely, ranging from severe (total inability to control bodily movements) to very mild (only a slight

speech impairment). Damage to the brain contributes to abnormal reflex development in the majority of individuals; this results in difficulty coordinating and integrating basic movement patterns. It is rare for damage to be isolated in a small portion of the brain. For this reason, the person commonly exhibits a multiplicity of other impairments, which may include mental retardation, seizures, speech and language disorders, and sensory impairments (especially those involving visual-motor control). CP can result from a myriad of prenatal, natal, or postnatal causes. Some of the more common causes are rubella, Rh incompatibility, prematurity, birth trauma, anoxia, meningitis, poisoning, brain hemorrhages or tumors, and other forms of brain injury that may result from accidents or abuse.

Incidence

According to the most recent figures published by United Cerebral Palsy Associations, Inc., it is estimated that as many as 700,000 Americans possess CP. There are now fewer infants born with CP because of the current low birth rate and better prenatal care in the United States. It is estimated that about 3,000 infants are born with CP each year, not to mention very young children who acquire the condition. Enhanced technology and treatment in neonatal intensive care units have led to a decrease in the number of "high-risk" infants who might have otherwise acquired the condition.

Classifications

Individuals with CP typically exhibit a variety of observable symptoms, depending on the degree and location of brain damage. Over the years, classification schemes have evolved that categorize CP according to *topographical (anatomical site), neuromotor (medical),* and *functional* perspectives (of which the functional classification is the most recent).

Topographical

The topographical classification is based on the body segments afflicted. Classes include

- monoplegia—any one body part involved,
- diplegia—major involvement of both lower limbs and minor involvement of both upper limbs,
- hemiplegia—involvement of one complete side of the body (arm and leg),
- paraplegia—involvement of both lower limbs only,
- triplegia—any three limbs involved (this is a rare occurrence), and
- quadriplegia—also known as total body involvement (all four limbs, head, neck, and trunk).

Neuromotor

Approximately 40 years ago, the American Academy for Cerebral Palsy adopted a neuromotor classification system to describe cerebral palsy. This system comprises six types.

Spasticity

Spasticity results from damage to motor areas of the cerebrum and is characterized by increased muscle tone (hypertonicity), primarily of the flexors and internal rotators, which may lead to permanent contractures and bone deformities. Strong, exaggerated muscle contractions are common, and in some cases muscles will continue to contract repetitively. Spasticity is associated with a *hyperactive stretch reflex.* The hyperactive reflex can be elicited, for example, when muscles of the anterior forearm (flexors) are quickly stretched to extend

the wrist. When this happens, receptors that control tone in the stretched muscles overreact, causing the stretched muscles to contract. This results in inaccurate and jerky movement, with the wrist assuming a flexed as opposed to an extended or midposition. If muscles of the upper limb are prone to spasticity, the shoulder will be adducted, the arm will be carried toward the midline of the body, and the forearm will be flexed and pronated. The wrist will be hyperflexed and the hand will be fisted.

Lower-limb involvement results in hip flexion, with the thigh pulling toward the midline, causing the leg to cross during ambulation. Lower-limb involvement causes flexion at the knee joint because of tight hamstring muscles. Increased tone in both the gastrocnemius and soleus muscles and a shortened Achilles tendon contribute to excessive plantar flexion of the foot. A scissoring gait characterized by flexion of the hip, knee, and ankle along with rotation of the leg toward the midline is exhibited (Figure 11.1). With their narrow base of support, people with a scissoring gait typically have problems with balance and locomotor activities. Because of increased muscle contraction and limited range of motion, they may have difficulty running, jumping, and throwing properly. Mental

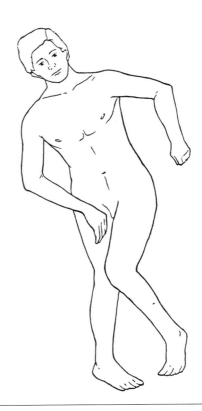

Figure 11.1 Person exhibiting spastic cerebral palsy.

retardation, seizures, and perceptual disorders are more common in spasticity than in any other type of CP.

Athetosis

Damage to the basal ganglia (masses of gray matter composed of neurons located deep within the cerebral hemispheres of the brain) results in an overflow of motor impulses to the muscles, a condition known as athetosis (Figure 11.2). Slow, writhing movements that are uncoordinated and involuntary are characteristic of this type of CP. Muscle tone tends to fluctuate from hypertonicity to hypotonicity; the fluctuation typically affects muscles that control the head, neck, limbs, and trunk. Severe difficulty in head control is usually exhibited, with head drawn back and positioned to one side. Facial grimacing, a protruding tongue, and trouble controlling salivation are common. The individual has difficulty eating, drinking, and speaking. Because lack of head control affects visual pursuit, individuals may have difficulty tracking thrown balls or responding to quick movements made by others in motor activity situations. They will have difficulty performing movements that require accuracy, such as throwing a ball to a target or kicking a moving ball. A lordotic standing posture, in which the lumbar spine assumes an abnormal anterior curve, is common. In compensation, the arms and shoulders are placed in a forward position. Athetoids typically exhibit aphasia (impairment or loss of language) and articulation difficulties. This type comprises approximately 20% of the entire population of individuals with CP.

Ataxia

Damage to the cerebellum, which normally regulates balance and muscle coordination, results in a condition known as ataxia (see Figure 11.2). Muscles show abnormal degrees of hypotonicity. Ataxia is usually not diagnosed until the child attempts to walk. When trying to walk, the individual is extremely unsteady because of balance difficulties and lacks the coordination necessary for proper arm and leg movement. A wide-based gait is typically exhibited. Nystagmus, a constant involuntary movement of the eyeball, is commonly observed, and those able to ambulate frequently fall. People with mild forms of ataxia are often considered clumsy or awkward. They will experience difficulty with basic motor skills and patterns, especially locomotor activities like running, jumping, and skipping. Ataxia occurs in about 10% of the entire population of individuals with CP.

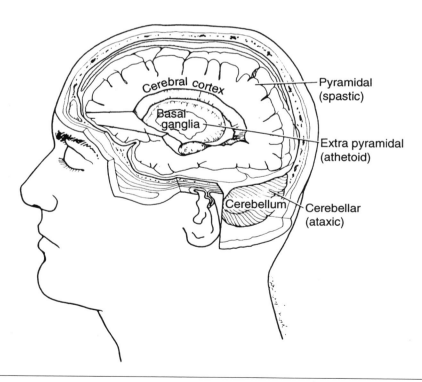

Figure 11.2 General areas of the brain involved in major neuromotor types of cerebral palsy.
From *Physically Handicapped Children: A Medical Atlas for Teachers* (2nd ed.), p. 67 by E.E. Bleck and D.A. Nagel (Eds.), 1982, New York: by Allyn and Bacon. Adapted by permission.

Tremor

Tremor results from damage to the basal ganglia (Figure 11.2) and is characterized by involuntary rhythmic movement. Voluntary movements tend to increase shaking and trembling of the affected limb. Tremor can be classified as either nonintentional (continuous) or intentional (only when movement is attempted). Nonintentional tremor is uncommon in children. People who have cerebral palsy of the tremor type have greater success with gross rather than with fine motor movements. Unlike gross motor activities, where general movement patterns predominate, fine motor activities require precision of movement. As a result, such activities as writing, drawing, archery, or pistol shooting will be difficult. Only about 2% of all individuals with CP exhibit tremor.

Rigidity

Rigidity is associated with diffuse damage to the brain, not damage to any specific area. It is considered a severe form of spasticity in which the stretch reflex is weak or absent. Severe hypotonicity and reduced range of motion are presented, and individuals usually have total body involvement (quadriplegic). The elbows, knee joints, and spine tend to remain in an extended position. Flexion movements are therefore difficult, and the rigid limb exhibits greater resistance to slow than to rapid movement. Some activities, like certain dances that require the person to perform slowly while bending the limbs and trunk, will be difficult if not impossible. Severe mental retardation is common; therefore, uncomplicated lead-up activities should be presented. Only about 2% to 4% of all individuals with CP are affected by rigidity.

Mixed

When an individual possesses two (usually spasticity and athetosis) or more of the above conditions in equal degrees, a rare mixed condition exists. People assigned to the mixed classification usually have total body involvement and have both spasticity and athetosis equally.

Functional

A *functional classification* scheme is commonly used today in the field of education. According to this classification system, persons are placed into one of eight ability classes according to the severity of the disability (see Table 11.1). Class I denotes severe impairment, while Class VIII denotes very minimal impairment. This scheme has important implications for physical education and sport, because individuals are categorized according to ability levels. For example, participants in Classes VII and VIII may be good candidates for inclusion in several regular physical education activities. Teachers and coaches can also use this system, as does the United States Cerebral Palsy Athletic Association (USCPAA), to equalize competition among participants. In activities requiring competition between two individuals, players of the same classification can compete against each other. In team activities, players of the same class can be placed on separate teams so that each team is composed of players of similar functional levels. These suggestions for equalizing competition can be followed in either integrated or nonintegrated settings.

General Educational Considerations

From a medical standpoint, treatment for CP is aimed at alleviating symptoms caused by damage to the brain. This consists of treating motor and other associated disabilities. Treatment for motor dysfunction usually entails developing voluntary muscle control, emphasizing muscle relaxation, and increasing functional motor skills. In some instances, braces and orthotic devices are used to help prevent permanent contractures or support affected muscle groups; this is especially true for those with spasticity. Surgery can be performed to lengthen contracted tendons (especially the Achilles tendon) or to reposition an unimpaired muscle to perform the movement of an impaired one. A repositioning operation known as the Eggar's procedure relieves flexion at the knee joint and helps to extend the hip by transferring the insertion of the hamstrings from the pelvis to the femur. In rare instances, brain surgery can alleviate extreme hypertonicity. A procedure known as **chronic cerebellar stimulation (CCS)**, in which electrodes are surgically implanted on the cerebellum, has recently been developed. CCS has demonstrated improvement; however, long-range effects on the central nervous system have not yet been documented and it seems that this procedure results in little direct clinical application at this time.

Because of central nervous system damage, many individuals with CP exhibit abnormal reflex development, which interferes with the acquisition of voluntary movement. If abnormal reflex patterns are present, young children with CP will most likely receive some type of physical therapy treatment designed to inhibit abnormal reflex activity in addition to enhancing flexibility and body alignment. However, recent scientific data show that passive activities and manipulations during the early years may not provide as much assistance in the remediation of abnormal reflex activity as

Table 11.1 Functional Classification Profile for Cerebral Palsy

	Class Description	Mode of Ambulation
I	Severe spasticity and athetosis in all extremities; poor to non-existent trunk control; poor functional range of motion and strength; only thumb and one finger for opposition; can grasp only bean bag.	Motorized wheelchair
II	Severe to moderate spastic and/or athetoid quadriplegic; poor functional strength in all extremities and poor trunk control; classified as Class II lower if one or two lower extremities are functional; otherwise, classified as Class II upper (can manipulate and throw a ball)	Propels wheelchair on level surfaces and slight inclines (lower Class II with legs only)
III	Moderate quadriplegic or triplegic; severe hemiplegic; fair to normal strength in one upper extremity; limited extension in follow through when throwing with dominant arm; normal grasp of round objects, but release is slow.	Can propel wheelchair independently, but may walk a short distance with assistance or assistive devices.
IV	Moderate to severe diplegic; good functional strength and minimal control problems in upper extremities and torso; normal follow through is evident when throwing.	Assistive devices used for distances; wheelchair is usually used for sport
V	Moderate to severe diplegic or hemiplegic; moderate to severe involvement in one or both legs; good functional strength; good balance when assistive devices are used; minimal control problems in upper limbs.	No wheelchair; may or may not use assistive devices
VI	Moderate to severe quadriplegic; fluctuating muscle tone producing involuntary movements in trunk and both sets of extremities; greater upper limb involvement when spasticity/athetosis present; running gait often shows better mechanics than walk.	Ambulates without aids.
VII	Moderate to minimal spastic hemiplegic; good functional ability on nonaffected side.	Walks and runs without assistive devices, but has marked asymmetrical gait
VIII	Minimal hemiplegic, monoplegic, diplegic, or quadriplegic; may have minimal coordination problems and good balance.	Runs and jumps freely with little or no limp

Note. From *United States Cerebral Palsy Athletic Association Sports Rules Manual* (4th ed.). (pp. A1–N22), 1991, Dallas, TX: USCPAA. Adapted by permission.

once thought. Treatment emphasis should be directed toward having individuals perform and refine motor tasks by active self-control. Functional motor skills such as walking, grasping, and throwing should be developed and attained.

Attention must also be given to the psychological and social development of individuals with CP. The various disabilities associated with CP increase the possibility of adjustment problems. Because of the negative reactions that other people may have to their condition, individuals with CP may not be totally accepted. As a result, guidance from psychologists or professional counselors should be sought for both parents and their children when emotional conflicts arise.

The primary concern should be for the *total* person. A team approach is recommended in which both medical and educational personnel work together with the parent and, when appropriate, the student.

TRAUMATIC BRAIN INJURY

Traumatic brain injury (TBI) refers to an insult to the brain that may produce a diminished or altered state of consciousness and that results in impairments of physical, cognitive, social, behavioral, and emotional functioning. Physical impairments include lack of coordination, planning and sequencing movements, muscle spasticity, headaches, speech disorders, paralysis, and seizures as well as a variety of sensory impairments (which include vision and hearing problems). Physical impairments often cause varying degrees of orthopedic involvement that require the use of crutches or wheelchairs. Even when individuals exhibit no loss of coordination, motor function deficits, or sensation, apraxia may be evident. Cognitive impairments often result in short- and/or long-term memory deficits, poor attention and concentration, altered perception, communication disorders such as reading and writing skills, and poor judgment. Social, emotional, and behavioral impairments may include mood swings, lack of motivation, self-centeredness, inability to self-monitor, difficulty with impulse control, depression, sexual dysfunction, excessive laughing or crying, and difficulty relating to others. Any or all of the above impairments vary greatly depending on the extent and location of damage to the brain and the success of the rehabilitation process. Therefore, impairments could range from mild to severe. However, with immediate and ongoing therapy these impairments may decrease in severity. Because of the developmental nature of the central nervous system, children with TBI recover motor and verbal skills faster than adults. However, children's head injuries tend to be more diffuse than focal. A diffuse injury may affect the entire range of academic achievement and therefore has significant educational implications for the child.

TBI is often referred to as the "silent epidemic" because impairments continue even though no external visible signs are present on or around the face and head area. TBI can result from motor vehicle, sports, and recreation accidents, child abuse, assaults and violence, and accidental falls. In addition, TBI can be caused from anoxia, cardiac arrest, or near drowning. Motor vehicle accidents are the leading cause of TBI, falls are second, and assaults are third. Since TBI is so common, it is now identified as a separate categorical condition in current federal legislation pertaining to the education of children and youth with disabilities (Individuals with Disabilities Education Act).

Incidence

According to the National Head Injury Foundation, TBI is the leading killer and cause of disability in children and young adults in the United States. Head injuries are 10 times more frequent than spinal cord injuries. Every year in the United States two million people sustain a TBI. Of this number, thousands will die. Of those who survive, approximately 70,000 to 90,000 will suffer a permanent loss of function. Twice as many males are likely to sustain a TBI than females, and the highest rate of injury is among young men between the ages of 15 and 24.

Classification

Generally there are two classifications of head injury: open and closed (National Head Injury Foundation, 1989). An open head injury may result from an accident, gunshot wound, or blow to the head by an object, resulting in a visible injury. On the other hand, a closed head injury may be caused by severe shaking, lack of oxygen (anoxia), or cranial hemorrhages. If the head injury is closed, damage to the brain is usually diffuse; however, if the head injury is open (e.g., bullet wound), damage is usually to a more limited area of the brain. In "Shaken Infant Syndrome," the brain is actually shaken back and forth within the skull. This type of injury either bruises or tears nerve fibers in the brain that send messages to other parts of the central nervous system and all parts of the body. TBI can range from very mild to severe. Severe brain injury is characterized by a prolonged state in which the person is unconscious (coma) and a number of functional limitations remain following rehabilitation. An injury to the brain can be considered minor when no formal rehabilitation program is prescribed and the person is sent directly home from the hospital. However, minor brain injury should never be treated as unimportant.

The Ranchos Los Amigos Hospital Scale describes eight levels of cognitive functioning and is typically used in the first few weeks or months following injury. These levels are (1) no response—deep sleep/coma; (2) generalized response—inconsistent and nonspecific response to stimuli; (3) localized response—may follow simple commands in an inconsistent and delayed manner, with vague awareness of self; (4) confused/agitated—severely decreased ability to process information, with poor discrimination and attention span; (5) confused/inappropriate—consistent response to simple commands, highly distractible, and needs frequent redirection; (6) confused/appropriate—responses may be incorrect due to memory but are appropriate to the situation, exhibits retention of tasks relearned, inconsistently oriented; (7) automatic/appropriate—appropriate and oriented behavior but lacks insight, exhibits poor judgment and problem solving, requires minimal supervision; and (8) purposeful/appropriate—ability to integrate recent and past events, requires no supervision once new activities are learned. This scale should not be used in later years as a gauge for improved function.

General Educational Considerations

Persons who possess TBI, depending on the severity of the injury, will need an individualized rehabilitative program. Persons suffering from severe injury will initially need to be provided acute rehabilitative programs where therapy begins as soon as they are medically stable. An interdisciplinary team of medical professionals such as physicians, nurses, and speech and occupational therapists provide such a program of therapy, which usually lasts for three to four months depending on the nature of the injury. For persons of school age, the acute rehabilitative program will take precedence over educational considerations. However, Ylvisaker, Hartwick, & Stevens (1991) suggest that medical personnel pursue the following shortly after admission: (1) obtain school records to understand the student's academic, intellectual, and psychosocial baseline; (2) initiate discussion with appropriate school officials if (when) special education programs are needed; (3) invite school personnel to visit the medical facility and observe the student's initial therapy program as soon as medically feasible; and (4) begin informal discussion of TBI, its possible outcome, and school services frequently needed.

Following the acute rehabilitation program, individuals will be provided a long-term rehabilitation program that offers a structured environment for those who make slow improvements. As long as progress is being made, the person will remain at this level of rehabilitation. Individuals of school age will typically receive their educational program within the hospital or rehabilitative facility.

Some persons, because of the severity of their injuries, will need extended therapy programs following long-term care. These extended and structured therapy programs usually last from 6 to 12 months following injury and usually emphasize cognitive skills, speech therapy, **activities of daily living (ADL)**, the relearning of social skills, recreation therapy, and prevocational and vocational training when appropriate. Individualized educational programming continues in this environment.

Only after persons have attained the maximum benefit of rehabilitation programs will they reenter their local educational environment. Both rehabilitation and educational personnel should work cooperatively to ensure the best possible transition from the rehabilitation facility to the school environment (Cohen, 1991). Approximately 4 to 8 weeks before discharge, Ylvisaker et al. (1991) suggest that the medical staff conduct the following: (1) explore all relevant educational variables such as scheduling, instructional materials, work expectations, and motivational variables; (2) prepare a videotape illustrating things such as behavior management, personal interaction with the student, use of therapeutic equipment, and physical handling; (3) visit the school to ascertain its physical layout and level of stimulation and cognitive needs; and (4) serve as members of the student's IEP planning team. In line with current educational guidelines, students need to be placed in as normalized an environment as possible. Once in an appropriate educational environment, students typically need to relearn skills previously acquired and not necessarily learn new skills for the first time.

The National Head Injury Foundation suggests a number of strategies for teachers. These include (1) redirecting the student when he/she appears "lost," shows signs of frustration, and is not able to keep up with classmates, (2) allowing for periods of rest to counteract fatigue, especially toward the end of the school day, (3) refraining from reprimands for lack of student attention because it may be partly caused by internal stimuli, (4) presenting material or instructions in a slower manner (students should be encouraged to ask the teacher to repeat, if needed), (5) encouraging and teaching the student to construct flowcharts, outlines, and graphs or to keep a diary/datebook to help organize information to facilitate memory processes, (6) teaching the student to use special techniques to remember material, and (7) breaking up a task into smaller and distinct parts so that they can be put together meaningfully at the end. A number of these strategies have direct implications for physical education and are discussed in detail in the section on program implications.

STROKE

Stroke (cerebral vascular disease) refers to brain tissue damage caused by faulty blood circulation. Stroke can seriously damage areas of the brain that control vital functions. These functions may include motor ability and control, sensation and perception, communication, emotions, and consciousness. In certain cases, stroke results in death. As a result, those persons who survive have varying degrees of disability, ranging from minimal loss of function to total dependency. Because of the nature of the cerebral arterial system, stroke commonly causes partial or total paralysis on either the left or right side of the body. This may be one limb (monoplegia) or body segment or the entire side (hemiplegia). Individuals with right-sided hemiplegia are likely to have problems with speech and language, and they tend to be slow, cautious, and disorganized when approaching new or unfamiliar problems. On the other hand, individuals with left-sided hemiplegia are likely to have difficulty with spatial-perceptual tasks (i.e., ability to judge distance, size, position, rate of movement, form and how parts relate to the whole) and tend to overestimate their abilities. They often try to do things they cannot do and that may be unsafe. This has significant implications for those performing in physical education, leisure, and sport settings.

A number of factors (risk factors) contribute to the occurrence of stroke. These include uncontrolled hypertension (high blood pressure), smoking, diabetes mellitus, diet, drug abuse (such as heroin and cocaine), obesity, and alcohol consumption. Many of these risk factors can be controlled through appropriate medical treatment. Over the past few years, there has been a substantial increase in the amount of knowledge regarding stroke and how it is treated, especially with regard to the promotion of healthful behaviors. As a result of better education and treatment, an increased number of people are living who otherwise might have died following a stroke.

Depending on the location of the damage, symptoms mirror those of cerebral palsy and TBI. Persons may exhibit cognitive and/or perceptual deficits, motor deficits, seizure disorders, and communication problems. While individuals with TBI and stroke can expect varying degrees of improvement following their injury, individuals with CP cannot. Research indicates that children show more improvement following brain trauma (TBI and stroke) than adults.

Incidence

According to recent figures (Bronstein, Popovich and Stewart-Amidei, 1991), more than two million people in the United States are living with neurological impairment caused by stroke. It is estimated that one or two people per 1000 experience a stroke each year. Stroke is the third largest cause of death in the United States, following heart disease and cancer. However, statistics indicate that the incidence of stroke is declining. Recent statistics also indicate that more than half of all individuals. will survive their first stroke, although only about 10% of these individuals will completely recover. Males have a higher incidence rate than females, and black persons are more prone to strokes than white persons. Typically, stroke affects older segments of the population. Stroke occuring in infants, children, and adolescents is rare when compared to adults. Nonetheless, the occurrences of stroke in infants, children, and adolescents have significant implications for educators.

Classification

Although there are many types, stroke can generally be divided into two distinct categories: hemorrhage and ischemia. Hemorrhage within the brain occurs when an artery loses its elasticity and ruptures, causing blood to flow into and around brain tissue. This type of hemorrhage is commonly called cerebral hemorrhage and is the most serious form of stroke. Ischemia, on the other hand, refers to the lack of blood to brain tissue. The lack of blood results from a blocked artery leading to or within the brain itself. Typically, the blockage results from a progressive narrowing of the artery or from an embolism. An embolism is usually a blood clot or piece of fat deposit (plaque) that may lodge in small arteries. An insufficient or absent blood supply means that oxygen, which is vital for proper brain functioning, is absent or diminished. This interruption may be permanent or for a brief period. If the attack is very brief, it is termed a transient ischemic attack (TIA). About 10% of all strokes are preceded by TIAs and may occur days, weeks, or months before a major stroke. This type of ischemia results in full recovery; however, it may indicate a future attack that is more severe. Aside from a TIA, whether a person experiences either hemorrhage or ischemia, brain tissue dies, which results in reduced brain function or death.

Educational Considerations

While many strokes occur without warning, some individuals will experience warning. Teachers and coaches should be aware of some common warnings signs of stroke. These are sudden weakness or numbness of the face or the arm and leg on one side of the body; sudden dimness or loss of vision in only one eye; sudden loss of speech or trouble understanding speech; sudden severe headaches with no apparent cause; and unexplained dizziness, unsteadiness, or sudden falls, especially with any of the previous symptoms. Teachers and coaches should have students seek medical attention immediately, especially if these students have heart and/or circulatory problems or have experienced previous brain injury.

Immediately following a stroke, persons surviving will need to be placed on a systematic and individualized rehabilitation program. However, the intensity and duration of the rehabilitation program will depend on the degree of disability. For example, a person who has **paresis** (muscle weakness) or paralysis in one limb and retains normal voluntary movement for the reminder of the body will need little in the form of intense therapy. On the other hand, a person exhibiting complete paralysis of all four limbs will need more intense therapy. From an educational standpoint, individuals of school age will follow a school reentry program very similar to those individuals with TBI, as described in the previous section.

AMPUTATIONS

Amputation refers to the loss of an entire limb or a specific limb segment. Amputations may be categorized as either acquired or congenital. Acquired amputations can result from disease, tumor, or trauma; congenital amputations result from failure of the fetus to properly develop during the first 3 months of gestation. In most cases, the cause or causes of partial or total congenital limb absence are unknown. Generally, there are two types of congenital deformities. In one type, a middle segment of a limb is absent, but the proximal and distal portions are intact; this is known as *phocomelia*. Here, the hand or foot is attached directly to the shoulder or hip without the remaining anatomical structures present. The second type of deficiency is similar to surgical amputation, where no normal structures, like hands or fingers, are present below the missing segment. In many cases, however, immature fingerlike buds are present; this deficiency is usually below the elbow and unilateral.

Incidence

Recent estimates indicate that 310,000 people in the United States are amputees, of whom more than two thirds are missing a lower limb. Of this number, about 7% are below 21 years of age. Unlike the general population of amputees, those below age 21 have a greater percentage of upper- than lower-limb losses. Congenital limb losses are approximately twice as prevalent as acquired losses for them.

Classification

Amputations can be classified according to the site and level of limb absence or from a *functional* point of view. Nine classes now in use by National Handicapped Sports (NHS) and the International Sports Organization for the Disabled (ISOD) are identified as follows:

- Class A1 Double above the knee (AK)
- Class A2 Single AK
- Class A3 Double below the knee (BK)
- Class A4 Single BK
- Class A5 Double above the elbow (AE)
- Class A6 Single AE
- Class A7 Double below the elbow (BE)
- Class A8 Single BE
- Class A9 Combined lower- plus upper-limb amputations

According to this system, Class A8 represents functional ability greater than Class A1.

General Educational Considerations

In nearly all cases, a *prosthetic device* is prescribed and selected for the amputee by a team of medical specialists. The prosthetic device is designed to compensate, as much as possible, for the functional loss of the limb. Devices are chosen according to the size of the individual and the area and extent of limb absence. Most authorities favor the use of a prosthetic device as early as possible following the loss of the limb because the device tends to be more easily incorporated into the person's normal body actions than if it were introduced later. Learning to use a device takes time and effort, and some individuals with more extensive lower-limb amputations need training with canes or crutches. With recent technological advances, new types of lower-limb prosthetic devices are now commonly used in sports to provide athletes with the most realistic sense of normal foot function. These devices provide an active push-off in which the device is propelling the body in a forward and/or vertical fashion. These prostheses, made of carbon graphite, possess a type of "dynamic response" in that they can store and release energy simulating the function of a normal foot. They respond smoothly, gradually, and proportionally to pressure applied by the user. Persons are fit individually with the assistance of computer-generated designs. As such, many athletes with both BK and AK amputations use these prostheses for competitive purposes in sports such as volleyball and basketball (which involve a significant amount of jumping), as well as sprinting and distance running (Figure 11.3). Several companies now offer these dynamic response devices commercially.

Individuals with limb deficiencies often have additional educational needs in the psychosocial domain that require attention. Many feel shame, inferiority, and anxiety when in a social setting—feelings that may result from the stares or comments of others. Individual counseling by a psychologist or professional counselor may be needed to foster healthy emotional functioning.

Figure 11.3 Todd Schaffhauser, a Paralympic Track Medalist, running with a dynamic response type prosthetic device.
Photo courtesy of artificial limb specialists C.A. Blatchford & Sons, Ltd., London, who sponsor Todd. Printed by permission.

DWARFISM

Dwarfism is a condition in which a person is of short stature (152.4 centimeters [5 feet] or less in height). When compared to the general population, people with dwarfism (also termed *little people*) are shorter than 98% of all other people. Generally, dwarfism may result from either the failure of cartilage to form into bone as the individual grows or from a pituitary irregularity. Aside from their short stature, people with dwarfism are considered normal.

Incidence

It is estimated that approximately 100,000 people in the United States possess some type of dwarfism. According to Crandall and Crosson (1994), 85–90% of all infants born with dwarfism are born to nondwarf, average-size parents. *Achondroplasia* is considered the most common type of disproportionate dwarfism.

Classification

Dwarfism can be classified as either proportionate or disproportionate. Proportionate dwarfism exhibits body parts that are proportionate but very short. This type of dwarfism results from a deficiency in the pituitary gland, which regulates growth. Disproportionate dwarfism, on the other hand, is characterized by short arms and legs with a normal torso and a large head. This type of dwarfism may be caused by a faulty gene, which results in failure of the bone to fully develop. Those persons with disproportionate dwarfism, or achondroplasia, are the most prevalent. *Achondroplasia* literally means the absence of normal cartilage formation and growth. It begins in utero, and may manifest itself in a waddling gait, lordosis, limited range of motion, and bowed legs. In more severe cases, where spinal involvement (such as scoliosis) as well as additional bone deformities are present, the individual with achondroplasia may require ambulation devices such as crutches.

Some persons with dwarfism who do not have achondroplasia may have cervical vertebrae abnormalities, similar to atlanto-axial instability in Down syndrome, which may lead to very serious neck injury. As such, the Dwarf Athletic Association of America (DAAA) requires a medical screening for all non-achondroplasic athletes before they can participate in running, jumping (basketball), and swimming (diving start) events.

General Educational Considerations

A physical education program for persons with dwarfism can and should follow the same guidelines as one developed for individuals without impairments. On an intellectual level, students with dwarfism do not function any differently than average-size students. Therefore, these individuals are to be treated the same as other students with regard to cognitive ability and academic achievement. People with dwarfism should have the opportunity to develop a positive self-image in a psychologically safe educational environment. Students with obvious physical differences and limitations are often held up to undue ridicule. It is the responsibility of the teacher to maintain an environment that encourages positive interactions and social contacts among all students.

LES AUTRES

Muscular Dystrophy

Muscular dystrophy is actually considered a group of inherited diseases characterized by progressive, diffuse weakness of various muscle groups. Muscle cells within the belly of the muscles degenerate and are replaced by adipose and connective tissue. The dystrophy itself is not fatal, but secondary complications of muscle weakness predispose the person to respiratory disorders and heart problems. It is quite common for individuals with dystrophy in advanced stages of the disease to die from a simple respiratory infection or as a result of myocardial infarction. Symptoms of the disease may appear any time between birth and middle age; however, muscular dystrophy usually strikes children.

There are various types of muscular dystrophy, including the *myotonic, facio-scapulo-humeral, limb-girdle*, and *Duchenne* types. Myotonic muscular dystrophy, also known as *Stienert's disease*, manifests itself through muscle weakness and affects the central nervous system, heart, eyes, and endocrine glands. It is a slowly progressing disease occurring between the ages of 20 to 40. Congenital myotonic dystrophy is rare, occurring almost exclusively in infants of mothers with the adult form. With appropriate care, their conditions often improve; however, delayed motor development and mental retardation in late infancy and early childhood are common. The facio-scapulo-humeral type initially affects muscles of the shoulders and face and, in some instances, the hip and thigh. Life

expectancy is usually normal because this type of dystrophy may arrest itself at any time. In limb-girdle muscular dystrophy, degeneration may begin in either the shoulder or the hip girdle, with eventual involvement of both. Unlike the facio-scapulo-humeral type, degeneration continues at a slow rate. Facio-scapulo-humeral dystrophy manifests itself during adolescence or adulthood. The limb-girdle type may be exhibited at any time from late childhood on, although it usually occurs during the teenage years. With both facio-scapulo-humeral and limb-girdle dystrophy, males and females are equally affected.

Duchenne muscular dystrophy is the most common and severe childhood form of the disease. It affects more boys than girls. Symptoms usually occur between ages 2 and 6. The Duchenne type is commonly referred to as *pseudohypertrophic muscular dystrophy*. A pseudohypertrophic appearance, especially of the calf and forearm muscles, is the result of an excessive accumulation of adipose and connective tissues within the interstitial spaces between degenerated muscle cells. It is yet to be determined precisely how this happens; however, the gene responsible for causing Duchenne dystrophy has been identified. Linked to this gene is a protein called dystrophin (dis-tro-pin). This protein (which is one of many) allows muscle cells to function properly; without it, the muscle cells eventually die. In persons with Duchenne dystrophy, this protein is absent. In an attempt to find a cure, researchers have recently transplanted healthy muscle cells into mice with Duchenne and have found that these muscle cells can actually produce dystrophin. However, a number of problems need to be overcome before this form of treatment can be offered to humans as a viable form of therapy.

Duchenne muscular dystrophy manifests itself in atrophy and weakness of the thigh, hip, back, shoulder girdle, and respiratory muscles. The anterior tibialis muscle of the lower leg becomes extremely weak, resulting in a *drop* foot where the foot remains angled in a downward manner; thus, the individual is prone to falling. Steady and rapid progression of the disease usually leads to the inability to walk within approximately 10 years after onset. The child exhibits characteristics that include

- a waddling gait,
- difficulty in climbing stairs,
- a tendency to fall, and
- difficulty in rising from a recumbent position.

An additional characteristic is a high level of creatine phosophokinase (CPK) in the blood.

Lordosis frequently develops from weakness of the trunk musculature. As the disease progresses, the individual eventually becomes confined to a wheelchair and grows obese. In addition, contractures may form at the ankle, knee, and hip joints, and muscle atrophy is extensive. Death often results in about the third decade of life. With continued research, such as muscle cell transplants, a cure for this type of dystrophy may be forthcoming. However, at present, no treatment exists to stop muscle atrophy; any treatment given is basically symptomatic. A major treatment goal is to maintain ambulation as long as possible through exercise and activity.

Physical education can play an important role in managing muscular dystrophy, especially when exercises and activities are performed during the initial stage of the disease. Muscular strength and endurance activities programmed on a regular basis can have a positive effect on muscular development and can serve to counteract muscular atrophy. Particular attention should be given to the development of the lower leg, hip, abdomen, and thigh since muscles of these areas are used for locomotion. For people with weak respiratory muscles, especially those confined to wheelchairs, breathing exercises and activities should be given priority and performed daily. Strength and endurance can be developed through aquatic activities, which utilize water as resistance. Performed on a regular basis, flexibility activities and exercises help to develop or maintain the person's range of motion so that permanent joint contractures do not develop; flexibility activities that keep the child's attention may be chosen. Low-intensity aerobic activities are also helpful in managing obesity, which is common in persons with muscular dystrophy. Various dance movements are particularly helpful for improving flexibility and cardiorespiratory efficiency. Arm and upper-body movements for those in wheelchairs can be performed to music. Postural exercises and activities help reduce lordosis and give the person an opportunity to perform out of the wheelchair.

Juvenile Rheumatoid Arthritis

Juvenile rheumatoid arthritis (JRA), or *Still's disease*, manifests itself in childhood and is one of several forms of juvenile arthritis. As with adult rheumatoid arthritis, the cause of JRA is unknown. Depending on the degree of involvement, JRA affects joint movement. Joints become inflamed, which results in reduced range of motion. In some cases, permanent joint contractures develop and muscle atrophy is pronounced. Some authorities suggest that joint inflammation results from abnormal antibodies of unknown origin that circulate in the blood and destroy the body's normal structures. The disease is not inherited, nor does it seem to be a result of climate, diet, or patterns of living. It may manifest itself as early as 6 weeks of age. According to current estimates from the Arthritis Foundation, as many as 165,000 children possess some form of arthritis to varying degrees. Of these, approximately 71,000 children in the United States possess JRA. The condition afflicts more girls than boys. JRA is characterized by a series of remissions and exacerbations (attacks). One cannot predict how long affected children will remain ill or the length of time they will be symptom-free. Generally, the prognosis for JRA is quite encouraging: Approximately 60% to 70% of children will be free of the disease with no permanent joint damage 10 years after onset. Others, however, will have severe and permanent functional disability.

At present, there is no cure for JRA. However, research is now being conducted in the areas of genetics and immunology. Treatment for severe periods of exacerbation consists of controlling joint inflammation through medicine, rest, appropriately designed exercises, and, in some cases, surgery. During acute stages, complete bed rest is strongly recommended, and excessive weight bearing by inflamed joints should be avoided. In some instances, surgery may be performed to remove damaged tissue from the joint in order to prevent greater deterioration to bone and cartilage. Total hip replacements are now performed in some cases with great success.

Even during acute stages of JRA, joints should be exercised through the greatest possible range of motion at least once or twice a day so that range of motion can be maintained. For individuals unable to exercise independently, teachers or therapists can provide partial or total assistance.

The physical education program should stress exercises and activities that help increase or maintain range of motion so that permanent contractures do not develop. Muscular strength and endurance activities should also be offered to decrease muscle atrophy. Isometric activities, such as hooking the fingers of both hands together and trying to pull them apart or placing the palms together and pushing, may be particularly helpful to encourage the development of hand muscles. Another hand exercise involves squeezing objects of various sizes and shapes. Hand exercises are most important to maintain appropriate manipulative skills. Most people with severe joint limitation or deterioration should refrain from activities that twist, jar, or place undue stress upon the joints; as such, activities like basketball, volleyball, and tennis may need to be modified accordingly.

Osteogenesis Imperfecta

Osteogenesis imperfecta, also known as *brittle bone disease*, is an inherited condition in which bones are imperfectly formed. An unknown cause produces a defect in the protein matrix of collagen fibers. The defect reduces the amount of calcium and phosphorus (bone salts), which in turn produces a weak bone structure. Bones are very easily broken. When healed, they take on a shortened, bowed appearance. Other affected body parts that include collagen are joint ligaments, skin, and the sclera (white portion) of the eye. Joint tissues exhibit abnormal elasticity, the skin appears translucent, and the thinning sclera takes on a blue discoloration as the choroid (underlying eyeball) is exposed. There are two types of osteogenesis imperfecta: *congenital* (present at birth) and *tarda* (with later onset). The congenital type is severe, while the tarda type is mild. Many students with the severe form require the use of crutches or wheelchairs. There is no cure for the disease. At the present time, surgery is the most effective treatment; it consists of reinforcing the bone by inserting a steel rod lengthwise through its shaft.

Physical education activities such as swimming, bowling (with some modifications), and the use of beach balls for striking and catching are safe to perform because they do not place undue stress upon the joints or bones. Because of abnormal joint elasticity, strength-building exercises and activities, which can increase joint stability, should be encouraged. This may be accomplished in a swimming environment. Most people with the disorder should not play power volleyball, basketball, or football unless the games are modified appropriately.

Arthrogryposis

Arthrogryposis, also known as *multiple congenital contractures*, is a nonprogressive congenital disease of unknown origin. Approximately 500 infants in the United States are born with arthrogryposis each year. The condition, which may affect some or all of the joints, is characterized by stiff joints (contractures) and weak muscles. Instead of normal muscle tissue surrounding the joints, fatty and connective tissue is present. The severity of the condition varies; an individual may be in a wheelchair or only be minimally affected. Limbs commonly exhibit deformities and can be fixed in almost any position. In addition, affected limbs are usually small in circumference, and joints appear large. Surgery, casting, and bracing are usually recommended for people with deformities. Most typically, upper limb involvement includes turned-in shoulders, extended and straightened elbows, pronated forearms, and flexed wrists and fingers. Trunk and lower-limb involvement includes flexion and outward rotation of the hip, bent or straightened knees, and feet that are turned in and down. Other conditions associated with the disease include congenital heart defects, respiratory problems, and various facial abnormalities. Individuals with arthrogryposis almost always possess normal intelligence and speech.

Because people with this disease have restricted range of motion, their physical education program should focus on exercises and activities that increase flexibility. In addition, they should be taught games and sports that use leisure time effectively. In most cases, exercises and activities that are appropriate for arthritic individuals are also acceptable for those with arthrogryposis. Swimming, an excellent leisure activity, encourages the development of flexibility and serves to strengthen weak muscles surrounding joints. Other activities, modified when needed, may include miniature golf, bowling, shuffleboard, boccie, and track and field events.

Multiple Sclerosis

According to the most recent data provided by the National Multiple Sclerosis Society, up to 350,000 people in the United States have multiple sclerosis (MS). It is a slowly progressive neurological disorder that may result in total incapacitation. Approximately two thirds of all those afflicted with the disease experience onset between the ages of 20 and 40. But the disease may manifest itself in young children or the elderly as well. It affects more women than men and more whites than blacks. MS is characterized by changes in the white matter covering (myelin sheath) of nerve fibers at various locations throughout the central nervous system (brain and spinal cord); the cause is unknown. However, scientists believe that the disease may be a result of a virus attack, an immune reaction, or a combination of both. Current research studies are focusing upon myelin formation and its changes, drug therapy, immunotherapy, and diagnostic tests. MS is diagnosed through such tests as neurological examination, blood tests, and magnetic resonance imaging (MRI), which can show lesions in the central nervous system.

In MS, the myelin sheath is destroyed and is replaced by scar tissue; a lesion may vary from the size of a pinpoint to about 1 or 2 centimeters in diameter. Individuals with MS may exhibit various symptoms, depending on the location of the damage. The most common symptoms are numbness, general weakness, double vision, slurred speech, staggering gait, and partial or complete paralysis. The early stage of the disease is characterized by periods of exacerbation followed by periods of remission. As scar tissue continues to replace healthy tissue, the symptoms tend to continue uninterrupted.

Because most people with MS are stricken in the most productive and enjoyable years of life, many are unable to cope emotionally with the disease. Additional stress results from the fact that there is no established treatment that can cure it. The main treatment objective is to maintain the person's functional ability as long as possible. Treatment should be directed toward preventing loss of range of motion (which would result in permanent contractures) and preserving strength and endurance. Often the disease progresses to a point where the person needs braces or a wheelchair. Intensive therapy or physical conditioning during acute phases of MS may cause general body fatigue. Therefore, physical activities should be judiciously programmed.

Mild forms of physical activity that emphasize strength and endurance should be performed for short periods of time. However, the duration and intensity of the activity should be programmed according to the individual's exercise tolerance level. Activities such as bowling, miniature golf, and table tennis are acceptable if regular rest periods are provided. In addition, a variety of stretching exercises is recommended to maintain adequate range of motion. Activities incorporating balance and agility components may prove to be helpful for those exhibiting staggering gait or varying degrees of paralysis. Many of these activities can be done in water.

Friedreich's Ataxia

An inherited neurological disease, Friedreich's ataxia usually manifests itself in childhood and early adolescence (boys and girls 7 to 13 years of age). The disease was first identified in the 1860s by German neurologist Nikolaus Friedreich, who described the disease as a gradual loss of motor coordination and progressive nerve degeneration. The sensory nerves of the limbs and trunk (peripheral nerves) are affected, and the disease may progress either slowly or rapidly. When the disease progresses rapidly, many people become wheelchair bound by their late teens and early twenties. Early symptoms may be poor balance and lack of limb and trunk coordination, resulting in a clumsy, awkward, wide-based gait almost indistinguishable from the gait of ataxic cerebral palsy. Fine motor control of the upper limbs tends to be impaired because tremors may be present. Atrophy is common in muscles of the distal limbs. Individuals typically exhibit slurred speech and are prone to seizures. Most will develop foot deformities such as clubfoot, high arches, and hammer toes, a condition in which the toes are curled because of tight flexor tendons of the second and third toes. As the disease progresses, spinal deformities such as kyphosis and scoliosis are common. The majority of individuals exhibit heart problems such as heart murmur, enlarged heart, and constriction of the aorta and pulmonary arteries. Diabetes develops in 10% to 40% of people with Friedreich's ataxia. Visual abnormalities include nystagmus and poor visual tracking. There is no known cure at this time; however, research is being conducted to find the gene(s) responsible for the condition. Therapy consists of managing foot and spinal deformities and cardiac conditions. Medication may be prescribed to control diabetes as well as cardiac, tremor, and seizure disorders.

Physical education activities should be planned to promote muscle strength, endurance, and coordination. Activities that develop muscles of the distal limbs such as the wrist, forearm, foot, and lower leg are recommended. The development of grip strength is essential for activities that utilize implements such as rackets and bats. Individuals exhibiting poor balance and lack of coordination are in need of balance training and activities that encourage development of fundamental locomotor movements. For those with fine motor control difficulties, activities may take the form of riflery, billiards, or archery. Remedial exercises are recommended for people with foot and spinal deviations. Games, exercises, and activities should be programmed according to individual tolerance levels for those with cardiac conditions, and those prone to seizures should be closely monitored.

Myasthenia Gravis

Myasthenia gravis is a disease characterized by a reduction in muscular strength that may be minimal or severe. Even when strength is greatly reduced, the individual still has enough strength to perform activities, but often this demands maximum or near maximum effort. In some cases, the disease is easily confused with muscular dystrophy because muscle weakness affects the back, lower extremities, and intercostal muscles. It affects twice as many females as males and occurs most often in the fourth decade, though some cases have shown that adolescent girls can exhibit the disease. Although the cause is unknown, some authorities believe that nerve impulses are prevented from reaching muscle fibers because of the production of an abnormal chemical compound at the distal end of the motor nerve.

One of the main symptoms is abnormal fatigue. Muscles generally appear normal except for some disuse atrophy. Weakness of the extraocular and lid muscles of the eye occurs in half of all cases; this results in drooping of the eyelid (ptosis) and double vision (strabismus). Because facial, jaw, and tongue muscles become easily fatigued, individuals may have problems chewing and speaking. Weakness of the neck muscles may cause the person not to hold the head erect. Back musculature may also be weakened; this leads to malalignment of the spinal column, which can further restrict movement. Muscle weakness makes the execution of the activities of daily living difficult and contributes to low levels of cardiorespiratory efficiency. The disease is not progressive; it may appear gradually, or it may be sudden. It commonly goes into remission for weeks, months, or years. Affected individuals therefore live in fear of recurrent attacks.

Physical education activities should focus on the development of physical fitness. Because people with myasthenia gravis fatigue easily, their activities should be programmed in a progressive manner and according to individual tolerance levels that take into account the duration, intensity, and frequency of the activity. When the muscles of respiration are weakened, breathing activities are strongly recommended. It is important to strengthen weak neck muscles, especially when the program includes such activities as heading a soccer ball or hitting a volleyball. Fitness levels can be maintained during acute stages through swimming activities. Poor body mechanics resulting from weak musculature will ultimately affect locomotor skills; therefore, remedial posture exercises and activities should be offered.

Guillain-Barré Syndrome

Guillain-Barré syndrome (also known as *infectious polyneuritis or infectious neuronitis*) is a neurological disorder characterized by ascending paralysis of peripheral and cranial nerves. Spinal and cranial nerves are affected, which results in acute and progressive paralysis. Initially, the lower extremities become easily fatigued, and numbness, tingling, and symmetrical weakness are present. Paralysis, which usually originates in the feet and lower legs, progresses to the upper leg, continues on to the trunk and upper extremities, and finally affects the facial muscles. Symptoms usually reach their maximum within a few weeks. When initially affected, people involved in locomotor activities of an endurance nature, such as distance running, typically find themselves stumbling or falling during the activity session as muscles of the feet and lower legs fatigue prematurely. The condition is frequently preceded by a respiratory or gastrointestinal infection, which suggests that a virus may be the cause. However, attempts to isolate a virus have not been successful. Some authorities believe that the syndrome is an autoimmune disease.

Guillain-Barré syndrome affects both males and females equally. It may affect both infants and the elderly, but it seems to cluster in childhood and middle age. While about one third of those stricken with the syndrome may die, the majority recover, either completely or with minimal paralysis. Acute stage treatment includes warm, wet applications to the extremities, passive range-of-motion exercise, and rest.

For people who have made a complete recovery, no restrictions in physical activities are needed. However, some individuals who do not completely recover exhibit weakness in limb and respiratory muscles. Their activities can focus on maintaining or improving cardiorespiratory endurance and strength and endurance of unaffected muscles. When a significant amount of weakness remains in the lower extremities, activities may need to be modified accordingly.

PROGRAM IMPLICATIONS

All people with cerebral palsy, TBI, stroke, amputations, dwarfism, or Les Autres conditions can benefit from physical education and sport activities. The type and degree of physical disability, motor educability, interest level, and overall educational goals will determine the modifications and adaptations that are needed. With these factors taken into account, the instructional program can be individualized and personalized.

General Guidelines

A number of general guidelines can be applied to programs for people with cerebral palsy, TBI, stroke, amputations, dwarfism, and Les Autres conditions. The guidelines that follow pertain to safety considerations, physical fitness, motor development, psychosocial development, and implications for sports.

Safety Considerations

All programs should be conducted in a safe and secure environment in which students are free to explore the capabilities of their own bodies and to interact with surroundings that will nurture their physical and motor development. Teachers and/or coaches should closely monitor games and activities especially for those individuals who are prone to seizures or lack good judgment (e.g., persons with TBI). Activity areas should always be well padded for those who are considered clumsy or who ambulate with assistive devices.

Students with more severe impairments will need special equipment, such as bolsters (to support the upper body while in the prone position), standing platforms (to assist them in maintaining a standing posture), orthotic devices, and/or seating systems to help them perform various motor tasks. However, students with mild impairments will need no specialized equipment. Because many persons with physical disabilities have difficulty maintaining an erect posture for extended periods, some activities are best done in a prone, supine, or sitting position. Persons with physical limitations should also be encouraged to experience as many different postures as possible. This is especially true for persons in wheelchairs. A positioning program for persons possessing severe physical disabilities should be designed by a team of persons responsible for the individual's education (Fraser, Hensinger, & Phelps, 1990).

Because of abnormal muscle tone and reduced range of motion, many individuals with neuromotor involvement have difficulty moving voluntarily. The teacher may need to assist in the following ways:

- Getting the person into and out of activity positions,

- Physically supporting the person during activity, and

- Helping the person execute a specific skill or exercise.

The teacher may also need to position students by applying various degrees of pressure with the hands to key points of the body such as the head, neck, spine, shoulders, elbows, hips, pelvis, knees, and ankles. An example is applying both hands symmetrically to the individual's elbows to reduce flexion at the elbow joints. However, these techniques should be performed only after instruction by a therapist or physician. The ultimate aim of handling, positioning, and lifting individuals with CP is to continually encourage them to move as independently as possible. This is accomplished by gradually reducing the amount of support to key points of the body. Teachers should consult with therapists whenever possible in an effort to coordinate these procedures. In addition, teachers should closely monitor the physical assistance that a student with a disability receives from peers. Peer assistance should be discouraged if it poses a safety risk.

Because all conditions described in this chapter are of medical origin, it is important that physical educators consult medical professionals when establishing programs to meet unique needs. This is especially important for students who possess TBI, or those who are receiving physical or occupational therapy such as students with CP and stroke, or those who are convalescing under the care of a physician.

Physical Fitness

Reduced muscular strength, flexibility, and cardiovascular endurance levels are common in students with physical handicaps, especially in comparison to the normal population. Winnick and Short (1982) found that young people with CP or spinal neuromuscular conditions exhibited physical fitness levels significantly below those of normal youth. Youngsters with paraplegic spinal neuromuscular conditions generally exhibited significantly inferior scores on items that included grip strength, flexed-arm hang, and pull-ups. Compared to able-bodied youngsters, those with CP scored significantly lower on sit-ups, leg lifts, sit-and-reach, grip strength, flexed-arm hang, pull-ups, and standing long jump. When compared to youngsters with spinal neuromuscular conditions, those with CP had lower levels of fitness. Both groups were more variable in their performances when compared to normal youngsters. This variability is probably due to the wide range in the severity of each impairment. On muscular strength and endurance measures, youngsters with CP generally performed between one and two standard deviation units below normal youngsters.

Winnick and Short (1982) found similar scores when comparing subjects with CP to able-bodied youth on skinfold measures. Nevertheless, there was a trend for those with paraplegic spinal neuromuscular conditions to exhibit skinfold measures greater than those of able-bodied youth. Individuals with higher skinfold measures may be in greater need of continuous aerobic activities (such as running, swimming, or wheeling for distance).

In general, youngsters with less severe impairments exhibited better fitness scores than those more severely impaired. Winnick and Short (1982) reported that, while nonimpaired youngsters increase fitness scores as they get older, this was not the case with youngsters possessing orthopedic impairments. In fact, in some instances, fitness levels decreased as youngsters with impairments increased in age. These data strongly suggest the need for physical fitness development for young people who are severely impaired. Recommended tests for *assessing physical and motor fitness* in persons with CP, amputations, TBI, strokes, and Les Autres conditions include the following:

- Project UNIQUE Physical Fitness Test
- Hughes Basic Gross Motor Assessment (for minor impairments only)
- Project ACTIVE Motor Ability Test for the Severely Multihandicapped

For students with low fitness levels, certain precautions may need to be taken as fitness programs are established. It is especially important that the teacher be sensitive to the frequency, intensity, and duration of exercises and activities. Fatigue may cause the person to become frustrated, which in turn adversely affects proper performance. The instructor should permit rest periods and player substitutions when endurance-related activities like soccer and basketball are offered. Because restricted movement is common for individuals whose conditions are described in this chapter, it is vitally important that strength and flexibility be developed to the maximum extent possible. Weak musculature and limited range of motion, if unattended, will lead to permanent joint contractures that result in significant loss of movement capability.

Motor Development

CP, TBI, stroke, amputations, dwarfism, and Les Autres impairments restrict individuals from experiencing normal movement patterns that are essential to normal motor development. As a result, delays in motor control and development are common. Individuals with CP typically exhibit motor delays because they either lack movement ability or have difficulty in controlling movements. Individuals with varying degrees of TBI and stroke may have difficulty planning and performing movements because of damage to the motor control and related areas of the cerebrum. Children with congenital amputations are frequently unable to execute fundamental movements in an appropriate manner. A child born missing a lower limb, for example, may be delayed in acquiring locomotor patterns such as creeping, walking, and running. Conditions that result in muscle atrophy, like muscular dystrophy or Friedreich's ataxia, prevent individuals from developing the strength and endurance levels needed to perform fundamental movements.

Physical education programs should encourage the sequential development of fundamental motor patterns and skills essential for participation in games, sports, and leisure activities. When attempting to enhance motor development, the physical educator should be concerned primarily with the manner in which a movement is performed rather than with its outcome. The goal of every physical education program should be to encourage individuals to achieve maximum motor control and development. *Motor development tests* recommended for use with younger students include the following:

- The Denver Developmental Screening Test II
- The Milani-Comparetti Developmental Chart
- The Peabody Developmental Motor Scale

Psychosocial Development

Many people with CP, amputations, TBI, stroke, dwarfism, and Les Autres conditions lack self-confidence, have low motivational levels, and exhibit problems with body image. An appropriately designed physical education program can provide successful movement experiences that not only motivate students but also help them gain the self-confidence needed to develop a positive self-image, which is vitally important for emotional well-being. A realistic body image can be developed even when the physical education teacher does not expect students to perform skills and activities perfectly. Rather, it is more important that the student perform the activity as independently as possible with a specified degree of competence. The teacher should promote the attitude that it is acceptable to fail at times when attempting activities because this is a natural part of the learning process. Physical activities perceived as fun and not as hard work can motivate students to perform to their maximum potential.

Implications for Sports

Teachers are encouraged to integrate many of the sport activities described in the "Adapted Sports" section of this chapter into their programs. For example, the club throw, a USCPAA field event, can be incorporated into a physical education program as a means of developing strength and as an opportunity for sport competition. Other events (included in USCPAA, NHS, USLASA, and DAAA) such as bowling, archery, cycling, and boccie can be taught. Team games and sports may include volleyball, basketball, soccer, and floor hockey.

Individual and dual activities may include tennis, table tennis, riflery, archery, badminton, horseback riding, billiards, and track and field. A rifle activity for individuals in wheelchairs can take the form of a biathalon. The object is to accurately shoot an air rifle at targets located at varying distances along a predetermined course. The distances and number of targets can be determined on an individual basis. The course is to be traversed as quickly as possible while at the same time attempting to achieve a high shooting score.

Winter activities, including ice hockey, ice skating, downhill and cross-country skiing, tobogganing, and sledding, are also popular in northern regions. All of the above games and sports can be offered with a view toward future competition or leisure activity.

Cerebral Palsy

Individuals with CP exhibiting inappropriate reflexive behavior typically have difficulty learning and performing various motor skills. When a child is receiving therapy, it is important for the physical educator to work in conjunction with therapists in an effort to foster the suppression of certain abnormal reflexes and the facilitation of righting and equilibrium reactions. While many physical education activities help in the development of righting and equilibrium reactions, others may elicit abnormal reflexes. When attempting to catch a ball, for example, the person may be unable to place both hands in front of the body because an abnormal reflex overrides this voluntary movement.

As the young student progresses in age, even with therapy, inappropriate reflexes will not be inhibited. Professionals responsible for the student's physical education program must therefore pursue attainment of functional skills, including sport skills. Such functional skills as creeping, walking, running, and throwing are important to future development and should be incorporated into the student's program. Asking students with CP to repetitively perform activities that elicit unwanted reflexes will not aggravate the condition of CP, as professionals once believed.

Because of either restricted or extraneous movements, an individual with CP may exert more energy than a person without an impairment to accomplish the same task. The added energy output requires a greater degree of endurance. As a result, the duration of physical activities may need to be shortened.

Strength

In addressing the development of strength, it is important to note that muscle tone imbalances between flexor and extensor muscle groups are common in persons with CP. For those with spastic tendencies, flexor muscles may be disproportionately stronger than the extensors. Therefore, strength development should focus on strengthening the extensor muscles. For example, even though students may have increased tone of the forearm flexors, they may very well perform poorly on pull-ups. This being the case, one should not continue to develop forearm flexors as opposed to forearm extensors. The goal is to develop and maintain a balance between flexor and extensor muscles throughout all regions of the body. Individuals with CP can benefit from rigorous strength training programs. Isokinetic resistance exercises are particularly useful for developing strength, probably because they provide constant tension through the full range of motion and aid in inhibiting jerky movements that are extraneous and uncontrolled. Moving limbs in diagonal patterns (e.g., moving the entire arm across the body in a diagonal plane) encourages muscle groups to work in harmony. Such movements can be elicited by involving individuals in a variety of gross motor activities that may include throwing, striking, or kicking movements.

Flexibility

Tight muscles in both the upper and lower limbs and the hip region contribute to reduced flexibility. If left unattended, restricted range of motion leads to contractures and bone deformities. Surburg (1986) recommends that more emphasis be placed on relaxing affected muscles than on stretching them. The instructor may wish to begin a flexibility program session by helping students relax target muscle groups. This can be accomplished by teaching students a variety of relaxation techniques which they then perform independently. A number of relaxation techniques appear in chapter 21. When stretching exercises are used, they should be of a static, as opposed to a ballistic nature, and they should be done both before and after strength and endurance activities. If an individual is participating in a ballistic type of activity, such as a club throw, ballistic stretching can be used, but it should be preceded by static stretching. Stretching exercises for more severely affected body parts should be done on a daily basis. Therefore, students should be encouraged to perform stretching exercises on their own whenever possible.

Speed

Many students with CP have difficulty with games and sport skills that include a speed component because quickly performed movements tend to activate the stretch reflex. However, an appropriate program can permit students with CP to increase their movement speed. Speed development activities for persons with CP will differ little from those for nonimpaired persons, except that such activities should be conducted more frequently than for students without impairments. Daily activities are recommended. Students with CP should be encouraged to perform movements as quickly as possible but to perform them in a controlled, accurate, and purposeful manner. Activities having a speed component include throwing and kicking for distance, running, and jumping. Initially, the student should concentrate on the pattern of the movement while gradually increasing the speed of its execution. To develop arm and leg speed, the student can be asked to throw or kick a ball (or some other object) in a "soft" manner to a target; gradually, the throw or kick can increase in speed.

Motor Coordination

Lack of coordination is common in individuals with CP and contributes to delayed motor control and development. Those who are significantly uncoordinated may have problems ambulating independently or with appliances and may need to wear protective headgear. Because they frequently fall, they should be taught, when appropriate, to fall in a protective manner. Because of abnormal

movements and posture, individuals with CP have difficulty with controlling balance and body coordination. Obstacle courses, horseback riding, bicycling and tricycling, and balance beam and teeter (stability) board activities can be offered to assist in controlling movements.

Motor control difficulties notwithstanding, persons with CP (as well as those with TBI and stroke) can learn to become more accurate in their performance. Since persons with CP can have difficulty planning movements involving accuracy, they should be allowed sufficient time to plan the movement before executing it. Many times, the use of a weighted ball, bat, or other implement will assist in decreasing abnormal flailing or tremor movements. Adding weight to the implement helps in reducing exaggerated stretch reflexes, which, in turn, aids in controlling movements. Individuals with CP possessing motor control deficiencies resulting from athetoid, tremor, or ataxic tendencies can be expected to throw or kick for distance better and to exhibit freer running patterns than others who have limited range of motion due to spastic or rigid tendencies.

Loud noises and stressful situations increase the amount of electrical stimulation from the brain to the muscles; this tends to increase abnormal and extraneous movements, which, in turn, make motor activities difficult to perform. In an attempt to deal with this situation, students should be taught to concentrate on the activity to be performed. Individuals exhibiting spastic tendencies tend to relax more when encouraged to make slow, repetitive movements that have a purpose, while those with athetoid tendencies perform better when encouraged to relax before moving. Highly competitive situations that promote winning at all costs may tend to increase abnormal movements. Therefore, competitive situations may need to be introduced gradually. The teaching of relaxation techniques, which consciously reduce abnormal muscle tone and prepare the student for activity and competition, has been found to be beneficial. Another way to help individuals with CP improve general motor control and coordination is to have them imagine the skill or activity prior to performance. This technique, called *mental imagery*, may help to integrate thoughts with actions.

In motor skill development for students with CP, the skills taught should be broken down into basic components and presented sequentially. This method is particularly useful for uncoordinated students seeking to learn more complex motor skills. However, because of the general lack of body coordination, activities should initially focus on simple repetitive movements rather than on complicated ones requiring many directional changes. Therefore, activities that help to develop basic fundamental motor skills and patterns, such as walking, running, jumping, throwing, catching, and so forth, should be taught.

Perceptual-Motor Disorders

Perceptual-motor disorders also contribute to poor motor performance. Because of these disorders, many children with CP exhibit short attention spans and are easily distracted by objects and persons in the immediate environment. Activities may therefore need to be conducted in an environment as free from distractions as possible, especially during early skill development.

Visual perceptual disorders are common among students with CP and can adversely affect activities and events that involve spatial relationships. These may include player positioning in team sports like soccer, remaining in lanes during track events, and determining distances between objects like boccie balls. Students may have difficulty with various accuracy and aiming tasks such as throwing, tossing, kicking, or pushing an object to a specified target, as well as with activities involving various degrees of fine motor coordination, such as crossbow target shooting, angling, or pocket billiards.

Traumatic Brain Injury and Stroke

Previous to brain trauma, individuals were once involved in learning and performing a host of gross and fine motor skills in a normal manner. It is commonly known that the learning of motor skills requires varying amounts of cognition depending on the level of difficulty. Skills that were once though to be quite simple to learn now require constant practice and planning by the person with TBI or stroke. Depending on the age of the individual at the time of the injury, some skills may have already been learned (e.g., running, throwing, catching), while other skills had yet to be acquired (e.g., specific sport skills). While some individuals with TBI or stroke may fully recover the motor skills lost, others with more significant and permanent injury may never regain them. In order for individuals with TBI and stroke to regain skills to their maximum potential, physical education and sport programs need to be individualized and offered on a regular basis.

Physical Fitness

Acquiring and maintaining an adequate level of physical fitness is important. This is especially true for persons who have been severely injured due to TBI and those who have been immobile for long periods of time following a stroke. Therefore, the physical education program should allow for activities to develop and maintain the fitness areas of muscular strength and endurance, flexibility, and cardiovascular endurance levels depending on individual need. Most students will fatigue easily especially as they begin their reentry into school. Therefore, fitness exercises and activities should be introduced on a gradual basis, and sufficient rest periods should be offered between activities, especially if the student attends physical education class toward the end of the school day.

Some persons who exhibit spasticity (similar to CP) will need to focus on relaxation and flexibility exercises and activities. Those who exhibit partial paralysis will need to maintain residual functioning through muscular strength and endurance exercises and activities. Universal gym equipment is both convenient and safe to use to develop strength and endurance since persons need not be concerned with placing free weights on barbells and dumbbells. Except for the bench press exercise, persons can stay seated in their wheelchairs, although getting out of the wheelchair is important and should be encouraged. Weight training and flexibility exercises and activities will not be new to the person recovering from TBI or stroke since physical and occupational therapy rehabilitation programs typically employ them. For those persons who can remove themselves from their chairs, either independently or with assistance, isokinetic equipment (e.g., Nautilus) is also beneficial. Since persons with more severe brain injury are more likely to be sedentary, aerobic activities that develop cardiorespiratory endurance levels can be performed. These may take the form of low-impact aerobics for persons who can ambulate or aerobics done from a sitting position for those using wheelchairs. Aquatic activities are especially good for developing physical fitness. It is recommended that individuals with TBI and stroke participate in physical fitness programs that address all areas of fitness.

Motor Control

Depending on the location and severity of injury, individuals with TBI or stroke have difficulty planning, initiating, and controlling gross and fine motor movements. Persons with TBI typically have difficulty performing movements sequentially. This has important implications for physical education and sport activities, especially when combinations of separate skills need to be linked in succession. Individuals with TBI or stroke typically need to relearn movements and movement patterns that were performed before the injury. To assist in this process, more complex skills should be broken down into simpler subskills, and the subskills should then be practiced sequentially. Since these individuals typically have problems processing information, a sufficient amount of time should be given following directions so that movements can be planned before they are executed.

Like those persons with CP, visual perception may also be affected in persons with TBI and stroke. As such, they may exhibit difficulty with activities requiring spatial relationships and those requiring object control, such as catching, kicking, and striking. Of course, activities incorporating object control will need to be individualized. Adolescents with TBI and stroke should be given choices as to the type of sport and leisure activities they wish to learn in physical education classes. This gives them the needed sense of independence and self-control.

Amputees

In general, a physical education program for persons with amputations can follow the same guidelines as one developed for able-bodied individuals. Aside from missing limb(s), people with amputations are considered able bodied. However, the location and extent of the amputation(s) may require modifications in some activities.

Most persons with amputations typically use prosthetic devices in physical education activities. A person with unilateral lower-limb amputation usually continues to use the device for participation in football, basketball, volleyball, and most leisure activities. As previously stated, more mechanically efficient devices are now being worn by athletes with unilateral lower-limb amputations. In some situations, a unilateral BE, AE, or shoulder amputee may consider the device a hindrance to successful performance and discard it during participation; this is common in baseball or softball. Such is the case with Jim Abbott, a professional baseball pitcher who does not wear a prosthetic device for his BE congenital amputation. Of course, in some activities the prosthetic device must be removed, as in swimming. Since 1978, the National Federation of State High School Athletic Associations has allowed athletes to wear prosthetic devices for interscholastic sports such as football, wrestling, gymnastics, soccer, baseball, and field and ice hockey (Adams and McCubbin, 1991). However, a device cannot be used if it is more dangerous to other players than a corresponding human limb or if it places the user at an advantage over the opponent. For football, the ruling is restricted solely to BK prosthetic devices; for field hockey and soccer, upper-limb and AK prostheses are allowed, though their use is discouraged.

Physical Fitness

Like people with other physically handicapping conditions, amputees may need to increase their levels of physical fitness. Muscular strength and endurance and flexibility should be developed for all parts of the body. For a person with only a partial limb amputation, such as an ankle or wrist disarticulation, exercises and activities should be programmed to encourage the most normal possible use of the remaining limb segment. Individuals with bilateral BK or AK amputations often have lower cardiovascular endurance levels than upper-limb amputees because their locomotor activities may be severely restricted. To encourage cardiovascular development, the physical educator should provide activities, such as marathon racing or slalom events, in which a wheelchair can be used. Using an arm-propelled tricycle is also recommended. Swimming is an excellent cardiovascular activity; the effect of limb absence can be minimized by the use of flippers to aid in propulsion. Both unilateral and bilateral AK amputees have a tendency to be obese and therefore should be encouraged to follow a weight reduction diet along with a program of regular, vigorous physical activity.

Motor Ability

Limb deficiency can affect the person's level of motor ability. The absence of a limb most often affects the center of gravity, to a greater degree in lower-limb amputees than in upper-limb amputees. The result is difficulty with activities requiring balance. Developing both static and dynamic balance is crucial to the performance of locomotor skills such as walking, running, hopping, or, for that matter, sitting in a wheelchair. Activities that foster the development of balance and proper body alignment should be encouraged; these may include traversing an obstacle course, performing on a minitrampoline, or walking a balance beam. Speed and agility may also be adversely affected, especially in those with lower-limb deficiencies. People with unilateral AK and bilateral BK or AK amputations are most affected and may have difficulty in locomotor activities that require quick change of direction, such as basketball, football, soccer, and tennis.

While unilateral BK or BE amputees can participate most effectively in physical education and competitive sports, those with bilateral upper or lower amputations will have specific activity restrictions. Bilateral upper-limb amputees can successfully engage in activities that involve the lower extremities to a significant degree (e.g., skating, soccer, and jogging).

Unilateral AK amputees can effectively participate in activities such as swimming, waterskiing, snow skiing, weight lifting, and certain field events like the shot put and javelin, which do not place emphasis on locomotion. Those with bilateral BK amputations will be more limited in activities like track events, football, or basketball, which involve jumping, hopping, or body contact. Bilateral AK amputees are much more restricted in their activities, usually relying part time on a wheelchair and using crutches at other times. Activities such as archery, badminton, and riflery, which can be performed from a sitting or prone position, are appropriate.

Dwarfism

Individuals with dwarfism should be encouraged to perform in regular physical education and sport activities. The development of physical fitness and motor ability are important aspects of any physical education program. As such, individuals with dwarfism should have the same opportunities to develop as other individuals. However, some considerations need to be addressed. Because of shorter limbs, the quality of movement may be affected in such activities as throwing, catching, and striking, and in such locomotor skills as running, jumping, and hopping. Furthermore, restricted range of motion and joint defects may predispose the individual to dislocations and joint trauma. Physical fitness and motor ability exercises and activities that place undue stress on weight-bearing joints should be avoided or modified to accommodate this limitation. For example, jogging can be replaced with walking in order to reduce stress on the hip joint, a common location of joint trauma. Swimming, which promotes flexibility and cardiovascular endurance, is an excellent activity for persons with achrondoplasia since it does not place undue stress on the joints.

INTEGRATION

Unless people with CP, TBI, stroke, amputations, dwarfism, and Les Autres conditions are severely impaired, most can be safely and effectively integrated into regular physical education programs. Those with mild degrees of impairment are, for the most part, integrated. In all cases, however, decisions about integrating must be made on an individual basis. The impairments described in this chapter primarily affect physical functioning; aside from some instances of CP, TBI, and stroke, mental impairments are rare. Most students with these conditions will understand verbal and written directions as well as rules and strategies for various games and sports. In certain cases, teachers may need to structure activities to suit the participants' abilities. For example, students impaired by CP, amputation, or other lower-limb deficiencies could play goalie in soccer or floor hockey and could pitch or play first base in softball.

ADAPTED SPORTS

At almost all age levels, people with CP, TBI, stroke, amputations, dwarfism, and Les Autres conditions now have the opportunity to become involved in competitive sports. The United States Les Autres Sports Association (USLASA), the USCPAA (individuals with stroke and TBI are also eligible to participate), the Dwarf Athletic Association of America (DAAA), and National Handicapped Sports (NHS) assist individuals in reaching their maximum potential in sport. NHS is responsible for organized competition for athletes with amputations. USLASA, USCPAA, DAAA, and NHS offer a variety of sporting events that in many cases have been modified for specific disabilities. Athletes are able to participate in these events on the basis of their functional abilities.

All four organizations are members of the Committee on Sports for the Disabled (COSD) of the United States Olympic Committee and members of the International Sports Organization for the Disabled (ISOD). Athletes from these sport organizations are eligible to participate in international competition governed by ISOD as long as they meet ISOD classification standards and qualify for events. ISOD oversees the Paralympic Games, World Championships, World Games, and World Cup competition. The Paralympic Games are organized every fourth year with competition in multidisabled games and sports. The World Championships are organized relative to a specific sport where single or multiple disabilities are present. More than one sport can be arranged at the same time and place. World Games, on the other hand, are organized relative to competition in one or more sports for specific disability groups (CP) or games that may deviate from existing rules. Finally, World Cup competition refers to international competition for national or club teams in team and individual sports.

Cerebral Palsy, Traumatic Brain Injury, and Stroke

Competition for athletes with CP, stroke, and TBI is based on the eight-level classification system shown in Table 11.1. Athletes are placed in a specific class through two testing procedures. In the first, a functional profile is established through observation and questioning regarding the person's daily living skills. The second testing procedure involves the measurement of speed, accuracy, and range of motion for upper extremity and torso function and, for ambulant athletes, the assessment for lower extremity function. Generally athletes compete within their designated classes in a variety of events. Table 11.2 identifies events and associated classification levels.

Each year the USCPAA holds a number of clinics for professionals and volunteers that focus on coaching, training, and officiating techniques. The association publishes a medically approved rules manual and a separate training guide.

Amputations

National and international competition is based on the nine-level classification system previously described. People with combinations of amputations not specified in the classification system are assigned to the class closest to the actual disability. For example, a combined AK and BK amputee would be placed in Class A1, whereas a combined AE and BE amputee would be in Class A5. People with single-arm paralysis are tested for muscle strength of the arms and hands. The following movements are tested and scored on a scale from 0 to 5 (5 being the greatest function):

- Shoulder flexion, extension, abduction, and adduction
- Elbow flexion and extension
- Wrist dorsal and volar flexion
- Finger flexion and extension at the metacarpophalangeal joints
- Thumb opposition and extension

Classification for participants with single-arm paralysis is limited to A6 (AE) or A8 (BE).

Amputee competition at both the national and international level takes place in track events such as 100-, 200-, and 400-meter dashes and 800- and 1,500-meter runs, and in field events such as shot put, discus, javelin, long jump, and high jump. National and international competition may also be offered in basketball, volleyball, lawn bowling, pistol shooting, table tennis, cycling, archery, weight lifting, and swimming (100-meter backstroke, 400-meter breaststroke, 100- and 400-meter freestyle, and 4 × 50-meter individual medley). Volleyball and basketball are offered in both sitting and ambulatory categories. In each sport, athletes of similar classifications compete with prostheses, except for those with double AK or combined upper and lower amputations. In addition to national and regional competitions sponsored by NHSA, amputees are eligible to compete in events sponsored by the Wheelchair Sports, USA, the National Wheelchair Basketball Association (NWBA), and the National Federation of Wheelchair Tennis (NFWT), as long as they have an amputation of the lower extremity and require the use of a wheelchair.

Dwarfism

The DAAA was established in 1985 for the purpose of providing organized sport competition to individuals with dwarfism. Eight primary sports are offered. These include track (15, 20, 40, 60, 100 and 4 × 100 meter relay), field (shot put, tennis and softball throw, discus, soft discus, and javelin), swimming (freestyle, backstroke, and breaststroke at 25, 50, and 100 meters), basketball, boccie (individual and team), volleyball, table tennis, and powerlifting. Separate competition is offered for men and women except for basketball, volleyball, and team boccie in which both men and women play on the same team. Soccer and equestrian are demonstration sports, and skiing is offered in the winter.

Individuals are classified for open division (ages 16 to 39) track, field, and swimming events. There are three classes for track alone, based on a ratio of standing height to sitting height, and three classes for field and swimming, based on the ratio of arm span to biacromial breadth. This system, which is now being refined, is used only for National DAAA events. For International events, the ISOD functional classification system is used.

To be eligible for competition, persons with disproportionate dwarfism must be equal to or less than 152.4 cm (5 feet in height), while persons with proportionate dwarfism must be equal to or less than 147.3 cm (4 ft 10 inches) in height. Individuals participate

Table 11.2   Classes Eligible for USCPAA Activities

Activities	Classes
Archery	I–VIII
Bicycling	V–VIII
Tricycling	II–VI
Boccia (wheelchair—individual and team)	I–II
Bowling	I–VIII
Cross country	VI–VIII
Equestrian	I–VIII
Power lifting (bench press)	I–VIII (according to weight)
Slalom	I–IV
Soccer (seven-a-side)	V–VIII
Wheelchair team handball	I–VI
Swimming	I–VIII
Table tennis	III–VIII
Target shooting—rifle	II–VIII
Track	I
Electric wheelchair slalom, 60m weave	
Wheelchair slalom	II–IV
20m, 60m	II (upper)
100m, 200m	II (upper), III–VIII
400m	II–VIII
800m	II, VI–VIII
1500m	IV, VII–VIII
3000m	VI–VIII
4 × 100m relay	II, II (upper), III–IV, VI–VIII
Field Events	I
High toss, soft shot, precision throw, soft discus	
Medicine ball thrust, distance kick	II
Club throw	II (upper), III–VI
Shot, discus	II (upper), III–VIII
Javelin throw	III–VIII
Long jump	VII–VIII

Note. From *United States Cerebral Palsy Athletic Association Sports Rules Manual* (4th ed.) (pp. 8–19), 1991, Dallas, TX: USCPAA. Adapted by permission.

in one of five divisions (open, junior, master, wheelchair, and futures). The futures division is for youth under 7 years of age. Here, a limited number of events is offered on a noncompetitive basis.

Les Autres

Historically, the Les Autres movement was associated with cerebral palsy sports. Les Autres

athletes performed at the National Cerebral Palsy Games in 1981 and 1983 along with CP athletes. At the National Cerebral Palsy/Les Autres games in East Lansing, Michigan in 1985, they participated in their own separate competition. In 1988 USLASA held a national competition in Nashville. Since then, national competitions havepbeen held regularly.

Under USLASA auspices, athletes compete mostly in the same general event categories as other sport organizations such as USCPAA. Track and field, swimming, volleyball, archery, boccie, cycling, shooting, table tennis, wheelchair team handball, and powerlifting are included. USLASA is in the process of revising its classification system to coincide with ISOD. Classes are divided into wheelchair and ambulatory sections. The number of eligible classes may vary with each event. For track and field competition, there are five wheelchair classes and five ambulatory classes with the recent addition of three jumping classes for certain field events.

SUMMARY

This chapter has described the conditions of CP, TBI, stroke, amputations, dwarfism, and Les Autres as they relate to physical education and sport. Physical and motor needs were described, and program and activity suggestions were presented. Recognizing the medical nature of these conditions, teachers and coaches are encouraged to plan activities on the basis of input from physicians and allied health professionals.

BIBLIOGRAPHY

Adams, R.C., & McCubbin, J.A. (1991). *Games, sports and exercises for the physically handicapped* (4th ed.). Philadelphia: Lea & Febiger.

Bronstein, K.S., Popovich, J.M., & Stewart-Amidei, C. (1991). *Promoting stroke recovery*. St. Louis: Mosby–Year Book, Inc.

Cohen, S. (1991). Adapting educational programs for students with head injuries. *Journal of Head Trauma Rehabilitation*, **6**(1), 56–63.

Crandall, R., & Crosson, T. (Eds.). (1994). *Dwarfism: The family and professional guide*. Irvine, CA: Short Stature Foundation and Information Center, Inc.

Fraser, B.A., Hensinger, R.N., & Phelps, J.A. (1990). *Physical management of multiple handicaps: A professional's guide* (2nd ed.). Baltimore: Brookes.

National Head Injury Foundation (1989). Basic questions about head injury and disability. Washington, DC: Author.

Scott, C.I. (1988). Dwarfism. *Clinical Symposia*, **40**(1), 2–32.

Surburg, P.R. (1986). New perspectives for developing range of motion and flexibility for special populations. *Adapted Physical Activity Quarterly*, **3**, 227–235.

Winnick J.P., & Short, F.X. (1982). The physical fitness of sensory and orthopedically impaired youth (final report, Project UNIQUE). Brockport: State University of New York College at Brockport. (ERIC Document Reproduction Service N. ED 240 764)

Ylvisaker, M., Hartwick, P., & Stevens, M. (1991). School reentry following head injury: Managing the transition from hospital to school. *Journal of Head Trauma Rehabilitation*, **6**(1), 10–22.

RESOURCES

Written

Fiegenbaum, E., Hanson, C., & Reed, P. (1991). *Traumatic brain injury: An educator's manual*. Salem: Oregon Department of Education. This manual presents educational information pertaining to traumatic brain injury. Topics include injury in children versus adults, the educational needs of students, school reentry, teaching strategies, and assessment.

Hughes Basic Gross Motor Assessment. This tool is appropriate for use with children having mild motor dysfunction and can be acquired from G. E. Miller, 484 South Broadway, Yonkers, NY 10705.

Knipe, B. (1993). *School reentry of students experiencing traumatic brain injury: Physical education considerations*. Johnston, IA: Heartland Area Educational Agency II. This paper provides current information regarding traumatic brain injury as it relates to physical education. An overview of TBI is provided along with information relative to assessment, teaching, and programming strategies as well as sport-related issues. This information can be acquired from Dr. Barbara Knipe, Heartland Educational Agency II, 6500 Corporate Drive, Johnston, IA 50131-1603.

Michael, J.W. (1989). New developments in prosthetic feet for sports and recreation. *Palaestra*, **5**(2), 21–22, 32–35. This article describes both conventional and new sophisticated prosthetic feet. Discusses the advantages and disadvantages of the new feet and their application to sports.

Audiovisual

A stroke survivor's workout [Videotape]. American Heart Association, 7272 Greenville Avenue, Dallas, TX 75231. This is a 28-minute video that shows a variety of flexibility and strength exercises. Some exercises are done from a standing position and, if needed, using the support of a chair, while other exercises are done while seated in a chair or wheelchair.

Traumatic brain injury (tape no. 16) [videotape]. Carle Foundation, Center for Health, Law, and Ethics, 110 West Main, Urbana, IL 61801. This 52-minute tape covers such topics as rehabilitative counseling, assistive technological devices, recreation and independent leisure lifestyles, transitional planning, and planning IEPs.

CHAPTER 12

Spinal Cord Disabilities

Luke E. Kelly

Sally "broke her back" in a car accident when she was 13. As a result, she lost all sensation and control of the muscles in her legs. When she returned to school in a wheelchair, her parents questioned why she should still attend physical education since she could no longer do most of the activities and probably could use the time better developing her abilities in areas like computer skills, which would help her get a job after the school years. If you were the physical education teacher, how would you respond to Sally's parents on this question? Mrs. Kamide, Sally's teacher, responded with the following points:

1. *Sally needs to learn wheelchair mobility skills so that she can use the wheelchair as her legs. These skills are important not only for Sally to participate in sport activities but also for her to move independently and safely in her environment.*

2. *With good wheelchair mobility skills, there is no reason why Sally should not be able to participate in most of the regular physical education units with little or no modifications.*

3. *Due to the loss of the large leg muscles, which are the body's major calorie burners, Sally has an even greater need for regular physical activity and a daily fitness routine.*

4. *With proper instruction and practice, Sally could develop the skills needed to participate in most of the leisure skills that individuals without disabilities participate in as adults (e.g., bowling, swimming, skiing, tennis, basketball).*

5. *If Sally is interested, she could also choose to compete at regional, national, and international levels in a variety of competitive sports (e.g., weight lifting, track and field, riflery).*

This chapter reviews the common spinal cord disabilities and the implications for physical education. After reading this chapter, you should be able to respond to questions like Sally's physical education teacher did and make appropriate accommodations to meet the needs of students like Sally.

Spinal cord disabilities are conditions that result from injury or disease to the vertebrae and/or the nerves of the spinal column. These conditions almost always are associated with some degree of paralysis resulting from damage to the spinal cord. The degree of the paralysis is a function of the location of the injury on the spinal column and the number of neural fibers that are subsequently destroyed. Five such spinal cord disabilities will be examined in this chapter: traumatic injuries to the spine resulting in **quadriplegia** and **paraplegia, poliomyelitis, spina bifida, spondylolysis, and spondylolisthesis**. In addition, this chapter will cover **orthotic devices** commonly associated with spinal cord disabilities as well as physical education and sport implications.

The physical education teacher should be aware of the different systems for categorizing spinal cord disabilities. Medical classifications are based on the segment of the spinal cord that is impaired, while sport organizations choose to classify people by their abilities in order to match similarly able athletes for competition.

Medical

As illustrated in Figure 12.1, spinal cord injuries are medically labeled or classified according to the segment of the spinal column (i.e., cervical, thoracic, lumbar, or sacral) and the number of the vertebrae at or below which the injury occurred. For example, an individual classified as a C-6 complete would have suffered a fracture between the sixth and seventh cervical vertebrae that completely severed the spinal cord. The location of the injury is important because it provides some insight into the functions that may be affected as a result. The extent of the spinal cord lesion is ascertained through muscle, reflex, and sensation testing.

The actual impact of a spinal cord injury is best understood in terms of what muscles can still be used, how strong these muscles are, and what can functionally be done with these muscles in the context of self-help skills (eating, dressing, grooming, toileting), movement (wheelchair, ambulation, transfers, bed), vocational skills, and physical education skills.

Table 12.1 provides a summary of the major muscle groups innervated at several key locations along the spinal column, with implications for the movements, abilities, and physical education activities that may be possible with lesions at those locations. The functional abilities remaining are cumulative as one progresses down the spinal column. For example, an individual with a lesion at or below T-1 would have all the muscles and abilities shown at and above that level.

Sport

Sport organizations that sponsor athletic events for individuals with spinal cord disabilities use different classification systems to equate athletes for competition. The most widely used system is the one used by Wheelchair Sports, USA. This system classifies athletes by functional ability into one of several classes based on the sport event, the degree of muscular functioning, and actual performance during competition. Muscular functioning includes the evaluation of such actions as arm function, hand function, trunk function, trunk stability, and pelvic stability in relation to their importance in performing a given sport event. This classification system provides an efficient way of equating

competition among a diverse group of athletes with varying types of spinal cord disabilities (Curtis, 1991). The Wheelchair Sports, USA functional classification system is illustrated in Table 12.2 on pages 198-201. It is important to note that while functional abilities are the key criteria in functional classification systems, there is a relationship between these sport classifications and the level of spinal cord damage. The approximate spinal cord lesion level associated with the National Wheelchair Basketball Association (NWBA) and several of the Wheelchair Sports, USA functional sport classifications are shown in Figure 12.2 on page 202.

CONDITIONS

Damage to the spinal cord can occur as a result of infectious diseases or from a variety of genetic and environmental causes. This section describes the common causes of spinal cord disabilities and the implications for planning and delivering physical education.

Traumatic Quadriplegia and Paraplegia

Traumatic quadriplegia and paraplegia refer to spinal cord injuries that result in the loss of movement and sensation. Quadriplegia is used to describe the more severe form, in which all four limbs are affected. Paraplegia refers to the condition in which primarily the lower limbs are affected.

The amount of paralysis and/or loss of sensation associated with quadriplegia and paraplegia is related to the location of the injury (how high on the spine) and the amount of neural damage (the degree of the lesion). Figure 12.1 shows a side view of the spinal column, accompanied by a description of the functional abilities associated with various levels of injury. The functional abilities indicated for each of the levels should be viewed cautiously because the neural damage to the spinal cord at the site of the injury may be complete or partial. If the cord is severed completely, the individuals will have no motor control or sensation in the parts of the body innervated below that point. This loss will be permanent because the spinal cord cannot regenerate itself. In many cases the damage to the spinal cord will only be partial, resulting in retention of some sensation and motor control below the site of the injury. In a case involving partial lesion, the individual may experience a gradual return of some muscle control and sensation over a period of several months following the injury. This is due not to regeneration of damaged

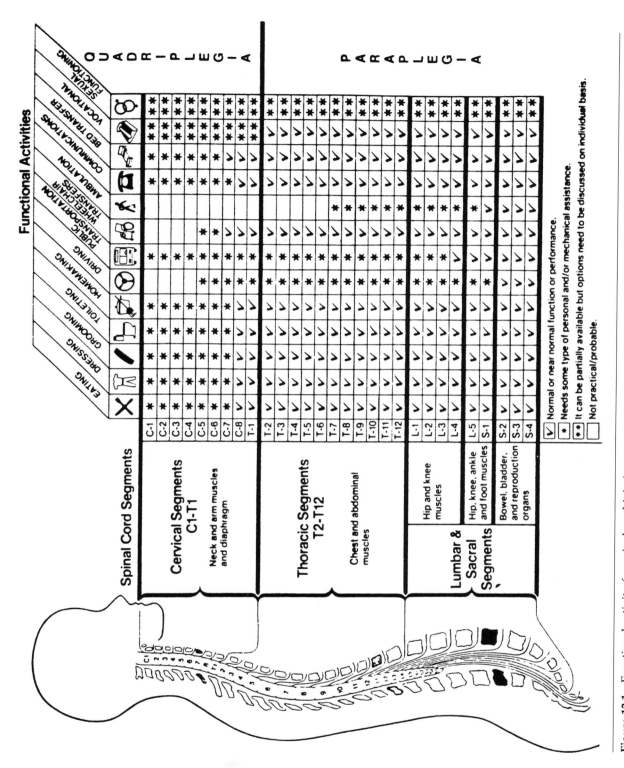

Figure 12.1 Functional activity for spinal cord injuries.

From *Games, Sports, and Exercises for the Physically Disabled* (4th ed.) (p. 150) by R.C. Adams and J.A. McCubbin, 1991, Philadelphia: Lea & Febiger. Courtesy of the Harmarville Rehabilitation Center, Pittsburgh, PA 15238. Reprinted by permission.

nerves but rather to the alleviation of pressure on nerves at the injury site caused by bruising and/or swelling.

Incidence

It is estimated that approximately 10,000 people suffer spinal cord injuries each year in the United States. Among the major causes are falls, automobile accidents, athletic injuries (e.g., football, gymnastics, diving), and bicycle accidents. Unfortunately, a large percentage of these injuries happen to students of high school age, with the incidence being greater among males than females. It should be noted that, when spinal cord injury is suspected, proper handling of the patient immediately after the injury can play a major role in minimizing any additional damage to the spinal cord.

The American Medical Association recommends the following procedures whenever a neck injury is suspected.

A neck injury should be suspected if a head injury has occurred. **Never** move a victim with a suspected neck injury without trained medical assistance unless the victim is in imminent danger of death (from fire, explosion, or a collapsing building, for example). **Warning**: Any movement of the head, either forward, backward, or side to side, can result in paralysis or death.

Immediate Treatment If the Victim Must Be Moved:

1. Immobilize the neck with a rolled towel or newspaper about 4 inches

Table 12.1 Potential Functional Abilities by Select Lesion Locations

Lesion locations	Key muscles innervated	Potential movements	Associated functional abilities	Sample PE activities
C-4	Neck Diaphragm	Head control Limited respiratory endurance	Control of an electronic wheelchair and other computer/electronic devices that can be controlled by a mouth opening operated joystick.	Riflery Bowling
C-5	Partial shoulder Biceps	Abduction of the arms Flexion of the arms	Can propel a wheelchair with modified rims, can assist in transfers, can perform some functional arm movements using elbow flexion and gravity to extend the arm.	Swimming
C-6	Major shoulder Wrist extensors	Abduction and flexion of the arms Wrist extension and possibly a weak grasp	Roll over in bed, may be able to transfer from wheelchair to bed, improved ability to propel wheelchair independently, partial independence in eating, grooming, and dressing using special assistive devices.	Billiards Putting
C-7	Triceps Finger extensions Finger flexions	Stabilization and extension of the arm at the elbow. Improved grasp and release, but still weak	Independent in wheelchair locomotion, bed, sitting up, and in many cases transferring from bed to wheelchair. Increased independence in eating, grooming, and dressing.	Archery Crossbow Table tennis
T-1	All upper extremity muscles	All upper body Lacks trunk stability and respiratory endurance	Independent in wheelchair, bed, transfers, eating, grooming, dressing, and toileting. Can ambulate with assistance using long braces, pelvic band, and crutches.	Any activities from a wheelchair

(continued)

Table 12.1 *(Continued)*

Lesion locations	Key muscles innervated	Potential movements	Associated functional abilities	Sample PE activities
T-6	Upper trunk muscles	Trunk stability Improved respiratory endurance	Lift heavier objects because of improved stability. Can independently put their own braces on. Can ambulate with low spinal attachment, pelvic band, long leg braces, and crutches using a "swing" to gait but still depend on wheelchair as primary means of locomotion.	Track & Field Bowling Weightlifting
T-12	Abdominal muscles and thoracic back muscles	Increased trunk stability All muscles needed for respiratory endurance	Can independently ambulate with long leg braces including stairs and curbs. Uses a wheelchair only for convenience.	Competitive swimming Marathon racing
L-4	Lower back Hip flexions Quadriceps	Total trunk stability Ability to flex the hip and left the leg	Can walk independently with short leg braces and bilateral canes or crutches.	Some standing activities
S-1	Hamstring and peroneal muscles	Bend knee Lift the foot up	Can walk independently without crutches. May require ankle braces and/or orthodic shoes.	Normal PE

wide wrapped around the neck and tied loosely in place. (Do not allow the tie to interfere with the victim's breathing.) If the victim is being rescued from an automobile or from water, place a reasonably short, wide board behind the victim's head and back. The board should extend to the victim's buttocks. If possible, tie the board to the victim's body around the forehead and under the armpits. Move the victim very slowly and gently. Do **not** let the victim's body bend or twist.

2. If the victim is not breathing or is having great difficulty in breathing, tilt his or her head **slightly** backward to provide and maintain an open airway.

3. Restore breathing and circulation, if necessary.

4. Summon paramedics or trained ambulance personnel immediately.

5. Lay folded towels, blankets, clothing, sandbags, or other suitable objects around the victim's head, neck, and shoulders to keep the head and neck from moving. Place bricks or stones next to the blankets for additional support.

6. Keep the victim comfortably warm. (pp. 191–192)

Treatment and Educational Considerations

The treatment of individuals with spinal cord injuries usually involves three phases:

- hospitalization,
- rehabilitation, and
- return to the home environment.

Although the three phases are presented as separate, there is considerable overlap between the treatments provided within each phase. During the hospital phase the acute medical aspects of the injury are addressed and therapy is initiated. Depending on the severity of the injury, the hospital stay can last up to several months. Many people with spinal cord injuries are then transferred from the hospital to a rehabilitation center. As indicated by its name, the rehabilitation phase centers on adjustment to the injury and mastery of basic living

Table 12.2 NWAA Functional Classifications

Sport/class	Description
Archery	
A1	Archers in a wheelchair with dysfunction with a need to use a mechanical release. The archer may use a release, compound, or recurve bow, strapping, and body support.
A2	Is an open class for wheelchair archers. The archers use equipment according to FITA rules, except those with balance problems who are allowed to use strapping or body support.
Field events	
F1	Have no grip with nonthrowing arm (use resin or adhesivelike substance for grip). These athletes have functional elbow flexors and wrist dorsiflexors. May have elbow extensors (up to power 3), but usually do not have wrist-palmar flexors. May have shoulder weakness. Have no sitting balance. Discus: have little control of the discus because finger movements are absent. Throw with a flat trajectory. Club: may throw forward or may throw backward over the head. Use thumb-and-index-finger, index-and-middle-finger, or middle-and-ring-finger grip.
F2	Have difficulty gripping with nonthrowing arm. These athletes have functional elbow flexors and extensors, wrist dorsiflexors, and palmar flexors. Have good shoulder-muscle function. May have some finger flexion and extension but not functional. Shot: unable to form a fist and therefore do not usually have finger contact with the shot at the release point. Unable to spread fingers apart. Discus: have no functional finger flexors. Have difficulty placing fingers over the edge of the discus but may do so with the aid of contractures or spasticity. Javelin: usually grip the javelin between the index and middle fingers, but may use the gap between the thumb and index finger or between the middle and ring fingers. These athletes may have slight function between the digits of the hand.
F3	Have nearly normal grip with nonthrowing arm. Have full power at elbow and wrist joints. Have full or almost full power of finger flexion and extension. Have functional but not normal intrinsic muscles of the hand. Shot: usually a good fist can be made. Can spread the fingers apart but not with normal power. Use some spreading of the fingers and can grasp the shot put when throwing. Discus: have good finger function to hold discus. Are able to spread and close the fingers but not with normal power. Javelin: usually grip javelin between the thumb and index finger. Have ability to hold javelin because of presence of hand muscles that spread and close the fingers.
F4	Have no sitting balance. Usually hold onto part of the chair while throwing. Have normal upper limbs. They can hold the throwing implement normally. They have no functional trunk movements. Have trunk movements, but hand function like F3.
F5	Normal upper-limb function. Have abdominal muscles and spinal extensors. May have nonfunctional hip flexors (grade 1). Have no adductor function. Three trunk movements may be seen in this class: off the back of a chair (in an upward direction), movement in the backward and forward plane, and some trunk rotation. They have fair-to-good sitting balance. They cannot have functional hip flexors (i.e., ability to lift the thigh upward in the sitting position). They may have stiffness of the spine that improves balance but reduces the ability to rotate the spine. Shot and javelin: tend to use forward and backward movements, whereas the discus predominantly uses rotatory movements.
F6	Have good balance and movement in the backward and forward planes. Have good trunk rotation. Can lift the thighs. Can press the knees together. May be able to straighten the knees. May have some ability to bend the knees.

(continued)

Table 12.2 *(Continued)*

Sport/class	Description
Field events (cont.)	
F7	Have good balance and movements in the backward and forward planes. Usually have very good balance and movements toward one side (side-to-side movements), due to presence of one functional hip abductor, on the side that movement is toward. Usually can bend one hip backward. Usually can bend one ankle downward. The side that is strong is important when considering how much it will help functional performance.
F8	Standing athletes with dynamic standing balance. Able to recover in standing when balance is challenged. For U.S. competitions there is also an F8 Sitting Class: have normal sitting balance and trunk movements in all planes. Usually are able to stand and possibly walk with braces or by locking knees straight. Are unable to recover balance in standing when balance is challenged and will fall when attempting throws with full effort in standing. For international competition, athletes must compete from a standing position in this class.
Track	
T1	Have functional elbow flexors and wrist dorsiflexors. Have no functional elbow extensors or wrist palmar flexors. May have shoulder weakness. May use elbow flexors to start (back of wrist behind pushing rim). Hands stay in contact or close to the pushing rim, with the power coming from elbow flexion.
T2	Usually use elbow flexors to start, but may use elbow extensors. Power from pushing comes from elbow extension, wrist dorsiflexion, and upper chest muscles. Additional power may be gained by using the elbow flexors when the hands are in contact with the back of the wheel. The head may be forced backwards (by the use of neck muscles), producing slight upper trunk movements.
T2A	Have functional pectoral muscles, elbow flexors and extensors, wrist dorsiflexors, radial wrist movements, some palmar flexors. Have no finger flexors or extensors.
T2B	Have functional pectoral muscles, elbow flexors and extensors, wrist dorsiflexors, and palmar flexors, radial and ulnar wrist movements, finger flexors and extensors. Do not have the ability to perform finger abduction and adduction.
T3	Have normal or nearly normal upper limb function. Have no active trunk movements. When pushing, the trunk is usually lying on the legs. The trunk may rise with the pushing action. Usually use a hand flick technique for power (friction technique). May use the shoulder to steer around curves. Interrupt pushing movements to steer and have difficulty resuming the pushing position. When braking quickly, the trunk stays close to pushing position.
T4	Have back extension, which usually includes both upper and lower extensors. Usually have trunk rotation (i.e., abdominal muscles). Have backward movement of the trunk. Usually have rotation movements of the trunk. May use trunk movements to steer around curves. Usually do not have to interrupt pushing-stroke rate around curves. When stopping quickly, the trunk moves toward an upright position. Use abdominals for power, particularly when starting but also when pushing.

(continued)

Table 12.2 *(Continued)*

Sport/class	Description
Basketball	
I	Class I athletes have no favorable sitting balance when sitting in a wheelchair and without support of a back. The trunk cannot be moved in any plane without the help of at least one arm.
II	Class II athletes have fair-to-good sitting balance. They are able to move their trunk in the horizontal plane when sitting upright without the support of the back. They cannot move their trunk forward maximally. They need at least one arm holding onto the wheelchair to perform trunk movements in the sagittal and frontal plane.
III	Class III athletes have an optimal sitting balance and optimal trunk movements in the horizontal and sagittal plane without the help of one arm holding any part of the wheelchair.
IV	Class IV athletes have an optimal sitting balance and optimal trunk movements in all planes. A significant limitation in movement to one side of the frontal plane must be tolerated.
Shooting	
SH I	All competitors who are able to stand and do not require a shooting stand to support the rifle in rifle events.
SH IIa	Sitting competitors who have good balance (i.e., have functioning abdominal muscles and spinal extensors) and/or fixed kyphoscoliosis (cobb 70–90 degrees). In this subclass, the backrest of the wheelchair, chair, or stool may have a maximum back-height of 15 cm.
SH IIb	Sitting competitors without balance.
SH III	ISMWSF Classes 1C and 2 or similar disability (without shooting stand).
SH IV	All competitors who are unable to support the weight of rifle at all and who therefore require a shooting stand.
SH IVa	Standing competitors with one nonfunctional upper limb or severe problems with both upper limbs (e.g., congenital amputees). Competitors in this class will use a type B stand in kneeling and prone competition. In standing competition, a type A stand may be used.
SH IVc	Sitting competitors with no trunk function. These competitors may use a high backrest and a type A shooting stand.
Swimming	S1–S10 Freestyle, backstroke, butterfly
S1	Very severe quadriplegic with poor head and trunk control.
S2	Tetraplegic, complete below C5/6, severe MD; amputation of four limbs.
S3	Tetraplegic, complete below C6; a lower tetraplegic with an additional handicap; severe MD.
S4	Tetraplegic, complete below C7; some incomplete C5; polio with nonfunctional hands for swimming; MD comparable with C7.
S5	Complete tetraplegic below C8, incomplete C7 or C6 with ability to keep legs horizontal and functional hands for swimming.
S6	Complete paraplegia below T1–T8, incomplete C8 with ability to keep legs horizontal.
S7	Complete paraplegia below T9–L1, double above-knee amputation shorter than 1/2.
S8	Paraplegia L2–L3 with no leg propulsion but ability to keep legs straight, double above-knee amputation, double below-knee amputation no longer than 1/3.
S9	Paraplegia L4–L5; polio with one nonfunctional leg; single above-knee amputation, double below-knee amputation no longer than 1/3.

(continued)

Table 12.2 *(Continued)*

Sport/class	Description
Swimming (cont.)	
S10	Polio or cauda equina lesion with minimal affection of lower limbs, single below-knee amputation, double fore-foot amputation.
	B1–B10 Breaststroke
B1	Tetraplegic, complete below C6; a lower tetraplegic with an additional handicap; severe MD.
B2	Tetraplegic, complete below C7; MD comparable with C1 complete tetraplegia with no finger extension.
B3	Complete tetraplegic below C8, complete paraplegic T1–T5, incomplete C7.
B4	Complete paraplegic T6–T10, incomplete C8, or comparable polio.
B5	Complete paraplegia below T10–L1, incomplete T5, double above-knee amputation shorter than 1/4.
B6	Paraplegia and polio L2–L3 with no leg propulsion, double above-knee amputation longer than 1/4.
B7	Paraplegia and polio L4, poor leg propulsion, double below-knee amputation shorter than 1/2.
B8	Paraplegia L5, polio with one nonfunctional leg, double below-knee amputation longer than 1/2, single above-knee amputation.
B9	Single below-knee amputation, less than 3/4.
B10	Single below-knee amputation longer than 3/4.

Note: From the *Official Rule Book of the Member Organizations of Wheelchair Sports, USA,* 1993, Colorado Springs: Wheelchair Sports, USA. Reprinted by permission.

skills (toileting, dressing, transfers, wheelchair use, etc.) with the functional abilities still available. Near the end of the rehabilitation phase, a transition is begun to move the individual back into the home environment. In the case of a student, the transition involves working with parents and school personnel to make sure that they have the appropriate skills and understanding of the individual's condition and needs and that they know what environmental modifications will be required to accommodate those needs.

The abilities outlined in Table 12.1 are those that can potentially be achieved by people with spinal cord injuries. Unfortunately, to achieve these abilities, individuals must accept their condition, not be hindered by any secondary health problems, and be highly motivated to work in rehabilitation.

One of the major secondary problems associated with spinal cord injuries is *psychological acceptance* of the limitations imposed by the injury and the loss of former abilities. *Counseling* is usually a major component of the treatment plan during rehabilitation. It should be recognized that the rate of adjustment and the degree to which different individuals learn to cope with their disabilities varies tremendously.

People with spinal cord injuries are susceptible to a number of *secondary health conditions.* One of their most common health problems is pressure sores or decubitus ulcers. These are caused by the lack of innervation and reduced blood flow to the skin and most commonly occur at pressure points of bony prominence close to the skin (buttocks, pelvis, and ankles). Because of the poor blood circulation, these sores can easily become infected and are extremely slow to heal. The prevention of pressure sores involves regular inspection of the skin, the use of additional padding in troubled areas, and regular pressure releases (changes in position that alleviate the pressure). Individually designed seat cushions can be made and are used by many people to help better distribute pressure and avoid pressures sores. Keeping the skin dry is also important because the skin is more susceptible to sores when it is wet from urine and/or perspiration.

A problem closely related to pressure sores is *bruising* of the skin. Because no sensation is felt in

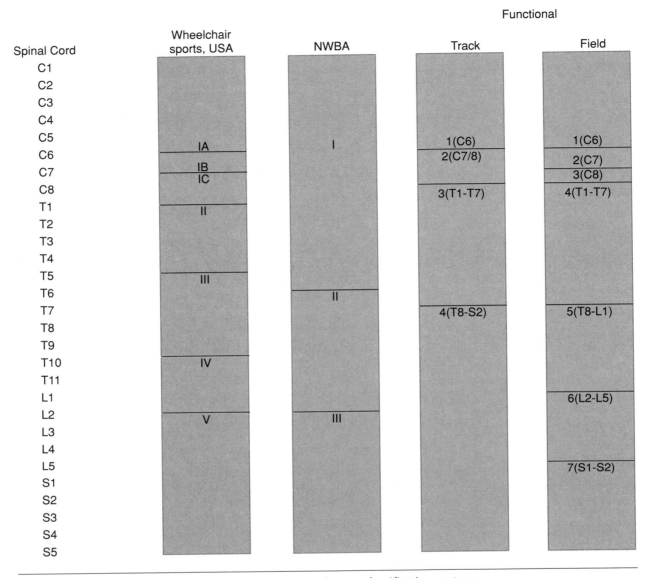

Figure 12.2 Spinal cord levels associated with functional sport classification systems.

the limbs that are not innervated, it is not uncommon for them to be unconsciously bruised or irritated from hitting or rubbing against other surfaces. Injuries of this nature are quite common in wheelchair activities like basketball if appropriate precautions are not taken. Because these bruises are not felt, they can go unnoticed and eventually can become infected.

A third health problem commonly encountered in individuals with spinal cord injuries is **urinary tract infection.** Urination is controlled by some form of catheterization on an established schedule. Urinary infections occur when urine is retained in the bladder and backs up into the kidneys. Urinary tract infections can be very severe and usually keep

the patient bedridden for a prolonged period of time, which is counterproductive for attitude, rehabilitation, and skill development. Bowel movements must also be carefully monitored to prevent constipation and incontinence. Bowel movements are usually controlled by a combination of diet and mild laxatives. In cases where bowel movements cannot be controlled by diet, a tube is surgically inserted into the intestine. The tube exits through a small opening made in the side and is connected to a bag that collects the fecal excretions.

Two other closely associated problems that frequently accompany spinal cord injuries are **spasticity** and **contractures.** Spasticity is increased tone in muscles that are no longer innervated because of the injury. This increased muscle tone can nullify the use of other, still innervated muscles. The term spasm is frequently used to describe sudden spasticity in a muscle group that can be of sufficient force to launch an individual out of a wheelchair. The best treatment for spastic muscles is to stretch them regularly, particularly before and after rigorous activity. Contractures can frequently occur in the joints of the lower limbs if they are not regularly, passively moved through the full range of motion. A high degree of spasticity in various muscle groups can also limit the range of motion and contribute to contractures.

The last problem commonly associated with spinal cord injuries is a tendency toward obesity. The loss of function in the large muscle groups in the lower limbs severely reduces the caloric burning capacity of people with spinal cord injuries. Unfortunately, a corresponding loss in appetite does not also occur. Many individuals with spinal cord injuries tend to resume their habitual caloric intake or even to increase it because of their sedentary condition. Weight and diet should be carefully monitored to prevent obesity and the secondary health hazards associated with it. Once weight is gained, it is extremely difficult to lose.

A major key to success in rehabilitation and in accepting a disability is motivation. Many individuals with spinal cord disabilities initially have great difficulty accepting the loss of previous abilities and subsequently are reluctant to work hard during the tedious and often painful therapy. Recreational and sport activities are commonly used in both counseling and therapy as reasons for working hard and as distractions. A physical educator should be sensitive to the motivational needs of a student returning to a program with a spinal cord disability. Although sport can be a motivator for many, it can also highlight the loss of previous skills and abilities.

The physical education teacher should anticipate needs in the areas of body image, upper body strength, range of motion, endurance, and wheelchair tolerance. These needs, together with the student's functional abilities, should be analyzed to determine what lifetime sport skills and wheelchair sports are most viable for future participation. These activities then become the annual instructional goals for the physical education program.

While an individual with a spinal cord injury is still learning to deal with the injury, the physical educator can assist by anticipating the person's needs and planning ahead. This may involve reminding the student to perform pressure releases at regular intervals (lifting the weight off the seat of the chair by doing an arm press on the arm supports of the chair, or just shifting the sitting position) or bringing extra towels to class to absorb extra moisture in the chair. Because spasticity and spasms are common, stretching at the beginning of class and periodically during the class is recommended. Finally, pads should be provided to prevent bruising in active wheelchair activities. As the student becomes accustomed to the condition, most of these precautions will become habits. A student who has an external bag should be reminded to empty and clean it before physical education class. In contact activities, care should be taken to protect the bag from contact. For swimming, the bag should be removed and the opening in the side covered with a watertight bandage.

Poliomyelitis

Poliomyelitis, commonly called *polio*, is a form of paralysis caused by a viral infection that affects the motor cells in the spinal cord. The severity and degree of paralysis vary with each individual and depend on the number and location of the motor cells affected. The paralysis may be temporary, occurring only during the acute phase of the illness (in which case the motor cells are not destroyed), or permanent if the motor cells are destroyed by the virus. Bowel and bladder control and sensation in the involved limbs are not affected by this condition.

Incidence

The occurrence of polio is rare in school-age children today because of the widespread use of the Salk vaccine.

Treatment and Educational Considerations

During the acute, or active, phase of the illness, the child is confined to bed. The illness is accompanied by a high fever and pain and paralysis in the affected muscles. After the acute phase, muscle tests determine which muscles were affected and to what degree. Rehabilitation is then begun to develop functional abilities with the muscles that remain.

Depending on the severity of the paralysis, a child may require instruction in walking with crutches or long leg braces and/or using a wheelchair. When the lower limbs have been severely affected, it is not uncommon for bone deformities to occur as the child develops. These deformities can involve the hips, knees, ankles, or feet and frequently require surgery to correct.

Specific activity implications are difficult to provide for children with polio because their range of abilities can be so great. Physical educators need to accurately evaluate the abilities and limitations imposed by the condition for each student and then make appropriate placement and instructional decisions.

Many children with only one involved limb or mild involvement of two limbs will already have learned to compensate for the condition and will do fine in the regular physical education program. Others with more extensive or severe involvement may require a more restricted adapted physical education program. Care should be taken not to totally remove these children from regular physical education. Whatever the degree of involvement, these children have normal IQs, typical play interests, and the desire to be with their classmates.

Regardless of the physical education placement, the emphasis should be on optimal development of the muscles the student does have. Priority should be given to lifetime sport skills and activities that can be carried over and pursued for recreation and fitness when the school years are past. Swimming is an excellent example of an activity that promotes lifetime fitness, provides recreation, and prepares one for other activities such as sailing and canoeing.

Spina Bifida

Spina bifida is a congenital birth defect in which the neural tube fails to close completely during the first four weeks of fetal development. Subsequently, the posterior arch of one or more vertebrae fails to develop properly, leaving an opening in the spinal column. There are three classifications of spina bifida, based on which structures, if any, protrude through the opening in the spine.

Myelomeningocele is the most severe and, unfortunately, the most common form of spinal bifida. In this condition the covering of the spinal cord (meninges), cerebrospinal fluid, and part of the spinal cord protrude through the opening and form a visible sac on the child's back (see Figure 12.3a). Some degree of neurological damage and subsequent loss of motor function are always associated with this form.

Spina bifida meningocele is similar to the myelomeningocele form, except that only the spinal cord covering and cerebrospinal fluid protrude into the sac (see Figure 12.3b). This form rarely has any neurological damage associated with it.

Occulta is the mildest and least common form of spina bifida. In this condition, the defect is present in the posterior arch of the vertebra, but nothing protrudes through the opening (see Figure 12.3c). No neurological damage is associated with this type of spina bifida.

Once detected soon after birth and surgically corrected, the meningocele and occulta forms of spina bifida have no adverse ramifications. The greatest threat in these conditions is from infection prior to surgery.

Incidence

Because some degree of neurological damage is always associated with the myelomeningocele type of spina bifida, it will be the form discussed in the remainder of this section. Approximately two children out of every 1,000 live births have spina bifida, and 80% of these children have the myelomeningocele form. The degree of neurological damage associated with spina bifida myelomeningocele depends on the location of the deformity and the amount of damage done to the spinal cord. Fortunately, spina bifida occurs most commonly in the lumbar vertebrae, sparing motor function in the upper limbs and limiting the disability primarily to the lower limbs. Bowel and bladder control are almost always lost. The muscle functions and abilities presented in Table 12.1 for spinal cord lesions in the lumbar region can also be used to ascertain what functional abilities a child with spina bifida will have.

In addition to the neurological disability associated with damage to the spinal cord, myelomeningocele is almost always accompanied by hydrocephalus. This is a condition in which the circulation of the cerebrospinal fluid is obstructed in one of the ventricles or cavities of the brain. If the obstruction is not removed or circumvented, the ventricle begins to enlarge, putting pressure on the brain and enlarging the head. If not treated, this condition can lead to brain damage, mental retardation, and ultimately to death. Today, hydrocephalus is suspected early in children with spina bifida and is usually treated surgically by insertion of a shunt during the first few weeks after birth (see Figure 12.4). The shunt, a plastic tube equipped with a pressure valve, is inserted into a ventricle and drains off the excess cerebrospinal fluid. The fluid is usually drained into either the heart (ventriculoatrial) or the abdomen (ventriculoperitoneal) to be reabsorbed by the body.

Treatment and Educational Considerations

As mentioned earlier, all forms of spina bifida are diagnosed and surgically treated soon after birth.

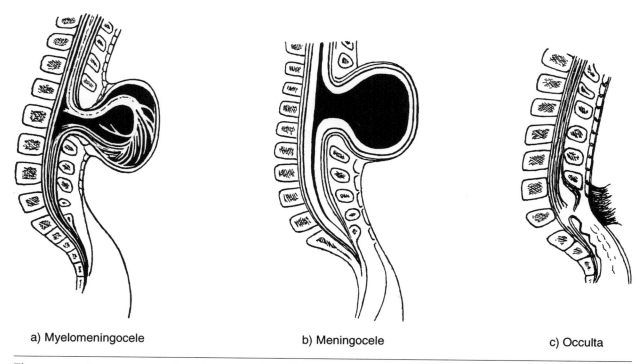

a) Myelomeningocele   b) Meningocele   c) Occulta

Figure 12.3   Diagram of the three types of spina bifida.
From "Spina Bifida" (p. 10) by G.G. Deaver, D. Buck, and J. McCarthy. In *1951 Yearbook of Physical Medicine and Rehabilitation.*
Copyright 1952 by Year Book Medical Publishers, Inc., Chicago.

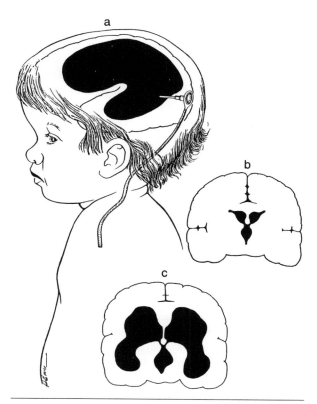

Figure 12.4   Illustration of a shunt being used to relieve hydrocephalus: (a) the shunt in place, (b) normal ventricles, (c) enlarged ventricles.

The major treatment beyond the immediate medical procedures involves physical and occupational therapy for the child and counseling and training for the parents. The therapy has two focuses: using assistive devices to position children so that they parallel the developmental positions (sitting, crawling, standing, etc.) through which a normal child progresses, and maintaining full range of motion and stimulating circulation in the lower limbs. In conjunction with their therapy, children with spina bifida are fitted with braces and encouraged to ambulate. Even if functional walking skills are not developed, it is very important for the child with spina bifida to do weight-bearing activities to stimulate bone growth and circulation in the lower limbs. Parents are counseled to try to provide the child with as normal and as many appropriate stimuli as possible. Many parents, unfortunately, frequently overprotect and confine their children with spina bifida, which results in further delays in growth and development.

There are several important similarities and differences in the treatments of spina bifida and of the spinal cord injuries discussed earlier in this chapter. The similarities concern the muscle and sensation loss and the common problems related to these deficits:

- Bone deformities
- Postural deviations
- Pressure sores
- Bruising
- Urinary infections
- Obesity

The differences are related to the onset of the conditions; different circumstances result in different emotional and developmental ramifications.

Generally, children with spina bifida have fewer emotional problems dealing with their condition than do children with acquired spinal cord disabilities, probably because the condition has been present since birth and they have not suffered the loss of any former abilities. However, this is not to imply that they do not become frustrated when other children can perform skills and play activities that they cannot because of their dependence on a wheelchair or crutches.

A second major ramification of the early onset of spina bifida is its effect on growth and development. The lack of innervation and subsequent use and stimulation of the affected limbs retards their physical growth. The result is a greater incidence of bone deformities and contractures in the lower limbs and a greater need for orthotics (braces) to help minimize these deformities and assist in providing functional support. A concurrent problem is related to sensory deprivation during the early years of development due to restricted mobility. This deprivation is frequently compounded by overprotective parents and medical problems that confine the child to bed for long periods.

Children with spina bifida are vulnerable to infections from pressure sores and bruises. Pressure sores are most common in those who are confined to wheelchairs. Bruising and skin irritation are particular concerns for children with spina bifida using crutches and long leg braces. These children have a tendency to fall frequently in physical activities and to be susceptible to skin irritations from their braces if the braces are not properly put on each time.

Bowel and bladder control present significant social problems for the child with spina bifida during the early elementary school years. Bowel movements are controlled by diet and medication, which are designed to prevent constipation. Urination is commonly controlled today by a regular schedule of catheterization, performed during the day by the school nurse or an aide (see Figure 12.5). This dependence on others for help with personal functions and the inevitable occasional accident in class can have negative social implications.

Finally, children with spina bifida have a tendency toward obesity. Several causes contribute to this tendency. The loss of the caloric expenditure typically made by the large muscle groups in the lower limbs limits the number of calories that can be burned. Caloric expenditure is frequently further limited by the sedentary environment of these children and their limited mobility during the early years. Control of caloric intake is essential to avoid obesity. Unfortunately, food is frequently highly gratifying to these children and is provided in abundance by indulging parents and caregivers. Obesity should be avoided at all costs because it further limits the children's mobility and predisposes them to a variety of other health problems.

Children with spina bifida will most likely be placed initially in some combination of adapted and regular physical education during the early elementary years and will be fully mainstreamed into the regular physical education program by the end of the elementary years. It is important not to remove these children unnecessarily from regular physical education. They have normal IQs and the same play and social needs as the other students in their classes. On the other hand, the primary goal of physical education, to develop physical and motor skills, should not be sacrificed purely for social objectives. If the children's physical and motor needs cannot be met in the regular class, they should receive appropriate support and/or supplemental adapted physical education to meet these needs.

In summary, children with spina bifida need to achieve the same physical education goals and objectives targeted for other students. Modifications will be needed to accommodate their mode of locomotion (crutches or wheelchair) and to emphasize their upper body development. Emphasis should be placed on physical fitness and the development of lifetime sport skills.

Spondylolysis and Spondylolisthesis

Spondylolysis refers to a congenital malformation of the neural arches of the fourth, or more commonly, the fifth lumbar vertebra. Individuals with spondylolysis may or may not experience any back pain, but they are predisposed to acquiring spondylolisthesis. Spondylolisthesis is similar to spondylolysis, except that in this condition, the fifth lumbar vertebra has slid forward. The displacement occurs because of the lack of the neural arch structure and the ligaments that normally hold this area in place. Spondylolisthesis can be congenital or can occur as a result

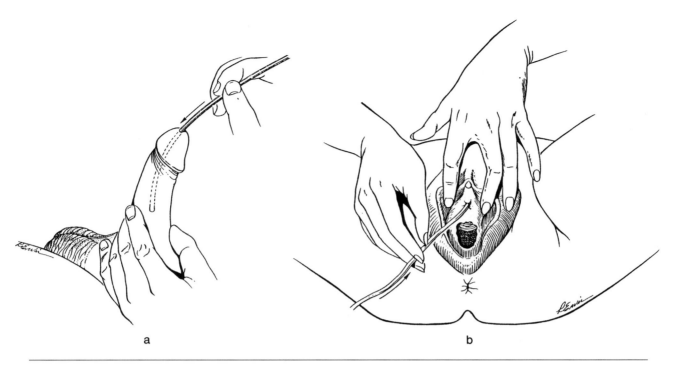

a   b

Figure 12.5 Illustration of male (a) and female (b) catherterization procedures used to remove urine using a lubricated plastic catheter.

of trauma to the back. It is usually associated with severe pain in the back and legs.

Treatment in mild cases involves training and awareness of proper posture. Individuals with spondylolisthesis frequently have an exaggerated lordotic curve in the back. In more severe cases, surgery is performed to realign the vertebrae and fuse that section of the spine.

Medical consultation should be pursued before any students with spondylolysis or spondylolisthesis participate in physical education. Children with mild cases may be able to participate in regular physical education with emphasis on proper posture, additional stretching, and avoidance of activities that involve severe stretching or trauma to the back. In more severe cases, adapted physical education may be required to provide more comprehensive posture training and exercises and to foster the development of physical and motor skills that will not aggravate the condition.

IMPLICATIONS FOR PHYSICAL EDUCATION

Assessment is the key to successfully addressing the physical education needs of students with spinal cord disabilities. Physical educators must work

as part of a team to obtain the assessment data they need to provide appropriate instruction. By consulting with each other, the physical educator and the physical and/or occupational therapist can share essential information about their goals and objectives for each student. The physical therapist can provide pertinent information about the muscles that are still innervated and those that have been lost, the existing muscle strength and the prognosis for its further development, the range of motion at the various joints, and the presence or absence of sensation in the limbs. The physical and/or occupational therapist can also provide useful information about adapted appliances (e.g., a device to hold a racket when a grip is not possible) as well as practical guidance on putting on and removing braces, adjusting wheelchairs, positioning and the use of restraints in wheelchairs, lifting and handling the student, and making transfers to and from the wheelchair.

Within the domain of physical education, the teacher must be able to assess the students' fitness and motor skills. Only one available physical fitness test, the Project UNIQUE Physical Fitness Test (Winnick & Short, 1985), was designed specifically to accommodate individuals with spinal cord disabilities and provides appropriate normative data for this population. Given the lack of norm-referenced tests for these individuals, physical educators should modify and use criterion-referenced tests to assess both motor skills and physical fitness for individuals with spinal cord disabilities.

In general, individuals with spinal cord disabilities have placed significantly below students without disabilities at their age level on physical fitness measures and in motor skill development. Winnick and Short (1985), for example, have reported that 52% to 72% of individuals with spinal cord disabilities in their Project UNIQUE study had skinfold measures greater than the median value for same-aged subjects who were not impaired, and only about 19% of the girls with spinal cord disabilities and 36% of the boys scored above the nonimpaired median on grip strength. Winnick and Short (1984) have also reported that youngsters with paraplegic spinal neuromuscular conditions have generally lower fitness levels than normal youngsters of the same age and gender, and that these youngsters do not demonstrate significant improvement with age or show significant gender differences like those found among normal youngsters. These results should not be misinterpreted to mean that people with spinal cord disabilities cannot develop better levels of physical fitness. Research has shown, on the contrary, that with proper instruction and opportunity to practice, these individuals can make significant improvements in physical fitness. The key is appropriate instruction and practice designed to address individual needs.

Fitness programs for individuals with spinal cord disabilities should focus on flexibility, strength, and endurance training. While flexibility in all joints should be a goal, particular emphasis should be placed on preventing or reducing contractures in joints where muscles are no longer innervated. These situations require a regular routine of passive stretching that moves the joints through the full range of motion.

Strength training should focus on restoring and/or maximizing the strength in the unaffected muscles. Care must be taken not to create muscle imbalances by overstrengthening muscle groups when the antagonist muscles are affected. Most common progressive resistance exercises are suitable for individuals with spinal cord disabilities with little or no modification. Posture and correct body mechanics should be stressed during all strength training activities.

One of the most challenging fitness areas with individuals who have spinal cord disabilities is cardiorespiratory endurance. Work in this area is frequently complicated by the loss of the large muscle groups of the legs, which makes cardiorespiratory training more difficult. In these cases, the principles of intensity, frequency, and duration must be applied to less traditional aerobic activities that use the smaller muscle groups of the arms and shoulders. A number of wheelchair ergometers and hand-driven bicycle ergometers have been designed specifically to address the cardiorespiratory needs of individuals with spinal cord disabilities. While it is more difficult to attain the benefits of cardiorespiratory training using the smaller muscle groups of the arms and shoulders, it is not impossible. There are a number of highly conditioned wheelchair marathoners who clearly demonstrate that high levels of aerobic fitness can be attained.

In addition to physical fitness and motor skill areas, physical educators should concentrate on *posture, body mechanics* and *weight control*. Individuals with spinal cord disabilities frequently have poor body mechanics as a result of muscle imbalances and contractures. Exercises and activities that contribute to body awareness and alignment should therefore be stressed. Another secondary problem that contributes to poor posture and has a general negative effect on both physical fitness and motor skill acquisition is obesity. Obesity is, unfortunately, very common in individuals with spinal cord disabilities, largely because the loss of the large muscle groups of the lower limbs diminishes their capacity to burn calories. Weight control is a function of balancing caloric intake with caloric expenditure. Because, in many cases, caloric expenditure is limited to a large degree by the extent of muscle damage and the subsequent activities that can be undertaken, the obvious solution is to control food intake.

In terms of sport skills, the most valuable activities are those that have the greatest carryover potential for lifetime participation. The selection of activities should provide a balance between warm- and cold-weather sports as well as indoor and outdoor sports. Preference should be given to sports that promote physical fitness and for which there are organized opportunities for participation in the community. Just about any sport (e.g., golf, tennis, swimming, skiing) can be adapted or modified so that individuals with spinal cord disabilities can participate.

The goal of assessment is to obtain the most accurate and complete data possible so that the most appropriate placement and instruction can be provided. Physical educators must be willing to devote both the time and the effort required to obtain this assessment data if they wish to help their students reach their maximum potential. Working cooperatively with a team is the key to maximizing staff efficiency and the benefits for the students.

ORTHOTIC DEVICES

Due to the neuromuscular limitations imposed by spinal cord disabilities, many individuals with these disabilities use orthoses to enhance their functional abilities. Orthoses are a variety of splints and braces designed to provide support, improve positioning, correct or prevent deformities, and reduce or alleviate pain. Although presented in this chapter, the use of orthotic devices is not limited to individuals with spinal cord disabilities. Orthotic devices are prescribed by physicians and fitted by occupational therapists, who also instruct users in wearing and caring for the devices. Examples of the more common orthoses are shown in Figure 12.6. They are used both by individuals who are ambulatory to provide better stability and by individuals in wheelchairs to prevent deformities. These devices are commonly referred to by acronyms that describe the joints they cover: AFO (ankle-foot orthosis), KAFO (knee-ankle-foot orthosis), and HKAFO (hip-knee-ankle-foot orthosis).

Many of the newer plastic orthoses can be worn inside regular shoes and under clothing. Under normal circumstances, orthoses should be worn in all physical education activities with the exception of swimming. In vigorous activities, physical educators should periodically check that the straps are secure and that no abrasion or skin irritation is occurring where the orthosis or straps contact the skin. Orthoses can also be used to improve positioning to maximize sensory input. Figure 12.7 shows a series of assistive devices often used with children with spina bifida. The purpose of these orthotics is to allow these children with spina bifida to view and interact with the environment from the normal developmental vertical postures which they cannot attain and maintain on their own. The last device is a parapodium (see Figure 12.7), or standing table. The parapodium allows individuals who otherwise could not stand to attain a standing position from which they can work and view the world. The parapodium frees the individual from the burden of balancing and bearing weight and also affords complete use of the arms and hands. The parapodium can be used effectively in physical education to teach a number of skills such as table tennis. In recent years, several companies have devised ingenious modifications of the parapodium that can be easily adjusted to a number of vertical and horizontal positions.

A secondary category of orthotic devices includes canes and walkers that are used as assistive devices for ambulation. The Lofstrand or Canadian crutches are most commonly used by individuals with spina bifida and spinal cord disabilities who ambulate with leg braces and crutches. Physical

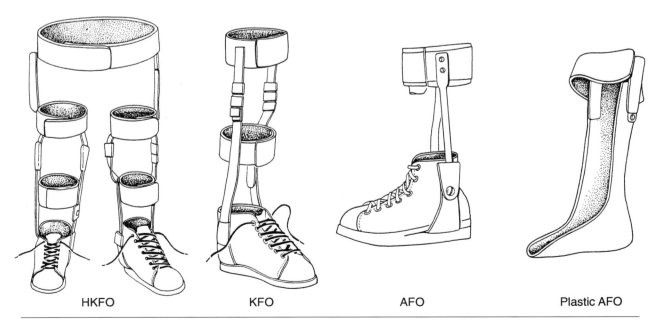

| HKFO | KFO | AFO | Plastic AFO |

Figure 12.6 Common orthotic devices worn by individuals with spinal cord disabilities.

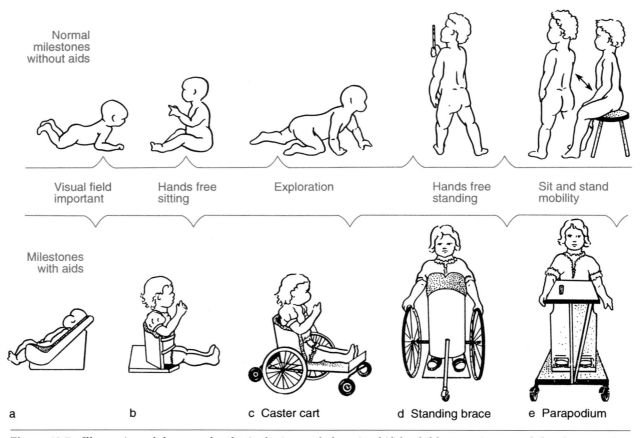

Normal milestones without aids

Visual field important | Hands free sitting | Exploration | Hands free standing | Sit and stand mobility

Milestones with aids

a   b   c Caster cart   d Standing brace   e Parapodium

Figure 12.7 Illustration of the use of orthotic devices to help spina bifida children attain normal developmental postures.

educators should be aware that a person using only one cane or crutch employs it on the strong side, thus immobilizing the better arm. This should be considered, and appropriate modifications (i.e., to maintain balance) should be made for skills in which use of the better arm is desired.

ADAPTED SPORT ACTIVITIES

Today, there is a large number of organizations that sponsor athletic programs and sporting events for individuals with spinal cord disabilities. Wheelchair Sports, USA (previously known as the National Wheelchair Athletic Association) is one of the oldest and most notable, sponsoring athletic events for people with neuromuscular disabilities resulting from spinal cord injuries, spina bifida, or polio. Wheelchair Sports, USA sponsors competitive events in pistol shooting, riflery, swimming, table tennis, weight lifting, archery, fencing, wheelchair slalom, and track and field. Competitors are classified into divisions by age and functional ability (see Table 12.2). There are two age divisions:

adult, for individuals aged 16 and older, and junior, for individuals 8 to 15. As discussed earlier in this chapter, there is growing interest in replacing the Wheelchair Sports, USA system with a functional classification system (see Table 12.2) that is now used for international competitions.

The National Handicapped Sports (formally the National Handicapped Sport and Recreation Association) plays a major role in organizing and sponsoring both competitive and noncompetitive winter sports events for individuals with disabilities. In addition, NHS is a leader in the development and dissemination of recreation/fitness and training materials related to sport and recreation for the individuals with disabilities. One example is the "Fitness Is for Everyone" program, which includes a series of aerobic dance videotapes designed especially to help individuals with paraplegia, quadriplegia, amputations, and cerebral palsy develop endurance, strength, and flexibility. NHS also serves as the official governing body for sport competitions for individuals with amputations.

Numerous special organizations sponsor athletic competitions in a specific sport. Although many of these organizations employ the Wheelchair Sports, USA classification system, the National Wheelchair Basketball Association (NWBA) has its own system. In the NWBA classification system, each player is classified as a I, II, or III, depending on the location of the spinal injury and the degree of motor loss. Internationally, a similar system with four classification levels is used (Labanowich, 1988). Each class has a corresponding point value of 1, 2, or 3. A team can comprise players in any combination of classes as long as the total point value for the five players does not exceed 12 and there are not more than three Class III players. The classifications are made according to certain criteria (NWBA, 1986, p. 7).

National Wheelchair Basketball Association Classification System

Class I: Complete motor loss at T-7 or above or comparable disability where there is total loss of muscle function originating at or above T-7.

Class II: Complete motor loss originating at T-8 and descending through and including L-2 where there may be motor power of hips and thighs. Also included are amputees with bilateral hip disarticulation.

Class III: All other physical disabilities as related to lower extremity paralysis or paresis originating at or below L-3. All lower-extremity amputees are included in this class except those with bilateral hip disarticulation.

The NWBA classification system provides an excellent model for equating team sport competition in physical education classes that include mainstreamed students with spinal cord disabilities. A similar classification system based on students' skill levels could also be designed and used in physical education classes.

In the past decade, wheelchair sports have evolved from recreation into events that are highly sophisticated and competitive. Many of the initial advances in wheelchair sports were the direct result of technical advances in wheelchair design and/or research related to the postural and body mechanics of wheelchair propulsion (see chapter 27). In recent years, attention has shifted to defining and improving training and conditioning programs for wheelchair athletes (Ferrara & Davis, 1990; Gayle & Muir, 1992; Horvat, French, & Henschen, 1986; Skuldt, 1984; Wells & Hooker, 1990).

Specialized, organized sport programs serve as an extension of the physical education curriculum. They provide students with spinal cord disabilities

with the same opportunity to gain the benefits and experiences all athletes derive from sport, and they act as an additional source of motivation. These activities also give participants an opportunity to meet and interact socially with others who have similar characteristics, interests, and needs. Finally, these sport experiences expose students with spinal cord disabilities to positive role models who demonstrate the difference between having a disability and being handicapped. To maximize the probability that students with disabilities will both attempt and succeed in sports, physical educators must ensure that the physical education curriculum provides both instruction in the fundamental sport skills and the appropriate transition from skill development to skill application in actual sport situations.

SUMMARY

Individuals with spinal cord disabilities need to achieve the same physical education goals as other students. To successfully meet the needs of these students, physical educators must have a thorough understanding of the nature of the disabilities and the functional abilities that can be attained. They can then build on this knowledge base to determine the most appropriate placement and instructional programming for each student. Particular emphasis in the program should be placed on body awareness, physical fitness, and the development of lifetime sport skills. Adapted sports, using functional ability classification systems, provide excellent opportunities for individuals with spinal cord disabilities to apply and practice the skills learned in physical education.

BIBLIOGRAPHY

American Medical Association. (1990). *Handbook of first aid and emergency care*. New York: Random House.

Curtis, K. (1991). Sport-specific functional classification for wheelchair athletes. *Sports 'N Spokes*, **17**(2), 45–48.

Ferrara, M.S., & Davis, R.W. (1990). Injuries to wheelchair athletes. *Paraplegia*, **28**, 335–341.

Gayle, G.W., & Muir, J.L. (1992). Role of sportsmedicine and the spinal cord injured: A multidisciplinary relationship. *Palaestra*, **8**(3), 51–56.

Horvat, M., French, R., & Henschen, K. (1986). A comparison of male and female able-bodied and wheelchair athletes. *Paraplegia*, **24**, 115–122.

Labanowich, S. (1988). Wheelchair basketball classification: National and international perspective. *Palaestra*, **4**(3), 14–54.

Lough, L.K., & Nielsen, D.H. (1986). Ambulation of children with myelomeningocele: Parapodium versus parapodium with Orlauswivel modification. *Developmental Medicine and Child Neurology*, **28**, 489–497.

National Wheelchair Basketball Association. (1986). *1985–1986 NWBA rules and case book*. Lexington, KY: Author.

Skuldt, A. (1984). Exercise limitations for quadriplegics. *Sports 'N Spokes*, **10**, 19–20.

Wells, C.L., & Hooker, S.P. (1990). The spinal injured athlete. *Adapted Physical Activity Quarterly*, **7**, 265–285.

Wheelchair Sports, USA. (1993). *Official rulebook of the member organizations of Wheelchair Sports, USA*. Colorado Springs, CO: Author.

Winnick, J.P., & Short, F.X. (1984). The physical fitness of youngsters with spinal neuromuscular conditions. *Adapted Physical Activity Quarterly*, **1**, 37–51.

Winnick, J.P., & Short, F.X. (1985). *Physical fitness testing of the disabled*. Champaign, IL: Human Kinetics.

RESOURCES

Written

Curtis, K. (1981a). Wheelchair sports medicine. Part 1: Basics of exercise physiology. *Sports 'N Spokes*, **7**(1), 26–30.

Curtis, K. (1981b). Wheelchair sports medicine. Part 2: Training. *Sports 'N Spokes*, **7**(2), 16–19.

Curtis, K. (1981c). Wheelchair sports medicine. Part 3: Stretching routines. *Sports 'N Spokes*, **7**(3), 16–20.

Curtis, K. (1982). Wheelchair sports medicine. Part 4: Athletic injuries. *Sports 'N Spokes*, **7**(5), 20–24.

This four-part series on sports medicine for wheelchair sports provides an excellent foundation for the beginning athlete and volunteer coaches working with wheelchair athletes for the first time.

Audiovisual

National Handicapped Sports and Recreation Association. (1986). *Fitness is for everyone* [Videotape]. Cleveland; Wyse Public Relations. NHS has developed a series of aerobic and strength-flexibility videotapes (each approximately 30 minutes in length) that are specifically designed for individuals with paraplegia, quadriplegia, cerebral palsy, and amputations. These are professionally made tapes. Each routine is demonstrated by a professional aerobics instructor and a person with a specific disability. Address for videotapes: NHS/Videotapes, 451 Hungerford Drive, #100, Rockville, MD 20850.

Project Fit. This is an 18-minute VHS video where individuals with disabilities explain why fitness is important. Available from YMCA Program Store, c/o Human Kinetics, Box 5076, Champaign, IL 61820. Cost $29.95.

CHAPTER 13

Other Health Impaired Students

Paul R. Surburg

When the public laws (PL 94-142 through PL 101-476) were discussed in earlier chapters, one of 11 official disabling or handicapping conditions identified was *other health impaired* (OHI). By design this category is a broad designation that provides coverage under the law for a variety of disabling conditions and diseases. While students may be eligible for special education services under the OHI classification, there are several reasons for this designation not being utilized.

First, a student with diabetes or asthma may not want to be labeled as disabled in the vernacular of certain school settings, "a special ed student." In many states the OHI designation must be officially diagnosed by a physician. A family physician may not want to confirm the diagnosis and place a certain stigma upon a student. Parents often intercede with the doctor to prevent the label of disabled being imposed upon their child.

Second, in many states the development of an individualized education plan (IEP) that deals exclusively with physical education is a rare situation. Without certain limitations on the part of a student in the academic learning environment, the probability of establishing an IEP only for physical education is low. Nevertheless, while OHI students may not be designated as disabled, regular and adapted physical educators must understand those students' conditions and the best way to provide meaningful physical education experiences for them.

DIABETES MELLITUS

Diabetes mellitus is a chronic disease characterized by insufficient insulin and disturbances of carbohydrate, protein, and fat metabolism. This disease affects approximately 11 million people in the United States. It is responsible for 50% of myocardial infarctions and 75% of all strokes; it is a major cause of new blindness and a causal factor for amputations (Duda, 1985). Ten percent of documented cases occur among school-aged children. This statistic has direct implications for physical education programs because there is an excellent chance of having a student with diabetes in class.

Insulin-dependent diabetes mellitus (IDDM) has, in certain cases, been linked to a viral origin; genetic or hereditary causes have also been associated with this type of diabetes. Also cited as a possible cause is an autoimmune reaction in which a virus may affect body cells, and the immune system no longer identifies these cells as part of the body. These cells, which may be beta cells in the pancreas, are then destroyed or rejected by the body. Several factors seem to increase the likelihood of developing IDDM:

- Obesity
- Emotional stress
- Pregnancy
- Oral contraceptives
- Medications such as corticosteroids

Types of Diabetes

There are two types of diabetes: (a) IDDM, also known as ketosis-prone or juvenile diabetes, and (b) non–insulin-dependent mellitus (NIDDM), also known as ketosis-resistant or maturity-onset diabetes. **Insulin-dependent diabetes mellitus** occurs most frequently before age 30 but may develop at any age. This type of diabetes requires daily insulin injections and dietary management. The treatment of non–insulin-dependent diabetes, by contrast, may be diet alone or in conjunction with insulin or hypoglycemic agents. It should be noted that 80% of persons with NIDDM are overweight (Helmrich, Ragland & Leung, 1991).

Because most school-age diabetics are insulin dependent, this section will deal exclusively with this form of the disease. With IDDM, insulin-producing cells known as islets of Langerhans degenerate and/or disappear; consequently, insulin production is diminished. Related complications are interference with the action of insulin at the cellular level, faulty storage of sugar in the liver, overproduction of sugar in the liver, and diminished utilization of sugar at the tissue level.

Insulin-dependent diabetes may become apparent dramatically, with ketoacidosis (or diabetic coma), or gradually with an asymptomatic status as in mild diabetes. With a deficiency of insulin the body cannot convert glucose to glycogen for storage in the liver, and an excess of sugar accumulates in the blood. Inadequate carbohydrate utilization also affects fat metabolism. When there is improper fat usage, waste products called ketones are formed, providing a condition called acidosis.

Be Watchful for Symptoms of Diabetic Coma and Insulin Shock

Symptoms of ketoacidosis or diabetic coma are extreme thirst, dry mucous membranes, labored breathing, weak and rapid pulse, sweet, fruity breath odor, vomiting, and high sugar content in the urine. This condition is a first-rank medical emergency and should be treated at a hospital with dosages of insulin and intravenous fluids for a dehydrated state.

A condition that may be corrected more easily is insulin shock of hypoglycemia, which occurs when glycogen stored in the liver is depleted. Symptoms of insulin shock or hypoglycemia are fatigue, excessive perspiration, hunger, double vision, tremor, and absence of sugar in the urine. If this condition is not in an advanced stage, the ingestion of fruit juice, a candy bar, honey, or a carbonated (not diet) drink should rectify the sugar imbalance. When shock is severe enough to result in unconsciousness, an injection of glucagon or dextrose is used to elevate the glucose level in the blood.

Physical Education and the Student With Diabetes

The observation of certain procedures and protocols should ensure students with diabetes successful involvement in physical education activities. Diabetes does not preclude exceptional achievement in sport activities, as evidenced by former professional sports greats Ron Santo of the Chicago Cubs, Catfish Hunter of the Oakland A's and New York Yankees, and hockey player Bobby Clarke.

Both the student and physical educator must be aware of the interrelationship of diet, insulin intake, and exercise. The site of the insulin injection may depend on the kind of exercise planned. Insulin is a protein that cannot be taken orally because the digestive juices would destroy it; therefore, it must be injected subcutaneously. Injections are needed once or twice a day and should be administered at sites where the muscles are not used extensively in a sport or physical activity. Thus, for a student who is participating in track, the injection site should be the stomach rather than the legs. Another important consideration is the interaction between exercise and insulin dosage. There is an inverse relationship between the intensity of activity and the amount of insulin needed. A heightened level of activity necessitates a reduction in insulin dosage. The physical educator must alert the diabetic student to any planned changes in kind or intensity of activity; in anticipation, the student will have to make appropriate adjustments in insulin dosage and/or diet.

Generally, the student with diabetes tries to keep three factors constant: *exercise, insulin usage,* and *diet.* A variation in one or more of these factors may precipitate a physiological imbalance. For example, a reduction in calories and an increase in exercise intensity may lead to insulin shock; an increase in calories and a reduction in insulin can lead to diabetic coma.

A student with diabetes must constantly monitor the sugar level in the body. Several times a day the student will use a urine sample or blood test to evaluate the sugar level; teachers should provide the time and privacy to conduct this test. A key to diabetes control is keeping the blood glucose level in the normal range. Close monitoring permits diabetics to determine how well they are managing their condition, and it is essential for safe participation in physical education or athletics.

There are some other factors or situations for both the physical educator and the diabetic to consider. A student involved in an intense exercise or training program should increase food intake rather than altering insulin dosage. Carbohydrate loading is not appropriate for diabetics; rather, they should take in carbohydrates during exercise because they lack the capacity for storing glycogen. As diabetics become older, circulatory problems may become a real concern. This should not exclude the school-age student from participating in contact or collision sports. Good skin care, however, should be encouraged by the physical educator.

Physicians today recognize the benefits for students with diabetes of participation in all kinds of physical activity, including contact sports. Moreover, we live in a society that is increasingly aware of fitness, and physical fitness for the student with diabetes should be part of the physical education program.

SEIZURE DISORDERS

Seizure disorders, convulsive disorders, and epilepsy are terms used to describe a condition of the brain that is characterized by recurrent seizures. These episodes are related to erratic electrochemical brain discharges. It is estimated that 1% to 2% of the population have some type of seizure disorder; the incidence is higher in families that have a history of such disorders. Possible causes of epilepsy are severe birth trauma, drug abuse, congenital brain malformation, infection, brain tumor, poor cerebral circulation, and head trauma. Between 50% and 70% of all cases are idiopathic, with no known cause and no structural damage to the nervous system. The Epilepsy Foundation of America claims that each year at least 200,000 Americans sustain seizure-producing head trauma.

Types of Seizure Disorders

Several systems have been developed to categorize seizure disorders. One approach dichotomizes this condition into generalized nonconvulsive and general convulsive seizures. Another system classifies seizures as grand mal, petit mal, jacksonian, focal epilepsy, psychomotor, jackknife seizures, and Lennox-Gastaul syndrome. The classification system endorsed by the Epilepsy Foundation of America has four categories: partial seizures, generalized seizures, unilateral seizures, and unclassified seizures.

Partial seizures originate from a localized area of the brain and usually are symptom specific. The traditional terms *psychomotor* and *jacksonian* would indicate seizures in this category. A jacksonian seizure begins as a localized seizure and may subsequently involve surrounding areas of the brain. It is manifested in jerky or stiff movements of an extremity, with tingling sensations in the limb. The seizure may start in a finger, spread to the hand, and finally affect the rest of the arm. Sometimes a partial seizure of this type becomes a generalized tonic-clonic (grand mal) seizure.

The complex partial seizure may have different types of symptoms, but generally purposeless behavior is in evidence. The person may exhibit a glassy stare, produce undiscernible speech, engage in purposeless wandering, and emit strange noises. After this type of seizure a person may seem confused and is sometimes mistakenly thought to be drunk or on drugs.

Myoclonic, atonic, generalized tonic-clonic, and absence seizures are forms of generalized seizures. Absence seizures (petit mal), often found in children, usually last from 1 to 10 seconds. There are no overt manifestations, such as postural changes or interruption of activities, but there is a brief change in the level of consciousness. A teacher may mistake this change in consciousness for daydreaming or inattentiveness. This type of seizure rarely occurs during exercise. Myoclonic seizures are characterized by brief, involuntary quivers of the body sometimes occurring in rhythmic fashion. An atonic seizure is sometimes called "drop attack" because the person falls to the floor and is unconscious for a few seconds; this brief episode may result in injury from the fall.

A generalized tonic-clonic (grand mal) seizure is the most common type of seizure. In many people it is preceded by a warning or an aura, an experience such as a dreamy feeling, nausea, a visual disturbance, or olfactory sensations. Sensations of this nature are probably the beginning of abnormal brain discharges.

A generalized tonic-clonic seizure may begin with a guttural cry, loss of consciousness and falling to the floor, boardlike rigidity changing to quivering and jerking, wild thrashing movements, foaming at the mouth, labored breathing, and incontinence. This series of events may last from 2 to 5 minutes; the person regains consciousness, may be somewhat confused, and may feel sleepy and fatigued.

The following factors seem to promote the occurrence of seizures:

- Alcohol consumption
- Psychological stress

- Increase in blood alkalinity
- Hyperventilation
- Menstrual period
- Constipation
- Flashing lights of a certain velocity

While the cause of many seizure disorders has not been determined, treatment is highly successful. Approximately 80% of people with seizure disorders can control the conditions by using anticonvulsant drugs. Medications frequently prescribed for epileptics include phenytoin, phenobarbital, carbomazeprine, and primidone. Phenytoin (Dilantin) is prescribed for generalized tonic-clonic seizures because it does not produce the side effect of drowsiness. In females, it may cause increased hair growth on the face and extremities. Phenobarbital (Luminal) is also used for generalized seizures but may produce hyperactivity with elementary-school-age students. For partial seizures ethosuximide (Zarontin) and trimethadione (Tridione) are often prescribed.

First-Aid Measures for a Generalized Tonic-Clonic Seizure

If a person with epilepsy displays indicators of an impending seizure, help the person into a supine position. Remove glasses and false teeth. Loosen tight-fitting clothes, and place a pillow or rolled-up cloth material under the head. If there is no warning, help the person into a lying position and follow the procedures just described. Clear the area of hard objects. Do not attempt to restrain movements or force anything into the person's mouth, because tongue blades or other objects may break teeth and lacerate the mouth. If the mouth is open, some authorities advocate placing a soft object such as a clean, folded handkerchief between the teeth. Turn the head to provide an open airway and allow saliva to drain from the mouth. After the seizure subsides, the person should be told what happened, be given reassurance, and, if tired, be allowed to rest.

If a seizure occurs, it is important to make a detailed written account of it. This information not only is important for the school system's incident reports but also provides input that lets the physician evaluate the severity and duration of the person's seizures and adjust drug dosages, if necessary.

Participation in physical education by students with seizure disorders has evolved through several stages. At one time physical education for this population was relatively passive, with activities like croquet, golf, and bowling being recommended. The next stage was a more vigorous program, with most activities being permitted except contact sports. Today, all activities including contact sports are deemed appropriate; the only stipulation is that the student's seizures be controlled and the activities be supervised (Cowart, 1986; Livingston & Berman, 1974). The possibility of a blow to the head causing a seizure does not seem to be a valid reason for exclusion. Another misconception is that physical activity will precipitate seizures; in reality, physical activity may elevate the seizure threshold. The extent to which seizures are controlled through medication is the key factor in the selection of physical education activities.

Frequently, students with seizure disorders do not exhibit normal levels of physical fitness and motor skill development. While progress has been made toward controlling seizures, social factors such as protective parents and the stigma associated with a seizure disorder contribute to a passive lifestyle. Physical educators may help these students become more actively involved in sports and physical activity.

A major concern of the physical educator is the student's safety. While students with seizure disorders may engage in most activities, certain precautions should be observed. To engage in aquatic activities, which are often an object of concern, students should have their seizures under control. For swimming, the buddy system should be standard operating procedure. Also, the physical educator should be sure that the medication is not causing a side effect that may compromise safety procedures. If seizures are not controlled or side effects pose a risk, then activities such as weight training, gymnastics, and rope climbing must be modified or excluded from the student's program. However, because 80% of all students with epilepsy have their seizures under control, most may engage in a varied and beneficial physical education program.

ASTHMA

The student with asthma may be apprehensive about participating in physical education class.

The regular or adapted physical educator should help to alleviate this anxiety; unfortunately, some physical educators have been inept in handling situations with asthmatic students. The purpose of this section is to provide guidance concerning the involvement of asthmatic students in physical education classes.

Thirty-five million Americans are affected by asthma; approximately 50% of all cases begin in children under the age of 10. Twice as many males as females are affected by this condition.

While there are various theories concerning the types and causes of asthma, the mechanisms for the obstructive symptoms are (a) spasm of the muscular layer in the bronchial walls, (b) swollen mucous membranes, and (c) mucus secretions in the airways. All three conditions reduce the diameter of the bronchial passages and impede air flow. Recently, asthma has been described as an inflammatory condition.

Systems for classifying asthmatic disorders are oriented toward causation. One system reflects a dichotomy of causes. Extrinsic or allergic asthma occurs in children or adults who have a history of allergic reactions. These people are allergic to such offending substances as dust, pollen, animal danders, mold spores, and certain drugs. Intrinsic or nonallergic asthma may be induced by excessive exercise or may be psychosomatic in nature. Some authorities contend that a person may suffer from a combination of both extrinsic and intrinsic types.

The student with asthma may present symptoms ranging from brief episodes of wheezing, shortness of breath, and coughing to breathlessness, which will cause the person to talk in one- to two-word sentences, to tighten neck muscles with inhalation, and to exhibit a blue or gray coloration of lips and nail beds. When a student with asthma has difficulty breathing, the physical educator should help establish an upright position with shoulders relaxed, advise the student to drink a lot of fluids, provide reassurance, and encourage the student to take appropriate medication if one has been prescribed for such occasions. The school nurse, parent, or physician should be notified if a prescribed medication does not seem to be effective.

Physical educators, especially, should be aware of a condition known as either *exercise-induced asthma* (EIA), or *exercise-induced bronchospasm* (EIB). McCarthy (1989) estimates that 80% of asthmatics experience EIA. Exercise of high intensity or duration seems to precipitate muscular contraction of the bronchial tubes, which results in an asthmatic attack. A commonly accepted hypothesis is that intrathoracic airways are cooled during exercise by air that has not been completely warmed. This is related to abnormal increases in the rate and depth of breathing because the coolness affects airway mast cells, which liberate bronchoconstrictive substances.

The following factors influence the occurrence of EIA:

- Exercise intensity
- Type of exercise
- Interval versus sustained exercise
- Absence of warm-up
- Condition of air
- Use of preexercise medication

Medication and Asthma

Recent advances in medication have helped markedly to prevent EIA and have permitted persons with asthma to be active in physical education and sport. Aerosol medication acts rapidly on the prime target area, the lungs. Cromolyn sodium and beta adrenergic agonists such as terbutaline are often the agents of choice, used singularly or in combination before exercise. These drugs should be administered 30 minutes to an hour before physical education class or sport participation. A word of caution must accompany the use of these pharmacological agents. First, there is concern among physicians that aerosols may be used to excess, and some recommend oral medication for children and certain adolescents. Excessive aerosol use can have deleterious effects; a relationship has been established between excessive use and an increase in mortality rate of asthmatics in Great Britain. Second, the use of certain drugs is prohibited in high-level competition. For example, use of isoproterenol or ephedrine would disqualify an athlete from Olympic competition.

Physical Education and the Students With Asthma

Integration of the student with asthma into the physical education class should follow these guidelines:

1. Consult the school nurse and/or the records to ascertain the status of the student's asthmatic condition. If no up-to-date information is available, a conference should be scheduled with the committee on adapted physical education (see chapter 3 for a discussion of this committee).

2. Together with the student, discuss feelings about exercise and collectively develop goals for physical education.

3. Conduct warm-up activities at the beginning of each class before bouts of vigorous activity. The purpose is to increase the body temperature until a mild sweat is developed. Warm-up might consist of walking, jogging, light mobilizing activities, and even some strengthening activities.

4. Classes should last from 30 to 40 minutes; unfit students should have shorter classes and interpolated rests initially.

5. If possible, asthmatic students should have class or engage in physical activity four or five times a week.

6. Gradually increase the level of exercise intensity. With an interval training regime, exercise intensity may be elevated to 70% of maximum heart rate. Rest intervals should be only brief enough to reduce the heart rate to 50% of maximum.

7. Administer preexercise medication as prescribed by the physician.

8. Establish emergency procedures for coping with EIA episodes.

9. End each class with a cool-down period. At no time should vigorous activity be stopped abruptly. The student should at least walk around the gymnasium until the heart rate returns to within 20 beats per minute of the resting level.

10. Short-burst (anaerobic) or short-duration activities should be the predominant type of curricular activity for asthmatic students. For example, softball is a short-burst activity; soccer would not fall into this category.

11. While general strengthening exercises are valuable for the asthmatic, special emphasis should be placed on developing abdominal, trunk, and shoulder muscles. Gymnastics may serve as a valuable adjunct to this strength development phase.

12. Class participation should emphasize cooperative endeavors and enjoyment of team play rather than winning.

13. Aquatic activities provide many benefits. Conducted in a warm, damp environment, they promote breath control and involve numerous muscle groups.

14. Other activities that emphasize breath control may be incorporated into the student's curriculum. Karate and various forms of dance are valuable in this regard.

15. A healthful environment should be maintained. The physical educator should regularly clean and air gym mats, and students should be responsible for keeping their uniforms, lockers, and gym shoes clean. Mats, shoes, and lockers harbor molds and dust.

16. While specific breathing exercises are a topic of controversy, activities that stress exhalation may be of value in a physical education class. Blowing Ping-Pong balls while on a gym scooter or in a swimming pool may help expiration and facilitate airflow out of the lungs. To help prevent hyperventilation, make sure students exhale twice as long as they inhale. Other activities that emphasize exhalation are balloon relays, blowing tissues in the air, and laughing.

17. Whether a student is on the gym floor, in the swimming pool, or on the softball field, provision should be made for disposing of coughed-up mucus. Tissues, some type of spittoon, or other conveniences should be available for the asthmatic student.

18. Finally, a well-conducted physical education program should not only help students learn to pace themselves but also help them experience the joy of physical activity.

CANCER

Approximately 350,000 Americans die of cancer each year; it is second only to cardiovascular disease as a cause of death. While cancer is often associated with advancing age, it is a leading cause of death among children. Only accidents claim more victims among this age group.

Types of Cancer

Cancer is usually categorized according to the tissue that is affected. Malignant tumors of connective, muscular, or bone tissue are called sarcomas, while neoplasms of the epithelial tissue that covers surfaces, lines cavities, and constitutes glands are referred to as carcinomas. A clear understanding has not been established concerning the mechanisms of cell division; cancer cells differ in size and multiply more rapidly than normal cells. This uncontrolled, rapid growth may originate at a primary site and spread, or metastasize, to other locations of the body. Certain substances such as asbestos, nitrogen mustard, and cigarette smoke have been identified as carcinogenic in nature. Among school-age students, leukemia and tumors of the central nervous system are the most common forms of cancer. Bone tumors are more common in children than adults, with peak ages between 15 and 19 years.

Treatment of neoplasms involves one or a combination of these therapeutic approaches: surgery, radiation, and chemotherapy. Surgery is used to remove a bulky tumor, relieve pain, correct obstructions, and/or reduce pressure on surrounding structures. Radiation is applied to impede cell multiplication and destroy cancerous cells; it may reduce tumor mass and help control pain. Ionizing radiation (gamma rays) and particle radiation (beta rays) are targeted at the cellular deoxyribonucleic acid (DNA). Radiation therapy may be delivered through external beam radiation or isotope implants. Chemotherapy involves a variety of drugs to inhibit tumor growth or impede metastasis. Chemotherapeutic agents inhibit cell growth by interacting with DNA, competing with metabolites, preventing cell reproduction by altering protein synthesis, and changing chemical susceptibility. While certain drugs may be effective in certain situations, chemotherapy may cause side effects of pain, anemia, hair loss, vomiting, and dermatitis.

A holistic approach for the terminally ill person is *hospice care*, which includes comprehensive physical, psychological, social, and spiritual care. Good hospice care emphasizes coordinating efforts of health care staff, maintaining quality of life in a homelike environment, and providing emotional support for both patient and family. In several large cities hospice programs have been established for children with leukemia.

Physical Education and the Student With Cancer

The involvement of the student with cancer in physical education is predicated on the following factors: the student's health status, the importance of physical activity as perceived by the oncologist, the kind of support available from parents, and the willingness of physical educators to cope with this type of student. The student with cancer would be eligible for the benefits of IDEA under the category of other health-impaired conditions.

Exercise as a maintenance or restorative technique for cancer patients holds promise. Buettner and Gavron (1981) reported that men and women who had a history of cancer benefited from an 8-week aerobic training program. When a sedentary control group was compared to the exercise group, the latter group exhibited significant improvement on five physiological measures. Another study compared an exercise group receiving chemotherapy for breast cancer with a control group (Winningham & MacVicar, 1985). Subjects in the exercise group exhibited more improvement on a graded exercise test than did the control group. Participants reported that their feelings of nausea decreased as the exercise session progressed.

While participation in exercise and physical education programs may be beneficial, each student's needs must be dealt with individually. The type of cancer, its status, and the general condition of the student determine the extent and intensity of the program. The physician must have input concerning the nature and intensity of activities. A person with lung cancer will definitely have respiratory restrictions, and a student with osteogenic sarcoma, a type of bone cancer, may not be allowed to jog or even walk because of a risk of fractures. While the physical well-being of a student with cancer cannot be minimized, psychological well-being is also important. Being mainstreamed into physical education and succeeding in this environment may greatly improve the student's self-image. To help minimize self-consciousness, the physical educator may let the student wear a ball cap or other head covering in class if hair loss has resulted from the medical treatment. Other variations in gym attire should be allowed when dermatological side effects are evident.

There may be days when chemotherapy or its side effects preclude active involvement in many activities. The following symptoms or situations are contraindications for exercise: pain in the legs or chest, unusual weakness, nausea during exercise, vomiting or diarrhea a day before class, sudden onset of labored breathing, dizziness or disorientation, and intravenous chemotherapy administered a day before class. On other days the student may be able to engage in many physical education activities.

Adaptations discussed in other sections of this book may be appropriate for students with certain types of cancer. The student with leukemia may profit from program modifications recommended for an anemic student or one with a cardiovascular problem. Adaptations for a student with Perthes disease or other orthopedic problems may be appropriate for the student with a bone tumor. A student with a tumor of the central nervous system may need the same adaptations as one who has cerebral palsy or muscular dystrophy. The key to physical education for the student with cancer, as for all students with unique needs, is the IEP.

CARDIOVASCULAR DISORDERS

The cardiovascular system, which comprises the heart, arteries, veins, and lymphatic system, may be considered the life-giving transportation system of the body. Disorders of this system appear during all stages of development and age periods. The following are major categories of cardiovascular disorders: congenital acyanotic defects, congenital cyanotic defects, acquired inflammatory heart disease, valvular heart disease, degenerative cardiovascular disorders, cardiac complications, and vascular disorders. An estimated 25 million Americans have some type of cardiovascular disease. While heart disease is the leading cause of death in people over 25, it is the sixth leading cause of death among people between 15 and 25.

A student with a cardiovascular disease or problem may be covered by IDEA under the OHI designation. While IEPs including physical education may be developed for certain students with cardiac conditions, other students with this type of condition may be integrated into regular physical education without the benefit of an IEP. In both situations, the physical educator must know how best to involve students who are or have been afflicted with some type of cardiovascular problem. This section will orient the reader to some cardiovascular problems commonly found among school-age or preschool-age children and will recommend procedures and techniques for the delivery of physical education services to these students.

Rheumatic Fever and Rheumatic Heart Disease

A condition included in the broader designation of acquired inflammatory heart disease is rheumatic heart disease. *Rheumatic fever* is a systemic inflammatory disease of children that may occur following an untreated or inadequately treated streptococcal infection. Rheumatic heart disease is the cardiac manifestation of rheumatic fever;

it is estimated that 500,000 young people between the ages of 5 and 19 are affected by this condition.

Rheumatic fever, which usually follows a strep throat, may be a hypersensitive reaction to the streptococcal infection, in which antibodies produced to combat the infection affect specific tissue locations and produce lesions at the heart and joints. Approximately 1% to 3% of strep infections develop into rheumatic fever. Some common symptoms of rheumatic fever are polyarthritis, motor awkwardness (chorea), pancarditis (myocarditis, pericarditis, and endocarditis), skin rash, and subcutaneous nodules near tendons or bony prominences of joints. While most of the symptoms are transitory in nature, the destructive effect of rheumatic fever lies in pancarditis, which develops in up to 50% of cases. Endocarditis causes a scarring of the heart valves, which may result in a stenosis or narrowing of valve openings; this scarring may also prevent the valve leaflets from completely closing, which causes a regurgitation between heart chambers. Both situations cause the heart to work more intensely, and if the damage is quite severe, congestive heart failure may occur. The mitral valve is more often affected in girls and the aortic valve in boys.

Treatment of rheumatic fever and *rheumatic heart disease* begins with eradicating the streptococcal infection, relieving symptoms, and preventing recurrence of the strep throat or rheumatic fever. During the acute stage of the disease, penicillin is often prescribed along with aspirin. With active carditis, bed rest may be indicated for as long as 5 weeks. Following the acute stage, penicillin may be prescribed to prevent recurrence. With severe valve damage, repair or replacement may be the treatment of choice. The physical educator may help with a very important aspect of combating rheumatic fever or rheumatic heart disease— namely, preventive measures. If a student presents symptoms of a cold with a severe sore throat, the student should be referred to the school nurse or advised to obtain a throat culture. A strep throat must be treated with antibiotics to ensure that it does not lead to rheumatic fever.

Physical Education and Students With Cardiovascular Conditions

Determining the appropriate intensity level for students with cardiovascular disorders is the key to their integration into a physical education class. An affected student who is attending school should be involved in some type of physical education program. Numerous systems have been developed to classify individuals with cardiovascular disorders into groups that provide a baseline for activity selection. The system most frequently used to determine levels of intensity is based on metabolic equivalents (MET). Physicians often refer to this system in recommending exercise programs. The level of intensity, at least initially, should be based on the recommendation of the physician.

One MET is the equivalent of the basal oxygen requirement of the body at rest, or 3.5 milliliters of oxygen per kilogram of body weight per minute. If a person's maximum MET capacity is determined to be 7.0, the exercise prescription for a person with a heart condition is approximately 70% of this value, or 4.9 MET units. Using this information the physical educator may consult a table that recommends appropriate activities for different MET levels (see Table 13.1).

While physical education programs for students with cardiovascular problems must be personalized, the following suggestions should help in the implementation of each student's program:

Table 13.1   Metabolic Equivalents for Selected Activities

MET[a]	Activities
3–4	Archery Bowling Billiards Croquet Table tennis
5–6	Dancing (troika, etc.) Golf (pulling cart) Roller skating Swimming (2 mph) Tennis (doubles)
7–8	Basketball (5-person teams) Cycling (10 mph) Running (12 minutes/mile) Tennis (singles) Touch football
9–10	Cycling (13 mph) Handball Racquetball Running (10 minutes/mile) Squash

[a]Metabolic equivalent (MET) is the body's basal oxygen requirement at rest.

1. Secure approval of the general framework of the physical education program (see chapter 3).

2. Gradually increase the level of intensity of all exercises and activities.

3. Stop all activity following pain in the sternal area, palpitation of the heart, cyanic appearance of the lips and nail beds, swelling of the ankles, or labored breathing.

4. Provide appropriate rest periods.

5. Reduce the intensity level of an activity if elementary children are squatting between activities or high school students are standing and breathing through their mouths.

6. Compare pulse rates before, during, and after exercise.

7. Reduce the intensity of certain exercises by having students perform them in a supine position.

8. Carefully monitor aquatic activities, which cause students to use a considerable number of muscle groups, thus placing greater demands on the cardiovascular system.

9. Reduce the highly competitive aspects of certain sport activities that may elevate stress levels.

10. Modify programs according to climatic conditions. Hot and/or humid weather, for example, necessitates a reduction in intensity level.

11. Include a warm-up period. Part of every student's program, it is even more important for students with cardiovascular problems.

12. Caution against extremes in temperature variations of ingested fluids.

13. Provide assistance in weight management. Added poundage places additional stress on the cardiovascular system.

14. Understand the possible interactions between medication and activity.

15. Modify intensity levels by the following means:

- Playing doubles in tennis and badminton and using the boundaries of the singles court

- Using courtesy runners in softball and kickball

- Allowing the ball to bounce more than the usual number of times in racquetball, volleyball, and tennis

- Reducing the velocity of balls by using a beachball in place of an official volleyball and using whiffle balls rather than regulation balls

ANEMIA

Anemia is a condition marked by a reduction in erythrocytes (red blood cells) or in the quality of hemoglobin, which is associated with oxygen transport throughout the body. A reduction in the oxygen-carrying capabilities of the blood necessitates increased cardiac output to compensate for the reduced amount of oxygen provided at the cellular level.

Characteristics of Anemia

Anemia may be an inherited condition or may be caused by hemorrhaging and dietary deficiencies. Hemorrhagic anemia may result from infections, severe trauma, postoperative or postpartum bleeding, and coagulation defects. Iron deficiency anemia is prevalent in young children, preadolescent boys, pubescent girls who are experiencing their first menstrual periods, and premenopausal women. Iron is a main component of hemoglobin and is needed in the production of red blood cells. Lack of adequate stores of iron in the body leads to depleted erythrocyte mass and decreased hemoglobin concentration.

Sickle-cell anemia occurs most commonly, but not exclusively, in Blacks. It results from defective hemoglobin, which causes red blood cells to have a sickle shape. This condition is linked to a recessive trait that produces defective hemoglobin molecules. About 1 in 10 Blacks carries this abnormal gene; this situation is referred to as sickle-cell trait. If both parents have the trait, the chances are one in four that their child will have the disease. It is estimated that 1 in every 400 to 600 Black children has sickle-cell anemia. Hypoxia seems to affect the abnormal or defective hemoglobin molecules in the red blood cells, which become insoluble. An end result is an elongation or sicklelike appearance of these erythrocytes. This sickling effect may result in cell destruction and may impair circulation in capillaries and small blood vessels. A vicious cycle may be set up, with circulation impairment causing anoxic changes, which may lead to additional sickling and obstruction. To date, treatment consists mainly in management of symptoms, with hospitalization for severe aplastic crises. In these crises, blood transfusions, oxygen administration, and fluid ingestion are used. Symptoms accompanying sickle-cell anemia are jaundice, labored breathing, aching bones, chest pains, swollen joints, fatigue, and leg ulcers.

Physical Education for the Students With Anemia

Many of the guidelines provided in the section dealing with cardiovascular disorders are applicable for the student with any type of anemia. The physical educator may be the first person to suspect that a student has anemia, observing lethargy, lack or loss of strength and endurance, irritability, and early onset of fatigue.

Excusing the anemic student from physical education is *not an appropriate option*. Lack of activity will aggravate the condition. It should be apparent to all concerned—parents, physician, teachers, and student—that a modified program of physical activity is in the student's best interest. Intensity levels in all activities must correlate with the student's physiological status. Initially, activities such as bowling and archery may be suitable. Conditioning may mean walking around the track and lifting light weights such as dumbbells. As the student's fitness improves through medical intervention and modified activity, the intensity level of activities may be elevated.

For the student with sickle-cell anemia, a coordinated effort between the physician and the physical educator is needed to design a safe and effective program. The physician must provide guidance on the level of intensity of physical fitness efforts, and the physical educator must select appropriate motor activities. Even with motor activities that stress balance, eye-hand coordination, and agility, the physical educator must note any sign of cardiorespiratory distress such as rapid pulse, labored breathing, any complaint of pain, and pale lips, tongue, or nail beds. Underwater swimming is usually avoided, and jumping activities should not be excessive because of possible joint inflammation. Both the student and the physical educator should monitor the condition of the student's skin, because skin ulcers may be a problem with this disorder.

HEMOPHILIA

Hemophilia is a hereditary bleeding disorder resulting from the inability of the blood to coagulate properly because of a deficiency of certain clotting factors. Hemophilia is the most common X-linked genetic disease and affects 1.25 in 10,000 live male births. Because of the genetic mode, females act as carriers; they have a 50% chance of transmitting the defective gene to each male child. There is also a 50% chance that each female child will likewise be a carrier of this defect.

Types of Hemophilia

Hemophilia A, which affects over 80% of all hemophiliacs, is caused by a deficiency of coagulation Factor VIII. Another type of hemophilia is sometimes called Christmas disease, or hemophilia B, resulting from a deficiency in Factor IX. The absence or deficiency of certain clotting factors is the reason for the vernacular designation, *bleeder's disease*.

Hemophilia may be classified as mild, moderate, or severe. The mild form may not appear until adolescence or adulthood. Its symptoms are a tendency to bruise, frequent nosebleeds, bleeding gums, and hematomas. Moderate hemophilia causes symptoms similar to those of the mild type, but bleeding episodes are more frequent, and there is occasional bleeding into the joints. Severe hemophilia is marked by spontaneous bleeding or severe bleeding after minor injuries. Bleeding into joints and muscles is more extensive than with the moderate type and causes pain, swelling, and extreme tenderness. Peripheral neuropathies may result from bleeding near peripheral nerves, with subsequent pain and muscle atrophy.

Physical Education for the Student With Hemophilia

The student with hemophilia may derive both physical and social benefit from participating in physical education if appropriate precautions and modifications are in place. The student's physician should provide guidance on suitable activities. The physician also may wish to be informed (or instruct that the school nurse be informed) if certain injuries to the head, neck, or chest occur. Some of these injuries may require special blood factor replacement. The physician may alert the physical educator to watch for signs of severe internal hemorrhage, which may include severe pain or swelling in joints and muscles, joint stiffness, and abdominal pain. *Students with hemophilia should wear a medical identification tag or bracelet at all times.* Because blood transfusions carry the risk of infection with hepatitis, the physical educator may observe early symptoms of that disease: headache, vomiting, fever, pain over the liver, and abdominal tenderness. At no time should a student with hemophilia take aspirin, because this drug exacerbates the tendency to bleed.

If a student with hemophilia sustains some type of trauma, apply ice bags and pressure to the injured area and elevate the part if possible. The student should be restricted from activity for 48 hours after the bleeding is under control.

Activities that enhance physical fitness should be part of this student's program. Swimming is an excellent activity for enhancing cardiorespiratory endurance, muscular strength, and flexibility without subjecting the student to possible trauma. Jogging or fast walking may be used to develop aerobic capacities. If a student has had a problem with bleeding in a joint such as the knee, isometric rather than isotonic exercises may be used. Contact and collision sports such as football, basketball, and soccer are contraindicated. However, developing certain skill components of these sports, such as passing a football and shooting free throws, is desirable. Dual and individual sports such as tennis, archery, and golf are fine; racquetball is not an appropriate sport because of the risk of being hit by the ball.

ACQUIRED IMMUNODEFICIENCY SYNDROME

Acquired Immunodeficiency Syndrome (AIDS) is a very serious health disorder that has reached epidemic proportions. It is caused by an infection with Human T-Cell Lymphotropic Virus Type III (HTLV-III), which is known as the *Human Immunodeficiency Virus* (HIV). As a result of HIV, people with AIDS have defective immune systems and cannot combat certain types of infections or rare malignancies. These persons may be severely incapacitated or relatively well. For each person with AIDS there are an undetermined number of individuals who carry the HIV virus; this is referred to as HIV-positive status. While these people have the potential to infect others, they are capable of participating effectively in activities of daily living, including physical activity, without any evidence of the syndrome. It is estimated that within 5 to 7 years of infection, 30% of the HIV carriers will develop a serious or life-threatening complication.

Characteristics of HIV Infection

The HIV virus has been found in such body fluids as blood, seminal fluid, vaginal secretions, saliva, and tears. It has not been documented that the last two fluids transmit this virus or that the disease can be airborne or spread by casual contact. Casual contact is defined as contact other than (a) sexual contact or (b) contact between mother and child during birth or breast feeding.

Two causal factors are associated with AIDS-infected children: (a) birth to a mother who has this disorder and (b) receiving blood or clotting factors containing HIV. Ryan White (Figure 13.1), a courageous young man who spent much of his short life destigmatizing children with AIDS, contracted the virus from contaminated blood.

Within the last decade there has been a dramatic rise in the incidence of HIV infection in infants and children (WHO, 1990). Researchers estimate that 65% of HIV-positive mothers in the United States transmit the virus to their offspring (Modlin & Saah, 1991). Authorities believe AIDS will soon be among the top five causes of death for children ages 1 to 4. It is not clear if the number of elementary-age children infected with AIDS will appreciably increase. While blood screening techniques have improved, a certain number of hemophilic children may still acquire AIDS. The Centers for Disease Control have reported that 6% to 8% of certain adolescent groups may have HIV.

Physical Education and Students With AIDS

The physician has a critical role to play in determining the student's placement in the school setting and in the physical education class. Most state departments of health will allow a student to attend school if the student behaves acceptably (e.g., does not bite) and has no skin eruptions or uncovered sores. If any of these conditions are seen in classes, the student should be removed immediately and sent to the appropriate school official. The same procedure should be followed if the student has a fever, a cough, or diarrhea.

The nature of the physical education program for students with AIDS depends on their physical capacities and motor abilities. Children with AIDS manifest some of the following symptoms: opportunistic infections, chronic lung disease, failure to thrive, and encephalopathy. As this last symptom progresses, there is evidence of delays or loss of motor milestones and pyramidal tract problems. Cognitive impairments are more evident in children with AIDS than in those who are HIV positive. Because some students with AIDS are hemophiliacs, the information provided in the sections on hemophilia and other cardiovascular problems is applicable to them.

If there is a bleeding episode in a physical education class because of an accident, an injury, or a situation involving any student, universal precautions should be followed. Blood or any body fluid should be treated with caution. Rubber gloves should be worn for cleaning up spills of any body fluid, and blood-soaked articles should be placed in leakproof bags for disposal or washing.

While universal precautions are required, AIDS necessitates fewer adaptations and modifications for students than some other types of disabling conditions. Students who are HIV carriers can successfully engage in physical activity and are often involved in competitive sports. According to Calabrese and Kelley (1989) there is increasing evidence that persons infected with HIV should remain physically active. For example, progressive resistance exercises during the nonacute stage of AIDS did not exacerbate the disease but provided improved muscle function (Spence, Galantino, Mossberg, & Zimmerman, 1990). A key to a physical education program for this type of student is carefully monitored activities.

Figure 13.1 Ryan White was a student with hemophilia who received contaminated blood and developed AIDS. Before his illness, Ryan participated in most physical education activities.
Photo by Mary Ann Carter. Used by permission.

STUDENTS AFFECTED BY SUBSTANCE ABUSE CONDITIONS

In the United States today there are approximately 1.2 million females of childbearing age who are taking one or more of the following drugs: alcohol, cocaine, nicotine, marijuana. The ingestion of these drugs in single or combination dosages increase the probability of producing an offspring with developmental difficulties (Chasnoff, 1986). A more alarming statistic is found in a survey by Adams (1988), who reported 8 million women of the 56 million in their childbearing years are taking one or more of these drugs.

An estimated 10% to 20% of pregnant women are using drugs during the child's gestation. According to Chasnoff, Landeress, and Barrett (1990), 375,000 newborns are exposed to drugs. After marijuana, cocaine is the second most frequently used drug, with approximately 2 million Americans addicted to this substance (Howze & Howze, 1989). "Crack" cocaine babies are found to exhibit tremors, hypertonicity, hyperreflexia, seizures, mood swings, vomiting, and hypersensitivity (Kronstadt, 1991). Cocaine-exposed toddlers manifest behavior patterns that are less mature or appropriate in comparison to their nonaffected peers (Roding, Beckwith, & Howard, 1990). The frequency, type, and time of drug usage during gestation as well as sociocultural factors do affect the early development of crack babies (Cratty, 1990). Roding et al. (1990) has observed with drug-exposed toddlers that their object manipulation skills are comparable to children with neurological problems. There still is a need for research to investigate how these students fare in academic and physical education settings as they progress through elementary and high school.

Fetal Alcohol Syndrome

Fetal alcohol syndrome (FAS) and fetal alcohol effects (FAE) were not truly diagnosed and given a label until 1973 (Niebyl, 1988). A combination of physical and mental defects that result from a mother ingesting excessive amounts of alcohol during pregnancy is referred to as FAS. FAE describes a child who has been exposed to alcohol in utero but does not manifest all the symptoms of an individual with FAS. To be classified as a person with FAS, at least one characteristic must be found in each of these categories: (1) retardation in growth before or after birth, (2) facial anomalies such as epicanthic folds, flattened nasal bridge, and thin upper lip, and (3) central nervous system dysfunction such as mental retardation, attention deficit disorder, and hyperactivity.

A brief synopsis of a student with FAS will be presented to help gain better insight into this condition. From a physical perspective these persons may exhibit altered facial features, limited range of motion in their joints, scoliosis, extra fingers and toes, hip dislocations, fusion of the radius and ulna, hollowed or depressed chest, ventricular septal defects, and poor performance of both fine and gross motor functions. While the range of mental disabilities varies with different individuals, many are in the mild range of mental disabilities. In the social domain they are also very much at risk. The mother-child relationship is often strained, which initially may preclude appropriate bonding, while in later life these children are more prone to be physically and sexually abused and to suffer neglect. There is also a higher risk of the child developing alcoholism than non-FAS persons. There is mounting evidence that FAS is not just a childhood disorder but a long-term disorder affecting the adolescent and adult. While facial features are less distinctive after childhood, these individuals tend to be short of stature and microcephalic in nature. Academic functioning is often equivalent to a fourth grader, and maladaptive behavior such as distractibility, poor judgment, and problems perceiving social cues are evident (Steissguth et al., 1991).

Physical Education for Students Affected By Substance Abuse

The key to providing these students with successful physical education experiences is to develop individualized physical education programs. Because of the heterogeneity of their conditions, a teacher must consider each student individually. One student with FAS may be quite hypertonic in nature and should receive programming for this condition, which is similar to the individual with spastic cerebral palsy. Another student with FAS may exhibit hypotonicity, and programming strategies similar to the hypotonic student with Down syndrome would be appropriate. Unfortunately, a certain percentage of these students will exhibit mental disabilities. Chapter 7 deals with this topic and will help to provide guidance for this type of student affected by substance abuse. For young children with FAS, early motor intervention programs have been found to counter developmental delays (Gianta & Steissguth, 1988). A real challenge for the physical educator will be to elicit a support system and a certain amount of continuity from the home environment. Many of these students come from single parent homes, have been put into foster homes, and have a parent who is dealing with a substance abuse problem, which is not conducive to helping these students with their limitations or disabilities.

SUMMARY

The focus of this chapter has been certain conditions that, under IDEA, are designated as *other health impaired*. Cancer, rheumatic heart disorders, diabetes, asthma, hemophilia, acquired immunodeficiency syndrome, and fetal alcohol syndrome are included in this category. Some students with these conditions (for example, students with asthma) may not have formal IEPs but may need certain modifications or adaptations in physical education. The real challenge in physical education is to integrate these students into the normal setting and provide programs for individualized needs.

BIBLIOGRAPHY

Adams, E. (1988). The multiple deficits of prenatal drug abuse. *Science Focus, 2,* 112–118.

Buettner, L.L., & Gavron, S.J. (1981, November). *Personality changes and physiological effects of a personalized fitness enrichment program for cancer patients.* Paper presented at the Third International Symposium on Adapted Physical Activity, New Orleans.

Calabrese, L.H., & Kelley, D. (1989). AIDS and athletes. *Physician and Sportsmedicine, 17,* 127–132.

Chasnoff, I.J. (1986). Perinatal addiction: Consequences of intrauterine exposure to opiate and nonopiate drugs. In I.J. Chasnoff (Ed.), *Drug use in pregnancy: Mother and child* (pp. 52–63). Boston: MTD Press.

Chasnoff, I.J., Landeress, H.J., & Barrett, M.E. (1990). The prevalence of illicit drug or alcohol use during pregnancy and discrepancies in mandatory reporting in Pinnella County, Florida. *New England Journal of Medicine, 26,* 1202–1206.

Cowart, V.S. (1986). Should epileptics exercise? *Physician and Sportsmedicine, 14,* 183–191.

Cratty, B.J. (1990). Motor development of infants subject to maternal drug use: Current evidence and future research strategies. *Adapted Physical Activity Quarterly, 7,* 110–125.

Duda, M. (1985). The role of exercise in managing diabetes. *Physician and Sportsmedicine, 13,* 164–170.

Gianta, L., & Steissguth, A.P. (1988). Parents with fetal alcohol syndrome and their caretakers. *Social Casework: The Journal of Contemporary Social Work,* Sect.: 453–459.

Helmrich, S.P., Ragland, V.R., & Leung, R.W., et al. (1991). Physical activity and reduced occurrence of non–insulin dependent diabetes mellitus. *New England Journal of Medicine, 325,* 147–152.

Howze, K., & Howze, W.M. (1989). *Children of cocaine: Treatment and childcare.* Fact sheets presented at the Annual Conference of the National Association for the Education of Young Children (Atlanta, November 2–5, 1989), 1–19.

Kronstadt, D. (1991). Complex developmental issues of prenatal drug exposure. *Future of Children, 1,* 36–49.

Livingston, S., & Berman, W. (1974). Participation of the epileptic child in contact sports. *Sports Medicine, 2,* 170–173.

McCarthy, P. (1989). Wheezing or breezing through exercise-induced asthma. *Physician and Sportsmedicine, 17,* 125–130.

Modlin, J., & Saah, H. (1991). Health and clinical aspects of HIV infection in women and children in the United States. In R. Faden, G. Geller, & M. Power (Eds.), *AIDS: Women and generation.* New York: Oxford University Press.

Niebyl, J.R. (1988). *Drug use in pregnancy.* Philadelphia: Lea & Febiger.

Roding, C., Beckwith, L., & Howard, T. (1990). Attachment in play in prenatal drug exposure. *Developmental and Psychopathology, 1,* 277–289.

Spence, D.W., Galantino, M., Mossberg, K.H., & Zimmerman, S.O. (1990). Progressive resistance exercise: Effect on muscle function and anthropometry of a select AIDS population. *Archives of Physical Medicine and Rehabilitation, 71,* 644–648.

Steissguth, A.P., Aase, J.M., Clarren, S.K., Randels, D.P., LaDue, K.A., & Smith, D.F. (1991). Fetal alcohol syndrome in adolescents and adults. *Journal of the American Medical Association, 265,* 1961–1967.

WHO revises global estimates of HIV: Has more deaths of women, children. (1990). *Infectious Disease in Children, 10,* 3.

Winningham, M.L., & MacVicar, M.G. (1985). Response of cancer patients on chemotherapy to a supervised exercise program. *Medicine and Science in Sports and Exercise, 17,* 292.

RESOURCES

Written

Adams, R.C., & McCubbin, J.A. (1991). *Games, sports, and exercises for the physically disabled.* Philadelphia: Lea & Febiger. Teachers will find this book to be an excellent guide to understanding various disabling conditions. An extensive portion of the book describes various ways to modify physical education activities.

Cratty, B.J. (1990). Motor development of infants subject to maternal drug use: Current evidence and future research strategies. *Adapted Physical Activity Quarterly, 7,* 110–125. Comprehensive information pertaining to infants exposed prenatally to drugs, including neurological implications of this condition.

Day, N.L. (1992). The effects of prenatal exposure to alcohol. *Alcohol Health and Research World, 16,* 238–244. The author integrates the latest research about fetal alcohol syndrome into an article that supplements the information in this chapter and provides additional insights into this condition. Factors such as dosage and timing of consumption are part of this focus.

Eichner, E. (1993). Sickle cell trait, heroic exercise, and fatal collapse. *Physician and Sportsmedicine, 21,* 511–564. This article gives an excellent overview of this condition and discusses clinical concerns. Taking into consideration the number of Black athletes, it is vital that people in physical education understand the "heroic exercise syndrome."

Parker, D.F., & Bar-Or, O. (1991). Juvenile obesity. *Physician and Sportsmedicine,* **19,** 113–125. This article illustrates the numerous ways that exercise helps the obese juvenile control weight. An area of emphasis is the challenge to the physician as well as the physical educator to provide suitable activity without causing any adverse effects.

Robbins, D.C., & Carleton, S. (1989). Managing the diabetic athlete. *Physician and Sportsmedicine,* **17,** 45–54. This article helps a person provide guidance for the student with diabetes who wants to be involved in competitive athletics. Discusses the benefits of exercise, regulation of insulin, and carbohydrate levels. Unique problems that this type of athlete might encounter are also addressed.

Audiovisual

Diabetic Fitness: Oh, What a Feeling [Videotape]. Coronet/ MTI Film and Video, 108 Wilmot Road, Deerfield, IL 60015. Physical activities that may enhance the overall fitness of the person with diabetes are presented. The routines could be incorporated into the curriculum of a student with this condition.

Epilepsy [Videotape]. Third annual Ed-MED Conference, Institute for the Study of Developmental Disabilities, Indiana University, Bloomington, IN 47408. A presentation for teachers that addresses types of seizures and strategies for dealing with students having seizures in the school setting.

Fetal Alcohol Syndrome (FAS) [Videotape]. Third annual Ed-MED Conference, Institute for the Study of Developmental Disabilities, Indiana University, Bloomington, IN 47408. This video reproduces a program on FAS that covered the following topics: history, characteristics, cause and effect, and examination of case studies.

CHAPTER 14

Nondisabled Students and Adapted Physical Education

Paul R. Surburg

As noted in chapter 3, students without a disability should have an individualized physical education program (IPEP). Students without disabilities also have unique needs that should be met in a physical education program. For example, a middle school student who has Osgood-Schlatter's condition may not be able to engage in all types of physical education activities. A person with a broken leg may be temporarily limited in the physical education setting (see Figure 14.1). People with long-term disorders will benefit from programs that are modified to meet their present unique needs.

Ironically, the information offered in this chapter to help students without disabilities may also be applicable to students with disabilities. A student with a deaf condition might break a leg, and information presented in this section on fractures would be useful for working with this student. Topics discussed under the heading of "Long-Term Disorders" are conditions that persons with disabilities may exhibit. Thus, the content of this chapter is applicable to both types of students.

ACTIVITY INJURIES

Students may sustain activity injuries in different settings. While some injuries may originate in a physical education class, more occur during free-time or recreational pursuits.

If an injury occurs in physical education class, immediate care should be provided in the RICE sequence: **Rest** should be given immediately to the

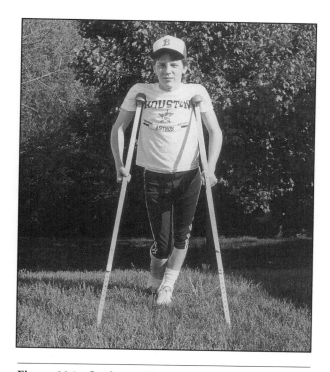

Figure 14.1 Student with a temporary limitation.

injured part or joint. **Ice** or a cold application should be administered immediately and removed after a 20-minute interval. Cold may be reapplied in 1 to 1-1/2 hours, depending upon the extent of injury. **Compression** and **elevation** reduce internal bleeding and swelling. Unfortunately, in the recreational or free-time setting, these procedures are not always followed, and the injury may be exacerbated. Without the ice and compression, intra-articular pressure from the swelling may stretch structures such as ankle ligaments in the same manner as if the joint had been purposely twisted. Some type of immobilization or rest is needed for musculoskeletal injuries; this rest facilitates healing and reduces the risk of prolonging recovery time.

Unless injured students are on an athletic team, there probably will be no type of rehabilitation service available to them. While physical educators cannot act in the capacity of athletic trainers, they may provide valuable assistance. If an injury is not being managed in an appropriate manner, the physical educator may recommend that the student see a physician or visit a sports medicine clinic. In addition, many hospitals employ sport physical therapists or athletic trainers.

If the injured student is progressing normally toward recovery, the physical education class may provide an opportunity for exercises or activities that will ameliorate the condition. See Tables 14.1 through 14.5 for activities or exercises for three joints—ankle, knee, and shoulder—frequently injured in sport and recreational activities.

Ankle

Ankle sprains are a risk for anyone who actively engages in sport or physical activity. Jumping and other movements may cause a person to roll over on the ankle and stretch the medial or lateral side of this joint. Eighty-five percent of all ankle sprains are of the inversion type, in which the ligaments on the lateral side of the ankle are stretched.

Table 14.1 provides an exercise protocol for inversion sprains after primary care and treatment have been administered. While eversion sprains are less frequent, this injury tends to be more serious and entails a longer recovery period. Most of the exercises listed in Table 14.1 could be used for an eversion sprain; the eversion exercises, however, should be eliminated.

While the primary focus of this chapter is on activity and exercise, the reader should be aware that other rehabilitative measures may have been or are currently being used. Hydrotherapy and/or cryotherapy are used to treat sprained ankles. Taping of the ankle may be in evidence in physical education class. Sports medicine practitioners differ on the value, duration, and methods of taping or strapping. If ankle taping has been prescribed by sports medicine personnel, compliance by the student should be encouraged. The physical educator, however, should not make a practice of taping ankles, for this could set a precedent for a time-consuming practice.

Knee

A variety of conditions and situations involving the knee may affect physical education performance. Several exercise protocols are available to deal with these conditions and situations. The first protocol (Table 14.2) is for a person who has a sprain of the medial collateral ligament. This is a common injury because forces are applied to the lateral part of the knee with subsequent stretching of ligaments on the medial side. The second protocol, the *daily adjustable progressive* resistance program (DAPRE) developed by Knight (1979), can be used for other joints or body parts where rehabilitation or strength improvement is desired (Table 14.3).

A third protocol (Table 14.4) is a patella protection program (Paulos, Rusche, Johnson, & Noyes, 1980). Because of the increased incidence of patella chondromalacia and other knee-related problems, short arc exercise programs like this one are being used in strength development and rehabilitation programs. *Short arc* refers to knee movement in the last 5° to 25° of extension. This program could be used with students who have iliotibial band syndrome, patella tendinitis, Osgood-Schlatter's condition, patellar subluxation, and rheumatoid joint disease.

Shoulder

The shoulder is composed of several major joints: sternoclavicular, acromioclavicular, scapulocostal, and glenohumeral. In many instances, activity-related strains or overuse syndromes involve the glenohumeral joint. Rotator cuff impingement syndrome, tendinitis, bursitis, and other glenohumeral problems may benefit from a general mobilizing and conditioning program for this joint (Table 14.5). This program is contraindicated for students suffering from anterior glenohumeral dislocation. In its chronic form, this condition is sometimes referred to as a "trick shoulder."

Mobilization for this condition consists primarily of adduction and/or internal rotation exercises. During the immobilization stage, isometric exercises are the exercises of choice; following immobilization, the exercise regimen may progress from isometric exercises, such as pulling against rubber tubing, to pulley or free-weight exercises that emphasize adduction and internal rotation. It should be noted that external rotation and abduction are

Table 14.1 Rehabilitation Protocol for a Moderate Inversion Sprain of the Ankle

Stage	Activity	Purpose
I. Control and decrease foot swelling and pain	A1. Flexion, extension, and spreading of toes	A1. Work on intrinsic muscles and certain muscles that go across the ankle
	2. Exercises for noninvolved leg and upper extremities	2. Keep rest of body in good condition
	3. Crutch walking with touch weight bearing	3. Involve ankle in a minimal amount of motion, yet replicate as closely as possible a normal gait pattern
II. Begin restoration of strength and movement	B1. Ankle circumduction movements	B1. Involve ankle in the four basic movements of this joint
	2. Toe raises	2. Begin to develop plantar flexors
	3. Eversion exercises—isometric then isotonic	3. Reinforce side of ankle that has been stretched
	4. Achilles tendon stretch in sitting position with toes in, out, and straight ahead	4. Improve dorsiflexion and slight inversion and eversion
	5. Shift body weight from injured side to uninjured side	5. Begin to retain proprioception
III. Restore full function to ankle	C1. Ankle circumduction	C1. Continue to improve range of motion (ROM)
	2. Achilles tendon stretching in standing position	2. Work on dorsiflexion
	3. Eversion exercises	3. Improve strength for protection
	4. Plantar, dorsiflexion, and inversion exercises	4. Develop main muscle groups of ankle
IV. Restore full function to ankle	D1-4. As in previous stage	D1-4. As in previous stage
	5. Tilt board exercises	D5. Work on proprioception
	6. Walk-jog	6–14. Develop functional and sport-specific activities
	7. Jog faster; stop	
	8. Run and sprint	
	9. Jog figure 8s	
	10. Run figure 8s	
	11. Cutting-half speed	
	12. Cutting-full speed	
	13. Run Z-shaped patterns	
	14. Backwards running	

Table 14.2   Rehabilitation Protocol for a Medial Collateral Ligament Sprain

Stage	Activity	Purpose
I. Control and decrease swelling and pain	A1. Isometric contractions of quadriceps muscles (quad setting) and hamstring muscles	A1. Prevent atrophy of muscles around knee
	2. Straight leg raises and dorsiflex the ankles	2. Work quadriceps muscles and stretch triceps surae
	3. Walk on crutches	3. Provide a method of ambulation
	4. General conditioning exercises for other three extremities	4. Keep rest of body in good condition
II. Begin to restore strength and movement at knee joint	B1. Isometric contraction of quadriceps and hamstring muscles	B1. Help to keep muscle tone
	2. Begin active range of motion (ROM) exercises	2. Need to have motion at the knee
	3. General conditioning exercises of other extremities	3. Keep rest of body fit
III. Restore full function to knee	C1. Do isotonic exercise (DAPRE)	C1. Need to have sufficient strength to do activities and protect knee
	2. Steps D5–14 as delineated in Table 14.1	2. Same as in Table 14.1

movements associated with causing anterior glenohumeral dislocations.

An important phase of many rehabilitation programs is the development of proprioception and kinesthesia. There is evidence (Smith & Bronolli, 1989) that after a glenohumeral dislocation, kinesthetic problems are evident. Because of this position sense deficit, a comprehensive rehabilitation and conditioning program should include proprioceptive and kinesthetic exercises such as proprioceptive neuromuscular facilitation (PNF) (Voss, Knott, & Iona, 1986) and practice with reproducing arm positions without looking at the extremity.

Selected Exercises

This section describes selected exercises for rehabilitation and conditioning (see Tables 14.1 through 14.5) that may not be familiar to the reader. Table 14.1 refers to tilt-board exercises to rehabilitate a sprained ankle. The apparatus used with this exercise, which is available commercially or could easily be constructed, is basically a circle of 3/4" plywood that is 1 foot in diameter (Figure 14.2). Attached to the center of the board is half of a pool ball or similar wooden ball. Standing with both feet on the board,

the user attempts to balance on the board. This apparatus could be used to develop proprioceptive capabilities following an injury to the lower extremity. This exercise would be appropriate for balance and proprioceptive training of students with and without disabilities.

Terminal extension exercises are listed as an intermediate strength exercise for quadricep development in the patella protection program (Table 14.4). Ideally, this exercise is done with a knee extension machine rather than a weight boot or weights wrapped around the ankle. The latter procedure pulls on the knee, which could stretch ligaments. Terminal extension exercises are initiated with the knee completely extended and resistance applied to the extremity (Figure 14.2). In subsequent exercise sessions, isotonic contractions are started with 5° of extension. Over a number of sessions, the degree of extension is increased until the person can extend against resistance through 25° of motion.

In Table 14.5 Codman's exercise is listed as an exercise to mobilize the shoulder. In this exercise, the participant bends over at the waist to achieve 90° of a trunk flexion and holds onto a chair or the end of a table. In this position the arm of the affected side should hang in a relaxed state. The

Table 14.3 Daily Adjustable Progressive Resistance Exercise (DAPRE)

Set	Weight	Repetitions
1	50% of working weight	10
2	75% of working weight	6
3	100% of working weight	Maximum
4	Determined by repetitions done in third set[a]	Maximum number determines working weight for next session

Working weight adjustments

Repetitions during third set[a]	Working weight for fourth set
0–2	Decrease 5–10 lb
3–4	Decrease 0–5 lb
5–7	Keep the same
8–10	Increase 2.5–5 lb
More than 10	Increase 5–10 lb

Repetitions during fourth set	Working weight for next session[a]
0–2	Decrease 5–10 lb
3–4	Keep the same
5–7	Increase 2.5–7.5 lb
8–10	Increase 5–10 lb
More than 10	Increase 10–15 lb

[a]From ''Rehabilitating Chondromalacia Patellae'' by K. Knight, 1979, *Physician and Sportsmedicine*, **1**, pp. 147–148.

person initiates motion in a flexion-extension direction, then adduction-abduction, and finally circumduction. All of these motions are pendular in nature without benefit of muscular contractions at the shoulder joint. Progressions in this exercise include wider circumduction motions and holding 2.5 and 5 pound weights as motions are performed (Figure 14.2). As with the tilt board for proprioceptive development, Codman's exercise may be used to enhance range of motion and flexibility of students with certain types of disabilities.

LONG-TERM DISORDERS

This section will deal with several conditions that are classified as long-term disorders. The designation

implies a condition or a problem that will last longer than 30 days. This time span is, to an extent, an arbitrary designation. A third-degree ankle sprain may not be totally rehabilitated within these 30 days. Three conditions will be the primary focus here, but certain principles and procedures relevant to these conditions may be applied to the integration of students with other long-term conditions into regular physical education classes.

Fractures

While most bones may be fractured in various types of accidents, bones in the upper and lower extremities are often fractured in activity-related accidents (e.g., in landing on an outstretched arm).

Table 14.4 Patella Protection Program

Stage	Activity	Purpose
I. Decrease inflammation and atrophy	A1. Isometric exercises (10 repetitions for 10 seconds; 10 seconds relax)	A1. Develop quadriceps muscles
	2. Flexibility exercises for lower extremity	2. Keep appropriate range of motion (ROM) in all major joints of leg
II. Develop strength without pain	B1. Terminal extension exercises[a]	B1. Continue to develop quadriceps muscles without undue stress on patello-femoral surfaces
III. Develop maximum strength and endurance	C1. Isotonic extension exercises relegated to 0–20°	C1. Maintain reduced stress on patello-femoral surfaces
	2. Isotonic flexion exercises through full ROM	2. Flexion exercises do not put undue stress on patello-femoral surfaces
	3. Flexibility exercises continued	3. Need to have full ROM at this joint and appropriate level of flexibility for future activities
	4. Endurance exercises in the form of swimming or bicycle ergometer work	4. Endurance components, both muscular and cardiovascular, need to be developed for future activities
IV. Restore full function to knee	D1. Continue strength and endurance exercises	D1. Need to increase these components to be comparable with nonaffected extremity
	2. Work on balance activities	2. Develop proprioception for this extremity
	3. Work on activities that are specific to sports or recreational activities	3. Address concept of task specificity

[a]To be explained in text under the heading "Selected Exercises"
Note. Adapted from "Patellar Malalignment: A Treatment Rationale" by L. Paulos, K. Rusche, C. Johnson, & F.R. Noyes, 1980, *Physical Therapy,* **60,** pp. 1624–1632.

While the focus of this chapter is on activity, readers should be aware that fractures may result from other situations such as child abuse and pathologic bone weakening conditions like cancer.

For physical educators, the student with a fracture presents two challenges: first, developing a program for a student immobilized in a cast; second, providing assistance to integrate the student into the regular physical education program after the cast is removed.

The first challenge must be dealt with from the perspective that the other three extremities have normal movement. A student with a broken arm has no problem concerning ambulation and can easily maintain a high level of cardiovascular fitness. Strength development of three extremities can be pursued with only minimal modification or adaptation. With a broken arm, certain lifts such as the bench press would have to be eliminated, but development of the triceps of the nonaffected arm could be accomplished through other exercises, such as elbow extension exercises. Involvement of the affected arm should be predicated on recommendations from the physician and on good judgment. For example, any type of isometric exercise involving muscles immobilized in a cast should be approved by the physician. Exercises, isotonic or isometric, involving joints above or below the cast area should also have physician approval; this, however, does not mean that exercises are contraindicated for these joints.

Participation in physical education is based upon the nature of the activities in the unit. While a track unit may mean little restriction for the student with a broken arm, a unit on gymnastic activities may require considerable restriction. For the

Table 14.5 Shoulder Exercise Protocol for the Glenohumeral Joint

I. During period of immobilization	A1. Isometric contractions of major muscle groups of shoulder	A1. Reduce muscle atrophy
	2. Isotonic wrist exercises of involved extremity	2. These muscles may be kept in condition without involving shoulder muscle
	3. General conditioning exercises for the other three extremities	3. These muscle groups should be kept in good condition
II. Mobilization of the shoulder	B1. Work on moving the shoulder through abduction and external rotation	B1. Begin to gain appropriate range of motion
	2. Codman's exercise[a]	2. Begins to enhance four motions of the shoulder
	3. Wall climbing exercise	3. Help to develop abduction and external rotation
	4. Continue conditioning other extremities	4. Improve body fitness
III. Development of shoulder	C1. Isotonic exercises that involve shoulder flexion, extension, abduction, adduction, medial rotation, and lateral rotation	C1. Develop muscles that cause specific motions
	2. Specific exercise involvement: bench press, pullovers, push-ups, parallel bar dips	2. Develop muscles for aggregate muscle action
	3. PNF exercises, replicate arm positions without the use of sight	3. Improve kinesthesis
	4. Resistance movements that replicate sport activities	4. Conform to the principle of specificity

Note. Not to be used with glenohumeral dislocations.
[a]Explained in text under the heading "Selected Exercises."

person with a broken radius of the nondominant arm, a badminton unit will need very little modification. An archery unit, while less vigorous, does require use of both upper extremities; the student could use a crossbow, which needs dexterity of one arm and could be mounted on a camera tripod. When unit activities preclude participation because of a fracture, physical fitness of the other three extremities may be the focus of the student's involvement in physical education class.

Once the cast is removed, the curricular focus should be on integrating the student into normal class activities. Part of this integration process may be to help develop range of motion, flexibility, strength, and muscular endurance in the affected limb. This assistance may be very important for students from low socioeconomic levels who may not have the benefit of appropriate medical services. Most students, regardless of socioeconomic

background, can benefit from a systemic reconditioning program. Activities and exercises described in the earlier section entitled "Activity Injuries" may be incorporated into this program. The student's total integration into the regular physical education program depends on a group of factors: the nature of the fracture, the extent of immobilization, the duration of the reconditioning period, and the nature of unit activities.

Osgood-Schlatter's Condition

A long-term condition that often presents a dilemma for the physical educator is Osgood-Schlatter's condition. Not a disease, as some books describe it, the condition involves incomplete separation of the epiphysis of the tibial tubercle from the tibia. O'Donoghue (1984) considers this condition to be more than just a single problem. Whether

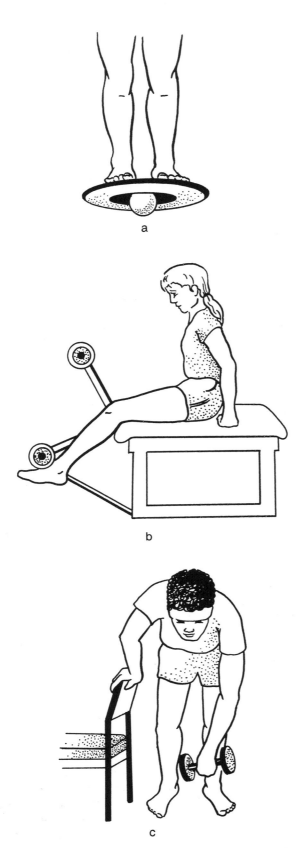

Figure 14.2 Selected rehabilitation exercises.

Osgood-Schlatter's condition has one or several causes, it primarily affects boys ages 13 to 15; incidence among girls has increased in recent years (Strauss, 1991). The treatment varies from immobilization in a cast to restriction of explosive extension movements at the knee, such as jumping and kicking. Variation in treatment depends on the severity of the condition and the philosophy of the attending physician.

The physical educator should help the student with this condition *during both its stages*, the acute stage of involvement and the recovery stage. Because 60% to 75% of all cases are unilateral (Mital & Matza, 1977), affected students may be considered to have normal status for three of their extremities. In essence, the approach discussed in the earlier section on fractures may be applied here. The comparison is applicable not only from a programmatic standpoint but also from a causality perspective, for with Osgood-Schlatter's condition there is a type of avulsion or fracture of bone from the tibial tuberosity. Involvement of the affected knee in activity must be based on a physician's recommendation. For example, certain physicians may approve isometric contractions of the quadriceps and stretching of the hamstrings in the affected extremity. Ankle exercises may also be considered appropriate. When all symptoms have disappeared and the physician has approved full participation, the student should begin a general mobilizing program in physical education class. Development of strength and flexibility of the affected limb should be part of the student's physical education program. Special attention should be given to the ratio of quadriceps to hamstring strength. The hamstrings should have 50% to 55% of the quadriceps' isotonic strength. The physical educator should evaluate (and improve where needed) the student's gait pattern following the occurrence of Osgood-Schlatter's condition.

Weight Control Problems

Many people associate weight control problems with the obese person going for the fourth serving at an all-you-can-eat smorgasbord. In reality there are two types of weight control problems: overweight and underweight. Both pose serious threats to a student's health. This problem may be the only condition a student must cope with, or it might be an accompanying condition or syndrome of a disability as defined by the public laws.

Underweight

Only recently have the terms **anorexia nervosa** and **bulimia** become familiar to the general public.

School staff and faculty, including physical educators, should realize that a coordinated effort among parents, student, physician, and school personnel is needed to deal with these problems.

Anorexia nervosa is a preoccupation with being thin that is manifested in willful self-starvation and may be accompanied by excessive physical activity. These individuals are 15% below what is considered normal for their weight and height, and they have a distorted body image. Females often develop primary or secondary amenorrhea. Ninety percent of all cases involve females, usually between the ages of 12 and 19 with a mean onset age of 16 years (Wichmann & Martin, 1993). During the early stages, both parents and student may be unaware that the condition is developing. As it progresses, the student becomes emaciated and hungry, but denies the existence of the problem. Anorexia nervosa is not to be regarded lightly, for mortality rates range from 5% to 15% among diagnosed anorexics. Death is the result of circulatory collapse or cardiac arrhythmias caused by electrolyte imbalance.

Bulimia is a condition associated with anorexia nervosa; it involves obsessive eating habits with ritualistic purging of ingested food by means of self-induced vomiting or laxatives. This practice also leads to electrolyte imbalance, impaired liver and kidney functioning, stomach rupture, tooth decay, and esophagitis.

The goals of treatment to promote weight gain in these conditions are simplistic in nature but challenging in execution. Hospitalization in a medical or psychiatric unit may be needed to initiate treatment, with a brief stay of 2 weeks or a longer period of several months. Treatment consists of behavior modification, vitamin and mineral supplements, appropriate diet, and psychotherapy for the student and family. Low self-esteem, guilt, and anxiety are often part of the student's underlying problem.

The physical educator may be one of the first to recognize these problems. Anorexics and bulimics present a profile of being compliant high-achievers. A preoccupation with thinness, obvious weight loss, and an increasing involvement in aerobic activities may be signs that referral to an appropriate health professional is needed. Whatever the stage of the student's disorder, physical education activities must be monitored to ensure an appropriate level of exertion. A caloric deficit—more calories being used than are taken in—should not be allowed to develop through or in conjunction with physical education activities. Fitness enhancement should be a gradual process, with strength gains achieved before cardiovascular endurance is attempted. Precautions or exercise contraindications for students with cardiovascular conditions are applicable in this situation. Dual and individual sports, some with certain modifications, are of suitable intensity and good for facilitating social interaction. A priority with the anorexic or bulimic student should be enhancement of self-esteem.

Overweight

A major health concern today is the number of overweight and obese students. Overweight is generally regarded as 10% over the appropriate weight, based on height and somatotype. *Obesity* is generally defined as at least 20% over appropriate weight. However, there are gender differences: females may be considered obese when they exceed the appropriate weight by 30% to 35%; for males the range is 20% to 25%. One out of four school-age children is overweight (Rosenbaum & Seibel, 1989). Both physical educators and adapted physical educators must cope with and provide suitable experiences for overweight and obese students.

The cause of this condition is multifaceted in nature. While an endocrine disorder may cause excessive weight gains, fewer than 10% of all cases can be attributed to this. Hypothalamic, pituitary, and thyroid dysfunctions are causes of endocrine obesity. In the case of the hypothalamic dysfunction, damping of the hunger sensation does not take place, and a person feels hungry after consuming sufficient calories. Certain medications such as cortisone and adrenocortical steroids may produce the side effect of appetite elevation, with concomitant weight gain. Emotional factors may result in overweight and obesity. Some people eat as a means of compensation or to reduce feelings of anxiety; others, however, eat excessively when content and happy.

Demographic variables related to obesity are gender, age, and socioeconomic level. Females are more likely than males to be obese at all age levels. The critical age range for obesity is between 20 and 50 years, and obesity is more prevalent among people from lower socioeconomic levels.

An increase in the number (hypertrophic obesity) or size (hyperplastic obesity) of the fat cells that make up adipose tissue may lead to obesity. There are two periods during which there are rapid increases in fat cell production: (a) the third trimester and the first year of life and (b) the adolescent growth spurt. Between these two periods the number of fat cells increases gradually. There is some evidence that vigorous exercise during childhood may reduce the size and number of fat cells (Saltin & Rowell, 1980).

Strategies for Weight Control

The physical educator is one member of a team who may help a student with a weight control problem. Just as exercise alone cannot remediate a weight problem, the physician educator alone cannot solve this problem. A team effort is needed, with the physician overseeing medical and dietary matters, the parents providing appropriate diet and psychological support, and the physical educator selecting the exercises and activities best for the obese or overweight student.

There are basically three ways to lose weight: diet, exercise, and a combination of the two. Diet alone is the most common method used by adults and is often the most abused method. The criterion frequently used to judge success with this approach is how quickly the maximum number of pounds can be lost. A crash diet may even trigger a starvation reaction, which causes the basal metabolic rate to diminish and may increase metabolic efficiency during physical activity. In this way, the body counteracts certain effects of the crash diet. A more gradual approach is a reduction of 500 calories a day, which in a week equals 3,500 calories—the number of calories needed to lose a pound of fat. Under the direction of a physician, an obese student may be on a diet that reduces intake by more than 500 calories per day.

Exercise helps with weight control, but it is a slow, difficult process if used as the sole method for weight reduction. On the other hand, exercise used in conjunction with a controlled diet may help to generate a negative caloric imbalance; this imbalance results when more calories are being used than are being consumed.

Physical Education and the Obese Student

A well-designed physical education program for overweight and obese students may contribute to increased caloric expenditure. There are, however, certain limitations or problems the physical educator must recognize and cope with in developing such a program.

Sherrill (1993) noted the following physical characteristics associated with obesity that may affect program planning:

- Distended abdomen
- Skeletal immaturity
- Mobility of fat rolls
- Edema
- Excessive perspiration
- Broad base in locomotor activities
- Galling between the thighs
- Fear of falling
- Postural faults
- Excessive buoyancy

Sherrill explains that the distended abdomen places excessive pressure on the diaphragm, with a resultant difficulty in breathing and a buildup of carbon dioxide. The consequence is a manifestation of drowsiness on the part of the obese student. The label of "lazy" may be unfair, for this student has a physiological disadvantage.

The physical education program should be developed to provide successful experiences for the obese student. Activities that require lifting or excessively moving the body weight will not result in positive experiences. Gymnastic activities, distance running, rope climbing, and field events such as long jump may need extensive modification for the obese student. Gradual enhancement of endurance capabilities should be part of the student's program. Fast walking, bicycle riding, and certain swimming pool activities may help to develop aerobic endurance. Aquatic activities are usually deemed appropriate for many types of special populations; with the obese student, activities such as water calisthenics may be quite appropriate because buoyancy may reduce stress on joints. Excessive buoyancy may be counterproductive, as Sherrill (1993) points out, because this force may keep parts of the body out of the water, thus impeding the execution of certain swimming strokes.

Many of the typical units covered in a physical education class will need considerable modification for obese students. A basketball or football unit may center on developing certain fundamental skills such as passing, catching, kicking, and shooting. Softball may include the development of fundamental skills and involve modification of some rules (e.g., allowing for courtesy or pinch runners). Dual and individual sports with modifications such as boundary or rule changes (e.g., the ball may bounce twice in handball) are appropriate activities. Golf, archery, and bowling need no modification, while tennis and racquetball may be feasible only in doubles play.

All curricular experiences should be oriented toward helping obese students develop a positive attitude about themselves and about activity.

Whether doing a caloric analysis of energy expenditures, learning to drive a golf ball, or being permitted to wear a different type of sport clothing than the typical gym uniform, physical education should help obese students cope with their condition and should contribute directly or indirectly to solving the problem. Finally, any strategy to improve self-image will help. Likewise, any strategy that changes the other students' attitude toward those with weight problems will facilitate integration of obese and overweight students into the social environment.

SUMMARY

This chapter has addressed conditions which students with disabilities as defined by IDEA and without these types of disabilities may exhibit. While activity injuries and long-term disorders may be found among students with and without disabilities, these conditions should not preclude participation in physical education class. Suggestions for appropriate physical education experiences have been provided for students with activity injuries, long-term disorders, and weight control problems.

BIBLIOGRAPHY

Knight, K. (1979). Rehabilitating chondromalacia patellae. *Physician and Sportsmedicine, 7*, 147–148.

Mital, M.A., & Matza, R.A. (1977). Osgood-Schlatter's disease: The pain puzzler. *Physician and Sportsmedicine, 5*, 60–73.

O'Donoghue, D. (1984). *Treatment of injuries to athletes.* St. Louis: Mosby.

Paulos, L., Rusche, K., Johnson, C., & Noyes, F.R. (1980). Patellar malalignment: A treatment rationale. *Physical Therapy, 60*, 1624–1632.

Rosenbaum, M., & Seibel, R.L. (1989). Obesity in childhood. *Pediatric Review, 11*, 43–55.

Saltin, B., & Rowell, L.B. (1980). Functional adaptation to physical activity and inactivity. *Federation Proceeding, 39*, 1506–13.

Sherrill, C. (1993). *Adapted physical education and recreation: A multidisciplinary approach* (3rd ed.). Dubuque, IA: Brown.

Smith, R.L., & Bronolli, J. (1989). Shoulder kinesthesia after anterior glenohumeral joint dislocation. *Physical Therapy, 69*, 106–112.

Strauss, R.H. (Ed.) (1991). *Sports medicine and physiology.* Philadelphia: Saunders.

Voss, D., Knott, M., & Iona, B. (1986). *Proprioceptive neuromuscular facilitation.* Philadelphia: Harper & Row.

Wichmann, S., & Martin, D.R. (1993). Eating disorder of athletes. *Physician and Sportsmedicine, 21*, 126–135.

RESOURCES

Written

Anderson, S.T. (1991). Acute knee injuries in young athletes. *Physician and Sportsmedicine, 19*, 64–76. This is a discussion of knee problems that a child or adolescent may develop. The focus of this area is with an age level that is younger in nature than traditional sports medicine articles dealing with knee problems.

Aronen, J.G., Chronister, R., Regan, K., & Hensien, M.A. (1993). Practical, conservative management of ileotibial band syndrome. *Physician and Sportsmedicine, 21*, 59–69. These authors discuss the means to treat the initial symptoms of what often is called Runner's knee. Suggestions focus on returning to complete activity.

Calvo, R.D., Steadman, S.R., Sterling, J.C., Holden, S.C., & Meyers, M.C. (1990). Managing plica syndrome of the knee. *Physician and Sportsmedicine, 18*, 64–74. Focuses upon the nature of this condition and the symptoms associated with this vestige of embryonic development. Presents methods to reduce the pain associated with this condition.

Surburg, P.R. (1986). New perspectives for developing range of motion and flexibility for special populations. *Adapted Physical Education Activity Quarterly, 3*, 227–235. The author provides new insights into developing range of motion and flexibility. While individuals with disabilities are the primary focus of this article, the principles of flexibility may be applied to any person with and without a disability.

Audiovisual

Nutrition for sports: Facts and fallacies [Videotape]. Dairy and Nutrition Council, 10255 W. Higgins Road, Suite 900, Rosemont, IL 60018-5616. Facts and fallacies of how nutrition influences health and performance.

Real people: Coping with eating disorders [Videotape]. Dairy and Nutrition Council, 10255 W. Higgins Road, Suite 900, Rosemont, IL 60018-5616. Insights into the causes of eating disorders, documented by stories of an anorexic, a bulimic, and a compulsive overeater.

PART III

Developmental and Early Childhood Topics in Adapted Physical Education

Part III begins with three chapters that discuss physical fitness, motor development, and perceptual-motor development. The information presented is intended to build on foundational knowledge related to growth and development and measurement and evaluation taken in a student's professional preparation program. In discussing these topics, particular emphasis is given to their relationship with persons with disabilities.

The last two chapters in this section deal with early childhood physical activity. The first emphasizes the infant and toddler population and includes a description of the population, the legislative basis for provision of services, and suggestions important for assessment, consultation, or direct service activities. The second chapter dealing with preschoolers presents best practices in planning and teaching preschoolers with disabilities, with particular attention given to assessment and program planning. Programs designed for early childhood physical education are themselves in their infancy in terms of identifying the role of physical education and physical educators in these programs and identifying goals, objectives, and approaches for meeting the needs of this population. Many advances are expected in the near future, and these chapters represent a good start.

CHAPTER 15

Physical Fitness

Francis X. Short

Two high school students, Neil and Tracy, were talking over lunch in the cafeteria. "What were you and Mrs. Speight talking about after PE class today?" asked Neil.

"I'm going to be an assistant coach for Gregory after school each day."

"The kid in the wheelchair? What sport does he do?"

"He competes in road races and marathons," said Tracy.

"Marathons? That must take forever in a wheelchair."

"Greg's times are faster than most of the able-bodied runners he competes with."

"You're kidding! He must use one of those motorized wheelchairs and lay rubber all over the course!"

"No, wiseguy, he uses a manual racing chair and he trains very hard to push it that fast."

"Yeah? What does he do?" asked Neil.

"Well, it depends on what he's training for, but Greg lifts weights regularly, works out on the speedbag like the boxers do, does a lot of roadwork in his chair, and sometimes uses an arm ergometer."

"What's that?"

"Kind of like a stationary bicycle you peddle with your hands instead of your feet."

"Cool."

Whether it is necessary to sit independently or to successfully complete a marathon like Gregory does, physical fitness is critical to the development of the disabled person. Activities for daily living (including self-help skills), job requirements, recreational opportunities, and reducing risk of developing health problems caused by inactivity all require certain levels of physical fitness. This chapter examines definitions, principles for development, and considerations for people with unique needs.

DEFINITION AND COMPONENTS OF PHYSICAL FITNESS

A universally acceptable definition of physical fitness does not exist. Traditionally, physical fitness has been defined as "the ability to carry out tasks with vigor and alertness, without undue fatigue, and with ample energy to enjoy leisure-time pursuits and to meet unusual situations and unforeseen emergencies" (Clarke & Clarke, 1978, p. 32). Caspersen, Powell, and Christenson (1985) defined physical fitness as a "set of attributes that people have or achieve that relates to the ability to perform physical activity" (p. 129). Furthermore, these authors suggest that the components of physical fitness can be categorized into two groups: one related to health and the other to skills that are necessary for athletic ability.

More recently, the American Alliance Board of Governors (AAHPERD, 1988) conceptualized physical fitness as a physical state of well-being that allows people to perform daily activities with vigor, reduce their risk of health problems related to lack of exercise, and establish a fitness base for participation in a variety of physical activities. Based on this definition AAHPERD (1988) developed *Physical Best*, a fitness test "that places major emphasis on health-related fitness" (p. 12). The health-related components included in both the Caspersen et al. and AAHPERD definitions are the same: body composition, muscular strength and endurance, flexibility, and aerobic capacity. Each of these components is addressed in the following paragraphs.

Body Composition

Body composition refers to the degree of leanness or fatness of the individual. Anthropometric measures such as skinfold and girth measurement and height and weight assessment can be utilized in field settings to gather information on body composition.

Muscular Strength and Endurance

Strength is the ability of the muscles to produce force at high intensities over short intervals of time. We can measure strength by using dynamometers or tensiometers, or by recording the maximum amount of weight that can be lifted in a single repetition. Muscular **endurance** refers to the ability to sustain repeated applications of force at low to moderate intensities over extended intervals of time. Sit-ups and flexed-arm hang are examples of field-based tests of muscular endurance.

Flexibility

Flexibility refers to the ability to move muscles and joints through their full range of motion. Because degree of flexibility is specific to the various joints in the body, a single test cannot reflect overall flexibility. Instruments such as goniometers and flexometers have been used to measure flexibility, but a popular field measure is the sit and reach test, which is an indicator of trunk-hip flexibility.

Aerobic Capacity

Aerobic capacity is defined as the highest rate oxygen can be taken up and utilized by the body during exercise. A number of factors contribute to efficient aerobic functioning, including the ability of the heart to pump blood, the ability of the respiratory system to process oxygen to the blood, and the ability of the muscles to utilize the oxygen delivered by the blood. A number of indices of aerobic capacity, including maximal oxygen consumption, are used in laboratory settings; however, distance runs are appropriate measures in field settings.

An emphasis on health-related physical fitness, as suggested by the American Alliance Board of Governors, certainly has relevance for adapted physical education. One of the accepted generalizations about disability is that it is usually associated with a sedentary lifestyle. Inactivity is considered to be an important risk factor in coronary heart disease, and there is evidence that instituting a physical activity program can guard against coronary heart disease and reduce the risk of dying in middle age (Blair, 1993). One of the challenges for adapted physical educators therefore is to develop appropriate exercise programs that will improve students' health-related physical fitness.

Physical education teachers, however, have another important responsibility to their students, namely, the development of skills that are necessary for successful performance in games and sports. Often athletic performance requires high levels of muscular strength and endurance, flexibility, and aerobic capacity, coupled with an appropriate body composition, to achieve success. In addition to these health-related components that help to establish a fitness base for many physical activities, the development of skill-related components is frequently necessary for athletic participation. Caspersen et al. (1985) included agility, balance, coordination, speed, power, and reaction time as the skill-related components of physical fitness. Throughout this chapter primary attention is given to development of health-related aspects of physical fitness, but teachers and coaches are reminded that developing the skill-related components also may be necessary to foster certain types of physical activity.

PRINCIPLES FOR DEVELOPMENT

A complete review of the principles of physical fitness development is beyond the scope of this chapter. Even the beginning physical educator, however, must understand that the progressions for the development of physical fitness revolve around the concepts of intensity, duration, frequency, and mode. These are the variables that the teacher must consider and manipulate when developing physical fitness programs.

- Intensity essentially refers to "how much." It describes the degree of effort that should be made in an exercise to bring about the desired training effect.

- Duration essentially refers to "how long." It describes the length of time an exercise should be performed at a given level of intensity.

- Frequency essentially refers to "how often." It describes the number of times per week the exercise should be performed at given levels of intensity and duration.

- Mode essentially refers to "what kind." It describes the type of exercise to be performed.

These four training variables differ for the various components of fitness. Table 15.1 summarizes the recommended levels of intensity, duration, and frequency for the four components of fitness.

PERSONALIZING PHYSICAL FITNESS

When programming for students with disabilities, the physical educator must first ask, "Physical fitness for what purpose?" Objectives may vary widely from student to student. Fitness objectives for a student with a disability can be influenced by a number of factors including, but not necessarily limited to, present level of physical fitness, functional motor abilities, physical maturity, age, nature of the disability (and how the disability affects activity selection), student interests and/or activity preferences, and availability of equipment and facilities. In adapted physical education, objectives can range from fitness for the execution of rudimentary movements (sitting, reaching, creeping, etc.) to fitness for the execution of specialized

movements (sport skills, recreational activities, vocational tasks) to fitness for the pursuit of a healthier lifestyle.

With the help of the student, as appropriate, teachers should design *personalized* fitness programs. In personalizing physical fitness, certain elements of the fitness program are emphasized for each student. For instance, for each student the teacher might ask the following questions:

- What are the highest priority fitness needs for this student?
- Which component(s) of health-related or skill-related physical fitness should be targeted for development given the identified needs?
- Which areas of the body will be trained? (For students with physical disabilities, the teacher must decide whether or not to train affected body parts.)
- Which tests will be used to measure physical fitness for this student and what standards will be adopted for evaluative purposes?

The following scenarios are presented to illustrate the notion of personalized physical fitness.

Scenario 1. Danny is a three-year-old boy with a severe form of mental retardation. He does

Table 15.1 Summary of Training Recommendations

Component	Intensity	Duration	Frequency
Body composition	Moderate	20–30 minutes per session	3–5 days per week
Muscular strength/ endurance			
Strength	4–10 repetitions[a] (heavy load)	10 seconds or less	3 times per session; 3–5 days per week
Muscular endurance	Minimum 20 repetitions[a] (lighter load)	30 seconds or more	2–3 times per session; 3–5 days per week
Speed	Maximal or near maximal (7/8) effort (moderate load)	1–30 seconds (emphasis on alactic system) 30–180 seconds (emphasis on lactic acid system)	1–3 times per session (at least 1 repetition per set); 3–5 times per week
Power	10–20 repetitions[a] executed (moderate to heavy load)	30 seconds or less	2–3 times per session; 3–5 days per week
Flexibility	5–10 repetitions at approximately 10% overstretch or to point of discomfiture	6–12 seconds per repetition	3 times per session; 3–7 days per week
Aerobic capacity	75% maximum heart rate	20–40 minutes per session	3–5 days per week

[a]Recommendations are for isotonic or isokinetic activity.

not have any physical disabilities, but he engages in very little purposeful voluntary movement and his present level of physical performance is essentially "prone lying." Parents and teachers agree that learning to creep is a high priority goal for Danny. The physical educator decides to emphasize the development of muscular strength and endurance to support creeping. Since motor development progresses in a cephalocaudal direction, the neck extensors are targeted first for training. Lifting the head from the floor is the first step in the developmental sequence that will lead to "all fours," the necessary posture for creeping (see Figure 15.1). Additional muscle groups will be targeted as progress in the developmental sequence is made. The physical educator selects test items from the Peabody Developmental Motor Scales (see chapter 4) that address the developmental sequence leading to creeping. Although the PDMS is not a physical fitness test per se, the selected items (e.g., "extending head," "extending trunk," "propping on extended arms," etc.) are directly related to creeping and require prerequisite levels of muscular strength and endurance in selected muscle groups for success. In essence, the teacher constructs a task analysis for creeping and measures whether necessary levels of fitness have been achieved by Danny's progress on the sequence of tasks. The standards for evaluation are the criterion-referenced standards associated with the PDMS, which are judged on a pass-fail basis.

Scenario 2. Twelve-year-old Kelly has spina bifida, is largely independent, and uses a wheelchair for activities for daily living. She is not interested in being an athlete, but she would like to be more physically fit. Her highest priority fitness need, in consultation with her teacher, is to attain minimal levels of health-related fitness. The components targeted for development are body composition, aerobic capacity, flexibility, and muscular strength and endurance with greatest emphasis placed on the first two. Upper-body exercises and activities are identified for training purposes since Kelly has virtually no lower-limb functional ability. A modified version of FITNESSGRAM (see chapter 4) is selected as the assessment instrument. Curl-ups and trunk lift are eliminated as inappropriate. Percent body fat, flexed arm hang, and shoulder stretch are tested, and the regular criterion-referenced standards are employed. The mile run is done in the wheelchair

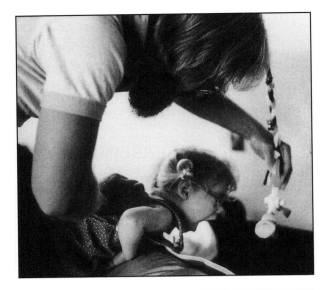

Figure 15.1 A physical educator works to improve the muscular strength and endurance of a student's neck extensors.

with teacher-generated standards serving as the criteria.

Scenario 3. Bobby is 17 years old. He is congenitally blind, but has been active his entire life. His goal is to win a medal in the 50-meter dash in competition sponsored by the United States Association of Blind Athletes. In consultation with his physical education teacher, it is decided that he will maintain at least minimal levels of health-related fitness, but his training will emphasize the development of the skill-related components of power and speed. FITNESSGRAM will serve as the test instrument for health-related fitness utilizing the regular criterion-referenced standards. (The pacer test will be modified to include a guide rope.) The 50-meter dash, as conducted by Project UNIQUE Physical Fitness Test (see chapter 4) procedures, will serve as an additional test item. The 85th percentile from the UNIQUE norms will be the standard that represents an intermediate step in the pursuit of a USABA medal.

PHYSICAL FITNESS FOR STUDENTS WITH UNIQUE NEEDS

The principles established for the development of physical fitness in the general population are also appropriate in many cases for the development of physical fitness for individuals with unique needs. This is particularly true for students with sensory, cognitive, or emotional disabilities, as well as for nondisabled students with low fitness. It should be emphasized, however, that when students begin programs with low levels of fitness, the intensity and duration of the activity may need to be reduced. Programs for those with low fitness should be characterized initially by limited intensity and duration followed by gradual progression.

One of the most common ways of assessing the intensity of aerobic exercise is to monitor heart rate. Maximum heart rate is often estimated using "Karvonen's formula" (220 − age). While this may be appropriate for most students, it is not applicable for all. For those with certain spinal cord injuries, for instance, heart rate does not accelerate during exercise to the same levels attained by able-bodied individuals (Shephard, 1990), and those with motor control problems (especially cerebral palsy) may not be able to monitor their pulse due to an unsteady hand (Birk & Mossing, 1988).

Borg's (1985) ratings of perceived exertion (RPE) scale provides a useful alternative to monitoring intensity via heart rate (see Table 15.2). This 15-point scale provides a subjective measure of exercise intensity related to such sensations as perceived changes in heart rate, breathlessness,

sweating, muscle fatigue, and lactate accumulation (Arnhold, Ng, & Pechar, 1992). The RPE scale has good utility for physical education settings and has been used successfully in research projects employing subjects with mental retardation, asthma, spinal cord injuries, and cerebral palsy. Burke and Humphreys (1982) have suggested that participants attempt to work at a 14 or 15 on the scale when training.

In whatever manner exercise intensity is monitored, it is important that the program be followed on a regular basis; otherwise, important gains may be lost. Canadian researchers, for instance, have reported that, following a rigorous training program, sightless adolescents were found to have aerobic power and body composition test scores that were comparable to those of normally sighted individuals. Following a 10-week summer vacation, however, these scores deteriorated to levels previously reported for untrained blind adolescents and well below the values for those with normal sight (di Natale, Lee, Ward, & Shephard, 1985). One implication is that students with disabilities must understand the value of regular physical activity, and teachers must give the students training ideas that are "transportable," that is, ideas that can be used outside the school environment.

Instructors who work with persons with unique needs may have to modify methodology to achieve satisfactory results. For instance, with students who have auditory impairments, a teacher will need to employ some alternate form of communication when describing activities; more demonstration may be necessary for students who are mentally retarded; and a behavior modification program may be necessary to increase the motivation of a student with an emotional problem.

In some cases, the *way* an activity is performed may need to be modified. For example, students with visual impairments can, and should, participate in running activities as long as some form of guidance is provided. For short-distance running (to develop power and speed), a guide wire or a rope is usually an appropriate way to supply the necessary guidance. For running over a longer distance (to develop aerobic capacity or to lose weight), tactual guidance provided by a sighted partner is usually the recommended method. Another way to modify an activity is to reduce its complexity by eliminating or adapting rules to increase participation by students with disabilities. (Readers are referred to other chapters for more specific discussions of modifications of methods and activities.)

Table 15.2 Borg's Ratings of Perceived Exertion Scale

6	No exertion at all
7	Extremely light
8	
9	Very light
10	
11	Light
12	
13	Somewhat hard
14	
15	Hard (heavy)
16	
17	Very hard
18	
19	Extremely hard
20	Maximal exertion

Note. From *An Introduction to Borg's RPE-Scale* by G. Borg, 1985, Ithaca, NY: Mouvement Publications. Copyright 1985 by Gunnar Borg. Reprinted by permission.

In the development of physical fitness programs in adapted physical education, the most significant modifications in intensity, duration, frequency, and mode will be made for students with physical disabilities. Considerations in fitness programming for those students, therefore, are discussed in greater detail in the following paragraphs. Although they are written specifically with the physically disabled person in mind, the reader may find that some of the material can be generalized to other students who exhibit poor fitness.

Body Composition and Aerobic Capacity

Because many of the activities suggested for both body composition (especially weight loss) and aerobic capacity are similar, they are combined here for discussion purposes. Youngsters with physical disabilities frequently have a unique need to improve body composition and to increase aerobic capacity resulting, at least in part, from a sedentary lifestyle. Research has demonstrated, for instance, that people with spinal injuries have a decreased lean body mass, a higher percent body fat, and a higher proportion of extracellular fluid when compared to the general population. Furthermore, resting oxygen consumption and cardiac output are reduced for those with spinal cord injuries. It is clear, however, that improvements in body composition and aerobic capacity are very possible. Studies conducted with wheelchair athletes as subjects suggest that the loss of lean body mass due to lower limb paralysis may be accommodated by an increase in lean body mass (hypertrophy) of the upper body. Furthermore, active wheelchair users may have better skinfold and maximum oxygen intake values than the inactive wheelchair user and comparable to the sedentary able-bodied population (Shephard, 1990).

Objectives for improved body composition and increased aerobic capacity will best be attained by utilizing a continuous aerobic training program. For those with lower-limb impairments, arm exercises rather than leg exercises will have to be employed. Cranking an arm cycle ergometer is one popular training activity. Although exercise guidelines (such as those depicted in Table 15.1) are fairly well established for the able-bodied, relatively few exist for those who are physically disabled. Lasko-McCarthey and Aufsesser (1990), however, have suggested an interval training program for spinal cord injured adults using arm ergometry (see Table 15.3).

Wheelchair training (e.g., "roadwork") is also appropriate and recommended for improved body composition and increased aerobic capacity. Readers are cautioned, however, that ordinary wheelchair ambulation alone is generally insufficient to induce a training effect. Wheelchair training should be regular (three to five times per week), continuous (20 to 60 minutes per training session), and challenging. Borg's scale or target heart rate should be used to estimate how "challenging" (i.e., intense) the program is. When calculating maximum heart rate, it is recommended that an additional 10 beats per minute be subtracted for arm exercises (Lasko-McCarthey & Aufsesser, 1990). Teachers and coaches are encouraged to closely monitor participants with spinal injuries during continuous aerobic activity, especially on warm or humid days. People with spinal cord injuries often have problems with thermoregulation (i.e., control of body temperature), so precautions should include such things as providing shade, wet towels, water to drink, sunscreens, hats, or other commonsense approaches to dissipating body heat.

Swimming is another excellent activity for enhancing physical fitness, particularly for students with physical disabilities. In cases where students have loss of muscle function or coordination, flotation devices may have to be provided so that exercise can be maintained for sufficient duration. Activities such as lap swimming and aerobic water games can enhance both body composition (when weight loss is indicated) and aerobic capacity. For students who use crutches or other assistive devices for ambulation, walking laps in chest-deep water may be an appropriate activity. The water simultaneously provides the support necessary for independent ambulation and the resistance necessary to increase the intensity of the task.

Bicycling activities also should be considered. When a student has sufficient leg function, stationary bikes and three-wheelers can be useful in designing a continuous activity of moderate to high intensity. In cases where the legs are impaired but the arms remain unaffected, hand-propelled bicycles can be used (see Figure 15.2).

Finally, the physical educator may wish to incorporate "mat activities" into the exercise program. Activities that require the student to pull the body along a mat are sometimes very challenging. In fact, having a student with cerebral palsy creep or crawl to a cone placed only 10 to 15 feet away may meet the intensity and duration requirements to elicit a training effect.

Table 15.3   Arm Ergometry Exercise Recommendations

Level of lesion (nerve root)	Cadence (rpm)	Duration	Intensity	Frequency (times/week)
C4 to C8	50–70	1 minute work, 1 in rest, until fatigue or 3 bouts of 2–4 minutes work, 1–2 minute rest	Heart rate max (~100–125 bpm) or use Borg's Perceived Exertion Scale	3–5
T1 to T6	60–70	3 bouts of 5 minutes work, 1 minute rest or 1 minute high load, 1 minute low load for 10–30 minutes	Use Borg's Perceived Exertion Scale	3–5
T7 and below	60–70	3 bouts of 5 minutes work, 1 minute rest or 1 minute high load, 1 minute low load for 10–30 minutes or continuous work for 15–30 minutes	60–80% of maximum heart rate reserve using Karvonen's formula	3–5

Note: From "Guidelines for a Community-Based Physical Fitness Program for Adults with Physical Disabilities" by P. Lasko-McCarthey and P.M. Aufsesser, 1990, *Palaestra, 7*(1), pp. 18–29. Reprinted by permission.

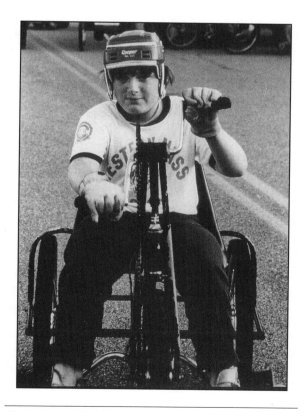

Figure 15.2   Hand-propelled bicycles can be used to develop aerobic capacity in youngsters with lower-limb disabilities.
Photo by Craig Huber.

Muscular Strength and Endurance

Research indicates that the muscular strength and endurance of most persons with disabilities is below that of their able-bodied peers. This is true despite the fact that, in many instances (muscular dystrophy being a notable exception), muscle physiology is normal and, consequently, the muscles of disabled youngsters will respond appropriately to training as long as innervation is intact.

When there is complete loss of muscle function due to spinal cord injury, no improvement in muscular strength and endurance can be attained through exercise. For people with partial loss of muscle function, exercise is recommended; however, the intensity of the activity must be modified radically. **Active** and/or **assistive exercises**, therefore, may have to be used in place of resistive exercises, although the overload principle must still be maintained to produce a training effect. An active exercise is one in which the participant independently works a muscle through the range of motion, with gravity providing the only resistance. An assistive exercise is one in which the participant works through the range of motion with some form of outside assistance. (A third alternative to resistive exercise is **passive exercise**, in which another individual moves the participant's limb through the range of motion. Because no muscle action is involved on the part of the participant, passive exercise is not recommended for the development of muscular strength and endurance, but it can be used to enhance flexibility.)

Principles of active and assistive exercises should also be applied to students who do not have nerve damage but who are unable to overcome even minimal resistance in exercise. For a student who is unable to do a sit-up, for instance, an inclined board can be used so that the student does "downhill" sit-ups. This is a less intense, assistive exercise where gravity provides the assistance. A pull-up task can also be modified with the use of an inclined board. By lying on a scooter placed on the inclined board, the student can perform pull-ups in a way in which the effects of gravity are reduced. It should be noted that, as levels of intensity are established for pull-ups or other tasks where the body provides resistance, the student's body weight and that of any braces or prosthetic devices being worn must be considered. The intensity of the task is more demanding for those who are heavier or who are wearing orthopedic devices.

Many muscular strength and endurance exercises can be done in a pool or on a mat. Teachers should be careful, however, to position the student in such a way that the targeted muscles are exercised at the most appropriate intensity. Knee flexion (hamstring) exercises, for example, are more difficult in a prone position than in a side-lying position because gravity provides more resistance when one is prone. Positioning of the student is also a consideration when reflexes are a problem. Activities that are appropriate for specific positions must be designed individually. An example would be exercises that allow the head to remain in the midline for an individual who exhibits the asymmetrical tonic neck reflex, a condition where turning the head in either direction causes extension of the limbs on the "face" side of the body and flexion of the limbs on the "skull" side.

When developing muscular strength and endurance, the physical educator must guard against creating muscular imbalances within the individual's body. Whenever possible and appropriate, therefore, both agonists and antagonists should be exercised. Muscular imbalance is a particularly important issue for students with spastic cerebral palsy. Ordinarily, attention should be given to the development of the extensors, abductors, and supinators of the student with spasticity because the flexors, adductors, and pronators tend to be hypertonic and dominate their antagonists. Muscle imbalance is also a problem for people with spinal cord injuries. Muscular strength and endurance activities should be selected to improve or maintain proper body alignment and to improve the capacity of the functional muscles. For those with

quadriplegia, exercise will usually involve the anterior deltoid, biceps, and lower trapezius; for those with paraplegia, exercise can be expanded to include the shoulder depressors (e.g., pectorals), triceps, and latissimus dorsi (O'Sullivan, Cullen, & Schmitz, 1981). Mat activities including modified push-ups, modified pull-ups, and log rolling are usually appropriate for students with spinal cord injuries.

The student with cerebral palsy requires some additional considerations with regard to muscular strength and endurance. Because of inefficiency of movement, individuals with cerebral palsy may tire more rapidly than other students in the class. Consequently, the duration of the activity may have to be modified; this is especially true with both muscular endurance and aerobic activities. When possible, isokinetic exercises are recommended over isotonic or isometric exercises because, with the former, resistance varies throughout the range of motion. Isokinetic exercise supplies a constant tension to the muscle, commensurate with muscle contraction, allowing for a more controlled exercise. McCubbin and Shasby (1985), for instance, have reported that isokinetic exercise can effectively improve torque and speed of movement in the elbow extensors of adolescents with cerebral palsy.

Flexibility

As with other components of physical fitness, research suggests that the flexibility of students with disabilities generally is inferior to that of their able-bodied peers. Although flexibility training is important for all students, its incorporation into physical fitness programs for physically disabled students is highly recommended. Increased flexibility will allow for improved functional movement and will help to combat contractures, a condition characterized by shortened muscles that may result in some physical deviation. Contractures are associated with a number of conditions including muscular dystrophy, juvenile rheumatoid arthritis, amputation, spinal cord injury, and cerebral palsy.

When severe restrictions in flexibility exist, the frequency and duration of training must increase significantly. In these instances it is recommended that flexibility training be provided at least three times per day and the duration of the training be up to 30–45 minutes per session (Winnick & Short, 1985). When this type of schedule is recommended, however, flexibility training will probably go beyond the scope of physical education programs (regular or adapted), and students must take responsibility for their own flexibility exercises outside of the school environment. For instance, youngsters with cerebral palsy whose legs are severely adducted should assume an abducted posture while doing homework or watching television at home, or they should become involved in appropriate recreation programs such as horseback riding.

Surburg (1986) has suggested that when flexibility training is incorporated into physical education programs (regular or adapted), it should be done toward the end of the class period when the muscles, and especially the collagenous tissues, are warm. He also has recommended that proprioceptive neuromuscular facilitation (PNF) techniques serve as the basis for flexibility training, and he discusses three approaches that have been used successfully:

- *Rhythmic stabilization:* the participant performs 10 rhythmical, alternating, isometric contractions of agonists and antagonists per set.

- *Contract—relax:* a partner or teacher passively stretches the muscle to elongation; the participant contracts the muscle against resistance provided by the partner/teacher until the body part has returned to its original/resting position; the muscle is relaxed for 5 seconds prior to next repetition.

- *Hold—relax:* a partner or teacher passively stretches the muscle to elongation; the participant then performs a 6-second isometric contraction in that position followed by a 5-second rest.

The physical therapist can serve as a valuable resource to the physical educator in identifying muscular imbalances and selecting appropriate activities for the development of flexibility. The flexors, adductors, and pronators, for instance, are usually the muscle groups requiring the greatest attention in development of flexibility among individuals with spastic cerebral palsy. For those with spinal cord injuries, flexibility of the arms and shoulders is important for functional efficiency. Attention to trunk flexibility, however, is not always recommended for those with spinal cord injuries because increased range of motion may interfere with necessary trunk stability (O'Sullivan et al., 1981).

Physical therapists also can provide additional flexibility training when the goals and objectives of the student's program cannot be met in physical education or when severe restrictions in flexibility prohibit the student from attaining other objectives in physical education. When there is complete loss of muscle function about a joint and passive exercise is needed to improve flexibility, it is recommended that the physical educator refer the student to the physical therapist.

GENERAL CONSIDERATIONS

When developing programs of physical fitness, the physical educator should be aware of students' initial levels of fitness and select activities accordingly. In all cases the procedure should be to start slowly and progress gradually. Students should be taught to warm up prior to a workout and cool down afterward. The physical educator should motivate students to pursue higher levels of fitness by keeping records, charting progress, and presenting awards. Selecting enjoyable activities will also help to maintain interest in physical fitness; for instance, charting a class's cumulative running distances on a map for a "cross-country run" will be more interesting and motivating than simply telling them to "run three laps." The physical educator should also be a good role model for students; this includes staying fit and participating in class activities whenever possible. Finally, the physical educator should view physical fitness as an ongoing part of the physical education program and not just one unit of instruction. Even though different units will be taught throughout the year, activities within a unit (exercises, games, drills, etc.) should be arranged to enhance, or at least maintain, physical fitness.

SUMMARY

Physical fitness is critical to the person with a disability. In addition to improved performance, health, and appearance, high levels of fitness can foster independence, particularly among individuals with physical disabilities. The goals of a fitness program for individuals with unique needs will depend upon the type and severity of the disability and current levels of physical fitness. Fitness for developing rudimentary, fundamental, or specialized movements or for pursuing a healthier lifestyle are all reasonable goals in adapted physical education. Fitness programs should be "personalized" to meet the goals of each student. Teachers must understand that, with few exceptions, disabled students will exhibit a favorable physiological response to training. In many cases the recommendations for frequency and duration of exercise do not differ significantly from those made for the nondisabled. The mode, or type of activity, and intensity, however, frequently must be modified to provide the student with an appropriate workout.

BIBLIOGRAPHY

American Alliance for Health, Physical Education, Recreation and Dance (1988). *Physical best*. Reston, VA: Author.

Arnhold, R., Ng, N., & Pechar, G. (1992). Relationship of rated perceived exertion to heart rate and workload in mentally retarded young adults. *Adapted Physical Activity Quarterly*, **9**, 47–53.

Birk, T.J., & Mossing, M. (1988). Relationship of perceived exertion to heart rate and ventilation in active teenagers with cerebral palsy. *Adapted Physical Activity Quarterly*, **5**, 154–164.

Blair, S.N. (1993). 1993 C.H. McCloy research lecture: Physical activity, physical fitness, and health. *Research Quarterly for Exercise and Sport*, **64**, 365–376.

Borg, G.A. (1985). *An Introduction to Borg's RPE-Scale*. Ithaca, NY: Mouvement.

Burke, E.J., & Humphreys, J.H. (1982). *Fit to exercise*. London: Pelham Books.

Caspersen, C.J., Powell, K.E., & Christenson, G.M. (1985). Physical activity, exercise, and physical fitness: Definitions and distinctions for health-related research. *Public Health Reports*, **100**, 126–131.

Clarke, H.H., & Clarke, D.H. (1978). *Developmental and adapted physical education*. Englewood Cliffs, NJ: Prentice Hall.

di Natale, J., Lee, M., Ward, G., & Shephard, R.J. (1985). Loss of physical condition in sightless adolescents during a summer vacation. *Adapted Physical Activity Quarterly*, **2**, 144–150.

Lasko-McCarthey, P., & Aufsesser, P.M. (1990). Guidelines for a community-based physical fitness program for adults with physical disabilities. *Palaestra*, **7**(1), 18–29.

McCubbin, J.A., & Shasby, G.B. (1985). Effects of isokinetic exercise on adolescents with cerebral palsy. *Adapted Physical Activity Quarterly*, **2**, 56–64.

O'Sullivan, S.B., Cullen, K.E., & Schmitz, T.J. (1981). *Physical rehabilitation: Evaluation and treatment procedures*. Philadelphia: Davis.

Shephard, R.J. (1990). *Fitness in special populations*. Champaign, IL: Human Kinetics.

Surburg, P.R. (1986). New perspectives for developing range of motion and flexibility for special populations. *Adapted Physical Activity Quarterly*, **3**, 227–235.

Winnick, J.P., & Short, F.X. (1985). *Physical fitness testing of the disabled*. Champaign, IL: Human Kinetics.

RESOURCES

Audiovisual

Fitness is for everyone (Videotape). National Handicapped Sports, 451 Hungerford Drive, Suite 100, Rockville, MD 20850. Tapes focusing on aerobic training are available for paraplegia, quadriplegia, amputation, and cerebral palsy. A strength and flexibility tape for all types of disabilities is also available.

CHAPTER 16

Motor Development

David L. Gallahue

Do you remember when you were young, about 4 or 5, and wanted to complete what now is a simple task, to just TIE your shoelaces? Back then, however, it was a monumental accomplishment. First, there were the fine motor requirements of the task itself (T). Second, there were the individual differences in the rate of learning among you and your preschool playmates (I). Finally, there were environmental factors, such as the fact that your mom or dad may have dressed you in shoes with velcro fasteners, and you had little need to learn how to tie laces (E). Motor development and the learning of new movement skills involves for all of us, able bodied and disabled, a transaction among the requirements of the specific task, with a variety of personalized factors within the individual and the environment itself. Keep the letters T, I, E in mind as you read this chapter, focusing on how the task, the individual, and the environment combine to determine the sequence, rate, and extent of learning any movement skill.

For years the topic of motor development has been of considerable interest to physical educators in general and adapted physical educators in particular. Knowledge of the process of development lies at the very core of education that is adapted to meet the needs of the individual, whether it be in the classroom, gymnasium, swimming pool, or on the playing field. Without sound knowledge of the learner's individual level of development, teachers can only guess at appropriate educational techniques and intervention strategies to be used to maximize one's learning potential. Educators, developmentally based in their instruction, incorporate learning experiences geared to the specific

needs of their students. They reject the all too frequent textbook ideal of students all being at the same level of development at given chronological age markers. In fact, one of the most valuable outcomes of studying human development has been less reliance on the concept of age appropriateness and more attention to the concept of individual appropriateness.

In a very real sense, adapted physical education is developmental education. Program content and instructional strategies, by their very nature, are designed to meet individual developmental needs. Unfortunately, human development is frequently studied from a compartmentalized viewpoint. That is, the cognitive, affective, and motor domains are viewed, by many, as unrelated entities. Although valid perhaps from the standpoint of basic research, such a perspective is of little value when it comes to trying to understand the learning process and devising appropriate intervention strategies. It is essential for teachers of students with developmental disabilities to be knowledgeable about the normal process of development in order to have a baseline for comparing the individuals with whom they are dealing. The totality and integrated nature of the individual must be recognized, respected, and accommodated in the educational process.

This chapter focuses on defining motor development and describing the categories of human movement. Developmental theory is briefly examined from the viewpoints of Dynamic Systems Theory and the Phases of Motor Development, two popular theoretical frameworks. The chapter concludes with common principles that emerge from the neuromaturational viewpoint of motor development.

MOTOR DEVELOPMENT DEFINED

Development is the continuous process of change over time, beginning at conception and ceasing only at death. Motor development, therefore, is progressive change in movement behavior throughout the life cycle. Motor development involves continuous adaptation to changes in one's movement capabilities in the never-ending effort to achieve and maintain motor control and movement competence. Such a perspective does not view development as being domain specific, nor does it view development as being stagelike or age dependent. Instead, a life-span perspective suggests that *some* aspects of one's development can be conceptualized into domains, as being stagelike and age-related, while others cannot. Furthermore, the concept of achieving and maintaining competence encompasses all developmental change, both positive and negative.

Motor development may be studied both as a process and as a product. As a process, it may be viewed from the standpoint of underlying factors that influence both the motor performance and movement capabilities of individuals from infancy through old age. As a product, motor development may be studied from a descriptive or normative standpoint and is typically viewed in broad time frames, phases, and stages.

Currently, Dynamic Systems Theory (Kamm, Thelen, Jensen, 1990; Thelen & Smith, 1993) is popular among developmentalists as a means of better understanding the process of development. On the other hand, the Phases of Motor Development (Gallahue & Ozmun, 1995) serve as a descriptive means for better understanding and conceptualizing the product of development. Both will be briefly discussed, but first a look at the categories of human movement.

CATEGORIES OF MOVEMENT

Both the process and products of motor development are revealed through changes in one's movement behavior across the life span. All of us—infants, children, adolescents, and adults—are involved in learning how to move with control and competence in response to the daily movement challenges we face. We are able to observe developmental differences in motor behavior by observing changes in body mechanics and motor performance scores. In other words, a "window" is provided through which the individual's actual movement behavior can be observed.

Observable movement takes many forms and may be grouped into categories. One technique involves three categories: stability, locomotion, and manipulation, and combinations of the three (Gallahue, 1993; Gallahue & Ozmun, 1995). Stability is the most basic form of movement, and it is present to a greater or lesser extent in all movement. A stability movement is any movement that places a premium on gaining and maintaining one's equilibrium in relation to the force of gravity. Gaining control of the muscles of the head, neck, and trunk are the first stability tasks of the newborn. Sitting with support, sitting unaided, and pulling oneself to a stand are important stability tasks of the normally developing infant. Standing without support, balancing momentarily on one foot, being able to bend and stretch, twist and turn, reach and lift are all important stability tasks of childhood through old age.

The locomotor movement category refers to movements that involve a change in location of the body relative to a fixed point on the surface. To walk, run, jump, hop, skip, or leap is to perform a locomotor task. In our use of the term, activities such as a forward or backward roll may be considered to be both locomotor and stability movements: locomotor because the body is moving from point to point, stability because of the premium placed on maintaining equilibrium in an unusual balancing situation.

The manipulative movement category refers to both gross and fine motor manipulation. The tasks of throwing, catching, kicking, and striking an object are all considered to be gross motor manipulative movements. Activities such as sewing, cutting with scissors, and typing are fine motor manipulative movements.

A large number of our movements involve a combination of stability, locomotor, and/or manipulative movements. In essence, all voluntary movement involves an element of stability. It is for this reason that stability is viewed as the most basic category of movement, and it is absolutely essential for progressive development in the other two categories. The individual with cerebral palsy, for example, is frequently encumbered in his or her walking gait because of difficulty in negotiating the problems of static and dynamic balance inherent in independent walking.

MOTOR DEVELOPMENT AS A DYNAMIC SYSTEM

Theory should undergird all research and science. The study of motor development is no exception. Motor development theory is based on the observation of individuals without disabilities as they acquire and refine movement skills. If applied wisely, this information provides insight into the influence of various developmental disabilities on the learning of new movement skills, thereby permitting adoption of appropriate instructional strategies.

To be of practical benefit, developmental theory must be both descriptive and explanatory. It is important to know about the products of development in terms of what people are typically like during particular age periods (description). It is equally important, however, to know what causes these changes (explanation). Many motor developmentalists are now looking at explanatory models in an attempt to understand more about the underlying processes that actually govern development. Dynamic Systems Theory is popular among many (Kamm et al., 1990; Caldwell & Clark, 1990; Thelen, 1989; Thelen & Smith, 1994).

In brief, the term **dynamic** conveys the concept that developmental change is nonlinear and discontinuous, rather than linear and continuous. Because development is viewed as nonlinear, it is seen as a discontinuous process. That is, individual change over time is not necessarily smooth and hierarchical, and it does not necessarily involve moving toward ever higher levels of complexity and competence in the motor system. Individuals, particularly those with disabling conditions, are encumbered by impairments that tend to impede their motor development. For example, children with spastic cerebral palsy are frequently delayed in learning to walk independently. When independent walking is achieved, the gait patterns will be individualized and achieved at a point in time appropriate for each. Although, by definition, development is a continuous process, it is also a discontinuous process. In other words, from a dynamical perspective, development is viewed as a "continuous-discontinuous" process. The dynamics of change occur over time, but in a highly individual manner influenced by a variety of critical factors within the system.

The term **systems** conveys the concept that the human organism is self-organizing and composed of several subsystems. It is self-organizing in that, by their very nature, humans are inclined to strive for motor control and movement competence. It is the subsystems, namely, the task, the individual and the environment, operating separately and in concert, that actually determine the rate, sequence, and extent of development. In other words, it is not some preprogrammed universal plan that unfolds on an inflexible schedule. Using our example of children with spastic cerebral palsy, they will, as a self-organizing system, develop their individually unique gait pattern in response to their capabilities in terms of meeting the achievement demands of the walking task.

Dynamic systems theory attempts to answer the "why?" or process questions that result in the observable product of motor development. That is: What are those enabling factors (termed *affordances*) that encourage or promote developmental change, and what are those inhibiting factors (termed *rate limiters*) that serve to restrict or impede development? For children with cerebral palsy, rate limiters are neurological and biomechanical in nature. Affordances may include assisted support, handholds, encouragement, and guided instruction.

For years, developmentalists have recognized the interactive role of two primary systems on the developmental process: heredity and environment. Many now, however, have taken this view one step further in recognizing that the specific demands of the movement task itself actually transact with the individual (i.e., hereditary or biological factors) and the environment (i.e., experience or learning factors) in the development of stability, locomotor, and manipulative movement abilities. Such a transactional model implies that factors within various subsystems of the task, the individual, and the environment not only interact with one another but also have the potential for modifying and being modified by the other as one strives to gain motor control and movement competence (Figure 16.1).

Both the processes and the products of motor development should constantly remind us of the individuality of the learner. Individuals have their own timetables for the development and extent of skill acquisition. Although our "biological clock" is rather specific when it comes to the sequence of movement skill acquisition, the rate and extent of development is individually determined and dramatically influenced by the specific performance demands of the task itself. Typical age periods of development are just that: typical, and nothing more. Age periods merely represent approximate time ranges during which certain behaviors may be observed for the mythical "average" individual.

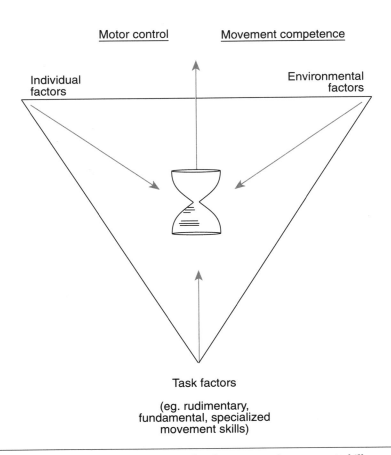

Figure 16.1 A transactional model of causality in motor development and movement skill acquisition.

Overreliance on these time periods would negate the concepts of continuity, specificity, and individuality in the developmental process, and these time periods are of little practical value when working with individuals with developmental disabilities.

THE PHASES OF MOTOR DEVELOPMENT

If movement serves as a "window" for viewing motor development, then one way of studying development is through examining the typical sequential progression in the acquisition of movement abilities. The Phases of Motor Development (Figure 16.2) and the developmental stages within each phase (Table 16.1) serve as a useful descriptive model for this study (Gallahue & Ozmun, 1995).

Reflexive Movement Phase

The very first movements are reflexive. **Reflexes** are involuntary, subcortically controlled movements. Through reflex activity the infant gains information about the immediate environment. The infant's reactions to touch, light, sounds, and changes in pressure trigger involuntary movements. These movements, coupled with the increasing cortical sophistication in the early months of life, play an important role in helping the child learn more about his or her body and the outside world, and are typically referred to as *primitive reflexes* and *postural reflexes*.

Primitive reflexes are information gathering, nourishment seeking, and protective responses. **Postural reflexes** resemble later voluntary movements and are used to support the body against gravity or to permit movement. See Tables 16.2 and 16.3 for a summary of common primitive and postural reflexes, respectively. The reflexive movement phase may be divided into two overlapping stages.

Information Encoding Stage

The information encoding (gathering) stage of the reflexive movement phase is characterized by observable involuntary movement during the fetal period until about the fourth month of infancy. During this stage lower brain centers are more highly developed than the motor cortex and are essentially in

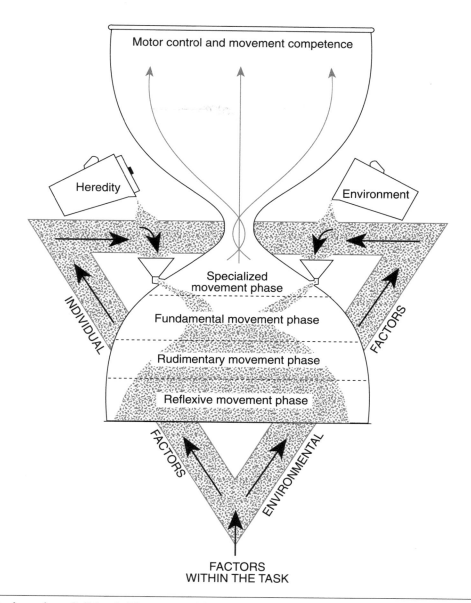

Figure 16.2   The hourglass: Gallahue's life span model of motor development.
From *Understanding Motor Development: Infants, Children, Adolescents, Adults* (p. 92) by D.L. Gallahue and J.C. Ozmun, 1995, Dubuque, IA: Brown & Benchmark. Printed by permission.

command of fetal and neonatal movement. These brain centers are capable of causing involuntary reactions to a variety of stimuli of varying intensity and duration. During this stage reflexes serve as the primary means by which the infant is able to gather information, seek nourishment, and seek protection through movement.

Information Decoding Stage

The information decoding (processing) stage begins around the fourth month of postnatal life. There is a gradual inhibition of many reflexes as higher brain

centers continue to develop. Lower brain centers gradually relinquish control over skeletal movements and are replaced by voluntary movement mediated by the motor area of the cerebral cortex. The decoding stage replaces sensorimotor activity with perceptual-motor behavior. That is, the infant's development of voluntary motor control involves processing sensory stimuli with stored information, not merely reacting to stimuli.

One means of diagnosing possible central nervous system disorders in the infant is through observation and reflex testing. The complete absence of a reflex is usually less significant than a reflex that remains

Table 16.1   The Phases and Stages of Motor Development

Phase of motor development	Approximate age periods of development	The stages of motor development
Reflexive movement phase	In utero to 4 months old 4 months to 1 year old	Information encoding stage Information decoding stage
Rudimentary movement phase	Birth to 1 year old 1 to 2 years old	Reflex inhibition stage Precontrol stage
Fundamental movement phase	2 to 3 years old 4 to 5 years old 6 to 7 years old	Initial stage Elementary stage Mature stage
Specialized movement phase	7 to 10 years old 11 to 13 years old 14 years old and up	Transition stage Application stage Lifelong utilization stage

Adapted from: David L. Gallahue and John C. Ozmun. *Understanding Motor Development*. 3rd ed. Copyright 1995 William C. Brown Communications, Inc.

Table 16.2   Sequence of Emergence of Selected Primitive Reflexes of the Newborn

Reflex	Onset	Inhibition	Stimulus	Behavior
Moro	Birth	Third month	Supine position. Sudden loud noise causes rapid or sudden movement of infant's head.	Stimulation will result in extension of the infant's extremities, followed by a return to a flexed position against the body.
Tonic neck (asymmetrical)	Birth[a]	Sixth month	Supine position. Neck is turned so head is facing left or right.	Extremities on side of body facing head position extend, those on side opposite flex.
Tonic neck (symmetrical)	Birth[a]	Sixth month	Supported sitting. Flexion or extension of infant's head.	Extension or flexion of neck will result in extension of arms and flexion of legs.
Grasping	Birth	Fourth to sixth month	Supine position. Stimulation of the palm of the hand or the ball of the foot.	Stimulation will result in a grasping action of the fingers or toes.
Babinski	Birth	Sixth month	Supine position. Stimulation by stroking the sole of the foot.	Stimulation will result in extension of the toes.
Sucking	Birth	Third month	Supine or supported sitting. Stimulus applied directly above or below the lips.	Touching area of mouth will result in a sucking action of the lips.

[a]Not seen in all children.

Table 16.3 Sequence of Emergence of Selected Postural Reflexes of the Newborn

Reflex	Onset	Inhibition	Stimulus	Behavior
Labyrinthine righting	Second month	Twelfth month	Supported upright position. Tilting of trunk forward, rearward, or to side.	Infant will attempt to keep head in an upright position by moving head in opposite direction from tilt.
Supportive reactions	Fourth month (arms) Ninth month (legs)	Twelfth month	Prone or upright supported. Movement of the child's extremities toward a surface.	Extension of the extremities to a position of support.
Pull-up	Third month	Fourth month	Upright sitting supported by hands. Tilting of child from side to side and front and back.	Infant will flex arms in an attempt to maintain equilibrium.
Stepping	Second week	Fifth month	Supported upright position. Infant is held in upright position and soles of feet are allowed to touch a surface.	Definite stepping action of only the lower extremities.
Crawling	Birth	Fourth month	Prone unsupported position. Stimulus is applied to sole of one foot.	Crawling action exhibited by both the upper and lower extremities.
Swimming	Birth	Fifth month	Prone held over water. Infant is held over or in water.	Swimming movements elicited in both the upper and lower extremities.

too long. Other evidence of possible damage may be found in a reflex that is too strong or too weak. Also, a reflex that elicits a stronger response on one side of the body than on the other may indicate central nervous system dysfunction. An asymmetrical tonic neck reflex, for example, that shows full arm extension on one side of the body and only weak extensor tone when the other side is stimulated may provide evidence of damage.

Examination of reflexive behaviors in the neonate provides the physician with a primary means of diagnosing central nervous system integrity in fullterm, premature, and at-risk infants. Furthermore, they serve as a basis for intervention by the physical and occupational therapists and by the adapted physical education specialist working with individuals displaying pathological reflexive behavior.

Rudimentary Movement Phase

The first forms of voluntary movement are rudimentary. **Rudimentary movements** are maturationally determined behaviors seen in the normally developing infant from birth to about age 2. They are heavily influenced by heredity and characterized by a highly predictable sequence that is resistant to change under normal conditions. The rate at which these abilities appear will, however, vary from child to child and relies on biological, environmental, and task-specific factors. The rudimentary movement abilities of the infant represent the basic forms of voluntary movement required for survival. See Table 16.4 for a descriptive profile of selected rudimentary stability, locomotor, and manipulative abilities.

The rudimentary movement phase may be subdivided into two stages that represent progressively higher orders of motor control and movement competence.

Reflex Inhibition Stage

The reflex inhibition stage of the rudimentary movement phase begins at birth. Although reflexes dominate the newborn's movement repertoire, the infant's movements are increasingly influenced by the developing cortex. Development of the cortex and the lessening of certain environmental constraints cause several reflexes to gradually disappear. Primitive and postural reflexes are replaced by voluntary movement behaviors. At the reflex inhibition level, voluntary movement is poorly differentiated and integrated. That is, the neuromotor apparatus of the infant is still at a rudimentary stage of development. Movements, though purposeful, appear uncontrolled and unrefined. If, for example, the infant desires to make contact with an object, there will be global activity of the entire hand, wrist, arm, shoulder, and even trunk. In other words, the process of moving the hand into contact with the object, although voluntary, lacks control.

Precontrol Stage

Around 1 year of age, normally developing children begin to bring greater precision and control to their movements. The process of differentiating between sensory and motor systems and integrating perceptual and motor information into a more meaningful and congruent whole takes place. The rapid development of higher cognitive processes as well as motor processes makes for rapid gains in rudimentary movement abilities during this stage. Children learn to gain and maintain their equilibrium, to manipulate objects, and to locomote throughout their environment. The maturational process may partially explain the rapidity and extent of development of movement control during this stage, but the growth of motor proficiency is no less amazing.

Fundamental Movement Phase

The fundamental movement abilities of early childhood are an outgrowth of the rudimentary movement phase of infancy. Fundamental movements are generally viewed as basic movement skills such as walking, running, throwing, and catching, which are building blocks for more highly developed and refined movement skills. This phase of motor development represents a time at which young children are actively involved in exploring and experimenting with the movement capabilities of their bodies. It is a time for discovering how to perform a variety of basic stabilizing, locomotor, and manipulative movements, first in isolation and then in combination with one another. Children who are developing fundamental patterns of movement are learning how to respond with motor control and movement competence to a variety of stimuli. Tables 16.5, 16.6, and 16.7 provide a descriptive overview of the typical development sequence of several fundamental stability, locomotor, and manipulative movements.

Several researchers and assessment instrument developers have attempted to subdivide fundamental movements into a series of identifiable sequential stages (McClenaghan & Gallahue, 1978; Haubenstricker & Seefeldt, 1986; Roberton & Halverson 1984; Gallahue & Ozmun, 1995). For the purposes of our model, we will view the entire fundamental movement phase as having three separate but often overlapping stages, namely, the initial, elementary, and mature stages.

Initial Stage

The initial stage of a fundamental movement phase represents the child's first goal-oriented attempts at performing a fundamental skill. Movement itself is characterized by missing or improperly sequenced parts, markedly restricted or exaggerated use of the body, and poor rhythmical flow and coordination. In other words, the spatial and temporal integration of movement is poor during this stage.

Elementary Stage

The elementary stage involves greater control and better rhythmical coordination of fundamental movements. The temporal and spatial elements of movement are better coordinated, but patterns of movement are still generally restricted or exaggerated. Children of normal intelligence and physical functioning tend to advance to the elementary stage primarily through the process of maturation. Many individuals, adults as well as children, fail to get beyond the elementary stage in many fundamental patterns of movement.

Mature Stage

The mature stage within the fundamental movement phase is characterized by mechanically efficient, coordinated, and controlled performances. The

Table 16.4 Developmental Sequence of Selected Rudimentary Movement Abilities

Movement pattern	Selected abilities	Approximate age of onset
Control of head and neck	Turns to one side	Birth
	Turns to both sides	1 week
	Held with support	First month
	Chin off contact surface	Second month
	Good prone control	Third month
	Good supine control	Fifth month
Control of trunk	Lifts head and chest	Second month
	Attempts supine-to-prone position	Third month
	Success in supine-to-prone roll	Sixth month
	Prone to supine roll	Eighth month
Sitting	Sits with support	Third month
	Sits with self-support	Sixth month
	Sits alone	Eighth month
	Stands with support	Sixth month
Standing	Supports with handholds	Tenth month
	Pulls to supported stand	Eleventh month
	Stands alone	Twelfth month
Horizontal movements	Scooting	Third month
	Crawling	Sixth month
	Creeping	Ninth month
	Walking on all fours	Eleventh month
Upright gait	Walks with support	Sixth month
	Walks with handholds	Tenth month
	Walks with lead	Eleventh month
	Walks alone (hands high)	Twelfth month
	Walks alone (hands low)	Thirteenth month
Reaching	Globular ineffective	First to third month
	Definite corralling	Fourth month
	Controlled	Sixth month
Grasping	Reflexive	Birth
	Voluntary	Third month
	Two-hand palmar grasp	Third month
	One-hand palmar grasp	Fifth month
	Pincer grasp	Ninth month
	Controlled grasping	Fourteenth month
	Eats without assistance	Eighteenth month
Releasing	Basic	Twelfth to fourteenth month
	Controlled	Eighteenth month

Note. From *Understanding Motor Development: Infants, Children, Adolescents, Adults* (pp. 173–176) by D.L. Gallahue and J. Ozmun, 1995, Dubuque, IA: Brown & Benchmark. Adapted by permission.

Table 16.5 Sequence of Emergence of Selected Fundamental Stability Abilities

Movement pattern	Selected abilities	Approximate age of onset
Dynamic balance Dynamic balance involves maintaining one's equilibrium as the center of gravity shifts.	Walks 1-inch straight line.	3 years
	Walks 1-inch circular line.	4 years
	Stands on low balance beam.	2 years
	Walks on 4-inch wide beam for a short distance.	3 years
	Walks on same beam, alternating feet.	3–4 years
	Walks on 2- or 3-inch beam.	4 years
	Performs basic forward roll.	3–4 years
	Performs mature forward roll.*	6–7 years
Static balance Static balance involves maintaining one's equilibrium while the center of gravity remains stationary.	Pulls to a standing position.	10 months
	Stands without handholds.	11 months
	Stands alone.	12 months
	Balances on one foot 3–5 seconds.	5 years
	Supports body in basic three-point inverted positions.	6 years
Axial movements Axial movements are static postures that involve bending, stretching, twisting, turning, and the like.	Axial movement abilities begin to develop early in infancy and are progressively refined to a point where they are included in the emerging manipulative patterns of throwing, catching, kicking, striking, trapping, and other activities.	2 months to 6 years

*The child has the developmental "potential" to be at the mature stage. Actual attainment will depend on task, individual and environmental factors.

Note. From *Understanding Motor Development: Infants, Children, Adolescents, Adults* (p. 227) by D.L. Gallahue and J.C. Ozmun, 1995, Dubuque, IA: Brown & Benchmark. Adapted by permission.

majority of available data on the acquisition of fundamental movement skills suggest that normally developing children can and should be at the mature stage by age 5 or 6 in most fundamental skills. Manipulative skills, however, which require tracking and intercepting moving objects (catching, striking, volleying), develop somewhat later because of the sophisticated visual-motor requirements of these tasks.

Specialized Movement Phase

The **specialized phase** of motor development is an outgrowth of the fundamental movement phase. Instead of continuing to be closely identified with learning to move for the sake of movement itself, movement now becomes a tool that is applied to a variety of specialized movement activities for daily living, recreation, and sport pursuits. This is a period when fundamental stability, locomotor, and manipulative skills are progressively refined, combined, and elaborated upon in order that they may be used in increasingly demanding situations. The fundamental movements of hopping and jumping, for example, may now be applied to jumping rope, performing folk dances, and performing the triple jump (hop-step-jump) in track and field.

The onset and extent of skill development within the specialized movement phase depends on a variety of task, individual, and environmental factors. Task/complexity, individual physical, mental, and emotional limitations, as well as environmental factors such as opportunity for practice, encouragement, and instruction are but a few. There are three

Table 16.6 Sequence of Emergence of Selected Fundamental Manipulative Abilities

Movement pattern	Selected abilities	Approximate age of onset
Reach, grasp, release Reaching, grasping, and releasing involves making successful contact with an object, retaining it in one's grasp, and releasing it at will.	Primitive reaching behaviors.	2–4 months
	Corralling of objects.	2–4 months
	Palmar grasp.	3–5 months
	Pincer grasp.	8–10 months
	Controlled grasp.	12–14 months
	Controlled releasing.	14–18 months
Throwing Throwing involves imparting force to an object in the general direction of intent.	Body faces target, feet remain stationary, ball thrown with forearm extension only.	2–3 years
	Same as above but with body rotation added.	3.6–5 years
	Steps forward with leg on same side as the throwing arm.	4–5 years
	Boys exhibit more mature pattern than girls.	5 years and over
	Mature throwing pattern.*	6 years
Catching Catching involves receiving force from an object with the hands, moving from large to progressively smaller balls.	Chases ball; does not respond to aerial ball.	2 years
	Responds to aerial ball with delayed arm movements.	2–3 years
	Needs to be told how to position arms.	2–3 years
	Fear reaction (turns head away).	3–4 years
	Basket catch using the body.	3 years
	Catches using the hands only with a small ball.	5 years
	Mature catching pattern.*	6 years
Kicking Kicking involves imparting force to an object with the foot.	Pushes against ball. Does not actually kick it.	18 months
	Kicks with leg straight and little body movement (kicks *at* the ball).	2–3 years
	Flexes lower leg on backward lift.	3–4 years
	Greater backward and forward swing with definite arm opposition.	4–5 years
	Mature pattern (kicks *through* the ball)*	5–6 years
Striking Striking involves sudden contact to objects in an overarm, sidearm, or underhand pattern.	Faces object and swings in a vertical plane.	2–3 years
	Swings in a horizontal plane and stands to the side of the object.	4–5 years
	Rotates the trunk and hips and shifts body weight forward.	5 years
	Mature horizontal pattern with stationary ball.	6–7 years

*The child has the developmental "potential" to be at the mature stage. Actual attainment will depend on environmental factors.

Note. From *Understanding Motor Development: Infants, Children, Adolescents, Adults* (p. 229) by D.L. Gallahue and J.C. Ozmun, 1995, Dubuque, IA: Brown & Benchmark. Adapted by permission.

Table 16.7   Sequence of Emergence of Selected Fundamental Locomotor Abilities

Movement pattern	Selected abilities	Approximate age of onset
Walking Walking involves placing one foot in front of the other while maintaining contact with the supporting surface.	Rudimentary upright unaided gait.	13 months
	Walks sideways.	16 months
	Walks backward.	17 months
	Walks upstairs with help.	20 months
	Walks upstairs alone—follow step.	24 months
	Walks downstairs alone—follow step.	25 months
Running Running involves a brief period of no contact with the supporting surface.	Hurried walk (maintains contact).	18 months
	First true run (nonsupport phase).	2–3 years
	Efficient and refined run.	4–5 years
	Speed of run increases, mature run.*	5 years
Jumping Jumping takes three forms: (1) jumping for distance; (2) jumping for height; and (3) jumping from a height. It involves a one- or two-foot takeoff with a landing on both feet.	Steps down from low objects.	18 months
	Jumps down from object with one foot lead.	2 years
	Jumps off floor with both feet.	28 months
	Jumps for distance (about 3 feet).	5 years
	Jumps for height (about 1 foot).	5 years
	Mature jumping pattern.*	6 years
Hopping Hopping involves a one-foot takeoff with a landing on the same foot.	Hops up to three times on preferred foot.	3 years
	Hops from four to six times on same foot.	4 years
	Hops from eight to ten times on same foot.	5 years
	Hops distance of 50 feet in about 11 seconds.	5 years
	Hops skillfully with rhythmical alteration, mature pattern.*	6 years
Galloping The gallop combines a walk and a leap with the same foot leading throughout.	Basic but inefficient gallop.	4 years
	Gallops skillfully, mature pattern.*	6 years
Skipping Skipping combines a step and a hop in rhythmic alteration.	One-footed skip.	4 years
	Skillful skipping (about 20%).	5 years
	Skillful skipping for most.*	6 years

*The child has the developmental "potential" to be at the mature stage. Actual attainment will depend on task, individual, and environmental factors.

Note. From *Understanding Motor Development: Infants, Children, Adolescents, Adults* (p. 228) by D.L. Gallahue and J.C. Ozmun, 1995. Dubuque, IA: Brown & Benchmark. Adapted by permission.

identifiable stages within the specialized movement phase.

Transitional Stage

Somewhere around the seventh or eighth year of life, children commonly enter a transitional movement skill stage. They begin to combine and apply fundamental movement skills to the performance of specialized skills in sport and recreational settings. Walking on a rope bridge, jumping rope, and playing kickball are examples of common transitional skills. These skills contain the same elements as fundamental movements, but greater form, accuracy, and control of movement are now required. The fundamental movement skills that were developed and refined for their own sake during the previous phase now begin to be applied to play, game, and daily living situations. Transitional skills are simply an application of fundamental movement patterns in somewhat more complex and specific forms.

Application Stage

From about age 10 to age 13, interesting changes take place in skill development. During the previous stage, children's limited cognitive abilities, affective abilities, and experiences, coupled with a natural eagerness to be active, caused the normal focus (without adult interference) on movement to be broad and generalized to "all" activity. During the application stage, increased cognitive sophistication and a broadened experience base enable them to make numerous learning and participation decisions based on a variety of factors. Children begin to make conscious decisions for or against participation in certain activities. These decisions are based, in large measure, on how they perceive the extent to which factors within the task, themselves, and the environment either enhance or inhibit chances for personal enjoyment and success.

Lifelong Utilization Stage

The lifelong utilization stage typically begins around age 13 and continues through adulthood. The lifelong utilization stage represents the pinnacle of the process of motor development and is characterized by the use of one's acquired movement repertoire throughout life. The interests, competencies, and choices made during the previous stage are carried over to this stage, further refined, and applied to a lifetime of daily living, recreational, and sports-related activities. Factors such as equipment and facility availability and physical and mental limitations affect this stage. Among other things, one's level of

activity participation will depend on talents, opportunities, physical condition, and personal motivation. One's lifetime performance level may range anywhere from the Paralympics and Special Olympics, to intercollegiate and interscholastic competition, to participation in organized or unorganized play, and important daily living skills such as toileting, grooming, and self-help.

In essence, the lifelong utilization stage represents a culmination of all preceding phases and stages and should be viewed as a lifelong process. One of the primary goals of adapted physical education programs is to help individuals to a point that they become happy, healthy, contributing members of society. The hierarchical development of the continuum of movement abilities embodied in the Phases of Motor Development serves as a primary means for achieving this goal. Only when we recognize that the progressive development of one's movement abilities in a developmentally appropriate manner is imperative to the balanced motor development of infants, children, adolescents, and adults will we begin to make significant contributions to the total development of the individual.

PRINCIPLES OF MOTOR DEVELOPMENT

The development and refinement of movement patterns and skills are influenced in complex ways. Both the process and product of one's movement are rooted in their unique genetic and experiential background, coupled with the specific demands of the movement task itself. Any study of motor development would be incomplete without a discussion of several of these influencing factors. The unique genetic inheritance that accounts for our individuality can also account for our similarity in many ways. One of these similarities is the trend for human development to proceed in an orderly, predictable fashion. A number of principles of motor development seem to emerge from this predictable pattern of development.

Developmental Direction

The principle of developmental direction was first formulated by Arnold Gesell (1954) as a means of explaining increased coordination and motor control as being a function of the maturing nervous system. Through observation, Gesell noted an orderly, predictable sequence of physical development that proceeds from the head to the feet (**cephalocaudal**) and from the center of the body to its periphery (proximodistal). The principle of developmental direction has, however, come into some criticism during the last few years, and should not be viewed as operational at all levels of development nor in all individuals. The observation of tendencies toward distinct developmental directions may not be an exclusive function of the maturing nervous system as originally hypothesized, but it may be due, in part, to the demands of the specific task itself. For example, the task demands of independent walking are considerably greater than those for crawling or creeping. There is less margin for error in independent walking than there is in creeping and, in turn, crawling. In other words, it is mechanically easier to crawl than it is to creep, and to creep than it is to walk. Therefore, the apparent cephalocaudal progression in development may not be simply due to maturation of the nervous system, but also to the specific performance demands of the task itself.

Rate of Growth and Development

One's growth rate follows a characteristic pattern that is universal for all and resistant to external influence. Even the interruption of the normal pace of growth is compensated for by a still unexplained process of self-regulatory fluctuation (Gesell, 1954) that comes into operation to help the growing child catch up to his or her age-mates. For example, a severe prolonged illness may markedly limit a child's gain in height and weight, but upon recovery from the illness there will be a definite tendency to catch up if the condition does not persist and treatment is administered. The same phenomenon is seen with low-birthweight infants. Despite this low weight at birth, there is still a tendency to catch up to the characteristic growth rate of one's age-mates in a few years.

Restricted opportunity for movement and deprivation of experience have been repeatedly shown to interfere with children's abilities to perform movement tasks that are characteristic for their particular age level. The effects of this deprivation of sensory and motor experience can sometimes be overcome when nearly optimal conditions are established for children (McGraw, 1939). The extent to which children will be able to catch up to their peers, however, depends on the duration and severity of deprivation and the age of the children, coupled with their individual genetic growth potential.

Differentiation and Integration

The coordinated and progressive intricate interweaving of neural mechanisms of opposing muscle systems into an increasingly mature relationship is characteristic of the developing child's motor behavior. Termed *reciprocal interweaving* by Gesell (1954), there are two different but related processes associated with this increase in functional complexity: differentiation and integration.

The process of **differentiation** is associated with the gradual progression from the gross globular (overall) movement patterns of infants to the more refined and functional movements of children and adolescents as they mature. For example, the manipulative behaviors of the newborn in terms of reaching, grasping, and releasing objects are quite poor. There is little control of movement, but as the child develops, control improves. The child is able to differentiate between various muscle groups and begins to establish control. Control continues to improve with practice until we see the precise movements of cursive writing, cutting with scissors, building with blocks, and playing the violin.

The process of **integration** refers to bringing various opposing muscle and sensory systems into coordinated interaction with one another. For example, the young child gradually progresses from ill-defined corralling movements when attempting to grasp an object to more mature and visually guided reaching and grasping behaviors. This differentiation of movements of the arms, hands, and fingers, followed by integration of the use of the eyes with the movements of the hand to perform eye-hand coordination tasks, is crucial to normal development.

Developmental Variability and Readiness

The tendency to exhibit individual differences is crucial. Each person is unique with his or her own timetable for development. This timetable is a combination of a particular individual's heredity and environmental influences. Although the sequence of appearance of developmental characteristics is predictable, the rate of appearance may be quite variable. Therefore, strict adherence to a chronological classification of development by age is without support or justification.

The "average" ages for the acquisition of all sorts of developmental tasks, ranging from learning how to walk to gaining bowel and bladder control, have been discussed in the professional literature and the daily conversation of parents and teachers for years. These average ages are just that and nothing more. They are merely approximations and are meant to serve as convenient indicators of developmentally appropriate behaviors in the normally developing individual. It is common to see deviations from the mean of as much as 6 months to 1 year or more in the appearance of numerous movement skills. The tendency to exhibit individual differences is closely linked to the principle of readiness, and it helps to explain why some individuals are ready to learn new skills when others are not.

Readiness refers to conditions within the task, the individual, and the environment that make a particular task appropriate for an individual to master. Physical and mental maturation, interacting with motivation, prerequisite learning, and an enriching environment, all influence readiness. At this juncture we simply do not know how to identify precisely when one is ready to learn a new movement skill. However, research suggests that early experience in a movement activity before the individual is ready is likely to have minimal benefits (Magill, 1993).

It is critical to recognize and respect the concepts of developmental variability and readiness, both among individuals and within individuals. We simply cannot deal with individuals with developmental disabilities on the basis of chronological age or grade level and expect to be successful in movement skill acquisition and fitness enhancement.

Critical and Sensitive Learning Periods

The principle of critical or sensitive learning periods is closely aligned to readiness, and it revolves around observation that there are certain time frames when an individual is more sensitive to certain kinds of stimulation. Normal development in later periods may be hindered if the child fails to receive the proper stimulation during a critical period. For example, inadequate nutrition, prolonged stress, inconsistent parenting, or a lack of appropriate learning experiences may have a more negative impact on development if introduced early in life rather than at a later age. The principle of critical periods also has a positive side. It suggests that appropriate intervention during a specific period of time tends to facilitate more positive forms of development at later stages than if the same intervention occurs later.

Current views of the critical period hypothesis reject the notion that there are highly specific time frames in which one must develop motor skills (Seefeldt, 1975). There are, however, periods during which development of certain skills is more easily accomplished. These are referred to as sensitive periods. A sensitive period is a broader time frame for development and is susceptible to modification. Learning is a phenomena that can continue throughout life.

Phylogeny and Ontogeny

Many of the rudimentary abilities of the infant and the fundamental movement abilities of young children are considered to be phylogenetic. That is, they tend to appear automatically and in a predictable sequence within the maturing child. Phylogenetic skills are resistant to external environmental influences. Movement skills such as the rudimentary manipulative tasks of reaching, grasping, and releasing objects, the stability tasks of gaining control of the gross musculature of the body, and the fundamental locomotor abilities of walking, jumping, and running are examples of phylogenetic skills.

Ontogenetic skills, on the other hand, are those that depend primarily on learning and environmental opportunities. Skills such as swimming, bicycling, and ice skating are considered to be ontogenetic because they do not appear automatically within individuals but require a period of practice and experience and are influenced by one's culture. Phylogeny and ontogeny need to be reevaluated in light of the fact that many skills, heretofore considered phylogenetic, can be influenced by environmental interaction.

SUMMARY

The acquisition of motor control and movement competency is an extensive process beginning with the early reflexive movements of the newborn and continuing throughout life. The process by which an individual progresses from the reflexive movement phase, through the rudimentary and fundamental movement phases, and finally to the specialized movement skill phase is influenced by factors within the task, the individual, and the environment.

Reflexes and rudimentary movement abilities are largely maturationally based. They appear and disappear in a fairly rigid sequence deviating only in the rate of their appearance. They do, however, form an important base upon which fundamental movement abilities are developed.

Fundamental movement abilities are basic movement patterns that begin developing around the same time that the child is able to walk independently and move freely through the environment. These basic locomotor, manipulative, and stability abilities go through a definite, observable process from immaturity to maturity. A variety of stages within this phase have been identified for a number of fundamental movements; these are the initial, elementary, and mature stages. Attainment of the mature stage is influenced greatly by opportunities for practice, encouragement, and instruction in an environment that fosters learning. These same fundamental skills will be elaborated on and refined to form the specialized movement abilities so highly valued for recreational, competitive, and daily living tasks.

The specialized movement skill phase of development is in essence an elaboration of the fundamental phase. Specialized skills are more precise than fundamental skills. They often involve a combination of fundamental movement abilities and require a greater degree of exactness in performance. Specialized skills have three related stages. From the transition stage onward, children are involved in the application of fundamental movement skills and their purposeful utilization in play, games, sport, and daily living tasks. If the fundamental abilities used in a particular activity are not at the mature stage, the individual will have to resort to the use of less mature patterns of movement.

Principles of development emerge as we study the process of growth and motor development. These principles serve as an avenue for theory formulation. Dynamic Systems Theory and the Phases of Motor Development serve as helpful means for conceptualizing both the process and the product of motor development. Individuals with developmental disabilities are more like their age-mates than they are unlike them. Therefore, it is essential that we understand and apply principles of normal development to the education of all individuals.

BIBLIOGRAPHY

Caldwell, G.E.., & Clark, J.E. (1990). The measurement and evaluation of skill within the dynamical systems perspective. In J.E. CLark & J.H. Humphrey (Eds.), *Advances in motor development research.* New York: AMS Press.

Gallahue, D.L. (1993). *Developmental physical education for today's children.* Dubuque, IA: Brown & Benchmark.

Gallahue, D.L., & Ozmun, J. (1995). *Understanding motor development: Infants, children, adolescents, adults.* Dubuque, IA: Brown & Benchmark.

Gesell, A. (1954). The ontogenesis of infant behavior. In L. Carmichael (Ed.), *Manual of child psychology* (pp. 335–373). New York: Wiley.

Haubenstricker, J.L., & Seefeldt, V.D. (1986). Acquisition of motor skills during childhood. In V.D. Seefeldt, *Physical activity and well-being* (pp. 42–102). Reston, VA: AAHPERD.

Kamm, K., Thelen, E., & Jensen, J.L. (1990). A dynamical systems approach to motor development. *Physical Therapy,* **70**(12), 763–774.

Magill, R. (1993). *Motor learning.* Dubuque, IA: Brown & Benchmark.

McClenaghan, B.A., & Gallahue, D.L. (1978). *Fundamental movement: A developmental and remedial approach.* Philadelphia: Saunders.

McGraw, M. (1939). Later development of children specially trained during infancy. *Child Development,* **10,** 1–19.

Roberton, M.A., & Halverson, L.E. (1984). *Developing children—their changing movement: A guide for teachers.* Philadelphia: Lea & Febiger.

Seefeldt, V. (1975). *Critical learning periods and programs of early intervention.* Paper presented to the National Convention of the American Alliance for Health, Physical Education and Recreation, Atlantic City.

Thelen, E. (1989). Dynamical approaches to the development of behavior. In J.A.S. Kelso, A.J. Mandell, & M.E. Schelsinger (Eds.), *Dynamic patterns in complex systems* (pp. 348–362). Singapore: World Scientific.

Thelen, E., & Smith, L.B. (Eds.) (1993). *A dynamic systems approach to development: Applications.* Cambridge, MA: MIT Press.

Thelen, E., & Smith, L.B. (1994). *A dynamic systems approach to the development of cognition and action.* Cambridge, MA: MIT Press.

RESOURCES

Beery, K.E. (1989). *Developmental test of visual-motor integration.* Chicago: Follett Educational. Short form, 15 figures and long form, 24 figures. Available to assess children's visual-motor skills. Thoroughly researched instrument.

Brigance, A. (1978). *The Brigance diagnostic inventory of early development.* Woburn, MA: Curriculum Associates. A criterion-referenced test suitable for very young children and those with developmental delays. Utilizes lists of progressively more difficult fine and gross motor tasks. A comprehensive motor development curriculum is also available.

Folio, M.R., & Fewell, R.R. (1983). *Peabody developmental motor scales.* Hingham, MA: Teaching Resources. A comprehensive program and assessment device for fine and gross motor skills from birth to 7 years of age. Extensive activity card file included.

Gallahue, D.L. (1993). *Developmental physical education for today's children.* Dubuque, IA: Brown & Benchmark. This text contains an expanded and updated version of the *Fundamental movement pattern assessment instrument* originally developed by McClenaghan & Gallahue in 1978. Assessment guidelines for conducting both total body configuration and segmental analysis are provided for 23 fundamental movement skills. Corresponding videotapes, developed by Arlene Ignico, are also available.

Gallahue, D.L. & Ozmun, J.S. (1995). *Understanding motor development: Infants, children, adolescents, adults.* Dubuque, IA: Brown & Benchmark. Contains a wealth of information on 23 fundamental movement skills. Line drawings depict initial, elementary, and mature stages of each.

Hammill, D.D., Pearson, N.A., & Voress, J.K. (1993). *Developmental test of visual perception*. Austin, TX: Pro-Ed. New edition of Marianne Frostig's popular *Developmental test of visual perception*. Eight subtests. Measures both visual perception and visual-motor integration.

Ulrich, D. (1985). *Test of Gross Motor Development*. Austin, TX: Pro-Ed. A 12-item test of selected fundamental movement skills. Norm-referenced and criterion-referenced interpretations.

Werder, J., & Bruininks, R.H. (1988). *Body skills: A motor development curriculum for children*. Circle Pines, MN: American Guidance Service. This program provides a systematic method for assessing and teaching gross motor skills. Can be implemented in any physical education curriculum without additional facilities or major equipment purchases.

Wessel, J. (1980). *I CAN: Pre-primary motor and play skills*. Northbrook, IL: Hubbard Scientific. Excellent curricular materials for preschool children in the regular or adapted physical education program.

CHAPTER 17

Perceptual-Motor Development

Joseph P. Winnick

Margaret is a totally blind 4-year-old who would like to move independently in her preschool gymnasium. Her teacher has encouraged Margaret to orient herself to play areas according to sound cues associated with each. In essence, she is encouraging Margaret to develop her auditory perceptual abilities to help compensate for her loss of sight. Do you feel that Margaret's teacher should help her develop her auditory perceptual abilities? If yes, which components of auditory perception should be developed, and what are some physical education activities that could help?

The ability to learn and function effectively is affected by perceptual-motor development. **Perceptual-motor ability** permits the human to receive, transmit, organize, integrate, and attach meaning to sensory information and to formulate appropriate responses. These responses are necessary for the individual to move, and to learn while moving, in a variety of environments. Thus, they have direct or indirect impact in physical education and sport.

Ordinarily, perceptual-motor development occurs without the need for formal intervention. In other instances, perceptual-motor abilities need attention because they have not developed satisfactorily. For example, deficits related to perceptual-motor ability are often named as characteristics of persons with learning disabilities. These deficits may include poor spatial orientation, poor body awareness, immature body image, clumsiness or awkwardness, coordination deficits, and poor balance. The higher incidence of perceptual-motor deficits among people with cerebral palsy or mental retardation is well

known. Perceptual-motor experiences are particularly important in cases where sensory systems are generally affected but where residual abilities may be enhanced, and in cases where perceptual-motor abilities must be developed to a greater degree to compensate for loss of sensory abilities. People with visual and/or auditory disabilities exemplify these situations.

In this introductory section it is important to comment on the influences of perceptual-motor programs. In the 1960s and early 1970s, such programs were strongly advocated and supported because of the belief that they led to a significant improvement in academic and intellectual abilities. Research recently conducted has not supported this notion. On the other hand, research indicates clearly that perceptual-motor abilities, as measured by various tests, may be attained through carefully sequenced programs (Winnick, 1979). For example, it is clear that balance, a perceptual-motor ability that is basic to movement skills, may be enhanced through systematic training. Since these perceptual-motor abilities are fundamental to many motoric, academic, and daily living skills, the nurturing and/or remediation of these skills is vital and relevant to adapted physical education.

After reading this chapter it should be clear that all the movement activities experienced in physical education are perceptual-motor experiences. When perceptual-motor abilities require nurturing or when they have developed inadequately, there may be a need to plan programs to enhance their attainment. This chapter is designed to serve as a resource for planning and program implementation.

OVERVIEW OF THE PERCEPTUAL-MOTOR PROCESS

In order to implement perceptual-motor programs most effectively, it is helpful to have an understanding of the perceptual-motor process. A simplified four-step schematic of perceptual-motor functioning is presented in Figure 17.1.

Sensory Input

The first step in the perceptual-motor process, *sensory input*, involves receiving energy forms from the environment and from within the body itself as sensory stimuli and processing this information for integration by the central nervous system. Visual (sight), auditory (hearing), kinesthetic (movement), vestibular (balance), and tactile (touch) sensory systems provide raw data for the central nervous system. These sensory systems serve to gain information that is transmitted to the central nervous system through sensory (afferent) neurons.

Sensory Integration

The second step in the perceptual-motor process involves *sensory integration*. Present and past sensory information is integrated, compared, and stored in short- and/or long-term memory. An important phase occurs as the human organism selects and organizes an appropriate motor output based on the integration. The resultant decision becomes part of long-term memory, which is transmitted through the motor (efferent) mechanisms.

Motor/Behavioral Output and Feedback

The third major step in the perceptual-motor process is *motor/behavioral output*. Overt movements and/or behaviors occur as a result of decisions from the central nervous system. As output occurs, information is also continually fed back as sensory input about the nature of the ongoing response by the human organism. This *feedback* constitutes step 4 and serves as sensory information to continue the process. As with sensory input, feedback in movement settings is usually kinesthetic, tactual, visual, or auditory. During feedback, the adequacy or nature of the response is evaluated or judged. If it is judged inadequate, adjustments are made; if it is successful, adjustments are not required.

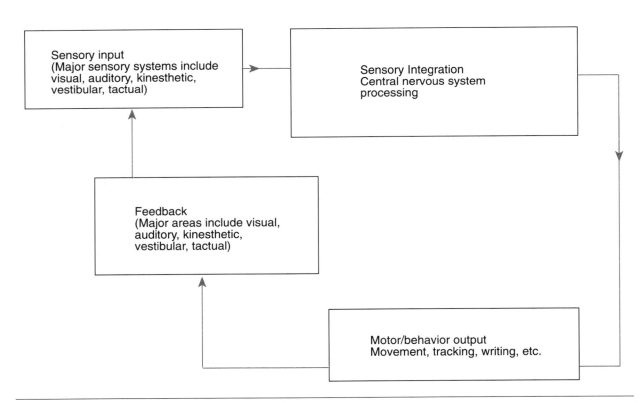

Figure 17.1 A simplified model of the perceptual-motor process.

Terms Associated With the Process

Terms associated with the perceptual-motor process are used in a variety of ways. The following are definitions of some terms used in this chapter.

Perception is the monitoring and interpretation of sensory data resulting from the interaction between sensory and central nervous system processes. Perception occurs in the brain and enables the individual to derive meaning from sensory data. **Perceptual-motor development** is the process of enhancing the ability to integrate sensory stimuli arising from or relating to observable movement experiences. It involves the ability to combine kinesthetic and tactual perceptions with and for the development of other perceptions, the use of movement as a vehicle to explore the environment and develop perceptual-motor abilities, and the ability to "perceive" tactually and kinesthetically. Perception occurs as sensory information is interpreted or given meaning. Because perceptual-motor includes both an individual's interpretation and response to sensory stimulation, it requires cognitive ability. On the other hand, sensorimotor activity occurs at a subcortical level and does not involve meaning, interpretation, or cortical-level functioning. Sensorimotor activity is characterized by motor responses to sensory input. The sensory integration process results in perception and other types of sensory data synthesis. Thus, perception is one aspect of sensory integration.

During the 1980s and continuing into the 1990s there has developed in physical education literature a view on perception that appears to have implication for perceptual-motor development. This view, known as the direct or *ecological approach* to perception, is based on the writings of J.J. Gibson (1977, 1979). This view emphasizes that perception is specific to each individual and that the environment is perceived directly in terms of its utility or usefulness for the perceiver. Persons perceive the environment in terms of the actions they can exert on it, that is, the *affordances* provided by the environment. For example, children may perceive a chair predominantly in terms of their ability to crawl under it, while adults perceive it as an object to sit on (although they may also recognize its other possibilities). Advocates of this orientation feel that perceptual deficits may be defined in terms of inadequate perception of affordances. Thus, perception may become a prime candidate in the search for potential rate-limiters in children with movement problems (Burton, 1990).

An Example of a Perceptual-Motor Skill

The perceptual-motor skill of batting a pitched softball can be used to illustrate these basic introductory concepts. As the pitched ball comes toward the plate, the batter focuses on the ball and tracks it. Information about speed, direction, spin, and other flight characteristics is picked up (stimulus reception) by the visual system (sensory input) for further processing. The information is transmitted via sensory neurons to the central nervous system, where it undergoes sensory integration. Because of various characteristics in the environment, the nature of the sensory information, and past experience, the incoming object is perceived as a softball (perception) to be struck (perceptual-motor). The batter's past experience will influence the ability to fixate and track the softball and process information about how to hit it. "How to hit it" involves comparative evaluations in which, for example, the arc of the ball is compared with that from previous instances when the act was performed.

The batter decides on the appropriate swing (decision about motor behavior) on the basis of earlier steps in the process. This decision becomes part of the long-term memory, to be used for future reference. During the pitch, the brain is constantly kept informed about the position of the bat and the body; and will use this information to enhance the overt behavior of swinging the bat. Once the nature of the motor behavior or response has been determined, messages are sent to appropriate parts of the body to initiate the response (motor output response). As the batter moves and completes the task, the information is provided on which to judge whether the response is successful or inadequate (feedback). If the pitch was missed, the batter may decide that adjustments are necessary in similar future instances; this information is stored in long-term memory and serves as a basis for learning. Perceptual-motor functioning is concerned with the entire process depicted in Figure 17.1 and described in this example; batting is thus one type of perceptual-motor skill.

If the ecological perspective on perception is applied to the "hitting of the pitch" example described above, the ball will be perceived by each observer in terms of ability to hit the ball or to hit the ball to a particular place on the field given one's body size and skill rather than a focus on the ball's velocity, spin, and so on. Thus, individuals will perceive the ball in terms of their ability to hit it, and based on this perception, they will decide what to do and respond accordingly.

Perceptual-Motor Deficits

Because Figure 17.1 depicts perceptual-motor processing, it is a useful reference for breakdowns in the process: breakdowns at the input, integration, output, and feedback sites. A breakdown at the *input* site may occur for a variety of reasons. For example, individuals with sensory impairments like blindness or deafness may not be able to adequately pick up visual or auditory information from the environment, with the result that this information does not appropriately reach the central nervous system. Students who are mentally retarded or autistic may not attend to, and thus may not receive, relevant information. People with neuromuscular impairments may be inhibited by the lack of appropriate kinesthetic, vestibular, or tactual information basic to quality input.

Sensory *integration* may be affected by factors such as mental retardation or neurological conditions that impair the functioning of the central nervous system. Also, sensory integration may be influenced by the quality of information received during sensory input. Motor *output* can be affected by inappropriate functioning during previous steps as well as conditions influencing movement, including transmission of information. Conditions associated with cerebral palsy, muscular dystrophy, and other neurological or orthopedic impairments are examples. Breakdowns at the *feedback* site can result from factors that affect earlier steps and any additional factors that bear on the ability to modify or correct behavior. The clumsy child, for example, may lack body awareness because of faulty kinesthetic perception; this would impair the adequacy of feedback.

Related to the ecological approach, Burton (1987, 1990) has suggested that the influence of perception be examined more closely when movement problems occur. Consistent with this view, it is suggested that perceptual judgments be assessed using actual performance as a criterion to determine if the motor outcomes are due to faulty perception. The game of golf provides a good example of this concept. In golf, the club used for a particular shot is selected on the basis of distance, height desired, and so on. If, after selecting a club, the golfer makes a shot short of the target, it is possible that this inadequate performance resulted from selecting the wrong club (faulty perception of shot requirements) rather than from poor skill. For example, the golfer may have underestimated the distance, wind resistance, and so on. Although the shortness of the shot may have been due to other reasons, the possibility for faulty perception exists and should be assessed.

Many of the factors causing perceptual-motor deficits are associated with student disabilities seen in the school environment. Due to the influence on perceptual-motor development, physical educators may need to develop programs to nurture development or remediate performance. The nature of an individualized program will depend on the cause of the perceptual-motor breakdown, the student's perception and abilities, and the purpose of the program. In the case of a student who is totally blind, for example, it may be necessary to focus on heightening auditory perceptual-motor components to improve orientation to school grounds and to focus on kinesthetic perception to enhance efficient movement in the environment. Table 17.1 presents an analysis of prominent perceptual-motor need and deficit areas as a function of specific impairments.

Facilitating Development

The teacher has an important role in nurturing or remediating perceptual-motor abilities. The exact role and teaching styles to be employed should vary with characteristics of the learner. Since perceptual-motor abilities appear to develop optimally between the ages of 2 and 7, movement exploration and guided discovery are the styles generally most appropriate up to development age 5. As children reach ages 6 and 7, more direct teaching styles may be effective. If the teacher believes that it is warranted, a diagnostic-prescriptive approach may be used to stimulate movement. A more direct teaching style may be appropriate even in the earlier years.

Burton (1987) suggested two implications for teaching to enhance perceptual skill which may have important potential for enhancing perceptual-motor development. First, he emphasized that teachers should provide *purposeful movement*. Movements are purposeful when they are performed as a means to an end rather than as the end itself. Key to the provision of purposeful movement is to select an activity involving an objective beyond the actual movement itself. For example, assume that the teacher wishes to improve the accuracy of throwing a ball overhand. A purposeful movement would be to toss a ball at a target that emits a light or sound when successfully hit. This is more motivating to the student than throwing a ball for the sake of throwing a ball.

A second teaching implication is for students to become more accurately attuned to *affordances in the environment* (Burton, 1987). One way this is

Table 17.1   An Analysis of Prominent Perceptual-Motor Need and Deficit Areas

Disability	Prominent need and deficit areas
Visual disability	Need to focus on the development of residual visual perceptual abilities and to help the child compensate for visual perceptual-motor deficits by enhancing auditory, vestibular, tactual, and kinesthetic perception. Give particular attention to input and feedback steps in the perceptual-motor process.
Auditory disability	Need to focus on the development of residual hearing and vestibular abilities (if affected) and help the child compensate by enhancing development associated with intact sensory systems. Give particular attention to input, integration, and feedback steps in the perceptual-motor process.
Haptic disabilities (primarily the clumsy child, children with orthopedic, neuromuscular, or neurological impairments)	Need to focus on the development of vestibular, kinesthetic, and tactual perception and to integrate motor experiences with visual and auditory perception. There may be a particular need to focus on input, motor response, and feedback steps.
Mental or affective disabilities (children with mental retardation or emotional disturbance)	Needs and focus based on assessment of perceptual-motor abilities. Involvement throughout the perceptual-motor process may exist.

done is by encouraging students to make perceptual judgments and to assess the accuracy of their judgments. Applied to a golf example, the question posed may be, "Can I hit the ball to the green using the nine iron?" In another example, a question posed may be, "Can I pass the ball to a teammate without it being intercepted by a defensive player?" In these situations the congruency between perception and action or movement is evaluated. The accuracy of one's perception of the environment or the affordances available is evaluated. In these situations the influence of perception on motor performance may be evaluated to determine whether poor performance results from faulty perception.

Although technically there are many sensory systems associated with perceptual-motor development, the remainder of this chapter discusses visual, auditory, kinesthetic, and tactual perception.

VISUAL PERCEPTUAL-MOTOR DEVELOPMENT

Visual perceptual-motor abilities are important in academic, physical education, and sport settings. In the academic setting, visual perceptual abilities are used in writing, drawing, reading, spelling,

and arithmetic. In physical education and sport they are important for catching, throwing, and kicking objects, playing tag, balancing, running, and performing fundamental movements. Age-appropriate visual perceptual-motor abilities are built on visual acuity, which affects the ability to see, fixate, track, and so forth, and thus is required for the input step. On the basis of input, the individual develops the abilities or components of visual perceptual-motor development associated with central nervous system processing and output. Components closely associated with movement include visual figure-ground perception, spatial relations, visual constancy, and visual-motor coordination.

Figure-Ground Perception

Figure-ground perception involves the ability to distinguish a figure from its background and give meaning to the forms or the combination of forms or elements that constitute the figure. It requires the ability to concentrate, differentiate, and integrate parts of objects to form meaningful wholes and to appropriately shift attention and ignore irrelevant stimuli. Visual figure-ground perception is called on when students are asked to pick out a specific letter of the alphabet from a field of extraneous items. In sport, visual figure-ground perception is clearly demonstrated in baseball because a batter must distinguish a white ball from a background in attempting to hit it. Students with inadequate perception may exhibit difficulties in differentiating letters, numbers, and other geometric forms, combining parts of words to form an entire word, or sorting objects. In physical education, figure-ground perception is required in games that depend on tracking moving objects and observing lines and boundaries and in activities requiring concentration on relevant stimuli. These include activities in which children move under, over, through, and around perception boxes, tires, hoops, or playground equipment, as well as activities in which they follow or avoid the lines and shapes associated with obstacle courses, geometric figures, maps, mazes, hopscotch diagrams, or footprints.

Spatial Relationships

The perception of spatial relationships means locating objects in space relative to oneself (egocentric localization) and locating objects relative to one another (objective localization). *Egocentric localization*, often referred to as perception of position in space, is demonstrated as youngsters attempt to move through hoops without touching them. Objective localization is seen as a player attempts to complete a pass to a guarded teammate.

Spatial relationship, which affects virtually all aspects of academic learning, involves knowing direction, distance, and depth. Position in space is basic to the solution of reversal or directional problems (such as the ability to distinguish *d*, *p*, and *q*, *36* and *63*, *saw* and *was*, *no* and *on*, etc.). Perception of spatial relationship also encompasses temporal ordering and sequencing. People who have difficulty putting objects in order will have difficulty in various academic areas, including arithmetic sequencing problems (performing operations in correct order). Some authors have contended that spatial awareness is preceded by body awareness, that the awareness of relationships in space grows out of an awareness of relationships among the parts of one's own body.

Visual Perceptual Constancy

Perceptual constancy is the ability to recognize objects despite variations in their presentation. It entails recognizing the sameness of an object although the object may in actuality vary in appearnace, size, color, texture, brightness, shape, and so on. For example, a football is recognized as having the same size even when seen from a distance. It has the same color in daylight as in twilight and maintains its shape even when only its tip is visible. Development of perceptual constancy involves seeing, feeling, manipulating, smelling, tasting, hearing, naming, classifying, and analyzing objects. Inadequate perceptual constancy affects the recognition of letters, numbers, shapes, and other symbols in different contexts. Physical education and sport provide a unique opportunity for the nurturing of constancy because objects are used and manipulated in a variety of ways and are viewed from many different perspectives.

Visual-Motor Coordination

Visual-motor coordination is the ability to coordinate vision with body movements. It is the aspect of visual perceptual-motor ability that combines visual with tactual and kinesthetic perception; thus, it is not an exclusively visual ability. Although coordination of vision and movement may involve many different parts of the body, eye-hand and eye-foot coordination are usually most important in physical education and sport activities. Effective eye-limb coordination is also important in academic pursuits, such as cutting, pasting, finger painting, drawing, tracing, coloring, scribbling, using the chalkboard, and manipulating clay and toys. It is particularly important in writing. Effective eye-limb coordination is also necessary for such basic skills as putting on and tying shoes, putting on and buttoning clothes, eating or drinking without tipping glasses and plates, and using simple tools.

Using and Developing Visual Perceptual-Motor Abilities

A wide variety of experiences in physical education and sport call on and may be used to stimulate visual perceptual-motor abilities. Although motor activities are not generally limited to the development of one specific ability, some activities are especially well suited for figure-ground development. These include rolling, throwing, catching, kicking, striking, dodging, and chasing a variety of objects in a variety of ways; moving under, over, through, and around perception boxes, tires, hoops, geometric shapes, ropes, playground equipment, pieces of apparatus, and other "junk"; following or avoiding lines associated with obstacles courses, geometric shapes, maps, mazes, hopscotch games, or grids; stepping on or avoiding footprints, stones, animals, or shapes painted on outdoor hardtops or floors; imitating movements as in Leapfrog, Follow the Leader, or Simon Says; and doing simple rope activities, including moving under and over ropes and jumping rope.

Spatial relationships are involved in trampolining, tumbling, swimming, rope jumping, rhythms and dance, obstacle courses, and the like. Activities particularly useful in helping the individual to develop spatial abilities include moving through tunnels, tires, hoops, mazes, and perception boxes. Elementary games like dodgeball, tag, and Steal the Bacon, in which one must locate objects in space relative to oneself (egocentric localization) or relative to one another (objective localization), foster perception of spatial relationships as well (Figure 17.2).

Visual-motor coordination is clearly important in physical education and sport. Games that include throwing, catching, kicking, and striking balls and other objects are among those activities requiring such coordination. Age-appropriate games are highly recommended because they enhance the purposefulness of movement.

AUDITORY PERCEPTUAL-MOTOR DEVELOPMENT

Age-appropriate auditory perceptual-motor abilities are built on auditory acuity. The ability to receive and transmit auditory stimuli as sensory input is the foundation of the development of auditory figure-ground perception, sound localization, discrimination, temporal auditory perception, and auditory-motor coordination. Educators should give much attention to auditory perception when working with students who have sensory impairments.

Figure-Ground Perception

Auditory figure-ground perception is the ability to distinguish and attend to relevant auditory stimuli against a background of general auditory stimuli. It includes the ability to ignore irrelevant stimuli (such as those in a noisy room or a room in which different activities are conducted simultaneously) and to attend to relevant stimuli. In situations where irrelevant stimuli are present, people with inadequate figure-ground perception may have difficulty concentrating on the task at hand, responding to directions, and comprehending information received during the many listening activities of daily life. They may not attend to a honking horn, a shout, or a signaling whistle. Their problems in physical education and sport may be associated with occasions when beginning, changing, or ending activities are signaled through sound.

Auditory Discrimination

Auditory discrimination is the capacity to distinguish different frequencies, qualities, and amplitudes of sound. It involves the ability to recognize and discriminate among variations of auditory stimuli presented in a temporal series, as well as auditory perceptual constancy. The latter is the ability to recognize an auditory stimulus as the same under varying presentations. Auditory discrimination thus involves the ability to distinguish pitch, loudness, and constancy of auditory stimuli. People with inadequate auditory discrimination may exhibit problems in games, dances, and other rhythmic activities that depend on this ability.

Sound Localization

Sound localization is the ability to determine the source or direction of sounds in the environment. Sound localization is used on the basketball court to find the open player who is calling for the ball, and it is basic to goal ball, in which blindfolded players attempt to stop a ball emitting a sound. Sound localization is vital to orientation and mobility for people with visual impairments. They often

Figure 17.2 An activity to learn spatial concepts, colors, shapes, and texture.

need to further develop their ability to locate sounds and may do so by reacting to various stimuli (bells, voices, horns, etc.).

Temporal Auditory Perception

Temporal auditory perception involves the ability to recognize and discriminate among variations of auditory stimuli presented in time. It entails distinguishing rate, emphasis, tempo, and order of auditory stimuli. Individuals with inadequate temporal auditory perception may exhibit difficulties in rhythmic movement and dance, singing games, and other physical education activities.

Auditory-Motor Coordination

Auditory-motor coordination is the ability to coordinate auditory stimuli with body movements. This coordination is readily apparent when a person playing goal ball reaches for a rolling ball (ear-hand coordination) according to where the player believes the ball is located. Linking auditory and motor activities is also demonstrated when a person responds to a beat in music (ear-foot coordination) or to a particular cadence when football signals are called out. Auditory-motor coordination is evident as a skater or gymnast performs a routine to musical accompaniment.

Development of Auditory Perceptual-Motor Abilities

Physical education and sport offer many opportunities to develop auditory perception. Participants may follow verbal directions or perform activities in response to tapes or records; the activities may be suggested by the music itself. For example, children may walk, run, skip, or gallop to a musical beat; they may imitate trains, airplanes, cars, or animals, as suggested by the music. Dances and rhythmic activities with variations in the rate and beat are useful, as are games and activities in which movements are begun, changed, or stopped in response to various sounds. Blind or blindfolded children may move toward or be guided by audible goal locators or play with balls that have bells attached to them. Triangles, drums, bells, sticks, or whistles may direct children in movement or serve as play equipment. A teacher conducting such activities should minimize distracting stimuli and vary the tempo and loudness of sound. It may be necessary to speak softly at certain times so that the participants must concentrate on listening.

PROPRIOCEPTION

Proprioception encompasses those perceptual-motor abilities that respond to stimuli arising within the organism. These include sensory stimuli arising from muscles, tendons, joints, and vestibular sense receptors. Such abilities emphasize movement and are discussed within the categories of kinesthetic perception and balance.

Kinesthetic Perception

It is apparent even to the casual observer that we use information gained through auditory and visual receptors to move within and learn from the environment. Just as we know a sight or sound, we also have the ability to know a movement or body position. We can know an action before executing it, or feel the correctness of a movement. The awareness and memory of movement and position is **kinesthetic perception**. It develops from impulses that originate from the body's proprioceptors. Because kinesthetic perception is basic to all movement, it is associated with visual-motor and auditory-motor abilities.

Like all perceptions, kinesthetic perceptions depend on sensory input (including kinesthetic acuity) provided to the central nervous system. The central nervous system, in turn, processes this information in accord with the perceptual-motor process. Certain diseases and conditions may cause kinesthetic perception to be impaired. For example, in the case of a person who has had an amputation, all sensory information that normally would be processed by a particular extremity could be missing. Cerebral palsy, muscular dystrophy, and other diseases or conditions affecting the motor system may result in a pattern of input or output that is different from that of an individual without disabilities. A youngster with a learning disability may have difficulty selecting appropriate information from the many sources in the organism. Inadequate kinesthetic perception may manifest itself in clumsiness due to lack of opportunity for participation in motoric experiences. Abilities closely associated with kinesthetic perception are body awareness, laterality, and verticality.

Body Awareness

Body awareness is an elusive term that has been used in various ways by writers representing different but related disciplines. Used here, **body awareness** is a comprehensive term that includes body schema, body image, and body concept or knowledge. *Body schema*, is the most basic component and is sometimes known as the sensorimotor component because it is dependent on information supplied through activity of the body itself. It involves awareness of the body's capabilities and limitations, including the ability to create appropriate muscular tensions in movement activities, and awareness of the position in space of the body and its parts. At basic levels, body schema helps the individual know where the body ends and external space begins. Thus, an infant uses feedback from body action to become aware of the dimensions and limitations of the physical being and begins to establish separateness of the body from external surroundings. As body schema evolves, higher levels of motor development and control appear and follow a continuous process of change throughout life.

Body image refers to the feelings one has about one's body. It is affected by biological, intellectual, psychological, and social experiences. It includes the internal awareness of body parts and how they function. For example, people learn that they have two arms and two legs or two sides of the body and that, at times, these work in combination and at other times function independently. Intellectual, social, and psychological factors enter into the perception of oneself as fast, slow, ugly, beautiful, weak, strong, masculine, feminine, and so forth.

Body concept, or body knowledge, is the verbalized knowledge one has about one's body. It includes the intellectual operation of naming body parts and the understanding of how the body and its parts move in space. Body concept builds on body schema and body image.

The importance of movement experiences for the stimulation and nurturing of body awareness and the importance of body awareness for movement are obvious. Movement experiences that may serve in the developmental years to enhance body awareness include those in which parts of the body are identified, named, pointed to, and innervated: imitation of movements, balance activities, rhythmic or dance activities, trampoline and scooter board activities, mimetic activities, movement and exploration, swimming games, activities conducted in front of a mirror, stunts and tumbling, and a variety of exercises. Virtually all gross motor activities involve body awareness at some level.

Laterality and Verticality

Laterality and verticality refer to internal awareness of right and left and up and down, respectively. **Laterality** is the internal awareness of the

sides of the body and their differences. It is believed that development of laterality normally proceeds from bilateral to unilateral activity. As described by Kephart (1960), laterality develops through experimentation with the movements of the two halves of the body, observing and comparing their differences, ascribing different qualities to each side, and then distinguishing the two sides.

Verticality refers to an internal awareness of up and down. Development of verticality is also believed to be enhanced through experimentation in upper and lower parts of the body. Laterality and verticality should be conceived as very much related to body awareness. Laterality and verticality are significantly included in many physical education activities, and nurturing these abilities enhances their successful development and performance. Examples include most balance, locomotor, and object control activities.

Balance

As mentioned previously, proprioception includes sensation pertaining to vestibular sense reception. The vestibular apparatus provides the individual with information about the body's relationship to gravitational pull and thus serves as the basis for balance or equilibrium. Vestibular sense perception combines with visual, auditory, kinesthetic, and tactual information to enhance attainment of static and dynamic balance.

It is well known that balance is a key element in the performance of movement activities. In relation to perceptual-motor development, balance was believed by Kephart (1960) to be the primary pattern yielding the differentiation of the parts of the body because balancing requires postural adjustment (muscular tension) to keep the center of gravity over the base, and it helps the individual identify the midline of the body as a reference point for separating the two sides. These postural adjustments or muscular tensions, Kephart believed, help a child develop an internal awareness of left or right, that is, laterality (Figure 17.3).

Many activities may be used to nurture or remediate balance during the perceptual-motor developmental years. These include activities conducted on tiltboards, balance boards, and balance beams. Mimetic activities, stunts and tumbling, and a variety of games may also be used to develop balance.

TACTUAL PERCEPTION

Tactual perception is the ability to interpret sensations from the cutaneous surfaces of the body.

Figure 17.3 Balance activities on a large ball stimulate postural adjustment and body awareness.

Whereas kinesthetic perception is internally related, tactual perception is externally related and responds to touch, feel, and manipulation. Through these aspects of the tactile system, the human experiences various sensations that contribute to a better understanding of the environment. For example, tactual perception enables one to distinguish wet from dry, hot from cold, soft from hard, and rough from smooth. The importance of tactual perception is evident as a student who is blind feels a lacrosse stick to understand what it is, tries to stay on a cinder track while running, or learns to move through the environment using cane travel. For all youngsters, learning is enhanced when they touch, feel, hold, and manipulate objects. The term *soft* becomes more meaningful and tangible as youngsters feel something soft and distinguish it from something hard.

Gross motor activities in physical education and sport offer many opportunities to use tactual perception. Relevant activities include those involving contact of the hands or the total body with a variety of surfaces. Tactual perception combines with kinesthetic sensations as youngsters crawl through a tunnel, walk along a balance beam, jump on a trampoline, climb a ladder, wrestle, or tumble. Individuals may walk barefoot on floors, lawns, beaches, balance beams, or mats or in swimming pools; they may climb ropes, cargo nets, ladders, and playground equipment. Swimming activities are particularly important because of the unique sensations that water provides.

SUMMARY

Perceptual-motor development is a process of enhancing the ability to integrate sensory stimuli arising from or relating to observable movement experiences. It is associated with all the sensory systems. This chapter has discussed visual, auditory, kinesthetic, and tactual systems in regard to perceptual-motor development. It has delineated the importance of these systems and has presented examples of how each is involved in, and can be enhanced through, physical education and sport.

BIBLIOGRAPHY

Burton, A.W. (1987). Confronting the interaction between perception and movement in adapted physical education. *Adapted Physical Education Quarterly,* **4**, 257–267.

Burton, A.W. (1990). Assessing the perceptual-motor interaction in developmentally disabled and handicapped children. *Adapted Physical Activity Quarterly,* **7**, 325–337.

Davis, W.E. (1983). An ecological approach to perceptual-motor learning. In R.L. Eason, T.L. Smith, & F. Caron (Eds.), *Adapted physical activity: From theory to application.* Champaign, IL: Human Kinetics.

Gibson, J.J. (1966). *The senses considered as perceptual systems.* Boston: Houghton Mifflin.

Gibson, J.J. (1977). The theory of affordance. In R. Shaw & J. Bransford (Eds.), *Perceiving, acting, and knowing: Toward an ecological psychology*. Hillsdale, NJ: Earlbaum.

Gibson, J.J. (1979). *The ecological approach to visual perception*. Boston: Houghton Mifflin.

Kephart, N.C. (1960). *Slow learner in the classroom*. Columbus, OH: Merrill.

Williams, H.G. (1983). *Perceptual and motor development*. Englewood Cliffs, NJ: Prentice Hall.

Winnick, J.P. (1979). *Early movement experiences and development: Habilitation and remediation*. Philadelphia: Saunders.

RESOURCES

Written

Capon, J. (1975). *Perceptual-motor lesson plans*. Byron, CA: Front Row Experience. Also, Capon, J. (1983). *Perceptual-motor lesson plans*. Byron, CA: Front Row Experience. These books present two levels of basic and practical lesson plans for perceptual-motor programs in preschool and elementary grades.

Cratty, B.J. (1986). *Perceptual motor development in infants and children* (3rd ed.). Englewood Cliffs, NJ: Prentice Hall. This comprehensive book provides a theoretical overview of perceptual-motor development and practical suggestions for programs.

Stillwell, J. (1990). *Perceptual motor activities for preschool and elementary children*. Great Activities, P.O. Box 51158, Durham, NC 27717.

Audiovisual

Cassettes, records, filmstrips, videos, and compact discs related to perceptual-motor development may be purchased from Kimbo Educational, Dept. S, P.O. Box 477, Long Branch, NJ 07740-0477 and from Educational Activities, P.O. Box 87, Baldwin, NY 11510.

Other

Perceptual-motor equipment and supplies can be ordered from J.A. Preston Corporation, P.O. Box 89, Jackson, MI 49204; Gopher Sport, 2929 West Park Drive, Owatonna, MN 55060; Flaghouse Rehab., 150 N. MacQuesten Parkway, Mt. Vernon, NY 10550.

CHAPTER 18

Infants and Toddlers

Bobby L. Eason

This chapter defines the role of the adapted physical educator as a direct service provider for infants and toddlers with disabilities (ITD). Providing instruction to ITD populations is different from that for older special education populations, and the content of this chapter reflects those differences. A Meaning Curriculum Framework (see Figure 18.1) has been developed to guide understanding of specific techniques for providing hands-on instruction for infants and toddlers considered at risk or with established risk.

The framework is best viewed from inside out. Inside the framework are concepts related to the actual teaching behaviors of assessment and programming. Convergent assessment, which defines a team approach, is the recommended assessment technique because it enables adapted physical educators to pool their information with team members from several disciplines.

Basic to both assessment and programming is a working knowledge of the motor traits and behaviors of infants and toddlers. The traits and behaviors have been grouped into related categories to form an infant and toddler motor taxonomy. This taxonomy is used to guide the selection of appropriate motor test items and for motor programming.

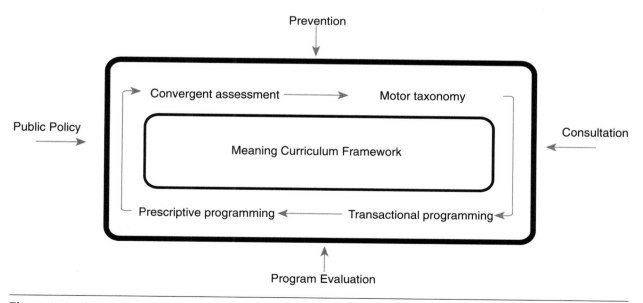

Figure 18.1 A meaning curriculum framework.

Two types of motor programming strategies are recommended within the framework: transactional and prescriptive. Transactional programming is child centered and allows the child and teacher to work together in determining the goals and objectives of a given lesson; it is suggested for an infant or toddler whose long-term prognosis is similar to that of typical children. Prescriptive programming is for children with established risk factors whose prognoses are more severe. Both types of programming are based on the assumption that children learn best when they are engaged in *meaningful* activities that require action, discovery, and problem solving.

Outside the framework are important but secondary concepts that include public policy, prevention, consultation, and program evaluation. This chapter provides a brief history of PL 99-457 and other public policies that were written to provide funding for state-initiated multidisciplinary intervention projects. The intervention goals of the adapted physical educator are twofold—prevent disabling conditions when possible; if not, reduce their severity.

But the adapted physical educator is not expected to work alone. Public policy states that intervention strategies are to be multidisciplinary and involve the child's family. Thus consultation is an important component of the framework, as the adapted physical education teachers will be expected to share their vast knowledge of motor development with family members and other practicing professionals. Moreover, public policy indicates that intervention programs must be routinely evaluated for effectiveness. Although detailed explanations of consultation and program evaluation are beyond the scope of this chapter, the framework provides a reminder that practicing adapted physical education professionals will be expected to provide consultation in addition to accountability for program effectiveness.

PUBLIC POLICY AND PREVENTION

The recent history of adapted physical education has been greatly influenced by public policies such as PL 94-142. The impetus for providing motor development experiences for infants and toddlers has been generated by legislation originally titled PL 99-457 (now known as Part H of IDEA 101-476). The objective of PL 99-457 was to provide early intervention to prevent or reduce the seriousness of diseases and conditions of children considered at risk or with established risk.

In addition to describing the infant and toddler population within the framework of public policy, this section will provide current definitions of the landmark legislation, the mandate for multidisciplinary intervention, and the role of the family and the Individualized Family Service Plan for the intervention process.

Describing the Infant and Toddler Population

Before initiating practice, the adapted physical educator should become familiar with the definitions and descriptions of the ITD population. Federal policy through Part H of IDEA has provided a general definition. An infant or toddler with a disability requires early intervention services due to (1) developmental delays in one of the following domains: cognitive, physical, language and speech, psychosocial, or self-help, (2) a condition such as Down syndrome that has a high probability of resulting in delay, and (3) being at risk medically or environmentally for substantial developmental delays if early education is not provided. (Federal Register, 1986).

Several categories have emerged to describe the ITD population. Garwood and Sheehan (1989) proposed a simple dichotomy—at risk and established risk. At-risk children are either biologically or environmentally vulnerable. Biological deficiencies include low birth weight, respiratory difficulties, prematurity, central nervous system involvement, and prenatal alcohol and/or drug abuse by the mother. Environmental at-risk factors include poverty, low maternal education or age, family instability, low social support systems, and weak parent-infant bonding.

Examples of established risk include such conditions as cerebral palsy, Down syndrome, and spina bifida. Delays may occur at any time during either prenatal (conception to birth), perinatal (during birth), and postnatal (after birth) periods (see Table 18.1 for an overview).

Because of improved medical technology (Ulrich, 1984), and changes in social patterns (Rist, 1990), the ITD population is rapidly expanding. Rist (1990) reported that cocaine abuse among New York's pregnant women has increased 3,000% over a 10-year period and 200,000 babies were born in 1991 with cocaine exposure. Often, these babies have birth defects such as deformed hearts, lungs, digestive systems, and limbs. Nearly all are small and underweight and suffer neurological damage.

Table 18.1   Typical Classifications and Descriptions of Infants and Toddlers With an Established Risk or Who Are Environmentally or Biologically at Risk

Established-risk conditions

1. **Cerebral palsy**: Cerebral palsy refers to symptoms rather than to a specific disease. Symptoms include paralysis, muscle weakness, and poor coordination. Most commonly **caused** by a lack of oxygen to the brain during birth.

2. **Down syndrome**: Down syndrome is associated with mental retardation. The syndrome is caused by a chromosomal abnormality, usually Trisomy 21. Infants and toddlers with Down syndrome are characterized by poor muscle tone and hyperflexibility of joints.

3. **Hydrocephalus**: Hydrocephalus refers to a condition in which there is an abnormal amount of cerebro-spinal fluid around the brain. The condition is linked to several medical diagnoses, the most common of which is spina bifida. Treatment for the problem often requires that a tubical shunt be surgically placed under the skin. Engagement in typical motor activities is indicated, but protective head gear may be recommended.

4. **Pediatric AIDS**: Acquired immunodeficiency syndrome, or AIDS, is caused by the transmission of the human immunodeficiency virus (HIV) from the infected mother. Early symptoms include fever, failure to thrive, and weight loss. As the condition progresses, children show lack of developmental milestone attainment, poor motor coordination, and progressive neurological disease.

5. **Muscular dystrophy**: Muscular dystrophy is the most common of all childhood muscular diseases. The condition is usually not detected during infancy, but by the toddler stage muscle weaknesses in the extremities may be detected. Affected toddlers may have trouble climbing stairs or moving from sitting to standing. The disease is genetic in origin.

6. **Seizure disorders**: Seizure disorders are an indication that the infant or toddler is undergoing a sudden and abnormal burst of electrical activity in the brain. Symptoms range from muscular twitching, localized stiffening of a body limb, alteration of consciousness, or total body convulsion. Epilepsy is a commonly diagnosed disorder that refers to an otherwise healthy child who experiences repeated bouts with seizures.

7. **Spina bifida**: Spina bifida is an incomplete closure of the spinal column. Of the three types, occulta is the least severe and is characterized by an opening in one or more of the vertebrae. Myelomeningocele is the most severe, featuring a protruding sac from an opening in both the vertebrae and spinal cord. The nerves are exposed and are not properly connected. The least common spina bifida condition is meningocele. It features a protruding sac, but spinal cord is intact. Poor muscle control, tactile sensitivity, and eventually scoliosis are major health problems.

Environmentally or biologically at risk

1. **Inadequate health care**: Inadequate health care places the infant/toddler at risk when available preventative practices are not followed, when health problems are not detected early, or when existing problems are not properly managed.

2. **Inadequate nutrition**: Inadequate nutrition will detrimentally affect growth and development.

3. **Low socioeconomic status**: Single parent families, teenage parents, financial constraints, and inferior housing and transportation are socioeconomic situations that place a child at risk.

4. **Poisons and toxins**: Poisoning from lead-based paints, cigarette smoking, and controlled drugs are factors that affect growth and development.

5. **Dysfunctional families**: Other environmental conditions include children from families from one or more of the following family situations: homeless, migrant, foster care, shelter, or institution; in a family where physical or emotional abuse is tolerated; and caregiver cannot consistently perform essential parenting duties.

6. **Genetic risk factors**: Genetic risk factors refers to chromosomal or single gene problems that are genetic in origin. Typical conditions include deafness, mental retardation, metabolic abnormalities, and muscular disorders.

(continued)

Table 18.1 *(Continued)*

Established-risk conditions

7. **Maternal risk factors**: Several characteristics of the mother are associated with prenatal development. Age below 16 and above 35 years, poverty and diet, educational level, spacing between pregnancies, chronic disease, and Rh incompatibility are some factors that place an unborn child at risk.

8. **Prenatal risk factors**: Viral infections such as rubella, hepatitis, and HIV pose the largest threat to the developing fetus.

9. **Perinatal and postnatal risk factors**: Inadequate oxygen to the brain during birth or later during an accident or near-drowning can result in growth and development problems. Chronic or prolonged illness, serious infection, trauma, and inadequate growth are other conditions that affect development.

The number of children born with fetal alcohol syndrome (FAS) is also increasing. FAS, the nation's third largest cause of retardation, was undocumented as late as 1978. Besides retardation, characteristics of FAS include seizures, poor eyesight, and faulty balance. Surburg (1988) has alerted educators to be ready for increasing numbers of children infected with the AIDS/HIV virus. Also, the number of babies born prematurely and small for chronological age are increasing because mothers are not receiving adequate prenatal care.

Landmark Legislation and Processes of Intervention

The adapted physical educator's intervention role for infants and toddlers with disabilities is guided by governmental regulations and by established intervention processes. This section will briefly explain landmark legislation including PL 101-476, the Individualized Family Service Plan, and variations of the multidisciplinary intervention process.

Individuals With Disabilities Education Act

In the United States, prevention was the stimulus for the passage in 1986 of the historic PL 99-457 legislation, which required all states to provide systematic intervention for disabled children between 3 and 5 years old. This bill also authorized Part H funding for states to develop comprehensive, multidisciplinary, coordinated, interagency programs for infants and toddlers with disabilities and their families. In 1990, PL 99-457 and PL 94-142 were subsumed with PL 101-476, the Individuals with Disabilities Education Act (IDEA).

The Multidisciplinary Process

Provisions in the IDEA resulted in different staffing patterns for the design of intervention services. Previously, a unidisciplinary approach, defined as independent evaluation and planning by a single professional, was the prevalent staffing strategy. Now, Part H requires a unified multidisciplinary intervention process. Under the direction of a team leader, the group provides an extensive assessment and, if necessary, creates an Individualized Family Service Plan (IFSP). Professions and disciplines typically selected for the team are drawn from one or more of the following: adapted physical education, audiology, child development, early childhood education, family studies, medicine, nursing, nutrition, occupational therapy, physical therapy, psychology, rehabilitation counseling, social work, speech and language, and special education.

Current "best practices" in early childhood theory have resulted in important refinements in the multidisciplined process. The term multidisciplinary, although still utilized within the legal language of IDEA, is not recommended as a practice of choice. A process that is truly "multidisciplinary" is considered flawed because it is conducted by professionals without regard to unified planning. As such, intervention goals are often redundant, conflicting, and confusing to the parents.

Of greater value for meeting the motor needs of the ITD population is an interdisciplinary process that involves a whole-child team approach. Team personnel, including family members, meet regularly to obtain a unified intervention strategy. However, a more highly recommended process is the transdisciplinary approach, which is also team oriented, but in which disciplinary boundaries are crossed and professionals share techniques. More-over, family members are encouraged to learn advanced intervention techniques and to become "co-therapists" (Bagnato & Neisworth, 1991). The adapted physical educator's role on the transdisciplinary team is to provide direct intervention for gross motor development and to consult with parents and other professionals concerning technique.

The Family and the IFSP

Placing "family" in the intervention plan signifies the family's central role in prevention and remediation. Deal, Dunst, and Trivett (1989) have written extensively about the role of family members. One goal is to assist family members to identify and work within available social networks to better meet the needs of their child. A second goal is to "empower" families to gain a sense of control over the manner and direction in which intervention occurs.

When working with families, the adapted physical educator must remember that each family has a distinct structure in terms of culture, individual roles, values, beliefs, and coping styles. Although many infants and toddlers with special needs come from dysfunctional families, the family has the right to choose the level and nature of recommended intervention.

Part H of IDEA requires a formal relationship between society and the child's family—the **Individualized Family Service Plan (IFSP)**. By legal mandate, the IFSP is determined after a multidisciplinary assessment has been conducted. Components of the IFSP must include the following:

- The developmental status of the child

- Strengths and needs of the family

- Expected outcomes with related procedures, criteria, and timelines

- The frequency, intensity, location, and description of recommended early intervention service

- Dates for initiation and termination of services

- Identification of a case manager

- A stated transition plan to begin at age 3

The most appropriate out-of-home location for intervention is not resolved. Hospitals will undoubtedly remain prominent for infants with established risks. Special day-care centers exist for toddlers. But these facilities are rapidly becoming overburdened as a result of the proliferation of disabled children and the time lag required to sufficiently train personnel. Thus, some states are expanding special education to include infants and toddlers, a trend with high opportunity for direct adapted physical education involvement.

CONVERGENT ASSESSMENT AND A MOTOR BEHAVIOR TAXONOMY

This section of the chapter explains the adapted physical educator's role in the assessment process for ITD populations. Assessment theory related to validity and objectivity and descriptions of specific screening and norm-referenced testing as discussed in chapter 4 will be expanded to include a taxonomy of movements specific to infants and toddlers. The motor behavior taxonomy is a guide to indicate which movements should be assessed. Also, a team approach to assessment, convergent assessment, will be discussed because of its importance in the interdisciplinary and transdisciplinary intervention processes.

A Motor Behavior Taxonomy

Gallahue's widely utilized motor classification taxonomy presents four phases of movement development: reflexive, rudimentary, fundamental, and specialized. The adapted physical education teacher should use this or some other acceptable taxonomy to provide direction for both assessment and activity selection. (See Tables 16.1 through 16.7 for an overview of Gallahue's model.)

The reflexive stage is divided into primitive and postural developmental stages. **Primitive reflexes,** which are present at birth, are phased out during the first year. Reflexes serve the primary function of obtaining nourishment and providing protection. Reflexes are involuntary and typically become integrated within the voluntary nervous system. **Postural reflexes** resemble later voluntary movement activity and serve to maintain equilibrium.

Rhythmic movements, known as **stereotypies,** occur during the same developmental period as reflexes. Thelen (1979) identified 47 separate movements and included kicking, waving, banging, rocking, and swaying. They appear to occur randomly, but may lay the foundation for full volitional motor control (Gallahue, 1989). Although children vary in frequency of occurrence of stereotypies, the teacher should observe the presence and frequency of a child's rhythmic movements.

Toward the end of the first year, the normally developing child begins to gain body control. Rudimentary abilities and skills are developed. Sufficient tone, muscular strength, and neurological control are adequate to allow postural stability, movement coordination, and balance; all are foundations for skills of locomotion and object manipulation (see Figure 18.2).

The components of postural stability include control of head and neck, control of trunk, sitting, and standing. As the child is adjusting to the forces of gravity, locomotion enables the child to explore aspects of the environment. Horizontal movements include scooting, crawling, creeping, and walking on all fours. From the upright position, the child goes from walking with support to independent walking. Eventually, the child is capable of backward and sideward walking.

The third component of rudimentary movements is a reach, grasp, and release stage. Reaching abilities advance from globular ineffective thrusts to controlled and accurate reaches. Voluntary grasping proceeds from palmar to pincer grasping. For infants, most movement is performed while they are lying down. Older infants and toddlers add upright and locomotor skills to their fundamental movement repertoire.

Convergent Assessment as a Process

This section of the chapter explains current theory concerning assessment relative to infants and toddlers with disability. With ITD populations, less importance is now placed on formal traditional norm- or criterion-referenced assessment, and greater reliance is placed on informal judgments of intervention team members. One highly recommended process is convergent assessment which enables the adapted teacher and other team members to compare their formal and informal observations to create a unified assessment profile of a given child.

Convergent assessment has five basic functions:

1. Screening
2. In-depth assessment
3. Assessment for activity selection
4. Monitoring change
5. Evaluation (Widerstrom, Mowder, & Sandall, 1991)

Screening and in-depth assessment utilize formal tests such as the Milani-Comparetti Motor Development Screening Test and the Peabody Developmental Motor scales (see chapter 4). Data from such tests as these provide a developmental motor age and help establish a legal basis for determining intervention practices. Less formal tests guide activity selection and help determine what adjustments, if any, may be required during the ongoing intervention period. At program's end, formal tests are again used to determine intervention effectiveness and what changes are necessary for future programs.

As stated, convergent assessment relies upon both formal and informal instruments. Standardized, norm-referenced, and criterion-referenced tests are considered formal (see chapter 4). Two widely utilized informal techniques include judgment-based and arena-based assessment and are the benchmarks of convergent assessment theory.

Components of Motor Activity

Elements	Functions	Skills
Tone	Postural stability	Sitting
Control	Movement coordination	Walking, running
Strength	Balance	Reaching, grasping

Figure 18.2 Components of motor activity within the Meaning Curriculum Framework.
From ''Pediatric Adapted Physical Education for Infants, Toddlers, and Preschoolers: Meeting IDEA-H and IDEA-B Challenges'' by J. Cowden and B. Eason, 1991, *Adapted Physical Activity Quarterly*, **8**, p. 271. Reprinted by permission.

Judgment-Based Assessment

When the adapted physical educator makes professional judgments about a child's ability without relying solely upon numeric scores, judgment-based assessment is being employed. Standardized test batteries provide quantifiable data for the diagnostic purpose of comparing a child to a noninvolved peer group and for determining the degree of developmental deficit. However, they may lack sensitivity for detecting the subtle abilities of infants and toddlers with special needs.

Hands-on experience is the best indicator of an adapted physical educator's ability to perform judgment-based assessment. However, there are guidelines and techniques that should be followed. One technique is to spend several familiarization sessions with the child before beginning assessment. Second, direct interaction should occur on the child's ''turf'' and in a natural setting.

Third, following familiarization, the teacher should learn how to ''engineer'' an environment, which requires careful selection of toys and situations to elicit both spontaneous and facilitated action. To the degree possible, it is important to allow the child to lead, but guide the action when necessary. Thus, when a child is familiar with the teacher, engineered activities performed in a natural setting provide observations that can be professionally judged with validity.

Arena Assessment

Because infants and toddlers are easily distractible, some teams create arenas for diagnostic assessment and intervention (Wolery & Dyk, 1984). Arenas are typically arranged with modules and learning centers. Modules are designed to assist assessment and practice for gross motor, fine motor, eating, and functional skills, and for language and cognitive development.

For assessment, arenas should be provided with videotape capabilities. As children play and interact with one or more of the team members, behavior is videotaped for later critique and analysis. The arenas may be equipped with one-way mirrors for unobtrusive observations. Also, microphones should be placed to receive and transmit sounds to the observation areas. After assessment, the team members meet to compare notes and view the recorded information for validation.

A MEANING CURRICULUM FRAMEWORK

Once screening and initial in-depth assessment have taken place, the adapted teacher must select or develop a curriculum framework to guide decisions regarding the selection, structuring, and sequencing of developmental movement. Since passage of PL 99-457, several frameworks for ITD populations have been published (see resource section). Characteristically, the models are medically oriented, based upon developmental milestone theory. They are highly prescriptive and feature hierarchically and sequentially arranged activities.

In this chapter, a different and uniquely physical education approach is recommended. The Meaning Curriculum Framework (MCF) draws heavily from experience gained from documenting the teaching style of successful adapted physical education teachers working with infants and toddlers with disability. To some extent, MCF also draws heavily from the Personal Meaning Curriculum Model of Jewett and Bain (1985) and Bricker and Cripe's (1988) Activity Based Curriculum for preschool children with disability. The assumption is that infants and toddlers with disabilities respond best to gross motor activities that combine elements of adventure, play, joy, and pretending, and that require action, discovery, and problem solving.

The basis for activity selection is the anticipated ''meaning'' that the infant or toddler is expected to derive from movement experiences. Intervention for prevention and normalization are vital goals of the MCF, but they may influence activity selection and methodology after the ''meaning'' component has been ensured.

When working with the ITD population, it is important to remember that these children are different in terms of the severity of their disabilities. Thus, the MCF is designed to accommodate levels of disability by providing two distinct intervention approaches—transactional and prescriptive. The transactional approach is for children with mild to moderate developmental delay, and the prescriptive approach is for children with severe disabilities.

Transactional MCF Model

The transactional MCF model (MCF-T) is recommended for individuals at risk or those who have mild established risks. It is ''child centered,'' which means that it does not overly rely upon developmental milestone theory. Developmental milestones are motor descriptions of normal development. The model assumes that children mature and change in a genetically predetermined manner. Thus, activity selection is highly structured, and the child's obtainment of the developmental milestones is the curriculum objective.

A dictionary definition of *transactional* provides a simple description of the child-centered process, for example, to actively participate, to complete tasks, to be about business. Thus, the transactional approach recognizes the importance of environmental context and the interplay between the infant and his or her surroundings (Thurman & Widerstrom, 1990).

The essence of the MCF-T is to create situations where children must interact and complete tasks in a natural environment. The model assumes that mild/moderate ITD learn more completely and naturally when engaging in activities that allow for the obtainment of personal "meaning" (see Figure 18.3). Or, as Jewett and Bain (1985) state about the Personal Meaning Curriculum framework: "The framework is based on the assumption that human beings of *all ages* [emphasis added] have the same fundamental purposes for moving. These purposes are unique ways of finding or extending personal meaning through movement activities" (p. 73).

Thus, the transactional MCF model is based on activity rather than on the attainment of developmental milestones. Bricker and Cripe (1988) defined activity-based instruction as a child-directed, transactional approach that embeds a child's individual goals and objectives into routine and planned activities. The embedding process, defined as "engineering," also incorporates goals and

Figure 18.3 A typical Transactional Meaning Curriculum Framework (MCF-T) activity.

objectives as deemed necessary by an interdisciplinary or transdisciplinary team.

Using the transactional MCF model, the adapted physical education teacher should conduct ecological assessment to ensure that selected environments are safe and to continually scrutinize an area's potential for providing meaningful situations. The MCF-T calls for the teacher to provide varied activities as well as locations.

During the infancy period, selected activities should involve sensorimotor challenges as well as rudimentary movements that lead to stable postures and control of the head, neck, and trunk. Positioning is an important aspect of the teaching process, and some situations will require the teacher to hold the child while performing activities. Other situations will require positioning to originate from prone, supine, and sidelying positions. It is during this stage of development that children are learning to inhibit primitive reflexes and integrate postural reflexes so that voluntary motor control is possible. It is the teacher who facilitates the process of correct positioning.

Toy selection should provide toys that are colorful, soft, and smooth and that require active involvement. Orange, yellow, and red enhance alertness, while blue, green, and purple have a calming influence. Toys with soft and smooth textures invite exploration, but rough, jagged, or scratchy toys are turned away. Toys that can be activated are those that squeak when squeezed, glide easily when pulled, swing when pushed, "pop-up" when twisted, or rattle when moved. These activities lead to the development of the rudimentary abilities of reaching, grasping, holding, and releasing.

As children approach the toddler stage, activities should be arranged for upright positioning, locomotion, and balance. For toddlers, lesson structuring for MCF-T emphasizes activities of pretending, adventure, and conquest. Children are challenged to climb over, around, under, and through obstacles in make-believe situations in which the teacher is actively involved with the child. Long tunnels, parachutes, mats, climbers, foam rings, balance platforms, oversized balls, plastic slides, monkey bars, and minitramps are typical MCF activities for the toddler with mild disabilities.

MCF-T relies upon intrinsic motivation gained from the meaning that comes from moving successfully and playing with significant others. When a self-selected or engineered goal is completed, the adapted physical education teacher reinforces the accomplishment by smiling and praising. However, the teacher should refrain from reinforcing too often and from taking the focus away from task accomplishment.

Prescriptive MCF Model

Infants and toddlers with moderate to severe established risks require a more structured or prescriptive meaning curriculum framework (MCF-P) to guide activity selection than what was recommended for infants and toddlers with at-risk or mild established risk characteristics. However, MCF-P is presented as an extension rather than as a substitute for MCF-T. Children with more severe risks are capable of experiencing meaning from movement, but they are less likely to self-select appropriate movement activities.

The adapted physical education teacher, working with a transdisciplinary team when possible, must define what motor activities should be selected during practice. However, the teacher should not abandon the MCF concepts of play, action, pretending, and adventure. Also, the principles of transactional MCF and prescriptive MCF are not mutually exclusive. Many of the methods and activities recommended for one population can also be utilized for the other.

Prescriptive MCF requires that each motor lesson possess three distinct intervention components: tone normalization, positioning and handling, and strength and motor control activity (Copeland & Kimmel, 1989).

Normalizing Tone

Children who experience developmental problems (see Figure 18.4) with muscle tone must be "normalized" prior to practice. Achieving relaxation is the goal if muscles are hypertonic (excessively stiff and rigid muscles). Hypertonicity and unresolved primitive reflexes are mutually compounding. Therapy ball exercises, massage, and proper positioning are recommended for achieving relaxed muscles.

Hypotonicity is insufficient tone. The term describes a child with an abnormal lack of resistance to movement. One common method for assessing tone is to gently shake the child's knees and elbows. If the feet or hands appear loose or "floppy," hypotonicity is indicated. Conversely, if the range of motion is limited and the joints allow little movement of the feet and hands, hypertonicity is indicated. A hypotonic child has difficulty holding the head up or the arms out for periods longer than a few seconds. Joints are easily hyperextended, which poses a risk for dislocations. Normalization requires muscle stimulation (e.g.,

bouncing on a therapy ball, gentle jostling up and down, joint compression, firm massage, and other activities).

Dystonia defines muscle tone that fluctuates between stiff and flaccid. Dystonia is typical of athetoid cerebral palsy. Normalization requires the monitoring of muscles during practice and interjecting appropriate relaxing or stimulating techniques as required.

The therapy ball is effective for normalizing muscle tone. To relax muscles, the child is placed prone over the ball with legs slightly separated and toes pointed outward. The child is held by the upper thighs and is rocked forward and backward. Hypotonic children may be placed in a supported sitting position while the ball is bounced to stimulate tone.

Other relaxation techniques involve the use of sideyling boards, bolsters, and rolled mats. Using one of these props, the child is placed in a slightly flexed sidelying position with hands at midline. The teacher gently rotates the shoulder forward and rotates the hip backward in a slow, rhythmic pattern.

Supine relaxation requires that the child's knees and hips be slowly "rolled" upward toward the stomach. After several rolls, the knees can then be rotated from left to right while flexed.

Body tapping, firm massage, and joint compression are also recommended for the child with hypotonia. Low tone muscles are mildly tapped to elicit additional tone. In massage, the muscles are stroked rather than tapped. Joint compression involves placing downward pressure on the vertebrae and other joints to elicit cocontraction. Never compress the joints of children with Down syndrome and atlanto-axial instability, a genetic weakness of the first and second vertebrae.

Positioning and Handling Skills

Most children with severe difficulties require transportation and positioning to achieve movement goals. Hold the child securely with the appropriate "key point of control." Points of control include the head and neck, the shoulder girdle, and the hips. When positioning or handling a child, the teacher should remember to maintain symmetry of the child's body parts.

Some children with severe established-risk conditions lack the intrinsic motivation to accomplish movements of a planned lesson. Others lack the requisite strength and control for a given movement. To nurture an appropriate response, the adapted physical education teacher should attempt to "woo," "prompt," or "coddle" a child

Watch your baby for these signs:

NORMAL DEVELOPMENT

DEVELOPMENTAL PROBLEMS

By 3 Months*

- pushes up on arms
- holds head up

- unable to lift head or push up on arms
- stiff legs

- pushing back with head
- constantly fisted hand and stiff leg on one side
- difficult to move out of this position

NORMAL DEVELOPMENT

DEVELOPMENTAL PROBLEMS

By 6 Months*

- sits with support
- holds head up
- straight back

- unable to lift head
- rounded back
- stiff arms

- arms held back
- stiff, crossed legs

NORMAL DEVELOPMENT

DEVELOPMENTAL PROBLEMS

By 8 Months*

- sits without support
- arms free to reach and grasp

- poor head control
- difficult to get arms forward
- arches back—stiff legs

- rounded back
- poor use of arms for play
- stiff legs, pointed toes

- poor ability to lift head and back
- will not take weight on legs

NORMAL DEVELOPMENT

DEVELOPMENTAL PROBLEMS

By 12 Months*

- pulls to stand

- difficulty getting to stand
- stiff legs, pointed toes

- cannot crawl on hands and knees
- uses only one side of body to move

NORMAL DEVELOPMENT

DEVELOPMENTAL PROBLEMS

By 15 Months*

- independent standing or walking

- walks on toes on one side of body
- holds arm stiffly and bent
- excessive tip-toeing when walking

- sits with weight to one side
- uses predominately one hand for play
- one leg may be stiff

* 90% of babies do this before these ages. Remember to correct your child's age for prematurity.

Figure 18.4   Comparative silhouettes of infants and toddlers following normal developmental patterns and those with developmental delays.
Reproduced by permission of the Illinois Chapter of the American Academy of Pediatrics and the Pathways Foundation.

into action. If these social prompts fail, the child should be passively positioned and moved to complete an engineered task. To passively move a child, assume one or more of the points of control and move the child through the necessary sequences of a prescribed movement. Encourage the child to "share" in the work required until the child can complete a movement task independent of the teacher.

Often, the infant or toddler with established risk will require the use of bolsters, wedges, pillows, or blankets to maintain proper positions. To overcome the downward pull of gravity, a wedge or bolster can be placed under the arms. From this position the head can be held up to enable focus on objects placed at midline.

Some positions and techniques are contraindicated. The familiar W sitting position should be avoided because it aggravates flexor hypertonicity. It is preferable for the child to sit in straight-leg or sailor style or, if possible, on a low bench.

Practice for Strength and Control

After the child has received tone normalization and has been correctly positioned, he/she should practice strength and motor control. For large muscles, typical strength and motor control goals involve head control, trunk control, protective extension reactions, sitting, mobility on the floor, rising to stand with support, and standing. After upright posture is developed, more advanced goals include walking, running, jumping, and stair climbing.

Practice for strength and control should occur in four positions: prone, supine, sidelying, and upright. In the prone position, the goal is to teach head and trunk control, which will culminate in the child's ability to move forward with creeping skills. Movement from the prone position begins with the child being placed stomach down on a flat firm surface, such as a blanket covered pallet or mat. The child's ability to raise the head and trunk against gravity is a prerequisite for crawling and creeping.

The development of head control from prone involves several sequential steps. Use an interesting toy to motivate the child to raise the head so that the nose and chin clear the blanket and allow the child to see or grasp the toy. Arms and legs should be in a flexed position. The child should learn to hold the position at 45 degrees or higher for approximately 20 seconds. During practice, the child should raise the arms and legs from the blanket for sustained periods. Head control should be practiced while the child is bearing weight on elbows in the prone position.

Practice for trunk control from the prone position involves rolling from stomach to back, exhibiting forward protective extension, pivoting, pulling, and precreeping skills. First, the child should be encouraged to roll from the prone to supine position. Verbal and passive prompts may be necessary. Second, plan reaching techniques with toys that will require the child to pivot. Reaching and pulling can be taught as the child, supported with one arm, reaches forward to bat or grasp an interesting toy. Slight resistance can be offered so that the child must pull the object to midline. Later, the child can be encouraged to grasp the object by reaching across the body's midline.

As the child gains experience, head control, and the prerequisite limb and trunk strength, creeping skills should be taught and nurtured from the prone position. The first objective is for the child to assume the classic front leaning position with arms extended and head held high. With experience, the child is then encouraged to assume the quad position with hands and knees readied for creeping. Initially the child should be encouraged to rock back and forth from this position.

The child should also receive practice in the supine and sidelying positions. Practice goals include helping the child perform movement tasks while maintaining stability of the neck, trunk, shoulders, and hips. From these positions the child should be taught to bring the arms and hands to midline for exploration. One caution: The supine position is not recommended for a child with excessively high or low tone. For hypertonic children, the supine positions allow muscles to stiffen and extend rather than relax and flex. For hypotonic children, the muscles become even more flaccid and limp. Thus, if children are excessively hypertonic or hypotonic, the sidelying and semireclined positions should be used but not the supine position.

With the head at midline, the hands should be allowed to come to midline and to the mouth. Encourage the child to repeatedly bend and straighten the arms and legs while in the supine position. Engage the child in active play so that the arms and legs are moved into both extended and flexed positions. It is important to smile and laugh with the child as activities are performed.

Mastering upright positions is the culminating goal of the MCF-P (see Table 18.2 for a sample lesson with the goal of achieving independent sitting). Important goals include standing, walking,

Table 18.2 Sample Prescriptive Meaning Curriculum Framework (MCF-P) Lesson for Gross Motor Development

Scenario:	Beth is 9 months old and is environmentally and biologically at risk. The case worker indicated that Beth was born prematurely, had low birth weight, and was tactile defensive. Her mom admitted to frequent cocaine and alcohol usage during the pregnancy. The mom works but is unmarried. Beth stays with her grandmother during the day. Beth cannot sit without support, but she can maintain a straight back and hold her head up.
Goal:	To achieve independent sitting.
Subgoals:	Tactile responsiveness, reaching, midline crossing with arms.
Objective:	To sit without support while using the arms to reach for a toy.
Environment:	Use a 4' × 8' padded and covered gym mat with a bright orange ball and a pop-up clown, Beth's favorites. The toys should be out of Beth's vision.
Prelesson consideration:	Gain Beth's confidence with socialization activities. Talk with her, smile, tell her how pretty she looks. Both the teacher and the grandmother "settle down" on the mat with Beth and assist her with the sitting posture. After a few minutes of playing, smiling, and laughing, the teacher lightly touches Beth on the nose, the shoulder, and the hand to help overcome Beth's tactile defensiveness.
Lesson:	With Beth in a playful mood, show her the ball. Ask her to reach for the ball. Ask her to return the ball. Make the ball disappear and reappear. Put the ball in different locations that will require Beth to reach forward and to the side and to pivot from the waist. Remind her grandmother to provide as little support as possible. Teach the grandmother how to sense Beth's muscles and when Beth can perform sitting without assistance. Discontinue the activity before Beth loses interest. Change Beth to a different sitting position. Put away the ball and introduce the pop-up clown. Encourage Beth to reach across her body's midline to touch the clown's nose. If necessary, ask her grandmother to gently hold the right arm and place the clown on Beth's right side. Ask Beth to reach for the clown with her left hand. Vary the procedure so that both arms are utilized in all directions.
Reinforcement:	Celebrate early reaching and sitting accomplishments with enthusiasm. As success is achieved, celebrate later success less frequently. Teach the child to gain satisfaction from task completion rather than to please the teacher or the grandmother. Continually increase the requirements for teacher celebration.
Criteria:	When the child can sit without support, arms free, back straight, and head held up for 5 minutes and can freely rotate at the waist, the child has mastered sitting.
New goal:	The child is ready to move to a new goal, such as pulling up to a stand.

running, and jumping. Balance and axial goals include bending, stooping, and maintaining and regaining balance.

Strength and control combined with the psychological boost gained from mastering prone and supine positions encourage the child to assume the upright posture. The teacher should be aware, however, that some ITD individuals will never achieve full independence for standing and walking.

From a seated position on a mat, the child should practice rising to a standing position. Initially the child will sit, using arms for support, then the child will learn to sit with the support of trunk muscles alone. Next, teach the child to pull to a standing position. A toy placed on a stable chair or table can provide the motivation. After a child has mastered standing, suggest sideward stepping while holding a support. With increased confidence, the child can be taught to stoop and pick up objects of interest, first with and then without support. The child then stands without the need for support. When furniture support is removed, the teacher may need to support the child's hips. Finally, the child walks independently.

Variations on basic walking include sideward and backward walking. One technique is to place a favorite push toy on a table. Sideward walking is reinforced as the child pushes the toy along the table. The teacher can invent other situations that require sideward and backward walking.

Advanced locomotor skills include running, stair climbing, and jumping. Running skills begin when the child can walk without support. At first, running will be stiff and awkward. Running for children with hypertonicity may be contraindicated if the behavior elicits excessive stiffening of the legs.

To foster climbing, 6-inch high by 6-inch deep climbing steps with railings may be used. Initially, the child can be allowed to climb and descend stairs one step at a time (marking time) while holding the rail. The objective is to ascend and descend without rail support, using cross lateral stepping.

Encourage the child to jump from low platforms and by performing jumping activities on rebound boards and minitramps. If the child is unable to imitate a jump demonstration, bend and extend the child's legs to teach the jumping motion.

Static and dynamic balance is nurtured and taught in conjunction with standing and locomotor practice. As a child gains confidence, he/she can be allowed to perform tasks that involve balance platforms, beams, and minitramps. Toys that require the toddler to perform axial movements that involve bending, reaching, stooping, and stretching can be strategically placed in the environment. Finally, activities that require the child to squeeze through openings, stoop and reach for objects, and stretch or bend to complete an "engineered" task can be arranged in obstacle courses.

For both transactional and prescriptive versions of the MCF, inspect the environment for safety and structure prior to use. Assemble toys, adaptive equipment, and other items necessary for the lesson. Have latex gloves, diapers, and disinfectants available for cleaning body fluids. If the strategy is transdisciplinary, the team should review the day's sequence of activities and determine each member's intervention role.

SUMMARY

For infants and toddlers a physical-education-oriented "meaning curriculum framework" is recommended for providing early motor intervention. The framework is activity- and child-centered and is based on the premise that all children learn best when engaged in personally meaningful motor activity that involves action and adventure, but that concurrently provides prevention and remediation. For best results, the MCF should be integrated into a transdisciplinary strategy that is team-based, includes parents as partners, focuses on family needs, and emphasizes collaborative decision making and convergent assessment and evaluation. For more severely disabled children, the MCF should incorporate tone normalization, positioning and handling techniques, and activities for muscular strength and motor control conducted in prone, supine, sidelying, and upright positions, but within the MCF philosophy.

BIBLIOGRAPHY

Bagnato, S., & Neisworth, J. (1991). *Assessment for early intervention: Best practices for professionals.* New York: Guilford Press.

Bricker, D., & Cripe, J. (1988). *An activity-based approach to early intervention.* Glenview, IL: Scott Foresman.

Copeland, M.E., & Kimmel, J.R. (1989). *Evaluation and management of infants and young children with developmental disabilities.* Baltimore: Brookes.

Deal, A., Dunst, C., & Trivett, C. (1989). A flexible and functional approach to developing individualized family support plans. *Infants and Young Children: An Interdisciplinary Journal of Special Care Practices,* **1**(4), 32–43.

Federal Register. (1986). Public Law 99-457: Education for the Handicapped Act Amendments of 1986, » 671 [a], 1146–1150.

Gallahue, D. (1989). *Understanding motor development: Infants, children, adolescent* (2nd ed.). Indianapolis: Benchmark Press.

Garwood, S., & Sheehan, R. (1989). *Designing a comprehensive early intervention system: The challenge of Public Law 99-457.* Austin, TX: Pro-Ed.

Jewett, A., & Bain, L. (1985). *The curriculum process in physical education.* Dubuque, IA: Brown.

Rist, M. (1990). The shadow children. *Research Bulletin,* 9. Bloomington, IN: Phi Delta Kappa, Center for Evaluation, Development and Research.

Surburg, P. (1988). Are adapted physical educators ready for the students with AIDS? *Adapted Physical Activity Quarterly,* **5**, 259–263.

Thelen, E. (1979). Rhythmical stereotypies in normal human infants. *Animal Behavior,* **27**, 699–715.

Thurman, S., & Widerstrom, A. (1990). A genetics primer for early service providers. *Infants and Young Children,* **2**(1), 37–48.

Ulrich, B. (1984). The effects of stimulation programs on the development of high-risk infants: A review of research. *Adapted Physical Activity Quarterly,* **1**, 68–80.

Widerstrom, A., Mowder, B., & Sandall, S. (1991). *At-risk and handicapped newborns and infants.* Englewood Cliffs, NJ: Prentice Hall.

Wolery, M., & Dyk, L. (1984). Arena assessment: Description and preliminary social validity data. *Journal of the Association for the Severely Handicapped*, **9**, 231–235.

RESOURCES

Curriculum Packages

Several commercial companies and publishing houses have developed complete curriculum sequences in the forms of guides, books, or kits. Most include a discussion of the following: theoretical frame of reference, developmental issues, an assessment system specific to the guide, recommended teaching activities. Some current resources include the following:

1. *Teaching the young child with motor delays: A guide for parents and professionals.* (1986). Pro-Ed, 5341 Industrial Oaks Boulevard, Austin, TX 78757.

2. *The Carolina Curriculum for Disabled Infants and Infants at Risk* (2nd ed.) (1991). Paul H. Brookes, P.O. Box 10624, Baltimore, MD 21285-0624.

3. *Gross motor activities.* (1984). Maryland State Department of Special Education. State Department Publications. Annapolis, MD 21400.

4. *System to Plan Early Childhood Services (SPECS).* (1990). American Guidance Service, Circle Pines, MN 55014-1796.

5. *Hawaii Early Learning Profile (HELP).* (1987). VORT, P.O. Box 60880, Palo Alto, CA 94306.

Equipment Companies

Many ideas for positioning, teaching relaxation, and motor activity selection can be gained from catalogs of equipment companies that feature products for infants and toddlers. Two helpful catalogs follow:

1. *ABC, Achieving Basic Concepts with products for sensory integration, inclusion, and instruction.* 1994 Catalog. J.A. Preston, P.O. Box 89, Jackson, MI 49204-0089.

2. *Rifton: For people with disabilities.* 1994 Catalog. P.O. Box 901, Rifton, NY 12471-0901.

CHAPTER 19

Preschool Adapted Physical Education

Dale A. Ulrich

It's 8:30 a.m. on September 1 and Ms. Cloyd, a new physical education teacher, is attending her first faculty in-service workshop. The workshop is designed to make any new teaching assignments and to have all teachers discuss the curricular modifications that have been made since the end of the previous year. It also provides time for teachers in each content area to share information that they have found helpful in working with specific students. Ms. Cloyd is given a copy of her teaching schedule, which includes 10 classes each day at Chapman Elementary School. She notices that Mrs. Cole's class is highlighted on her schedule and that it meets three times a week. She asks Mrs. Riggen, the principal, if there is anything special about this class. Mrs. Riggen replies that Mrs. Cole's class is the new preschool class for young children who have developmental disabilities. Eight students are enrolled in the class, and one paraprofessional has been assigned to assist Mrs. Cole. The children are ages 3 to 5. Mrs. Riggen tells Ms. Cloyd that her responsibility is to provide the motor development services three days a week for 30 minutes each session and to provide Mrs. Cole with lessons that can be implemented on the other two days. She also recommends that she meet with Mrs. Cole during the workshop to learn more about the children. While meeting with Mrs. Cole, Ms. Cloyd learns that two of the children have Down syndrome, one has cerebral palsy, one exhibits characteristics common to autism, one has a hearing disability, and three have communication disorders. She also learns that minimal information

is available concerning the current level of performance in the motor domain for most of the children. Mrs. Cole attempts to comfort Ms. Cloyd by telling her that they will have to learn more about the children as the year progresses. As Ms. Cloyd sits through the rest of the workshop, she realizes that she has less than a week to prepare.

At 1 a.m. Ms. Cloyd is trying to get to sleep, but she keeps tossing and turning, thinking about her new job and specifically about the preschoolers with developmental disabilities. Given that she has not taught preschoolers before and that she only has minimal experience working with children with disabilities, anxiety results in a restless night. After breakfast she recalls having an adapted physical education course two years earlier and that she purchased a textbook for the course. After looking through her box of old textbooks she recalls selling the book back to the bookstore. After another restless night she decides to call the professor she had for that course at Indiana University, Dr. Collier, and ask him two important questions: What skills do I teach these preschoolers, and what are the best teaching practices to employ?

This chapter is designed to address the two questions posed by Ms. Cloyd concerning the design, implementation, and evaluation of quality motor development services for preschool children with developmental disabilities in the typical elementary school building. Given that this is the fastest-growing program in U.S. public schools, more elementary physical education teachers will be given responsibility for implementing the motor development services for this population. Developmental disability as defined in Public Law 101-476 is a severe, chronic disability initiated prior to the age of 22 that continues throughout a person's life, resulting in significant functional limitations in several developmental areas (cognition, motor, social, communication). Children who experience mental retardation, Down syndrome, autism, and cerebral palsy usually have developmental disabilities. This chapter will discuss current practices in assessment and programming that are appropriate for young children. It is important to recognize that children ages 3 to 5 with disabilities are extremely heterogeneous, making it impossible to recommend strategies that will prove effective for *all* children under *all* conditions. General goals of the preschool program can include such areas as the development of fundamental motor skills and patterns, preacademic skills, social and play skills, and communication skills. This chapter begins with information on assessment because it is an important element for implementing quality programs to preschoolers with disabilities. It should not be interpreted that all preschool programs are totally diagnostic and prescriptive in nature. Assessment provides a good foundation for making instructional decisions.

ASSESSMENT

Assessment is a primary teaching competency that must be acquired by all teachers regardless of the content that is taught. Assessment is defined as the collection of student information to aid in making accurate decisions about a child (McLoughlin & Lewis, 1990). The most common decisions that must be made concerning a young child with a disability relate to screening, eligibility, program planning, and monitoring progress. Screening involves all children in a school district where you look for youngsters who appear to exhibit motor skill problems. Children who are identified during screening are referred for more in-depth evaluation. As a result of the evaluation, a decision is made regarding their eligibility status. If their motor performance indicates that they are experiencing a significant deficit in their motor skills (e.g., more than 1.5 standard deviations below average for their age), they will become eligible for adapted physical education services. For program planning, it is necessary to determine a child's current level of performance in the motor domain. In general, the primary task is to determine which

motor behaviors a child can currently perform (stand, walk, run, jump, climb, etc.). In monitoring progress, an attempt is made to document improvement in skill level and to record new motor behaviors that have emerged since instruction was initiated.

All these assessment tasks can and should be employed with all students, not just those with disabilities. The remainder of this section will address several practices that can be employed in determining current level of performance that should result in quality program planning. Other assessment ideas have been presented in chapters 3 and 4.

ASSESSING CURRENT LEVEL OF PERFORMANCE

The determination of a child's current level of performance in the motor domain can be achieved by administering a standardized test or through informal behavior observation. Current professional guidelines and federal special education laws encourage teachers to combine both approaches in making decisions about a child's entry-level performance.

Standardized Tests

Given that most physical education teachers working at the preschool and elementary level have many classes scheduled each day, the administration of a standardized test offers a method of assessment that is easier and less time-consuming than informal motor behavior observation. The teacher arranges the environment so that it matches the standardized conditions established for each motor skill test item, then scores the child's performance under those conditions. The standardization of testing conditions permits a teacher to make performance comparisons across children.

The **Test of Gross Motor Development (TGMD)** (Ulrich, 1985) is a good example of a test that can be used in determining the current level of performance. This test was designed to measure a child's movement pattern when performing 12 locomotor and object control skills. A mature pattern consisting of three or four specific movement behaviors was established for each of the 12 skills. The teacher is required to observe the child perform three trials of each skill and determine whether the child's performance matches the movement behaviors listed for the mature pattern at least two out of three trials. The test assumes that the teacher has developed adequate observation skills and is able to distinguish when a motor behavior is demonstrated correctly. Figure 19.1 provides an example of a completed score sheet for the TGMD.

Statements concerning a child's current level of performance can consist of a percentile score or a listing of motor behaviors that the child can perform. A percentile score of 10 on the locomotor subtest of the TGMD suggests that when compared to other children of similar age, this child currently displays only a few motor behaviors. A listing of motor behaviors that were performed correctly will provide more specific information for planning instruction. When the teacher notices that the child displays additional motor behaviors, these behaviors can be added to the list. This method meets the requirements for developing a quality individualized education plan (IEP), as discussed in chapter 3.

Informal Motor Behavior Observation

The primary criticism against the use of a test with standardized conditions for assessing young children with developmental disabilities is that children do not live, work, or play under standardized conditions. Early childhood special educators suggest that assessment procedures and conditions should match real world conditions if you want to get a valid measure of what the child typically does during play activity. Based on this suggestion it is more appropriate to use informal procedures that can be modified for individual children when observing their physical activity. The two most promising best practices for informal assessment of motor skills (and many other developmental skills) include play-based assessment (Linder, 1990) and ecological inventories (Brown, Nietupski, & Hamre-Nietupski, 1976).

Play-based assessment (PBA) is a very functional approach to assessing and programming for children with developmental deficits. PBA is conducted in an environment that elicits motor behavior and that is familiar to the child. A good example would be the elementary school playground with swings, slides, climbing equipment, and sandboxes. This same environment usually has a variety of balls available. The stimuli present in most playgrounds will elicit play behavior from most preschool children and provides the necessary motivation children need to display their best motor performance. This cannot be said about the standardized conditions of most tests. Young children

typically get bored before the test is completed. In the PBA approach, the professional who is responsible for completing the observation of a specific child will take a position so they can see and hear everything that takes place. The task of the observer is to record the motor behaviors displayed by the child and to record the environmental conditions (physical and social) that elicited the motor behavior. Figure 19.2 presents the results of a PBA for a 5-year-old child with Down syndrome. The results of PBA are easily transformed into individualized instructional objectives. For the child who was observed in Figure 19.2 it would be appropriate to work on improving his stair climbing pattern and to provide many opportunities for Devon to initiate positive social interactions with his peers while playing in the sandbox.

Linder's 1990 book on transdisciplinary play-based assessment provides a wealth of information for setting up and implementing a PBA session. She assists professionals in observing the current level of performance in the cognitive, social, communication, and motor domains. This book should be required reading for all professionals responsible for assessing young children with or without disabilities. It provides insightful suggestions for maintaining a high level of flexibility in the assessment procedures used with young children, which is the most important characteristic needed by professionals.

An ecological inventory is an assessment strategy that provides information on which skills the young child displays while encountering specific environments. A global play environment that most children encounter 5 days each week is the preschool or elementary school playground. The global environment consists of multiple subenvironments: sandbox, asphalt game area, grassy field, climbing equipment, slides, and swings. Figure 19.3 reflects common pieces of play equipment found on most playgrounds. This particular play equipment provides a stimulus for climbing, jumping, swinging, sliding, and hanging. When conducting an ecological inventory it is necessary to determine which skills are needed by all children to participate in specific subenvironments such as the play equipment area. To participate in activity on the play equipment found in Figure 19.3, the child would need to be able to climb up, over, through, and off equipment, jump off flat surfaces, swing on a tire, slide down a slide, and take turns. Once the skills are identified for a subenvironment, the next task is to determine which skills the young child with a disability can perform. It will be very

The Test of Gross Motor Development

			LOCOMOTOR SKILLS		
Skill	Equipment	Directions	Performance Criteria	1st	2nd
RUN	50 feet of clear space and masking tape, chalk, or other marking device	Mark off two lines 50 feet apart. Instruct student to "run fast" from one line to the other	1. Brief period where both feet are off the ground 2. Arms in opposition to legs, elbows bent 3. Foot placement near or on a line (not flat footed) 4. Nonsupport leg bent approximately 90 degrees (close to buttocks)	1 0 1 0	
GALLOP	A minimum of 30 feet of clear space	Mark off two lines 30 feet apart. Tell student to gallop from one line to the other three times. Tell student to gallop leading with one foot and then the other	1. A step forward with the lead foot followed by a step with the trailing foot to a position adjacent to or behind the lead foot 2. Brief period where both feet are off the ground 3. Arms bent and lifted to waist level 4. Able to lead with the right and left foot	0 1 0 0	
HOP	A minimum of 15 feet of clear space	Ask student to hop three times, first on one foot and then on the other	1. Foot of nonsupport leg is bent and carried in back of the body 2. Nonsupport leg swings in pendular fashion to produce force 3. Arms bent at elbows and swing forward on take off 4. Able to hop on the right and left foot	0 0 0 0	
LEAP	A minimum of 30 feet of clear space	Ask student to leap. Tell him/her to take large steps leaping from one foot to the other	1. Take off on one foot and land on the opposite foot 2. A period where both feet are off the ground (longer than running) 3. Forward reach with arm opposite the lead foot	0 0 0	
HORIZONTAL JUMP	10 feet of clear space and tape or other marking device	Mark off a starting line on the floor, mat, or carpet. Have the student start behind the line. Tell the student to "jump far"	1. Preparatory movement includes flexion of both knees with arms extended behind the body 2. Arms extend forcefully forward and upward, reaching full extension above head 3. Take off and land on both feet simultaneously 4. Arms are brought downward during landing	1 0 1 0	
SKIP	A minimum of 30 feet of clear space, marking device	Mark off two lines 30 feet apart. Tell the student to skip from one line to the other three times	1. A rhythmical repetition of the step-hop on alternate feet 2. Foot of nonsupport leg is carried near surface during hop 3. Arms alternately moving in opposition to legs at about waist level	0 0 0	
SLIDE	A minimum of 30 feet of clear space and masking tape or other marking device	Mark off two lines 30 feet apart. Tell the student to slide from one line to the other three times facing the same direction	1. Body turned sideways to desired direction of travel 2. A step sideways followed by a slide of the trailing foot to a point next to the lead foot 3. A short period where both feet are off the floor 4. Able to slide to the right and to the left side	0 1 0 1	
			LOCOMOTOR SKILLS SUBTEST SCORE	7	

Figure 19.1   An example of a completed score sheet from the TGMD.

The Test of Gross Motor Development (cont.)

			LOCOMOTOR SKILLS			
Skill	Equipment	Directions	Performance Criteria	1st	2nd
TWO-HAND STRIKE	4-6 inch light-weight ball, plastic bat	Toss the ball softly to the student at about waist level. Tell the student to hit the ball "hard." Only count those tosses that are between the student's waist and shoulders.	1. Dominant hand grips bat above non-dominant hand 2. Nondominant side of body faces the tosser (feet parallel) 3. Hip and spine rotation 4. Weight is transferred by stepping with front foot	*1* 0 0 0	
STATIONARY BOUNCE	8-10 inch play-ground ball, hard, flat surface (floor, pavement)	Tell the student to bounce the ball three times using one hand. Make sure the ball is not underinflated. Repeat three separate trials.	1. Contacts ball with one hand at about hip height 2. Pushes ball with fingers (not a step) 3. Ball contacts floor in front of (or to the outside of) foot on the side of the hand being used	0 0 0	
CATCH	6-8 inch sponge ball, 15 feet of clear space, tape or other marking device	Mark off 2 lines 15 feet apart. Student stands on one line and the tosser on the other. Toss the ball underhand directly to student with a slight arc and tell him/her to "catch it with your hands." Only count those tosses that are between student's shoulders and waist.	1. Preparation phase where elbows are flexed and hands are in front of body 2. Arms extend in preparation for ball contact 3. Ball is caught and controlled by hands only 4. Elbows bend to absorb force	*1* 0 0 0	
KICK	8-10 inch plastic or slightly deflated playground ball, 30 feet of clear space, tape or other marking device	Mark off one line 30 feet away from a wall and one that is 20 feet from the wall. Place the ball on the line nearest the wall and tell the student to stand on the other line. Tell the student to kick the ball "hard" toward the wall.	1. Rapid continuous approach to the ball 2. The trunk is inclined backward during ball contact 3. Forward swing of the arm opposite kicking leg 4. Follow through by hopping on the nonkicking foot.	*1* 0 0 0	
OVERHAND THROW	3 tennis balls, a wall, 25 feet of clear space	Tell student to throw the ball "hard" at the wall	1. A downward arc of the throwing arm initiates the wind-up 2. Rotation of hip and shoulder to a point where the nondominant side faces an imaginary target 3. Weight is transferred by stepping with the foot opposite the throwing hand 4. Follow-through beyond ball release diagonally across body toward side opposite throwing arm.	*1* 0 0 0	
			LOCOMOTOR SKILLS SUBTEST SCORE	*3*	

Figure 19.1 *(Continued)*

Child's Name: Devon
Play Environment: Arlington Elementary School Playground
Time of Observation: 10-10:20 Recess

BEHAVIORS OBSERVED	ENVIRONMENTAL CONDITIONS	COMMENTS
A. Locomotion 1. Walking	Hallway, asphalt and grass surface	Alternating pattern, good control, head tilted forward
2. Descending stairs	Hallway stairs (3)	Did not use alternating step pattern but marks time
3. Crawling	Sandbox, retrieving a plastic truck	Alternating pattern, good control
4. Ascending stairs	Hallway stairs (3)	Did not use alternating step pattern but marks time
B. Object Manipulation 1. Two hand grasp 2. Two hand underhand toss 3. Right hand grasp 4. Left hand grasp	8 inch playground ball 8 inch playground ball Small truck, sandbox Small truck, sandbox	Uses right hand for objects on right side of body. Uses left hand for objects on left side of body.
C. Playground Equipment Used 1. Sandbox	Various plastic trucks	Isolated play with trucks while 2 other children were near by
D. Postures Used for Play 1. Standing 2. Sitting 3. Squatting	Hallway, grass and asphalt surface Grass surface, sandbox Sandbox	Wide base of support. One hand support and unsupported. Good Control
E. Social Interactions 1. Teacher 2. Peers	Teacher initiates vocal interaction. 2 other children in sandbox area	Child responds to teacher's question. Child plays alone. Child watches others play

Figure 19.2 Results of a play-based assessment for a preschooler with Down syndrome.

Figure 19.3 An example of common playground equipment that provides a stimulus for many skills.

helpful to note which skills the child performs independently, which skills the child can perform with some physical assistance, and which skills the child cannot perform even with physical assistance. The latter two groups of skills should be the emphasis of your motor skills instruction program. This ecological inventory process should be completed for all subenvironments that are considered relevant on the playground. Other major physical activity environments that the child encounters should also be considered. An example would be the playground area in the child's neighborhood. It will be necessary to involve the child's parents in helping to collect the needed information for this area. Most parents of young children with a disability hold strong aspirations for their child to play with other children in the neighborhood. Most parents will be willing to collect information if a professional provides some guidelines in the form of questions to help focus their observations. Questions could include: Does your child climb up on play equipment? Does your child jump off equipment? Does your child use the slide? Does your child use the swing? Does your child take turns using a busy piece of equipment? Does your child maintain his balance when playing on the equipment? How often did your child fall while playing for 10 minutes? How often did your child initiate verbal interaction with his peers while playing for

10 minutes? Interaction with parents for the purpose of assessment and programming is rapidly becoming an essential best practice.

PROGRAMMING

Programming includes three primary elements: planning, teaching, and monitoring progress. This process can be employed with all children. This section of the chapter will concentrate on providing current best practices in planning and teaching preschoolers with disabilities. Monitoring progress can be completed by following the suggestions given earlier for assessing current level of performance. When monitoring progress you generally observe performance on those skills that were included in the child's IEP. Decisions can be made about future instructional procedures based on the results of monitoring progress.

PROGRAM PLANNING

The most important element in maximizing the rate and amount of learning in preschoolers with disabilities is the quality of planning that takes place prior to and during instruction. Professionals who are involved in teaching young children with disabilities must plan for teaching the *whole* child, including all developmental domains (motor, social, cognitive, and communication). This is the most challenging demand physical educators will face when teaching preschoolers with disabilities. Besides planning specific motor development goals and objectives for each child, the physical educator must be knowledgeable about the goals and objectives identified in the other developmental domains. For example, knowing that a specific child is trying to increase her social interaction skills with peers will help the physical educator know that when this child initiates social contact with a peer, the teacher should provide positive reinforcement. The teacher should also prompt the child to make social contact with other children during the motor activities (performing "high fives" is a good example of social contact). The remainder of this chapter will present information on four best practices that should guide the planning and teaching of motor activities for preschoolers with disabilities.

Selection of Skills With Present and Future Utility

Given that preschoolers with developmental disabilities frequently possess constraints that reduce their rate of learning (an example is mental retardation), it is very important that program planning should identify movement and social skills that the child can use immediately and that will help to develop future skills needed in elementary school. Functional skills have immediate usefulness (Baily & Wolery, 1989) and help to make the child more independent. Functional skills should also facilitate integration of young children with disabilities into games and play activities with normally developing peers. Selection of functional skills should be individualized for each child. Examples of typical functional skills for young children with disabilities are presented in Table 19.1. All of these skills are necessary to maximize the probability of success in kindergarten and early elementary school. Other examples of skills that are appropriate for preschool physical education can be found in the professional literature (Dummer, Connor, & Goodway, in press). Teachers should consult the parents of a child with a disability to determine what aspirations they have for skill acquisition. They are generally a good source of information.

Activity-Based Approach to Instruction

The fundamental concept of activity-based instruction (ABI) is to teach skills in the context of a common activity. Consideration must be given to the activity context in which the skills are typically displayed. For example, the physical education teacher can teach the object projection skills of throwing, kicking, and batting during a kickball and teeball activity. The teacher can teach the skill of rolling a ball in a bowling activity where a small playground ball is used to knock down milk cartons. Ascending and descending stairs can be taught when traveling to and from the playground. The rationale of ABI is that skills are not performed in isolation but rather are integrated with specific games, activities, and routines. Teaching skills in isolation has been shown to result in splinter skills that children with mental retardation or autism will not generalize to functional activities that they encounter outside the gymnasium. One advantage to adopting an ABI approach is that multiple skill objectives across several developmental domains can be embedded in a single activity (Bricker & Woods-Cripe, 1992). In a bowling activity, a preschooler with Down syndrome could work on several functional skills presented in Table 19.1. This activity is appropriate for learning to (1) project objects, (2) manipulate objects of various sizes (require the child to roll various balls), (3) demonstrate independent locomotion (require the child to retrieve the rolled ball), (4) model the teacher rolling a ball, (5) play with peers (have two or three children taking turns bowling), and (6) initiate positive interactions with peers (have the child hand the ball to peers and display a "high five" after hitting the bowling pins). This approach requires that the teacher be aware of the various skill objectives in the preschooler's program plans. This can be facilitated by keeping a note card close by for each child that lists the individual program objectives.

Preschool physical activities can involve movement exploration, swimming, games, dances, and partner activities. The primary intent is to improve the amount of control that children display over their body movements. Appropriate activities for a preschool motor development program are presented in Table 19.2. These activities can be modified for individual children.

The major difference in teaching preschoolers rather than older children will be in the teaching style that is employed. When teaching elementary physical education teachers are more inclined to expect children to learn a mature pattern of movement (throw, kick, bat). Teachers provide feedback to children on their movement patterns during activities. Teachers direct the activity more during this level of education. With preschoolers, it is

Table 19.1 Examples of Functional Skills for Preschool-Aged Children With Disabilities

Functional skills
Ability to demonstrate independent locomotion
Ability to control posture in various positions
Ability to receive and control objects in a game activity
Ability to manipulate objects of various sizes and textures
Ability to project objects in a game activity
Ability to project the body on a three-wheeler
Ability to model teacher and peer behavior
Ability to ascend and descend stairs
Ability to play with peers
Ability to communicate needs
Ability to initiate positive interactions with peers
Ability to follow simple directions
Ability to sit still for brief periods during instruction

more advisable to allow the child to explore various ways or patterns of movement for accomplishing a task. For example, if the goal is to project a ball toward a target, children may choose to throw overhanded, underhanded, or two-handed. They may also choose to kick the object or strike it with their hands. All of these movement patterns are acceptable. The teacher's objective is to have children explore all the possibilities for achieving the task and allow them to choose the ones that are best for them. In other words, the teacher should exert less direction and promote experimentation. The teacher must remember that there is no right or wrong way. The important factor is whether the task is achieved; in other words, did the child project the object to the goal? It is also critical that, when planning activities for preschoolers, the teacher end each session with an exercise to calm the children down before returning them to the preschool classroom. A good example would be to have all the students sit down in a circle while one or two children demonstrate or explain what they learned that day or what they liked most about the activities.

Vary Task Difficulty for Individual Preschoolers

Teachers should expect to find greater levels of variability in performance among preschoolers with developmental disabilities than in those without

disabilities. The range of skill levels will be great in most preschool classes serving children with disabilities. The level of difficulty that a preschooler experiences in completing a movement task is determined primarily by the child's developmental level in many biological systems and the task conditions under which the child is asked to perform (Keogh & Sugden, 1985). The human body is comprised of many biological subsystems that interact when performing a movement. Those most likely involved in movement include the muscles, nerves, skeleton, vision, proprioception, posture, and motivation. These subsystems develop at various rates. A child may exhibit a less mature movement pattern (e.g., jumping) because one or more of the biological subsystems are delayed and act as a constraint to performing at a higher level of coordination. For example, if the child is delayed in developing appropriate strength (muscular subsystem), he or she will have trouble jumping. The physical education teacher's task is to look for biological constraints that affect performance, then change the task conditions so the child can achieve the task most of the time. In jumping, the teacher who notices that the child is not strong should ask the child to jump over an obstacle that is lower than for other children. As the child develops strength, the obstacle can be raised. Many novice physical education teachers require all preschoolers to perform a movement task under identical task conditions. A best instructional practice is to vary the task conditions for each child based on

Table 19.2 Examples of Typical Activities for Preschool-Aged Children

Activity	Description
Copy cats	Children imitate movements of others.
Moving to music	Various locomotor movements performed to music.
Over, under, around, and through	Children move through various obstacle courses.
Tightrope walker	Children walk on tape placed on floor pretending to be tightrope walkers.
Milk carton dice	Children role the dice to determine the number of times to perform a movement.
Milk carton soccer	Children dribble their milk carton across the room and kick it into a goal.
Simon Says	When Simon says to perform a movement, all children should attempt the movement.
Bowling	Set up milk cartons or two-litter jugs as pins and have pairs of children alternate as bowler and pin setter.
Carpet square activity	Children jump and leap over squares, play musical squares, and toss newspaper balls to children standing on their square.
Going for a ride	Children ride three- and four-wheelers while negotiating obstacle courses.
Duck, Duck, Goose	Children sit in a circle with one child walking around the outside of the circle touching each child on the head saying "duck." When the child says "goose," that child stands up and chases after the other child, trying to tag her before she gets back to the open seat.
Box activity	Children climb in and out of various sized boxes. Boxes can also be used as targets for throwing and kicking.
Balloon activity	Children perform movements with balloons. Balloons also serve as targets for throwing.
Hoop activity	Hoops are used while performing various locomotor movements. Hoops are also used as targets for throwing and kicking.

his or her changing levels of development. This practice of individualizing task conditions will result in a higher level of motivation and learning.

Promote Social Interaction With Peers

The Council for Exceptional Children has stated that any educational program designed for preschoolers with disabilities should be implemented in integrated, community-based environments (Division of Early Childhood, 1987). Preschoolers with disabilities receive the services and programming they need in the school located in their neighborhood. In this context most preschoolers are not disabled, and

the necessary supports and assistance to teachers, children, and families are provided (Institute for the Study of Developmental Disabilities, 1990). Social learning theory suggests that children with disabilities will imitate the more advanced skills modeled by their normally developing peers (Vincent, Brown, & Getz-Sheftel, 1981). Research indicates that simply placing children with and without disabilities together does not automatically result in social interaction between the two groups. Teachers must promote desired levels of social interaction.

The first strategy to increase social interaction is to prompt the student with a disability to initiate social contact with normally developing peers and then provide positive reinforcement (Devoney, Guralnick, & Rubin, 1974; Strain, Schores, & Kerr, 1976). Second, structure activities so that social interaction is required. Students can perform an activity in pairs. Tossing a ball or a bean bag to a classmate or playing a game where one student takes a turn bowling while the other sets up the pins requires social interaction. Third, prompt and reinforce normally developing peers to initiate social interaction with their disabled peers. The physical education teacher should include a periodic measure of social interaction as part of the instructional assessment program. This can be achieved by noting the frequency of social interactions that take place between preschoolers with and without a disability within a set interval of time.

SUMMARY

More elementary physical education teachers will be required to provide services to preschool classes serving children with disabilities. These preschool classes will consist of a heterogeneous group of children with a variety of disabilities. The teacher must be prepared to determine each child's present level of motor performance employing standardized motor skill tests and informal motor behavior assessment procedures. Play-based assessment and ecological inventories are appropriate methods for determining what developmental skills the child possesses. The motor development instruction will be founded on functional goals and objectives that will improve the children's independence and help prepare them for kindergarten and elementary school. Many preschoolers with disabilities will need to learn how to play; therefore, instruction should be planned to facilitate the development of play skills. Physical education teachers will need to be concerned about helping children learn skills in all developmental areas, not just the motor domain. Teachers will also need to facilitate social interaction between preschoolers with and without disabilities. Activities that promote social interaction will need to be planned, and when interaction occurs, children should be reinforced.

BIBLIOGRAPHY

Baily, D.B., & Wolery, M. (1989). *Assessing infants and preschoolers with handicaps*. Columbus, OH: Merrill.

Bricker, D., & Woods-Cripe, J.J. (1992). *An activity-based approach to early intervention*. Baltimore: Brookes.

Brown, L., Nietupski, J., & Hamre-Nietupski, S. (1976). The criterion of ultimate functioning. In M.A. Thomas (Ed.), *Hey, don't forget about me!* Reston, VA: CEC Information Center.

Devoney, C., Guralnick, M.J., & Rubin, H. (1974). Integrating handicapped and nonhandicapped preschool children: Effects on social play. *Childhood Education, 50*, 360–364.

Division of Early Childhood. (1987). *Least restrictive environment and social integration for young children with handicaps*. DEC White Paper. Reston, VA: Council for Exceptional Children.

Dummer, G.M., Conner, F.J., & Goodway, J.D. (in press). A physical education curriculum for preschool and preprimary impaired students. *Teaching Exceptional Children*.

Institute for the Study of Developmental Disabilities. (1990). *Best practices in integration*. Bloomington: Indiana University.

Keogh, J., & Sugden, D. (1985). *Movement skill development*. New York: Macmillan.

Linder, T.W. (1990). *Transdisciplinary play-based assessment*. Baltimore: Brookes.

McLoughlin, J.H., & Lewis, R.B. (1990). *Assessing special students* (3rd ed.). New York: Macmillan.

Strain, P.S., Schores, R.E., & Kerr, M.M. (1976). An experimental analysis of "spillover" effects on the social interaction of behaviorally handicapped preschool children. *Journal of Applied Behavior Analysis, 9*, 31–40.

Ulrich, D.A. (1985). *The test of gross motor development*. Austin, TX: Pro-Ed.

Vincent, L.J., Brown, L., & Getz-Sheftel, M. (1981). Integrating handicapped and typical children during the preschool years: The definition of best educational practice. *Topics in Early Childhood Special Education, 1*, 17–24.

RESOURCES

Bos, C.S., Vaughn, S., & Levine, L.M. (1990). *Instructional activities for children at risk (motor domain)*. Allen, TX: DLM. An excellent resource for instructional activities for children ages 2–6.

Craft, D.H. (1994). Implications of inclusion for physical education. *Journal of Physical Education, Recreation and Dance, 65*(1), 54–55. Discusses various reasons for including children with disabilities in regular physical education programs.

Eichstaedt, C.B., & Lavay, B.W. (1992). *Physical activity for individuals with mental retardation: Infancy through adulthood*. Champaign, IL: Human Kinetics. Chapter 9 in this book presents valuable information on preschool programs for children with mental retardation.

Gable, R.A., & Warren, S.F. (1993). *Strategies for teaching students with mild to severe mental retardation*. Baltimore: Brookes. This book presents information on teaching strategies that generalize to instruction in all developmental domains.

Gilmore, P.J. (1993). *Kids in motion: An early childhood movement education program.* Tucson, AZ: Therapy Skill Builders. Specific goals, objectives, and activities are provided for young children.

Hanson, M.J., & Harris, S.R. (1986). *Teaching the young child with motor delays.* Austin, TX: Pro-Ed. This book presents many excellent suggestions for teaching children with physical disabilities. Positioning and handling techniques are presented.

Johnson-Martin, N.M., Attermeier, S.M., & Hacker, B. (1990). *The Carolina curriculum for preschoolers with special needs.* Baltimore, MD: Paul H.Brookes, Provides curricular materials for preschoolers with special needs including materials encompassing motor development.

McCall, R. (1994). An inclusive preschool physical education program. *Journal of Physical Education, Recreation and Dance,* **65**(1), 45–47. An example of an integrated preschool program is presented.

Sher, B. (1992). *Extraordinary play with ordinary things: Recycling everyday materials to build motor skills.* Tucson, AZ: Therapy Skill Builders. Many examples of physical activities using homemade equipment are presented.

Taylor, R.L. (1993). *Assessment of exceptional students: Educational and psychological procedures.* Needham Heights, MA: Allyn & Bacon. A discussion of current assessment procedures for children with disabilities is provided.

Trimble, S. (1992). *Positioning and handling for the child with physical disabilities.* Bloomington, IN: Indiana University, Institute for the Study of Developmental Disabilities. Presents excellent suggestions for managing the child with physical disabilities.

Werder, J.K., & Bruininks, R.H. (1988). *Body skills: A motor development curriculum for children.* Circle Pines, MN: American Guidance Service. Specific goals, objectives, and activities are provided. An assessment scale is also included.

Wessel, J.A. (1980). *I CAN preprimary motor and play skills.* East Lansing, MI: Michigan State University. Specific goals, objectives, activities, and assessment procedures are included.

Activities for Students With Unique Needs

Part IV builds upon and extends from Part III and covers activities associated with adapted physical education and sport. It includes separate chapters on body mechanics and posture; developmental and remedial exercises and activities; rhythms and dance; aquatics; team sports; individual, dual, and cooperative sports; winter sports; and wheelchair performance. Although the exact topical coverage of each chapter is influenced by the nature of the activities discussed, there are several common threads. First, to the extent relevant and appropriate, the chapters identify skills, lead-up activities, modifications, and variations. In many instances these include ideas associated with or procedures currently used in established organized sport programs. Second, some chapters provide information on organized sport programs. Third, most of the chapters address the integration of disabled and nondisabled youngsters in activities.

The reader's attention is directed to the many techniques that can be used, separately or in combination, in adapting activities. These include, but are not limited to, modifying or reducing skill or effort demands of an activity; "giving handicaps"; sharing responsibilities; providing physical assistance or assistive devices; reducing space and distance requirements; modifying facilities, equipment, or rules; and modifying activities to emphasize abilities rather than disabilities. These and other techniques have many interesting applications. Examples include striking stationary rather than moving objects, throwing light rather than heavy objects, striking with large rather than small implements, bowling with a handrail guide or ramp, playing on a shortened field, using hand rather than foot cranks or pedals to move a tricycle, and running or responding to a sound cue instead of a visual cue. The importance of the use of wheelchairs in physical education and sport is recognized by including an entire chapter on ways of enhancing performance when using wheelchairs. In reading the chapters, record all the techniques for modifying activities that you can find; then use these techniques in adapting activities for students with unique needs.

CHAPTER 20

Body Mechanics and Posture

Luke E. Kelly

Have you ever noticed individuals wearing shoes where one shoe has a thicker sole than the other or individuals who appear to have one shoulder higher than the other? Have you ever heard the terms *pigeon-toed* or *hump-backed?* These are examples of common postural deviations. The purpose of this chapter is to describe the common postural deviations that physical educators will encounter as well as the roles they should play in screening for and correcting these deviations.

The term *good posture* implies appropriate alignment of body segments and body mechanics. Optimal body mechanics are desirable because they allow individuals to maximize their efficiency and minimize the strain placed upon the body, both of which are important for safe and successful performance in physical education and sport. Posture refers to appropriate body mechanics, whether the body is stationary or moving. It should not be thought of only as correct body alignment in standing or sitting. Good posture is a relative term. There are acceptable variations among individuals resulting from differences in body build and composition, and there are marked deviations that clearly require professional attention. Physical educators should be able to identify postural deviations and, where appropriate, to correct them in class.

Mild postural deviations are common and can often be remedied through proper instruction and practice. It is estimated that 70% of all children have mild postural deviations and that 5% have serious ones. The prevalence of serious postural deviations is, unfortunately, much greater among students with disabilities.

Poor posture can result from any one or a combination of factors, such as ignorance, environmental conditions, genetics, physical and/or growth abnormalities, or psychological conditions. In many cases children are unaware that they have poor postures because they do not know what correct postures are and how their postures differ. In other cases, postural deviations can be traced to simple environmental factors such as poorly fitting shoes. In students with disabilities, poor posture can be caused by factors affecting balance (e.g., visual impairments), neuromuscular conditions (e.g., spina bifida and cerebral palsy), or congenital defects (e.g., bone deformities and amputations). Finally, poor posture can occur as a result of attitude or self-concept. Pupils who have a poor body image or lack confidence in their ability to move tend to display defensive postures characterized by poor body alignment.

Physical educators should play an important role in identifying and treating postural deviations. They are often the only teachers in their schools with the opportunity and background to identify and address such problems. Unfortunately, postural screening and treatment are often neglected. This is ironic because the development of kinesthetic awareness and proper body mechanics is fundamental to teaching physical education and is clearly within the domain of physical education as defined in IDEA.

Several excellent posture screening tests are available that involve minimal preparation and equipment to administer. Three examples are the Posture Grid (Adams & McCubbin, 1991), the Iowa Posture Test (Scott & French, 1959), and the New

York Posture Rating Test (New York State Education Department, 1966). Posture screening should be an annual procedure in all physical education programs. Particular attention should be paid to children with disabilities. The appropriate school personnel, as well as the parents or guardians of all children identified as having present and potential postural problems, should be informed and invited to pursue further evaluation. The instructor can remediate most mild postural deviations within the regular physical education program by educating children about proper body mechanics and suggesting exercises that can be performed both in and out of class. Sample exercises are described late in this chapter.

The purpose of the remainder of this chapter is to review some of the specific postural deviations that occur in the spinal column and lower extremities. Implications for adapted physical education, as well as procedures for assessment and treatment, will be discussed for each deviation.

SPINAL COLUMN DEVIATIONS

Viewed from the back, the spinal column should be straight with no lateral (sideways) curves. Any lateral curvature in the back is abnormal and is referred to as *scoliosis*. Viewed from the side, the spinal column has two mild curves. The first natural curve occurs in the thoracic region, where the vertebrae are concave forward (curving slightly in a posterior or outward direction). An extreme curvature in this region is abnormal and is known as *kyphosis*. The second natural curve occurs in the lumbar section, where there is mild forward convexity (inward curvature) of the spine. An extreme curvature in this region is also abnormal and is called *lordosis*. An exaggerated lumbar curve is natural but should disappear by the age of 8.

Scoliosis

Lateral deviations in the spinal column are generally classified according to whether the deviation is structural or nonstructural. Structural deviations are generally related to orthopedic impairments and are permanent or fixed changes in vertebrae alignment that cannot be altered through simple physical manipulation, positioning, or exercise. Nonstructural or functional deviations are those in which the vertebrae can be realigned through positioning and/or removal of the primary cause—such as ignorance or muscle weaknesses—which can be remedied with practice and exercise.

Structural scoliosis is also frequently classified according to the cause of the condition. Although scoliosis has many possible causes, the two most common are labeled *idiopathic* and *neuromuscular*. Idiopathic means that the cause is unknown. Neuromuscular means that the scoliosis is the result of nerve and/or muscle problems.

Structural idiopathic scoliosis occurs in only 2% of all school-age children. Scoliosis usually occurs during the early adolescent years, when children are growing rapidly. This form of scoliosis is characterized by an **S-shaped curve**, usually composed of a major curve and one or two minor curves. The major curve is the one causing the deformity. The minor curves, sometimes referred to as secondary or compensatory curves, usually occur above and/or below the major curve and are the result of the body's attempt to adjust for the major curve. Although both genders appear to be equally affected by this condition, a greater percentage of females have the progressive form that becomes more severe if not altered. The cause of this progressive form of scoliosis is unknown, but there is some evidence that suggests a possible genetic link in females.

A second type of structural scoliosis, more commonly found in children with severe disabilities, is caused by neuromuscular problems. This form of scoliosis is usually characterized by a **C-shaped curve**. In severe cases this form of scoliosis can lead to balance difficulties, pressure on internal organs, and seating problems (pressure sores) for students in wheelchairs.

Nonstructural scoliosis has a number of known causes, primarily skeletal or muscular, and can be characterized by either an **S-** or a **C-curve**. An example of scoliosis with a skeletal cause would be a curve that has resulted from one leg being shorter than the other. An example of scoliosis with a muscular cause would be a curve that has resulted because the muscles on one side of the back have become stronger than those on the other side and have pulled the spinal column out of line. Fortunately, nonstructural scoliosis can usually be effectively treated by correcting the imbalance (e.g., inserting a lift in the child's shoe to equalize the length of the legs or strengthening and stretching the appropriate muscle groups in the back).

Assessment of Scoliosis

Early identification is extremely important for both structural and nonstructural scoliosis so that help can begin and the severity of the curve can be reduced. Scoliosis screening should be conducted annually for all children, particularly from the 3rd through the 10th grade, when the condition is most likely to occur. If a child is suspected of having scoliosis, the parents or guardians as well as other appropriate school personnel should be notified and further evaluation conducted. Students suspected of having scoliosis should be monitored more frequently, approximately every 3 months, to ascertain if the condition is progressing. A scoliosis assessment, which can be performed in less than a minute, involves observing the student shirtless. The assessments should be done individually and by an assessor of the same gender as the children being assessed because children of these ages are usually self-conscious about the changes occurring in their bodies and about being seen undressed.

To perform a scoliosis assessment, check the symmetry of the child's back while the child is standing and then while the child is bent forward. First, from a posterior view with the child standing erect, look for any differences between the two sides of the back, including the following points (see Figure 20.1, rows A–D):

1. Does the spinal column appear straight or curved?

2. Are the shoulders at the same height, or does one appear higher than the other?

3. Are the hips at the same horizontal distance from the floor, or does one appear higher?

4. Is the space between the arms and trunk equal on both sides of the body?

5. Do the shoulder blades protrude evenly, or does one appear to protrude more?

Then ask the child to perform the Adam's position, bent forward at the waist to approximately 90° (Adam's Test; see Figure 20.2). Examine the back from both a posterior and an anterior view for any noticeable differences in symmetry, such as curvature of the spine or one side of the back being higher or lower than the other, particularly in the thoracic and lumbar regions.

Care and Remediation of Scoliosis

The treatment of scoliosis depends on the type and the degree of curvature. Nonstructural scoliosis can frequently be corrected when the cause is identified and the condition remedied through a program of specific exercises and body awareness. With structural scoliosis, the treatment varies according to the degree of curvature. Children

with mild curvatures (less than 20°) are usually given exercise programs to keep the spine flexible and are examined regularly to make sure the curves are not becoming more severe.

Children with more severe curves (20–40°) are usually treated by means of braces or orthotics, which force the spine into better alignment and/or prevent it from deviating further. The Charleston Bending and Milwaukee braces shown in Figure 20.3 are the two most effective and commonly used braces for the treatment of scoliosis. A number of cosmetic braces developed in recent years are made of molded orthoplast and are custom fitted to the individual. These braces are effective in treating mild and moderate curves. One of the major advantages of the orthoplast braces is that they are less conspicuous and tend to be worn more consistently. These braces must be worn continuously until the child reaches skeletal maturity—in many cases, for 4 or 5 years. The brace can be removed for short periods for swimming and bathing. The treatment of scoliosis in persons who are wheelchair bound may also involve modifying the chair to improve alignment and to equalize seating pressures.

In extreme cases of scoliosis, where the curve is greater than 40° or does not respond to bracing, surgery is employed. This usually involves fusing the vertebrae in the affected region by means of bone grafts and implanting a metal rod. Following surgery, a brace must be worn for about a year until the fusion has solidified.

Kyphosis and Lordosis

Abnormal concavity forward (backward curve) in the thoracic region (kyphosis) and abnormal convexity forward (forward curve) in the lumbar region (lordosis) are usually nonstructural and the result of poor posture (see Figure 20.1, rows G–M). These deformities are routinely remedied by exercise programs designed to tighten specific muscle groups and stretch opposing muscle groups and by education designed to make students aware of their present posture, proper body mechanics, and the desired posture.

The physical educator can assess kyphosis and lordosis by observing children from the side under the conditions described previously for scoliosis screening. Look for exaggerated curves in the thoracic and lumbar regions of the spinal column. Kyphosis is usually characterized by a rounded appearance of the upper back. Lordosis is characterized by a hollow back appearance and a protruding abdomen.

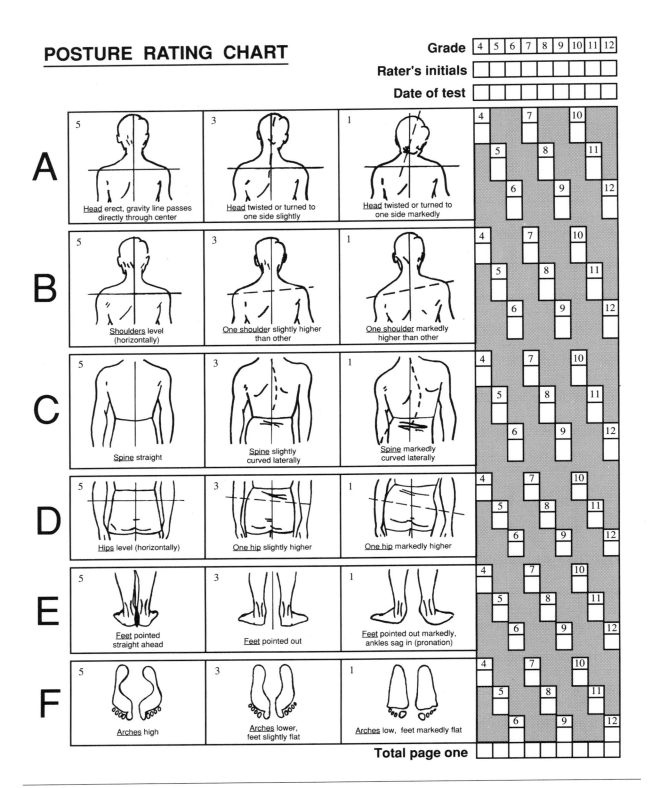

Figure 20.1 The New York State Posture Rating Chart.

From *New York State Physical Fitness Test for Boys and Girls Grades 4–12* by New York State Education Department, 1966, Albany, NY. Copyright by New York State Education Department. Reprinted by permission.

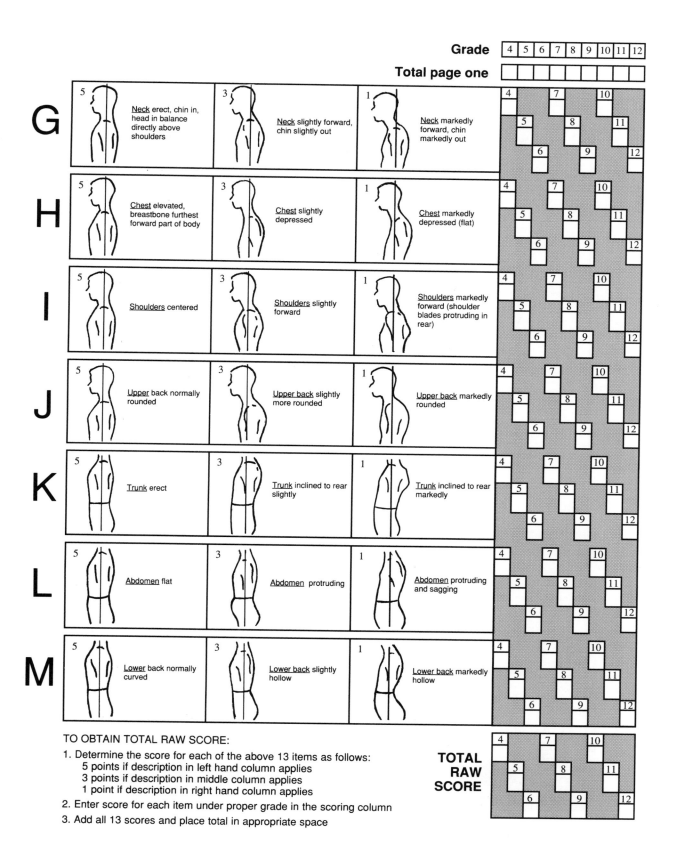

Grade | 4 | 5 | 6 | 7 | 8 | 9 | 10 | 11 | 12 |

Total page one

G
5   Neck erect, chin in, head in balance directly above shoulders
3   Neck slightly forward, chin slightly out
1   Neck markedly forward, chin markedly out

H
5   Chest elevated, breastbone furthest forward part of body
3   Chest slightly depressed
1   Chest markedly depressed (flat)

I
5   Shoulders centered
3   Shoulders slightly forward
1   Shoulders markedly forward (shoulder blades protruding in rear)

J
5   Upper back normally rounded
3   Upper back slightly more rounded
1   Upper back markedly rounded

K
5   Trunk erect
3   Trunk inclined to rear slightly
1   Trunk inclined to rear markedly

L
5   Abdomen flat
3   Abdomen protruding
1   Abdomen protruding and sagging

M
5   Lower back normally curved
3   Lower back slightly hollow
1   Lower back markedly hollow

TO OBTAIN TOTAL RAW SCORE:

1. Determine the score for each of the above 13 items as follows:
    5 points if description in left hand column applies
    3 points if description in middle column applies
    1 point if description in right hand column applies
2. Enter score for each item under proper grade in the scoring column
3. Add all 13 scores and place total in appropriate space

TOTAL RAW SCORE

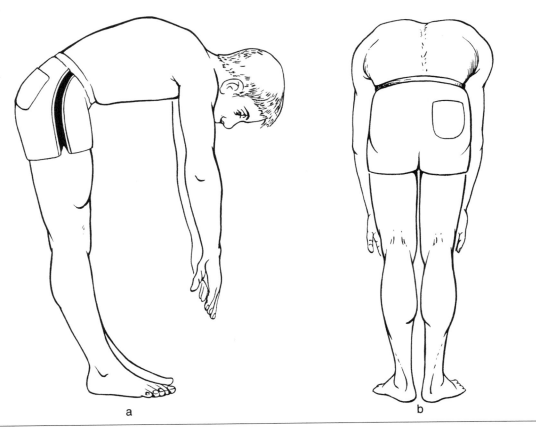

Figure 20.2 Illustration of the Adam's position.

Figure 20.3 The Charleston Bending brace and two forms of the Milwaukee brace used to treat scoliosis.

Structural kyphosis, sometimes referred to as Scheuermann's disease or juvenile kyphosis, is similar in appearance during the early stages to the nonstructural form described earlier, but it results from a deformity in the shape of the vertebrae in the thoracic region. While the cause of this vertebral deformity is unknown, it can be diagnosed by X-rays. This form of kyphosis is frequently accompanied by a compensatory lordotic curve. The prevalence of this deformity is not known, but it appears to affect both genders equally during adolescence.

Early detection and treatment of structural kyphosis through bracing can correct this condition. The treatment typically involves wearing a brace continuously for 1 or 2 years until the vertebrae reshape themselves. A variety of braces and orthotic jackets have been developed, and the Milwaukee brace is considered one of the most effective for treating this form of kyphosis.

Implications for Adapted Physical Education

As discussed earlier, physical educators can play a major role in screening for postural deviations in the spinal column. Children identified as having mild, nonstructural posture problems should receive special instruction and exercises to remedy their problems. A physical educator should consider the following guidelines when designing, implementing, or monitoring an exercise program to correct postural deviations.

1. Establish and follow policies and procedures for working with students suspected of having structural or serious postural deviations of the spinal column.

2. In an exercise program, the objective is to strengthen the muscles used to pull the spinal column back into correct alignment and to stretch or lengthen the muscles that are pulling the spinal column out of alignment. The stretching program should be performed at least twice a day, and strengthening exercises should be performed at least every other day.

3. All programs should begin and end with stretching exercises, with greatest emphasis on static stretching. Stretches should each be performed five times and held for a count of 15.

4. Proceed with mild, low-intensity exercises that can be easily performed by the children. Increase the intensity gradually as the children's strength and endurance improve.

5. In most cases, individual exercise programs should be initiated and taught in adapted physical education. After students have learned the exercise routine, they can perform it in the regular physical education class, monitored by the regular teacher. First, explain to the students the nature of the postural deviation being addressed, the reasons that good posture is desirable, and the ways in which the exercises will help. The exercises should then be taught and monitored until it is clear that the students understand how to perform them correctly. The importance of making students aware of the difference between the present posture and the desired posture cannot be overemphasized. Many children with mild postural deviations are simply unaware of the problem and therefore do not even try to correct their posture. Mirrors and videotape are useful media for giving students feedback. When working with students with visual impairments, the teacher will need to provide specific tactile and kinesthetic feedback to teach them the feeling of the correct postures. Cratty (1971) has described a tactile posture board, composed of a series of movable wooden pegs projecting through a vertical board, which can be placed along a student's spine to provide tactual feedback related to both postural deviations and desired postures.

6. Children should follow their exercise programs at home on the days they do not have class. They should use some form of monitoring system, such as a log or progress chart. Periodically they should be evaluated and given feedback and reinforcement to motivate them to continue working on their exercise programs.

7. Exercises that make the body symmetrical are recommended. The use of asymmetric exercises, especially for children being treated for scoliosis, should be used only following medical consultation.

8. When selecting exercises to reduce one curve (i.e., the major curve), take care that the exercise does not foster the development of another curve (i.e., the minor curve).

9. The exercise program should be made as varied and interesting as possible to maintain the student's motivation and involvement. Alternating between routine exercises and activities like swimming and rowing will usually result in greater compliance and motivation. Setting

the routines to music and using reward systems are also recommended. Motivation is an even greater concern with students with mental disabilities, who may not comprehend why they need to exercise or why better posture is desirable; they will require more frequent feedback and reinforcement. Showing students periodic Polaroid snapshots is a good technique for keeping their attention on their posture and rewarding them when they are displaying the desired posture.

10. Students wearing braces such as the Milwaukee brace can exercise and participate in physical education, although activities that cause trauma to the spine (e.g., jumping and gymnastics) may be contraindicated. As a general rule, the brace will be self-limiting.

Recommended Exercises

Using the guidelines just presented and drawing on an understanding of the muscles involved in a spinal column deviation, a physical educator should be able to select appropriate exercises and activities. The following lists include sample exercises for the upper and lower back that can be used in the remediation of the three major spinal cord deviations discussed in this chapter. Several resources that provide additional exercises and more detailed descriptions of their performance are listed at the end of this chapter.

Sample Upper-Back Exercises

Listed here are several common exercises used in the remediation of postural deformities involving the upper back.

1. Symmetrical swimming strokes such as the backstroke and the breaststroke. If a pool is not available, the arm patterns of these strokes can be performed on a bench covered with a mat. Hand weights or pulley weights can be used to control the resistance.

2. Rowing using either a rowboat or a rowing machine. The rowing action can also be performed with hand weights or pulley weights.

3. Various arm and shoulder lifts from a prone position on a mat. Small hand weights can be used to increase resistance.

4. Hanging from a bar. This is a good stretching exercise.

5. Lateral (sideways) trunk bending from either a standing or a kneeling position. Forward bending should be avoided.

Sample Lower-Back Exercises

This list describes several common exercises used to remediate postural deformities involving the lower back.

1. Any form of correctly performed sit-ups commensurate with the student's ability. Emphasis should be placed on keeping the lower back flat and performing the sit-ups in a slow, continuous action, as opposed to performing a high number of repetitions. Raising of the hips and sudden jerky movements should not be allowed.

2. Pelvic tilt. This can be done from a supine position on a mat or standing against a wall.

3. Alternating or combined knee exchanges (bringing the knee to chest) from a supine position on a mat.

4. Doing a bicycling action with the legs from a supine position on a mat.

5. Leg lifts. Any variation is appropriate as long as the lower back is kept flat and pressed against the floor.

LOWER EXTREMITY AND FOOT DISORDERS

Deviations in the alignment of the hips, legs, and feet are common and can result in pain, loss of efficiency, and other postural problems. The correct alignment of the hips, legs, and feet is shown in Figure 20.4. The assessment of postural alignment of the lower extremities is included in the general posture screening instruments presented in the first part of this chapter.

The purpose of this section is to review some of the common deviations found in the hips, legs, and feet. Many of these problems are related and frequently occur together. As with the spinal column deviations discussed earlier, deviations in the alignment of the lower extremities can be either structural or nonstructural. Structural deviations are usually caused by skeletal or neuromuscular problems, which may be congenital or acquired. Nonstructural deviations are typically the result of muscle imbalances that, if not treated, may eventually become structural deviations.

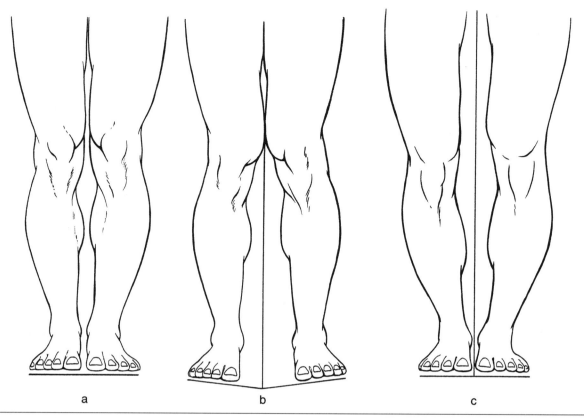

Figure 20.4 Illustration of alignment of the lower extremities: (a) normal, (b) knock-knees, and (c) bowlegs.

Hip Deformities

Four common deformities occur at the hip joint. The first two (*coxa valga* and *coxa vara*) are the result of the angle between the head of the femur and the shaft of the femur and can occur in anyone. The third and fourth deformities involve hip dislocations, which are caused by congenital abnormalities in the formation of the hip joint or are acquired during trauma or gradual deformation of the hip joint.

Coxa Valga

The alignment of the upper leg results from the way the head of the femur articulates with the hip socket and the angle between the head of the femur and the shaft of the femur. In *coxa* (hip) *valga* (out), the angle between the head of the femur and the shaft is greater than normal, which results in the upper leg appearing abducted or bowed. The increased angle also causes the affected leg to be longer. This condition is structural and usually congenital and cannot be corrected by attention, exercise, or activity in physical education.

Coxa Vara

This deformity is the opposite of *coxa valga*. In *coxa vara*, the angle between the head of the femur and the shaft is smaller than normal, which results in the upper leg bending inward. This condition, more common than *coxa valga*, can be either congenital or acquired. The acquired form, which occurs most frequently in males during the adolescent growth spurt, is usually caused by trauma or dislocation of the hip. If identified early, the condition is usually treated by several weeks of abstention from weight bearing. If the condition is allowed to progress, bracing and surgery may be required to correct it.

Hip Dislocations

Hip dislocation is the situation in which the head of the femur is separated from the hip socket. Hip dislocations can be classified as either congenital or acquired. Congenital dislocations, sometimes referred to as developmental hip dislocations, result from deficits in prenatal development and abnormal birth conditions. The cause of this condition is unknown, but there is some relatively strong evidence of a hereditary link. The condition is more prevalent in females and occurs most frequently in the left hip.

Depending on the severity of a congenital hip dislocation, it may be detected immediately after birth or, in mild cases, not until the child begins to walk. Other observable symptoms are decreased range of adduction of the hip on the affected side and asymmetrical fat folds on the upper legs. If the condition is not detected early, older children exhibit additional symptoms of exaggerated lordotic and scoliotic curves, pain, and fatigue. Treatment of congenital hip dislocations varies with the degree of the dislocation and the age at which it is detected. In mild cases involving very young children, dislocation can be successfully treated with splints. In more severe cases, a combination of casts, traction, and even surgery may be required.

In most cases, congenital hip dislocations will have been treated and corrected before the child enters school and will require no special attention in physical education. Occasionally, a case will be encountered where the condition was detected late and the child needs postural training and muscle conditioning in the hip region. The physical educator should consult with the appropriate medical personnel to coordinate the child's physical education objectives with the objectives being worked on in rehabilitation.

Acquired hip dislocations can be either acute or gradual. Acute dislocations are caused by trauma or injury to the hip. Gradual dislocations are caused by a progressive deformation of the hip joint and are common in many children with neuromuscular conditions such as cerebral palsy and spina bifida, who spend a majority of their time sitting in wheelchairs. These children are born with normal hip joints that are gradually deformed because of unbalanced muscle forces placed on the joint. Hip dislocations in these children frequently occur with very little associated pain. When the hip is dislocated, the affected leg will appear shorter and will be rotated inward in a scissoring position. Physical educators should be aware of these signs and of the potential for this problem in children with neuromuscular disabilities. They should consult regularly with the medical personnel on the status of students with potential hip dislocations and on physical education activities that might aggravate this condition and therefore should be avoided.

Hip dislocation conditions can be treated prior to the actual dislocation by surgery that cuts the muscles, tendons, and/or nerves of the muscles exerting the inappropriate force on the joint. This usually involves the adductor muscles and tendons and the obturator nerve. After the hip has actually been dislocated, more extensive surgery is required involving restructuring of the hip joint.

Knee Deformities

A number of alignment problems referred to as knee deformities are the result of muscle imbalances, compensatory actions resulting from hip deviations, or abnormalities in the lower leg (tibia and fibula).

Bowlegs

Bowlegs, or *genu* (knee) *varum* (inward), is the condition in which the lower legs bow inward, resulting in the knees being separated when the ankles are touching (Figure 20.4c). The bowing can occur in either the femur or the tibia but is most common in the tibia. One or both legs can be affected. This condition is a common nonstructural problem in many young children. It usually corrects itself by the time a child reaches the age of 3. If not, it must be treated with braces, or it will most likely become a permanent structural deformity. This structural deformity is frequently accompanied by compensatory deformities in the feet. By school age, bowlegs cannot be corrected by activity or exercises. The physical educator's major responsibility, when the condition is suspected in the lower elementary grades, is to refer the child to a physician for possible treatment through bracing. Most children with this deformity, although sometimes appearing awkward in their movements, can successfully participate in all regular physical education activities.

Knock-Knees

Knock-knees is the opposite of bowlegs. In this deviation the lower legs bow outward, with the result that the ankles are forced apart when the knees are touching (Figure 20.4b). This condition is usually nonstructural and common in very young children, and it frequently corrects itself. In young children, the deviation can be treated through bracing. If not treated, the deformity will eventually become structural. Knock-knees is a common postural deviation in obese children. Poor alignment of the knee results in a disproportionate amount of weight being borne by its medial aspect and predisposes the joint to potential strain and injury. Physical educators should carefully consider this point when selecting physical education and/or athletic events for students with this condition.

Activities that increase the possibility of trauma to the knee—such as jumping from heights, running on hard or uneven surfaces, and games and sports where the knees could be hit laterally—should be carefully evaluated.

Tibial Torsion

Tibial torsion is the result of an inward rotation of the lower leg (tibia). This condition can result in toeing in or can be caused by a foot deformity. The condition, caused by a muscle imbalance that twists the tibia inward, frequently occurs in young children who are in a non-weight-bearing position for a prolonged period as a result of injury or illness. When it is not contraindicated by the injury or illness, children should be encouraged to bear weight on their legs each day. Attention should be focused on maintaining the legs in proper alignment and stretching the muscles that pull the tibia inward. If identified early in children, this deformity can be treated through bracing. In more severe cases, a combination of surgery and bracing may be required.

Knee Flexion Deformity

Knee flexion deformity is common in children with neuromuscular disabilities such as cerebral palsy who are confined to wheelchairs. It is characterized by the legs being permanently bent or contracted in a sitting position. This often painful condition makes the legs harder to manage and prevents children from using standing tables or attempting ambulation even with the aid of braces and crutches. The condition is initially treated with splints and typically requires surgical lengthening of the hamstring tendons in which their insertions are repositioned. Physical educators can assist in preventing this condition by encouraging wheelchair-bound students to move their knees through the full range of motion. This might mean having the students leave their wheelchairs and perform a stretching routine on a mat while the other class members are doing other stretching exercises.

Foot Deformities

Although foot deformities can be caused by skeletal and neuromuscular abnormalities, the majority are caused by compensatory postures required to offset other postural misalignments in the legs, hips, and spine. As a result, the feet are typically the most abused structure in the body. Most foot deformities are identified and treated before children enter school. Occasionally mild deformities

can go unnoticed by parents and will be identified by the physical educator when the student complains of pain or avoids certain activities.

Physical educators should review the medical files and be aware of any students who have foot deformities. In most cases, the students will require no special consideration and will be able to participate normally in the regular physical education setting. When appropriate, the physical educator may need to monitor specific students to make sure they are wearing their braces and/or orthotics and performing any exercises prescribed by their physicians. Several of the common foot deformities found in children are described in the following paragraphs to provide physical educators with a basic understanding of the conditions and how they are treated.

Clubfoot

Clubfoot, or *talipes*, refers to a number of deformities in the foot in which the foot is severely twisted out of shape. This condition is usually congenital or acquired as the result of a neuromuscular condition. The term *talipes* is usually followed by one or more descriptors indicating the nature of the deformity: *equinus* (toe walking caused by tight heel cords), *calcaneus* (opposite of equinus and caused by loose heel cords, resulting in the foot being flexed), *varus* (toes and sole of the foot are turned inward, causing the individual to walk on the outside edge of the feet), and *valgus* (toes and sole of the foot are turned outward, causing the individual to walk on the inside edge of the feet). Mild forms of the conditions are treated with braces and orthopedic shoes. More severe forms require a combination of corrective surgery and braces.

Pronation

Pronation is a foot deformity in which the individual walks on the medial (inside) edge of the feet. The condition is frequently accompanied by toeing out. Pronation is usually acquired and can be cured, if identified early, through corrective shoes and exercises.

Flatfoot

Flatfoot, or *pes planus*, may be acquired or congenital and may be caused by a fallen or flat longitudinal arch. Flatfoot is considered a postural deviation only when it is acquired as a result of poor body mechanics. In such cases, the structure of the foot is altered, which reduces its mechanical efficiency in absorbing and distributing force. This postural deviation, in turn, can cause pain in the longitudinal arch and result in other postural deviations as well. This condition is common in children with visual impairments (probably due to their shuffling gait) and children who are obese. Treatment can involve prescriptive exercises and orthotics (inserts in the shoes).

Hollowfoot

Hollowfoot, or *pes cavus*, the opposite of flatfoot, is characterized by an extremely high longitudinal arch. This condition is usually congenital and is frequently associated with clubfoot. As in *pes planus*, the change in the foot's alignment due to the extremely high arch reduces the foot's ability to absorb and distribute force. The condition can be treated with orthopedic shoes and, in severe cases, with surgery.

Morton's Toe

Morton's toe refers to a deformity caused by a fallen metatarsal arch. The fallen arch puts pressure on surrounding nerves, which makes this condition very painful. The condition is caused by a disproportional amount of weight and stress being placed on the ball of the foot over a prolonged period of time. The treatment usually involves identifying and removing the cause, introducing appropriate exercises, and inserting an arch support in the shoe.

Hallux Valgus

Hallux valgus is a condition in which the big toe is bent inward toward the other toes. The condition is caused by pressure forcing the big toe inward, usually as a result of poorly fitting shoes. If the condition persists, a bunion forms, and eventually a calcium deposit builds up on the head of the first metatarsal. Treatment involves removing the bunion and calcium deposit and fitting the individual with appropriate shoes.

SUMMARY

All children can benefit from good posture and body mechanics to safely and efficiently participate in physical education and athletics. Poor posture and body mechanics predispose children to

injury. Physical educators, given the nature of their position and preparation, can play an important role in identifying and correcting postural deviations. Postural screening should be an annual event in all physical education programs. Awareness and understanding of proper body mechanics should be taught to all children so that they may monitor and evaluate their own postures.

BIBLIOGRAPHY

Adams, R.C., & McCubbin, J.A. (1991). *Games, sports, and exercises for the physically disabled* (4th ed.). Philadelphia: Lea & Febiger.

Cratty, B.J. (1971). *Movement and spatial awareness in blind children and youth.* Springfield, IL: Charles C Thomas.

New York State Education Department. (1966). *New York State physical fitness test for boys and girls, grades 4–12.* Albany, NY: Author.

Scott, M.G., & French, E. (1959). *Measurement and evaluation in physical education.* Dubuque, IA: Brown.

RESOURCES

Films and videotapes on posture screening can be obtained from the Scoliosis Research Society, P.O. Box 20001, Park Ridge, IL 60068.

Other

Iowa Posture Test (1959). In M.G. Scott & E. French, *Measurement and evaluation in physical education* (pp. 414–421). Dubuque, IA: Brown.

New York Posture Rating Test (1966). In *New York State physical fitness test for boys and girls, grades 4–12.* Albany: New York State Education Department. This test can be obtained by writing to the State Education Department, Division of Health, Physical Education, and Recreation, Albany, NY 12224.

Posture Grid. (1991). In R.C. Adams & J.A. McCubbin, *Games, sports, and exercises for the physically disabled* (pp. 155–162). Philadelphia: Lea & Febiger.

These are three examples of posture screening tests that are accessible to physical educators and are applicable for use in physical education classes.

CHAPTER 21

Developmental and Remedial Exercises and Activities

David L. Porretta

This chapter discusses developmental and remedial exercises and activities that can be incorporated into physical education and sport programs. Although many of the activities presented are of an individual nature, they can and should be used in a group setting whenever possible. This not only motivates participants to develop physically but also encourages them to socialize with one another.

RELAXATION

The primary focus of relaxation is the conscious control of the body and its various functions. When used appropriately, relaxation activities help people with physical and motor needs to consciously release muscular tension in various regions of the body.

Many individuals with disabilities are particularly in need of relaxation training. For people with increased muscle tone or general hyperactive behavior, relaxation techniques used *prior* to gross motor or sport activities prepare them to perform to the best of their ability. For individuals with cerebral palsy who exhibit increased muscle tone, relaxation training helps to reduce tone, thereby allowing greater capability of controlled movement. Some people have difficulty returning to a relatively calm state, especially after highly competitive or exciting activities. This is common for those exhibiting hyperactive or perseverative behavior. In such cases, relaxation techniques used as an immediate *follow-up* to gross motor or sport

activities prepare individuals for the return to a normal resting state by helping to bring about a reduction in many physiological responses like heart rate, breathing, and muscle tenseness. Relaxation following vigorous physical activity is particularly helpful in public school settings, where students must return to a normal resting state in order to resume sedentary classroom activities. There are cases, however, where relaxation activities should not be offered: people who are lethargic or have low levels of physical vitality do not need them.

A number of relaxation methods have proven to be successful. Some of the more popular, which will be discussed in the following subsections, include the Jacobson relaxation method, the imagery (association-set) method, and a relatively new method known as biofeedback. Two Eastern methods, Hatha yoga and tai chi (tie jee), while not discussed in detail, are also excellent forms of relaxation that focus on the concept of mental, spiritual, and physical health. Both methods advocate the harmonious functioning of mind and body. Hatha yoga emphasizes maintaining specific body positions, whereas tai chi emphasizes the feel of moving from one position to the other. Relaxation activities may use one of these methods exclusively or may combine varying aspects of two or more of them. This choice is left to the discretion of the teacher or coach and, where appropriate, the student. The manner in which the methods are taught and the amount of time devoted to their use will depend greatly upon the student's age and the degree and type of disability, as well as the type of gross motor activity and the amount of time devoted to physical education class or sport practice. However, whatever methods are used, a number of general principles apply to all. These are (1) practice the technique often and in a quiet place; (2) assume a comfortable position; (3) focus your attention; and (4) don't force the response.

Teaching relaxation techniques to individuals with disabilities can also provide them with a feeling of self-control. Historically, individuals with disabilities have been made to feel dependent upon others. Once individuals realize they can control their thoughts and physiological responses, they can become more independent and responsible. This can extend beyond physical education and sport arenas and into the person's everyday life.

Jacobson's Relaxation Method

The Jacobson method of relaxation was first developed over 50 years ago by Edmund Jacobson, a physician interested in tension control (Jacobson, 1970). Jacobson's method, still popular today, is based on consciously relaxing tense muscles. Information on the state of muscle activity is sent via proprioceptors to the arousal system located in the reticular area of the brain. Muscle relaxation brings about a reduction in neural activity of the reticular area, thereby reducing one's level of arousal.

The Jacobson method involves voluntarily contracting and then relaxing a specific group of muscles three times in succession. This is done progressively; the individual contracts and relaxes various muscle groups in a prescribed manner in a specific order. The progression begins with muscle groups in the left arm and then the right arm, followed by the left leg and then the right leg, proceeding to the trunk, back, neck, and face. The individual focuses on one region of the body at a time. Once a region, such as the right arm, has been relaxed, muscles in that region should remain relaxed as attention progresses to other regions of the body. Initially, progressive relaxation training should be done with the eyes closed from a supine position with legs together, arms at the sides, and palms facing upward. Once the technique has been learned in this position, the individual can use it in a sitting position.

Today this method is successfully used to relax individuals with hyperactivity and those with conditions such as mental retardation, cerebral palsy, learning disabilities, and emotional disturbances. For example, the Special Olympics Motor Activities Training Program (MATP) uses a modified

Sample Relaxation Routine

The following is a sample routine showing how a modification of the Jacobson method can be used *following* physical education and sport activities for individuals with disabilities. The session takes approximately 10 minutes once participants have been introduced to the method. This sample session incorporates a slight modification based on the method suggested by Landy and Landy (1993) and is intended as a cool-down activity. Before the session begins, the instructor has participants lie in a supine position on a mat, arms to the sides, legs slightly apart, and eyes closed with relaxing music being played. Students are asked to tighten various muscle groups as hard as they can for 10 seconds, then relax them for about 30 seconds on command.

Lie on your back and listen to the quiet music playing. Relax every part of your body by thinking of something pleasant. Press your head to the mat very hard; and then relax. Now, frown and move only your scalp upward. Yawn very slowly and then relax. Next, press your shoulder blades together very hard; then relax them completely. Make tight fists with both your hands and squeeze them hard as you would a sponge; then relax. Tighten your tummy muscles very hard. Can you feel them tighten? Now relax them completely. Next, squeeze your buttocks together real tight; then relax. Press your legs to the floor very hard; then relax. Point your toes away from you as hard as you can; now relax. Next, pull your toes toward you as hard as you can; now relax. Breathe in all the way, then slowly let all the air out, breathe in again, then let all the air out slowly again with a long hissing sound. Repeat this five times. Without making a sound, open your eyes, stand up very slowly and stretch as tall as you can. Now walk very slowly and quietly to the exit door. (Landy & Landy, 1993, p. 400)

---

version of Jacobson's method for participants with severe mental impairments (Special Olympics, 1989). Many persons with severe impairments possess muscular reflexes and imbalances that significantly reduce their range of motion and limit their ability to perform motor skills and activities. As part of a total warm-up program, participants are taught to relax specific body parts. This form of relaxation training is coupled with easy, rhythmic breathing. The MATP procedure is as follows:

- Pair one motor activities trainer with one to three participants.

- Remove participants from wheelchairs and place them on a mat.

- When necessary, support the participant's head, shoulders, and body.

- Dim lights if possible and play soft music.

- Face the participant to gain attention.

- Talk softly to participant and tell him/her which body part to relax. To cue the participant, point to or gently touch the body part.

- Ask participant to look at the body part and try to relax it (e.g., calm the body part, let all the air out of it, make it go to sleep, let it float, etc.). The following muscle groups should be relaxed: neck, shoulders, arms, front of leg, back of leg, feet and toes, and hands and fingers.

- Repeat with all major muscle groups.

- Encourage the participant to breathe easily and rhythmically; breathe with him/her to establish a rhythm.

- Muscles should be contracted for 5 seconds and then slowly relaxed for 15 seconds.

- The entire session should last at least 5 minutes.

Imagery (Association-Set) Relaxation Method

Imagery is a method of relaxation in which the individual produces a mental picture or image conducive to a relaxed state. This method is also known as association-set, mind-set, or autogenic training because the user voluntarily produces a mental image and continues to focus upon it. The image can be generated internally by the individual, or it can be suggested by the teacher or coach. Mental images may be elicited by words, phrases, or quiet music. The type of image used depends on age, mental capacity, and personal preference. Young children respond well to words and phrases

---

Sample of Imagery Training

Vealey (1986) recommends using imagery training daily for approximately 10 minutes. It can be used either before the practice or game, to create a proper frame of mind for participation, or afterward, to reemphasize key situations or plays. Imagery exercises are specific to the activity or sport and must therefore be tailored to each participant's need. The following exercise, suggested by Vealey for enhancing performance, is the type recommended for use in adapted physical education or sport programs.

Either sit or lie comfortably with eyes closed. Begin by placing yourself in a relaxed state by slow deep breathing of one to two minutes. Now, choose a piece of equipment in your sport such as a ball, racquet, club, etc. Try to imagine very fine details of the object. Turn it over in your hands and examine every part of the object. Feel its outline and texture. Now imagine yourself performing with the object. First focus on seeing yourself very clearly performing an activity. Visualize yourself repeating the skill over and over. Next try to hear the sounds that accompany this particular movement. Listen carefully to all the sounds that are being made as you perform this skill. Now put the sight and sound together. Try to get a clear picture of yourself performing the skill and also hear all of the sounds involved. (Vealey, 1986, p. 217)

---

such as melting like snow, floating like a cloud, or sleeping like a kitten. Older children and adults respond to various colors or scenic surroundings (e.g., lying on the beach) to produce a relaxing state. This method is best used in a restful environment free from noise or other distractions, with participants in a sitting or recumbent position with eyes closed. Imagery relaxation may be of limited benefit in some cases, especially for students who have mental retardation, emotional disturbances, or central nervous damage so severe as to interfere with the production of and continued focus on a realistic image.

Recently, sport psychologists have employed imagery as a means of improving the performance of athletes. With this method, individuals either produce a mental picture of themselves (external imagery) successfully performing a particular skill or feat (e.g., scoring a soccer goal) or feel themselves (internal imagery) actually performing the skill or movement correctly. According to sport psychologists, imagery is more successful when the image is vivid or the feeling is more accurate. Not all athletes can imagine to the same degree. However, with practice those with less ability can improve their imagery and as a result enhance performance. Imagery holds great promise for enhancing the performance of athletes with disabilities and is now receiving increased attention from coaches and researchers alike. For example, imagery has been shown to assist in the acquisition of both throwing and striking tasks in adolescents with mild mental retardation. For imagery to be successful for individuals with mental retardation, it is suggested that they be somewhat familiar with the skill being imaged.

Biofeedback

Biofeedback is a recommended form of relaxation therapy. A relatively new procedure, **biofeedback** uses a combination of modern technology and individual training to bring about physiological changes in such parameters as heart rate, body temperature, and muscular activity through conscious control. Through training, an individual can learn to reduce abnormal muscle tension. However, because of the lack of supporting research, it remains uncertain whether the clinical use of biofeedback is significantly better than muscle relaxation therapy in reducing hyperactivity (Winnick, 1984).

Of the various forms of biofeedback, **electromyographic (EMG) feedback** is the most often used in the rehabilitation process. Through the use of sophisticated electronic technology, a body signal like a muscle impulse is picked up by way of electrodes strategically placed on or in the muscle and is fed back to the person in the form of a tone, light, or number representing the muscle impulse. The person then tries to alter the intensity or duration of the signal, which in turn changes the physiological response. Finally, through practice, the person is taught to consciously control the response (muscle impulse) with the aim of reducing muscular tension.

Until recently, biofeedback has been employed primarily in medicine and psychotherapy. Through

---

A Sample Biofeedback Relaxation Program

The following is a description of a sample program to obtain muscle relaxation of the dominant upper arm. The person is seated comfortably in a chair. Surface electrodes are then placed on the person's biceps muscle. When the feedback apparatus is on, the person will begin to hear a clicking sound. Initially, the person should be allowed time to experiment with controlling the clicking sound. For example, the trainer might ask the person, "What makes the clicking less frequent? What happens when you think of throwing a ball as far as you can? What happens when you think of your arm floating on water?" Further direction are as follows:

Tighten your muscle very hard. As you tighten your muscle, you should hear the sound of the biofeedback machine increasing in the number and frequency of clicks. Now try to completely relax the muscle. As you relax, the number and frequency of clicks should diminish. (The tightening and relaxing of the muscle should be repeated so that the person can actually feel the muscle contracting and relaxing.) Now think of how limp and heavy your entire arm can be. Concentrate on reducing the clicking sound to a lower and lower level. Remember, you are in control of your muscles.

The person is to repeat the phrase "my arm is limp and heavy" three times aloud and then repeat the phrase silently. If concentration should happen to be completely lost, ask the person to rest for a short time and try again.

---

these avenues, biofeedback has been shown to be of benefit in the rehabilitation process for persons with spinal cord injuries, strokes, cardiovascular disorders, and low back pain (Basmajian, 1989). In addition, beneficial effects can be realized in persons with paralysis and spasticity resulting from brain damage. Realizing its great potential for the self-regulation of muscle responses in people with disabilities, teachers and coaches are now utilizing biofeedback as a method of relaxation. Although it has limits as a practical tool for physical education classes, its use as a training device in competitive sport and rehabilitation settings is virtually unlimited. Because of the complexity of the electronic technology and the training methodology, however, biofeedback to promote better performance can best be used outside the regular class or practice period. It is recommended that biofeedback training initially be conducted three to four times per week for a period of approximately 30 to 40 minutes. As one becomes more proficient in controlling the specific body functions of concern, training can be conducted less frequently for a period of 10 to 15 minutes. In addition, the participant should be instructed to supplement biofeedback training with progressive relaxation activities at home. When voluntary control is obtained at the desired level, monitoring by the biofeedback apparatus will no longer be needed.

PHYSICAL FITNESS

This section describes exercises and activities directed toward the development or remedy of physical fitness components crucial to successful performance in physical education and sport. In recognition of individual needs, modifications of exercises and activities are also presented. Many of these exercises and activities can be performed in an aquatic environment: Water provides buoyancy, which assists in movement, and also a degree of resistance for developing muscular strength and endurance.

The exercises and activities described fall into four areas (components) of physical fitness: flexibility, muscular strength and endurance, cardiorespiratory endurance, and body composition. Exercises and activities related to the fitness component of body composition will be presented in conjunction with cardiorespiratory activities because many of the latter activities also promote the regulation of fatness. Exercises and activities that develop cardiorespiratory endurance also provide the frequency, intensity, and duration levels needed to increase caloric expenditure and thus help reduce body fat. In the sections that follow, exercises and activities for the flexibility and the muscular strength and endurance components are grouped according to areas of the body targeted. Often these exercises can be performed to music; this helps maintain participants' interest. Individuals with mental disabilities respond particularly well to exercises using music. This section includes muscular strength and endurance exercises not typically found in weight training programs.

Flexibility

Exercises to develop flexibility are usually performed from a stationary position and are designed to improve joint range of motion and prepare the individual for more vigorous physical activity. Upper-body and upper-extremity exercises may include the following:

- Head rotations
- Face stretch (different ways to twist face muscles)
- Arm circles
- Arm hang from a horizontal bar
- Shoulder stretch
- Shoulder bracing

Exercises and activities for the trunk, hips, back, and thighs may include the following:

- Trunk twist
- Elephant walk
- Leg lifts from a prone position or lying on side
- Toe touches
- Alternate knee flexion
- Bent-knee sitting position (with back against wall)
- Head-and-chest raise from a prone position
- Groin stretch (Figure 21.1)

Figure 21.1 Groin stretch.

Lower leg and ankle exercises and activities may include the following:

- Toe and foot circles
- Dorsiflexion stretch
- Walking on heels, toes, lateral or medial aspect of foot
- Curling and extending toes

In some instances, individuals with partial paralysis or very poor range of motion will need to be assisted through an exercise by the teacher or coach. Students unable to exercise in a standing position, particularly those with cerebral palsy or traumatic brain injury, may perform the exercises from a sitting or lying position. For example, head rotations and arm circles can be performed from either a standing or sitting position, while leg lifts can be performed from either a prone or supine position. In flexibility exercises for individuals with cerebral palsy, Surburg (1986) suggests placing a greater emphasis on relaxing target muscle groups than on stretching them. In addition, it may be helpful for some students (e.g., those with juvenile rheumatoid arthritis) to perform exercises in a therapeutically warm pool. Upper-body stretching exercises can also be done with the assistance of a broom handle (Figure 21.2). With this type of exercise, the person is in full control of the amount of stretching that takes place.

Kennedy (1988) recommends a number of guidelines when performing flexibility exercises and activities. While Kennedy's guidelines were initially developed for persons in wheelchairs, they have been slightly modified here so that they can be followed by most persons with disabilities.

- Stretching should occur prior to and after vigorous activity.
- Performing exercises several times a day is most effective.
- Breathing normally while performing stretching exercises is recommended.
- Exercising should be done slowly and in a controlled manner.
- The final stretching position should result in no pain or strain.
- Performing flexibility exercises that resemble the movements in games or sports are the most effective.

Muscular Strength and Endurance

To increase the amount of force a specific muscle or muscle group can exert and the length of time it can continue working, muscular strength and endurance exercises can be used. Exercises and activities to develop the upper body and upper extremities may include the following:

- Modified push-ups (performed with knees touching the floor)
- Chin-ups with a horizontal bar (from a supine position on the floor)

a

Figure 21.2 Upper body stretches such as (a) the shoulder stretch and (b) the trunk twist can be performed with the assistance of a broom handle.

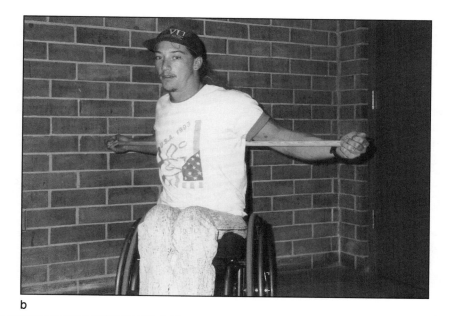

b

Figure 21.2 *(Continued)*

- Flexed-arm hang
- Using an overarm stroke while seated in chest-deep water
- Floor ladder pull
- Straight-arm support
- Squeezing balls of various sizes with both hands
- Squeezing play dough into various shapes with both hands
- Rope pull (seated or prone position on a carpet square) across gym floor
- Crab walk
- Rope climb
- Seal walk
- Medicine ball throw
- Pushing a weighted ball (Figure 21.3)
- Tug-of-war

Trunk, hip, back, and thigh exercises may include the following:

- Bent-knee sit-ups with arms folded across chest
- Squat-jumps
- Leg wrestling (with partner)
- Curl-ups

Exercises and activities for lower legs and ankles may include the following:

Figure 21.3 Pushing a weighted ball.

- Heel raises
- Foot dorsiflexion
- Moving an object (like a heavy ball or toy) across the floor with medial and lateral aspects of the foot

Students with unilateral upper-limb amputations can perform one-arm push-ups from a kneeling position, while those with greater initial strength can do regular push-ups with one arm by turning the body from the prone to the side position. Individuals in wheelchairs, such as those with traumatic brain injury, can perform pull-ups, chin-ups, flexed-arm hang, and straight-arm support exercises from the chair. Various weighted objects can be substituted for a medicine ball. Tug-of-war can be played from a standing, sitting, kneeling, or prone position on the floor. Those with poor abdominal strength can do bent-knee sit-ups on an incline mat, where the head and shoulders are placed at the top of the incline, or they may wish to use the arms to assist with sit-ups. Students with poor overall strength and endurance can do the crab walk supported by a scooter. Heel raises and the foot dorsiflexion exercise can be performed from a standing, sitting, or lying position. A partner or the instructor can help by providing resistance with the hand to either the instep (dorsiflexion exercise) or the ball of the foot (heel raises).

Cardiorespiratory Endurance and Body Composition

For efficient heart and lung function and for adequate caloric expenditure, exercises and activities usually incorporate fully body movement sustained over a long period of time. Exercises and activities may include the following:

- Mountain climbing or hiking
- Inverted cycle (performed from a supine position)
- Roller skating or roller blading over distance
- Bench stepping
- Stair climbing or stepping (Figure 21.4)
- Exercycling (Figure 21.4)
- Rope skipping
- Walking or jogging on a treadmill (Figure 21.5)
- Jogging in place
- Jogging over distance
- Swimming over distance
- Walking or jogging over distance through waist-deep water
- Wheeling over distance
- Low-impact aerobics
- Obstacle courses

Figure 21.4 Performing on an exercycle and stair stepper.
Photo courtesy of the Ohio State School for the Blind, Columbus, OH. Printed by permission.

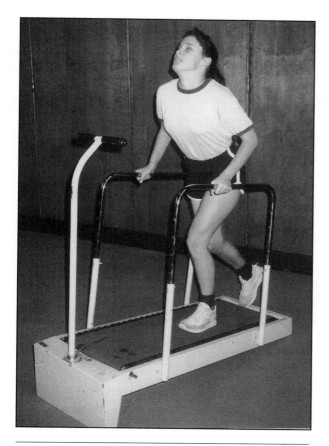

Figure 21.5   Jogging on a treadmill.
Photo courtesy of the Ohio State School for the Blind, Columbus, OH. Printed by permission.

- Fitness trails
- Cross-country skiing
- Canoeing or sculling over distance
- Bicycling or tricycling
- Jumping on a trampoline
- Arm cycling (Figure 21.6)
- Speed bag
- Tag games
- Scooter activities
- Relays
- Aerobic dance routines

Students who are visually impaired may have difficulty with activities that require running or moving specified distances without assistance. Increasingly, schools are using treadmills, exercycles, and stair stepping machines as part of cardiorespiratory development for youngsters with disabling conditions, especially those with visual impairments. With such equipment, the duration and intensity of the exercise can easily be set. Activity partners can provide assistance in jogging, while guide ropes may be helpful for distance swimming. In addition, a person with a visual impairment can run alongside a bike being pedaled by a sighted person, holding the bicycle's handlebar with one hand as long as the biker is not traveling too fast. People in wheelchairs can increase their cardiorespiratory endurance by participating in wheelchair marathoning or using an arm ergometer, a hand-propelled tricycle, or a speed bag. For individuals with asthma or cardiopathic conditions, activities performed on an intermittent basis—similar to an interval training regimen—are advised. Here, activities that require running short distances, like softball and volleyball, are preferable to continuous running activities.

BREATHING EXERCISES AND ACTIVITIES

For students with asthma, cystic fibrosis, or other conditions resulting in abnormal respiration or weak respiratory muscles (especially those with muscular dystrophy), breathing exercises and activities are of paramount importance. Breathing exercises and activities help people with asthma get air into and out of the lungs; for those with cystic fibrosis, these exercises and activities help eliminate excess mucous from the respiratory tract. Appropriately designed exercises can assist in increasing vital lung capacity and allowing the cardiorespiratory system to work more effectively. The respiratory muscles (such as the intercostals, major and minor pectorals, diaphragm, and abdominals) are exercised, and this enhances the movement of air into and out of the lungs.

Following are some examples of breathing exercises and activities that can be incorporated into any physical education program. For students with upper respiratory dysfunction, it is recommended that exercises and activities be conducted either daily or every other day for a period of 20 to 30 minutes. Frequency of the activity will depend on individual need. Breathing activities, as opposed to exercises, provide enjoyment, motivation, and competition for those who need daily sessions.

- *Forward flexion:* From a sitting or standing position and with arms relaxed, slowly bend forward at the waist while exhaling through the mouth. Bending forward as far as possible,

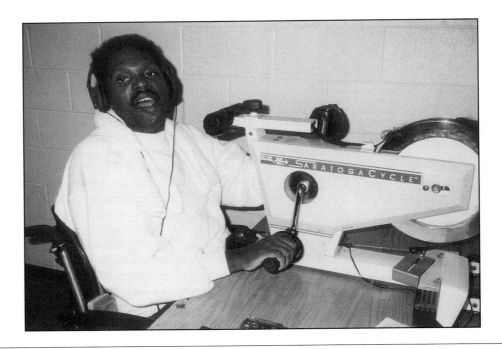

Figure 21.6 Using an arm cycling device.

forcefully expel as much air as possible and hold for a count of three. Slowly bring the trunk and head to an upright position while inhaling through the nostrils. This can be repeated as many times as desired.

- *Chest expander:* In a supine position with hips and knees flexed (so that feet are flat on the floor and approximately 30 centimeters from the buttocks), place one hand on the chest and the other on the abdomen. Inhale slowly through the nostrils, trying to expand only the chest to the maximum extent possible. Hold for a count of two or three and then slowly exhale through the mouth with pursed lips until air is expelled. This can be repeated as many times as desired.

- *Elbow rotation:* From a sitting or standing position, place fingers on the shoulders so that elbows are bent and out to the sides. At the same time, slowly move both elbows in a circular fashion. Beginning with an upward and then backward motion of the elbows, inhale through the mouth. As elbows complete the circle and move downward and to the front, exhale through the mouth. This can be repeated as many times as desired.

- *Balloon keep-up:* Two players stand facing each other about 1 meter apart. One player tosses a balloon into the air directly in front of the other player. The players blow the balloon to each other. They attempt to keep the balloon in the air as long as possible without touching it or letting it hit the ground.

- *Ping-Pong soccer:* Two players sit facing each other at a small table (approximately 1 meter long). A Ping-Pong ball is placed in the middle of the table. On command, each player attempts to blow the ball toward the opponent's goal. A goal is scored when the ball falls off the opponent's side of the table. Players are not allowed to rise from the sitting position.

- *Lights out:* Each player sits at the end of a long table directly in front of a lighted candle. The player attempts to blow out the flame at progressively greater distances. The player who extinguishes the flame at the greatest distance is the winner.

- *Breathing activities in an aquatic environment:* Breathing activities in water are popular and are most helpful in motivating students. Some activities include fully inhaling and exhaling air in neck- or shoulder-deep water, blowing bubbles with the face submerged in waist-deep water, and blowing a Ping-Pong ball across the width of the pool or over a specified distance.

WEIGHT TRAINING AND BODYBUILDING

Weight training programs utilize various exercises designed to develop muscular strength and endurance of specified muscle groups. In addition, many people seek to develop muscular power through weight training. The development of power is important for games and sports that require explosive movements like the long jump or spiking in volleyball.

Weight training is a very popular form of physical activity and is found in a variety of programs and environments. It is commonplace in health clubs, fitness centers, and recreational facilities as well as in schools. Some individuals use weight training for the purpose of bodybuilding (developing maximum muscle size and definition), while others use it for developing and maintaining physical fitness. Weight training is taught as an activity in many physical education programs, and it is commonly included as part of overall conditioning regimes for athletes at all competitive levels in nearly every sport.

Physical rehabilitation programs regularly incorporate weight training exercises to help people regain muscular strength and endurance following traumatic injury or illness. Anyone who has experienced physical rehabilitation can attest to the importance of weight training in restoring appropriate levels of muscular strength and endurance. Many individuals with physical disabilities continue to pursue weight training following medically prescribed rehabilitation programs. In fact, weight lifting (of which the bench press is the most popular activity) is a sanctioned event in all levels of competition for persons with disabilities.

Weight training programs for prepubescent children should follow the same principles as programs for adults. However, for children, maximal or near-maximal resistances should not be lifted, and overhead lifts with free weights should be avoided. High resistances can damage growth areas of bones or cause bone fractures. Fleck and Kraemer (1987) suggests that a well-organized and well-supervised training program for prepubescent children should not last longer than 30 to 60 minutes per session, three times per week. They recommend that prepubescent children be involved in training programs that use one's own body weight as resistance (e.g., toe raises, self-resistance arm curls, push-ups) or programs that use *some* resistance training equipment.

Isokinetics and Accommodating Resistance Training

A form of weight training that has recently become popular is **isokinetics**. Here, the rate at which the exercise is performed can be controlled with variable resistance provided throughout the full range of movement. With this type of training, the resistance automatically increases or decreases in a manner directly proportional to increases or decreases in muscle force. Isokinetic training can closely match normal speeds of performance while, at the same time, producing lower incidences of muscle and joint pain following workouts. Nautilus equipment, which incorporates principles similar to those of isokinetic training, can be adjusted to allow for very fast or very slow movements (Figure 21.7).

This type of training, involving accommodating resistance, has tremendous possibilities, especially in developing muscles for specific sports that require powerful and fast movements. In Nautilus training, Westcott (1983) suggests that optimum strength gains can be realized with only one set of 8 to 12 repetitions with maximum weight for each exercise, as opposed to three sets recommended for training **isotonically**. Even though it is costly, some school districts and recreation centers and most athletic clubs now have

Figure 21.7 Using a Nautilus machine for upper-body exercise.

isokinetic or accommodating-resistance equipment. Nautilus equipment is popular and offers a number of advantages. It can be adjusted to fit persons of various sizes and physiques. It is safe, durable, and designed so that the user has control over the exercise. Training partners are recommended, especially for persons with physical disabilities, but are not necessary for operating the machine. Unlike exercises with free weights, movement patterns are fixed.

Other Forms of Weight Training

In addition to Nautilus-type equipment, weight training can be performed with free weights, a Universal gym, or various weighted objects. These methods seem to be most feasible and cost-effective to date. Most schools and recreational and training facilities now have, in addition to free weights, at least one Universal gym. Universal gym equipment is arranged so that a number of people can perform a variety of exercises in a relatively small area. The Universal gym is preferable to the use of free weights in weight training programs for individuals with disabilities for the following reasons:

- It is safer than free weights because weights cannot be dropped on the floor, nor can one lose balance, as when lifting a heavy barbell.
- It saves time because weights can be changed by the simple use of a pin, whereas free weights must be continually placed on or removed from bars.
- It is convenient, especially for individuals with physical disabilities such as amputation or paralysis.

Most weight training exercises can be performed with Universal equipment. Exercises that develop the upper body and upper extremities include the following:

- Military press
- Bench press
- Pull-downs
- Biceps curls
- Forearm curls

Exercises that develop the back, hips, and abdomen include the following:

- Bent-knee curl-ups with arms folded across chest, on inclined board
- Back arch

Lower extremity exercises include the following:

- Leg press
- Knee extensions
- Knee curls
- Foot plantar flexion

In a weight training program for children of elementary school age, various weighted objects can be used in place of free weights or Universal gym equipment. Stuffed animals, beanbags, or balls are desirable because the weight of these objects can initially be light and adjusted in small increments and can keep the child's attention.

Modifications of Weight Training Exercises

People with unilateral upper- or lower-limb amputations can perform modified exercises with the nonaffected limb. For example, a person with a unilateral upper-limb amputation may find it easier to perform a military press using a dumbbell instead of Universal equipment. Those with below-the-elbow, below-the-knee, or wrist or ankle disarticulations can exercise with free weights strapped to the remaining limb segment. Most people in wheelchairs can perform exercises in their chairs (except for the bench press, where assistance may be needed for transfer and the person may need to be strapped to the bench).

RECOMMENDATIONS FOR DEVELOPMENTAL AND REHABILITATIVE ACTIVITIES

The following general program recommendations, designed to enhance performance, have been taken in part from Winnick and Short (1985).

- Exercises and activities with a rehabilitative purpose should be conducted under the supervision of a physician and in coordination with physical therapists, occupational therapists, and/or other professional support personnel.
- Program activity sessions should take place on a regular rather than a sporadic basis.
- A variety of exercises and activities should be offered to allow as many parts of the body as possible to be active.
- The frequency, intensity, and duration of activity sessions should be programmed on an

individual basis according to the person's tolerance level. AAHPERD (1980) suggests that activity levels should not be increased more than 10% each week.

- Individuals with more severe impairments may need exercises and activities with greater frequency than can be offered within the adapted physical education program. Therefore, exercises and activities performed at home or outside of the program are encouraged.

GUIDELINES FOR COMMUNITY-BASED FITNESS PROGRAMS

The ultimate goal of any physical education program is to provide pupils with disabilities with the sport and leisure skills needed to function effectively and safely in a community setting. In order for this type of integration to occur, guidelines for developing and implementing such programs are highlighted. Lasko-McCarthey and Aufsesser (1990) have developed a series of guidelines for physical fitness programs for adults with physical disabilities based on a fitness clinic at San Diego State University. The following guidelines have been adapted from this program:

- Participants need to obtain a medical examination from a qualified physician and complete a detailed intake form (Figure 21.8).
- Following medical clearance, physical fitness is comprehensively assessed. This includes muscular strength and endurance, cardiovascular endurance, flexibility, and gross motor skills.
- Based on assessment results, and information obtained from the participant's medical history, an individualized exercise program is then developed.
- Program implementation includes selected exercises along with recordkeeping (exercise program card) and program evaluation (from community and medical advisory boards).

These physical fitness guidelines are general enough to apply to almost any person with a disability.

SUMMARY

This chapter dealt with exercises and activities for relaxation and physical fitness. It stressed the importance of relaxation in preparing people both physically and psychologically for activity and in assisting in the recovery from injury. It focused on exercises and activity modifications that can improve physical fitness levels in persons with unique needs. Further, along with an overview of weight training and bodybuilding, it presented program principles as well as exercises and activities that can be appropriately modified for persons with unique needs. Finally, it offered guidelines for community-based physical fitness programs for adults.

BIBLIOGRAPHY

American Alliance for Health, Physical Education, Recreation and Dance (1980). *Health-related physical fitness manual*. Washington, DC: Author.

Basmajian, J.V. (Ed.) (1989). *Biofeedback: Principles and practices for clinicians* (3rd ed.). Baltimore: Williams & Wilkins.

Fleck, S.J., & Kraemer, W.J. (1987). *Designing resistance training programs*. Champaign, IL: Human Kinetics.

Jacobson, E. (1970). *Modern treatment of tense patients*. Springfield, IL: Charles C Thomas.

Kennedy, S.O. (1988). Flexibility training for wheelchair athletes. *Sports 'N Spokes*, **13**(5), 43–46.

Landy, J.M., & Landy, M.J. (1993). *Ready-to-use PE activities for grades 5–6*. West Nyack, NJ: Parker.

Lasko-McCarthey, P., & Aufsesser, P.M. (1990). Guidelines for a community-based physical fitness program for adults with physical disabilities. *Palaestra*, **6**(4), 18–29.

Special Olympics. (1989). *Special Olympics motor activities training program*. Washington, DC: Author.

Surburg, P.R. (1986). New perspectives for developing range of motion and flexibility for special populations. *Adapted Physical Activity Quarterly*, **3**, 227–235.

Vealey, R. (1986). Imagery training for performance enhancement. In J. Williams (Ed.), *Applied sport psychology: Personal growth to peak performance* (pp. 209–234). Palo Alto, CA: Mayfield.

Westcott, W.L. (1983). *Strength fitness: Physiological principles and training techniques*. Newton, MA: Allyn & Bacon.

Winnick, J.P. (1984). Recent advances related to special physical education and sport. *Adapted Physical Activity Quarterly*, **1**, 197–206.

Winnick, J.P., & Short, F.X. (1985). *Physical fitness testing of the disabled*. Champaign, IL: Human Kinetics.

RESOURCES

Written

Brosnan, B. (1982). *Yoga for handicapped people*. London: Souvenir Press. This book describes how yoga can

MEDICAL HISTORY/HEALTH HABIT QUESTIONNAIRE

PRESENT MEDICAL HISTORY

Date of Interview _____ Interviewer _____

Name _____ Age _____ Birthdate _____

Address _____ Zip Code _____

Phone Numbers: Day _____ Evening _____

Soc. Sec. No. _____ Vehicle Lic. No. _____

Place of Birth _____

Height _____ Weight _____ Sex _____ Race _____

Resting Heart Rate _____ Resting Blood Pressure _____

In Case of Emergency Contact: _____

Phone _____ Address _____

1. LIST ALL MEDICATIONS PRESENTLY TAKING

Medicine	Dose	Purpose	Duration	Side Effects

2. MEDICAL DIAGNOSIS: (Include date of onset or occurrence)

_____

_____

_____

3. PRESENT MEDICAL CONDITION:

_____

_____

_____

4. EXERCISE CONTRAINDICATIONS:

_____

_____

_____

5. OPERATIONS: (Since onset or occurrence of disablility)

Type	Reason	Date	Complications

6. THERAPY RECEIVED DURING PAST YEAR:

Type	Reason	Duration	Where

7. LIST YOUR PHYSICIANS

Name _____ Specialty _____ Phone _____

Address _____ Zip _____

Frequency of visits _____ Reason _____

Name _____ Specialty _____ Phone _____

Address _____ Zip _____

Frequency of visits _____ Reason _____

Figure 21.8 San Diego State University Medical History/Health Habit Questionnaire.
From "Guidelines for a Community-Based Physical Fitness Program for Adults With Physical Disabilities," *Palaestra*, **7**(1), p. 21. Copyright 1990 by *Palaestra*. Reprinted by permission.

be performed by people with a variety of disabilities. Specific exercises and positions are included with illustrations.

Fitness for students with developmental disabilities: A 7-module program. (1992). Learner Managed Designs, 2201-K W. 25th Street, Lawrence, KS 66047. This is a comprehensive fitness program designed by the Schiefelbusch Institute for Life Span Studies and the Kansas University Affiliated Program at Parsons. The program, which is designed to be used as a fitness curriculum, is composed of instructor's guides, teacher's guides, and videotapes. Module topics include fitness routines, teaching strategies, fitness testing, and safety.

Orlick, T. (1990). *In pursuit of excellence: How to win in sport and life through mental training.* Champaign, IL: Human Kinetics. This book describes such topics as self-assessment, choosing a self-control strategy, imagery, relaxation, concentration, and cases in self-control.

Shepard, R. (1990). *Fitness in special populations.* Champaign, IL: Human Kinetics. Discusses fitness assessment, training programs, and program design.

Audiovisual

Groden, J., & Cautela, J. (1993). *Imagery procedures for people with special needs: Breaking the barriers II* [Videotape]. Distributed by Research Press, 2612 North Mattis Avenue, Champaign, IL 61821. This is the second and more recent of two videotapes. It is 32 minutes in length designed for practitioners interested in teaching imagery techniques to individuals with disabilities with the focus on controlling specific behaviors. The video shows how persons with lower cognitive abilities can be taught imagery through the use of pictures (to help imagine the scene), prompts, or tangible reinforcers. A written guide detailing the procedures accompanies the video.

Groden, J., Cautela, J., & Groden, G. (1989). *Relaxation techniques for people with special needs: Breaking the barriers* [Videotape]. Distributed by Research Press, 2612 North Mattis Avenue, Champaign, IL 61821. This 23-minute video shows a number of persons with developmental disabilities learning relaxation techniques and using them in integrated settings. Both young and old people with developmental disabilities are featured learning self-control techniques of which relaxation is one. A free copy of the book *Relaxation: A comprehensive manual for adults, children, and children with special needs* by J. Cautela and J. Groden is included with the purchase of the video.

National Handicapped Sports. (n.d.). *A strength and flexibility exercise program for individuals with all types of physical disabilities* [Videotape]. Richard Sirianni & Associates, 248 East 48th Street, New York, NY 10017. This video presents both a strength program and flexibility program for persons with all types of physical disabilities. Each program is approximately 30 minutes in duration and participants perform to music.

National Handicapped Sports. (n.d.). *An aerobic exercise program designed for individuals with paraplegia, quadriplegia, cerebral palsy, leg amputations* [Videotape]. 451 Hungerford Drive, Suite 100, Rockville, MD 20850. This video presents four 30-minute segments on aerobic exercise programs for individuals with paraplegia, quadriplegia, cerebral palsy, and leg amputations. Individuals with these disabilities are shown performing each program.

Richard Simmons Reach Foundation. (n.d.). *Reach for fitness* [Videotape]. Karl-Lorimar Home Video: Irvine, CA. This 40-minute video was developed in conjunction with leading physicians and health educators for persons with physical impairments. Individuals with disabilities are shown performing a variety of exercises.

CHAPTER 22

Rhythms and Dance

Ellen M. Kowalski

Billy sat on the bleachers watching the other children. The class was square dancing. Billy was one of those clumsy kids with two left feet. In first grade, he had a lot of trouble with his coordination and rhythm activities, especially when the class danced. He could never seem to hear the music like the other children and always was the one who clapped off-beat. It was frustrating trying to perform the steps the way the teacher did. He always went the wrong way or did the wrong movement, stepping on toes and bumping into others. When this happened, the other children laughed and made fun of him. This year, whenever the class dances and performs rhythm activities, Billy refuses to participate. "I don't want to dance," he says. "I hate dance. I'll just mess it up."

THE VALUE OF TEACHING RHYTHM AND DANCE

Many children, able-bodied and disabled, are like Billy. Almost 80% of school-age children are uncomfortable moving to music, following a visual movement demonstration, and expressing themselves rhythmically (Weikart, 1989). Rhythm is a functional component of all aspects of life, from the beating of the human heart to the rhythm inherent in movement skills. Few teachers realize the contribution that rhythm and dance activities can make to the psychological and motor development of children and to the long-term well-being of adults (Schmitz, 1989). Rhythm is the connecting thread that enhances the development of skills and abilities, develops self-esteem, promotes social interaction, and allows children of all ability levels to participate in activity. At the basic level, rhythmic activities help develop auditory, visual, and tactile/kinesthetic decoding skills, timing, creative movement and language, and comfort with movement (Weikart, 1989).

The medium of rhythm is particularly valuable to children with disabilities, since it provides the opportunity to participate in activities that are educational, lifetime-recreational, and therapeutic in nature. "Dance is all inclusive—respecting individuals for what they bring to the moment; their abilities, and their strengths" (Schwartz, 1989). Dance does not discriminate between age or ability level, high functioning or low, ambulatory or not. Many children with disabilities display developmental delays in self-esteem, body and spatial awareness, and coordination, exhibiting deficits in spatial awareness, motor sequencing, and timing. Linked to theoretical concepts of sensory integration (Ayres, 1972), dance provides an excellent medium for developing perceptual-motor skills and spatial awareness, offering opportunities to explore the abilities and limitations of the physical self. Through dance, children cultivate the development of accurate body image, kinesthetic awareness, and position and movement in space. Dance provides a connection between the mental and physical self. Children's perceptions and feelings about themselves, their identity, and self-esteem are largely influenced by how well their bodies move (Marsh & Shavelson, 1985). Rhythm and dance activities focus on children becoming comfortable with their bodies and therefore play a crucial role in developing self-concept.

Children with disabilities often have difficulty with self-expression, creative movement, and interpretation. Dance, by the nature of its definition, encourages children to express themselves through movement. Dance is a living, moving language that offers a medium for self-discovery, self-expression, and creativity, despite limitations imposed by a disability (Pesetsky & Burack, 1984). Creative movement is important to all students, especially those with disabilities. It helps them investigate new movement patterns and explore their bodies' capacity for movement (Riordan, 1989). Creative dance is a wonderful medium to encourage expressive movement because, unlike many other activities in physical education, there is no right or wrong (Joyce, 1980). Dance needs no words, thus serving as an excellent way to develop communication and expression for children who are nonverbal or have limited verbal capacity. Through creative dance activities, those who have little physical movement or language are given the opportunity to express their feelings, to communicate, and to interact with others in a nonthreatening environment.

Dance is a functional, lifetime activity that enables individuals to enjoy movement and to laugh with others in a leisure activity. Children need to develop basic rhythmic skills that allow them to enjoy social activities in a leisure setting, especially as they reach adulthood. Sometimes it is difficult to motivate children with disabilities to move, especially those at severe and profound levels. In addition to being a lifetime activity, at the basic level rhythm and music can be used to facilitate movement. Rhythm and music can be powerful motivators to encourage hesitant children into the gymnasium and to maximize movement during instructional time.

THE DIFFERENCE BETWEEN ADAPTED DANCE AND DANCE THERAPY

Both educators and dance therapists use rhythm and dance in their programs for individuals with disabilities. However, a distinction needs to be made between adapted dance and dance therapy. Although adapted dance can be an art form, an educational modality, and therapeutic in nature, it cannot be considered therapy. Up until the middle 1960s, rhythmic movement and dance for individuals with disabilities was referred to as dance therapy, with no differentiation made between terms. The **American Dance Therapy Association (ADTA)**, formed in 1966, defines **dance/movement**

therapy as "the psychotherapeutic use of movement as a process which furthers the emotional and physical integration of the individual. Dance therapy is distinguished from other utilizations of dance . . . by its focus on the nonverbal aspects of behavior and its use of movement as the process for intervention" (Sherrill, 1993). Dance therapy is a specific treatment modality used as a nonverbal psychotherapy with individuals exhibiting psychological, emotional, and behavioral problems. Though similar to adapted dance, dance therapy is more closely aligned with physical or occupational therapy and can only be conducted by a certified dance therapist. **Adapted dance**, which parallels the definition of adapted physical education, refers to rhythmic movement instruction designed or modified to meet the unique needs of individuals with disabilities. "The purpose of adapted dance . . . is to facilitate self-actualization, particularly as it relates to understanding and appreciation of the body and its capacity for movement" (Sherrill, 1993, p. 402).

RHYTHM AND DANCE IN THE PHYSICAL EDUCATION PROGRAM

Rhythmical movement experiences are important to the motoric development of children with disabilities. Dance is an integral part of physical education and should be given major emphasis. Unfortunately, this is not always the case. Many physical educators have a limited background in dance and are uncomfortable teaching rhythmic activities. Consequently, these teachers tend to include few rhythm and dance experiences in their programs or to eliminate them altogether. As a result, students lack adequate experiences for rhythm and dance to become a natural part of their movement repertoire. Compounding the problem, teachers often unknowingly introduce dance activities at too high a level, beginning with movements that are too complex. Dance "steps" that involve the coordination of several body parts require a level of integration, kinesthetic awareness, and motor sequencing that is often difficult for children to perform.

Participation in rhythm and dance activities can often be frustrating for children with disabilities, especially in an integrated setting. Because the growth and maturation of their motor patterns is often different, basic motor skills may not develop fully or may develop as splinter skills, resulting in difficulty when performing rhythmic movements and dance steps. Unfortunately, minimal exposure such as a two-week dance unit does not develop the necessary skills. Dance and rhythmic activities need to be threaded throughout the entire physical education curriculum. With well-designed and developmentally sequenced rhythm and dance activities, participation can be both successful and fulfilling.

Begin With Rhythm Awareness

Helping individuals feel comfortable with their bodies is important. If children have basic rhythm awareness, they are much more likely to participate in and enjoy rhythmic activities in physical education classes and in social settings. Inherent in almost any piece of music, rhythm involves three components: beat, tempo, and accent. At the basic level, rhythmic movement requires the ability to effectively use time and space. Many children with disabilities lack rhythm awareness and thus are unable to respond naturally to pulse beats or to the time intervals between beats (Sherrill, 1986). **Rhythmic competency**, or basic timing, is composed of two abilities, **beat awareness** and **beat competency** (Weikart, 1989). Beat awareness is defined as the ability to feel and express the steady beat of a rhyme, song, recorded musical selection, and so on, using nonlocomotor movements. Beat competency involves the ability to walk to a beat in self-space or general space. Weikart (1989) suggests a teaching progression to help students attain a basic level of rhythmic competency. The first task is feeling and moving to a steady beat, such as rocking, patting, or clapping. The second task involves organizing and repeating two nonlocomotor movements to the beat. Children may be able to tap their knees to a beat but not be able to bend their knees rhythmically while clapping. The third task involves walking to a beat. The addition of mobility requires greater integration and coordination of body parts. Beat awareness activities involve simple movements to a beat creating a bonding to rhythm by providing a link between sound and movement (Bornell, 1989; Weikart, 1989). Following simple guidelines can assist teaching rhythmic competency to all age groups and ability levels, including individuals with disabilities.

- Begin with the individual. It is challenging enough to follow a beat by oneself without attempting to coordinate one's movements with another. Many children with mobility impairments or temporal perception problems experience difficulty moving to an external rhythm (Krebs, 1990). Allow children to move to their own rhythm initially. Children then imitate a steady beat created by the teacher using simple movements such as clapping or rhythm instruments. When using music, be sure to reinforce the heavy or even beat, which is much easier to hear.

- Activities should begin with nonlocomotor movements: sitting by oneself, with a partner, or with objects such as balls, bean bags, and so on. When standing, use movements such as bending, twisting, rocking, or walking in place. Eventually incorporate marching in place, walking, and other locomotor movements into rhythm activities.

- Initially use whole body movements (rocking, bending at waist), individual body parts (one arm), or same body part on both sides of body (bend both knees/elbows). Change alternating single movements (lift right arm, then left). Eventually incorporate two or more body parts, either sequentially or simultaneously (i.e., two slaps each on floor, knees, shoulders, head). Bending knees to a beat is much simpler rhythmically than bending knees and clapping.

Once basic beat awareness is obtained individually, students can work on performing movements with a partner where they have to coordinate their own movements with the movements of another. Activities include children clapping hands (double patty cake) and mirroring each other's movements to a beat or sitting in a choo-choo train tapping the beat on the back of the person in front of them. To increase level of difficulty, teachers add equipment such as bean bags, balls, or ribbon sticks to the rhythmical movement. Children must coordinate the movement of an external object to the movement of their bodies. When using equipment, teachers should begin with activities involving nonlocomotor movements.

Teaching the Elements of Movement

Although developing beat competency and rhythm awareness should be the first objective, rhythmic and dance activities can also focus upon the **elements of movement**. All dance is composed of elements of movement, space (shape, level, size, pathway), time (beat, accent, pattern), force (light or strong), and flow (free or bound). Laban (1963) grouped movement into 16 basic themes. Each theme corresponds to the progressive unfolding of movement in the growing child. Both creative and modern dance expand upon the elements of movement to allow all students to test the limits of their bodies' capabilities, especially those who are motorically challenged. By focusing on the elements of movement through creative dance and movement education (exploration and guided discovery), teachers can enhance body image and spatial awareness, language development through associations between words and movement, creativity, and emotional expression. Preston (1963) simplified Laban's themes into seven movement themes for organizing educational dance content. Building on beat awareness, these themes provide teachers with guidelines for developing rhythm and dance progressions and activities. A valuable tool in an integrated setting, these themes can assist the teacher to individualize activities, allowing students to work at their own level. These seven themes are referred to throughout the remaining portions of the chapter.

Theme 1. Awareness of the body (total body actions and actions of individual body parts)

Theme 2. Awareness of weight and time (contrasting qualities)

Theme 3. Awareness of space (areas, directions, levels, pathways, and extensions)

Theme 4. Awareness of flow of movement (use of space and time)

Theme 5. Awareness of adaptation to partners and small groups (simple forms of relationships)

Theme 6. Awareness of body (emphasis on elevation, body shapes, and gestures)

Theme 7. Awareness of basic effort actions (rhythmic nature of time, weight, and space)

Once children learn the basic content of a theme, experiences may be designed to combine previous themes with the newly learned content. Modified to incorporate the early childhood age group, Table 22.1 outlines a dance program that continues through age 12 (Logsdon et al., 1984).

Steps for Teaching a Dance

As children develop rhythmic awareness, teachers can introduce simple dance steps and movement sequences. No matter what the age group or the disability, teachers should follow a simple progression when teaching a dance. Classes should be given the opportunity to listen to the entire piece of music first to give them a feeling of the rhythm and tempo, then they can be asked to tap or clap to the beat. Without music first, teachers should teach dance steps by having children verbally rehearse/label each step. **Verbal rehearsal/labeling** involves active learning where verbal labels are spoken in the same timing in which the movement is performed. Documented as an effective teaching strategy (Kowalski & Sherrill, 1992; Weiss & Klint, 1987) verbal rehearsal/labeling assists encoding and integration of information, improving the ability to plan, sequence, and perform a motor pattern. Children with disabilities are often motorically awkward, displaying difficulties in integrating movement, motor memory, and motor sequencing. For children who have difficulty encoding and decoding visual and auditory information and then translating it into smooth coordinated movement, verbal rehearsal creates a concrete link between movement and thought and enhances motor sequencing and motor memory.

One such progression for enhancing motor sequencing and memory is the **Say & Do method** (Weikart, 1989), designed to teach dance by connecting language and movement. Verbal labels identifying the body part, locomotor movement, or motion are spoken in the same timing in which the movements are performed. The four-step language process begins with (a) no movement and no music, just chanting the movement labels out loud to a rhythm set by the teacher; (b) no music, chanting out loud while simultaneously performing the movements; (c) adding music, whispering chant while simultaneously performing the movements; and (d) thinking the words while simultaneously performing movements to music.

SUGGESTED RHYTHM AND DANCE ACTIVITIES

Rhythm and dance activities provide children with disabilities wonderful opportunities to become involved with their able-bodied peers. To ensure successful and enjoyable participation, activities must be appropriate to the group's age. Selecting appropriate activities requires careful consideration of the group's developmental level as well as accurate assessment of each individual's skill level. With young children, teachers must be careful that movement activities designed for the age group

Table 22.1 Suggested Dance Progression by Theme and Age

Theme	Age in years									
	3	4	5	6	7	8	9	10	11	12
1. Awareness of body	————	————	————	————	————	————	*****	*****	*****	*****
2. Awareness of weight and time	————	————	————	————	————	————	————	*****	*****	*****
3. Awareness of space				······	······	————	————	————	*****	*****
4. Awareness of flow				······	————	————	————	————	————	*****
5. Awareness of adaptation to partners and small groups	······	······	······	————	————	————	————	————	————	————
6. Awareness of the body	······	······	······	————	————	————	————	————	————	————
7. Awareness of the basic effort actions	······	······	······	————	————	————	————	————	————	————

Key:

———————— Theme is developmentally appropriate in physical education program.

********* Theme may be appropriate but used less frequently.

·············· More advanced themes to increase complexity in a physical education program.

Note. From *Physical Education for Children: A Focus on the Teaching Process* (2nd ed.) (p. 161) by B.J. Logsdon, K.R. Barrett, M.R. Broer, R. McGee, M. Ammons, L.E. Halverson, and M.S. Roberton, 1995, Philadelphia: Lea & Febiger. Copyright 1993 by Bette J. Logsdon. Adapted by permission of the author.

are not too difficult, resulting in repeated failure (Weikart, 1989). Although older, adolescents and adults may still need to experience and develop the simplest levels of rhythmic competency. Although the focus and objectives remain the same, it is extremely important that selected rhythmic activities are appropriate for the age group. Because of developmental level, selecting age-appropriate activities is particularly difficult for persons with severe and profound disability. Even so, nursery songs such as "Ring Around the Rosie" or "The Wheels on the Bus" are unacceptable for use with older students and adults.

Early Childhood

Rhythmic activities for children ages 3–5 should emphasize body awareness (theme 1) and fundamental spatial concepts (themes 2 & 3). Especially for children with perceptual-motor deficits, all rhythmic activities should combine chanting with movement (Jensen, 1983). For example, chanting and tapping various body parts (i.e., head, head, head, head; knees, knees, knees, knees) or performing simple movements (push, push, push, push) helps create a strong word-movement association. Action songs such as "Head, Shoulders, Knees, and Toes" are popular for teaching body

part names and locations or simple movement concepts about space, effort, and time (bent/straight, big/small). Teachers can also create action songs to familiar tunes (e.g., "Skip to My Lou") by substituting words (shake, push, tap, jump, etc.) relevant to the action or body part being taught. On a simpler level, **single bilateral symmetrical movement**, such as moving both feet or hands in a single movement (Weikart, 1989), is recommended because at this level bilateral integration is yet unrefined and even simple integrated movements are often too complex. Young children need and enjoy activities that are simple and extremely repetitive in nature. Use activities that are primarily nonlocomotor and allow each child to perform in their own space. Locomotor skills should be limited to simple walks or marches. Most importantly, whether using music or a simple rhythm instrument, action song, or chant, teachers should not be concerned with students moving "correctly" to an external beat. They should allow them to move to their own rhythms (Weikart, 1989).

Primary

Rhythmic activities for children ages 5–7 expand upon activities taught in early childhood. Although activities are still focused on body and space awareness (themes 1, 2, 3) and are repetitive in nature, teachers can begin to combine movements (themes 1, 4, 6). Rhythmic activities help children with disabilities to recognize variation of movement force and flow (theme 4) and to discriminate between even and uneven rhythm and various tempos (theme 2). Action songs and chants remain a foundation for rhythmic activities, involving isolated body parts (themes 2 & 3) and total body movement (themes 1, 4, 6, 7). Increased coordination and ability to combine rhythm with locomotor and axial movement allow activities to contain a greater variety of movement and utilize words that involve total body coordination rather than body parts. Percussive instruments (tambourines, drums, shakers, etc.) or other equipment (ribbon sticks, bean bags, lummi sticks) are an excellent way to increase coordination requirements and bridge rhythmic movement from nonlocomotor (sitting) to locomotor skills (marching). Simple dance steps and formations should be introduced as early as possible. Individual, or nonpartner, dances (e.g., "Hokey Pokey," "Alley Cat," and "Bunny Hop") are the easiest to start with because they do not require coordination of one's own movements with the movements of another. Children of this age level have wonderfully active imaginations. Rhythmic activities and action songs enhance creative movement (themes 1, 2, 3) by stimulating play such as imitating people, animals, and things or acting out nursery rhymes, poems, stories, and songs (Krebs, 1990).

Late Childhood and Early Adolescence

Children ages 8–11 demonstrate increased levels of attention and cognitive functioning, balance, coordination, perceptual-motor abilities, and social interaction. Children are ready to be challenged by adding the use of objects such as balls, hoops, ribbon sticks, and ropes to rhythmic activities. Socially, children should begin to work cooperatively with partners and in small groups. Line dances, simple folk and square dances, and activities using improvisation (Theme 6) provide older children with the fundamentals to learn more complex dance movements (Krebs, 1990) important to successful participation in integrated social settings later in life.

Adolescence and Young Adulthood

Adolescence brings a shift in the demands of the school environment, where social behavior becomes a central focus of a student's life. These social demands are no different for adolescents with disabilities. Interest is on the "cool" way to dress or learning the latest dance everyone's doing to the most recent popular music. Rhythmic programs during the adolescent years should be predominantly geared toward teaching social dance skills and lifetime fitness activities.

More than any other age, adolescents with disabilities need to be provided opportunities to participate in age-appropriate, integrated activities. Teachers need to keep up with current trends in music and social dances (i.e., "Hip Hop," "The Electric Slide," "Achy Breaky Heart") often seen at school dances and social gatherings. Adolescents with disabilities may not have the opportunity to learn these current dances because of motoric difficulty or lack of exposure. More fundamental than learning current dance steps, students need to feel good about expressing themselves rhythmically. Frequently seen at school dances and social gatherings is **free style dance**, which is no dance in particular but simply moving rhythmically in a way that fits the music and reflects the individual. Students can create their own dance style by taking a few simple movements, performing them to the beat, then changing the direction, emphasis, or tempo (themes 3, 4, 6, 7). When rhythmic competency and simple dance steps are mastered, teachers can help students with disabilities learn to express themselves through movement and develop their own styles.

Rhythmic programs should also include aerobic dance, now popular in many physical education programs. Aerobics, which combines simple locomotor and nonlocomotor activity, is social activity easily modified for an integrated group (see Figure 22.1). Though more formal than freestyle or aerobic dancing, everyone from young to old can enjoy integrated rhythmic activities through folk and square dance. Folk dances provide valuable insight into many cultures and customs. Whether it be freestyle, aerobic, folk, or square dance, adolescents with disabilities can participate in age-appropriate, integrated activities and feel good about themselves.

MODIFYING RHYTHM AND DANCE ACTIVITIES FOR PERSONS WITH DISABILITIES

With only slight modification, all individuals can enjoy rhythm and dance activities. One of the most significant benefits of using rhythmic activities and

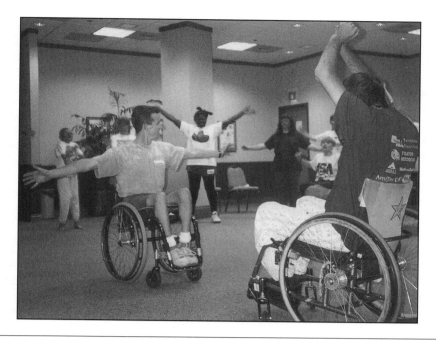

Figure 22.1 Aerobics is a social fitness activity easily modified for all age groups and ability levels. Photo courtesy of National Handicapped Sports.

dance with disabled individuals is that it can be used to work on all levels of movement control. For students who have difficulty processing multi-part directions and sequencing movements, break dance steps into small movement phrases and teach separately first, then in combination. Teachers may initially need to slow the tempo down or manually assist students' movements to help them feel the beat or tempo. Although specific modifications and techniques are associated with various disabling conditions, teachers should follow a few general guidelines: (a) keep movement sequences short and within the comprehension level and physical tolerance of the group, (b) place less emphasis on verbal explanation and greater emphasis on manual guidance, and (c) select music containing a strong, steady beat.

When teaching students with mental retardation, it is important to be very concrete. Because of the abstract nature of language, understanding verbal directions is often difficult. Emphasize visual and manual guidance to help students learn movement sequences. Footprints and arrows on the floor, numbers on cones, enlarged pictures and diagrams, as well as visual demonstrations focus attention and clarify directions. Props such as hoops, balls, elastic bands, sandpaper, and scarves help students focus their energy and develop concepts through concrete experience. For example, teachers can use hula hoops as a prop for stretching

overhead or scarves for experiencing lightness of movement (Silk, 1989). When teaching action songs, use short, simple melodies with repeated phrases (Krebs, 1990). Teach the words to the melody first, followed by the movements or steps without partners or groups.

Children with learning disabilities often have difficulty planning, organizing, sequencing, and remembering movement because of problems in information processing and motor planning (Lazarus, 1990). For children exhibiting motor awkwardness, rhythmic activities should focus on developing temporal perception and body localization (Schmitz, 1989). It is important to incorporate rhythm awareness using simple bilateral movements that require a low level of coordination. If processing deficits are apparent, it is crucial to provide for maximum repetition and focus children on relevant cues through verbal labeling. Children with learning disabilities should be taught to verbalize their movements in all activities, thus helping them to encode movement sequences by connecting language and movement at basic levels of processing (Kowalski & Sherrill, 1992). For children displaying social imperception, using activities that focus on expressive movement helps children learn to interpret and express feelings accurately. Pantomime and creative dance can also be instrumental in the development of appropriate social behavior.

Children with mental illness and behavior disorders characteristically have difficulty with self-expression, interpretation, and interpersonal relationships. Although they may understand and appreciate their bodies and derive great pleasure from exploration of space, they still may be unable to use movement to convey their needs, wishes, feelings, and moods to others (Sherrill, 1986). Often used with emotional disturbance and mental disabilities, dance therapy is an effective intervention because it focuses on nonverbal communication through movement and allows children to reflect their thoughts in a nonthreatening way. Teachers can apply principles of dance therapy in rhythmic activities to help students with emotional problems to develop a better perspective about themselves and their feelings. Initially, teachers should mimic the student's movement rather than being the one initiating movement. Eventually students can reflect the movement patterns of others. Through creative expression and modern dance, activities should focus on the expression of feelings rather than on specific steps or movements. Dances should be created that encourage children to use their bodies in different ways, experiment with opposites in movement, and explore movement through space.

Although students with hearing impairments may be unable to hear music, this does not mean they cannot dance. Although hearing does make it easier, profoundly deaf and hearing impaired students can learn to dance as well as their hearing peers. Avoid high-frequency music, since many students will be unable to hear it. Music should be amplified and contain a heavy bass. In addition, place speakers face down on a wood floor to increase the intensity of the vibrations and bass tones. When integrating hearing and deaf students in dance activities, it is important that all information be presented visually (Hottendorf, 1989). All forms of communication should be utilized: written directions on poster board and blackboards, gestures, and pantomime, as well as the spoken word. Teachers should always face students when giving instructions and allow them to place themselves where they can see best. Walking around and talking makes it extremely difficult for students to lipread. The rhythm of music should be consistently demonstrated visually by beating a drum, clapping hands, tapping a leg, or counting with the fingers. Teachers should demonstrate dance steps with their backs to the students, making it easier to mimic right and left movements (Krebs, 1990).

When teaching students with visual impairments, rhythmic activities should be modified by replacing visual cues with tactile and/or kinesthetic cues. Totally blind students, paired with a partially sighted or sighted partner, can acquire a kinesthetic sense of force, flow, timing, and space by placing their hands on the partner's shoulders, arms, or hip. Teachers and students can mark dance steps and patterns by moving the hands on the floor. Dances can be modified so that either contact is maintained continuously (circle, line, square) or dancers are totally separate from each other in their own defined space (Krebs, 1990). Complex dance movements should be replaced with simpler forward, backward, and side steps. Teachers can enhance residual vision by using brightly colored tape to mark position and indicate direction or space and establish boundaries by adding surface textures to the floor (thin mats, taping down news/butcher paper). Especially when teaching students with visual impairments, it is important to make sure that the sound system and acoustics are clear and that any distracting or competing noises are eliminated. For example, when leading/cuing aerobics, music that is too loud drowns out the instructor's voice.

Characteristically, children with mobility impairments (cerebral palsy, muscular dystrophy, spina bifida, etc.) have difficulty performing movements smoothly and with control. When teaching rhythmic activities and dances, independent movement and control should be emphasized. To modify activities, the tempo may need to be slowed, movements simplified, and timing of coordinated steps adjusted (Harris, 1989; Krebs, 1990) to allow students to focus on controlling a movement or holding a position. For ambulatory students, walking and nonlocomotor movements (swaying, swinging arms, balancing) can be substituted for dance steps that are too fast or complex. Students who use wheelchairs may substitute upper-body, arm, and head movements for leg movements and rolling for locomotor skills (Kindel, 1986). Although limited motorically, physically challenged students need to be given opportunities for creative expression as much as their able-bodied peers. Rather than being limited to traditional activities such as wheelchair square dancing, students should be encouraged to explore and create new movements or patterns made possible by the chair (Riordan, 1989).

THEATRICAL DANCE AND PERFORMANCE PROGRAMS

Beginning during childhood and adolescence, many students become interested in formalized dance (tap, ballet, jazz, modern), attending weekly dance lessons and performing in recitals. Students with disabilities also need to experience formal dance, both as a participant and as an observer (Boswell, 1989; Schmitz, 1989). It is important for children to be exposed to role models with disabilities who demonstrate high levels of skill, not only in sport but in dance. For example, within Gallaudet University for the Deaf, a professional-level dance company performs ballet, modern dance, and jazz. Other examples include improvisational dance troupes such as Sunrise: A Special Company (composed of individuals with developmental delays) and Sunrise Wheels (composed of individuals using wheelchairs). Led by Ann Riordan, the Sunrise troupes have performed in several states. If live performances are not possible, videotapes of performances are available (see the Resources at the end of this chapter).

From a different perspective, dance is a valuable facilitator of social integration. Although dancers with disabilities are important in serving as role models, if children are exposed to dance recitals performed exclusively by individuals with disabilities, social integration will not be facilitated. To encourage social integration, all children need to experience and observe integrated dance performances (see Figure 22.2). One example is an integrated social-dance troupe that originated in the Federal Republic of Germany in 1974. Social-integrative wheelchair dancing clearly demonstrates how the movements of the wheelchair and the steps of the "pedestrian" are coordinated so that the couple dances in harmony.

Figure 22.2   Margit Quell and Carsteu Lenz, European Social Integrative-Wheelchair Dance Champions, 1991.
Photo courtesy of Dr. Gertrude Krombholz, Munich, Germany.

SUMMARY

Rhythmic movement and dance are valuable forms of communication and creative expression that enrich one's life in many ways and contribute to motor and psychological development. Children with disabilities can benefit greatly through a modified dance curriculum in which activities are designed to meet their unique needs. Benefits of rhythmic and dance activities include development of mind/body connections, body image, and spatial awareness; improvement of mobility, strength, coordination, and flexibility; enhancement of self-image; and development of social skills and cooperation (Schmitz, 1989). Rhythm awareness and basic rhythm skills, such as locomotor and nonlocomotor movements, are prerequisite to successful participation in many games and activities taught in integrated settings. The recent trend toward inclusion in education today only increases the value and significance of rhythms and dance in physical education classes. If children with disabilities are to be integrated with their able-bodied peers, physical educators must ensure opportunities for reaching their full potential by threading dance and rhythmic activities throughout the entire curriculum.

BIBLIOGRAPHY

Ayres, J. (1972). *Sensory integration and learning disorders.* Los Angeles: Western Psychological Services.
Bornell, D. (1989). Movement discovery linking the impossible to the possible. In S. Grosse, C. Cooper, S. Gavron, & J. Stein (Eds.), *The Best of Practical Pointers* (pp. 120–138). Reston, VA: AAHPERD Publications.
Boswell, B. (1989). Dance as creative expression for the disabled. *Palaestra,* **6**(1), 28–30.

Harris, C. (1989). Dance for students with orthopedic conditions: Popular, square/folk, modern/ballet. In S. Grosse, C. Cooper, S. Gavron, & J. Stein (Eds.), *The Best of Practical Pointers* (pp. 155–172). Reston, VA: AAHPERD Publications.

Hottendorf, D. (1989). Mainstreaming deaf and hearing children in dance classes. *Journal of Physical Education, Recreation and Dance*, **60**(9), 54–55.

Jensen, M. (1983). Composing and guiding creative movement. *Journal of Physical Education, Recreation and Dance*, **54**(1), 85–87.

Joyce, M. (1980). *First steps in teaching creative dance to children* (2nd ed.). Mountain View, CA: Mayfield.

Kindel, M. (1986). Wheelchair dancer. *A Positive Approach: A National Magazine for the Physically Challenged*, **1**(1), 41–43.

Kowalski, E., & Sherrill, C. (1992). Motor sequencing of learning disabled boys: Modeling and verbal rehearsal strategies. *Adapted Physical Activity Quarterly*, **9**, 261–272.

Krebs, P. (1990). Rhythms and dance. In J. Winnick (Eds.), *Adapted physical education and sport*. Champaign, IL: Human Kinetics.

Laban, R. (1963). *Modern education dance* (2nd ed.). Revised by L. Ullman. New York: Praeger.

Lazarus, J. (1990). Factors underlying inefficient movement in learning disabled children. In G. Reid (Ed.), *Problems in movement control* (pp. 241–261). New York: Elsevier.

Logsdon, B., Barrett, K., Broer, M., McGee, R., Ammons, M., Halverson, L., & Roberton, M. (1984). *Physical education for children: A focus on the teaching process* (2nd ed.). Philadelphia: Lea & Febiger.

Marsh, H., & Shavelson, R. (1985). Self-concept: Its multifaceted, hierarchical structure. *Educational Psychologist*, **20**, 107–125.

Pesetsky, S., & Burack, S. (1984). *Teaching dance for the handicapped: A curriculum guide*. Michigan Dance Association.

Preston, V. (1963). *A handbook for modern educational dance*. London: McDonald & Evans.

Riordan, A. (1989). Sunrise wheels. *Journal of Physical Education, Recreation and Dance*, **60**(9), 62–64.

Schmitz, N. (1989). Children with learning disabilities and the dance movement class. *Journal of Physical Education, Recreation and Dance*, **60**(9), 59–61.

Schwartz, V. (1989). A dance for all people. *Journal of Physical Education, Recreation and Dance*, **60**(9), 49.

Sherrill, C. (1986). *Adapted physical education and recreation* (3rd ed.). Dubuque, IA: Brown.

Sherrill, C. (1993). *Adapted physical activity, recreation, and sport* (4th ed.). Madison, WI: Brown & Benchmark.

Silk, G. (1989). Creative movement for people who are developmentally disabled. *Journal of Physical Education, Recreation and Dance*, **60**(9), 56–58.

Weikart, P. (1989). *Teaching movement and dance: A sequential approach*. Ypsilanti, MI: High/Scope.

Weiss, M., & Klint, K. (1987). "Show and Tell: in the gymnasium: An investigation of developmental differences in modeling and verbal rehearsal of motor skills. *Research Quarterly for Exercise and Sport*, **58**, 234–241.

RESOURCES

Written

Crain, C. (1981). *Movement and rhythmical activities for the mentally retarded*. Springfield, IL: Charles C Thomas. This book provides basic knowledge and information, as well as activities for teaching individuals with mental retardation.

Fitt, S., & Riordan, A. (Eds.) (1980). *Dance for the handicapped: Focus on Dance IX*. Reston, VA: American Alliance for Health, Physical Education, Recreation and Dance. A useful resource for those teaching older children and adolescents, this book shares different approaches, techniques, activities, and ideas for teaching dance to individuals with disabilities. Provides information on developing a conceptual framework as well as suggestions for teaching dance to various populations.

Gander, F. (1985). *Father Gander's nursery rhymes*. Santa Barbara, CA: Advocacy Press. Excellent for use with young children, this book provides a wealth of rhymes from which teachers can easily develop action songs with basic movements.

Hill, K. (1976). *Dance for physically disabled persons: A manual for teaching ballroom, square, and folk dances to users of wheelchairs and crutches*. Reston, VA: American Alliance for Health, Physical Education, Recreation and Dance. Appropriate for those teaching adolescents and adults, this book provides basic information helpful to teaching dance to individuals with physical challenges.

Pica, R. (1991). *Preschoolers moving and learning* and *Early elementary children moving and learning*. Champaign, IL: Human Kinetics. Great for children of all ages, these are comprehensive programs involving skills and activities arranged in a developmental progression and focusing on locomotor skills, body awareness, and spatial concepts. Lesson plans and cassettes of music/songs designed for each lesson.

**Weikart, P. (1989, 1990). *Movement plus music: Movement to a steady beat*. Most appropriate for 3–7 year olds, but may be adapted for older children. These booklets provide useful activities for developing rhythmic competency.

**Weikart, P. (1988). *Movement plus rhymes, songs, and singing games*. Most appropriate for 3–7 year olds, but may be adapted for older children. This booklet provides lesson plans that combine key movement experiences with familiar folk activities.

Audiovisual

Recordings

*Greg & Steve. (1986). *Kidding around with Greg and Steve.* Good for children, stimulates positive interactions through movement and song. (Recording No. YM7)

*Palmer, H. (1989). *Rhythms on parade.* Good for children of all ages, this recording provides a variety of music. (Recording No. EA 633)

*Sharon, Lois, & Bram. (1980). *In the schoolyard.* Includes sing-a-longs and silly rhymes from which teachers can easily create action songs. Good for older children. (Recording No. ER 8105)

*Stewart, G. (1987). *Preschool playtime band.* Ranges from ragtime to rock melodies with activities to encourage learning about rhythm. (Recording No. KIM 9099)

*Weikart, P. (n.d.). *Rhythmically moving.* A record series designed to complement activity booklets. Appropriate for all children.

Teaching Videos

Boswell, B. (1987). *Teaching creative dance to children with disabilities.* Physical Education Department, East Carolina University, Greenville, NC 27834, (919) 757-4632. Designed to assist educators in teaching movement elements of force, flow, and time to children with mental retardation.

**Weikart, P. (1988, 1989, 1991). *Movement and dance: A sequential approach instructors video. Folk dances I, II, III, and IV.* Useful for older children, adolescents, and adults, this video demonstrates 55 dances with the Say & Do process with the music.

Participation Videos

Gallaudet Physical Education Department. (1989). *Sign 'N Sweat.* Gallaudet University Press, 800 Florida Ave, NE, Washington, DC 20002-3695, (800) 451-1073. Designed for adolescents and adults with hearing impairment. Instructors use total communication as they lead an aerobic workout and conditioning exercises.

National Handicapped Sports. (1985). *An aerobic exercise program designed for individuals with paraplegia, quadriplegia, cerebral palsy, and leg amputations.* 451 Hungerford Dr, Suite 100, Rockville, MD 20850, (301) 217-0960. Four videos, one for each condition. Great for promoting independent functioning.

Performance Videos

Boswell, B. (1989). *Shake, rattle, and roll wheelchair dancing.* Physical Education Department, East Carolina University, Greenville, NC 27843, (919) 757-4632.

Fitt, S., & Riordan, A. (1978). *A very special dance.* National Dance Association, 1900 Association Dr., Reston, VA.

Very Special Catalog(s)

*Starred recordings are available from Kimbo Educational Catalog, Department P, P.O. Box 477, Long Branch, NJ 07740-0477, (800) 631-2187.

**Starred materials are available from High/Scope Press, 600 N. River St., Ypsilanti, MI 48198; (313) 485-2000.

CHAPTER 23

Aquatics

E. Louise Priest

*Why aquatics? Ask Denny, the little boy standing in the corner of the pool. Corners are "neat": there are two walls to lean against, and if you have cerebral palsy, that makes it much easier to stand alone. Denny rested there, and then looked up at his teacher, his blue eyes shining and a grin on his bright face. "You know something? This pool is the only place in the world where I can **walk!**" And he proceeded to do so, the joy in his independence showing in chuckles and grins. You didn't need to explain the benefits of aquatics to Denny: he truly understood them. And suddenly the teacher understood, too, more than ever before.*

Aquatics provides many of the best lifetime activities available to people who are disabled, particularly because most activities are individual in nature and thus easily adapted to individual differences. Aquatic activities can be therapeutic, educational, recreational, and sport-participatory, and thus offer a broad scope of benefits to people with physical or cognitive impairments. Aquatics itself is an extremely varied field, with activities ranging from simple learn-to-swim programs to aquatic sports such as canoeing, water skiing, scuba diving, sailing, and other types of boating. Competitive programs are available in most of these sports. Both competitive and noncompetitive programs offer individuals opportunity for peer interaction, achievement, success, improved self-concept, and lessened evidence of (and effect of) disability. In aquatics, these programs also offer a lifetime activity.

SWIMMING

When asked to define swimming, most people will describe a stroke such as the crawl or the breaststroke. Swimming, in actuality, is moving independently through the water, and as so defined, it is a skill within reach of most people.

Some general benefits of swimming are the same for all people: improved cardiovascular fitness, increased muscle strength and flexibility, and improved general physiological function. While these benefits can accrue to all participants, they may be of much greater importance to disabled persons, who may have a functional deficit in one of these areas. They may also be more readily achieved in the aquatic environment. A person with balance problems may find walking much easier in the water because of the support of the water and the buoyancy of the body. These two factors, buoyancy and support, are doubly important when weight-bearing activities are impossible or inadvisable. There are, in fact, many individuals who can engage in aerobic levels of activity only in the water; thus, swimming can be essential to the development of fitness and a healthy lifestyle. In addition, flexibility and muscle strength can often be increased by aquatic activity, and these factors are most important to daily living skills.

Some components of psychomotor development are also important to consider in the context of aquatics. Many children have deficits in perceptual motor performance—such factors as balance, kinesthetic awareness, and eye-hand coordination—and aquatic activities can be used to improve performance in these areas. In fact, structuring aquatic classes around components of perceptual-motor performance can be therapeutic for a child with a disability and concurrently can be developmental for a child who is not disabled: the approach is thus a logical one for use in a mainstream (inclusive) setting.

Safety is an important consideration as well. Swimming ability is essential for safe participation in all other water sports. All participants should be comfortable in water and learn simple self-help and rescue skills. The safety of the participants must be of primary concern. According to the American Red Cross (1974, 1992), it is absolutely essential that there be a lifeguard on duty at all times in aquatic programs.

General Teaching Suggestions

Every teacher must have a degree of expertise in task analysis, the process of analyzing a task or skill and identifying its component parts. Often an aquatic skill cannot be taught effectively until the teacher understands the component parts and their effects upon the performance of the whole skill. An example is the beginner skill of recovery from the **prone float**. Superficially, it might seem to be an action that could be elicited by the simple command "stand up." Many beginners have trouble, however, in initial stages because they omit some of the component parts of the action or do them in the wrong sequence.

The Task: Recovery from the prone float.

The Components:

1. Tuck legs
2. Thrust extended arms downward
3. Extend legs to bottom of pool
4. Lift head
5. Straighten trunk to balanced stand

Doing the actions in proper sequence makes the skill easy; doing them out of sequence makes it difficult or impossible. When teaching this skill to any student, it may be necessary to incorporate several steps into each component. For example, the learner may do the tuck and extension of the legs while holding the poolside with both hands, then with one hand, then while holding the teacher's hands, then while being held at the waist by the teacher. Similarly, the arm action may be practiced with decreasing support, before being combined with the tuck and stand. This analysis and sequencing of components is absolutely essential to teaching in adapted programs.

Much of the motor performance and adapted physical education literature will be helpful to the aquatics teacher in understanding how the body moves. Aquatic teaching materials that contain some information on task analysis include *Adapted Aquatics* (American Red Cross, 1977a), *Methods in Adapted Aquatics* (American Red Cross, 1977b), *Swimming and Diving* (American Red Cross, 1992), *Adapted Aquatics* (Canadian Red Cross Society, 1989), and *Competitive Swimming for New Champions* (Van Rossen & Woodrich, 1979).

Knowledge of reflexology and other aspects of human development can be extremely useful to the swimming teacher. Sometimes a reflex pattern can look very much like a fear response, and it can be important for the teacher to discriminate between the two and react appropriately. Some individuals who have cerebral palsy or are developmentally delayed exhibit reflexes that are normal in very young children but are sometimes misinterpreted when seen in older children. Knowledge of reflexes can also be useful in eliciting a desired response. For example, if a child with cerebral palsy has one leg extended and one leg flexed, stimulation of the sole of the foot of the flexed leg will cause the leg to extend. This extensor thrust reflexive reaction can be used to cause leg extension. Some individuals with cerebral palsy retain a "startle reflex" throughout their lives, and any sudden loud noise (and some other stimuli) will cause them to extend and then flex the arms. This reflex would not indicate fear of the water per se, but the movement pattern is sometimes interpreted as that. Swimming teachers with students who are developmentally delayed or have cerebral palsy are well advised to learn about reflexes and human development sequences.

Adapting Swimming Skills

Adapting swimming skills to individuals of varying capabilities requires several competencies on the part of teachers. The aquatics teacher must understand swimming skills and the actions that are effective in balancing and moving a body through the water. The teacher must also understand specific impairments and how they affect an individual in swimming (or in motor skills in other aquatic activities). Of primary importance is the teacher's competency in individual assessment—the ability to look at student movement, assess capabilities, and say, "I believe I can teach this skill with this or that adaptation or change." Of course, not all skills will need to be adapted; many students can perform aquatic skills with no adaptations. In fact, most people with physical impairments could do most aquatic skills if instruction were based on goals, not on the methods of achieving those goals. (For instance, the skill "**flutter kick** for 50 yards" is not achievable by a paraplegic or a double-leg amputee. But if the requirement is stated in terms of the goal—"move 50 yards independently"—the method of doing so is irrelevant, and the paraplegic and the amputee could achieve that goal.)

The purpose of adaptation in aquatics is to facilitate movement through the water. This is done by either adjusting the student's body position or increasing the effectiveness of propulsive action. An adaptation may also necessitate deletion of a skill component, as in the deletion of the **breaststroke kick** for individuals who have an amputation or are paralyzed. In any case, the stroke or skill is adapted to the student's ability.

Looking at physical disability and inferring incompetence (both physical and mental) is a common—and very bad—habit. The aquatic educator must learn to think in positive terms, to look at an individual and say, "This person can move this way, so he or she can do these skills or do this skill in this way." For example, in assessing an individual with limited shoulder and elbow flexibility, the teacher should not think, "Well, I can't teach the **back crawl** to this person," but rather, "The **beginner crawl** will give this person mobility." Even such things as residual reflexive actions can be used in positive rather than negative ways.

Adapting may also mean incorporating the use of flotation aids or weights for counterbalance: these somewhat simple modifications may greatly enhance the swimmer's balance and movement capacity. Any change or adaptation that helps the swimmer achieve is appropriate. The nature of the change becomes critical only in those agency or competitive programs requiring skills to be performed in specific ways.

Orientation to Water

If a student hesitates to enter the water for any reason, there are several things an instructor can and must do.

1. Provide support, either tactile or artificial. The student may need to feel the handclasp of the instructor to be reassured that help is there. Sometimes artificial supporters such as **water wings** or **foam mats**, with the instructor standing close by, will be effective (see Figure 23.1).

2. Do simple activities first. Usually, walking in the water and maintaining contact with either the poolside or the instructor is a useful activity for developing "water comfort."

For the young child, toys and sponges are often most helpful in facilitating water orientation. The student who cannot walk can be supported in slow patterns of movement.

3. Continue to provide support until the student can regain balance in the water when it is lost.

As research has shown (Lawrence & Hackett, 1975; Priest 1976b, 1976c) many games of low organization and movement exploration activities are easily adapted to the aquatic environment and are useful in facilitating water orientation for children. The following activities are fun, and at the same time they enhance participants' social, emotional, and physical development. The challenge can be enjoyed by both able-bodied swimmers and those with various impairments, because the required movements and concepts can be adapted to the swimmers' abilities.

Obstacle Course

An obstacle course may be set up in a pool with equipment such as

- a post or standard to go around;
- a hoop or snapwall to go through;
- two ropes, one to go under and one to go over; and
- several hoops or snapwalls to go in and out.

Negotiating the obstacle course is enjoyable and helps reinforce basic movement concepts. A child who is not ambulatory may be carried through the course, and a child who is hesitant may be accompanied by the teacher. However, maximum benefit from the standpoint of movement exploration will be derived only if a child does the activity or movement independently. An obstacle course

- reinforces concepts of around, in/out, over/under, up/down,
- improves ability to follow directions,
- sharpens awareness of the environment and objects in it, and
- improves the child's ability to move through water in varying directions.

Dive and Collect Relay

For this group game, a variety of sinkable objects are tossed into the pool. At the start signal, players sit or surface dive and collect as many objects as possible, until all are collected or a stop signal is

Figure 23.1 Buoyancy aids can help build confidence and encourage independent mobility.
Photo courtesy of the Council for National Cooperation in Aquatics.

given. The player with the most objects wins. The relay incorporates an academic element if the players are asked to identify/quantify/qualify the objects. This game

- enhances fine motor control,
- improves ability to follow directions,
- enhances target location ability,
- enhances spatial orientation,
- improves ability to open eyes and swim underwater, and
- improves breath control.

Object Relay

In this relay a variety of objects are placed on the pool deck in two matching stacks, one for each team. The leader stands in the pool at any distance from the side, holding two hula hoops floating in the water. The leader gives a directive to the first students in line, such as, "Bring me something that floats. Ready. Go." The child chooses the object and takes it to the hula hoop. A new directive is given for each team member. In addition to promoting water comfort, this activity

- enhances discrimination among certain objects,
- exposes children to competition on a simple level,

- requires following a task with several steps,
- teaches different and faster methods of moving, and
- improves understanding of the buoyancy of objects.

Introductory Level Skills

For some individuals with a disability, it is advisable to begin with simple skills, where all participants can achieve early success. Such a skill breakdown usually includes such actions as

- entering and leaving the pool with assistance,
- walking in the water with assistance,
- walking in the water unassisted,
- bobbing up and down to chin level,
- blowing bubbles with the mouth and nose in water,
- entering and leaving the pool unassisted,
- putting the face in the water and blowing bubbles,
- kicking the legs while assisted,
- kicking the legs while being "towed" by the instructor,
- sitting on the pool bottom assisted,

- sitting on the pool bottom and regaining standing balance assisted, and
- sitting on the pool bottom and regaining standing balance unassisted.

It is important to reinforce completion of the skill with specific feedback. In teaching the introductory skills, and in moving from these into a structured skill progression and more advanced skills, the instructor should take into consideration the motor complexity of a skill. For instance, a synchronous bilateral activity, one in which both arms or both legs move in the same plane and at the same time, is more easily executed (or at a lower developmental level) than is an alternating bilateral activity. Thus, the crawl stroke is more complex motorically than are the elementary backstroke and the breaststroke. The crawl is, in fact, a very complex motor activity: the arms are moving in one alternating activity and the legs are moving in a different alternating activity while, in addition, the head is moving in a very specific way and in a different rhythm. It is a demanding stroke motorically, and some individuals with developmental delay would find other strokes easier to execute.

Facility Considerations

There are several aspects of a facility that can affect an individual's participation in aquatic activities. Water and air temperatures, especially if they are below 82° F, can adversely affect a student who is new to water experience. A water temperature of 86° to 90° F is desirable, with air temperature a few degrees higher. These higher temperatures are especially beneficial for individuals who have cerebral palsy and for very young children. However, they are not recommended for people with multiple sclerosis, for whom the water temperature should be 85° F or lower.

Few pools in the United States are built for easy access. Even many newer pools are not ideally constructed. Fortunately, adaptation can be made with removable ramps and other devices, and equipment (see Figure 23.2) is available for facilitating transfers and water entry.

The ideal teaching facility has different water depths so that swimmers of any height can touch bottom while walking. Some pools are designed with an adjustable bottom. With a portion of the bottom constructed to move up and down on hydraulic lifts, water depth can be easily and rapidly varied. This feature is ideal in programs for persons who have motor performance deficits or other mobility impairments.

Many other devices have been developed to accommodate smaller individuals in pools lacking sufficient shallow water. Some devices are available commercially. An example is the Tot Dock, designed for adapting a deep-water pool for use by small children (see Figure 23.3). Constructed and assembled in sections, the Tot Dock can be varied in size and in height. For information on other aspects of facility design that should be considered and modified if necessary, consult the list of resources at the end of this chapter.

Specific Techniques

Some disabilities can cause difficulties for students in water adjustment and skill performance. The effects of the disabilities will be discussed briefly in this section, with suggestions for helping the teacher adapt the skill so that the student can be successful. Obviously, all impairments cannot be dealt with here. Where effects or appropriate teaching methods are similar, impairments are grouped. Although generalization is necessary, it should always be remembered that no generalization applies to all individuals within a group. For this and other reasons, actual practice teaching of students with unique needs is a necessity. Hands-on experience is essential for beginning teachers.

Cerebral Palsy

The extent to which cerebral palsy affects an individual in the water depends on the degree of involvement. A person who is severely involved will have problems with breath control, balance, coordination, and lack of flexibility. In addition, the person may have extreme hip flexion and exhibit some reflex patterns that make swimming more difficult. Warm water (90° F plus) is highly desirable. Assessing the student's movement capability on land will help the teacher know what movements to expect in the water; however, many people who use a wheelchair for mobility on land can walk unaided in the water. This independent mobility is greatly rewarding to the individual and may in fact contribute to greater independence on land. Generally speaking, the teacher should follow these guidelines with students who have cerebral palsy:

- Assess the student's ability to control head position. The prone position is unsafe, and even the supine position difficult, until the student can (a) control breathing, (b) lift the

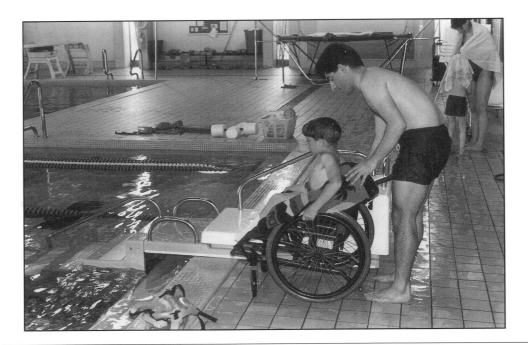

Figure 23.2   A Transfer Tier facilitates water entry.
Photo courtesy of Triad Technologies.

Figure 23.3   Shallow water can be a great asset to instructional programs, and a Tot Dock can make it possible.

head voluntarily and independently, or (c) signal the teacher for assistance in rising to an upright position.

- Let the student adjust to the water in a vertical position. This position is usually most restful for individuals with cerebral palsy. Provide tactile support and reassurance (see Figure 23.4).

- Spend time during each lesson on breath control. This is difficult for many individuals with cerebral palsy because it involves the oral musculature.

- Be aware that the student with cerebral palsy will probably be more comfortable on the back because of breathing freedom, but will have less effective movement patterns in that position because of limited shoulder and arm flexibility and increased hip flexion. Thus, it is better to start the student in supine position, then—when breath control is effective—move to prone position for greater mobility.

- Be alert to balance problems. A student who cannot recover a balanced stance when balance is lost requires one-on-one attention.

- Work toward increasing range of motion and mobility. Most individuals will be nonbuoyant, and the use of buoyancy aids may be desirable. Many people with cerebral palsy are unable to do a motionless float but can nevertheless swim effectively.

It is important to encourage independent action: walking and swimming with or without flotation devices or aids. The general physical fitness level may be low, and specific activities to increase strength and endurance should be included in the aquatic program. Students who are severely involved will have limited range of movement and, sometimes, immobile joints and contractures. Teachers must be able to assess differing movement patterns and establish attainable goals.

Cognitive Disabilities

The most common characteristic of cognitive impairment is slowness in learning; thus, the main effect of the impairment in aquatics may be a necessary modification in the teacher's style and approach. Where learning is slow, more repetition is necessary; where attention span is limited, a greater variety of activities must be included. Lawrence and Hackett (1975) and Priest (1976a) have demonstrated aquatic activities to be useful in academic reinforcement. Individuals with mild or moderate impairment usually have the motoric ability to do most swimming skills. Activities and instructions may have to be repetitive. Sometimes flotation aids will help in water adjustment and in overcoming reluctance in new situations (see Figure 23.5). The teacher may need to simplify some terminology or descriptions to allow for lower cognitive functioning. However, the movement patterns and skills may need no adaptation. A reminder here: even in simplifying, age-appropriate vocabulary should be used.

In contrast, individuals who have severe cognitive impairment usually do have motoric involvement. (The motoric deficit may be partially due

Figure 23.4 Providing support and reassurance: important functions of the teacher.
Photo courtesy of the Council for National Cooperation in Aquatics. Frank Demma, photographer.

Figure 23.5 Flotation aids often help overcome reluctance in new aquatic situations.
Photo courtesy of the American Red Cross. Printed by permission.

to inactivity.) They also have greater difficulty in learning, so repetition is essential. A multisensory approach is most effective, stimulating as many senses as possible in the learning situation. These students may also have speech defects, and swimming teachers should utilize parallel talk, describing aquatic activities while guiding the individual through them.

Water adjustment will ordinarily be less rapid because of the fear of new situations. The teacher needs to be reassuring, while spending much time on water adjustment and facility orientation. Tactile modeling, guiding the student's body part through a movement pattern, can be effective. Fear of new situations is not unusual, but conversely, because some severely mentally retarded individuals seem to lack self-preservation awareness, extra care must be taken for their safety.

Most individuals with cognitive disability will be capable of skills found in the traditional (American Red Cross, YMCA, or National Safety Council) courses. As the Special Olympics program has shown, many can excel in both skill and competition. U.S. Synchronized Swimming, the national governing body for that sport, reports that several states have synchronized swim teams for persons with cognitive disability.

Orthopedic Impairments

Similarities in functional problems and in teaching considerations make it convenient to group these impairments under a common heading. Orthopedic impairments may adversely affect a person's balance, buoyancy, and range of movement in aquatic activities.

Balance

Most humans float in a vertical position, with the water at about eye level. Most of us can also learn to float in a supine position, or at least lie in that position with a minimum of motion. Once learned, balance is relatively easy to maintain. A person who has an arm or a leg missing will not float as easily in this position: the absent weight of the arm or leg causes the body to roll, with the side of the amputation high. Thus, the person must apply the principles of counterbalance, turning the head to the side of the amputation and swinging the remaining arm or leg laterally to provide some support. Counteracting an undesirable action or effect with another action or movement is a necessary principle in aquatics for a person with an orthopedic impairment. This may be as simple as turning the head and rotating an arm, or it may involve the need for more forceful sculling with

the arms to overcome the drag of nonfunctional legs. Balance in the water changes as body composition changes, and balance must be relearned if the body changes drastically.

Buoyancy and Range of Movement

Orthopedic impairments also affect buoyancy. A person with no legs will float higher in the water than a person who has paralyzed legs: both individuals will have to adjust the direction and force of their arm pull to compensate and achieve a comfortable position. Some people find that, because of a gain in weight (adipose tissue), they have too much buoyancy for swimming in ways previously learned, and must change their head position or arm pull in compensation.

Most people with lower-body involvement have stronger upper bodies because they use their arms more. Some, however, have decreased general strength and greater susceptibility to fatigue. Activities to improve cardiovascular efficiency are often advisable. Sensory responses may be low or absent in the extremities of paraplegics and quadriplegics, and weight-bearing activities may be inadvisable for some individuals. The aquatic instructor should follow these guidelines:

- Individualize instruction. This is absolutely essential because impairments differ, and every "body" will move differently.

- Provide support until balance is learned and until the student can recover to an upright position from prone or supine.

- Spend time on water adjustment and watermanship. Comfort in the water is important.

- Be alert to signs of fatigue and chilling.

- Allow independent action wherever possible. Don't overprotect.

Individuals with orthopedic impairments should learn all basic strokes, determining from experience which they prefer or can do more easily. Any adaptation is acceptable. Generally speaking, students with good upper-body strength and shoulder flexibility will do well with the crawl stroke and backstroke, and those with balance difficulty will do less well with the sidestroke. A stroke with underwater recovery, such as the elementary backstroke or beginner crawl, will be more easily executed by an individual with either balance or buoyancy difficulties because such strokes minimize changes caused by lifting the arms out of the water.

Sport participation and competition today are such that people with orthopedic impairments have almost unlimited opportunity to compete and to excel. A strong foundation of swimming skill and watermanship will help ensure their safety as they participate in available water sports.

Seizure Disorders

Most seizures can be controlled by medication, and people with seizure disorders participate in most aquatic activities. The medical community is not in agreement about the effect of head-impact sports on seizure incidence, but a few physicians say that diving should be avoided. Some individuals find that increased fatigue affects them adversely, and aquatic instructors need to be aware of their students' fatigue level. There does seem to be general agreement that people who are subject to seizures should not scuba dive (although some do), but other water sports are not a problem. It is obvious, however, that a person whose seizures are not controlled should be accompanied by someone who knows how to handle a seizure in the water. If an individual has a tonic/clonic seizure while in the water, the instructor, guard, or aide should do the following:

- Support the person, keeping the head above water and tilted back to maintain an open airway.
- Keep the person away from the poolside and any equipment.
- Remove the person from the water after the seizure, using a mat or appropriate lift.
- Place the person on his or her side to rest briefly.
- Provide privacy, if desired.
- Tell the person (if an adult) or the parent or supervisor (if a child) that the seizure occurred.

In some aquatic programs, a person who has a seizure is not allowed to return to the water the same day. That is not always the case, however, and instructors need to know the policies of the program in which they are teaching. It is always true, however, that someone who has multiple seizures, especially if the seizures last 10 minutes or more, is in danger of status epilepticus. If this occurs, the person should certainly not return to the water, and medical help should be obtained.

Other than the possibility of a seizure, epilepsy will probably have little effect on an individual's participation in aquatic activities. There is no need to adapt skills, but there is need for the aquatic instructor to know how to handle the seizure emergency.

Vision and Hearing Impairments

Vision or hearing loss does not essentially affect a person in the performance of aquatic skills. Students having these sensory impairments create a challenge in communication for the aquatic instructor. When one sensory capacity is impaired, communication through the other senses must be maximized.

Visual Impairment

Students who are blind should be given the opportunity to measure their environment by walking around the pool and dressing rooms and learning the shape and location of things through auditory and tactile input. When there is doubt about whether or not help is needed, it is appropriate to ask the individual. Many people are self-reliant and prefer to function independently, but some will appreciate and accept help with some tasks. Generally speaking, people with visual impairment will not be able to profit visually from demonstrations but will benefit from tactile modeling (having the motion guided by the instructor's hands, or feeling the action while someone else is executing it). In aquatics, as in all activities for persons with visual impairment, the teacher must speak with verbal accuracy and specificity. Teaching suggestions for use with persons who have visual impairment can be found in *Adapted Aquatics: Promoting Aquatic Activities for All* (Canadian Red Cross Society, 1989), *Aquatics for Special Populations* (YMCA of the USA, 1987), and *Aquatic Recreation for the Blind* (Cordellos, 1976).

Hearing Impairment

People with impaired hearing rely heavily on visual cues and are particularly adept at imitating actions they view. The child who uses manual communication will usually delight in teaching sign language words to the teacher who does not know that language. Children with hearing impairment usually have no motoric or perceptual problems other than the hearing deficit and can become skilled swimmers. Some must wear ear molds while swimming.

There are various schools of thought regarding education for hearing-impaired individuals, and it is important that the aquatics program not conflict with the educational or therapeutic program. If children are enrolled in an oral program (where manual communication is not taught), it is essential that, in the swimming program, only those signs essential to safety be used. Teachers should speak clearly, and with normal (not exaggerated) lip movement, to facilitate speech-reading. When speaking to students, teachers must remember to face the student and to have the student face them. Demonstrations are essential because fewer than one third of the speech sounds in the English language are visually discernible, and teachers cannot assume that even adept speech-readers will understand all of what is said to them. Additional teaching suggestions may be found in American Red Cross (1977), Canadian Red Cross (1989), and YMCA (1987) materials.

Swimming as a Competitive Sport

Not everyone, whether disabled or nondisabled, wishes to participate in competitive events. For many people, the feeling of individual achievement, mastery of a skill, and a sense of independence provide exhilarating rewards. There are, after all, several kinds of competition, and competition with oneself in achieving a goal may be all the competition some people desire. Some, however, may wish to compete with others, and swimming competitively can have great rewards (see Figure 23.6).

People with disabilities have opportunities to compete in swimming at local, regional, national, and international levels. Wheelchair Sports, USA, the national governing body for regional and national wheelchair competition, has rules and guidebooks available for many sports, including swimming. Many authors, including Miller (1985), have shown that wheelchair sports have been effective in motivating adults who have a disability and in contributing to public awareness of disabled people as people of ability.

In swimming, as in other competitive sports for disabled persons, participants are classified according to degree of disability. Competition is regulated by classification to maintain fair competition for people with all degrees of disability, in both men's and women's divisions. In wheelchair sports, rules are kept as close as possible to those used in regular amateur competition. National rules are used, with only minimal adaptation.

OTHER AQUATIC SPORTS

Water sports offer disabled persons greater independence, enhanced leisure and recreation activities, and opportunity to develop their abilities in an increasing variety of ways. Persons with disabilities are participating in almost all water sports,

and for most of them, little adaptation is needed. According to the U.S. Coast Guard, more than 100,000 physically handicapped persons participate in boating activities in the United States. Coast Guard surveys show that people who are paraplegics, amputees, hearing-impaired, blind, and partially sighted operate power boats, race sailboats, and paddle canoes and kayaks on rivers and in wilderness areas—most with few modifications. Since the mid-1960s, people with physical impairments have engaged in scuba diving and water-skiing. Rowing and sculling have gained recently in popularity through the active participation and promotion of some championship rowers who are disabled. Whole books are devoted to some of these activities, and it is not possible to thoroughly cover all aquatic sports in one chapter. However, the more popular activities will be discussed in this section. The list of resources at the chapter's conclusion will guide those interested to further appropriate reading.

Lead-Up Skills for Boating Programs

Skills needed for operation of boats are type-specific—that is, a person needs one type of skill for paddling a canoe and another skill for sailcraft. However, there are some generalized lead-up skills, many of which can be taught in pools.

Use of Personal Flotation Devices (Life Jackets)

Federal law requires either the use of a **personal flotation device** (PFD) by every passenger or the availability of one for every passenger in every craft. To effectively use a PFD, a person must first understand its importance and then be able to wear it properly. All students should be given an explanation and demonstration of PFD use. Students who are too physically impaired to take an active part in this process should still be encouraged to give accurate instructions to whoever is helping them with the PFD and should always check to see that it is properly secured.

Students should also have the opportunity to learn for themselves that the PFD will really keep them afloat in deep water. From practicing a back float in shallow water while wearing the PFD, the student should progress to floating in deep water and eventually to falling off the dock or deck into deep water until he or she is comfortable in relying on, and convinced of the necessity for, the PFD.

Craft Familiarization

Canoes, kayaks, and small sailboats can be brought to the pool for initial familiarization. This is often

Figure 23.6 Blind athletes at the USABA National Games.
Photo courtesy of the Council for National Cooperation in Aquatics. Printed by permission.

done in colder climates or where initial instruction takes place in winter to prepare for outdoor participation.

Boarding and Debarking

Boarding, debarking, and even elementary handling techniques can be taught in a pool or on quiet water. Boarding and debarking are often the most difficult part of boat operation for disabled people.

Capsize Procedures

Practice of capsize procedures can be difficult, and the initial trial should be closely supervised by the instructor. Although an able-bodied individual might be able to react quickly to avoid getting hurt when a craft capsizes, a boater who is physically impaired, cannot see or hear, or has slower cognitive processing may be at a disadvantage. A supervised capsize of a stationary craft, with the instructor either on board or in the water, is a good way to start. The instructor initiates the capsize by submerging the near gunwale. As the boat comes over, the instructor catches the far gunwale to keep it from hitting any of the students and then assists them to supporting positions on the craft. This procedure results in a much slower capsize, giving the students a chance to understand what is happening and to react accordingly. As the students become familiar with what occurs during a capsize, the instructor can let them tip their craft independently in simulation of an actual emergency.

Canoeing and Kayaking

Canoeing and kayaking experiences can vary from a quiet and leisurely paddle on a lake to an exhilarating and breathtaking ride through the rapids of a giant river, and people with disabilities do both of these things. Participation in the sport requires the ability to sit and maintain balance and the ability to use the arms and hands. White water kayaking and canoeing require better balance and upper-body control than activities on flat water. Many amputees and paraplegics are expert white water kayakers and participate in demanding wilderness trips. Backrests or special seats are often used to reduce fatigue and aid balance. Basic canoeing and kayaking skills are best taught in warm pools, although in warm climates many programs are conducted completely out-of-doors. There is competition, including Olympic competition, in paddling sports, but most canoeing and kayaking, for both disabled and able-bodied people, is done for personal challenge and enjoyment. Adaptive equipment includes such items as high-back seats, custom-made hand grips and mitts, devices for one-arm paddling, and special docks with loading slings. There are hundreds of local canoe clubs that now have persons with disabilities among their membership. The American Canoe Association, Outward Bound, and Vinland Center all have programs that actively support the involvement of disabled persons. There are also excellent programs sponsored by universities, the Department of Education, and such organizations as the Council for Exceptional Children.

Sailing

Sailing offers freedom, fresh air, the exhilaration of speed, motion, and the sounds of the sea, and an opportunity to either participate or compete on equal terms with able-bodied people. Small sailboats can be handled with ease by many persons with a disability, and there are individuals who are amputees and paraplegics who ocean race. Sailing instruction for the blind has been available for years in England, Canada, and the United States.

It is often true that, for individuals with a disability, the only uncomfortable or risky part of sailing is getting on and off the boat. Boats, piers, and embarking procedures and facilities, like so many things in our society, were made for individuals having unimpaired mobility. Mobility is useful in other aspects of small boat sailing: handling the tiller, coming about, and changing positions to effect trim, to name a few. Nevertheless, obstacles can be overcome and adaptations made so that disabled people can sail competently. In England, several special seats have been developed that allow easy movement from one side of the boat to the other. The British Sports Association for the Disabled (1983) has done considerable work in the area of aquatic sports, and its book, *Water Sports for the Disabled*, is a fine reference on many aspects of aquatic sports, sailing in particular.

Rowing

Rowing is often seen as an ''Ivy League'' sport, largely associated with East Coast colleges. While colleges and prep schools in that region often do have rowing teams, the activity is certainly not confined there. Recreational rowing is growing greatly in popularity, and colleges all over the United States have rowing teams. Stoll (1986) reported on a program of U.S. Rowing, the national governing body for the sport. Through its program Rowing in the Mainstream, U.S. Rowing is promoting the sport by initiating programs that are community centered and accessible to all populations. Most of the communities selected had rowing programs, but none of the programs combined the activities of able-bodied and mobility-impaired individuals. Rowing in the Mainstream is an outgrowth of an earlier University of Michigan program called Freedom on the River, which involved amputees, quadriplegics, and other mobility-impaired individuals. The boats used in these rowing programs are stable recreational shells. For use by persons who are disabled, the shells are outfitted with a fixed molded fiberglass seat, a seat belt, and a chest strap for those with high-level spinal injuries. Mitts and straps are used for quadriplegics. Rowing can be excellent exercise. Enjoyment of this sport certainly is not limited to East Coast college students but can be available to anyone, disabled or nondisabled.

Waterskiing

Norway has conducted international ski competition, including trick skiing, for athletes who are blind. Slalom, barefoot, and jump skiing are well within the capacity of water-skiers who are blind. Wide tow bars, or two bars that can be coupled and detached, are often used in teaching blind or amputee skiers. Ski booms are used for more advanced practice. A sling device attached to a harness around the shoulder is used by some single-arm amputees, thus equalizing the pull between the arm and the body. (There is a quick release device for both the skier and the boat operator.) Opportunities for individuals who are disabled to engage in waterskiing have been expanding for more than 20 years. Many clubs have had activities for individuals who are blind or have impaired mobility, and the development of the sit-ski (a sled-like device) and the ski seat opened the sport to paraplegics. In general, a strong back and strong legs are desirable for skiing, although many single-leg amputees and unilateral amputees ski well. Both the American Water Ski Association and the British Disabled Water Ski Association have ongoing activities and instructors trained to teach skiing to disabled persons. Cordellos (1981) says that it was the excitement, freedom, and movement of waterskiing that caused him to disregard his blindness and changed his life. In his earlier work (1976), Cordellos discussed waterskiing and sailboarding for the blind, as well as many other water sports. Organizations such as the Christian Family Ski School in Winter Haven, the Cypress Gardens Ski School, and the Water Ski Club of San Francisco teach waterskiing on a regular basis to individuals who are disabled.

Scuba Diving

The number of people with disabilities involved in scuba diving has increased considerably in the past few years, although there have been diving clubs for disabled persons since the early 1970s. While both the medical and diving communities posed considerable resistance to the entrance into the sport by persons who are disabled, scuba diving proved to be an area where disabled persons intended to be involved, regardless of opposition (Priest, 1985). While it may be true that people subject to seizures should not engage in scuba diving, many other disabilities do not interfere with safe participation. Scuba is, of course, a high-risk sport, and particularly because more research is needed on several factors, the risks need to be made clear to participants. However, as Robinson (1986a) has shown, some of the greatest hurdles to overcome have been the attitudes of society about disabled persons. As she has also shown (Robinson 1986b), there are many effective techniques for adapting skills and equipment to enable people with disabilities to enjoy the underwater world. With modified techniques and equipment, risk can be maintained within acceptable limits.

One of the problems surrounding the involvement of disabled people in scuba diving has been the wording of course requirements in the training programs of certifying agencies. A 50-yard flutter kick is manifestly impossible for a paraplegic or a quadriplegic. Priest (1985) and others have suggested that criteria should be reworded to reflect performance *goals* rather than specific skills. In an example of this concept, the British Sub-Aqua club specifies a "level of competence" to be expected of disabled divers. The competencies include the following:

- Ability to drive to the dive site
- Ability to look after diving equipment
- Ability to swim unaided, dive, adjust equipment, perform safety exercises, swim in the company of a buddy diver, execute a controlled ascent, and swim to a boat on the surface

Scuba diving for individuals who are disabled is now being actively encouraged by certifying agencies such as the National Association of Underwater Instructors (NAUI), the Professional Association of Diving Instructors (PADI), and the YMCA in the United States and Canada. The Handicapped Scuba Association in California continues to promote scuba for disabled persons through activities, films, and printed materials. Scuba diving is an example of a sport providing personal challenge in a unique environment (see Figure 23.7).

SUMMARY

This chapter has offered an overview of aquatics for individuals who have a disability. The benefits

Figure 23.7 Scuba diving has become a popular adventure sport for people with disabilities.
Photo courtesy of Curt Barlow. Printed by permission.

of aquatics have been stressed, teaching suggestions given, and some specific disabilities examined in relation to function in the water. In addition to swimming, other aquatic sports have been discussed, including boating, waterskiing, and scuba diving. In these and other physically demanding sports, many individuals have shown ingenuity in adaptation, stamina and tenacity in participation, ability to overcome physical and psychological obstacles, and tremendous drive for achievement. Aquatic sports, with all their concomitant benefits, are pathways to achievement and normalization in the lives of disabled individuals.

BIBLIOGRAPHY

American Red Cross. (1974). *Basic rescue and water safety.* Washington, DC: Author.

American Red Cross. (1977a). *Adapted aquatics.* New York: Doubleday. (May be available only from local Red Cross chapters)

American Red Cross. (1977b). *Methods in adapted aquatics.* Washington, DC: Author. (May be available only from local Red Cross chapters)

American Red Cross. (1992). *Swimming and diving.* Washington, DC: Author.

British Sports Association for the Disabled. (1983). *Water sports for the disabled.* West Yorkshire, England: EP.

Canadian Red Cross Society. (1989). *Adapted aquatics: Promoting aquatic activities for all.* Ottawa, ON: Author.

Cordellos, H. (1976). *Aquatic recreation for the blind.* Berkeley, CA: LaBuy.

Cordellos, H. (1981). *Breaking through.* Mountain View, CA: Anderson World.

Lawrence, C., & Hackett, L. (1975). *Water learning: A new adventure.* Palo Alto, CA: PEEK.

Miller, B. (1985). Coaching the wheelchair athlete. *National Aquatics Journal*, **1**(2), 10–12.

Priest, L. (1976a). Academic remediation in aquatics. *Therapeutic Recreation Journal*, **10**(2), 35–37.

Priest, L. (1976b). Movement exploration in aquatics. *Therapeutic Recreation Journal*, **10**(2), 35–37.

Priest, L. (1976c). Developmental pool activities for fun. *Challenge*, **11**(3), 5.

Priest, L. (1979). Integrating the disabled into aquatics programs. *Journal of Physical Education and Recreation*, **50**(2), 57–59.

Priest, L. (1983). Instructor training in adapted aquatics. *National Association for Girls and Women in Sport Guide.* Reston, VA: American Alliance for Health, Physical Education, Recreation and Dance.

Priest, L. (1985). Diving for the disabled. *National Aquatics Journal*, **1**(1), 14–15.

Robinson, J. (1986a). Diving with disabilities. *National Aquatics Journal*, **2**(1), 8–9.

Robinson, J. (1986b). *Scuba diving with disabilities.* Champaign, IL: Human Kinetics.

Stoll, E. (1986). Rowing in the mainstream. *National Aquatics Journal*, **2**(3), 8.

Van Rossen, D., & Woodrich, B. (1979). *Competitive swimming for new champions.* New York: McGraw-Hill.

YMCA of the USA. (1987). *Aquatics for special populations.* Champaign, IL: Human Kinetics.

RESOURCES

Written

American Red Cross. (1992). *Swimming and Diving.* St. Louis: Mosby–Year Book. This book describes all skills in the American Red Cross swimming program. Teaching suggestions are in the companion book, *Water Safety Instructor's Manual*, also published by Mosby–Year Book, 7250 Parkway Dr., Suite 510, Hanover, MD 21076.

Council for National Cooperation in Aquatics. (1986). *Swimming pools: A guide to their planning, design, and operation.* Champaign, IL: Human Kinetics. This comprehensive book on planning and operating swimming pools has a chapter on pools for disabled persons.

Audiovisual

Allen, J. (Director), & Priest, L. (Technical Advisor). (1974). *Focus on ability* [Film]. American Red Cross, 431 18th St., NW, Washington, DC, 20006. The film offers an overview of the benefits of aquatic activity for disabled persons, with teaching suggestions for instructors. (May be available only from selected Red Cross chapters)

Handicapped Scuba Association. (1986). *Freedom in depth* [Videotape]. Handicapped Scuba Association, 1104 El Prado, San Clemente, CA 92672. An action-packed film made by disabled scuba divers.

Lawrence, Connie (Producer). (1969). *Splash* [Film]. This production shows benefits of aquatic activities and academic reinforcement through aquatics for severely handicapped children. Active Learning Films, Saratoga, CA 95070.

Other

American Canoe Association, 7432 Albon Station Blvd., Suite B226, Springfield, VA 22150. This membership organization promotes canoe and kayak education and participation.

American Red Cross, 431 18th St., NW, Washington, DC 20006. The American Red Cross develops aquatic materials and promotes aquatic education and instructor training through 3,000 local chapters.

American Water Ski Association, 799 Overlook Drive, P.O. Box 191, Winter Haven, FL 33882. This organization promotes safety education for recreational waterskiing.

Council for National Cooperation in Aquatics (CNCA), P.O. Box 351743, Toledo, Ohio 43635. This is a non-profit educational organization promoting all aspects of aquatics and aquatic education. A quarterly journal is available to members.

Handicapped Boaters Association, P.O. Box 1134, Ansonia Station, New York, NY 10023. This association develops materials and promotes programs in boating for disabled persons.

Handicapped Scuba Association, 1104 El Prado, San Clemente, CA 92672. The HSA conducts training programs for scuba instructors and disabled divers.

National Association of Underwater Instructors, P.O. Box 14650, Montclair, CA 91763. This certifying agency for scuba instructors develops resource material for instructors.

Professional Association of Diving Instructors, 1243 East Warner Avenue, Santa Ana, CA 92705. Another certifying agency for scuba instructors, this association develops resource material for instructors.

U.S. Rowing, 201 S. Capitol, Suite 400, Indianapolis, IN 46223. The national governing body for competitive rowing in the United States promotes recreational and competitive rowing.

United States Synchronized Swimming, 201 S. Capitol, Suite 510, Indianapolis, IN 46223. The national governing body for synchronized swimming in the United States develops materials and promotes the sport.

YMCA Scuba Program, 6083 Oakbrook Parkway, Norcross, GA 30093. This agency regulates and promotes the teaching of scuba diving in YMCAs.

CHAPTER 24

Team Sports

David L. Porretta

Team sports are a popular way for individuals with disabilities to become involved in physical activity. In elite or integrated settings, individuals with disabilities excel in amateur as well as professional team sports, and many interscholastic and recreational sport programs encourage participation of persons with disabilities on an integrated basis.

Fully integrated sport is especially encouraged for people with auditory impairments. In fact, as early as the late nineteenth century, people with auditory impairments were excelling in sport with nonimpaired persons. For example, William ''Dummy'' Hoy was a major league baseball player from 1888 until 1902 and was noted as the first person with deafness to become a superstar in the game as well as the person to invent hand signals used by umpires for calling balls and strikes. Today, Kenny Walker, deaf since the age of 2, is a successful professional football player. While playing defensive end, he gets his signals before each play by the defensive coordinator. In floor hockey, basketball, and volleyball, which are played in a relatively small area, very few modifications may need to be made. In volleyball, the beginning or ending of play may be signaled by an official pulling the net. On the other hand, sports played out-of-doors on a large field may require somewhat more modification. For instance, in football and soccer, flags and hand gestures can supplement whistles as signals. For deaf players, a bass drum on the sideline may signal the snap of the ball instead of the quarterback's verbal cadence. There are teams composed entirely of deaf players who compete against nondisabled individuals.

A number of organizations now provide sport programs for athletes with disabilities. The American Athletic Association for the Deaf (AAAD), one such organization, offers competition solely for those with hearing impairments. Team events include volleyball, soccer, and basketball, in which athletes are classified according to gender and degree of hearing loss. These sports are regularly featured at the World Games for the Deaf and follow international sports federation rules with some minor adjustments. Because few modifications are needed for people with hearing impairments to effectively participate in team sports, the focus in the remainder of this chapter will be on people with other types of disabilities.

Other sport organizations, such as the United States Cerebral Palsy Athletic Association (USCPAA), the National Beep Baseball Association (NBBA), and Special Olympics have been formed to meet the needs of individuals with disabilities for segregated sport competition. However, Special Olympics now promotes team sports competition by persons with mental retardation in totally integrated settings. This program is known as Unified Sports. Beep baseball, goal ball, wheelchair soccer, and wheelchair softball are relatively new team sports that have been designed for players with disabilities.

Only the significant modifications of each sport are presented in this chapter. Detailed descriptions of the rules and regulations for each sport should be obtained from each sponsoring sport organization.

BASKETBALL

Basketball is a popular activity in both physical education and sport programs. It incorporates the skills of running, jumping, shooting, passing, and dribbling. Varying or modifying skills, rules, and/ or equipment can allow individuals with disabilities to effectively participate in the game. Generally, most ambulatory persons can participate in basketball with few or no modifications. However, those with severe mental disabilities or mobility problems may need more restrictive settings, including segregated competition (e.g., basketball for people in wheelchairs).

Game Skills

Shooting and Passing

Bounce passing is advised for partially sighted players because the sound of the bounce lets them know from what direction the ball is coming. Bounce passing also provides more time for players with unilateral upper-limb involvement to catch the ball. One-hand shots and passes should be encouraged for players who use crutches or have upper-limb amputations. Players in wheelchairs find the one-hand pass useful for long passes; when shooting at the basket, however, they often prefer the two-hand set shot (especially for longer shots) because both arms can put more force behind the ball. For people with ambulation difficulties, a net placed directly beneath the basket during shooting practice facilitates return of the ball. Players with upper-limb involvement may find it helpful to trap or cradle the ball against the upper body when trying to catch a pass.

Dribbling

For players with poor eye-hand coordination or poor vision, dribbling can be performed with a larger ball. For those with poor body coordination, it may be necessary to permit periodic bouncing while running or walking, although they can dribble the ball continually while standing still. Players in wheelchairs may need to dribble to the left or the right of the chair and carry the ball in their laps when wheeling.

Lead-Up Games and Activities

Horse

Two or more players may play this shooting game, competing from varying distances from the goal. To begin, a player takes a shot from anywhere on the court. If the shot is made, the next player must duplicate the shot (type of shot, distance, etc.).

Failure to make the shot earns that player the letter H. If, however, the second player makes the shot, an additional shot may be attempted from anywhere on the court for the opponent to match. Players attempt shots that they feel the opponent may have difficulty making. The first person to acquire all of the letters H-O-R-S-E loses.

Circle Shot

This activity involves shooting a playground ball in any manner to a large basket approximately 1.1 meters (45 inches) high from six different spots on the floor, ranging from approximately .64 meters (2 feet) to 1.5 meters (5 feet) away surrounding the basket. Two shots are attempted from each spot, for a total of 12 shots. The player's score is the number of shots made.

Other Activities

Other basketball lead-up activities may include bouncing a beach ball over a specified distance, shooting a playground ball into a large barrel, or dropping a tennis ball into a large container.

Variations and Modifications

Sport

Basketball is an official sport of the **Dwarf Athletic Association of America (DAAA)**. The only modification to the game is that players use a slightly smaller ball (the size used in international play by women) for better control in dribbling and shooting situations.

In Special Olympics competition, the game follows rules developed by the **Federation Internationale de Basketball Amateur (FIBA)** for all multinational and international competition (Special Olympics, 1992). The significant modifications are as follows:

- Fouls are called only in rough contact.
- A smaller basketball 72.4 centimeters (28.5 inches) in circumference and .51 kilograms (18 ounces) to .75 kilograms (20 ounces) in weight may be used.
- A shorter basket 2.4 meters (8 feet) may be used for junior division play.
- Players may take two steps beyond what is allowable.

The **National Wheelchair Basketball Association (NWBA)** has also modified the game for people confined to wheelchairs (Figure 24.1) (NWBA, 1992). These are the major rule modifications:

- The wheelchair is considered part of the player.
- Offensive teammates are not allowed in the free throw lane before the ball is given to the offensive player throwing the ball in from out-of-bounds.
- Players must stay firmly seated in the chair at all times.
- Offensive players may not remain in the key more than 5 seconds.
- Dribbling consists of simultaneously wheeling the chair and dribbling the ball; however, the player may not take more than two consecutive pushes without bouncing the ball.
- Three or more pushes result in a traveling violation.
- The ball is awarded to the other team if the footrest or antitip casters of the player's wheelchair touch the floor while the player has possession of the ball.

Skill Events

Special Olympics offers individual skills competition in shooting, dribbling, and passing for individuals with lower ability levels, not for athletes who can already play the game. Scores for all three events are added together to obtain a final score.

The shooting competition is called *spot shot* and measures the athlete's skill in shooting a basketball. Six spots are marked on the basketball floor; three spots to the left of the basket and three spots to the right. The athlete attempts two shots from each of the six spots. The first six shots are taken from the right of the basket and the second six shots are taken from the left of the basket. Points are awarded for every field goal made. The farther the spot is from the basket, the higher the point value. For any shot that hits the backboard and/or rim and does not go into the basket, one point is scored. The athlete's score is the sum of all 12 shots.

The 10-meter event requires the athlete to dribble with one hand as fast as possible for a distance of 10 meters (32 feet 8 inches). If control of the ball is lost, the athlete can recover the ball. If, however, the ball goes outside of the designated 1.5 meter (4 feet 9 inch) lane, the ball may be retrieved or a back-up ball placed outside the lane 5 meters (16 feet 4 inches) from the start of the event may be picked up. Points are awarded depending upon how long it takes to dribble the entire 10 meters. A 1-second penalty is added for each illegal (two-handed) dribble. Two trials for this event are allowed. The athlete's score is the best of the two trials.

In the target pass event, the athlete must stand within a 3 meter (9 feet 8 inch) square and pass the ball in the air to a 1 meter (3 feet 3 inch) square

Figure 24.1   Wheelchair basketball.
Photo courtesy of *Sports 'N Spokes* © 1986, Paralyzed Veterans of America. Printed by permission.

target 1 meter in from the floor from a distance of 2.4 meters (7 feet 8 inches). Five attempts are allowed. The athlete receives three points for hitting the inside of the target, two points for hitting the lines of the target, one point for hitting the wall but no part of the target, and one point for catching the ball on the return from the wall. The final score is the sum of all five passes.

Other Variations and Modifications

Game rules may be simplified by reducing the types of fouls players are allowed to commit. A playground ball may be used, and the basket can be lowered and/or enlarged. The game area may be restricted to half-court for players with mobility impairments, such as those using lower-limb prostheses. Shorter play periods and frequent substitutions may be incorporated into the game for players with cardiac or asthmatic conditions. Lighter balls can be used by those with insufficient arm strength.

FLOOR HOCKEY

The game of floor hockey is gaining popularity in physical education and sport programs across the country. Game skills include stick handling, shooting, passing, checking, and goalkeeping. With appropriate variations and modifications, the game can be played by most individuals with disabilities.

Game Skills

Stick Handling

The key to successful stick handling is being able to keep the head up. This allows the player to pay attention to the field of play and opponents rather than to the puck. To facilitate better stick handling, the stick blade can be enlarged for players with motor control problems or visual impairments. The size and length of the stick are important factors for some individuals. Lighter sticks should be available for smaller players and those with muscle weaknesses, and shorter sticks for those in wheelchairs. Players with crutches may use the crutch as a stick to strike the puck as long as sufficient balance can be maintained. Those with crutches or leg braces can hit the puck more successfully from the stationary position. Players with unilateral upper-limb deficiencies or amputations can control the stick with the nonimpaired limb because sticks are light in weight. However, for those with poor

grip, arm, or shoulder strength, the stick can be secured to the limb with a Velcro strap. Players in wheelchairs may need to stress passing or shooting rather than trying to dribble past opponents. When moving the chair, they usually place the stick in the lap.

Shooting and Passing

Shooting and passing in floor hockey require speed, accuracy, eye-hand coordination, and skill in shooting the puck while moving. In the initial stages of learning to take a pass, the feet can back up the stick and serve to stop the puck. When passing or shooting on goal, players with visual impairments can push the puck with the stick rather than attempting a backswing before striking the puck. They will find playing with a larger, brightly colored puck very helpful. It is also helpful if a coach or a sighted teammate calls to them when the puck is passed in their direction.

Checking

Checking requires the player to gain control of the opponent's puck. Here, the player positions the stick under the opponent's stick and attempts to lift the opponent's stick away from the puck. Once the opponent's stick is raised, the puck can be controlled. Players should first practice slowly checking in a stationary position, then gradually increase their speed. The highest level of checking is when both players are moving.

Goalkeeping

Goalies try to keep the puck from going into the goal and, as such, need to make quick movements. They may stop the puck a number of ways by blocking it with their body, feet, or stick or catching it. Once the puck is controlled, it may be put back into play by using the stick or actually throwing it into the playing area. Goalies need to wear a facemask, pads, and gloves and use a larger stick. Players with asthma or poor cardiorespiratory endurance levels can be successful at the goalie position because little running is needed.

Lead-Up Games and Activities

Shooting Activity

The player attempts 10 shots on goal from a distance determined by the teacher or coach. A goalie is not used. However, Indian clubs, tires, or cones are placed at various locations along the goal line.

The player must score a goal without hitting these objects.

Puck Dribble Race

The player starts the race from behind a starting line. On command, the player dribbles the puck forward as quickly as possible for a distance of 10 meters.

Other Activities

Additional activities may include pushing a puck to the goal as fast as possible using a shuffleboard stick, kicking the puck with the feet as fast as possible to the goal, dribbling the puck as quickly as possible around a circle of cones, and shooting a sock stuffed in the shape of a ball (sock ball) with a poly hockey stick under the legs of a table and into a large box turned on its side.

Variations and Modifications

Sport

As played under 1990 Special Olympics rules, floor hockey is very similar to ice hockey (Figure 24.2). The game can be played on any safe, level, properly marked surface. Six players compose a team (one goalkeeper, two defenders, and three forwards). All players wear helmets and distinctive team markings. Players use sticks that resemble broom handles, except for the goalie, who uses a regulation ice hockey stick. The goalie must wear a mask and helmet; pads and gloves are optional. The puck is a circular felt disc (approximately 20 centimeters [8 inches] in diameter) with a 10 centimeter hole in the center. The end of the stick is placed in the hole to control the puck. Face-offs, offsides, and minor and major violations are part of the game. Games consist of three 9-minute periods of running time, with a 1-minute rest between periods. For penalties, "frozen" puck situations, time-outs, and substitutions, the clock is stopped.

Poly hockey, very similar to floor hockey, is also played in Special Olympics competition. The number of players is the same as in floor hockey. However, poly hockey is played on a gymnasium floor used for basketball. Equipment includes a plastic hockey set, a set of goals, and a goalie mask with helmet and throat protector. Pucks must be hard plastic "Safe Shot" or "Hot Shot" pucks. Positions include two forwards, two defenders, a center, and a goalie. Forwards must remain on their offensive side of the floor and defenders must stay on their defensive side. The center is the only player to move the full length of the court. The game is composed of three 9-minute periods with a 1-minute rest between periods. Penalties are similar to those called in floor hockey.

Skill Events

Special Olympics offers individual skills competition in shooting (two events), passing, stick handling, and defense. A final score is determined

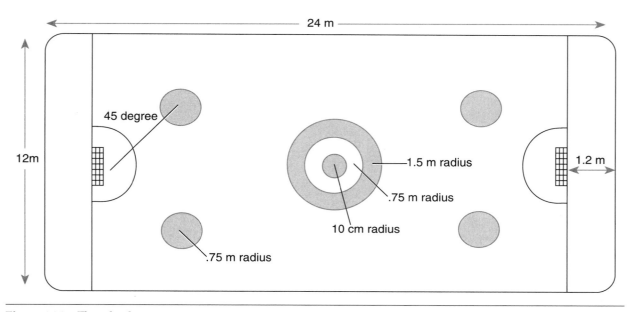

Figure 24.2 Floor hockey court.
From *Special Olympics Winter Sports Rules* (p. 66) by Special Olympics, 1990, Washington, DC: Joseph P. Kennedy, Jr. Foundation. Copyright 1990 by Special Olympics. Printed by permission.

by adding the scores of all five events. Shooting competition has two events, "Shoot Around the Goal" and "Shooting for Accuracy." In the shooting around the goal event, the athlete takes one shot from five different locations around the goal with each location being 6 meters (19 feet 7 inches) from the goal. The athlete has 10 seconds to shoot all the pucks. One puck will be at each location before the athlete starts shooting. Each puck that goes into the goal is worth five points. The score is the total of the five shots. In the shooting for accuracy event, the athlete takes five shots from directly in front of the goal from a distance of 5 meters (16 feet 4 inches). The goal is divided into the following point sections: five points for a shot entering the goal in either of the upper two corners, three points for a shot entering the goal in either of the lower two corners, two points for a shot entering the goal in the upper middle sections, one point for a shot entering the goal in the lower middle section, and no points for a shot not entering the goal.

The passing event requires that the athlete makes five passes from behind a passing line located 8 meters (26 feet) from two cones placed 1 meter (39 inches) apart. The athlete is awarded five points each time the puck passes between the two cones, while three points are awarded whenever the puck hits a cone. The total score is the sum of the scores for the five passes made.

In the stick handling event, the athlete stickhandles the puck past six cones 3 meters (9 feet 8 inches) apart for a distance of 21 meters, then shoots the puck at the goal. The time elapsed from the beginning of the event to the shot on goal is subtracted from 25. One point is also subtracted for each cone missed, and five points are added to the score if the goal is made.

In the defensive event, the athlete gets two attempts to steal the puck from two opponents who try to keep it away from the athlete within a 12 meter (39 feet 4 inch) square area. Fifteen seconds are allowed on each attempt. Each steal is worth 13 points. If the puck is not stolen, the athlete may score up to three points for pressing the opponents, trying to stick check the opponent with the puck, trying to stay between opponents, and touching the puck but not gaining control.

Other Variations and Modifications

To accommodate players with varying abilities, the game may be played on a smaller playing surface with larger or smaller goals. To make the game less strenuous, a whiffle ball, a sock ball, a yarn or Nerf ball, or a large reinforced beanbag may be used. If players have impaired mobility, increasing the number of players on each team may be helpful. Body contact can be eliminated for players with bone or soft tissue conditions such as juvenile rheumatoid arthritis or osteogenesis imperfecta. Penalties may be imposed on players who deliberately bump into opponents in wheelchairs.

SOCCER

Soccer is included in many physical education and sport programs. Skills in soccer include running, dribbling, kicking, trapping, heading, and catching (goalie only) the ball. Because of its large playing area and continuous play, soccer requires stamina. However, the game can be varied or modified so that persons with disabilities can participate in any setting. For those with very minimal impairments (e.g., mild learning disability), no modifications in the game are necessary. Where full inclusion is not feasible, Special Olympics and USCPAA provide segregated competition for individuals in this popular sport.

Game Skills

Kicking

Whether for dribbling, passing, or shooting, kicking is of paramount importance in the game of soccer. People with upper-limb amputations can learn to kick the ball effectively, but they may have difficulty with longer kicks because the arms are normally abducted and extended to maintain balance. Individuals with unilateral lower-limb amputations may use a prosthesis for support when passing or shooting the ball. Players may be unable to kick the ball with a prosthetic device; however, crutches can be used to "kick" the ball. Wheelchair users will be able to dribble the ball by using the footrests of the chair to contact the ball and push it forward. They can also be allowed to throw the ball because they do not have use of their lower limbs.

Heading

Most players can learn to head the ball successfully, although heading should not be encouraged for players with such conditions as traumatic brain injury or atlantoaxial instability. Players with mental or visual impairments may find using a balloon or beach ball helpful for learning to head because these balls are soft and give players time to make body adjustments prior to ball contact. Players with upper-limb amputations can be very effective in heading the ball. Players in wheelchairs will be able to head the ball effectively as long as it comes directly to them. However, the distance the ball can be headed will be limited because the chair's backrest and the sitting position limit the player's ability to exert force on the ball.

Trapping and Catching

Most players can effectively learn to trap the ball. Foam balls are good to use with players who are hesitant to have the ball hit the body. Persons in wheelchairs may have some difficulty trapping because the sitting position impedes the reception of the ball on the chest and abdomen. However, some players learn to trap the ball in their laps. When playing goalie, those in wheelchairs can catch effectively as long as upper-limb involvement is minimal. Most players with one arm will find it difficult to catch while in the goalie position. In this case, they should be encouraged to slap, trap, or hit the ball.

Lead-Up Games and Activities

Circle Soccer

The game may be played on a playground with two teams, preferably of 8 to 10 players each. Each team forms a semicircle, then both teams join to form a complete circle approximately 9 meters (29 feet 5 inches) in diameter. Players of each team try to kick a soccer ball below shoulder level past their opponents. After each score, players on both teams rotate one position to the right. A team scores one point each time the ball passes the opponents' semicircle, and one point is scored against players who use their hands to stop the ball.

Accuracy Kick

This activity involves kicking a playground ball into a goal area 1.5 meters (5 feet) wide (with flag-sticks at each end) from a distance of 3 meters. A player is allowed three kicks from either a standing or a sitting position. The player receives three points each time a ball is kicked into the goal, two points each time the ball hits a flag-stick but does not pass through the goal, and one point each time the ball is kicked in the direction of the goal but does not reach the goal. Following three kicks, players' scores are compared.

Other Activities

Additional activities may include heading a beach ball into a large goal area from a short distance, dribbling a soccer ball in a circular manner around stationary players as fast as possible, throwing the ball in-bounds for distance, keeping a balloon in the air by kicking it, punting a soccer ball for distance, and playing scooter soccer.

Variations and Modifications

Sport

Modifications in the sport of soccer have been introduced by the USCPAA. That organization has developed rules for competition in both wheelchair soccer (wheelchair team handball) and seven-a-side soccer (USCPAA, 1991).

In wheelchair team handball (Figure 24.3) players in Classes II–VI must participate in nonelectric wheelchairs. Chair movement must be accomplished by use of the hands and/or feet. The following are some modifications applied to team handball:

- Teams must include at least one player each from Classes I and II, two from Class III or VI (athetoid), and any combination of players (but not more than five) from Classes IV–VI.
- The game should be played on a gymnasium floor with boundaries not less than 15.2 meters (50 feet) wide and 28.6 meters (94 feet) long or not more than 15.2 meters wide and 30.5 meters (100 feet) long.
- A 25.4 centimeter (10 inch) circumference rubber playground ball is used.
- The goal area is 1.7 meters (5 feet 6 inches) high, 2.7 meters (9 feet) wide, and 1.2 meters (4 feet) deep.
- Goalies are not required to remain in the goal area.
- Players may not touch the playing surface while in possession of the ball.
- The wheelchair, a limb, and/or any part of the body can be used to move the ball.
- Dribbling the ball with both hands simultaneously is permitted.
- A maximum of 3 seconds is permitted for a player to hold or maintain possession of the ball before attempting a pass, dribble, or shot.
- Unnecessary roughness and holding or ramming into another wheelchair results in penalties.

Figure 24.3 Wheelchair team handball.
Photo courtesy of Jerry McCole and the Disabled Sports Association of North Texas. Printed by permission.

Players in Classes V-VIII who ambulate are eligible to play seven-a-side, or ambulatory soccer. Rules generally follow Federation Internationale de Football Amateur (FIFA) standards. Along with the seven-player limit, some modifications are as follows:

- Each team must field one Class V or Class VI player and one must be on the field at all times.

- No more than four Class VIII players are allowed.

- No offside rule is applied.

- An underhand throw-in is permitted.

- The field dimensions are 77.3 meters (84.5 yards) by 59.9 meters (65.5 yards).

In Special Olympics, the sport is played as either 11-a-side or 5-a-side soccer, and rules follow FIFA standards (Special Olympics, 1992). There are no major modifications for 11-a-side soccer. The following modifications, among others, are applied for 5-a-side soccer:

- The field dimensions must be a maximum of 50 meters (164 feet) by 35 meters (114 feet 9 inches) and a minimum of 40 meters (131 feet) by 30 meters (98 feet 4 inches). The smaller field is recommended for lower ability teams.

- The goal area must be 4 meters (13 feet) by 2 meters (6 feet 6 inches).

- A ball over the sideline results in a kick-in by a player from the opposing team to the player who last touched it.

Skill Events

Special Olympics offers individual skills competition in dribbling, shooting, running, and kicking for athletes with lower ability levels. Athletes perform each of the three events twice, and all scores are then added for a total score. In the dribbling event, the player dribbles the ball 15 meters (49 feet 2 inches) while staying in a 5 meter (16 feet 4 inch) wide lane into a 5 meter (16 feet 4 inch) finish zone. The finish zone is marked with cones. The clock is stopped when both the player and the ball are stopped inside the finish zone. If the player over dribbles the finish zone, he/she must dribble it back in the zone to finish. The time it takes to do this is converted into points. The maximum number of points that can be obtained is 60 and the minimum is 10, less a deduction of 5 points each time the ball runs over the sideline or the player touches the ball with the hands. If the ball runs over the sideline the referee places another ball in the center of the lane opposite the point at which the ball went out.

In the shooting event, the player walks, jogs, or runs forward a distance of 2 meters and then kicks a stationary ball into a 4-meter wide by 2-meter deep goal from a distance of 6 meters. Once the kick is made, the player returns to the starting line. A total of five kicks are allowed, and each successful kick is worth 10 points.

In the run and kick event, the player stands 4 meters from four balls (one to the left, one to the right, one in front, and one in back). The player begins by running to any ball and kicking it 2 meters through a target gate 2 meters wide made of cones. This continues until all four balls have been kicked. The total time in seconds from when the player starts until the last ball is kicked is recorded. The time is then converted into points. The maximum number of points is 50 and the minimum number is 5. In addition, a bonus of 5 points is added for each ball kicked successfully through the target.

Other Variations and Modifications

For a simplified game, fewer than 11 players can participate and field dimensions can be reduced. For players with low stamina, a partially deflated ball (which does not travel as fast as a fully inflated ball) can be used, and frequent rest periods, substitutions, or time-outs can be incorporated into the game. A soft foam soccer ball can be used; in some cases, a cage ball can replace a soccer ball. Players with upper-limb deficiencies may be allowed to kick the ball in-bounds on a throw-in. Additional players may be situated along the sidelines to take throw-ins for their teams. Penalty kicks can be employed for penalties occurring outside goal areas. To avoid mass conversion on the ball, players can be required to play in specific zone areas.

SOFTBALL

Softball uses the skills of throwing, catching, fielding, hitting, and running. With certain modifications, the game can be played in an integrated setting by most persons with disabilities, though players with visual or mobility impairments may find competing in a segregated setting more appropriate. The National Wheelchair Softball Association (NWSA) sponsors competition for athletes in wheelchairs, NBBA sponsors competition for players with blindness, Special Olympics sponsors competition for players with mental retardation, and the DAAA sponsors competition for players with dwarfism. The DAAA follows American Softball Association rules with no modifications.

Game Skills

Throwing

People with visual impairments will throw more accurately if the person receiving the ball communicates verbally with the thrower. For players with small hands or hand deformities, the use of a smaller or foam ball is recommended. Individuals with cerebral palsy, because of control problems, may find using a slightly heavier ball more advantageous. Individuals with lower-limb disability will be able to throw the ball quite well. However, they will have difficulty throwing for distance because rotation of the body may be limited. A player with one upper limb will be able to throw the ball without much difficulty.

Catching

Players with visual impairments will more easily learn to catch if a large, brightly colored ball is initially rolled or bounced. A beep baseball, described in this section under the heading "sport," will be most helpful. Persons using wheelchairs and those with crutches or with braces may wish to use a large glove. Players with one upper limb will be able to catch with one hand as long as eye-hand coordination is well developed. A glove is helpful to most players with one arm who have a remaining segment of the affected limb, provided they have mastered the technique of catching the ball and then freeing it from the glove for a throw. (After the catch, the player removes the glove with the ball by placing it under the armpit of the limb segment; the hand is then quickly drawn from the glove to grasp the ball for the throw). This technique is currently used by Jim Abbott, a major league pitcher.

Fielding

An oversize glove can facilitate fielding for players with poor eye-hand coordination. Fielders should face the direction from which the ball is being hit, and players with visual impairments should be encouraged to listen for a ground ball moving. Players with assistive devices or in wheelchairs can be paired with sighted, able-bodied players for assistance in fielding. While a fielder in a wheelchair should be able to intercept the ball independently, the assisting player can retrieve it from the ground after interception and hand it to the player with a disability for the throw.

Batting

Players with one upper limb will be able to bat as long as the nonimpaired limb possesses enough strength to hold and swing the bat. To facilitate hitting, the player may use a lighter bat, grasping it not too close to the handle. Players in wheelchairs or on crutches must rely more on arm and shoulder strength for batting because they will be unable to shift their body weight from the back leg to the front leg to provide power for the swing. Plastic bats with large barrels will be helpful for people with poor arm and grip strength or poor eye-hand coordination. In this case, a large whiffle ball should also be used.

Lead-Up Games and Activities

Home Run Softball

The game is played on a softball field with a pitcher, a catcher, a batter, and one fielder. The object of the game is for the batter to hit a pitched softball into fair territory, then run to first base and return home before the fielder or pitcher can get the ball to the catcher. The batter is out when three strikes are made, a fly ball is caught, or the ball reaches the catcher before the batter returns home.

Lead-Up Team Softball

The game is played in any open area, with six players constituting the team. Players position themselves in any manner approximately 3.6 meters (12 feet) apart. To begin play, the first player throws the ball to the second player. Each player attempts to catch the softball and throw it (in any manner) accurately to the next one. The sixth player, on catching the ball, attempts to throw it to a target 1 meter from a distance of 4 meters (13 feet). Following that throw, players rotate positions until each player has had an opportunity to throw the ball to the target.

Other Activities

Additional activities may include throwing beanbags in an underarm manner through a hoop suspended from the floor, hitting balls for distance from a batting tee, punching a volleyball pitched in an underarm manner, keeping a balloon in the air by hitting it with a plastic stick, and batting a ball suspended from the ceiling or a tetherball pole.

Variations and Modifications

Sport

Beep baseball, designed for the athlete with a visual impairment, has recently gained popularity.

It is sanctioned by the NBBA. The object of the game is for the batter to hit a regulation 16-inch audio softball equipped with a special sound-emitting device and to reach base before an opposing player fields the ball. (The Telephone Pioneers of America distribute the balls nationwide. To obtain one, contact the local telephone company and request the address of that organization.) Teams are composed of six players. Each team may have two additional sighted players on the roster; they may play blindfolded only when no other player with an impairment is available to play. The sighted players function as the pitcher and catcher, while on offense. The pitcher throws the ball in an underarm motion to the batter in an attempt to "give up" hits. The pitcher must give two verbal cues to the batter before the pitch. These are "ready" and "pitch" (or "ball"). The catcher assists batters by positioning them in the batter's box and retrieving pitched balls. On defense, one or both sighted players (spotters) stand in the field and assist their six teammates in fielding the ball by calling out the number of the defensive player closest to the ball. Usually, the numbering system to identify each of the six players is as follows: first base (1), right field (2), middle field (3), left field (4), third base (5), and back field (6). The spotters cannot field balls themselves. If a hit ball might injure a player, the spotter may yell a warning. Also, a spotter may knock down an unusually hard hit ball headed directly toward a player; however, a run will be awarded to the offensive team. A batter gets four strikes before being called out. A batter may allow one ball to go by without penalty; additional balls shall be called strikes. Each side has three outs per inning; there are six innings to an official game unless more innings are needed to break a tie.

Upon hitting the ball beyond the foul line, the batter runs to one of two cone-shaped bases. (The Telephone Pioneers of America also distribute bases nationwide.) Bases contain battery-powered, remote-controlled buzzers; before the ball is hit, the umpire predetermines which buzzer is to be activated by a hand signal to the operator. To score a run, the batter must touch the appropriate base before an opposing player cleanly fields the ball. However, if the opposing player fields the ball before the batter reaches base, the batter is out (Figure 24.4). A ball that travels 54.9 meters (180 feet) in the air is considered a home run.

The game of softball has been modified by the NWSA for players in wheelchairs. The game is played under official rules for 40.6-centimeters (16-inch) slow-pitch softball with the following major modifications ("Wheelin' Softball," 1977):

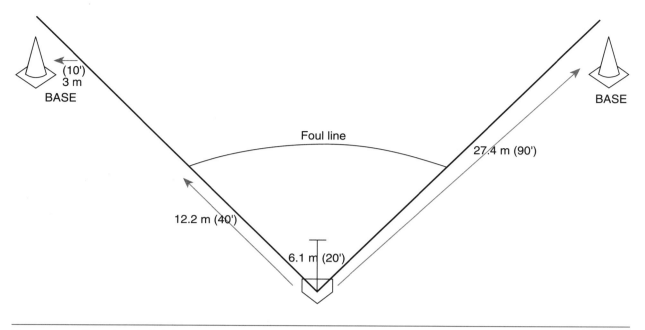

Figure 24.4 Beep baseball field.

- The field is a smooth, level surface of blacktop or similar material.

- Bases (1 foot square) are flush with the playing surface.

- Players are not allowed to leave their chairs to gain an advantage.

The game of softball is also modified for Special Olympics play (Special Olympics, 1992). Official events include slow-pitch team competition and tee ball competition. Both events follow Federation Internationale de Softball (FIS) rules. The following are some modifications that are used for the slow-pitch game.

- The distance from home plate to the pitching rubber can be modified to a distance of 12.2 meters (40 feet).

- Ten players play defense at any one time.

- An extra player may be used. If one is used, he/she must play the entire game. The extra player may be replaced at any time.

- If an extra player is used, all 11 players must bat and any 10 are allowed to play defense.

- If the batter has two strikes and fouls off the third pitch, the batter is out.

Skill Events

Special Olympics offers individual skill competition designed for lower ability athletes (not for athletes who can already play the game) in four events: base race, throwing, fielding, and hitting. The scores for each of the four events are added together to obtain the athlete's final score. In the base running event, the player must start at home plate, run around the bases, which are positioned 19.8 meters (65 feet) apart, and return home as fast as possible. The time needed to run the bases is subtracted from 60 to determine the point score. A 5-second penalty is given for each base missed or touched in an improper order. The best of two trials is counted.

In the throwing event, the object is to throw a softball as far and as accurately as possible. Two attempts are given, and the player's score is the distance of the longest throw (measured from the restraining line to the point where the ball first touches the ground). The score reflects the throwing distance in meters minus the error distance (the number of meters the ball landed to the left or right) of a perpendicular throwing line marked from the restraining line. A distance throwing event (without an accuracy component) is offered in competition sponsored by NWAA, which includes the Junior National Wheelchair Games.

Similar events sponsored by USCPAA include a beanbag toss and an Indian club throw for distance.

The fielding event requires the player to stand between two cones 3.05 meters (10 feet) apart and catch a total of 10 ground balls (five attempts per trial for a total of two trials) thrown by an official from 19.8 meters (65 feet) away. The throw from the official must hit the ground before traveling 6.1 meters (20 feet). The athlete can move aggressively to the thrown ball. Five points are received for catching the ball in the glove or trapping it against the body but off the ground, two points for a ball that is blocked, and no points for a missed ball.

The hitting event requires the player to bat for distance by hitting a softball off a batting tee. Three attempts are allowed, and the longest hit is the player's score. The distance is measured in meters from the tee to the point where the ball first touches the ground. If the score falls between meters, the score is rounded down to the lower meter.

Other Variations and Modifications

To accommodate players' varying ability levels, the number of strikes a batter is allowed can be increased. In some cases, fewer than four bases can be used and distances between bases can be shortened. Half-innings may end when three outs have been made, six runs have been scored, or 10 players have come to bat. In addition, lighter and large bats may be used. For players with poor eye-hand coordination, such as those with cerebral palsy or traumatic brain injury, the ball may be hit from a batting tee. A larger ball or restricted-flight softball, which travels a limited distance when hit, may be used. For more players with more severe impairments, the ball may be rolled to them down a groove or tubelike channel when they are at bat. A walled or fenced area is recommended for players with mobility impairments so that distances to be covered can be shortened. In addition, a greater number of players on defense may be allowed, especially if players have mobility problems. The game can also be modified so that it is played in a gymnasium with a whiffle ball and bat.

FOOTBALL

Football utilizes the skills of passing, catching, kicking, blocking, and tackling. Most individuals can participate effectively in football or some variation of it. The regulation game of tackle football can be played by people with mild impairments who are in good physical condition. A small number of players possessing partial sight do participate on high school and collegiate teams. However, people with total blindness will be unable to play the regulation game. Those with unilateral amputations either below the knee or above or below the elbow will be able to participate in regulation football as long as their prostheses do not pose a safety risk. Flag or touch football is more commonly offered in physical education and recreation sport programs. Most individuals with mental impairments, except those with severe or profound impairments, can safely be integrated with other players. Individuals with significant physical impairments may find modified, or less integrated, participation more suitable.

Game Skills

Passing

Players possessing partial sight are able to pass the ball as long as distances are short and receivers wear brightly-colored clothing. For players with poor grip strength, pronounced contracture of the hand or wrist, or crutches, a softer and smaller ball may be used to facilitate holding and gripping. People in wheelchairs will be able to effectively pass the ball if they have sufficient arm and shoulder strength. Wheelchair users will find it almost impossible to perform an underhand lateral pass while facing the line of scrimmage; therefore, this type of pass must be performed while facing the receiver.

Catching

Players with partial or no available sight as well as those in wheelchairs should be facing the passer when attempting to catch the ball. Instead of trying to catch with the hands, players should be encouraged to cradle the ball with both hands or to trap it in the midsection. The ball should be passed from short distances without great speed; a foam ball should be used for safety purposes. Players who have unilateral arm deformities or amputations or who use crutches should catch the ball by stopping it with the palm of the nonimpaired hand and trapping it against the body. Wheelchair users will be able to catch effectively if the ball is thrown accurately; confinement to a chair limits one's catching range.

Kicking

Players with partial or no available sight may be encouraged to practice punting without shoes so they can feel the ball contacting the foot. In learning this punt, players should be instructed to point the toes (plantar flex the foot) while kicking. A player with unilateral arm amputation can punt the ball by having it rest in the palm of the nonimpaired hand. A punting play may begin with the player already holding the ball rather than with a snap from center.

Lead-Up Games and Activities

Kickoff Football

The game is played on a playground 27.4 meters (30 yards) by 54.8 meters (60 yards) by two teams of six to eight players each. The object of the game is to return the kickoff as far as possible before being touched. The football is kicked off from the center of the field. The player with the ball returns it as far up the field as possible without being touched by opposing team members. The team returning the ball may use a series of lateral passes to advance it; forward passes are not permitted. Play stops when the ball carrier is touched. The other team then kicks off from the middle of the field. The winner is the team advancing farthest up the field.

Football Throw Activity

A player attempts to pass a football from a distance of 9.1 meters (30 feet) through the hole of a large rubber tire suspended 1.2 meters (4 feet) from the ground on a rope. Ten attempts are given; the player's score is the number of successful passes out of 10.

Other Activities

Other lead-up activities may include placekicking or punting the ball for distance, centering the ball to a target for accuracy; performing relays in which players hand the ball off to each other, and guessing the number of throws or kicks it will take to cover a predetermined distance.

Variations and Modifications

Sport

Wheelchair football has steadily gained in popularity since it began in 1948. The game is played by six on-the-field players on a hard, flat surface 20.1 meters (22 yards) by 54.8 meters (60 yards) and, with few exceptions, is very similar to touch football. Rule modifications as described by Brasile

(1975) as well as an organization that has sponsored wheelchair football tournaments for the past 14 years (Santa Barbara Parks and Recreation Department, 1993) are as follows:

- The ball carrier (not the wheelchair) must be touched above the knees with two hands simultaneously (quadriplegics are allowed a one-hand touch).
- All players on the team are eligible pass receivers.
- Blocking into the larger rear wheel constitutes "clipping."
- Ball throwing is substituted for kicking.
- Offense has five downs to advance the ball 13.7 meters (15 yards) for a first down.
- The ball is put into play at least 9.1 meters (10 yards) from the sideline.
- Direct runs are illegal. One exchange of the ball (in addition to the quarterback snap) must occur before the ball is advanced over the line of scrimmage by a run.

Skill Events

Various skill events can be offered. A catching event may require a player to run a specified pattern (e.g., down and out) and catch the ball. Five attempts are given, with the total number of catches constituting the player's score.

In a field goal kicking event, players attempt to placekick a football over a rope suspended 2.4 meters (8 feet) from the ground between two poles 15.2 meters (50 feet) apart. Kicks may be attempted from 4.6, 9.1, 13.7, 18.3, or 22.9 meters (5, 10, 15, 20, or 25 yards) from the rope. Ten kicks are given, and players may kick from any or all of the five distances. Points are awarded according to the distance kicked. The points are as follows: one point for a 5-yard kick, two points for a 10-yard kick, three points for a 15-yard kick, four points for a 20-yard kick, and five points for a 25-yard kick. The total number of points from 10 successful kicks is the player's score.

Other Variations and Modifications

Simplified game situations that include only the performance of specific game skills can be used. For example, the game may be played to allow only passing plays. The field can be both shortened and narrowed, and the number of players on each team can be reduced. In addition, first-down yardage can be reduced to less than 10 yards. For players possessing partial sight, a plastic football containing bells or a brightly colored foam ball may be used. The game may also be played with a kickball or volleyball by people of low skill. Individuals with arm or leg deformities as well as those with visual impairments can play most line positions.

VOLLEYBALL

Volleyball is a popular game included in most programs. Game skills include serving, passing, striking, and spiking the ball. Most persons with disabilities can be integrated into the game. However, for players with severe mental disabilities, or those with significant visual or mobility impairments, the game may require modifications.

Game Skills

Serving

Players with disabilities can learn to serve quite effectively. It will be helpful to begin with an underhand serve: the nondominant hand is beneath the ball, while the dominant hand (fisted) strikes the ball in an underhand motion. Very young players or those with insufficient arm and shoulder strength can move closer to the net. As players develop coordination, they can switch to the overhand serve. Players with one functional arm can serve overhand effectively by tossing the ball into the air with the nonimpaired arm and then hitting it with the same arm. Wheelchair users will be able to perform both the underhand and overhand serves, though for the underhand serve, it is important to be in a chair without armrests.

Striking

Players with visual impairments can competently hit the ball with two hands if the ball is first allowed to bounce. This gives the player more time to visually track the ball. Because of limited mobility, players in wheelchairs—like those on crutches—will need to learn to return the ball with one hand. However, players in wheelchairs can use both hands to return the ball within their immediate area. As these players become more adept at predicting the flight of the ball, they will be able to make a greater percentage of returns.

Lead-Up Games and Activities

Keep It Up

The game is played by teams forming circles approximately 4.6 to 6.1 meters (15 to 20 feet) in diameter. Any number of teams, of six to eight members each, may play. To begin the game, a team member tosses the volleyball into the air within the circle. Teammates, using both hands, attempt to keep hitting the ball into the air (it must not hit the ground). A player may not strike the ball twice in succession. The team that keeps the ball in the air the longest scores one point, and the team with the most points wins the game.

Serving Activity

A player hits a total of 10 volleyballs, either underhand or overhand, over a net and into the opposite court. Point values are assigned to various areas within the opposite court, with areas farther away from the net having higher values. The player's score is the point total for all 10 serves.

Other Activities

Additional activities may include setting a beach ball or large balloon to oneself as many times as possible in succession, serving in the direction of a wall and catching the ball as it returns, and spiking the ball over a net that is about 30.8 centimeters (1 foot) higher than the player.

Variations and Modifications

Sport

National Handicapped Sports (NHS, formerly known as the National Handicapped Sports and Recreation Association), the **United States Les Autres Sports Association (USLASA)**, as well as the DAAA offer team sport competition in volleyball. Two modifications of the sport under DAAA auspices consist of a slightly lowered net and court dimensions that are used by ISOD for seated amputee competition. Under NHS governance, players with amputations participate under the following rules. Six players for each team participate on the court. A point system is used to allow for equal distribution of players' abilities. Players are assigned one, two, three, or four points according to two criteria: (a) classification into one of nine classes and (b) the results of a muscle strength test. At all times, players on the court must represent a total of 13 or more points. Sitting volleyball is offered for players in classes A1–A9, while standing volleyball is played by athletes in classes A2–A4 and A6–A9.

The following are some of the more significant modifications (Cherenko, 1978) applied to the game of wheelchair volleyball:

- The court dimensions are 6.1 by 12.2 meters (20 by 40 feet), and the net is set at a height of 1.8 meters (6 feet).

- A team is composed of six on-court players (five players face the net to pass or spike the ball, while the sixth player is the setter and plays at the net to receive passes and set up spikers).

- A team is allowed a maximum of three contacts to return the ball over the net.

The game is also modified for Special Olympics play (Special Olympics, 1992). Rules are based upon Federation Internationale de Volleyball (FIVB) rules and regulations. One significant modification is that the ball may be hit with any part of the body on or above the waist.

Skill Events

Special Olympics competition includes three skill events: overhead passing (volleying), serving, and passing (forearm). These events are designed for athletes with lower ability levels, not for those who can already play the game. Scores obtained in each of the three events are added together to obtain a final score. For the overhead passing event the player stands 2 meters (6 feet 7 inches) from the net and 4.5 meters (14 feet 9 inches) from the sideline on a regulation size court. A tosser provides the player with 10 two-handed underhand tossed balls from the backcourt 4 meters (13 feet) from the baseline and 4.5 meters (14 feet 9 inches) from the sideline in the left back position. The player sets the tossed ball to a target (a person standing 2 meters [6 feet 7 inches] from the net and 2 meters [6 feet 7 inches] from the front left sideline position). If any toss is not high enough for the player to set, it is repeated. The peak of the arc of each set should be above net height. The height of each set is measured. One point is awarded for setting the ball 1 meter above the athlete's head, three points for setting the ball above net height, and no points for illegal contact, a ball that goes lower than head height or that goes over the net outside the court. The final score is the sum of all the points awarded for each of 10 attempts.

In the forearm passing event, the athlete stands on a regulation court at the right back position 3 meters for the right sideline and 1 meter from the baseline. A two-hand overhead toss is made by a tosser standing on the same side of the net in front center court 2 meters from the net. The athlete returns the toss with a forearm pass to a target (person standing on the same side of and 2 meters

from the net and 4 meters from the side away from the tosser. Varying point values are marked on the front court. This is repeated with the athlete at the left back position. To receive the maximum number of points, the peak of the arc of the pass must be at least net height. A ball landing on a line is assigned the higher point value. One point is received if the ball passes below net height. The final score is determined by adding together the five attempts from both the left and right sides.

Serving competition requires the athlete to serve a ball into the opponent's side of the court. That court is divided into three areas of equal size, and a point value is assigned to each area. One point is awarded for a serve landing in the area of the opponent's court closest to the net. Three points are awarded for a serve landing in the middle third area, and five points for a serve landing in the area closest to the opponent's end line. For serves that land on a line, the athlete receives the higher point value. The final score is the total number of points made in 10 serves.

Other Variations and Modifications

Volleyball is easily modified for most players with disabilities. Most often, court dimensions are reduced, the net lowered, and the serving line brought closer to the net to accommodate the varying abilities of players. Balls may be permitted one bounce before players attempt to return them over the net, or an unlimited number of hits by the same team may be allowed before the ball is returned. Players with arm or hand deficiencies can be allowed to carry on a hit or return. To serve, players may throw the ball over the net rather than hitting it, and they may catch the ball before returning it. Players may have greater success by using a large, colored beach ball or a foam ball. Players with mobility problems, such as those using crutches or walkers, may play the game from a seated position, or the number of players on each team may be increased.

GOAL BALL

Goal ball, a sport originating in Europe, was created primarily for persons with visual impairments to increase auditory tracking ability, agility, coordination, and team-mindedness. The game is played in a silent arena where blindfolded players attempt to score goals by rolling a ball across an opponent's goal line. Game skills are throwing, shot blocking, and ball control. Goal ball follows rules established by the International Blind Sports Association (1990).

Males and females compete separately. To remove any advantages for players possessing partial sight, all players are blindfolded, even those who are totally blind. A hard rubber ball 76 centimeters (29 inches) in circumference and weighing approximately 1.13 kilograms (2.8 pounds) is used. Each ball contains bells that allow players to track it during play. (Information on obtaining goal balls may be obtained from the USABA, 33 N. Institute, Colorado Springs, CO 80903.)

Coaches are not permitted to communicate with their players outside of half-time or during official time-outs. Spectators must also remain silent so that players may hear the ball. However, the rules permit communication between players in the form of talking, finger snapping, and/or tapping on the floor.

The game consists of two 7-minute periods and half-time lasts three minutes. Running time is not used; rather, the clock is stopped at various points in the game (e.g., a scored goal). Three 45-second team time-outs are allowed during regulation play. Whistles used to communicate clock times to players. Each team is allowed a total of six players. Three players are on the court at any one time, and each team is allowed three substitutions per game.

Players must remain within their respective play zones. Boundaries are marked with white tape approximately 5.1 centimeters (2 inches) wide. Various textured tapes are used so that the players can distinguish boundaries and zones (Figure 24.5).

Play begins with a throw by a designated team. During the game, the ball must touch the floor at least once in the team area or landing area. If not, the throw will be disallowed. The ball may be passed twice before each throw on goal.

All three players may play defense. Defensive players may assume a kneeling, crouching, or lying position to contact the ball, but they cannot drop onto the playing surface until the ball has been thrown by an opponent. Defenders may move laterally within their team area. However, they cannot rush forward into the throwing area to intercept the ball except to follow a deflection. A player must throw the ball within 8 seconds after defensive control has been gained.

The USABA encourages and promotes goal ball development camps across the country and provides technical assistance and professional support to members in regions throughout the country who are interested in offering these camps. The camps are designed to assist new players in learning the game.

Game Skills

Throwing

Throwing can be accomplished easily by most players. The ball is usually thrown underhand so that it rolls along the ground. Individuals with poor upper-body strength or poor motor control may need to use a lighter ball. Players with one arm can effectively throw the ball, while players with orthopedic impairments who use scooters may need to push the ball with both hands along the ground rather than throwing it underhand. In other cases, players on scooters can "throw" the ball by striking it with a sidearm motion when it is located at their side.

Blocking and Ball Control

Blocking and ball control are essential skills because defensive players must stop the ball from entering the goal area. Once the ball is blocked, it is brought under control with the hands so that a throw can be made. It may be helpful to have players who possess mental retardation see the ball when learning the skill of blocking so that they can more effectively coordinate body movement with the sound of the ball. Players with amputations can wear prosthetic devices to assist in blocking, as long as the ball does not damage the device or vice versa.

Lead-Up Games and Activities

Heads-Up

This game involves one-on-one competition with players positioning themselves in their half of the arena. A player is given possession of the ball with the object of scoring a goal. The ball must be continuously rolled as the offensive player moves about; the player cannot carry the ball. The defensive player can take control of the ball from the offensive player by deflecting or trapping a shot on goal. The first player to score three goals wins the game.

Speedy

This game involves two teams of three players each who play within an enclosed area. Players on each team assume a crouching or kneeling position and form a triangle with a distance of 3.7 meters (12 feet) between players. Players position themselves on small area rugs and face the middle of the triangle. On command, a designated player

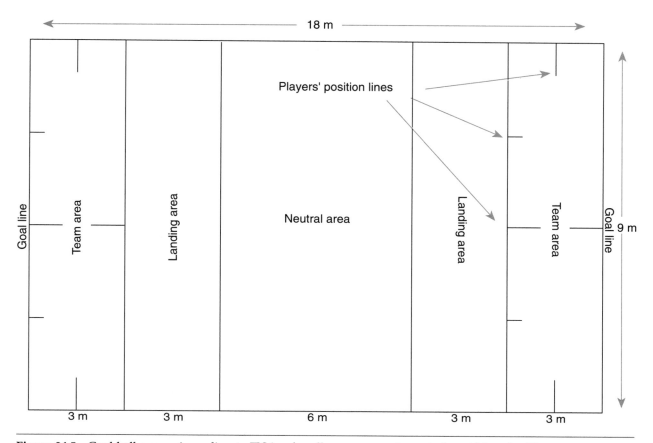

Figure 24.5   Goal ball arena. According to IBSA rules all measurements are to be within +/− .05 meters.

rolls a goal ball as quickly as possible to the player on the immediate right, who controls the ball and throws it to the next player on the right, and so on. In the event the ball is not controlled by a player to whom it was thrown, that player must retrieve the ball and return to the area rug before throwing to the next player. Each time the ball returns to the player who started the game, a point is scored. The team scoring the most points in 1 minute wins the game. Teams compete one at a time so that players can hear the ball.

Other Activities

Other activities may include throwing for accuracy to the goal and passing the ball as quickly as possible between two players for a specified period of time.

Variations and Modifications

Sport

Goal ball is quickly gaining popularity in the United States and has become an official competitive sport of the USABA. People with other types of disabilities as well as people without impairments can participate in the game as long as blindfolds are worn.

Other Variations and Modifications

The game may be modified by increasing or decreasing the size of the play arena and the number of players on a side. People with mobility problems may play on scooter boards, and for those with poor upper-arm and shoulder strength, a lighter ball may be used.

INTEGRATION

Most players with disabilities can be successfully and safely integrated into the regulation sports of basketball, floor hockey, soccer, football, softball, and goal ball as long as certain techniques are applied. One technique is to match abilities and positions; teachers and coaches should attempt to assign specific positions on the basis of ability. In football, players with mild mental retardation possessing good catching skills could play end positions, while others with good speed could play the backfield. Players with upper-arm impairments can serve as placekickers in football. In specific instances, a physical disability can be used to advantage. For example, Tom Dempsey, whose partial amputation of the kicking foot allowed for a broader surface with which to kick the ball, was a very successful placekicker in the National Football League.

Integration can also be enhanced by teaching to the players' abilities. When teaching or coaching players with mental retardation, one should emphasize concrete demonstrations more than verbal instructions. When used, verbal instructions should be short, simple, and direct as when coaching first and third base in softball. In football and basketball, a few simple plays that have been overlearned can encourage success. In sports like football or basketball the player holding the ball can shout or call out to help a partially sighted player with ball location.

Modification to equipment can also foster integration. The teacher or coach can place audible goal locators in goal areas in sports such as basketball, soccer, and floor hockey for players with visual impairments. Goals, when used, can be brightly painted or covered with tape. For example, the crossbar and goalposts in soccer could be brightly painted. In games played on an indoor court, such as floor hockey or basketball, mats may be placed along the sidelines to differentiate the playing surface from the out-of-bounds area.

Special Olympics now promotes competition with nondisabled persons provided Special Olympics athletes have demonstrated the ability to participate in team sports. This ability includes not only the attainment of certain skills but also teamwork and team strategy (Special Olympics, 1989). Special Olympics provides a detailed handbook that covers the philosophy of Unified Sports, research and evaluation results, and field implementation as well as sports rules for basketball, bowling, soccer, softball, and volleyball.

SUMMARY

This chapter described the more popular team sports included in physical education and sport programs. Team sports included in AAAD, DAAA, NBBA, NHS, NWBA, Special Olympics, USABA, USCPAA, and USLASA competition were also discussed. Game skills, along with variations and modifications specific to each sport, were identified. Also presented were lead-up games and activities, as well as rules

and strategies, corresponding to those found in programs for individuals without disabilities. Finally, suggestions for integrating persons with disabilities into sport were offered.

BIBLIOGRAPHY

Brasile, F.M. (1975). Football wheelchair style! *Sports 'N Spokes,* **1**(3), 1–2.

Cherenko, D. (1978). Volleyball. *Sports 'N Spokes,* **4**(2), 17–18.

International Blind Sports Association. (1990). *IBSA goalball rules.* Madrid: Author.

National Wheelchair Basketball Association. (1992). *1992–93 NWBA official rules and case book.* Lexington, KY: Author.

Santa Barbara Parks and Recreation Department. (1993). *Rules for the Blister Bowl wheelchair football tournament.* Santa Barbara, CA: Author.

Special Olympics. (1989). *Unified sports handbook.* Washington, DC: Special Olympics International.

Special Olympics. (1990). *Official Special Olympics winter sports rules.* Washington, DC: Special Olympics International.

Special Olympics. (1992). *Official Special Olympics summer sports rules.* Washington, DC: Special Olympics International.

United States Cerebral Palsy Athletic Association. (1991). *United States Cerebral Palsy Athletic Association sports rules manual.* Dallas: Author.

Wheelin' softball. (1977). *Sports 'N Spokes,* **3**(3), 15.

RESOURCES

Written

American Athletic Association for the Deaf. *Deaf Sports Review.* A quarterly publication by AAAD, 3607 Washington Blvd., Suite 4, Ogden, UT 84403-1737. Initiated in 1991, this periodical covers a variety of sports for the deaf. It features outstanding athletes and coaching tips, sports medicine topics, along with information on current and upcoming sport competitions.

National Wheelchair Basketball Association. (1993). *Constitution, bylaws, and executive regulations of the National Wheelchair Basketball Association.* Lexington, KY: Author. This document describes principles for the conduct of the game, membership, player eligibility, make-up of committees, and tournaments. It is intended for those interested in forming a team or for those teams who need to keep abreast of NWBA regulations.

Special Olympics. *Sports skills program* (1985). Washington, DC: Author. Separate manuals have been published for basketball, hockey, soccer, softball, and volleyball. Manuals include goals and objectives, skill assessment, task analyses, team tactics, modified games, and rules.

Audiovisual

Floor hockey [Videotape]. (n.d.). Washington, DC: Special Olympics. Approximately 13 minutes. The video highlights seven skills used in the game of floor hockey and a number of professional hockey players who support Special Olympics floor hockey. The skills include running, checking, stickhandling, shooting, passing, face-off, and goalie skills.

Goal ball: An introductional videotape [Videotape]. (n.d.). Winnipeg, MB: Communication Systems Distribution Group, University of Manitoba. This tape examines the sport of goal ball. It can be purchased or rented.

Soccer sports video [Videotape]. (1991). Washington, DC: Special Olympics. The 11-minute video features the 1991 International Summer Games. Segments include preliminaries, team preparation, coaching, finals competition, and awards.

Unified sports/basketball [Videotape]. (n.d.). Washington, DC: Special Olympics. Approximately 5 minutes. This tape features the Indianapolis Unified Basketball League, which is a pilot program. Teams are sponsored by local businesses and players and coaches are interviewed.

CHAPTER 25

Individual, Dual, and Cooperative Activities and Sports

E. Michael Loovis

This chapter presents a variety of individual, dual, and cooperative activities and sports in which persons with unique needs can participate successfully. Participation will be analyzed from two perspectives: within the context of sanctioned events sponsored by sport organizations, and as part of physical education programs in the schools. In terms of organized competition, discussion will be limited to the rules, procedural modifications, and adaptations that are in use and that are the only approved vehicle for participation. The remainder of the chapter will be a compendium of modifications or adjustments for a variety of activities and sports. The incorporation of each sport by major sports organizations will be discussed, if applicable.

TENNIS

Because of the nature of the game itself and the available variations and modifications, tennis or some form of it can be played by all persons except the most severely disabled. Because the game can be either a singles or doubles event, the skill requirements (both psychomotor and cognitive) can be modified in numerous ways to encourage participation. Regardless of the variations or modifications, the basic objective remains the same: to return the ball legally across the net and to prevent one's opponent from doing the same.

Sport Skills

Typically, tennis can be played quite adequately with the ability to perform only the forehand and backhand strokes and the service. For the ground strokes, good footwork (for ambulatory players) or effective wheelchair mobility (Figure 25.1) along with good racket preparation—moving the racket into the backswing position well in advance of the ball's arrival—is fundamental to execution. Under normal circumstances, movement into position to return the ball and racket preparation are performed simultaneously.

Lead-Up Activities

Adams and McCubbin (1991) describe an elementary noncourt lead-up game, Target Tennis, that is appropriate for wheelchair-bound as well as ambulatory students and that can be played indoors with limited space. Basically, the players position themselves behind the end zone line, which is 10 feet from a target screen. The screen has five 10-inch-diameter openings, which serve as the targets. The player tosses a tennis ball into the air and, with an overhand swing, attempts to bounce the ball midway between the end zone line and the target so that the ball goes through one of the five openings. A bonus serve is permitted for every point scored. No points are awarded if the ball bounces twice.

Special Olympics (1992) provides four developmental events that can serve as lead-up activities:

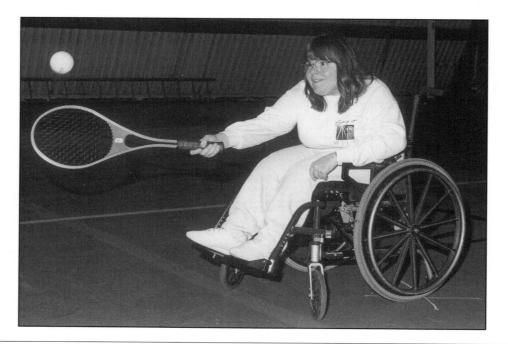

Figure 25.1 Wheelchair tennis competitor.

target stroke, target bounce, racket bounce, and **return shot**. In target stroke, the athlete attempts to drop hit the ball within the boundaries of the opponent's singles court. Target bounce consists of having the athlete bounce a tennis ball on the playing surface using one hand; the score is the highest number of consecutive bounces in two trials. In racket bounce, the athlete bounces the ball off the racket face as many times consecutively as possible; the score is the most consecutive bounces in two trials. Return shot involves attempting to return a tossed ball over the net and in-bounds; the score is the total for two trials.

Variations and Modifications

Sport

In 1980 the National Foundation of Wheelchair Tennis (NFWT) was founded to develop and sponsor competition in that sport. In 1981 the Wheelchair Tennis Players Association (WTPA) was formed under the aegis of the NFWT with the purpose of administering the rules and regulations of the sport. The rules for wheelchair tennis are the same as for regular tennis except that the ball is allowed to bounce *twice* before being returned (WTPA, 1990). The first bounce must land in-bounds, while the second bounce may land either in-bounds or out-of-bounds.

The WTPA (1990) sanctions the following divisions: men's and women's Open, A and B, men's C, men's and women's E (Quad) Open, men's and women's E (novice), and boys' and girls' junior. The E Quad division was established for individuals with limited power, mobility, and strength in at least three limbs as a result of accidents, spinal cord injuries, or other conditions. Also included in this division are walking quads, power wheelchair users, and triple amputees.

Other Variations and Modifications

If mobility is a problem, the court size can be reduced to accommodate persons with disabilities. This might be accomplished by having able-bodied players defending the entire regulation court while persons with disabilities defend one-half of their court. It could likewise be accomplished by permitting players to strike the ball on the second bounce. Variations in the scoring system can facilitate participation. An example is scoring by counting the number of consecutive hits, which, in effect, structures the game as cooperative rather than competitive. If the player with a disability has extremely limited mobility, then the court could be divided into designated scoring areas, with those closest to that player receiving higher point values. Racket control may be a concern for some students because the standard tennis racket may be too heavy.

There are several solutions to this problem, including shortening the grip on the racket, using a junior-size racket, or substituting a racketball racket. In the case of an amputee, the racket can be strapped to the stump, provided there is a functional stump remaining to allow for effective leverage and racket use.

If mobility and/or racket preparation are problematic, then reduction of court size, at least initially, will assist in learning proper racket positioning and stroking because footwork will be minimal. If still unsuccessful, the player can be placed in the appropriate stroking position with the shoulder of the nonswinging arm perpendicular to the net. At this point, all that is necessary is to move into and swing at the ball.

In service, the ball is routinely tossed into the air by the hand opposite the one holding the racket. In preparation for striking the ball at the optimal height, the racket is moved in an arc from a position in front of the body down to the floor and up to a position behind the back. At this point the racket arm is fully extended to strike the ball as it descends from the apex of the toss. For some individuals who lack either the coordination or strength to perform the service as described, an appropriate variation is to bring the racket straight up in front of the face to a position in which the hand holding the racket is approximately even with the forehead or slightly higher. Although serving in this manner reduces speed and produces an arc that is considerably higher than normal, it does allow for service on the part of some persons who might otherwise not learn to serve correctly. To accomplish the toss, a single-arm amputee may grip the ball in the racket hand by extending the thumb and first finger beyond the racket handle when gripped normally and hold the ball against the racket. The ball is then tossed in the air and stroked in the usual way. A double-arm amputee having the racket strapped to the stump uses a different approach. The ball lies on the racket's strings, and with a quick upward movement the ball is thrust into the air to be struck either in the air or after it bounces. In the case of Quad tennis, another individual may drop the ball for an E player who is unable to serve in the conventional manner (WTPA, 1990).

TABLE TENNIS

Like tennis, table tennis or some version of it can be played by all persons except the most severely disabled. It too can be played in singles or doubles competition and, although the requisite skills are less adjustable than in tennis, the mechanical modifications that are available make this sport quite suitable for persons with disabilities. Regardless of the variations and modifications, the basic objective of the game remains the same: to return the ball legally onto the opponent's side of the table in such a way as to prevent the opponent from making a legal return.

Sport Skills

As in tennis, the basic strokes are the forehand and backhand. Unlike tennis, the service is not a separate stroke. A serving player puts the ball in play with either a forehand or a backhand stroke. The ball is required to strike the table on the server's side initially before striking the table on the receiver's side. In addition, servers must strike the ball outside the boundary at their end of the court.

Lead-Up Activities

Appropriate for use in physical education programs is an adapted table tennis game that originated at the Children's Rehabilitation Center, University of Virginia Hospital. Two or four people can play this game, called **surface table tennis**. This game involves hitting a regulation table tennis ball so that it moves on the surface of the table and passes through a modified net. The net is constructed from two pieces of string attached 1/2 inch apart to the top of official standards, and two or three pieces of string 3/4 inch apart at the bottom (Adams & McCubbin, 1991). At the start of play, the ball is placed on the table. A player strikes it so that it rolls through the opening in the net into the opponent's court. Points are awarded to the player who last made a legal hit through the net. Points are lost when a player hits the ball over the net either on a bounce or in the air, when the ball fails to pass through the net, or when a player hits the ball twice in succession.

Another lead-up game, **Corner Ping-Pong,** was developed at the University of Connecticut (Dunn & Fait, 1989). It is played in a corner, with an area 6 feet high and 6 feet wide on each side of the corner. One player stands on either side of the center line. The server drops the ball and strokes it against the floor to the forward wall. The ball must rebound to the adjacent wall, then bounce onto the floor of the opponent's area. If the server fails to deliver a good serve, one point goes to the opponent. The ball may bounce only once on the floor before the opponent returns it. The ball must be stroked against the forward wall within the opponent's section of the playing area so that it rebounds to the adjacent wall and onto the floor in the server's area. Failure to return the ball means a point for the server. Scoring is similar to that for table tennis. Each player gets five consecutive serves. A ball that is stroked out of bounds is scored as a point for the other player. Game is 21 points, and the winner must win by 2 points.

Special Olympics provides three developmental events that can serve as lead-up activities. They are target serve, racket bounce, and return shot (Special Olympics, 1992). In target serve, the athlete serves five balls from the right side and five balls from the left side of the table; a point is awarded for each ball that lands in the correct service area. In racket bounce, the athlete bounces the ball off the racket as many times consecutively as possible in 30 seconds; the score is the most consecutive bounces in two trials. Return shot involves attempting to return a tossed ball to the feeder's side of the table; one point is awarded if the ball is successfully returned while five points are earned if the ball lands in one of the services boxes. The athlete attempts to return five balls with a maximum of 25 points possible.

Variations and Modifications

Sport

Table tennis is included as a sport in competitions offered by both Wheelchair Sports, USA, the United States Cerebral Palsy Athletic Association (USCPAA), National Handicapped Sports (NHS), the Dwarf Athletic Association of America (DAAA), the United States Les Autres Sports Association (USLASA), the American Athletic Association of the Deaf (AAAD), and Special Olympics. For the most part, competition is based on the rules established by the International Table Tennis Federation and ISOD (International Sports Organization for the Disabled). Some modifications are permitted. For example, DAAA (1991) permits the use of a riser. The USLASA uses the rule book of the (ISOD) and therefore incorporates many of the rules highlighted in the subsequent sections. In Wheelchair Sports, USA competition, the following rules apply (NWAA, 1993):

- Competitors' feet may not touch the floor.
- Athletes in certain classes (IA, IB, and IC) may have the racket secured to their hands, may serve with or without upward projection of

the ball or bounce the ball on the table, are not penalized for volleying a ball that would otherwise clearly miss the table, and may not impart spin on the ball during service.

The following rules apply in competition sanctioned by USCPAA (1991):

- Wheelchair participants (Divisions 1 and 2) must sit with their feet resting on the foot pedals and not touching the floor; they must also have one hip in constant contact with the seat.
- A serve, if it would have continued on course, would have crossed the baseline between the sidelines at the receiver's end to be good; if not, it is considered a let; all divisions are required to use a normal serve.
- Division 3 athletes may compete with assistive devices or a wheelchair, but they may not use the table for support; using the table for support during a volley or service results in forfeiture of the point.
- Competitors with spasticity in one arm may use a device to hold the ball to assist in serving.
- There are no exceptions to the playing rules for players who stand.

Other Variations and Modifications

Several assistive devices are available for individuals with severe disabilities such as muscular dystrophy and other disorders that weaken or affect the shoulder. A ball bearing feeder provides assistance for shoulder and elbow motion by using gravity to gain a mechanical advantage and makes up for a loss of power resulting from weakened muscles. The bi-handle paddle, which consists of a single paddle with handles on each side, was designed to encourage greater range of motion for participants in adapted table tennis. Its greatest asset is increased joint movement resulting from the bilateral nature of hand and finger positioning. A strap-on paddle has been designed for players with little or no functional finger flexion or grasp. The paddle is attached to the back of the hand with Velcro straps. The major disadvantage is that it precludes use of a forehand stroking action. The Table Tennis Cuff is useful with individuals who have limited finger movement and grip strength. It consists of a clip that attaches to a metal clamp on the paddle's handle; a Velcro strap then holds the cuff securely to the hand (Adams & McCubbin,

1991). Another device, the space ball net (Figure 25.2), can replace the paddle for players who are blind (Dunn & Fait, 1989). This device, held in two hands, consists of a lightweight metal frame that supports a nylon lattice or webbing. The net is large enough and provides an adequate rebounding surface to make participation feasible by persons who are blind.

ANGLING

The American Casting Association (ACA) is the governing body for tournament fly and bait casting in the United States. It sets the rules by which eligible casters may earn awards in registered tournaments. None of the contemporary sports organizations for disabled people sponsors competition in angling, and it is likewise not found very often in physical education programs. It is more likely to be used as a recreational sport.

Lead-Up Activities

Angling requires the mastery of casting and other fishing skills. In terms of lead-up activities, there are at least two casting games that deserve mention. Skish involves accuracy in target casting at various distances. Each participant casts 20 times at each target. One point is awarded for each direct hit (plug landing inside target or similar goal). Three targets can be used simultaneously to speed up the game, with players changing position after each has cast 20 times at a target. The player with the greatest number of hits at the end of 60 casts is the winner. The second game, speed casting, is a variation of skish, Each player casts for 5 minutes at each target. The player with the high score at the end of 15 minutes is the winner (Adams, Daniel, McCubbin, & Rullman, 1982).

Variations and Modifications

Major assistive devices for use in angling have become very popular in recent years. For example, the freehand recreation belt (Figure 25.3), a specially designed harness into which one inserts rod and reel, permits reeling and fighting fish one-handed. Other devices include the Ampo Fisher I, Van's EZ cast, Batick Bracket, and Handi-Gear. There are also several lines of electronic fishing reels (Adams & McCubbin, 1991).

ARCHERY

Under normal circumstances, shooting the longbow is a six-step procedure. The steps, in order of occurrence, are assuming the correct stance, nocking the arrow, drawing the bowstring, aiming at the target, releasing the bowstring, and following through until the arrow makes contact with the target. One or more of these steps may be problematic and may require some modification in the archer's technique.

Figure 25.2 Space ball net.

Figure 25.3 Freehand recreation belt.

Variations and Modifications

Sport

Target archery is an athletic event sponsored by USCPAA, Wheelchair Sports, USA, USLASA, and NHS. These groups observe the rules established by the Federation of International Target Archery, with certain modifications. In the case of USLASA, all competitors are in the same class as described in the ISOD rules. The following are modifications that may be employed to encourage participation by individuals in wheelchairs (NWAA, 1993):

- An adjustable arrowrest and arrowplate and a draw check indicator on the bow may be used, provided they are not electric or electronic and do not offer any additional aid in aiming.

- Archers may use an adaptive equipment archery body support.

The NWAA (1993) and USCPAA (1991) share two modifications:

- Only archers with quadriplegia may have the bow bandaged or strapped into the hand and a splint may be bandaged to the bow arm; they may also have a person load their arrows into the bow.

- Quadriplegic archers may use compound bows; classes 1 and 2 are allowed to use a mechanical release aid with recurve and compound bows.

Other Variations and Modifications

Several assistive devices are available to aid the archer who has a disability. These include (1) the **bow sling,** commercially available from most sports shops, which helps stabilize the wrist and hand for good bow control; (2) the **below-elbow amputee adapter device** (Figure 25.4), which is held by the terminal end of the prosthesis and requires a slight rotation of the prosthesis to release the string and the arrow; (3) the wheelchair **bowstringer,** which consists of a post buried in the ground with two appropriately spaced bolts around which the archer who is disabled places the bow in order to produce enough leverage to string it independently; and (4) the **elbow brace,** which is used to maintain extension in the bow arm when the archer has normal strength in the shoulder but minimal strength in the arm, possibly because of contractures (Adams & McCubbin,

1991). Additionally, the **vertical bow set** can accommodate individuals with bilateral upper-extremity involvement (Wiseman, 1982).

Other program adjustments include use of the crossbow with the aid of the tripod assistive device for bilateral upper-extremity amputees. Various telescopic sights are also commercially available for the partially sighted archer.

Although the United States Association for Blind Athletes (USABA) does not sponsor competition in archery, several modifications can facilitate participation by individuals with visual impairments (Hattenback, 1979). These include

- using foot blocks to ensure proper orientation with the target,

- placing an audible goal locator behind the target to aid in directional cuing,

- using a brightly colored target for partially sighted individuals, and

- placing balloons on the target as a means of auditory feedback.

BADMINTON

Special Olympics (1992) sponsors competition in badminton but only as a demonstration sport. Competition is based on the rules of the International Badminton Federation (IBF). The game is, however, ideally suited for individuals with disabilities and is played routinely in physical education class.

Sport Skills

Badminton can be played quite adequately using only the forehand and backhand strokes and the underhand service. Beyond these strokes, development of the clear, smash, drop shot, and drive will depend on the participant's ability.

Lead-Up Activities

There are at least two lead-up games that deserve mention. **Loop badminton** (Dunn & Fait, 1989) is played with a standard shuttlecock, table-tennis paddles, and a 24-inch loop that is placed on top of a standard 46 inches in height. The object of the game is to hit the shuttlecock through the loop, which is positioned in the center of a rectangular court 10 feet long and 5 feet wide. Scoring is done as in the standard game of badminton. Loop badminton is well adapted for individuals with restricted movement who wish to participate in an

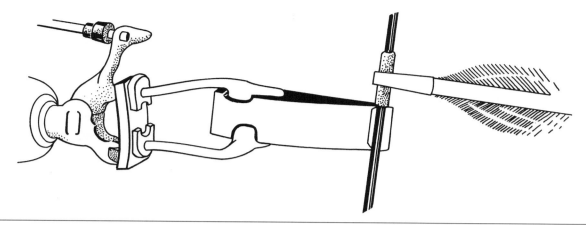

Figure 25.4 Amputee adapter device for archery.

active game that requires extreme accuracy. A second modified game is called **balloon badminton** (Adams & McCubbin, 1991). In this game a balloon is substituted for the shuttlecock, and table-tennis paddles are used instead of badminton rackets. The game can also be played by people with visual impairments if a bell is placed inside the balloon to aid in directional cuing.

Special Olympics provides three developmental events that serve as lead-up activities. They are **target serve, target stroke,** and **return serve** (Special Olympics, 1992). In target serve, the participant has 10 chances to hit the shuttlecock within the boundaries of the opponent's singles court; one point is awarded for each successful hit. In target stroke, the athlete has 10 chances to hit the shuttlecock to the opponent's empty court; one point is awarded for each successful hit. Return serve involves attempting to return a serve to anywhere in the opponent's court; one point is awarded for each successful return up to a maximum of 10 points.

Variations and Modifications

In Special Olympics competition, the following rules apply to wheelchair athletes (Special Olympics, 1992):

- Athletes have the option of serving an overhand serve from either right or left serving areas.

- The serving area is shortened to half the distance.

Some standard modifications are routinely used. These include, but are not limited to, reducing court size, strapping the racket to the stump of the double-arm amputee, and using Velcro on the butt

end of the racket and on the top edge of the cork or rubber base of the shuttlecock to aid in retrieval (Weber, 1991). Several assistive devices are used to facilitate participation in badminton. The **extension-handle racket** involves splicing a length of wood to the shaft of a standard badminton racket. This is helpful for a wheelchair player or one with limited movement. Another device is the **amputee serving tray** (Figure 25.5). Attached to the terminal end of the prosthesis, it permits easier service and promotes active use of the prosthesis.

BOWLING

Bowling is an activity in which both ambulatory and wheelchair-bound people can participate with a high

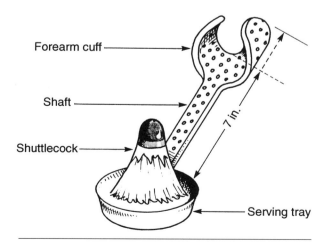

Figure 25.5 Amputee serving tray.
From *Games, Sports, and Exercise for the Physically Handicapped* (4th ed.) (p. 254) by R.C. Adams and J.A. McCubbin, 1991, Philadelphia: Lea & Febiger. Copyright 1991 by Lea & Febiger. Adapted by permission.

degree of success. Usually the ambulatory bowler demonstrates a procedure that incorporates the following actions: approach (which may be modified if lower-extremity involvement exists); delivery, including the swinging of the ball; and release. A wheelchair-bound bowler will eliminate the approach and will either perform the swing and release independently or will use a piece of adapted equipment to assist this part of the procedure. Two organizations that have made a significant impact on the lives of bowlers with disabilities are the American Blind Bowlers Association (ABBA) and the American Wheelchair Bowling Association (AWBA).

Lead-Up Activities

Special Olympics (1992) sponsors two developmental events that qualify as lead-up activities. The two events are target roll and frame bowl.

Target Roll

This event consists of rolling two 2-pound bowling balls in the direction of two regulation bowling pins positioned on a standard bowling lane that is modified to equal half its normal length. Participants bowl five frames utilizing the standard scoring systems of the American Bowling Congress (ABC).

Frame Bowl

In this event the bowler rolls two frames and has two 30-centimeter diameter plastic playground balls per frame. The object is to knock down the greatest number of plastic bowling pins from a traditional 10-pin triangular formation. The lead pin is set 5 meters from a restraining line. Bowlers may either sit or stand and may use either one or both hands to roll the ball; the ball must be released behind the restraining line. Pins that are knocked down are cleared between the first and second rolls; pins are reset for each new frame. A bowler's score equals the number of pins knocked down in two frames. Five bonus points are awarded when all pins are knocked down on the first roll of a frame, and two bonus points are awarded when all remaining pins are knocked down on the second roll of the frame.

Variations and Modifications

Sport

Bowling is a sanctioned event in the competitions of USCPAA and Special Olympics. Both follow the rules of the American Bowling Congress (ABC). The USCPAA (1991) has developed the following procedures and/or rules for its competition:

- There are four divisions; two chute and two nonchute.

- Nonchute divisions include Class 3 through 8 bowlers who do not use specialized equipment; the retractable ball handle is permitted in these divisions.

- Chute divisions are for Class 1 through 6 bowlers using specialized equipment. There are two divisions: closed chute, for Class 1 and 2 bowlers, who need assistance with equipment (wheelchair, chute, or ball), and open chute, for Classes 3 through 6 bowlers, who do not require assistance with their equipment.

- All bowlers must be able to bowl each ball independently within a 60-second period.

Special Olympics (1992) sponsors competition in bowling and follows the rules established by the ABC and the Women's International Bowling Congress. Modified rules for use in Special Olympics are as follows:

- Ramps and other assistive devices are permitted for singles competition only.

- Bowlers using ramps shall compete in separate divisions; there are two classifications of ramp bowling: unassisted and assisted.

- Bowlers are permitted to bowl three consecutive frames.

Other Variations and Modifications

Several assistive devices are used by ambulatory bowlers. The handle grip bowling ball, which snaps back instantly upon release, is ideal for bowlers with upper-extremity disabilities and for individuals with spastic cerebral palsy, especially those who have digital control difficulties. The American Bowling Congress has approved the handle grip ball for competitive play. Upper-extremity amputees who use a hook can utilize an attachable sleeve made of neoprene to hold and deliver a bowling ball. The sleeve can be made to compress by use of a spring and to expand for release with the identical action used to open the conventional hook. Stick bowling, which is similar to use of a shuffleboard cue, was designed for individuals with upper-extremity involvement, primarily grip problems. The AWBA permits stick bowling in its national competitions, provided the bowlers apply their own power and direction to the ball.

Wheelchair-bound bowlers have several assistive devices that facilitate participation. Although not approved by the AWBA for national competition, ramp or chute bowling has become extremely popular with bowlers who are severely disabled. The counterpart of stick bowling for the wheelchair-bound bowler is the adapter-pusher device, which was originally designed for wheelchair bowlers lacking sufficient upper-arm strength to lift the ball. The handlebar-extension accessory, used in conjunction with the adapter-pusher device, assists ambulatory bowlers who lack sufficient strength to lift the ball.

Although USABA does not sponsor competition in bowling, there are several modifications that can enhance participation in the sport by people with visual impairments. These modifications include

- the use of a bowling rail for guidance, which is the standard method employed by most bowlers in the ABBA National Blind Bowling Championship Tournament,
- the use of an auditory goal locator placed above or behind the pins, and
- a scoring board system that tactually indicates the pins that remain standing after the ball is rolled.

FENCING

Sport Skills

Fencing as a competitive event for people with disabilities began with the Stoke Mandeville Games in Stoke Mandeville, England. The object is to score by touching the opponent's target and to avoid being touched. Because of a lack of participants, fencing as a sanctioned event for athletes who are disabled in the United States is nonexistent. Several years ago it was an exhibition event for Wheelchair Sports, USA but subsequently was discontinued. If fencing is included in physical education, a number of variations and modifications make participation in this activity feasible for those with disabilities.

Variations and Modifications

Sport

Competition in fencing for wheelchair-bound individuals is normally conducted according to the rules of the International Stoke Mandeville Games Federation. In international competition the following classes are recognized: A2 (single AK), A3 (double BK), A4 (single BK), A6 (single AE), A8 (single BE), and A9 (combined lower- plus upper-limb amputations). Accordingly, Les Autres athletes are classified as L Fe 1, L Fe 2, and L Fe 3. Where appropriate, fencers in the above classes with significant loss of grip or control of the sword hand may bind the sword to the hand with a bandage or similar device (ISOD, 1990). Among the modified rules that have been written to ensure equal opportunity for all participants in wheelchair fencing, the following are important to note:

- A fencing frame must be used.
- Fencers cannot purposively lose their balance, leave their chairs, rise from their seats, or use their legs to score a hit or to avoid being hit; the first offense is a warning, with subsequent offenses penalized by awarding one hit for each occurrence; accidental loss of balance is not penalized.
- The legs and trunk below the waist are not valid target areas.

Other Variations and Modifications

Fencing is ordinarily conducted on a court measuring 6 by 40 feet; however, to accommodate wheelchair participants, it is suggested either that the dimensions of the standard court be changed to 8 by 20 feet or that a circular fencing court with a diameter of 15 to 20 feet be used (Adams et al., 1982). Fencers who are blind will require a smaller, narrower court, which may conceivably be equipped with a guide rail (Dunn & Fait, 1989).

Basically, the only piece of adaptive equipment is the lightweight sword, which permits independent participation, especially for individuals with upper-extremity disabilities. In cases where no modification is necessary, the epée is recommended for ease of handling rather than the foil or sabre (Orr & Sheffield, 1981).

HORSEBACK RIDING

The North American Riding for the Handicapped Association (NARHA), founded in 1969, is the primary advisory group on riding for the disabled in the United States and Canada. NARHA does not sponsor competition; however, it encourages its riders to compete in open shows such as the Annual Handicapped Riders Event of the Devon

Horse Show and at shows sponsored by Special Olympics, USCPAA, and the International Paralympic Equestrian Committee. The United States is represented in the World Championships of Horse Riding for the Disabled by a team that is determined through national competitions.

Sport Skills

The Cheff Center in Augusta, Michigan, houses the largest instructor training program for therapeutic riding in the United States. It also has an active riding program with an average of 150 students receiving lessons each week. Horseback riding involves, among other skills, mounting, maintaining correct positioning on the mount, and dismounting. At the Cheff Center students with disabilities receive a six-phase lesson. The phases include **mounting, warm-up, riding instruction, exercises, games,** and **dismounting** (McCowan, 1972). Special consideration should be given to the selection and training of horses used for therapeutic riding programs (Spink, 1993). Horses should be suitably sized—that is, small—because children are less likely to be fearful of smaller animals. In addition, smaller horses permit helpers to be in a better position for assisting unbalanced riders; the shoulder of the helper should be level with the middle of the rider's back.

Lead-Up Activities

Several possibilities exist for using games in the context of horseback riding instruction. The origin of some of these games is **pole bending,** which is common in Western riding and is used to teach horses how to bend and teach riders how to perform the movement. One game that encourages stretching of the arms involves placing quoits over the poles; this activity is conducted in relay fashion, with two- or three-member teams competing. Another game consists of throwing balls into buckets placed on a wall or pole. The traditional game of Green Light, Red Light can be played as a way of reinforcing certain maneuvers, such as halts, which are taught to riders.

Variations and Modifications

Sport

Special Olympics and USCPAA each have their own equestrian competition or show. The USLASA also sanctions equine competition; it is regulated, however, by USCPAA rules.

Special Olympics (1992) offers the following events: dressage, English equitation on the flat, stock seat equitation, working trail horse, rodeo events including pole bending and barrel racing, drill teams of twos or fours, prix caprilli, showmanship at halter/bridle classes, and team relays. There are eight divisions to which riders are assigned based upon a Rider Profile that is completed by the coach for each rider prior to any competition. The divisions are S-3, S-2, S-1, C-2, C-1, B-2, B-1, and A. Distinctions between divisions range from S-3 requiring a horse handler and one or two sidewalkers to act as spotters to A where a rider is not allowed any horse handler or sidewalkers and is expected to compete with no modifications to national governing body rules. Special Olympics (1992) has designated the following specific rules:

- Riders who must wear other footwear as the result of a physical disability must submit a physician's statement with their entry; English tack style riders must use Peacock safety stirrup or S-shaped stirrups; Western tack style rider must use tapaderos.

- All riders must wear protective SEI-ASTM approved helmets with full harness.

- Riders may use adaptive equipment without penalty, but must in no way be attached to the horse or saddle.

The USCPAA and USLASA offer competition in the following events: dressage including walk, beginning walk/trot, and intermediate walk/trot, training level 1, first level 1, and classes in pairs to music and musical free-style; obstacle including walk, intermediate walk/trot, and advanced walk/trot; and equitation including walk, beginning walk/trot, intermediate walk/trot, and walk/trot/canter. The USCPAA (1991) has the following specific rules:

- Athletes with cerebral palsy will compete separately from Les Autres athletes.

- Leaders and/or sidewalkers are permitted; leaders may only walk beside the horse; no aide is permitted to speak to a rider during event; coaches or family members are not allowed to act as aides for their riders.

Other Variations and Modifications

Mounting is the single most important phase of a riding program for individuals with disabilities. Because for some people with disabilities the typical method of mounting is impossible (i.e., placing the left foot in the stirrup, holding onto the cantle, and springing into the saddle), there are alternatives based upon the rider's abilities. Several basic types of mounting procedures are used by riders who are disabled; these range from totally assisted mounts, either from the top of a ramp or at ground level, to normal mounting from the ground (McCowan, 1972).

Once mounted, individuals with disabilities have available to them numerous pieces of special equipment that can make riding an enjoyable and profitable learning experience. One commonly used item is an **adapted rein bar**, which permits riders with a disability in one arm to apply sufficient leverage on the reins with the unaffected arm to successfully guide the horse; it is faded as soon as the rider learns to apply pressure with the knees. Another adaptation is the **Humes rein**, consisting of large oval handholds fitted on the rein; this allows individuals with involvement of the hands to direct the horse with wrist and arm movement. **Body harnesses** are used extensively in riding programs for the disabled. They consist of web belts approximately 4 inches wide with a leather handhold in the back, which a leader can hold onto to help maintain a rider's balance. Most riders who are disabled also use the **Peacock stirrup** (Figure 25.6), which is shaped like a regular stirrup except that only one side is iron while the other side has a rubber belt attached top and bottom. This flexible portion of the stirrup releases quickly in case of a fall, reducing the chance that a foot could get caught. The **Devonshire boot** is used frequently if a rider has tight heel cords or weak ankles. Designed much like the front portion of a boot, it prevents the foot from running through the stirrup, and consequently it encourages keeping the toes up and heels down, which can be invaluable if heel cord stretching is desirable.

GYMNASTICS

Gymnastics has enjoyed considerable popularity in recent decades because of its visibility in the Olympic Games. As a result, individuals with disabling conditions have likewise begun to participate in gymnastic programs where opportunities have been available. For example, people with orthopedic involvements can participate and have participated in gymnastics programs for able-bodied persons (Winnick & Short, 1985).

Sport Skills

Beyond possessing the physical attributes necessary to participate in gymnastics (e.g., strength, agility, endurance, flexibility, coordination, and balance), participants must learn to compete either in one or more single events or in all events, referred to as the all-around. Under normal conditions men compete in the following events: pommel horse, rings, horizontal bar, parallel bars, and floor exercise. Women compete in balance beam, uneven parallel bars, vaulting, and floor exercise. In both men's and women's competitions, participation in all events qualifies athletes for a chance to win the all-around title.

Lead-Up Activities

The closest thing to lead-up activities related to gymnastics can be found in the Special Olympics Sports Skills Program and in select developmental events that are offered as part of the Special Olympics Games. In its sports skills program manual, *Gymnastics* (Special Olympics, n.d.), general conditioning exercises with emphasis on flexibility and strength are recommended. Doubles tumbling and balance stunts are also suggested. As an introductory experience, educational gymnastics, which uses a creative, problem-solving approach, can be used to teach basic movement concepts. This could eventually enable participants to compete in more advanced forms of gymnastic competition. Beyond these suggestions, the Special Olympic program (1992) incorporates level A events (formerly referred to as developmental) that include the **wide beam walk, vaulting, tumbling,** and **floor exercise**.

Variations and Modifications

Sport

The USABA offered competition in women's gymnastics until 1992; it no longer offers this sport to its members. Gymnastics is offered in the Special Olympics Games. Events for men include vaulting, parallel bars, pommel horse, horizontal bar, rings, and floor exercise. Women's events include vaulting, uneven parallel bars, balance beam, and floor exercise. Both men and women can compete in the all-around competition. Only women compete in rhythmic gymnastics in the following events: ribbon, ball, rope, and hoop. Exceptions are levels A and B, which are coeducational. No significant rule modifications are required, and each participant's performance is judged according to the rules established for that event by the FIG and the NGB (Special Olympics, 1992).

Figure 25.6 Peacock stirrup.

Modifications of rules used to ensure equitable competition include the following:

- Gymnasts who are blind have the option of performing the vault with no run, a one-step or a multiple-step approach, or a two- or three-bounce takeoff; verbal or sound cues may be given by the coach during any part of the vault without penalty.
- Gymnasts who are blind can have the balance beam lowered without penalty; coaches or spotters may warn a gymnast without penalty if they believe the athlete is about to fall off the end of the beam; gymnasts may execute the approach for the mount with hand trailing the beam.
- Gymnasts who are blind may use audible cues during floor exercise; music may be played at any close point off the mat, or the coach may carry the music source around the perimeter of the mat.
- Gymnasts in levels A and B perform their rhythmic gymnastics routines while seated; gymnasts who are blind can have audible cues during competition; athletes who are deaf can have a visual cue to start with music without penalty.

Other Variations and Modifications

Few modifications are used in gymnastics competition. If gymnastics is used in physical education programs, all of the modifications observed by the sports organizations in the conduct of their competitions would be valid.

WRESTLING

The sport of wrestling requires considerable strength, balance, flexibility, and coordination. If individuals with a disability possess these characteristics and if they can combine a knowledge of specific techniques with an ability to demonstrate them in competitive situations, then there is no reason that wrestling cannot be a sport in which persons with disabilities experience success.

Sport Skills

Wrestling consists of several fundamentals and techniques that are essential for success. These include takedowns, escapes and reversals, breakdowns and controls, and pin holds. When learned and performed well, these maneuvers assist in accomplishing the basic objective in wrestling, which is to dominate opponents by controlling them and holding both shoulders to the mat simultaneously for 1 second.

Lead-Up Activities

The development of specific lead-up activities for wrestling has apparently not been an area of creative activity. If lead-up activities are desirable, then one can conceivably use certain traditional elementary physical education self-testing activities that have some relationship to wrestling. Two such activities are listed in the following paragraphs.

Hand Wrestling

While standing, two people face each other and grasp right hands; each person raises one foot off the ground. On signal, each attempts to cause the other to touch either the free foot or hand to the ground.

Indian Leg Wrestle

Two people lie side by side but facing in opposite directions. Hips are adjacent to the partner's waist. Inside arms and legs are hooked. Each person raises the inside leg to count of three; on the third count they bend knees, hook them, and attempt to force the partner into a backward roll.

Variations and Modifications

Sport

Both USABA and AAAD sponsor wrestling competitions. The USABA competition takes place in one division known as the Open Division and is contested according to international freestyle rules. Competition is held at the following weight classes: 91, 98, 105.5, 114.5, 125.5, 136.5, 149.5, 163, 180.5, 198, 220, and unlimited. The 91 and 98 weight classifications are reserved for competitors between the ages of 13–18. Competition is governed by the rules of United States of America Wrestling. The following modifications have been instituted to render conditions more suitable for visually impaired athletes:

- All authorized signals utilized by the referee must be given both verbally and visually at the same time when cautioning/warning or awarding points to either wrestler.

- Opponents begin the match in the neutral standing position with finger touch. Initial contact is made from the front unless waived by both competitors. When contact is broken, the match is interrupted and restarted in the neutral position at mat center (USABA, 1990).

Both Greco-Roman wrestling (which prohibits holds below the waist and use of the legs in attempting to take opponents to the mat) and freestyle wrestling are sanctioned events in competitions governed by AAAD. These events are conducted according to the rules established by the International Federation of Wrestling.

Competition in Judo is also sanctioned by USABA. It is contested according to the rules of the International Judo Federation. In the Paralympic Games, World Championships, and Regional Championships, competition for all weight classifications shall be combined for Classes B1, B2, and B3.

Other Variations and Modifications

Wrestling is not for everyone. For people with disabilities who want to attempt this sport, there are several modifications that can be used. For those with lower-extremity difficulties that prevent ambulation, all maneuvers should be taught from the mat with emphasis on arm technique. Bilateral upper-extremity involvement will probably restrict participation in all but leg wrestling maneuvers. After removal of prostheses, single-arm amputees can participate with emphasis placed on arm maneuvers.

TRACK AND FIELD

Because all major sports organizations for the disabled offer competitive opportunities in track and field, this section will focus on the rules modifications that have been enacted in order to make participation maximally available. For each organization the track portion will be discussed first, followed by the field events. No attempt will be made to examine sport skills, variations and modifications, and lead-up activities, except as related to Special Olympics.

Wheelchair Sports, USA

Track and field competitions are governed by the rules of The Athletic Congress (TAC). The Wheelchair Sports, USA sponsors a classed division for field events and classed and open divisions for track events. Classes include IA, IB, IC, II, III, IV, and V. All classes compete in 100-, 200-, 400-, 800-, and 1,500-meter races; class IA also competes in a 60-meter race. Relays are run at 400-, 800-, and 1,600-meter distances. The open division competes at the same distances and also runs a 5,000-meter race. In field events all classes compete in the discus, shot put, and javelin, except class IA, which substitutes the club throw for the javelin event. Additionally, all classes compete in the pentathlon, which consists of five individual events. Three events—javelin, shot put, discus—are similar across all classes. Classes IA, IB, and IC race at 100- and 800-meter distances, while classes II through V race at 200- and 1500-meter distances.

The NWAA (1993) has designated the following specific rules:

- Wheelchairs with rigidly attached handrims are the rule in national championships; local competitions may waive this rule by including a separate competitive division for wheelchairs with handrims or equivalent devices that are not rigidly attached to the large wheel; the use of chain-driven or geared equipment is not permitted in any sanctioned Wheelchair Sports, USA competition.

- Batons are not exchanged in relay races; incoming racers use their hands to touch the back, shoulder, arm, or hands of the outgoing racers.

- Competitors may not secure any portion of their bodies to any part of the wheelchair in any fashion.

- Approved hold-down devices can be used to stabilize competitors' chairs in field events; sitting on the wheel is specifically prohibited; raising both buttocks from the seat before releasing the implement is illegal.

- Competitors in the club throw can hold and throw in any manner, including overhand or underhand or a combination; however, the throw can only be made with one hand.

USABA

International Amateur Athletic Federation rules are employed in track and field competitions. Within the USABA (United States Association for Blind Athletes) structure there are three visual classifications: B1, B2, and B3. The following events are provided for males and females across all three classes: 100-, 200-, 400-, 800-, 1,500-meter races. In addition, women run a 3,000-meter race, while men run 5,000 meters; there are two relays for men and women: a 4×100 meter and a 4×400 meter with combined visual classes. Both men and women in all three classes compete in long jump, high jump, triple jump, discus, javelin, and shot put. There are pentathlons that are contested by all classes and by men and women. Both men and women compete in the long jump, discus, and 100-meter events. Men throw the javelin while women put the shot. Men run a 1,500-meter event, and women run a 800-meter race. A 10,000-meter road

race, open to all USABA classifications as well as the general public, may also be held. The USABA (1990) has determined that the following rule modifications are necessary to provide more suitable competition for visually impaired athletes:

- Class B1 sprinters may run the 100-meter with the help of not more than two callers, one of whom must remain behind the finish line; the second caller, if one is used, may not cross the finish line ahead of the athlete.

- Guides are allowed for B1 and B2 in 200-meter through 5,000-meter events. When guides are used, there is an allowance of two lanes per competitor.

- Competitors may also decide what form guidance will take. They may choose an elbow lead, a tether, or to be free; at no time will the guide push or pull the competitor, nor will the guide ever precede the athlete; the runner may receive verbal instructions from the guide.

- Acoustic signals are permitted for B1 and B2 athletes in field events.

- No visual modifications to the existing facilities are permitted for Class B1 athletes; such modifications are permitted for B2.

- Class B1 high jumpers may touch the bar as an orientation prior to jumping.

- Class B1 shot put, discus, and javelin throwers may enter the throwing circle or runway (runup track) only with the assistance of a helper, who must leave the area prior to the first attempt.

AAAD

Track competition for men includes races at standard distances from 100-meter through 25-kilometer road racing. It also includes 110- and 400-meter hurdles, 3,000-meter steeple-chase, and 20-kilometer walk. Along with the standard field events, AAAD (American Athletic Association for the Deaf) provides competition in pole vaulting and hammer throw. Women's competition in track and field parallels that described for women in USABA with one exception, 100-meter hurdle.

Special Olympics

Special Olympics offers a greater number and diversity of track and field events than any other sport organization for people with disabilities. Included in the list of possible events that can be offered at a sanctioned competition are 100-, 200-, 400-, 800-, 1,500-, 3,000-, 5,000-, and 10,000-meter races. There are walking races of 100, 400, and 800 meters; women compete in 100-meter hurdles while men compete in 110-meter hurdles. Additionally, there is a mile run along with a 4×100- and 4×400-meter relays. In field competition the following events are contested: long jump, high jump, shot put, and pentathlon. There are also track and field events for athletes in wheelchairs. Long-distance racing and walking events have been added, including a marathon. International Amateur Athletic Federation rules are employed in competitions sanctioned by Special Olympics (1992). Modifications to those rules include the following:

- In running events a rope or bell can be utilized to assist athletes who are visually impaired; a tap start can only be used with an athlete who is deaf and blind.

- In race walking events, athletes are not required to maintain a straight support leg while competing.

- In the softball throw, athletes can use any type of throw.

Special Olympics (1992) comes closer than the other organizations to describing lead-up activities. It does this through the provision of 17 developmental events including 25- and 50-meter dashes or walks, the 10-, 25-, and 50-meter assisted walk, softball throw, 10- and 25-meter wheelchair races, a 30-meter wheelchair slalom, a 4×25-meter wheelchair shuttle relay, 30- and 50-meter motorized wheelchair slaloms, a 25-meter motorized wheelchair obstacle race, a tennis ball throw for distance, and the standing long jump.

USCPAA

Competition sanctioned by the USCPAA (United States Cerebral Palsy Athletic Association) is governed by rules established by TAC. Events are contested via an eight-class system and consist of races as short as 60-meter (weave) for Class 1 athletes in electric wheelchairs up to 3,000 meters cross-country running for Class 5 through 8. There is a 4×100-meter open relay for Classes 2 through 8. The following events constitute the field portion: shot put, discus, javelin, club throw, and long jump. Additional events include the **precision throw, soft shot, distance kick, high toss,** and **medicine ball thrust**.

Modifications of rules (USCPAA, 1991) used to ensure equitable competition include the following:

- Class 5 athletes who use canes or crutches must use their assistive devices in a manner such that they make contact with the surface of the track a minimum of one time approximately every 10 meters.

- Athletes in wheelchair relays must make personal contact with a team member to complete a successful changeover. This contact can be on any part of the outgoing teammate or the teammate's chair; baton exchanges are required in relays for Classes 5 (without assistive devices) through 8.

The USCPAA (1991) incorporates the following additional modifications in its field events:

- An attendant or approved fixing apparatus may secure the chair in place; however, neither an attendant nor the apparatus may be inside the throwing area.

- The soft shot (5-inch-diameter cloth weighing maximum of 6 ounces), precision throw, high toss, and soft discus (Spungedis) are used for Class 1 only.

- Distance kick and medicine ball thrust are offered for Class II athletes who cannot engage in routine throwing events. In the distance kick a 13-inch playground ball is placed on a foul line; the competitors initiate a backswing and then kick the ball forward while remaining seated in their chairs. Distance of the kick is the criterion. In the medicine ball thrust, a 6-pound medicine ball is used. Competitors may not kick the ball; rather, the foot must remain in contact with the ball throughout the entire movement until release.

USLASA

Track and field competition sponsored by US-LASA (United States Les Autres Sports Association) is governed by ISOD (1990). As a result, the events and rules that govern competition for Les Autres athletes is similar to those of USCPAA. There are some exceptions:

- In track for wheelchair classes, there are 5,000-meter, 10,000-meter (men), and marathon events; for standing classes, there are 3,000-meter (women) and 5,000- and 10,000-meter events for men. There are also relay events for both wheelchairs and ambulatory classes contested at 4 × 400-meter.

- In terms of field events, the major addition in the standing classes is the inclusion of high jump and triple jump for men.

DAAA

The following events are sanctioned by DAAA (Dwarf Athletic Association of America) for track: 15-meter run for children under 7 years of age (futures); 20-meter run for juniors, 7–9 years; 40-meter run for juniors, 7–9 and 10–12 years; 60-meter run for juniors, 10–12 and 13–15 years and athletes over 40 years of age (Master). There is also a 100-meter open, wheelchair race and a 4 × 100-meter relay. The rules of TAC and wheelchair competition are typically adhered to.

Field events that are contested in DAAA competition include shot put, discus, and javelin in open and master's classes. Juniors (13–15) may participate in shot put and discus. Other juniors events include softball throw, flippy flyer (soft discus), and tennis ball throw for futures (DAAA, 1991).

Beyond the traditional track and field events sponsored by the sports organizations for the disabled, there are several special events that are unique to these competitions. Wheelchair Sports, USA, USCPAA, USABA, and AAAD hold pentathlons. Additionally, the USABA sponsors a standard marathon competition. The NWAA and the USCPAA offer slalom course competition. According to NWAA (1993), the slalom course is no longer than 100 meters, with no single straightaway longer than 5 meters. It contains a series of obstacles (e.g., ramps, tilt boards, curbs), directional changes (minimally 10 directional changes 180 degrees each), and varied surfaces (including gravel, grass, and water).

GOLF

Golf has been incorporated as an exhibition event into the major sport competitions of Special Olympics and USCPAA. It is also an activity that can be included in physical education programs for individuals with disabilities.

Sport Skills

Golf, as it is normally played, requires a person to grasp the club and address the ball using an appropriate stance. Being able to swing the golf club backwards, then forward through a large arc including follow-through are also requisite tasks.

Lead-Up Activities

An appropriate lead-up activity is miniature golf. This very popular version of golf is quite suited to persons with disabilities. For many, this may represent the extent to which the golf experience is explored. Holes should range from 8 to 14 feet from tee mat to hole with a width of 3 feet, which accommodates reaching a ball lying in the center of the course from a wheelchair.

Variations and Modifications

Sport

Special Olympics (1992) has created rules based upon the *Rules of Golf* as written by the Royal and Ancient Golf Club of St. Andrews. Official events include an individual skills contest (level 1), a partners team competition (level 2), and individual stroke play competition (level 3). The individual skills content is designed to train athletes to compete in basic golf skills. Competition is held in short putting, long putting, chipping, pitch shot, iron shot, and wood shot. The partners team competition involves pairing two Special Olympics athletes with two coaches. The format is a nine-hole tournament that is played as a modified four-person scramble. Level 3 competition enables athletes to play in regulation 18-hole golf competition.

Other Variations and Modifications

Because of various limitations experienced by persons with disabilities, the essential sport skills are often problematic. Dunn and Fait (1989) have detailed many practical considerations necessary for successful participation by golfers who are disabled. These include

- using powered carts for those who lack stamina to walk around the golf course but who can physically play the game;
- having a player whose right arm is missing or incapacitated play left-handed, or vice versa;
- providing a chair for players who cannot balance on one crutch or who are unable to stand; those using a chair or sitting in a wheelchair should have the chair turned so they are facing the ball;
- eliminating the preliminary movement of the club (waggle) for blind golfers because this

could produce an initial malalignment of the club with the ball. Additionally, information about distance to the hole can be provided by tapping on the cup or by telling golfers how far they are positioned from the cup; and

- for some wheelchair players, using extra long clubs to clear the foot plates.

The Putter Finger is an assistive device that consists of a molded rubber suction cup designed to fit on the grip end of any putter. It is used to retrieve the ball from the hole (Adams & McCubbin, 1991). Another adaptation that enables golfers who are blind to practice independently was developed by Huber (personal communication, January 1971). Three pieces of material, all of which produce a different sound when struck, are hung 15 to 20 feet in front of golfers while they practice indoors. Golfers are instructed about the positions of the different pieces of material and the sound made by each. Because feedback about the direction of the ball's line of flight is available, they can determine whether the ball went straight, hooked, or sliced. The golf chirper (Cowart, 1989), is used to develop independent putting skills; it serves as a cup locator and audio feedback device. The amputee golf grip developed by Synergetic Muscle-Powered Prosthetic Systems fits any standard prosthetic wrist. It permits full rotation during backswing, squared club face at impact, and complete follow-through.

POWERLIFTING

Powerlifting has developed over the years as an extremely popular sport for people with disabilities. In this chapter powerlifting as a sport is distinguished from routine weight training.

Sport Skills

Three events are usually considered in powerlifting; these include the bench press, squat, and deadlift. Participants are classified by weight; however, braces and other devices are not counted in the total weight. Wheelchair Sports, USA makes adjustments to recorded weight according to the site of an amputation.

Lead-Up Activities

Special Olympics (1992) offers three events that provide meaningful competition for athletes with lower ability levels. The modified push-up is executed in the kneeling position. As many push-ups as possible are performed in 60 seconds; legal push-ups consist of lowering the head and upper back to the floor, touching the chin to the floor, and returning to the starting position. The athlete may not receive assistance, and push-ups do not have to be performed continuously. *Sit-ups* are performed in the supine position with knees bent and feet held flat on the floor. The athlete folds arms across the chest with hands grasping opposite shoulders; one of the elbows must touch the participant's knee or thigh for the sit-up to be legal. In the *exercycle*, the athlete sits on the bike with feet on the pedals. Assistance may be provided to stay on the bike but not for pedaling. The athlete begins pedaling at the sound of the starting whistle and pedals a distance of 1 kilometer; the score is the amount of time it takes to pedal the distance.

Variations and Modifications

Competitive powerlifting programs are offered by DAAA, Wheelchair Sports, USA, USCPAA, USAAA, USABA, and Special Olympics as a demonstration event. All organizations but two restrict their competitions to the bench press. The USC-PAA, NHS, and USLASA follow the ISOD rules and provide events for men and women; DAAA (1991) makes no modifications in its competition. The USABA (1990) sanctions three events: bench press, squat, and deadlift. Special Olympics (1992) offers benchpress, deadlift, and squat. It also offers two combination events: benchpress and deadlift and benchpress, deadlift, and squat. Each organization has specific rules that accommodate its athletes. Some of the more significant modifications are the following:

- A safety device engineered to protect lifters against the "clasp knife reflex" is mandatory in all sanctioned events (USCPAA, 1991).

- Strapping the legs above the knees to the bench is permissible as long as it is done with the strap provided by the organizing committee (NWAA, 1993).

- A lifter who is also physically disabled may be strapped to the bench either between the naval and nipples and/or between the naval and ankles (Special Olympics, 1992).

- Les Autres competitors must be at least 16 years of age; full extension of the arms must be between 165 and 180 degrees (ISOD, 1990).

- Lifting with a prosthesis is allowed, and orthoses with shoes will be allowed for Les Autres (ISOD, 1990).

CYCLING

Cycling, whether bicycle or tricycle, is a useful skill from the standpoint of a lifelong leisure pursuit. It can likewise be a strenuous sport that is pursued for its competitiveness. To compete, participants must develop a high level of fitness and learn effective race strategy.

Sport Skills

Under most circumstances cycling requires the ability to maintain one's balance on the cycle and to execute a reciprocal movement of the legs to turn the pedals. Technological advances have enabled persons to cycle who would never have thought previously about cycling as a leisure pursuit or as a competitive event.

Variations and Modifications

Sport

The AAAD sponsors three events, which include the 1,000-meter sprint, a road race, and a time trial race on the road. Both NHS and USLASA, using ISOD (1990) rules, offer four events, a 35–45-kilometer for class 4, a 45 to 55-kilometer for class 3, a 55–65-kilometer for class 2, and a 65–75-kilometer for class 1 athletes. The USCPAA sponsors both tricycle and bicycle events. The tricycle events include a 1,500-meter for Classes 2 through 5 and 3,000- and 5,000-meter races for classes 4 and 5. The bicycle events include a 1,500- and 3,000-meter for class 5 and 6; 5,000-meter for classes 5 through 8; 10,000-meter for classes 7 and 8; and a 20,000-meter road race for class 8. Hand-propelled tricycles are not permitted in USCPAA competitions (USCPAA, 1991).

The USABA (1990) offers five events at each of two distances. These include 100-kilometer tandem for men and women, 100-kilometer tandem mixed (men/women), 100-kilometer tandem open event that combines any blind/visually impaired stoker and sighted pilot, 40-kilometer single men and women; the same events are also provided at a distance of 10-kilometers. With few exceptions the rules for USABA cycling are the same as those for the United States Cycling Federation. These exceptions are as follows:

- The pilot (front rider) in tandem riding events must be sighted, with vision to exceed 6/60; the stoker (back rider) can be from any vision class.
- Single riders must have a visual classification of B2 or B3.
- There are racing classes with competition taking place in one division and with no separation by visual class.
- Both the 10- and 100-kilometer courses will adhere to the following specifications: a paved road course that does not cross itself, has no hairpin turns, and is closed to at least one lane of traffic.
- At 100-kilometers, if there are more than 10 riders, a staggered start is used; at 10-kilometers bikes are started at intervals of 30 seconds.

Special Olympics offers the following events: 500-meter time trial, 1-, 5-, and 10-kilometer time trials, and 5-, 10-, 15-, 25-, and 40-kilometer road races. Two unified cycling events are also offered: a tandem time trial with one Special Olympics athlete and a Special partner and either a two-person or four-person team road race. All events are governed by the rules established by the International Federation of Amateur Cycling (Special Olympics, 1992).

Other Variations and Modifications

Riding a bicycle can be a difficult task. Individuals with impaired balance or coordination may require some adaptation. Three- and four-wheeled bicycles with or without hand cranks can facilitate cycling for disabled persons. If riding a two-wheeled bicycle is the desirable approach, then training wheels suitable for full-size adult bikes can be constructed. Additionally, tandem cycling can be used in cases where total control of the bicycle is beyond the ability of the person with a disability, e.g., the visually impaired. The **Cycl-One 48**, which attaches in only a moment, is a device that converts a wheelchair into a handcycle. It is available from Access Designs, Inc.

BOCCIE

Boccie, the Italian version of bowling, is generally played on a sand or soil alley 75 feet long and 8 feet wide. The playing area is normally enclosed at the ends and sides by boards that are 18 inches and 12 inches high, respectively.

Sport Skills

The game requires that players roll or throw wooden balls in the direction of a smaller wooden ball or "jack." The object is to have the ball come to rest closer to the "jack" than any of the opponent's balls. To do this, players try to roll balls in order to protect their own well-placed shots, while knocking aside their opponent's balls.

Lead-Up Activities

The New York State Games for the Physically Challenged have adopted a new game, **Crazy Bocce**, as a demonstration activity. This game consists of throwing two sets of four wooden balls alternately into various size rings for specified point totals. Three smaller rings sit inside one large ring, which is 13 feet in circumference. Points are awarded only if the ball remains inside a ring. If the ball lands inside the large ring (but not in any of the smaller rings), 1 point is awarded. If the ball lands inside the small blue or red ring, 2 points are earned. Landing inside the small yellow ring nets 3 points. The game is usually played with the large ring in a small wading pool (see Figure 25.7). The large ring can also be attached to swimming pool sides, using a suction cup attachment that is provided. The game can also be played in the snow, on the beach, on the lawn, and on carpet. Crazy Bocce is enjoyed by young and old alike.

Variations and Modifications

Sport

Both individual and team boccie are sanctioned events in the national competition of NHS, USC-PAA, DAAA, and USLASA. A minor adjustment to established rules permits the use of ramps/chutes by DAAA athletes. In international competition Les Autres athletes and athletes with amputations are combined in two groups designated as sitting and standing (ISOD). Additionally, US-LASA athletes follow the rules established by USC-PAA. Major modifications to the rules in either USCPAA (1991) or DAAA (1991) sanctioned events include the following:

- The court is laid out on a tile or wood gymnasium floor or asphalt surface and measures 12.5 by 6 meters.

- An assistant is allowed to adjust ramps/chutes and player's chair position within the throwing box; however, all direction for adjustments must be initiated by the player.

- Assistants to players with impaired vision who need light or sound signals may enter the playing court during the game, but they must leave the court immediately after the throw; systems must be approved in advance of the game.

Figure 25.7   Playing Crazy Bocce.
Photograph courtesy of A. Conforti. Printed by permission.

- Players who have difficulty holding or placing the balls can receive assistance; however, they must throw, kick, or roll the ball independently.

- The design of the boccie ramp must permit the player to control the release of the ball; this does not require the player's hand or body to be in direct contact with the ball.

- All balls must be thrown, rolled, or kicked into the court; use of a head pointer, chin, or pull lever is acceptable.

Individual and team boccie are governed by identical rules, with the following major exceptions that apply to the individual sport:

- Competition includes a ramp division for players classified 1 and 2 who use ramps/chutes and separate divisions for class 1 and class 2 athletes who do not use ramps/chutes.

- Competition consists of four rounds as compared to six rounds in the team event.

Other Variations and Modifications

There are several ways to modify boccie for participation by people with disabilities. A major concern is a lack of sufficient strength to propel the ball toward the jack. In such cases, substitution of a lighter object, such as a Nerf ball or balloon, or reduction of the legal court size would facilitate participation. Another area of concern is upper-extremity involvement, which could prohibit rolling or throwing the ball. This concern can be overcome if the individual is permitted to kick the ball into the target area or perhaps, as in regular bowling, to use a bowling cue/stick.

COOPERATIVE GAMES

For over 20 years the use of cooperative play and games in physical education to nurture prosocial behavior has been gaining momentum. Many who have written books on the subject have done so to supplement the competitive goals and activities that characterize many physical education programs. Seeing a need for attention to socialization and self-concept, they have provided cooperative game and play activities as an alternative to competitive ones. Prominent publications on cooperative play and games have been authored by Terry Orlick (1978, 1982) and the New Games Foundation (Fluegelman, 1976, 1981).

As an example of the breadth of game possibilities, several will be described. The following games are contained in resources listed at the end of this chapter:

Cooperative Badminton

The object of this game is to keep the shuttlecock in play for as long as possible. Twenty serves make up a game, 10 for each person or team in the case of doubles. The score is a running total of volleys, and the team score is the total number of volleys made in the 20 serves. A fault on either side ends a serve (Orlick, 1982).

Human Spring

Two people stand facing each other with feet spread shoulder width. They stand an arm's length apart. Hands are held up with palms facing forward. Keeping arms rigid, both people lean forward at the same time, catching each other with their palms and rebounding to a standing position. After doing this a few times, they move slightly farther apart, and the activity is repeated. This should be played on a soft surface, e.g., a grass field or mats (Fluegelman, 1981).

Catch the Dragon's Tail

This is a very active game for a dozen people or more. Participants line up one behind the other. The last person in line, the dragon's tail, places a handkerchief in his back pocket or belt. On the signal the dragon begins chasing its tail. The object is for the first person in line—the head of the dragon—to capture the handkerchief. The interesting aspect of this game is that the dragon's head and tail are in obvious competition; however, the people in the middle aren't certain. Once the head captures the handkerchief from the tail, the head becomes the new tail and the second person from the front becomes the new head. A variation is to have two dragons trying to capture each other's tails (Fluegelman, 1976).

Triangle Tag

This game involves groups of four people. Three people form a triangle by holding hands and facing each other; one person volunteers to be the target. The fourth person is the chaser and stands outside the triangle. The object of the game is quite simple: the chaser attempts to tag the target. This game is unique in that the people in the triangle move and shift cooperatively in an effort to protect the target from the chaser. Rules specify that the target cannot be tagged on the hands or arms or from across the triangle. Variations include having the people in the triangle touch each other's shoulders rather than hold hands or using one chaser and two or more triangles, each with a target (Fluegelman, 1981).

Cooperative Musical Hoops

This is a good game for introducing the idea of cooperation to young children between the ages of 3 and 4. Children are divided into pairs, with each pair standing inside a hula hoop, holding it at waist or shoulder level. Music is played and the children staying in their hoop move around the room using a designated locomotor pattern, such as skipping. In order for the children to move in the same direction and at the same pace, the children must cooperate with each other. Every time the music stops, children from two different hoops combine by stacking their hoops and getting inside. This process continues until as many children are inside and holding up as many hoops as possible (Orlick, 1978).

ADVENTURE ACTIVITIES

Another programmatic area that has gained considerable momentum over the past 25 years is the adventure curriculum. Perhaps the best known program is Project Adventure, started by R. Lentz in 1971. Project Adventure uses a sequence of activities that encourage the development of individual and group trust, cooperation, confidence, courage, independence, and competence. These themes or goals are achieved through trust activities, cooperative games, initiative problems, rope course elements, and high ropes courses. Over the years it became clear that these experiences would benefit individuals with disabilities just as they benefit those who are not disabled. In 1992, with the encouragement of Project Adventure, Havens published *Bridges to Accessibility*. The major theme of this text is the provision of integrated adventure experiences—experiences that are accessible rather than adapted—for persons with all abilities.

Persons with disabilities engage in other adventure activities that are considered by many to be high-risk, nontraditional experiences. These include canoeing (Wachtel, 1987), whitewater rafting (Roswal & Daugherty, 1991), kayaking (Kegel &

Peterson, 1989), rock climbing (Roos, 1991) (Figure 25.8), and backpacking (Huber, 1991). Many of these activities are conducted in a one-day format. Also available is the adventure or wilderness trip that may last for days or weeks. Several organizations provide separate wilderness experiences for persons who are disabled while others offer integrated experiences for people of all abilities. The more prominent organizations providing these experiences include

- S'PLORE—Special Populations Learning Outdoor Recreation and Education, 27 West 3300 South, Salt Lake City, UT 84115.
- C.W. HOG—Cooperative Wilderness Handicapped Outdoor Group, Idaho State University, Student Union, Box 8118, Pocatello, ID 83209.

Figure 25.8 Mountaineering descent by wheelchair. Photography courtesy of NICAN (Australia). Taken from a film by Outward Bound Australia.

- Wilderness Inquiry II—202 2nd St. N.W., #101, East Grand Forks, MN 56271.

- P.O.I.N.T.—Paraplegics On Independent Nature Trips, 4101 Cummings, Bedford, TX 76021.

- B.O.E.C.—The Breckenridge Outdoor Education Center, P.O. Box 697, Breckenridge, CO 80424.

- Bradford Woods—5040 State Road 67 North, Martinsville, IN 46151.

INTEGRATION

The variations and modifications that have been highlighted in this chapter reflect what is considered good practice in physical education as well as in sanctioned sports programs (e.g., limiting the play area is an adaptation technique used in several sports such as tennis, badminton, and boccie).

Individual, dual and cooperative sports and activities provide a unique opportunity for encouraging integration of people with disabilities with their able-bodied peers. From elementary school through high school, variations and modifications can be utilized to alter a sport in subtle ways (e.g., maintaining physical contact while wrestling). As a result of this approach, students with disabilities can participate and/or compete in integrated physical education and sport programs and not only derive the benefits of instruction in activities that are themselves normalizing but also receive that instruction in the least restrictive environment. Because of the reduced temporal and spatial demands of most of the individual, dual, and cooperative sports and activities, there is every reason to believe that success in activities such as those highlighted in this chapter will be readily attainable within accessible programs in integrated settings.

SUMMARY

For the most part, this chapter presented those individual and dual sports that are currently available as part of the competitive offerings of the major sport organizations serving athletes who are disabled. In each case, the particular skills needed in the able-bodied version of the game or sport were detailed. Additionally, lead-up activities were suggested, as well as variation and modifications for use in competitive sport or for use in physical education programs. Space limitations prevented discussion of other games and sports such as riflery and air pistol, shuffleboard, darts, and billiards; information on these activities can be found in Adams and McCubbin (1991). Also highlighted were cooperative games and activities including the use of accessible adventure activities.

BIBLIOGRAPHY

Adams, R.C., Daniel, A.N., McCubbin, J.A., & Rullman, L. (1982). *Games, sports, and exercises for the physically handicapped* (3rd ed.). Philadelphia: Lea & Febiger.

Adams, R.C., & McCubbin, J.A. (1991). *Games, sports and exercises for the physically handicapped* (4th ed.). Philadelphia: Lea & Febiger.

Cowart, J. (1989). Golf chirper for the blind. *Palaestra*, **5**(3), 34–35.

Dunn, J.M., & Fait, H. (1989). *Special physical education: Adapted, individualized, developmental* (6th ed.). Dubuque, IA: Brown.

Dwarf Athletic Association of America. (1991). *Athletic handbook*. Lewisville, TX: Author.

Fluegelman, A. (Ed.) (1976). *The new games book*. San Francisco: Headlands Press.

Fluegelman, A. (Ed.) (1981). *More new games*. Tiburon, CA: Headlands Press.

Hattenback, R.T. (1979). Integrating persons with handicapping conditions in archery activities. In J.P. Winnick & J. Hurwitz (Eds.), *The preparation of regular physical educators for mainstreaming* (pp. 50–54). Brockport: State University of New York, College at Brockport. (ERIC Document Reproduction Service No. ED 222 028)

Havens, M.D. (1992). *Bridges to accessibility: A primer for including persons with disabilities in adventure curricula*. Hamilton, MA: Project Adventure.

Huber, J.H. (1991). An historic accomplishment: The first blind person to hike the Appalachian trail. *Palaestra*, **7**(4), 18–23.

International Sports Organization for the Disabled. (1990). *ISOD handbook*. Aylesbury, England: Author.

Kegel, B., & Peterson, J. (1989). Summer splash: A water sports symposium for the physically challenged. *Palaestra*, **6**(1), 17–19.

McCowan, L.L. (1972). *It is ability that counts: A training manual on therapeutic riding for the handicapped*. Olivet, MI: Olivet College Press.

National Wheelchair Athletic Association. (1993). *Official rulebook of the National Wheelchair Athletic Association*. Colorado Springs: Author.

Orlick, T. (1978). *The cooperative sports and games book: Challenge without competition*. New York: Pantheon Books.

Orlick, T. (1982). *The second cooperative sports and games book*. New York: Pantheon Books.

Orr, R.E., & Sheffield, J. (1981). Adapted epée fencing. *Journal of Physical Education, Recreation and Dance*, **52**(6), 42, 71.

Roos, M. (1991). Pass the adrenalin, please. *Palaestra*, **8**(1), 44–46.

Roswal, G.M., & Daugherty, N. (1991). Whitewater rafting: An outdoor adventure activity for individuals with mental retardation. *Palaestra*, **7**(4), 24–25.

Special Olympics. (n.d.). *Gymnastics*. Washington, DC: Author.

Special Olympics. (1992). *Official Special Olympics summer sports rules*. Washington, DC: Author.

Spink, J. (1993). *Developmental riding therapy: A team approach to assessment and treatment*. Tucson, AZ: Therapy Skill Builders.

United States Association for Blind Athletes. (1990). *Official 1990 Rules*. Colorado Springs: Author.

United States Cerebral Palsy Athletic Association. (1991). *Sports rules manual* (4th ed.). Dallas: Author.

Wachtel, L.J. (1987). Thoughts on a wilderness canoe trip. *Palaestra*, **3**(4), 33–40.

Weber, R.C. (1991). Using Velcro to assist badminton players who are disabled or elderly. *Palaestra*, **7**(3), 10–11.

Wheelchair Tennis Players Association. (1990). *Wheelchair Tennis Players Association regulations*. San Clemente, CA: Author.

Winnick, J.P., & Short, F.X. (1985). *Physical fitness testing of the disabled*. Champaign, IL: Human Kinetics.

Wiseman, D.C. (1982). *A practical approach to adapted physical education*. Reading, MA: Addison-Wesley.

RESOURCES

Written

Adams, R.C., & McCubbin, J.A. (1991). *Games, sports, and exercise for the physically handicapped* (4th ed.). Philadelphia: Lea & Febiger. This excellent resource provides in-depth suggestions concerning traditional and nontraditional games and sports that are suitable for participation by disabled persons. Included are suggestions for modifying existing sport or game structures, rules, and procedures.

Fluegelman, A. (1981). *More new games*. Tiburon, CA: Headlands Press. Makes suggestions about how to adapt games more readily to a wide range of players.

Fluegelman, A. (Ed.) (1976). *The new games book*. San Francisco: Headlands Press. This book from the New Games Foundation contains a variety of games and activities that encourage cooperative play.

Grosse, S. (Ed.) (1991). *Sport instruction for individuals with disabilities: The best of practical pointers*. Reston, VA: AAHPERD. This book contains previously published *Pointers* as well as new articles on increasing opportunities for those with disabilities to participate in instructional sport programs. Adaptations are presented for students with crutches and with unilateral and bilateral upper-arm amputations in badminton, golf, archery, bowling, tennis, and table tennis.

Havens, M.D. (1992). *Bridges to accessibility: A primer for including persons with disabilities in adventure curricula*. Hamilton, MA: Project Adventure. This text provides the philosophical and practical wherewithal to include persons with disabilities in adventure programming.

Orlick, T. (1978). *The cooperative sports and games book: Challenge without competition*. New York: Pantheon Books. This book contains many cooperative games that are relevant for affective stimulation.

Orlick, T. (1982). *The second cooperative sports and games book*. New York: Pantheon Books. Orlick's second book of cooperative games contains several hundred games different from those in the 1978 text and modifies and refines versions of games presented in the earlier work.

Paciorek, M.J., & Jones, J.A. (1994). *Sports and recreation for the disabled*. Carmel, IN: Cooper. Perhaps the most comprehensive resource currently available, this manual uses a cross-categorical approach in discussing sports and recreation for people with disabilities. Information is provided on sport governing bodies, both able-bodied and disabled. An overview of each sport, along with adapted equipment suppliers and manufacturers, accompanies each description.

Rohnke, K. (1977). *Cowstails and cobras*. Hamilton, MA: Project Adventure. This book presents a broad range of natural outdoor activities, including cooperative group games and activities that may be selected to stimulate affective development. It also describes Project Adventure, a nationally validated project designed to further the spread of adventure programs throughout the country.

Rohnke, K. (1984). *Silver bullets: A guide to initiative problems, adventure games, stunts and trust activities*. Hamilton, MA: Project Adventure. This book presents innovative activities to bring people together and to build trust.

Rohnke, K. (1989). *Cowtails and cobras II: A guide to games, initiatives, ropes courses, and Adventure curriculum*. Dubuque, IA: Kendall/Hunt. This book is a major revision of the original text. It provides a much more comprehensive guide for those implementing an adventure curriculum in the physical education and recreation fields.

Audiovisual

Carnes, K. (n.d.). *How to race* [Videotape]. Author, 291 Comfort Drive, Henderson, NV 89014. This 30-minute video details chair setup and maintenance. It also provides information on pushing techniques, sitting positions, use of compensators, transferring to and from chairs, and preliminary training techniques.

Special Olympics. (n.d.). *Making of a champion: Track and field* [Videotape]. Author, 1350 New York Avenue, N.W., Suite 500, Washington, DC 20005. This video can be used as a training aid for athletes. It provides instruction on various techniques used to prepare athletes for competition.

United States Association for Blind Athletes. (n.d.). *Summer sports officials/coaches training video* [Videotape]. Author, 33 N. Institute Street, Colorado Springs, CO 80903. This video provides information about fundamentals, basic rules and their modifications from companion sports for able-bodied athletes. It addresses special equipment and adaptations. Sports include track, field, gymnastics, powerlifting, and wrestling.

CHAPTER 26

Winter Sport Activities

Luke E. Kelly

A major goal of physical education for students both with and without disabilities is to provide the knowledge, skills, and experiences they need to live healthy and productive lives. At the completion of their school physical education program, students should have the basic physical fitness and motor skills required to achieve this goal. It would be logical to assume that the emphasis on various sport skills in the school curriculum would reflect the students' needs in terms of carryover value and the likelihood of continuing participation after the school years. However, one area, that of winter sport skills, is frequently underrepresented in the physical education and sport curriculum. This is a serious omission for all students, especially those with disabilities. In many parts of the country, the winter season is the longest season during the school year. Winter sport activities provide opportunities for individuals with disabilities to

- maintain or improve their physical fitness levels,

- participate in many social/community recreation activities, and

- pursue athletic competition.

Failure to provide youngsters with disabilities with winter sport skills limits their recreational options during the winter months, which, in turn, may both affect their fitness and isolate them from many social activities and settings.

The purpose of this chapter is to introduce the reader to a number of winter sport activities that can be included in physical education and sport programs for persons with disabilities. It is not within the scope of this chapter to cover in detail how each winter sport skill should be taught. Instead, general guidelines are provided, along with a brief description of each winter sport activity and some specific adaptations for various participants with different disabilities.

Given proper instruction and practice, individuals with disabilities can pursue and successfully participate in a variety of winter sports such as alpine (downhill) skiing, cross-country skiing (nordic), ice skating, ice picking, sledding, curling, and hockey. Instructional programs for individuals with disabilities should be guided by equal attention to safety, motivation (fun), and skill development. Safety concerns should encompass the areas of physical and motoric readiness, appropriate clothing and equipment, and instructor qualifications.

ALPINE SKIING

Downhill skiing is a winter sport in which most individuals with disabilities can participate with little or no modification. Skiing frees them from many of the limitations that hinder their mobility on land and allows them to move with great agility and at great speeds. For many individuals with physical, mental, and sensory impairments, skiing offers a unique opportunity to challenge their environment (see Figure 26.1).

The key to learning to ski is controlling one's weight distribution and directing where the weight is applied on the surface (edges) of the skis. The goal of any introductory ski program is to provide

Figure 26.1 A paraplegic uses a mono-ski and outriggers to practice chairlift unloading under the guidance of Mark Andrews and Dara Kuller of Massanutten Adaptive Ski School, Harrisonburg, VA.
Photo courtesy of Michael W. Reilly, Daily News Record.

students with the basic skills needed to enjoy and safely participate in the sport. The basic skills of downhill skiing can be grouped into six categories:

1. Independence in putting on and taking off one's equipment
2. Independence in using rope and chair lifts
3. Falling and standing
4. Walking (sidestepping, herringbone)
5. Stopping (wedge, parallel)
6. Turning (wedge, parallel)

Instruction

It is strongly recommended that actual ski instruction be preceded by a conditioning program and the development of basic skills such as falling and standing. When the actual ski instruction begins, the skill sequence must be matched to the needs and abilities of the learners to both ensure safety and maximize enjoyment. While independent recovery (standing back up on one's skis) is ultimately a required skill for independent skiing, it may not be appropriate to concentrate on this skill during early learning. For many individuals with disabilities, learning to stand up on skis is very strenuous and often a frustrating experience. Students who are made to master this skill first are

likely not to experience much success or fun and will soon become disenchanted with the idea of learning to ski. Initial instruction should focus on learning actual skiing skills such as a wedge stop, and the instructor should provide assistance to compensate for the lack of other skills, such as the ability to independently recover from falls. This form of instruction will provide students with confidence and some of the thrills of moving on skis (Figure 26.2). As skill and enjoyment increase, the students will become more motivated to work on mastering the other essential skills such as independent recovery.

Assistive Devices

A number of assistive devices have been developed to offset some of the limitations imposed by various disabilities or to compensate for the general low fitness and/or poor motor coordination found in many individuals with disabilities. The most commonly used device is the **ski-bra** (Figure 26.3), which is mounted to the tip of the skis and serves two primary functions. First, it stabilizes the skis while still allowing them to move independently. Second, it assists the skier in positioning the skis in a wedge position, which improves balance and facilitates stopping and turning. The ski-bra can be used as a temporary learning device for any skier (e.g., mentally

Figure 26.2 A quadriplegic learns to use a bi-ski tethered by Mark Andrews of Massanutten Adaptive Ski School, Harrisonburg, VA.
Photo courtesy of Michael W. Reilly, Daily News Record.

retarded, visually impaired, orthopedically impaired) during the early stages of learning, to assist with balance and control of the skis. The ski-bra may also be used as a permanent assistive device for individuals with lower extremity orthopedic impairments who lack sufficient strength and/or control of their lower limbs.

Canting wedges are another common modification. Small, thin wedges are placed between the sole of the ski boot and the ski. The wedges adjust the lateral tilt of the boot and subsequently affect the distribution of the weight over the edges of the skis. Canting wedges are commonly used to assist skiers who have trouble turning to one side or the other.

Outriggers (Figure 26.4) are common assistive devices used by skiers with amputations and other orthopedic impairments who require additional support primarily in the area of balance. The outriggers are made from a **Lofstrand crutch** with a short ski attached to the bottom. The ski on the end of the crutch can be placed in a vertical (up) position and used as a crutch or positioned in a horizontal position for use as an outrigger. **Three-track** and **four-track skiing** are common terms used to describe the use of outriggers. Three-track skiing refers to individuals who use only one ski and two outriggers (e.g., single-leg amputees). Four-track skiing refers to those who use two skis and two outriggers.

Sit-skiing may be more accurately described as a form of sledding, but it is included here because it is performed on ski slopes and is the method used by skiers with paraplegia and quadriplegia to ski. Sit-skiing involves the use of a special sled (see Figure 26.5). The person with paraplegia is strapped into the sled, which contains appropriate padding and support to hold the skier in an upright sitting position. The top of the sled is covered by a water-repellent nylon skirt to keep the skier dry. The bottom of the sled is smooth, with a metal runner or edge running along each side. Skiers control the sled by shifting their weight (over the edge) in the direction they want to go. The skier can use a single kayak-type pole or two short poles to assist in balancing and controlling the sled. Special mittens are available to allow individuals with limited grip strength to hold onto the poles. For the protection of both the sit-skier and other skiers on the slope, the beginner sit-skier should always be tethered to an experienced ski instructor (as shown in Figure 26.2). Modified sit-skis are also available and can be used by persons with paraplegia for cross-country skiing.

Ski instructors use various forms of physical assistance to help and guide skiers with different disabilities. Instructors must be able to provide sufficient physical assistance during early learning to ensure both safety and success. Providing physical assistance to a moving beginner skier requires specific skills that must be learned and perfected. As the skills of a skier with a disability increase,

Figure 26.3 Photograph of a ski-bra.
Photo courtesy of Dave Burton, Kluge Children's Rehabilitation Center, University of Virginia. Printed by permission.

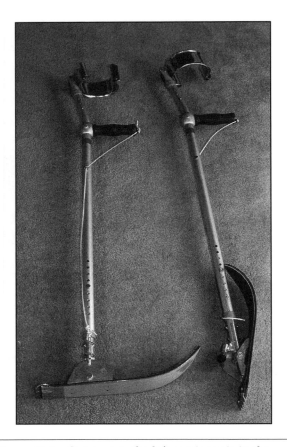

Figure 26.4 Outriggers: the left outrigger is in the down position for skiing; the right outrigger is in the up position and can be used as a crutch.
Photo courtesy of Mark Andrews, Massanutten Adaptive Ski School, Harrisonburg, VA. Printed by permission.

the instructor must also know how to gradually reduce the physical assistance to verbal cues and finally to independence.

In addition to the more universal assistive devices described above, numerous others have been created to address specific needs of skiers with disabilities. Special prosthetic limbs, for example, have been developed to allow single and double-leg (mono-ski) amputees to ski. Many of these devices are homemade by ski instructors trying to help specific individuals. Watching a national handicapped ski competition will clearly demonstrate that there is no limit to the devices that can be created to assist skiers with various disabilities.

CROSS-COUNTRY SKIING

Cross-country skiing in recent years has become a very popular winter sport. It is an excellent physical fitness and recreation activity. Because both the arms and the legs are used in cross-country skiing, this

activity develops total body fitness. Two other advantages of the sport are that it costs nothing after the initial equipment is purchased and that it can be done almost anywhere (e.g., golf courses, parks, open fields). The major disadvantage of cross-country skiing for many individuals with disabilities, when compared to downhill skiing, is that the skier must create the momentum to move. This difference eliminates many individuals with more severe orthopedic impairments who lack either the strength or the control to generate the momentum. However, because the activity is performed on snow and does not require that the feet actually be lifted off the ground, many individuals with cerebral palsy who have difficulty walking (shuffle gait) can successfully cross-country ski.

A complete cross-country skiing outfit (skies, poles, shoes, and gaiters) can be purchased for approximately $150. Waxless (fishscale or step pattern) skis are recommended over wax skis for beginners. Waxless skis require no maintenance or

Figure 26.5 Sit-skiing sleds. View of an athlete with a spinal cord injury in a stationary sit-ski.
Photo courtesy of Mark Andrews, Massanutten Adaptive Ski School, Harrisonburg, VA. Printed by permission.

preparation prior to use, and they provide more than sufficient resistance and glide for learning and enjoying cross-country skiing.

Initial instruction should take place in a relatively flat area with prepared tracks. Most beginning cross-country skiers tend to simply walk wearing their skis, using their poles for balance. This, unfortunately, is incorrect and very fatiguing. The key in learning to cross-country ski is getting the feel of pushing back on one ski while the weight is transferred to the front foot and the front ski is slid forward. Instructors should focus on demonstrating this pattern and contrasting it with walking. A very effective technique is to physically assist the beginning skier through this pattern so that the learner can feel what it is like. This works particularly well with skiers with mental and visual impairments. Cross-country skiers with visual impairments must be accompanied by sighted partners who usually ski parallel to them and inform them of upcoming conditions (e.g., turns, changes in grades). The forward push and glide technique is the preferred pattern for most skiers with disabilities, as opposed to the more strenuous and skill-demanding skating technique used by world-class nordic skiers.

COMPETITIVE SKIING FOR INDIVIDUALS WITH DISABILITIES

Skiing for individuals with disabilities is sponsored by a number of sport associations that conduct local, state, and national skiing competitions. Three of the largest and most prominent are Special Olympics, which sponsors ski competitions for individuals with mental retardation; the National Handicapped Sports (NHS), which sponsors national skiing competitions for individuals with disabilities; and the United States Association for Blind Athletes (USABA), which sponsors an annual national competition for skiers with visual impairments.

Special Olympics sponsors local, state, and national ski competitions. Competition is offered in both alpine and nordic events. The alpine events include downhill, giant slalom, and slalom races. The nordic events include the 50-meter, 100-meter, 500-meter, 1-kilometer, 3-kilometer, 5-kilometer, 7.5-kilometer, and 10-kilometer races, as well as 3 × 1-kilometer relay. Athletes are classified for competition into one of three levels—novice, intermediate, or advanced—on the basis of preliminary time trials in each event. There are no age or gender divisions. Special Olympics also offers developmental (noncompetitive/participation) alpine and nordic events. The developmental alpine events include a 10-meter glide and a 10-meter ski walk. The nordic developmental events include a 10-meter pole walk (no skis), a 10-meter ski walk (no poles), a glide event, and a 30-meter snowshoe race.

NHS sponsors the Handicapped National Ski Championships each year. The nationals are preceded by a series of regional meets where athletes must qualify for the nationals. The national meets involve competition in three categories: alpine (downhill, slalom, giant slalom), nordic (5-kilometer, 10-kilometer, 15-kilometer, 20-kilometer, 30-kilometer, biathlon, and relays), and sit-skiing (as listed for alpine and nordic). Athletes are classified according to the site and severity of their disability and the type of adapted equipment used in skiing. Skiers with orthopedic impairments are divided into 12 classes, described briefly as follows:

Class 1 4-track: disability of both legs, skiing with outriggers and using two skis or one ski using a prosthesis

Class 2 3-track: disability of one leg, skiing with outriggers and one ski

Class 3 Two skies with poles: disability in both legs

Class 4 Two skies with poles: disability in one leg

Class 5/7 Two skis with no poles: disability of both arms or hands

Class 6/8 Two skis with one pole: disability of one arm or hand

Class 9 Disability of arm and one leg (athletes can use equipment of their choice)

Class 10/12 Disability in both lower limbs and skiing with a sit-ski of your choice

Functional Classifications 10–12:

Class 11 All athletes who meet the Group 1 Class in Sledge Sports (above T-10 inclusive) and all athletes who meet the Group 1, 2, 3 Class with major disability of one arm

Class 12 All athletes who meet the Group 2 Class in Sledge Sports (below T-10 to L1 inclusive)

Class 13 All athletes who meet the Group 3 Class in Sledge Sports (below L1, double AK amputation)

Skiers with visual impairments are divided into three classes on the basis of visual acuity with maximum correction. The classifications are as follows (U.S. Ski Association, 1989).

Class B1 Totally blind: can distinguish light and dark but not shapes

Class B2 Partially sighted: 20/600 acuity or visual field of less than 5°

Class B3 Partially sighted: visual acuity between 20/600 and 20/200 and/or field of vision between 5° and 20°

The USABA, for its national ski competition, uses the three vision classifications just described for NHS. USABA offers giant slalom and downhill alpine events as well as 5-kilometer, 10-kilometer, and 25-kilometer nordic events. Separate competitions are offered for each gender within each classification; there are no age divisions. Sighted guides are used in all of the events to verbally assist the skiers who are visually impaired. USABA also sponsors approximately five nordic skiing training camps each year to promote skiing for individuals with visual impairments. In addition to the USABA, Blind Outdoor Leisure Development (BOLD) provides satellite training programs in downhill skiing, and the Ski for Light organization sponsors approximately 20 weekend nordic ski instructional programs around the country each year.

In addition to the classifications just described, there are three age divisions: children under 18 (juniors), ages 19 through 40, and ages 41 and over (seniors). Separate competitions are offered for each gender in each age division except when there are not enough participants of one gender to compose a heat. The same classifications apply for both alpine and cross-country skiing. The only difference between the men's and women's events is that females are limited to the 5-kilometer and 10-kilometer cross-country events.

Sit-skiing competition is conducted only in the United States; therefore, athletes competing in this category are not classified according to the international system. Sit-skiers are classified into one of two groups. Group 1 is composed of athletes with disabilities in the lower limbs, with injury between T5 and T10 inclusive. (Athletes with higher injuries, above T5, typically are not able to sit-ski.) Group 2 is for athletes with all other disabilities resulting from injury below T10 and conditions such as spina bifida, amputation, cerebral palsy, polio, and muscular dystrophy.

ICE SKATING

Ice skating is another inexpensive winter sport that is readily accessible in many regions of the country. Most individuals with disabilities who can stand and walk independently can learn to ice skate successfully. For those who cannot, a modified form of ice skating, ice picking, is available. While skating is common in many areas on frozen lakes and ponds or water-covered tennis courts, the preferred environment for teaching ice skating is an indoor ice rink. An indoor rink offers a more moderate temperature and a better quality ice surface, free from the cracks and bumps commonly found in natural ice. Ice rinks can frequently be used by physical education programs during off times such as daytime hours on weekdays.

Properly fitting skates are essential for learning and ultimately enjoying ice skating. Ice skates should be fitted by a professional experienced in working with and fitting individuals with disabilities. Either figure or hockey skates can be used. The important consideration is that the skates provide good ankle and arch support so that the skater's weight is centered over the ankles and the blades of the skates are perpendicular to the ice when the skater is standing.

As discussed earlier in this chapter, instruction should be guided by safety and success. The greatest obstacle in learning to ice skate is the fear of falling. Although falling while first learning to skate is inevitable, steps can and should be taken to minimize the frequency and severity of the falls and, consequently, the apprehension. At the same time, the early stages of learning must be associated with success, which gives learners confidence that they will be able to learn to skate. It is recommended that padding be used around the major joints most likely to hit the ice during a fall. Knee and elbow pads reduce the physical trauma of taking a fall and also provide a form of psychological security that alleviates the fear of falling. When teaching adults with mental impairments to ice skate, I have used football pants with knee, hip, and sacral pads along with elbow pads and have found them to be very beneficial during the early stages of learning.

The locomotor skill of ice skating is very similar to walking. The weight, the center of gravity, is transferred in front of the base of support and from side to side as the legs are lifted and swung forward to catch the weight. The back skate is usually rotated outward about 30° to provide some resistance to sliding backward as the weight is transferred to the forward skate. Because success during the early lessons is essential, one-on-one instruction from an experienced instructor is highly recommended.

The primary aid used in teaching ice skating is physical assistance. Some individuals with orthopedic and neuromuscular impairments may benefit from the use of polyproplylene orthoses to stabilize their ankles. Ankle-foot orthoses are custom made and can be worn inside the skates. The most universal skating aid is the Hein-A-Ken skate aid, which is simply a walker modified to be used

on ice. This device does not interfere with the skating action of the legs, and it provides the beginning skater with a stable means of support independent from the instructor. The skate aid can be used for temporary assistance during the early stages of learning for students who need a little additional support or confidence; it can also be a more permanent assistive device for skaters with more severe orthopedic impairments. I have found it beneficial to add some foam padding to the top support bar in the front of the skate aid to further reduce the chance of injury from falls. If skate aids are not available, chairs can be used in a similar fashion.

Ice picking is a modified form of ice skating in which the participant sits on a sledge, a small sled with blades on the bottom, and uses small poles (picks) to propel the sledge over the ice. Ice picking can be performed by almost anyone and is particularly appropriate for individuals who only have upper-limb control (e.g., paraplegics or those with spina bifida). Ice picking is an excellent activity for developing upper-body strength and endurance. All skating activities and events (speed skating and skate dancing) can be modified and performed in sledges. Because both able-bodied and individuals with disabilities can use the equipment, ice picking offers a unique way to equalize participation and competition in integrated settings.

Special Olympics sponsors ice skating competitions in two categories: figure skating and speed skating. The figure skating events include singles, pairs, and ice dancing; the speed skating events include the 100-, 300-, 500-, 800-, 1,000-, and 1,500-meter races. For each event, athletes are divided into three classifications—novice, intermediate, and advanced—on the basis of preliminary performance and time trials. Developmental (noncompetitive/participation) ice skating events are also offered. These include the slide for distance, the 10-meter assisted skate, the 10-meter unassisted skate, and the 30-meter slalom.

The USABA sponsors two speed skating events (5,000 and 10,000 meter) in conjunction with the national ski competition. The skaters with visual impairments are assisted by sighted guides who provide verbal cues from in front of, beside, or behind the skater.

SLEDDING AND TOBOGGANING

In snowy regions of the country, sledding and tobogganing are two common recreational activities that are universally enjoyed by children and adults. Many individuals with disabilities, however, avoid these activities because they lack the simple skills and confidence needed to successfully take part in them. The needed skills and confidence can easily be addressed in a physical education program. Given proper attention to safety and clothing, almost all children with disabilities can participate in sledding and tobogganing. Sleds and toboggans can be purchased and/or rented at minimal cost. Straps and padding can be added to commercial sleds and toboggans to accommodate the specific needs occasioned by individuals with different disabilities. Even the individuals with the most severe disabilities can experience the thrill of sledding or tobogganing when paired with an aide who can control and steer the sled.

HOCKEY

Ice hockey is a popular winter sport in the northern areas of the United States and is the national sport of Canada. The game is played by two teams who attempt to hit a puck into the opposing team's goal using their hockey sticks. Hockey is a continuous, highly active, and exciting sport. Because of these features, numerous modifications and adaptations have been made to ice hockey to accommodate players with disabilities. The major modifications include

- playing the game on a solid, less slippery surface, like a gymnasium floor or tennis court;
- using soft plastic balls, plastic pucks, or doughnut-shaped pucks instead of the traditional ice hockey pucks;
- using shorter and lighter sticks made of plastic, which are more durable, easier to handle, and less harmful to other players;
- changing the boundaries, the number of players per team, and the length of the playing periods to accommodate the ability of the players; and
- changing the size of the goals.

Modifications can easily be made to permit sticks to be held by players with physical impairments or used from wheelchairs. A wide range of abilities can be accommodated in a game if the teams are balanced and the players' abilities are matched to the various positions.

Special Olympics sponsors local, state, and national competition in floor hockey and poly hockey. These two games are basically the same except for the sticks and pucks used in each. In floor hockey, a stick similar to a broomstick with a vinyl coating on the end is used in conjunction with a doughnut-shaped puck. In poly hockey, plastic sticks similar to regular hockey sticks are used along with a plastic puck shaped like a regulation puck. The goalkeeper in both versions uses a regular hockey goalie stick. Although there are some minor variations in the skills related to each version due to the differences in equipment, the basic skills are the same for both games.

Sledge hockey is a modified form of ice hockey. The only difference from the regulation game is that this game is played from a sledge and the puck is struck with a modified stick called a pick (see Figure 26.6). The pick is approximately 30 inches in length. On one end it has metal points that grip the ice and allow the athlete to propel the sledge. The other end, called the butt, is rubber coated. The butt is held while the sledge is being propelled. When the athlete wants to hit the puck, the hand is slid down the shaft of the pick to cover the spiked end, and then the butt end of the pick is used to strike the puck.

Sledge hockey is an excellent recreational and fitness activity. Using sledges is also an ideal way of equating able-bodied students and those with orthopedic impairments in the same activity.

Figure 26.6 Sledges and picks used in sledge hockey. Photo courtesy of Mark Andrews. Printed by permission.

Logical modifications should be made to the regulation game of hockey to accommodate beginners, such as reducing the playing area, increasing the number of players on each team, increasing the size of the goal, playing without goalkeepers, or changing the size or type of puck (e.g., substituting a playground ball). The goal of all modifications should be to maximize participation and success in the basic sledge and hockey skills while gradually progressing toward the regulation game.

CURLING

Curling is a popular recreational activity and sport in Europe and Canada. The playing area is an ice court 46 yards long and 14 feet wide, with a 6-foot circular target, called a *house*, marked on the ice at each end. The game is played by two teams of four players, with pieces of equipment called *stones* (a kettle-shaped weight 36 inches in circumference and weighing approximately 40 pounds, with a gooseneck handle on top). A game is composed of 10 or 12 rounds, called *heads;* a round consists of each player delivering (sliding) two stones. Players on each team alternate delivering stones until all have been delivered. After each stone is delivered, teammates can use brooms to sweep frost and moisture from the ice in front of the coming stone to keep it straight and allow it to slide farther. At the end of a round, a team scores a point for each stone they have propelled closer to the center of the target than the other team. The team with the most points at the end of 10 or 12 rounds is the winner. If the score is tied, an additional round is played.

Curling can easily be modified to accommodate individuals with just about any disability. The distance between the houses and the weight of stones can be reduced to facilitate reaching the targets. The size of the targets can also easily be increased to maximize success. Audible goal locators can be placed on the houses to assist players with visual impairments. The sweeping component of the game may be difficult to modify to include players who are nonambulatory or who have visual impairments. In these cases, mixed teams could be formed of players with different disabilities so that each team had a few members who could do the sweeping. Finally, assistive devices like those used in bowling (ramps and guide rails) could be used to help players with more severe disabilities deliver the stones.

SUMMARY

Winter sports, in general, are excellent all-around activities. They develop motor skill, strength, and physical fitness while at the same time providing participants with functional recreational skills they can use for the rest of their lives. For many individuals with disabilities, winter sports performed on snow and ice allow them to move with agility and speed not possible under their own power on land. Winter sports, therefore, should be an essential component in the physical education and sport programs of all students, especially those with disabilities. For this reason, activities have been discussed in this chapter with particular focus on ways to modify them for people with unique needs.

BIBLIOGRAPHY

Adams, R.C., & McCubbin, J.A. (1991). *Games, sports, and exercises for the physically disabled* (4th ed.). Philadelphia: Lea & Febiger.

Paciorek, M.J., & Jones, J.A. (1989). *Sports and recreation for the disabled: A resource manual.* Indianapolis: Benchmark Press.

United States Ski Association. (1989). *Alpine skiing competition guide.* Park City, UT: Author.

RESOURCES

Altschul, C. (1989). National disabled ski championships provide preview of 1990 world event. *Palaestra,* **5,** 20–23.

Axelson, P. (1988). Hitting the slopes . . . Everything you ever wanted to know about mono-skis and mono-skiing. *Sports 'N Spokes* **14**(4), 22–34.

Caldwell, J. (1976). *The new cross-country ski book* (4th ed.). Brattleboro, VT: Stephen Green Press.

Cob, M. (1975). Skiing is for everyone. *Therapeutic Recreation Journal,* **9,** 18–20.

Cottrell, J. (1980a). *Special Olympics dry land ski school.* Washington, DC: Joseph P. Kennedy, Jr. Foundation.

Cottrell, J. (1980b). *Skiing for everyone.* Winston-Salem, NC: Hunter.

Crase, N. (1983). 1983 National handicap ski championships. *Sports 'N Spokes,* **9,** 36–39.

Fagerkie, A., Graff, H., Mathiesen, G., & Torheim, A. (1987). *Winter activities for the mentally and physically handicapped.* Norwegian Ministry of Cultural and Scientific Affairs, Norwegian University Press.

Fay, T., & Maddock, K. (1989). Disabled nordic skiers meet the challenge: The 1989 SUBARU/USSA cross-country ski championships. *Palaestra,* **5,** 24–29.

Krag, M.H., & Messner, D.G. (1982). Skiing for the physically handicapped. *Clinics in Sports medicine*, **1**, 319–332.

Leonard, E., & Pitzer, N.L. (1988). Special problems of handicapped skiers: An overview. *Physician and Sportsmedicine*, **16**(3), 77–82.

McKinley, N. (1982). The wilderness experience. *Sports 'N Spokes*, **7**, 10–12.

O'Leary, H. (1989). *Bold tracks: Skiing for the disabled* (M. Meinig, Ed.). Evergreen, CO: Cordillera Press.

O'Leary, H. *The Winter Park amputee ski teaching system.* Winter Park, CO: Winter Park Handicap Ski Program. Describes the program used to teach people with amputations how to ski. This manual is a must for anyone planning to work with amputees in a ski program. Winter Park is an excellent resource for up-to-date information and techniques.

Orr, L.F. (1983). Cross-country sled skiing. *Sports 'N Spokes*, **9**, 18–20.

Rappoport, A. (1982). Sledge hockey: The alternative to ice hockey for the disabled. *Sports 'N Spokes*, **7**, 24–25.

Seaton, D.C., Schmottlach, N., Clayton, I.A., Leibee, H.C., & Messersmith, L.L. (1983). *Physical education handbook* (7th ed.). Englewood Cliffs, NJ: Prentice Hall.

Sledge Hockey Ice Picking Association. (1984). *Official sledge hockey rules and regulations manual.* Alberta: Author.

Special Olympics. (1990). *Official Special Olympics winter sports rules.* Washington, DC: Joseph P. Kennedy, Jr. Foundation.

Special Olympics. (n.d.). *The alpine skiing sports skills instructional program* and *The hockey sports skills instructional program.* Washington, DC: Joseph P. Kennedy, Jr. Foundation.

These two Special Olympics manuals provide a how-to approach for teaching the basic skills involved in alpine skiing and hockey. Teaching suggestions, as well as sample drills and activities, are provided for each skill.

CHAPTER 27

Enhancing Wheelchair Sport Performance

Colin Higgs

An official yelled, "He's not part of the race. We don't count him!" when Bob Hall's wheelchair unofficially crossed the finish line of the Boston Marathon in 1975. Two years later Hall became the first wheelchair athlete to officially complete the race. His time of 2 hours, 40 minutes, 40 seconds was considerably slower than the 2 hours, 14 minutes, 46 seconds recorded by the able-bodied winner, Jerome Drayton. By 1993, able-bodied runners had improved their performance by 4 minutes and 13 seconds while the wheelchair athletes, led by Jim Knaub, had improved their time by more than 78 minutes to an almost unbelievable 1 hour, 22 minutes, 17 seconds.

For runners the two-hour marathon remains an elusive and distant goal, while those in wheelchairs have their sights firmly set on completing the 26-mile marathon in under 1 hour within the foreseeable future.

There has been a rapid and profound transition from wheelchair sport as a mode of therapy in the rehabilitation of persons with disabilities, to wheelchair sport as a legitimate expression of athletic excellence. This transition has been spearheaded by athletes themselves, and they have been instrumental in developing many of the innovations in equipment and technique that have occurred.

Coupled with innovations in equipment and technique has been increased specialization by the athletes. It was once possible for an athlete to compete at World Championship level in a number of sports, but this is no longer the case. Sport for athletes with disabilities now parallels the able-bodied world, and to reach the highest levels athletes must find the sport (and often the event) for which they are best suited. Suitability for specific sports is most commonly determined by body size and shape and by the physiological makeup of the athlete.

BODY SHAPE AND WHEELCHAIR PERFORMANCE

Body shape is most often described in terms of the athlete's somatotype (Sheldon, Dupertuis, & McDermott, 1954). Somatotyping is a system in which an athlete is scored on each of three independent body shape measures (see Figure 27.1). The first body shape component is called **endomorphy** and represents the degree of "bulk" of the athlete. Endomorphy scores were originally given a value between 1 (low bulk) and 7 (very high bulk), although in recent years scores higher than 7 have been recorded. The second component is **mesomorphy**, or degree of musculature. A person with a high mesomorphy score has large well-developed musculature, while a low score represents weak or underdeveloped musculature. The final component is **ectomorphy**, a measure of "linearity." People with high ectomorphy scores are tall in comparison to their width. Individual athletes are given a three-number score such as 2-7-4, which represents, respectively, that athlete's level of endomorphy, mesomorphy, and ectomorphy. Figure 27.1 shows a somatograph on which the extreme scores of 7-1-1 (endomorph), 1-7-1 (mesomorph), and 1-1-7 (ectomorph) are shown along with the endo-mesomorphic body shape associated with high performance in the power throwing events, and the ecto-mesomorphic body shape associated with success in track racing events.

TYPES OF SPORT WHEELCHAIRS

Specialization of body type for different activities, called somatic specialization, has driven the development of specialized wheelchairs, both to suit the size and shape of the athlete and to meet the special needs of each athletic event. There are three major types of wheelchair: (a) general sport wheelchairs for ballgames such as quad rugby and wheelchair basketball, racquetball, and tennis, (b) field event (throwing) wheelchairs, and (c) racing wheelchairs (see Figure 27.2).

General Sport Wheelchairs

General sport wheelchairs are the most popular specialized wheelchairs. For many individuals, these have become daily-use chairs as well as vehicles for athletic performance. Shown in Figure 27.2(a) is a typical "sport" wheelchair. Major design features are the relatively high seating position, lack of armrests/supports, and the cambered (inward sloping) main wheels. The cambered, 24-inch (0.61 meter) diameter mainwheels make the chair stable and easy to turn, while at the same time making it easier for the athlete to reach and apply force to the handrim to propel the wheelchair. The handrim (push-rim) is relatively large, usually 20 to 22 inches (0.51 to 0.56 meter) in diameter, which allows the athlete to start, stop, turn, and accelerate the wheelchair with ease, but which limits the potential top speed (Coutts, 1990). Small front wheels (castors) are designed for ease of turning. Built with quick release hubs on the mainwheels, and with removable cushioning on the seat, the wheelchair can be taken apart for easier transportation. The cost for a high performance "sport" wheelchair from a major manufacturer is approximately $2,000.

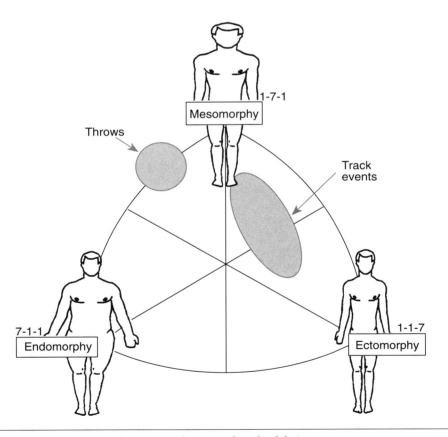

Figure 27.1 Certain body shapes are better suited to specific wheelchair events.

a

b

c

Figure 27.2   (a) General sport wheelchair. (b) A ''throwing'' wheelchair in which the wheels are only used for ease of transportation. (c) Kenny Carnes in a modern high-performance racing wheelchair.

Throwing Chairs

Field event, or throwing, wheelchairs are the latest sport wheelchair development, designed to provide the most rigid, stable base from which the athlete can throw the club, shot, discus, or javelin. Since the chair is firmly anchored to the ground during the throw, there is no need for wheels and, as can be seen in Figure 27.2(b), they are no longer part of the throwing chair design. The heavy metal frame is designed to provide stability for the athlete and to provide anchor points so that the chair can be tied down to prevent chair movement during throws. The seat is built as high above the ground as the rules allow, and since cushioning absorbs some of the power of the throw, the seat is usually hard.

Racing Wheelchairs and Their Design

Racing wheelchairs (Figure 27.2(c)) are designed to go fast, but chairs designed for speed suffer from a lack of maneuverability. There are many rules that govern the design of racing wheelchairs for national and international competition, and care must be taken to ensure that racing chairs do not contravene the rules of the competition in which they are used. Racing wheelchairs are constantly and rapidly evolving, and the interested reader should see LaMere & Labanowich's 1984 history of racing wheelchairs for details. Early racing wheelchairs were built with two main wheels and two front wheels (castors), but modern designs are usually three-wheeled.

Number of Wheels

A wheelchair remains stable as long as the center of gravity of the athlete plus the chair remains inside the wheelchair's base of support. The base of support is the area of ground marked by the points at which the wheels contact the surface. In four-wheeled designs, the base of support is rectangular with the base a little narrower at the front than at the rear, while in three-wheeled designs, the base of support is triangular. This means that as the weight of the athlete moves forward (as he or she leans forward to cut down air resistance) the center of gravity gets nearer to the edge of the base of support of the three-wheeled chair and the chair becomes less stable. This lack of stability can be a problem for less experienced athletes, but for those who can handle them, three-wheeled chairs are faster. They are faster because there is less resistance to passage over the ground for three rather than four wheels (Higgs, 1992a), and three-wheeled designs also have considerably less wind resistance than four-wheelers under most wind conditions (Higgs, 1992b).

The Wheelchair Frame

The wheelchair frame performs one major function. It holds the other components—the seat, the mainwheels, and front wheel(s)—in their proper relative positions. Perhaps the most important design consideration in building a wheelchair frame is to make it as light and as stiff as possible. It needs to be as light as possible so that the athlete has to propel as little weight as possible during athletic performances, and it needs to be rigid so that the energy that the athlete applies to the wheelchair is used to drive the chair forward, rather than to bend and deform the frame. Frame flexing absorbs energy directly, but because the wheel alignment of the wheelchair changes as the frame flexes, additional energy is lost when the mainwheels do not point straight ahead in the direction of travel. In addition, the frame must be matched to the body size and shape of the athlete.

Fitting the Wheelchair to the Athlete

Proper fitting of the wheelchair to the athlete is critical for high levels of athletic performance. The two most critical dimensions for the frame are the width and the relative positions of the seat and wheels. If the frame is too narrow for the athlete, there will be insufficient clearance between the wheels and the athlete, which results in the wheel rubbing the athlete's body. This both slows the chair and produces frictional injury to the athlete. If the frame is too wide, the handrim will be difficult to reach and even more difficult to push effectively.

Seat Height

The most effective seat height is a function of the athlete's trunk and arm length and of the handrim size that is selected. Higgs (1983) reported that in athletes at the 1980 Paralympic games, superior performances were recorded by those with lower seats. Experimental work by Traut (1989) showed greater propulsion efficiency when a "relatively low" seat position was used, and experimental work by Meijs, Van Oers, Van de Woude, & Veeger (1989) and by Van de Woude, Veeger, & Rozendal (1990) showed that there was a relationship between the elbow angle (when the athlete was sitting upright in a general sport wheelchair with hands placed on the top center of the handrim) and propulsion efficiency. Their results showed that efficiency was greatest when the elbow angle was 80 degrees and that the energy cost of sitting too high in the chair was greater than the penalty paid for sitting too low.

Anterior Posterior Seat Position

Little is known about the optimum anterior-posterior position of the wheelchair seat, although this position affects both the chair's stability and the effectiveness of application of force to the handrim. If the athlete is too far toward the rear of the wheelchair, there is a tendency for the chair to become unstable (particularly when going uphill) and for the athlete to "flip" out the back. A rear seat position also makes it difficult for the athlete to apply force to the front of the handrim where the most effective application of driving force can be made. If, on the other hand, the seat is too far forward, the wheelchair (particularly if it is a three-wheeler) becomes less stable during downhill turns, and a greater percentage of the athlete's weight is carried by the front wheel(s), which increases the rolling resistance of the chair. Optimum positioning is usually achieved by trial and error.

Seat Orientation

The seat orientation, particularly the angle of the seat bottom and back, has changed rapidly in recent years. Modern racing chairs now orient athletes so that they are leaning forward at 20–25 degrees, with much of the trunk weight supported by their thighs and knees. This forward leaning body position decreases the aerodynamic drag on the athlete while allowing a more effective stroke action.

Wheels

The rear wheels of racing wheelchairs are larger in diameter and narrower in cross-section than those used in general sport chairs. Unless the athlete is very small, the mainwheels are usually high-quality racing bicycle wheels in the European 700C or North American 27-inch size. For road racing, the narrowest possible tires (19 millimeters or less) are used, while for track racing there appears to be some benefit to using wider 23–28 millimeter tires. Since additional weight in the wheels of a wheelchair slows the athlete down twice as much as additional weight in the frame of the chair, racing wheels should be as light, strong, and rigid as possible. The recent trend for front wheel(s) has also been to use as large a wheel as the rules allow, and 18 and 20 inch (0.46 and 0.51 meter) diameter front wheels are now common. Although athletes have experimented with both disk and three-spoke airfoil wheels, there have been no demonstrated performance gains—probably because of their greater weight and poorer performance in cross-wind conditions.

Camber Angle

The mainwheels of a racing wheelchair are cambered for a number of reasons, of which the most important is to allow maximum application of force to the pushrim. Figure 27.3 shows a rear view of a wheelchair athlete in a racing wheelchair. With the wheels cambered, the hands fall naturally to the handrim. The majority of athletes use camber angles between 6 and 12 degrees, with 8 to 10 degrees being most popular.

Mainwheel Alignment

To allow the wheelchair to roll with the least resistance, it is critical that the mainwheels point straight ahead. If the mainwheels point slightly outward (toe-out) or slightly inward (toe-in), it significantly slows down the wheelchair. O'Reagan and co-workers (1981) showed that, for some tires, toe-in or toe out of as little as 3 degrees increased rolling resistance tenfold. Since the front wheels (castors) are free to move to allow turning to take place, they are not subject to the same toe-in/tow-out problems as mainwheels. They do, however, increase rolling resistance greatly when their bearings become worn (Van de Woude, 1991).

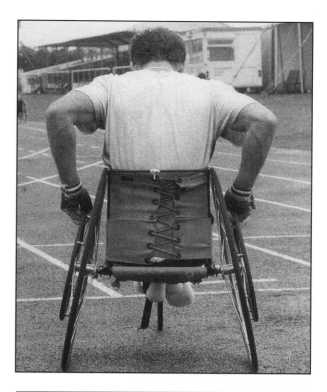

Figure 27.3 A suitable camber angle allows the hands to fall naturally to the handrim.

Handrims

The handrims are the point at which the energy produced by the wheelchair athlete is transmitted to the wheelchair, and as such they are critical to producing optimal performance. The three most important aspects of the handrim are its diameter, its width, and the material with which it is covered.

Handrim Diameter

The handrim acts like the gearing for the wheelchair. If a small diameter handrim is used, the athlete has selected a "high" gear that produces poor acceleration but a high top speed. Conversely, if a large diameter handrim is used, the benefit is greater acceleration at the cost of a lower top speed. In general, stronger athletes are able to effectively push smaller diameter handrims, and thus the optimum handrim diameter is a function of the size of the athlete, the relative importance of acceleration and top speed in the race being run, and the strength of the athlete. Most handrims are between 14 and 16 inches (0.35 and 0.41 meter) in diameter, and athletes usually experiment to determine what works best for them.

Handrim Width

If the handrim is made of relatively wide tubing, it is easier to grasp, which makes starts and uphill climbing easier. On the other hand, there is some evidence to suggest that narrower tubing encourages higher wheeling speeds because the athlete is more likely to "strike" the handrim, rather than hold it and push. In the absence of research studies, athletes determine their optimum handrim diameter by trial and error.

Handrim Material

The handrim covering is of great importance since it is this material that the hand strikes during propulsion. If it is too smooth or shiny, the hand will slip when power is applied. For this reason, a number of materials have been used for handrim covers. Many athletes have found that a child's bike tire glued over the handrim has the right combination of cushioning and surface friction that they are looking for, while others use crépe rubber, which is particularly effective under wet weather conditions. Many athletes use tape wrapped around the handrim, since the tape not only has good frictional properties, but the overlapping layers of tape form ridges that help the hand get an instant grip on contact. Lastly, commercial handrims are often "wet-dipped" in molten plastic so that a thin, uniform film of high-friction plastic is applied.

Although the frictional grip of the handrim is important, it is only half of the hand-wheelchair interface, and the hand covering used by the athlete is of equal or greater importance. Most athletes wear gloves that have been sculptured to their exact requirements by the application of hundreds of layers of adhesive tape. This glove and tape combination provides protective cushioning and high, instant grip between the hand and the handrim.

Accessories

Racing wheelchair accessories are almost as numerous as the wheelchair athletes who use them, but almost all racing wheelchairs incorporate at least a steering device, a compensator, and a computer. With downhill racing speeds reaching more than 40 mph (64 kph) the need for a steering mechanism to help the athlete negotiate corners is obvious, and the usual steering device is a small handle attached directly to the front wheel mounting. This lever can be moved left or right to steer the wheelchair, although steering only occurs when the lever is held in place. Once released, the front wheel returns (under spring action) to a neutral, straight ahead position. This process is called active steering, since turning only occurs when steering input is applied by the racer. In addition to this active

steering mechanism, the wheelchair also incorporates a compensator.

The purpose of the compensator is to permit small, long-term adjustments to the direction in which the chair moves, and it is most important in road racing. Most road races are held on public roads that are designed with a high crown along the midline with the road falling away for drainage toward the curb. A chair propelled along the crown would go straight, but a chair wheeled near the curb for safety would be moving forward on a sideways sloping surface. The front of the chair would be constantly "falling away" from the crest of the crown, and the chair would tend to steer into the curb. A compensator applies a small offset to the front wheel to allow the chair to move straight ahead without the athlete having to make constant small corrective steering adjustments. The second function of a compensator is to resist the effects of the front wheel(s) hitting bumps. The compensator uses counterbalanced springs to hold the front wheel pointing in the chosen direction, and when the wheel hits a bump and is deflected, the springs return the wheel to its original selected position. In keeping a small steering offset to compensate for the slope in the road, and in returning the front wheel(s) to the chosen position after hitting bumps, the compensator allows the athlete to concentrate on driving the wheelchair forward at top speed, rather than on keeping it heading in the right direction.

In recent years bicycle computers have dropped in price and increased in performance to such a degree that they are almost universally found on racing wheelchairs. In a bicycle computer a small magnet is attached to one of the wheelchair's wheels, and a small sensor is attached to the frame. As the wheelchair moves, the magnet passes the sensor, which times the intervals between passage of the magnet. Based on the time per revolution and the circumference of the mainwheel, the 2–3 ounce (0.1 kilogram) computer displays a variety of information including current speed, top speed reached, average speed, and distance covered. This information is valuable in helping the athlete maintain an accurate training and racing log.

High-performance racing wheelchairs are precision masterpieces of engineering and construction in which the goal is to build ever lighter, stronger, and more rigid frames and wheels. To this end manufacturers have turned to space-age materials, and it is now common to find wheelchairs made of a combination of aircraft-grade titanium, carbon fiber, and even more exotic materials.

PROPULSION TECHNIQUE

Coupled with the evolution of the racing wheelchair has been the development of ever more efficient propulsion techniques. A six-phase technique (see Figure 27.4) is most frequently used, although not all athletes use each phase with the same degree of effectiveness.

The Basic Stroke

The propulsion cycle starts with the hands drawn up as far above and behind the handrim as is possible given the seating position and flexibility of the athlete. The hands are then accelerated as rapidly and forcefully as possible (acceleration phase) (see points A on Figure 27.4) until they strike the handrim. The moment of contact is the impact energy transfer (point B on Figure 27.4) phase, during which the kinetic energy stored in the fast moving hand is transferred to the slower moving handrim. With the hand in contact with the handrim there is a force application, or push, phase (points C on Figure 27.4), and this continues until the hands reach almost to the bottom of the handrim. During the force application phase, most of the propulsion comes from the muscles acting around the elbow and shoulder. As the hands reach the bottom of the handrim, the powerful

muscles of the forearm are used to pronate the hand, which allows the thumb to be used to give a last, powerful "flick" to the handrim. This last flicking action is reversed by a few athletes who use supination in the rotational energy transfer phase (points d on Figure 27.4) to flick the handrim with the fingers rather than the thumb. Immediately following the rotational energy transfer, the hands leave the handrim during the cast-off phase (see point e on Figure 27.4). Here it is important that the hand be moving faster than the handrim as it pulls away, since a slower hand will act as a brake to the wheelchair. Often the athlete will use the pronation or supination of the rotational energy transfer phase to accelerate the hand and arm and thus allow them to be carried up and back under ballistic motion. This upward and backward motion is called the backswing phase (points f on Figure 27.4) and is used to get the hands far enough away from the handrim to allow them to accelerate forward to strike the handrim at high speed at the start of the next stroke.

This basic propulsion stroke is modified by the terrain over which the athlete is wheeling, by the tactics of the race, and by the athlete's level of disability. On uphill parts of a course, the athlete shortens the backswing and acceleration phases so as to minimize the time during which force is not applied to the handrim and during which the chair

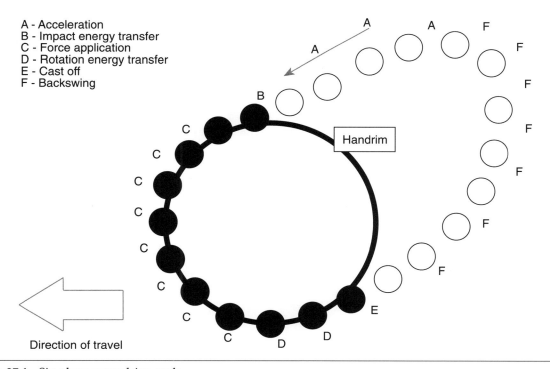

A - Acceleration
B - Impact energy transfer
C - Force application
D - Rotation energy transfer
E - Cast off
F - Backswing

Direction of travel

Figure 27.4   Six-phase propulsion cycle.

could roll backwards. Conversely, on the downhill stretch of a race, it is very difficult for the athlete to accelerate the hand rapidly enough to make it travel faster than the handrim, and thus the acceleration, impact, and backswing phases are exaggerated while the other phases are downplayed.

Tactically, the athlete is either wheeling at constant speed or is making an attack and needs to accelerate. The basic stroke described above is used at steady speed, while during bursts of acceleration the major change in stroke takes place during the backswing. At steady speeds the backswing is a relatively relaxed ballistic movement in which the velocity at cast-off is used to raise the hand to its highest and most rearward position. This relaxed backswing is efficient and allows a brief moment of rest during each stroke. During acceleration, however, the major change in stroke dynamics is to increase the number of strokes from approximately 80 per minute to more than 120 per minute. This is achieved by a rapid reduction in the time taken for a more restricted backswing. This shorter backswing is no longer ballistic, but rather a forced action taking considerable muscular energy, and it is the increased speed of the backswing, rather than the shorter distance, that allows for the approximately 50% increase in stroke rate.

Differences in stroke mechanics with differing degrees of disability are widespread, and are due mostly to the more severely disabled athletes being unable to bring their hands back and high enough to accelerate them onto the handrim. Since a more restricted backswing and acceleration phase limits the transfer of impact energy to the handrim, a radically different style of propulsion has been developed, particularly by high-lesion quadriplegics. This technique, the backhand stroke, applies lower levels of force to the handrim for longer periods of time per stroke in an attempt to maximize the impulse (force × time) applied to the wheelchair.

In the backhand stroke the posterior surface of the hand is used to strike the top outside surface of the handrim, which is pushed forward and down until the hand reaches the bottom of the stroke. During the downward portion of the stroke, the hands are supinated so that at the bottom the palms face forward, since the hand can then be used to pull up on the inside surface of the rear half of the handrim. In those who have sufficient musculature in the shoulder girdle, this action is supplemented by drawing the hands up and away from the handrim at the top of the stroke so that there can be an acceleration and impact phase to the stroke cycle.

The Start

In short races, the start is critical and a good start can provide the margin of victory. Critical aspects of the start are the upper-body action and modifications to the first few strokes.

Newton's third law, the law of action and reaction, confirms that if the upper body is thrown forward at the starting gun there will be a reaction of the lower part of the body (plus the front of the wheelchair) rising up to meet it. Then, as the upper body pushes down on the handrim and moves back up, the legs and the wheelchair will return to the ground, and only then will the chair start to move forward. This is clearly inefficient, and for this reason it is critical that athletes start with their bodies as far forward as possible and that, at the gun, the arms drive the wheelchair forward while the athletes try to prevent the chest and head from rising. In this way maximum energy is transferred to the forward motion of the wheelchair.

The stroke is also modified during the start. Since the wheelchair is stationary, the hands grip the handrim (rather than striking it) and for the first few strokes the arc of pushing is very restricted with as rapid as possible a recovery. The key is to get three or four short, hard strokes in before making the transition to a striking rather than pushing stroke. The next few transition strokes follow the six-phase pattern outlined previously, but with initially restricted backswing and acceleration phases that are gradually increased until the full stroke is achieved.

Some athletes, taking advantage of the lower gearing available, start with their hands pushing the tire directly, rather than pushing the handrim. This seems to provide a more rapid movement off the line, but there is usually a break in the flow of the stroke when the athlete changes from pushing the wheel to pushing the handrim. This break appears to nullify the benefits achieved by starting on the wheel, and there is no clear evidence as to which method of starting is more effective. Athletes need to experiment with both methods and decide for themselves which is best for them.

RETARDING FORCES AND OVERCOMING THEM

While the athlete provides the energy to drive the wheelchair forward, the twin retarding forces of rolling resistance and aerodynamic drag act to slow it down. When propulsive forces are greater than resistance, the wheelchair accelerates, and when the retarding forces are greater, the chair is slowed. Obviously reductions in rolling resistance and aerodynamic drag translate directly into higher wheeling speeds and improved athletic performance.

Rolling Resistance

In recent years considerable research has been undertaken into ways to reduce the rolling resistance of bicycles, and much of this research is directly applicable to wheelchair road racing. It must be noted however, that wheelchair track racing takes place under very different conditions, since athletic tracks are very much softer than the typical road surface on which bicycles and wheelchairs race.

On a hard, smooth surface the majority of rolling resistance of a wheelchair wheel occurs at the point where the tire is in contact with the ground. As the tire rotates, each part is compressed as it passes under the hub and is in contact with the road surface, and then rebounds as it begins to rise again and contact with the surface is broken. Not all the energy used to compress the tire is recovered on the rebound, and the energy loss (called *hysteresis*) is the major determinant of rolling resistance. Obviously the thicker and less flexible the wall of the tire, the greater the hysteresis energy loss. If the tire wall can be prevented from flexing, then energy losses will be reduced, and this is exactly what happens when the air pressure in the tire is increased.

Experiments have confirmed (Higgs, 1993) the theoretical expectation that, on a hard, smooth surface, rolling resistance will decrease as tire pressure increases. Thus, the road racing athlete should inflate tires to the highest safe pressure for best performance.

Theoretical work also suggests that rolling resistance decreases as the diameter of the wheel increases, and for this reason athletes use the largest wheels permitted by the rules. There is also some evidence to suggest that wider tires have lower rolling resistance than similarly constructed narrow tires. But since they also have higher aerodynamic drag, it is not clear if they offer higher overall performance in road racing.

On the track hysteresis energy losses still occur in the tires when they are compressed and allowed to rebound, but the tires also cut into the surface of the track and produce surface deformation energy losses. If tire pressures are very high, the hysteresis energy losses in the tire will be low, but the hard inflation pressure will cut deeply into the track

and surface deformation losses will be high. Conversely, at low tire pressures the "flatter" tire will spread the weight load of athlete and chair over a greater area and reduce surface deformation losses. At the same time, however, the tire hysteresis energy losses will increase. Best athletic performance will occur at the tire pressure that minimizes the combined energy losses from both hysteresis and surface deformation.

Experiments have been conducted (Higgs, 1993) which indicate that moderate tire pressures of approximately 90 pounds per square inch give the best results on synthetic athletic tracks, and that the penalty for overinflation of the tire is greater than the penalty for underinflation. The same series of experiments also indicated that wider, 28-millimeter (1.10-inch) tires had lower rolling resistance and better track performance than similarly constructed 20-millimeter (0.78-inch) tires. Additional work is required to determine performance differences between tires from different manufacturers, and between tires with different profiles and tread patterns.

Rolling resistance of racing wheelchairs is also affected by the mainwheel's camber angle, although the relationship is complex. Theoretical analysis suggests that lowest rolling resistance will occur when the wheels are aligned vertically and that rolling resistance will increase with increasing camber angle. Although experimental data support this theory for zero and very high camber angles, the findings for intermediate camber angles are confused. In experiments, 6 degrees of camber gave lower rolling resistance values than 3 or 9 degrees, and it has been suggested that this is because this camber angle allowed the tire to run on both the crown and sidewall, effectively increasing the width of the tire. Since wider tires have been shown to have lower rolling resistance than narrow tires, this greater effective tire width might have decreased rolling resistance by more than the increase from the greater camber angle.

While the evidence concerning rolling resistance and camber angle is confused, the finding with regard to longitudinal wheel alignment could not be clearer. Wheels that are not parallel and pointing straight ahead dramatically increase the rolling resistance of a wheelchair, and athletes should do everything in their power to check and adjust alignment prior to every important race—particularly in light of the damage to racing wheelchair frames caused by poor handling by airline baggage handlers and others.

Aerodynamic Drag

The problems of aerodynamic drag of racing wheelchairs and athletes are unique in the field of sport because of the relatively low speeds at which events take place. Coutts & Schutz (1988) have calculated that races on the track take place at average speeds between 3 and 7 meters/second (6.65 and 15.75 mph), which is considerably slower than the speeds found in cycling and running. This creates special low speed aerodynamic conditions. Aerodynamic drag is caused by two separate but interrelated forces called surface drag and form drag. Surface drag is caused by the adhesion of air molecules to the surface of an object passing through it, and it is very powerful at low speeds. Form drag, on the other hand, is caused by the difference in air pressure between the front and the back of an object, which in turn is created by the swirls and eddy currents formed as the wheelchair and athlete pass through the air.

For wheelchair racers the problem is that smooth surfaces increase surface drag while decreasing form drag—and at the speeds at which wheelchair track events take place, there is uncertainty as to which type of surface gives the best overall result.

Some aspects of aerodynamic drag reduction are beyond doubt, and those are to reduce both surface and form drag by minimizing the drag producing areas of the wheelchair and athlete's clothing. To reduce surface drag there is a need to reduce the exposed surfaces of the chair and athlete. When an athlete's trunk is resting on his or her knees, the air is unable to flow over the top surface of the thigh and the front surface of the chest and this reduces the surface area on which molecules of air can exert their retarding influence. Likewise, elimination of all trailing cords, belts, and straps acts to reduce both exposed surface area and surface drag. Loose and trailing clothing should also be eliminated.

Form drag is mostly reduced by ensuring that all of the exposed components of the wheelchair are streamlined, and that the chair and athlete have the lowest possible frontal area. Frontal area is the area of the body and chair perpendicular to the flow of air; this is what would be seen in silhouette if you looked head-on at an approaching athlete. Tipping the upper body forward (like the position taken by a racing cyclist) and eliminating loose clothing are the two major ways in which frontal area is reduced. Hedrick, Wang, Moeinzadeh, & Adrian (1990) have shown that frontal area can be reduced by up to 44% by adjustment of body position.

Drafting

Because aerodynamic drag represents approximately 40% of the force acting to slow down a wheelchair racer, methods of cheating the wind pay considerable dividends. The single most effective way in which drag can be reduced is by the process of drafting. Drafting occurs when a wheelchair follows closely behind another wheelchair that acts as a wind deflector. The second wheelchair may experience aerodynamic drag forces less than half of those that would occur under nondrafting conditions. In still air or in a headwind the following wheelchair gains greatest benefit when it follows directly behind the lead chair and as closely as possible. If a choice must be made between dropping back farther but remaining directly behind the lead chair, or staying closer and moving out to one side, the evidence (Pugh, 1971) is overwhelming that it is better to stay directly behind. If racing occurs under sidewind conditions, maximum benefit is achieved by the drafting wheelchair staying behind and to the downwind side of the leader.

At the end of long races, the energy saved by drafting can be a critical determinant of race outcome, and modern race tactics confirm this. Frequently teams will work together, taking turns at both leading and drafting, so that their overall performance will be increased. When a number of athletes draft together, there is no greater benefit from being number three in the line than from being number two—everyone except the leader has approximately the same advantage. Surprisingly, even though the leader has to perform more work than any of the drafting athletes, he or she expends slightly less energy than if wheeling alone.

THE ATHLETE

While advanced wheelchair designs are important, it is the athlete who ultimately determines the quality of performance. To compete at the highest levels, athletes must undertake rigorous long-term training with particular emphasis on strength, power, and both muscular and cardiovascular endurance.

Training

Training the cardiovascular system presents a problem to some wheelchair athletes. Cardiovascular endurance is produced by stressing the heart and respiratory system through the use of major muscle groups, which expend large amounts of energy over prolonged periods of time. For able-bodied athletes, running, cycling, and swimming use the large muscles of the trunk and lower limbs and are excellent modes of exercise. The wheelchair athlete, however, is limited to using the relatively small muscles of the arm and, in some cases, the muscles of the trunk. This smaller working muscle mass places lower demands on the heart and lungs and makes cardiovascular endurance training more difficult. In addition, the wheelchair athlete propels the wheelchair using a relatively small range of motion at the shoulder and elbow, and this action is asymmetrical in that the forces of extension (during propulsion) are far greater than the muscular forces used in recovery. This asymmetry can lead to muscle imbalance around the shoulder joint, which in turn may cause serious overuse injury.

Because of the small muscle mass involved in wheelchair propulsion, and the asymmetry of the propulsion movements, systematic strength and flexibility training is critical. Stretching, both before and after exercise, appears more important for athletes with disabilities than for the able bodied.

Training regimens for athletes with disabilities parallel those for the able bodied and, in many cases, appear identical. Where modifications are necessary, it is usually due to the smaller active muscle mass and to the lack of alternate modes of training available. The runner can train the legs through running, jumping, stair climbing, cycling, or weight training. Wheelchair athletes are usually limited to weight training, pushing their chairs, or arm cranking if they have access to this specialized equipment. This makes repetitive overuse injuries more prevalent and makes the incorporation of rest into the training plan critical.

Medical Concerns

Wheelchair athletes face several disability-specific sports medicine problems, of which the most important are those associated with thermal regulation. Damage to the spinal cord presents problems at both high and low ambient temperatures since impairment of sensory nerves means that athletes are often unable to feel heat, cold, or pain. Thus, in cold weather, they receive no sensory warning that body extremities (usually the feet) are becoming frozen. Coupled with reduced blood flow to the inactive feet, frostbite becomes an ever present danger against which the athlete must guard.

At high ambient temperatures the problem is damage to the nerves that initiate and control sweat production. The problem is particularly severe in quadriplegics, many of whom have little or no body sweat production, and thus no way of reducing their core temperature. Failure to sweat is particularly dangerous for athletes involved in longer distance races where metabolic heat from active muscles is added to the thermal stress of high ambient air temperature and absorption of radiant heat from exposure to sunlight. The provision of shade, adequate drinking fluids, and wet towels for surface temperature reduction can help alleviate this problem.

In recent years abrasive damage to the feet has become a problem. Many athletes now use one-piece lycra tights that cover the feet instead of pants and shoes. Frequently the feet are tucked under the athlete's seat, and are held in position by restraining straps. If these straps become loose or undone during a race, the feet can fall, and usually the toes then scrape the road surface. In the absence of sensation from the lower limbs, the toes can drag for some time before the athlete is aware that a problem exists—by which time the toes can be worn down to the bone! Abrasions on the medial surface of the upper arm are also common, and are caused when the skin is brought into contact with the lateral surface of the rotating tire.

The most recent medical problem to surface in wheelchair sport is the life-threatening but deliberate precipitation of autonomic dysreflexia by quadriplegics, a process they refer to as "boosting." Autonomic dysreflexia is a medical condition characterized by hypertension, piloerection, headaches, and bradycardia, and associated with very high levels of catecholamine. Autonomic dysreflexia is unique to individuals with spinal cord injury above the major splanchnic outflow at the sixth thoracic vertebrae.

Quadriplegic wheelchair athletes believe that "boosting" increases their athletic performance, and recent experimental evidence (Burnham et al., 1993) supports this view. Eight elite quadriplegic road racers performed a simulated 7.5 kilometer race under both normal and "boosted" conditions and race times improved by 9.7% under the "boosted" condition. National and international sports groups are aware of both the use of "boosting" and its dangers, although to this date there has been no attempt to prohibit the practice.

THE FUTURE

Somatic specialization and technological advances have changed the look of wheelchair sport dramatically, even though historically we are still in the early stages of the development of sport for athletes with disabilities. The opportunities are endless. New sports are constantly being adapted to meet the needs of those with disabilities, and, with each new sport, come the needs for specialized equipment designed to meet that sport's unique demands.

The demands of each sport and the needs of athletes involved in the sport must be systematically assessed, and suitable equipment must then be designed and built. There are hundreds, probably thousands, of different shoes on the market to meet the very specialized needs of able-bodied athletes in every conceivable sport, but at this stage we have only three or four basic wheelchair designs to meet the equally diverse needs of athletes with disabilities engaged in the same range of sports. Greater equipment and technique specialization is the wave of the future in wheelchair sport. Great strides have been made, but much remains to be done.

SUMMARY

This chapter has dealt with information for optimum performance in wheelchair sport, particularly wheelchair racing. It dealt with somatic specialization—the matching of body size and shape to the demands of a sport—and with the basic types of sport wheelchair. Wheelchair racing was used as an example of the type of scientific research that can shed light on sport performance. Wheelchair design and propulsion techniques were covered in some detail, followed by a discussion of the retarding forces of aerodynamic drag and rolling resistance. The chapter concludes with a discussion of some differences between the training of able-bodied athletes and athletes with disabilities and with basic information on the sport medicine problems faced by athletes with disabilities.

BIBLIOGRAPHY

Burnham, R., Wheeler, G., Bhambhani, Y., Cumming, D., Maclean, I., Sloley, B.D., Belanger, M., Eriksson, P., & Steadward, R. (1993). Performance enhancement in elite quadriplegic wheelchair racers through self-induced autonomic dysreflexia. Vista '93 Conference, May 14–20, Jasper, AB.

Coutts, K.D. (1990). Kinematics of sport wheelchair propulsion. *Journal of Rehabilitation Research and Development*, **27**(1), 21–26.

Coutts, K.D., & Schutz, R.W. (1988). Analysis of wheelchair track performance. *Medicine & Science in Sport and Exercise*, **20**, 188–194.

Hedrick, B., Wang, Y.T., Moeinzadeh, M., & Adrian, M. (1990). Aerodynamic positioning and performance in wheelchair racing. *Adapted Physical Activity Quarterly*, **7**(1), 41–51.

Higgs, C. (1983). An analysis of racing wheelchairs used at the 1980 Olympic Games for the Disabled. *Research Quarterly for Exercise and Sport*, **54**(3), 229–233.

Higgs, C. (1985). Propulsion of racing wheelchairs. In M. Ellis & D. Tripps (Eds.), *Proceedings of the 1984 Olympic Scientific Congress, Eugene, Oregon*. Champaign, IL: Human Kinetics.

Higgs, C. (1992a). Racing wheelchairs: A comparison of three- and four-wheeled designs. *Palaestra*, **8**(4), 28–36.

Higgs, C. (1992b). Wheeling the wind: The effect of wind velocity and direction on the aerodynamic drag of wheelchairs. *Adapted Physical Activity Quarterly*, **9**(1), 74–87.

Higgs, C. (1993). *The rolling resistance of racing wheelchairs: The effect of rolling surface, rear-wheel camber and tire pressure*. Final report, Applied Sport Science Program, Fitness and Amateur Sport, Government of Canada.

LaMere, T.J., & Labanowich, S. (1984). The history of sport wheelchairs—Part III: The racing wheelchair 1976–1983. *Sports 'N Spokes*, **10**(2), 12–16.

Meijs, P.J.M., Van Oers, C.A.J.M., Van de Woude, L.H.V., & Veeger, H.E.J. (1989). The effect of seat height on the physiological response and propulsion technique in wheelchair ambulation. *Journal of Rehabilitation Science*, **2**, 104–107.

O'Reagan, J.R., Thacker, J.G., Kauzlarich, J.J., Mochel, E., Carmine, D., & Bryant, M. (1981). Wheelchair dynamics. In *Wheelchair Mobility 1976–1981*. Rehabilitation Engineering Center, University of Virginia, 33–41.

Pugh, L.G.C.E. (1971). The influence of wind resistance in running and walking and the mechanical efficiency of work against horizontal and vertical forces. *Journal of Physiology* (London), **213**, 795–808.

Sheldon, W.H., Dupertuis, C.W., & McDermott, E. (1954). *Atlas of Men*. New York: Harper.

Traut, L. (1989).Gestaltung ergonoisch relevanter Konstruktionsparameter am Antriebssysteem des Greiffreifenrollstuhls—Teil 1. *Orthopedaedie Technik*, **7**, 394–398.

Van de Woude, L.H.V., Veeger, H.E.J., & Rozendal, R.H. (1990). Seat height in hand rim wheelchair propulsion: A follow up study. *Journal of Rehabilitation Science*, **3**, 79–83.

RESOURCES

Written

Clark, R. (1986). *Wheelchair sports: Techniques and training in athletics*. Cambridge, England: Woodhead-Faulkner. This book, translated into English by Kristina

Ehrenstrale, is a very basic introduction to wheelchair sports. It is well suited for use by young athletes, those just starting in the sport, and those seeking a nontechnical, easily read introduction to the topic.

LaMere, T.J., & Labanowich, S. (1984). The history of sport wheelchairs—Part III: The racing wheelchair 1976–1983. *Sports 'N Spokes*, **10**(2), 12–16. A brief history of the development of the modern racing wheelchair. Most of the landmark developments are covered, and the reader is left with a vivid impression of the relentless drive of the athletes to improve their equipment.

Audiovisual

Carnes, K. (1992). *You feel the need for speed*. K.C. Racing, 291 Comfort Drive, Henderson, NV 89014. This instructional video, available in both North American and European VHS formats, covers all the basics of wheelchair racing. Adjustment and operation of a new chair, propulsion techniques, maintenance, and many tricks-of-the-trade are covered. The narrator and producer of the video is Kenny Carnes, one of the top racers in the United States.

APPENDIX A

Rating Scale for Adapted Physical Education

Developed by Joseph P. Winnick

SUNY College at Brockport
Brockport, New York 14420
January 1994

NAME OF SCHOOL:_____

ADDRESS: _____

LEVEL:_____   NUMBER OF PUPILS ENROLLED IN ADAPTED P.E._____

PRINCIPAL:_____

DIRECTOR OF PHYSICAL EDUCATION:_____

REVIEWED BY:_____   DATE:_____

Introduction

The purpose of the rating scale is to assist school personnel to improve the adapted physical education program.

When properly guided and developed, physical education becomes a purposeful and vital part of a student's school education. It aids in the realization of those objectives concerned with the development of favorable self-image, creative expression, motor skills, physical fitness, knowledge, and understanding of human movement. The individual, to become a fully functioning individual, needs many opportunities to participate in well-conceived, well-taught learning experiences in physical education. To achieve this objective, the essentials of a quality program of physical education need to be identified.

The rating scale is designed for self-appraisal.

Use and Interpretation of the Scores

The rating scale comprises a series of ratings on the major areas that should concern the school personnel relative to the adapted physical education program. There are seven sections to the rating scale: Curriculum, Required Instruction, Attendance, Personnel, Facilities, and Administrative Procedures.

The person(s) making the assessment should consider the criteria statement in terms of the degree of achievement that exists for the program. The rating score is on a scale from *0* to *4, 0* meaning inadequate achievement and *4* meaning fully achieved with excellent results. Each section can be rated by the total section score, and a program overall rating can be obtained by totalling all sections of the rating scale.

A careful analysis should be made of each statement, section, and overall rating to determine the areas in need of improvement. The interpretation of the score for each statement is as follows:

0 = INADEQUATE/extremely limited

1 = POOR/exists but needs a great deal of improvement

2 = FAIR/adequate but needs some improvement

3 = GOOD/well done and only needs periodic review

4 = EXCELLENT/has achieved outstanding results

RATING SCALE FOR ADAPTED PHYSICAL EDUCATION

	Inadequate (0)	Poor (1)	Fair (2)	Good (3)	Excellent (4)
Section I - Curriculum					
1. The goals and objectives of the school district plan for physical education encompasses adapted physical education.					
2. Provision is explicitly made for adapted physical education in the school district physical education plan.					
3. There exists a definition of adapted physical education which is in accord with state, federal, and professional laws, regulations, or practices.					
4. Adapted physical education may include pupils with disabilities as well as pupils without disabilities.					
5. Various activities exist to meet unique pupil needs.					
6. Instruction is based upon a curriculum guide that encompasses adapted physical education content.					
7. Instruction for all pupils is distributed among the following areas in accord with students' needs and abilities.					
a. Basic movement					
b. Creative movement					
c. Rhythms and dance					
d. Games and sports					
e. Gymnastics					
f. Outdoor living skills					
g. Motor skills					
h. Perceptual-motor skills					
i. Physical fitness					
j. Aquatics					
8. Appropriate literature and other resource materials regarding adapted physical education are made available to professional staff.					
9. Pupils with disabilities are provided equivalent opportunities in intramural, extramural, or extraclass activities.					

	Inadequate (0)	Poor (1)	Fair (2)	Good (3)	Excellent (4)
Section I - Curriculum *(continued)*					
10. There is an annual evaluation of the instructional program in adapted physical education.					
11. Guidelines pertaining to adapted physical education are evaluated at least every five years.					
12. There is a procedure for reporting pupil status and progress.					
13. The progress of pupils is continuously measured.					
14. Cumulative records pertaining to the physical education of each pupil are maintained.					
Section II - Required Instruction					
1. All pupils not receiving regular physical education have an adapted physical education program.					
2. No pupil is excused from physical activity or excused from adapted physical education because of participation in extraclass programs unless approved by the school's Committee on Adapted Physical Education or similar committee or unless approved in a pupil's individualized education program (pupil with a disability).					
3. Instruction in adapted physical education is conducted with a time allotment which is in accord with state regulations and in a frequency and duration that is comparable to chronological-aged peers in the school district.					
4. Class periods are scheduled in time lengths that are appropriate to pupil needs and achievement of instructional objectives.					
5. Time allotment for physical education meets state requirements.					
6. Physical education instruction is made available to every pupil with a disability.					
Section III - Attendance					
1. Physical education is required of all pupils, ages 3-21, and adapted physical education is provided for pupils who exhibit unique physical education needs.					

	Inadequate (0)	Poor (1)	Fair (2)	Good (3)	Excellent (4)
2. Credit is provided for adapted physical education in accord with regular physical education credit.					
Section IV - Personnel					
1. Instruction in adapted physical education for pupils ages 3-21 is provided by a certified physical education teacher.					
2. Physical education for infants and toddlers is provided by an adapted physical educator.					
3. Physical educators teaching adapted physical education who have not completed at least 12 semester hours of formal higher education in adapted physical education have access to appropriate resource personnel.					
4. Extraclass activities are provided under the supervision of personnel meeting state requirements and approved by the Board of Education.					
5. Physical educators teaching adapted physical education for more than 50% of their teaching load have completed at least 12 semester hours of formal study in adapted physical education, have a concentration in adapted physical education from an accredited college or university, or have a state credential or endorsement in adapted physical education.					
6. Supervision and coordination of all phases of adapted physical education (instruction, intramurals, extraclass programs, interscholastic athletics) are provided by a director certified in physical education and in administrative and supervisory services.					
7. Aides are provided for instructional classes in physical education.					
8. The qualifications of aides is in accord with appropriate state and/or local regulations.					
9. A physician delegated by a district submits to appropriate committees/personnel areas of the program in which a pupil may participate when medical reasons are given to limit participation.					
10. Teachers of adapted physical education are involved in individualized education programming and placement decisions.					
11. Teachers of pupils requiring adapted physical education are involved in assessment, setting goals and objectives, and determining unique needs of pupils receiving adapted physical education.					

	Inadequate (0)	Poor (1)	Fair (2)	Good (3)	Excellent (4)
Section V - Facilities					
1. Pupils receiving adapted physical education have equal access to facilities required to provide equal opportunity for programmatic benefits.					
2. Indoor facilities for adapted physical education					
a. Have adequate clear activity space.					
b. Provide a safe environment for activity.					
c. Have appropriate flooring and satisfactory finish.					
d. Have adequate lighting.					
e. Have adequate acoustical treatment.					
f. Have protective padding on walls.					
g. Have sufficient ceiling clearance.					
h. Have adequate ventilation.					
3. Equipment and supplies required for reasonable accommodations are provided.					
4. For pupils receiving adapted physical education, the dressing, showering, and drying areas include					
a. Adequate space for peak load periods.					
b. Floors constructed to facilitate ambulation and maintenance of safe and clean conditions.					
c. Lockers of proper type and sufficient quantity.					
d. Sufficient number of shower heads.					
e. Adequate ventilation.					
f. Adequate lighting.					
g. Adequate heating.					
h. Adequate benches, mirrors, and toilets.					
i. All facilities are clean, sanitary, and in operable condition.					
5. The outdoor adapted physical education facilities are designed for effective instruction and safety. They are					
a. Readily accessible.					

	Inadequate (0)	Poor (1)	Fair (2)	Good (3)	Excellent (4)
b. Free from safety hazards (glass, holes, stones).					
c. Properly fenced or enclosed for safety and efficient usage.					
d. Properly surfaced, graded, and drained.					
e. Laid out and marked for a variety of activities.					
f. Properly equipped (playground structures, backstops, physical fitness equipment, etc.).					
6. Qualified supervision of areas and facilities is provided during use.					
Section VI - Administrative Procedures					
1. Class sizes for adapted physical education are equitable to those specified for special education classroom teaching.					
2. Class load for adapted physical education teachers is equitable to that for special education teachers.					
3. Adapted physical education teachers receive support staff on the same student/teacher ratio as special education teachers.					
4. The Committee on Special Education and the Committee on Preschool Special Education use certified physical educators to assess physical education status for IEP development when unique physical education needs are suspected.					
5. Pupils with disabilities are integrated into regular physical education classes to the maximum extent appropriate.					
6. Pupils with disabilities are provided reasonable accommodations in physical education classes.					
7. Provisions are made for physical educators to refer to the CSE or CSPE all pupils with disabilities suspected of having unique needs in physical education.					
8. The physical education teacher is involved with individualized program development of all pupils who participate in physical education outside of regular or integrated classes.					
9. Physical education is included in the IEP of every pupil with a disability.					

	Inadequate (0)	Poor (1)	Fair (2)	Good (3)	Excellent (4)
Section VI - Administrative Procedures *(continued)*					
10. Pupils are referred to the CSE or CSPE and receive adapted physical education on the basis of objective criteria.					
11. The physical education abilities of all pupils not participating in regular physical education are assessed by a physical educator.					
12. Staff implementing adapted physical education are provided in-service education on at least an annual basis.					
13. School districts provide placement settings that permit individualized attention in the most appropriate environment.					
14. The annual budget request for adapted physical education is prepared on the basis of an inventory of needs of the program, including needs specified in individualized education programs.					
15. The adapted physical education budget includes state and federal monies earmarked for instruction of pupils with disabilities if such pupils are receiving an adapted physical education program.					
16. A variety of up-to-date reference materials are provided for teachers providing adapted physical education.					
17. The school library contains materials on adapted physical education that are sufficient and appropriate.					
18. Budgets for instructional, intramural, extramural, and athletic programs for pupils with disabilities are equitable to those for nondisabled pupils and reflect at least a double weighting in favor of the pupils with disabilities.					
19. The school district plan includes provisions for regular extraclass programs for qualified pupils with disabilities.					

APPENDIX B

Definitions Associated With the Individuals With Disabilities Education Act (IDEA)[1]

There are several definitions associated with infants, toddlers, and children with disabilities. To a great extent, the definitions used in this book are based on those from IDEA. Those definitions are summarized here.

INFANTS AND TODDLERS WITH DISABILITIES

The term "infants and toddlers with disabilities" means individuals from birth to age 2, inclusive, who need early intervention services because they

(1) are experiencing developmental delays, as measured by appropriate diagnostic instruments and procedures in one or more of the following areas: cognitive development, physical development, language and speech development (hereafter in this part referred to as 'communication development'), psychosocial development (hereafter in this part referred to as 'social or emotional development'), or self-help skills (hereafter in this part referred to as "adaptive development"), or

(2) have diagnosed physical or mental condition that has a high probability of resulting in developmental delay.

Such term may also include, at a state's discretion, individuals from birth to age 2, inclusive, who are at risk of having substantial developmental delays if early intervention services are not provided.

CHILDREN WITH DISABILITIES

The term "children with disabilities" means those children having mental retardation, hearing impairments including deafness, speech or language impairments, visual impairments including blindness, serious emotional disturbance, orthopedic impairments, autism, traumatic brain injury, other health impairments, specific learning disabilities, deaf-blindness, or multiple disabilities, and who because of those impairments need special education and related services.

The term "children with disabilities," for children aged 3 through 5 may, at a state's discretion, include children

• who are experiencing developmental delays, as defined by the state and as measured by appropriate diagnostic instruments and procedures, in one or more of the following areas: physical development, cognitive development, communication development, social

---

[1]These definitions were taken from the September 29, 1992 issue of the *Federal Register*, Vol. 57, No. 189.

or emotional development, or adaptive development; and

- who, for that reason, need special education and related services.

- The terms used in this definition are defined as follows:

1. "Autism" means a developmental disability significantly affecting verbal and nonverbal communication and social interaction, generally evident before age 3, that adversely affects a child's educational performance. Other characteristics often associated with autism are engagement in repetitive activities and stereotyped movements, resistance to environmental change or change in daily routines, and unusual responses to sensory experiences. The term does not apply if a child's educational performance is adversely affected primarily because the child has a serious emotional disturbance.

2. "Deaf-blindness" means concomitant hearing and visual impairments the combination of which causes such severe communication and other developmental and educational problems that they cannot be accommodated in special education programs solely for children with deafness or children with blindness.

3. "Deafness" means a hearing impairment that is so severe that the child is impaired in processing linguistic information through hearing, with or without amplification, that adversely affects a child's educational performance.

4. "Hearing impairment" means an impairment in hearing, whether permanent or fluctuating, that adversely affects a child's educational performance but that is not included under the definition of deafness in this section.

5. "Mental retardation" means significantly subaverage general intellectual functioning existing concurrently with deficits in adaptive behavior and manifested during the developmental period that adversely affects a child's educational performance.

6. "Multiple disabilities" means concomitant impairments (such as mental retardation-blindness, mental retardation-orthopedic

impairment, etc.) the combination of which causes such severe educational problems that they cannot be accommodated in special education programs solely for one of the impairments. The term does not include deaf-blindness.

7. "Orthopedic impairment" means a severe orthopedic impairment that adversely affects a child's educational performance. The term includes impairments caused by congenital anomaly (e.g., clubfoot, absence of some member, etc.), impairments caused by disease (e.g., poliomyelitis, bone tuberculosis, etc.), and impairments from other causes (e.g., cerebral palsy, amputations, and fractures or burns that cause contractures).

8. "Other health impairment" means having limited strength, vitality or alertness, as due to chronic or acute health problems such as a heart condition, tuberculosis, rheumatic fever, nephritis, asthma, sickle cell anemia, hemophilia, epilepsy, lead poisoning, leukemia, or diabetes that adversely affects a child's educational performance.

9. "Serious emotional disturbance" is defined as follows: (i) The term means a condition exhibiting one or more of the following characteristics over a long period of time and to a marked degree that adversely affects a child's educational performance:

   A. An inability to learn that cannot be explained by intellectual, sensory, or health factors

   B. An inability to build or maintain satisfactory interpersonal relationships with peers and teachers

   C. Inappropriate types of behavior or feelings under normal circumstances

   D. A general pervasive mood of unhappiness or depression

   E. A tendency to develop physical symptoms or fears associated with personal or school problems

   (ii) The term includes schizophrenia. The term does not necessarily apply to children who are socially maladjusted, unless it is determined that they have a serious emotional disturbance.

10. "Specific learning disability" means a disorder in one or more of the basic psycho-

logical processes involved in understanding or in using language, spoken or written, that may manifest itself in an imperfect ability to listen, think, speak, read, write, spell, or to do mathematical calculations. The term includes such conditions as perceptual disabilities, brain injury, minimal brain dysfunction, dyslexia, and developmental aphasia. The term does not apply to children who have learning problems that are primarily the result of visual, hearing, or motor disabilities, mental retardation, emotional disturbance, or environmental, cultural, or economic disadvantage.

11. "Speech or language impairment" means a communication disorder such as stuttering, impaired articulation, a language impairment, or a voice impairment that adversely affects a child's educational performance.

12. "Traumatic brain injury" means an acquired injury to the brain caused by an external physical force, resulting in total or partial functional disability or psychosocial impairment, or both, that adversely affects a child's educational performance. The term applies to open or closed head injuries resulting in impairments in one or more areas, such as cognition; language memory; attention; reasoning; abstract thinking; judgment; problem-solving; sensory, perceptual, and motor abilities; psychosocial behavior; physical functions; information processing; and speech. The term does not apply to brain injuries that are congenital or degenerative, or brain injuries induced by birth trauma.

13. "Visual impairment including blindness" means an impairment in vision that, even with correction, adversely affects a child's educational performance. The term includes both partial sight and blindness.

Index

About the Authors

Diane H. Craft received a doctorate in adapted physical education from New York University and is a professor of physical education at the State University of New York, College at Cortland, where she teaches undergraduate and graduate courses in adapted physical education. Her research and writing focus on preparing teachers to instruct all children, including those with disabilities, in inclusive physical education classes.

Bobby L. Eason has a bachelor's and master's degree from Texas Tech University, and a doctorate from the University of Houston. He is professor and chair of the Department of Human Performance and Health Promotion at the University of New Orleans. He was executive director of the 3rd International Symposium on Adapted Physical Activity and president of the Louisiana AAHPERD. His line of research is midline crossing and special populations.

David L. Gallahue is a professor of kinesiology at Indiana University in Bloomington. He holds degrees from Indiana University (B.S.), Purdue University (M.S.), and Temple University (Ed.D.). Dr. Gallahue is active in the study of motor development, sport, and fitness education of children. He is author of several textbooks, numerous journal articles, and edited book chapters. Dr. Gallahue is a past president of the National Association for Sport and Physical Education (NASPE) and former chair of the Motor Development Academy and the Council of Physical Education for Children (COPEC). He is a recognized leader in children's motor development and developmental physical activity. His research focuses on environmental influences on the motor performance of young children across cultures.

Colin Higgs is a professor of physical education at Memorial University of Newfoundland. He received his master's and doctoral degrees from the University of Oregon, and he has published and lectured extensively on the biomechanics of wheelchair sport. Most recently he has worked for the Commonwealth Games Association of Canada on a sport and physical education development project in the Eastern Caribbean based in Barbados.

Luke E. Kelly received his doctorate from Texas Woman's University and his bachelor's and master's degrees from the State University of New York, College at Brockport. He is an associate professor at the University of Virginia, where he directs graduate programs in adapted physical education. Dr. Kelly works extensively with public schools to design and revise their curricula using the Achievement-Based Curriculum model so that they accommodate all students. Dr. Kelly is also the project director of the Adapted Physical Education National Standards Project.

Ellen M. Kowalski earned her bachelor's degree from SUNY, College at Geneseo, her certification in physical education from SUNY, College at Brockport, her master's from the University of Connecticut, and her doctorate in adapted physical education from Texas Woman's University. She is an assistant professor at Adelphi University in New York, where she prepares teachers in the undergraduate and graduate programs. Her research focuses on the infusion of disabilities knowledge throughout the entire teacher preparation curriculum to improve student competency to teach in an inclusive environment.

Patricia L. Krebs is the chief executive officer of Maryland Special Olympics. She earned her doctorate from the University of Maryland in 1979. Formerly professor in the undergraduate and graduate adapted physical education programs at Adelphi University and director of education for Special Olympics International, Dr. Krebs now administers Special Olympics year-round sports training, competition, and marketing events throughout Maryland to support more than 6,000 athletes.

E. Michael Loovis is an associate professor of health, physical education, recreation, and dance at Cleveland State University. He assists the Greater Cleveland Educational Development Center in the College of Education in delivering staff development activities to teachers from a consortium of over 70 school districts in Northeast Ohio. His research centers on development of "grounded" theory as it relates to instructional delivery in adapted physical education, including the use of ethnography.

David L. Porretta received his bachelor's degree in physical education from Niagara University, his master's from Ithaca College, and his doctorate from Temple University. He is an associate professor of physical education at The Ohio State University and is responsible for training graduate-level adapted physical education specialists. Dr. Porretta has been successful in obtaining funds to support the graduate program from the U.S. Department of Education. His research focuses primarily on variables that affect the motor performance of individuals with disabilities, especially those individuals with mental retardation.

E. Louise Priest is an independent consultant in aquatic safety. She also serves as volunteer executive director of the Council for National Cooperation in Aquatics (CNCA). She has worked as a professional in aquatics for the YMCA, the ARC, and CNCA. She spent 7 years at ARC national headquarters developing aquatic materials, including the text *Adapted Aquatics*. As executive director of CNCA, she developed the *National Aquatics Journal* and continues as managing editor. A graduate of the University of Southern Indiana, she did graduate work at George Mason University in Virginia.

Sarah M. Rich received a doctorate in adapted and developmental physical education, under the guidance of Dr. Claudine Sherrill at Texas Woman's University. She is an associate professor at Ithaca College (NY), where she is the coordinator of the adapted physical education and therapeutic recreation concentrations. She recently traveled to Niger, Guatemala, and Ecuador to provide training in adapted physical activities.

Francis X. Short is an associate professor of physical education and sport at the State University of New York, College at Brockport. He teaches courses in adapted physical education and in growth and development. He also coaches the women's intercollegiate volleyball team. He has authored and coauthored a number of publications and presentations related to the physical fitness of individuals with disabilities. Dr. Short holds degrees from Springfield College and Indiana University.

Paul R. Surburg earned a BS at Concordia Teachers College and a PhD from the University of Iowa. He is a professor at Indiana University and director of the adapted physical education program. He is a licensed physical therapist and has published research and pedagogical articles in sports medicine. His other research area is the motor functioning of individuals with mental retardation, with a focus on factors influencing information processing.

Dale A. Ulrich earned his doctorate at Michigan State University majoring in adapted physical education. He is an associate professor at Indiana University. He specializes in the assessment of motor skills in children, and he wrote the Test of Gross Motor Development. He is involved in motor development research designed to reduce the consistent delay in the onset of walking in infants with Down syndrome.

Joseph P. Winnick serves as a professor of physical education and sport at the State University of New York, College at Brockport. He received his bachelor's degree from Ithaca College and his master's and doctoral degrees from Temple University. Dr. Winnick developed and implemented America's first master's degree professional preparation program in adapted physical education at Brockport in 1968 and has secured funds from the U.S. Department of Education for over 20 years to support the program. He has and continues to be involved in research related to the physical fitness of persons with disabilities. Dr. Winnick has received the G. Lawrence Rarick Research Award and the Hollis Fait Scholarly Contribution Award.

Additional resources for adapted physical educators

Disability and Sport

Karen P. DePauw, PhD, and Susan J. Gavron, PED

1995 • Cloth • 312 pp • Item BDEP0848
ISBN 0-87322-848-0 • $35.00 ($48.95 Canadian)

This book is the first comprehensive reference of the past, present, and future of disability sport. It brings together under one cover the most current information available on this emerging and important field.

In *Disability and Sport,* the authors describe the historical context for disability sport today and trends for the future, provide an understanding of the issues and complexity of disability sport, increase the awareness of sport modifications and the multitude of sport opportunities available worldwide to athletes with disabilities, and present biographical sketches of athletes with disabilities who have excelled in sport.

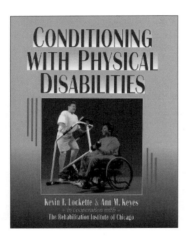

Conditioning With Physical Disabilities

Kevin F. Lockette PT, CSCS, and Ann M. Keyes, PT, CSCS

In cooperation with the Rehabilitation Institute of Chicago

1994 • Paper • 288 pp • Item PLOC0614
ISBN 0-87322-614-3 • $22.95 ($30.95 Canadian)

"The most current reference and most useful resource regarding exercise for people with physical disabilities."
> Kirk Bauer
> National Director
> National Handicapped Sports

Conditioning With Physical Disabilities is the first practical, authoritative exercise guide for people with all classifications and levels of physical disabilities. This highly readable fitness manual contains safe, easy-to-use exercises, accompanied by step-by-step descriptions and more than 250 helpful illustrations.

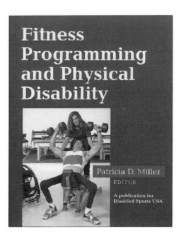

Fitness Programming and Physical Disability

A Publication for Disabled Sports USA

Patricia D. Miller, Editor

1995 • Paper • 208 pp • Item BMIL0434
ISBN 0-87322-434-5 • $29.00 ($40.50 Canadian)

"This is the most amazing book. I'm overwhelmed with how thorough and knowledgeable it is."
> Joanie Greggains
> Health and fitness expert
> Star of TV's "Morning Stretch"
> Host of KGO radio talk show (San Francisco)

In *Fitness Programming and Physical Disability,* 12 authorities in exercise science, physical disabilities, and adapted exercise programming show you how to safely and effectively modify your existing fitness programs to enable individuals with disabilities to participate—*without* changing the quality or nature of the activity.

Prices subject to change.

Human Kinetics
The Information Leader in Physical Activity

2335